Families as They Really Are

Third Edition

Families as They Really Are

Third Edition

EDITED BY

VIRGINIA E. RUTTER
Framingham State University

KRISTI WILLIAMS
Ohio State University

BARBARA J. RISMAN
University of Illinois at Chicago

W. W. NORTON & COMPANY
Celebrating a Century of Independent Publishing

W. W. NORTON & COMPANY has been independent since its founding in 1923, when William Warder Norton and Mary D. Herter Norton first published lectures delivered at the People's Institute, the adult education division of New York City's Cooper Union. The firm soon expanded its program beyond the Institute, publishing books by celebrated academics from America and abroad. By midcentury, the two major pillars of Norton's publishing program—trade books and college texts—were firmly established. In the 1950s, the Norton family transferred control of the company to its employees, and today—with a staff of five hundred and hundreds of trade, college, and professional titles published each year—W. W. Norton & Company stands as the largest and oldest publishing house owned wholly by its employees.

Editor: Sasha Levitt
Editorial Assistants: Quinn Campbell and Aidan Windorf
Project Editor: Layne Broadwater
Managing Editor, College: Marian Johnson
Production Manager: Jane Searle
Media Editor: Eileen Connell
Associate Media Editor: Alexandra Park
Assistant Media Editor: Caleb Wertz
Media Project Editor: Colette Nolan
Managing Editor, College Digital Media: Kim Yi
Ebook Producer: Lily Edgerton
Marketing Director: Julia Hall
Designer: Juan Paolo Francisco
Director of College Permissions: Megan Schindel
Permissions Manager: Joshua Garvin
Composition: Six Red Marbles
Manufacturing: CJK Group/Sheridan Printing

W. W. Norton & Company, Inc., 500 Fifth Avenue, New York, NY 10110
WWNORTON.COM

W. W. Norton & Company Ltd., 15 Carlisle Street, London W1D 3BS

1 2 3 4 5 6 7 8 9 0

To Stephanie Coontz, for her life's
ongoing dedication to families as
they really are

Contents

Part Two: How Did We Get Here?

Part Three: What Do We Talk about When We Talk about Diversity of Family Forms?

Part Four: Intimacy in the Twenty-First Century

Part Five: How Does Policy Link to Personal Lives?

Part Seven: Leveling the Playing Field

How Do We Know What We Know?

1

This We Know: Things Change

An Introduction

Virginia E. Rutter and Kristi Williams

Families as They Really Are is a brilliant title. We didn't come up with it, so we can say so. It says efficiently what this book is about. The first edition of *Families as They Really Are* was published in 2010, the brainchild of our co-editor Barbara Risman, who gave it this name. The title was a play on historian Stephanie Coontz's paradigm-shifting 1991 book, *The Way We Never Were: The American Family and the Nostalgia Trap. Families as They Really Are*, like Coontz's classic, focuses on debunking myths, elevating reliable research, and activating readers with lively writing, with an aim toward empowering wide audiences with its ideas.

Families as They Really Are supports the work of the Council on Contemporary Families (CCF), a group of scholars who are committed to including everyone in conversations about families in the world. In turn, CCF—with work from top scholars—publishes free, open-access, accurate, engaging, and easy-to-read research. Many of the contributors to this volume are senior scholars with CCF.

CCF engages wider audiences to spread knowledge, and we want to guide others—like you—to join us in doing so. A first step is absorbing the wide range of ideas and perspectives on families as they really are. As an active reader, you become part of this knowledge and understanding project. This is important because the topic of "families as they really are," like the title, implies the centrality of change in our lives and in knowledge itself.

This new third edition has been *extensively* updated. Why? In recent years, social change has accelerated, even as we find ourselves in dire need of *usable* information. We don't want to waste your time and attention. Your understanding of family diversity and family change is crucial to the future—as a student, a scholar, a worker, and a person who lives your life in and among families.

In this book of forty chapters, seventeen are new and seventeen more have been intensively revised. Our chapters are not reprints; they were written for this edited volume. Chapters offer original data, tackle new topics, and provide updated perspectives on parenting, marriage, couples, gender, queer and LGBTQ experiences, critical race theory, COVID-19's impact, and the remarkable struggle we are witnessing with the notion of "truth."

Revisions were rigorous, as authors labored to update existing material to reflect new and evolving situations of families today. The authors are at the top of their fields as scholars, yet they were selected because they care about social change—including the social change that begins with readable, current, and relevant chapters for students and other scholars.

The updates to the third edition of *Families as They Really Are* don't end there. Throughout this book you'll also find thirty-three very brief articles titled "In Other Words." These CCF research reports and blog posts apply new perspectives while linking to ideas presented in the chapters. These articles pull no punches; they are direct and personal and frank. We hope these pieces together with the chapters will inspire and inform class discussions, dinner table conversations, and conversations with people in your lives.

Today, when struggles over what is *true* dominate the news and public debate thinking about what "really is" has never been more important. You are studying families at a time when ways to make a family or be a family are expanding. At the same time, political divisions about these very families have widened. You are doing this as new generations—you!—are ushering in magnificent change in how people express themselves, find connection, and imagine themselves as part of a better world. Our new generations deserve thoughtful *guidance* about the world, including clear insights about families as they *really* are.

But What's It *Really* About?

Our contributors have diverse writing styles, and their topics are wide-ranging. In Chapter 14, Jenifer Bratter uses personal stories about her interracial family to highlight connections to what scholars have learned to be true about families. Others highlight new data, including Pamela Quiroz's Chapter 28 on international adoption and Kathleen Gerson's Chapter 36 on couples, housework, and "having it all."

Many authors bring forward perspectives that are not heard in everyday life, such as Amy Brainer's Chapter 15 on the challenges faced by queer college students during the pandemic. Other chapters explore the realities of families across a great spectrum of experience, including childfree families (Blackstone et al., Chapter 11), stepfamilies (Ganong et al., Chapter 12), and LGBTQ families (Goldberg, Chapter 13). We wrote this book with the hope that every person who picks it up discovers something that is new, important, and valuable to them.

Within that diversity, common features and themes appear across the chapters and articles. The book begins with an emphasis on what scholars call *epistemology*. That's a fancy and useful word that means "how we know what we know." Once you understand that how we know something is an important topic in the study of families, the conversation gets deeper and even more interesting.

Starting with epistemology helps you to recognize a priority in all our chapters: examining *how* we can know what is true—and what the limits are to those claims of truth. In Chapter 2, Philip Cohen helps us grapple with truth as scholars see it. You'll see that it really is within your own powers of understanding to grapple with truth too. As the book continues, authors share how they found their knowledge. For example, Adina Nack writes from personal and research perspectives about sexually transmitted infections (Chapter 17). Authors such as Georgiann Davis (Chapter 29) show you *how* to question knowledge claims and remind you of the costly impact of misinformation, in this case as it relates to intersex children and their families. You'll learn the wide variety of ways that scholars use careful methods to derive critical perspectives on families as they really are.

Other chapters share in common a commitment to advancing areas that are understudied; they not only cover the topics but also highlight the consequences of neglecting them. Xavier Guadalupe-Diaz shines a light on the experiences of intimate partner violence among transgender people (Chapter 34); Elizabeth Whalley challenges how we think about gender in her discussion of family sexual violence and displays the power of using a queer perspective (Chapter 40). Emily Via and colleagues examine what happens when nonbinary people come out to their families (Chapter 27); Patricia Sanchez-Connally shares original research on schooling experiences that marginalize immigrant children and devalue the resources that their families provide (Chapter 32); Cassaundra Rodriguez lays bare the struggles and trauma of mixed-status immigrant families when death or disease occurs during a separation (Chapter 33).

How Is the Book Organized? An Overview by Section

Part One (How Do We Know What We Know?) tackles how scholars decide what is true. You'll learn about qualitative and quantitative methods. You'll learn how recognizing historical bias is also part of our methods and that using critical race theory can be a powerful tool for finding truth.

Part Two (How Did We Get Here?) helps to illustrate how families are socially constructed and that there is no one, true family form. You'll learn how myths and nostalgia dominate the evolution of families in the United States and around the world. We cover families in U.S. and world history, dig into the rich history of Black families and present-day attitudes toward gay and lesbian families, and examine the historic links between labor unions and family.

Part Three (What Do We Talk about When We Talk about Diversity of Family Forms?) explores a range of "new families" (though we don't cover them all!). You'll learn about families that are intentionally childfree. You'll get updates on stepfamilies and details on LGBTQ people as they become parents. You'll learn how interracial families are coded and experienced and how queer young people cope and rely on chosen family—in and after a pandemic.

Part Four (Intimacy in the Twenty-First Century) examines sex and intimate relationships—since these are part of our family lives too. Chapter topics include explanations for contradictory American attitudes toward sex, how intimacy is challenged by sexually transmitted infections, the gender gap in orgasms among college students, and insights about equality in lesbian couples. This section underscores how even our most intimate experiences are influenced by the social world.

Part Five (How Does Policy Link to Personal Lives?) draws your attention to the social and institutional contexts of families. The focus of these five chapters is policy—the agreed-upon institutional rules or programs that govern how family life unfolds. You'll read chapters on family process research, public policies on marriage, public debates on divorce, racial inequality in access to resources in childhood, and the impact of workplaces on couples and parents during COVID-19. One thing you'll see again and again in this section—and elsewhere in the third edition—is that claims about the existence of one ideal family structure are not supported by evidence. Looking at policies can help us identify the stakeholders who might be interested in sustaining that myth.

Part Six (How Parents and Kids Relate) focuses on what happens between generations. These six chapters look at the experiences of Latina mothers and daughters; how parents today support their transgender children; the process of coming out to family as nonbinary; parents' and children's rights in international adoption; finding new resources for parents of an intersex child; and the unique challenges of parenting adult children. These intergenerational stories show readers how complex—and consequential—parenting is.

Part Seven (Leveling the Playing Field): Families aim to support their children and help them become healthy adults. But how does that *really* work in a time of spiraling inequality? The five chapters in Part Seven examine student loans and the transition to adulthood; how American schools devalue and overlook the resources that families of immigrant students provide to their children; the trauma for mixed-status immigrant families of dealing with death and illness while separated; how addressing intimate partner violence can—but has not—included the experiences of transgender people; and the impact of mass incarceration on families in the United States.

Part Eight (Unfinished Gender Revolution) looks at couples and inequality at home and at work; how immigration status influences equity in mixed-sex relationships; how gender inequality in mixed-sex couples played out during the pandemic; how "guy moms"—transgender men who are moms—challenge the gendering that often happens in families; and how updating and "queering" the meaning of gender can lead to greater care in the case of family sexual violence. Throughout the book you will see how taking a critical view—even a queer theory view—of gender gets us closer to the true story of families as they really are. Part Eight brings that message home to you.

How about Some Recognition?

You might want to keep reading the rest of this chapter—because learning how a book actually gets made will help you as you create things yourself! We started this book around January 2020 . . . and then the world changed as the COVID-19 pandemic took over our lives. Each of us—just as each of you—managed work and family and the human struggles that are portrayed in the pages of this book on a personal level, as workers, teachers and students, and family members. The pandemic wasn't (isn't) the only challenge. As we tell our students, it was a five-part crisis that really had six parts. Along with COVID-19, we experienced recession and joblessness, the growing struggle for Black lives, the climate crisis, and the troubled political climate. The sixth? The struggles each person we meet has had in life as these things unfolded.

We *feel* deeply the uncertainty created by these many crises. Now more than ever we need to recognize the importance of each student, each faculty member, each scholar, each reader as we do the work of understanding families as they really are and addressing the problems we believe need fixing.

All that explains why we took our time to bring this book to you. We benefited enormously from the wisdom we inherited from founding editor Barbara Risman. We built much of our material on the excellent work of our CCF colleagues Stephanie Coontz, Arielle Kuperberg, and Alicia Walker, whose work has made all the difference. Indeed, much of the CCF "In Other Words" articles in here are thanks to these people.

For the past twenty years, CCF's brief reports (which you can explore freely at www.contemporaryfamilies.org) have been edited and curated by historian

Stephanie Coontz (see Chapter 6) along with one of this volume's co-editors (Virginia Rutter, Chapter 22). The CCF blog at the Society Pages (www.the societypages.org/ccf) extends that coverage. The blog was founded by Rutter, who edited it for many years. More recently, Arielle Kuperberg (see Chapter 31) led the production of superb, wide-ranging, and fresh material. Currently, Alicia Walker—whom you will read about in In Other Words 16.2—is the curator of the blog and continues this valuable work.

There's more to the story of how we got here: Deep in the background— though not to us—is the remarkable Jennifer Glass, who, while producing award-winning scholarship on family diversity and family change, has kept CCF running. By Jennifer's side was Michael Garcia, who did remarkable work as a research assistant. Early in the book's creation, Virginia's student assistant Tyler Risteen kept us moving with curiosity and commitment. A gift to this book was finding an astonishing, expert editorial assistant in Ruby Alberti. Even as a high school senior, she carefully edited and queried many of the authors in this book; her mark is on every page.

And then there is also the big-brained, can-do guidance from Sasha Levitt, our editor at Norton. We love Norton because it has great people and because it is worker-owned. We received great support in earlier editions from Karl Bakeman, who also helped found the Society Pages.

Finally, we wish all people working on joint projects, or working indepen- dently, to have supportive, reliable collaborations. The two of us (Virginia and Kristi) have had the chance to work together creatively and consistently over this strange time of Zoom calls, publishing puzzles, and unpredictable crises. We've had the equally reliable support and input from our founding editor, Barbara. We hope you see that all this work was done in an environment of compassion for the pressures we are all under and for the concerns that our student readers have. We hope you will bring compassion and a spirit of collaboration to yourself and to your reading of this work. Finally, we hope that the ideas in this book help you to imagine what the world is—and what it can be. Thank you for reading, thinking, and trying.

2

How Do We Tell What's True?

Philip N. Cohen

Don't call bullshit carelessly—but if you can, call bullshit when necessary.

—Carl T. Bergstrom and Jevin D. West

What is true? *True* in general means "in accordance with fact or reality." Truth is the basis of knowledge. *Being* true is also important in families, and especially romantic relationships, where we value loyalty and dedication. People today think of *true love* as meaning love that is real and authentic, not fake or superficial. That understanding comes from the historical meaning of true as *faithful*; being true to a marriage referred to sexual or romantic fidelity (not having sex with or loving anyone else). The connection between knowledge and love also appears in the Torah, where a man "knowing" a woman meant having sex with her. Was it meaningful when Adam knew Eve, in Genesis Chapter 4—was it true? Yes, we are told. It was the opposite of what a spouse caught cheating often protests: "But it didn't *mean* anything!"

Nowadays, *fidelity* also means the degree to which something is accurately—faithfully—reproduced, like a picture or a sound recording. Fidelity is not just important to people in their romantic relationships, but also to people who like art, music, or data. If you're using *Wi-Fi* right now, incidentally, that's because the term sounded cool to people who marketed the wireless protocol in 1999. It rhymed with "Hi-Fi," short for "high fidelity," which is what people used to call their music-playing machines when I was a kid. Like, "Whoa, that's a cool Hi-Fi!" Fidelity matters.

You can think of true ideas or facts as those that accurately reproduce reality—that are faithful to reality. Facts have fidelity. And the question for us—as students, teachers, researchers, and citizens—is, how can we tell what's true? This book is about getting at what is true. It asks you to think about family diversity and family change—and also about how we know what we know about these topics. This is especially important when studying families, because the issues that arise in this area involve contentious debates about how to describe and interpret the rapidly changing realities that so many of us experience in our daily lives. In short, a lot of people are telling tall tales about families, and the stakes are high. From marriage equality and reproductive rights to parenting and gender identity, to make decisions that matter we need to have a handle on "families as they *really* are."

PEER REVIEW AND SYSTEMS OF EXPERTISE

Because I'm a professor, you might expect me to answer my question—how can we tell what's true?—by saying, "Peer review!" When research is *peer reviewed,* that means other scholars with expertise in the same field of study have evaluated the work and declared it to be true. Or at least that's the ideal. We most commonly encounter research that has been peer reviewed in academic journals and books, and many college instructors ask their students to focus on these works for their assignments.

Why is peer review necessary? In a world of highly specialized training, it's impossible for individuals intent on learning something to verify all the information they encounter. That applies whether we are doctors deciding what medications to prescribe, airline manufacturers deciding what materials to use, or regular people deciding whether a viral outbreak means it's not safe to hug our grandchildren. We need experts. That's why "Do your own research," which pretends to be a call to independent thought, is actually the mantra of know-nothing conspiracy theorists. It signals a disregard for systems of expertise, and opens a back door to the dark world of ignorance (Sagan 1997).

Our modern life requires systematically trusting people who know more about something than we do and who have the legitimate role of exercising that expertise. We could seek out individual experts—asking them what food to eat, medicines to take, bridges to drive over, water to drink, and air to breathe. But there are too many decisions to make about whom or what to trust. Instead we rely on *institutional systems of expertise* in which groups of experts evaluate the information we need (even if we don't know we need it). This "trust in expert systems," which we learn to do without thinking, has become a key component of the modern personality, in the view of social theorist Anthony Giddens (1990). We are socialized to live under the protection of anonymous experts whose judgment is a daily matter of life and death. Although it might seem reassuring to have so much trust, there is also an inherent anxiety to this existence, because so much is out of our control. Still, we are forced to accept this protection in order to survive in the modern world.

The experts who conduct peer review have training related to that of the people whose work is under scrutiny—that's why we call them "peers." Engineers assess bridge design, doctors test medicines, chemists evaluate toxic hazards, family sociologists scrutinize family sociology research (I'll refer to all these people as "scientists" in this essay). Among the millions of people laboring in the global scientific enterprise, peer review has been elevated to a defining principle, and for good reason. Only people with relevant skills and knowledge can effectively evaluate work in specialized topics. The stakes are high, for scientists and their careers and for the people who live or die by the veracity of scientific research.

Evaluating science is part of the machinery of science, and it occupies a large part of the collective work of the scientists at universities around the world. In a recent year, almost 14 million peer reviews of research articles were conducted, requiring 69 million hours. That's the equivalent of 33,000 reviewers working full time for the entire year (Publons 2018). Most of those thousands of reviewers—including me and many of the authors who contributed to this book—do this work as part of our jobs, without additional pay, in service to our academic institutions and disciplines. These academics have a vested interest in contributing to the system, because scientists and readers of science benefit from the trust it generates. Or so we hope. For people outside of academic disciplines, peer review is also seen as a core, fundamental process—part of the definition of science many people learn. It has become part of the social contract between scientists and the public.

TRUST, NOT FAITH

This social contract presents a puzzle: How do we trust experts while thinking critically about expertise? Albert Einstein, a professional scientist who wanted people to believe his theories, nevertheless wrote that "a foolish faith in authority is the worst enemy of truth" (Isaacson 2007). As a scientist committed to truth, Einstein didn't want people to have *faith* in science as an authority—like the religious authorities whose leadership he rejected—but rather to have *trust* in science. You can think of "trust" as something that comes from evidence and conscious deliberation; "faith" is something we don't need to think about to believe in. Religious faith may play a positive role in the lives of many people, but you can see why Einstein—a Jewish man who renounced his German citizenship and fled the country after Hitler took over the government there—would be against "foolish faith in authority."

In sum, we can continue to trust what deserves to be trusted while keeping a critical eye on the process and the people involved. But how? We simply can't stand up alone to a firehose of information and judge what's good and what's bad. Thinking critically about expertise requires us to build trust in one another and our knowledge communities. And this commitment needs to run both ways, between experts and the communities they serve. Experts must earn the trust required to do their work effectively, and one way they do that is by engaging with the public in responsible and respectful ways.

A History of Peer Review

Despite its mystique as the one true way of publishing science, academic peer review in its current form is a recent innovation. For most of scientific history, the editors of academic journals decided what to publish and consulted with additional experts at their discretion (sometimes anonymously, sometimes not). The term *peer review* became common only in the 1970s in the wake of mid-century trends in science. There was an explosion of research after World War II, and federal funding for that research threatened to put power in the hands of government bureaucrats instead of academic researchers, so scientists sought to institutionalize their influence. Insisting on peer review meant scientists had to be involved at all levels (Moxham and Fyfe 2018; Baldwin 2018). In the major U.S. sociology journals, the assumption that papers would be reviewed by outside reviewers (that is, beyond the editor and editorial board members) did not become universal until the 1980s. The main purpose of the change, rather than stemming from ethical or intellectual concerns, was to involve more professors in the work of handling the rising tide of papers and the growing technical specialization required to review them (Merriman 2021).

Many people consider peer review to be the pinnacle of modern knowledge creation. Whether or not that's true, a word of caution is important here: Putting peer review on a pedestal happens to be exactly what the companies that sell research publications want you to do. Have you ever hit a paywall while tracking down an article for school or a project? Then you have encountered these big businesses—I call it Big Publishing—and experienced firsthand how they profit off specialized research. The five biggest publishers collectively publish more than 12,000 academic journals (Nishikawa-Pacher 2022). One of the biggest, Elsevier, published 600,000 articles in 2021 alone, and its parent company, RELX, turned a profit of $1.6 billion that year (RELX 2021). The people of Big Publishing, and the academic establishment more generally, are happy to control the definition of truth and sell it to us. And some of them have gotten ridiculously rich as a result. That doesn't automatically make them wrong, but we need to think critically about this system too. The companies that publish science play an important role, especially by organizing peer review and disseminating research. Similarly, the companies of Big Pharma develop and produce many of the valuable medicines that we rely on today. Critics of these systems have to wrestle with how to accomplish the good parts of what the profiteering companies do, while reining in the harmful practices that follow from their profit motive.

Regardless of its origins, review of research by other experts often serves both the research and the researcher well. Using peer review, we often improve our research and stop bad or erroneous research before it finds a wider audience. Being a responsible researcher involves aiming to stop faulty research, including one's own, from misleading or confusing the public. Peer review is a way for us to work together toward this end. In addition, peer review helps establish priorities in the field—that is, to rank the importance of different work—and judge people's work to decide who should get jobs, promotions, and prizes.

Equally important, perhaps, the existence and reputation of the peer-review system helps establish the legitimacy of the scientific enterprise in the eyes of the public (Cohen 2019). In our highly contentious social and political milieu, where researchers are sometimes depicted as just another interest group competing to establish their own self-serving version of the truth, peer review sends an important signal that scientists aren't afraid of independent scrutiny and assessment of our work. This is especially crucial when the public doesn't have the training to understand the science and is being asked to take our word for it.

THE REAL WORLD AND MORE WAYS THAT INFORMATION IS CREATED

The idealized form of peer review of research articles—in which anonymous professional academics conduct "blind" reviews to help editors decide what to publish in academic journals—doesn't apply to all the ways information is created. That's partly because of technology. Publishing used to mean having something printed in a paper journal or book. A decision to publish something implied a substantial cost, so publishers had to be selective, as did the libraries and bookstores that stocked and archived the written word. Now these items may still end up in print, but they begin online, and whole bodies of research now exist solely online. As a result, the cost of disseminating information has plummeted. We now need ways of identifying quality among the endless supply of available work. Often, in this new world, research is judged after it's published rather than before. Because so much is posted and published, peer review is no longer used to determine what people can read. Instead, it helps people decide what to believe.

This is important because it democratizes the process. A lot more people can be involved in assessing research—for better and for worse. The sooner we recognize that the importance of peer review extends beyond the decision of whether to publish research, the sooner we can improve our own contributions—as individuals and communities—to the massive, endless undertaking of global information quality control.

If the essence of peer review is experts using their expertise to review work that other readers aren't qualified to review, there are a lot of ways this can happen— not all of them equally trustworthy. Consider this disparate set of apparently factual recent statements about poverty in the United States that were produced by various combinations of academics, non-academic organizations, and people with different kinds of formal and informal training—and axes to grind:

- The U.S. Census Bureau reported that the poverty rate in 2021 fell to a historic low: 7.8 percent (according to the Supplemental Poverty Measure). The report was based on a large sample survey, written by a team of analysts, and subjected to strict quality review within the bureau before it was released (Creamer et al. 2022).

- I made a graph using the Census Bureau data showing the trend in poverty rates for children and posted it on Twitter (Cohen 2022).

- The *New York Times* also reported on the falling poverty rates, creating their own graphs with the Census data, which were then interpreted by half a dozen professors and researchers the *Times* reporters interviewed, who all agreed the big drop in poverty came from government assistance during the pandemic (DePillis and DeParle 2022).

- Brad Wilcox, a conservative scholar at the American Enterprise Institute and a University of Virginia sociology professor devoted to promoting marriage, testified before Congress in 2020 that "child poverty would be markedly reduced if the nation enjoyed 1970s marriage levels" (Wilcox 2020). What he didn't say, in his effort to turn back the clock, was that he based that claim on research conducted in 1995, using data collected in 1989—thirty-one years earlier. Since then, child poverty has fallen drastically despite no increase in marriage rates.

- Sociologists Deadric Williams and Regina Baker published an article in the peer-reviewed journal *Social Problems*, reporting that racial stratification, more than family structure, is a systemic cause of poverty in the United States (Williams and Baker 2021).

In these examples, you can see different systems of review and evaluation at work, each of which could be considered a kind of peer review. At the Census Bureau, highly trained experts collect and analyze data, and their reports go through further expert review before being published. When I tweet a data graph, you know it's from me—a professor with a PhD and a publication record—and I link to my data sources. You also know from my social media feeds or my *Family Inequality* blog that I am a progressive who favors liberal social policies. The *New York Times* also links to the data its reporters present and identifies the experts they consulted in their reporting. Brad Wilcox cites his sources, allowing a critical reader to see how weakly they support his case. And if we are aware of the highly partisan political nature of the American Enterprise Institute, we can approach his work cautiously with an eye toward identifying bias. Finally, the sociologists Williams and Baker, publishing in a peer-reviewed journal, offer the purest form of what we normally call peer review. The journal does not have a transparent process—we don't know who the reviewers were or how thorough their review was—but we can decide to trust it based on its long institutional reputation and the credentials of the authors. In each of these cases, we can make some judgments about the trustworthiness of the information—based on the reputations of the individuals and their institutions and their documented credentials. Before we make important decisions based on this information, we might want to investigate the sources and potential biases and discuss the work with others who have some expertise to gain a deeper understanding of the research and its context.

I could list many other examples of scholarly experts involved in knowledge (or disinformation) production outside the idealized system of peer review. There is a lot of important research working its way into the public eye outside the scrutiny of the academic peer-review system—such as the first three examples above—often having been reviewed by experts in ways not normally understood to be peer review. All the more reason not to put academic journals on a pedestal.

Academic journal peer review doesn't always work, of course. Bad actors sometimes get their work out under cover of peer review even when it either wasn't really reviewed or was reviewed in corrupt ways—a problem exacerbated by the fact that most journals conduct their peer review in secret, and anonymously. That was the case with a racist article authored by the political scientist Lawrence Mead, who wrote in the journal *Society* that "cultural difference . . . best explain(s) why minorities—especially blacks and Hispanics—typically respond only weakly to chances to get ahead through education and work . . . [and] the ultimate solution to poverty is for the poor themselves to adopt the more inner-driven individualist style" (Mead 2020). Only after hundreds of people complained (the article had no evidence to support his claims) did the journal retract the article and admit it was "published without proper editorial oversight."

Family research has seen its share of deceptive or shoddy research published after peer review. In particular, there has been a long campaign by activists on the religious right to undermine same-sex marriage and parenting rights by publishing research claiming to show harms caused to children raised by same-sex couples. That research includes a number of papers by sociologists and tenured professors Mark Regnerus and Paul Sullins, whose research was widely criticized, including by me, for its low quality and clear bias. Nevertheless, the papers ended up being used to support court challenges to same-sex marriage and parental rights. In the case of several Sullins papers, the journals published the peer reviews, which is unfortunately rare, revealing that they were never seriously scrutinized by qualified experts (Cohen 2015). Research labeled "peer reviewed" is not necessarily a reliable source of true information, especially in cases of deliberate manipulation.

Even when peer review works more like it should, the system has serious problems. During the COVID-19 pandemic, peer review buckled under the pressure of urgent demands for scientific output and the rush of scientists generating results. Papers were backed up for months waiting for reviewers to volunteer for the job and complete their work. Scientists posted tens of thousands of papers as preprints—made public before peer review—in the first months of the pandemic alone (Fraser et al. 2021). In some cases, that was great; important work got where it needed to go much faster as a result. There were some bad papers as well, but some of those were improved based on feedback to the drafts posted.

During the pandemic, we also saw the dramatic rise of a group of public health experts, epidemiologists, physicians, and related scientists speaking directly to the public on social media. Their tweets weren't peer reviewed, but their expertise was on public display, along with their credentials. And they worked with science journalists and their editors and producers in the news media. Many of those non-peer-reviewed papers posted on preprint platforms got run through a wringer of overworked, overtired peers who felt compelled to publicly evaluate them as rapidly as possible—especially if they were generating significant attention. Dozens of such experts had more than 100,000 followers on Twitter by 2022, as the public demanded information as quickly as possible (Murray n.d.). This was a kind of rapid-response peer-review system.

The constantly churning crew of experts (and people who think they're experts) unspooling capacious threads about the latest research on social media—where tempers are short and the incentives favor extreme positions—has many counterproductive aspects. But then again, "traditional" peer review produced hundreds of pandemic-related research articles that were subsequently retracted by their journals (there is a list maintained by a nonprofit called Retraction Watch here: retractionwatch.com/retracted-coronavirus-covid-19-papers/). The pandemic—and all the chaos in the information ecosystem that came with it—clearly showed we can't just choose to live in an idealized world of verified truths.

GET INVOLVED

In my role as a public intellectual, I encourage other scholars to get involved in the public debates of the day, not shrink from the controversy or dismiss the discussion simply because the venue or format does not match the review process we were trained to respect. If I say, "This paper is bad!" on social media, about a piece of scholarship I am qualified to evaluate, I might not be living up to the highest standards of peer review. But it would still be part of the stream of discourse we call peer review in the broader sense, and it might be better than nothing.

My expansionist view of peer review—which is not shared by all academics—should not be taken to diminish the more formal (and slow!) processes described earlier. In fact, being inefficient—slowing down the production of information and imposing quality hurdles—is important for impeding the spread of bad information (Bak-Coleman et al. 2021). But we should not kid ourselves about the formal peer-review process, elevating it to an unrealistically sacred status. There are trade-offs to different kinds of review and commentary, and there are no easy solutions.

Peer review—formal or informal—has many advantages. We need people with different kinds of expertise to get involved in the process of evaluating and communicating about new knowledge as it is produced and disseminated. But peer review alone can't stop misinformation. Time and again, anti-vaccine conspiracies and other campaigns to undermine our public health response ripped through social media during the pandemic (Germani and Biller-Andorno 2021). We can't stop it, but we can respond (Bergstrom and West 2020). We can be responsible consumers—as well as producers—of information, carefully deciding what information to spread and when to raise a ruckus in protest. We all have expertise on something, if only our own experience, and we should bring that knowledge to our communication networks and our reputations as responsible citizen scholars to the scrum of public debate. We can be engaged, as individuals and as communities.

The quality of our information is vitally important, and there are no easy solutions to the problem of deciding where to place our trust. But we have some safeguards, and you can be part of those safeguards. We can ask whether the research we're reading is peer reviewed, but that's not the whole story. As educated (and educating) readers, we can ask more: How was it peer reviewed, and by whom? If it's not in an academic publication, was it produced by other people with real expertise or experience that lends it authority in our eyes? Is there some system of accountability in place to correct or respond if it turns out to be wrong? And crucially, can we use our knowledge and skills to help others evaluate and respond to what we're reading?

When we decide whether something is true, we often use the word *tell*, as in, "I can tell that's true." To tell something is to know it, as well as to communicate about it. We have a social obligation to tell the truth about what we can tell is true. That requires listening and learning but also talking and writing. In the end, the way we tell what's true is to speak up.

In Other Words

NEIGHBORHOOD SOCIAL COHESION NOT IN DECLINE, BUT CONCERNING DISPARITIES PERSIST

Kira England, December 6, 2022 / CCF@TSP

"Hey, Eli, can you watch the kids on Friday while I run to a doctor's appointment?"

"Sure, Maria! By the way, would you mind getting my mail next week while I visit my sister?"

While it's easy to imagine similar conversations between neighbors occurring all around the country every day, there's a widespread belief that these conversations have become less common, that neighbors have grown apart, and that the bonds between neighbors have weakened. Yet, in recent research, colleagues and I find that connections among neighbors are more stable than many may expect.

Neighborhood social cohesion, which is the extent of mutual trust and support among neighbors, is an important predictor of a wide range of outcomes, including both kids' and adults' well-being.[1] Researchers have hypothesized that neighborhood social cohesion has been declining for decades due to factors like changes in communication technology, leisure activities, and economic organization.[2] This is commonly referred to as the "community lost" hypothesis.

Yet, research on whether changes in perceived neighborhood social cohesion have actually occurred is lacking, and despite the far-reaching body of research that considers neighborhood social cohesion, gaps in the literature remain. Studies on the topic frequently use data from a single city (often those near large research universities, like Chicago or Boston), leaving a large gap in our knowledge of what is happening throughout the country.[3] Furthermore, few studies examine how perceptions of neighborhood social cohesion vary by individual and neighborhood characteristics, and those that do have produced conflicting findings. For example, some studies suggest that less-resourced neighborhoods may be more cohesive, while others suggest that higher-resourced neighborhoods are more cohesive.[4]

In a recent research article, my colleagues and I addressed these gaps in the research by focusing on trends in neighborhood social cohesion across the entire country and whether perceptions of neighborhood social cohesion differ by individual and neighborhood characteristics. We used two different data sets in our study, including data that focuses on families with children, as neighborhood social cohesion is particularly important for families with children. Households with children are also the most common type of household in the United States.

The first data set is the Survey of Income and Program Participation (SIPP), which allowed us to look at nationwide trends from 1997 to 2011 in neighborhood social cohesion. The second data set is the Fragile Families and Child Wellbeing Study (FFCWS), which followed a group of families in the early 2000s though 2017, allowing us to examine whether individuals' perceptions of neighborhood social cohesion have changed and whether neighborhood characteristics are associated with differences in neighborhood social cohesion. In both data sets, respondents shared how much they agreed with statements related to neighborhood social cohesion, such as "There are people I can count on in this neighborhood" and "This is a close-knit neighborhood." We examined responses to individual statements and also combined the statements and their responses into a single scale representing overall cohesion.

Findings:

Both data sets:

- Across the different outcome measures, neighborhood social cohesion either remained stable or increased over time.

SIPP data:

- Reported cohesion was greater for respondents who are homeowners, married, non-Hispanic White, college educated, middle-aged, higher income, or living in nonmetro areas.

FFCWS data:

- Cohesion was greater for respondents who are homeowners, higher income, college educated, and not living in public housing.
- Cohesion was greater for non-Hispanic Blacks compared to non-Hispanic Whites for some measures. Cohesion was lower for other non-Hispanic races and identities compared to non-Hispanic Whites for most measures.
- Cohesion was lower for respondents in neighborhoods with higher percentages of unemployed residents, housing units that are rented, and households receiving public assistance.

In sum, we used different data sources with different strengths and found multiple consistent patterns that all point to overall stability in neighborhood social cohesion across time and across individual and neighborhood differences. We found that neighborhood social cohesion has not decreased and in fact has increased in certain ways. Our findings contradict the popular "community lost" hypothesis, at least for families with children. However, we did find notable disparities in neighborhood social cohesion depending on individual and neighborhood characteristics. We found lower levels of neighborhood social cohesion for respondents who had incomes below the poverty line, lived in disadvantaged neighborhoods, or were racial and ethnic minorities, renters, or unmarried. Since higher neighborhood social cohesion is associated with greater well-being for both adults and children, our findings suggest that less-resourced and/or marginalized families may face a well-being disadvantage linked to lower neighborhood social cohesion. While we do not find evidence that neighborhood social cohesion has decreased in recent years, concerns about certain families experiencing lost community are not unfounded.

Notes

1. Christyl T. Dawson, Wensong Wu, Kristopher P. Fennie, Gladys Ibañez, Miguel Á. Cano, Jeremy W. Pettit, and Mary Jo Trepka, "Perceived Neighborhood Social Cohesion Moderates the Relationship between Neighborhood Structural Disadvantage and Adolescent Depressive Symptoms," *Health & Place* 56 (2019): 88–98; Jennifer W. Robinette, Susan T. Charles, Jacqueline A. Mogle, and David M. Almeida, "Neighborhood Cohesion and Daily Well-Being: Results from a Diary Study," *Social Science & Medicine* 96 (2013):174–182; Jennifer W. Robinette, Jason D. Boardman, and Eileen Crimmins, "Perceived Neighborhood Social Cohesion and Cardiometabolic Risk: A Gene x Environment Study," *Biodemography and Social Biology* 65, no. 1 (2018): 1–15; Neika Sharifian, Briana N. Spivey, Afsara B. Zaheed, and Laura B. Zahodne, "Psychological Distress Links Perceived Neighborhood Characteristics to Longitudinal Trajectories of Cognitive Health in Older Adulthood," *Social Science & Medicine* 258 (2020): 113125, doi:10.1016/j.socscimed.2020.113125.

2. Adam Boessen, John R. Hipp, Emily J. Smith, Carter T. Butts, Nicholas N. Nagle, and Zack Almquist, "Networks, Space, and Residents' Perception of Cohesion," *American Journal of Community Psychology* 53 (2014): 447–461; Taylor Dotson, *Technically Together: Reconsidering Community in a Networked World* (Cambridge, MA: MIT Press, 2017); Barry Wellman, "The Community Question: The Intimate Networks of East Yorkers," *American Journal of Sociology* 84, no. 5 (1979): 1201–1231; Barry Wellman and Barry Leighton, "Networks, Neighborhoods, and Communities: Approaches to the Study of the Community Question," *Urban Affairs Quarterly* 14, no. 3 (1979): 363–390.

3. Nicole M. Schmidt, Eric J. Tchetgen, Amy Ehntholt, Joanna Almeida, Quynh C. Nguyen, Beth E. Molnar, Deborah Azrael, and Theresa L. Osypuk, "Does Neighborhood Collective Efficacy for Families Change over Time? The Boston Neighborhood Survey," *Journal of Community Psychology* 42, no. 1 (2014): 61–79.

4. Danya Keene, Michael Bader, and Jennifer Ailshire, "Length of Residence and Social Integration: The Contingent Effects of Neighborhood Poverty," *Health & Place* 21 (2013): 171–178; Robert J. Sampson, Jeffrey D. Morenoff, and Felton Earls, "Beyond Social Capital: Spatial Dynamics of Collective Efficacy for Children," *American Sociological Review* 64, no. 5 (1999): 633–660. ∎

3

When Is a Relationship between
Facts a Causal One?

Philip A. Cowan

More than 18 million American children (almost one in four) live in a home without a resident father.[1] These children are more likely to have social-emotional adjustment problems,[2] to have failing grades at school,[3] and to become involved in the juvenile justice system.[4] These facts have been cited as proof that an absent father is a prime cause of contemporary childhood difficulties. They have also been used to support the decision to provide substantial federal and state funding for programs that encourage fathers to become and remain positively involved with their young children.

A summary of research on mass shootings in America indicates that almost all perpetrators have a history of diagnosable mental illness.[5] This fact has been cited in support of the widely held belief that mental illness plays a causal role in leading (mostly) males to become mass shooters. The assumption that mental illness causes shooter behavior was the rationale for the Bipartisan Safer Communities Act. Passed by Congress in 2022, the act provides nearly $250 million in funding for community-based violence prevention initiatives and additional funding to protect schools and increase mental health services.

These two examples illustrate the fact that inferences about causality from empirical studies can have substantial real-world consequences in terms of government policies, service delivery programs, and family decisions. What I want to point out in this brief chapter is that the inferences about what causes what are very often incorrect and misleading and may point policy makers and program providers in the wrong direction.

This problem is not the sole property of the political left or political right. Both sides are too quick to draw support from social science research when the correlations support their cherished conclusions. For example, I personally favor decisions to devote funds to encourage father involvement and to increase mental health funding for school-based programs, but I will show that the facts in these two examples do not support some of the conclusions that have been drawn.

In my view there are two major kinds of errors in making causal inferences from empirical studies. First, it is not possible—not ever—to determine causal connections from correlational data. I will propose instead that correlational studies be conducted as a necessary first step in establishing whether an intervention that targets a given variable is likely to produce the desired effects. Second, not just any intervention design can test whether the hypothesized causal connection between outcomes is valid. I will discuss the problem with using data from an intervention study that has no control or comparison group to conclude that the intervention had an impact on the participants. (See Rutter, Chapter 22, for examples in divorce research.)

Problems with Causal Interpretations of Correlational Data

Most social science studies attempt to determine whether there is some kind of relationship between two or more variables (e.g., family conflict and child aggression). Most often the variables are measured at a single point in time. The investigator is attempting to determine whether there is a correlation between them—an association such that variation in one is reliably associated with variation in the other. There is nothing wrong with this research strategy to understand connections between variables, except when the investigator concludes that one variable is the *cause* of variation in the other.

1.   Causality always implies a direction of effects—the cause, A, comes before the effect, B. But statements based on statistical correlations can *never* tell us about which comes first. For example, it is a fact that there is an association between being married and having better-functioning lives and between non-marriage and financial or emotional difficulties.[6] But we do not know whether marriage produces the partners' better functioning or whether better-functioning partners tend to marry. That is, correlations between variables measured at the same time cannot reveal the sequence in which the variables of interest emerge.

2. Longitudinal studies don't solve the problem. Some investigators attempt to determine sequencing by following people or families over time — measuring one variable earlier and another variable later. Those who focus on the assumption that early family experience plays a causal role in children's later adjustment buttress their argument with longitudinal studies that assess conflict between parents when children are young and then measure children's adjustment when they are in elementary school.[7] This strategy seems to establish a sequence in which parental conflict comes first, but this is just an illusion related to the investigator's choice of when to measure the variables they are interested in. It is entirely possible that the parents who are in conflict early on are still in conflict when the child's adjustment is assessed; it is also possible that the earlier parental conflict was caused by a difficult toddler. In either case, longitudinal measures simply produce correlations in which the direction of effects cannot be determined.

3. Social trend data pose the same problem. Researchers and social commentators often make causal statements about changing social trends. For example, increases in the proportion of mothers of young children in the workforce occurred in the mid-twentieth century around the same time that the divorce rate went up. On the basis of these two facts alone we cannot point to women's working as a cause of the increase in divorce. Why not? First, these data are simply correlations with the added problem that we don't know whether divorce occurred more often in the families of women who went to work and less often in the families of women who did not.

4. Correlations can result from a third variable that produces the association between them. It is a fact that children whose parents are divorced, or who live with a single parent, tend to have more emotional, behavioral, and academic difficulties than children whose parents are married. It is possible, though, that some of the effects of divorce and single parenthood come from the fact that these households have lower incomes and that reduced resources are responsible, at least in part, for the children's difficulties.

5. Reasoning backward about causality produces backward thinking. Now we get to the specific flaw in causal reasoning illustrated by the examples that introduced this chapter — the logical fallacy of reasoning backward from outcomes to causes. Compared with children whose fathers are resident in the home, a higher proportion of children who have behavior problems tend to have absent fathers; therefore, it is claimed, the absence of fathers in the home is the source of children's problematic behavior. But what this ignores is that if we reason forward, and consider all families with absent fathers, we find that only a minority of them have children with

problems; most fatherless children grow up to be reasonably well adjusted.[8] Blaming fathers for children's behavior problems allows policy makers to ignore other systemic social and financial factors that impede children's development. Similarly, most mass shooters have long-standing mental health issues, but only an infinitesimally small number of people with diagnosed mental illness become mass shooters. There are many good reasons to increase funds for mental health programs, but there is no reason to believe that this will lower the incidence of mass shootings. We should note here that accepting mental illness as a prime cause of mass shootings allows legislators to ignore possible third variables influencing the association between mental illness and shooting behavior—for example, the effect of easy access to firearms on lethal violence.

THE NEED FOR RESEARCH ON INTERVENTION TRIALS WITH CONTROL GROUPS

There are many reasons why investigators want to describe correlations between variables. The examples here are motivated by the desire to identify causes of negative outcomes in order to plan more effective interventions. For example, if father absence is a cause of children's behavior problems, then an intervention that increases fathers' involvement with their children could provide direct proof of the hypothesis that there is a causal connection.

But here we have a dilemma. I have argued that the correlational data do not support a causal hypothesis, and in the late twentieth century there were no interventions that successfully enhanced father involvement and assessed the outcomes for the children. That is, we did not have proof of the causal connection before attempting to intervene. In my view, correlational studies are a necessary first step to creating hypotheses about causal relationships, which can only be validated with systematic intervention research.[9]

But not just any intervention design will do. In the current political climate, with a scarcity of funds allocated to health and mental health services, there has been an increasing demand that funded programs be "evidence-based."[10] This demand has led to increasing attention to program evaluation—measuring participants at baseline and again after the intervention to determine whether they have made changes in the areas of functioning that the program was designed to produce.

The information from what is usually called a pre–post assessment design, in which participants improve after intervention, is useful and may help to buttress the service providers' hopes that they are on the right track. But it does not provide evidence that the intervention produced the positive changes (i.e., that there is a causal connection between what the intervention targets and the outcome achieved). What if the participants in a job-training program have a statistically significant higher income a year after the program ends? How can we rule out the possibility that these results were the product of an economic boom in which most families have higher incomes a year later? That is, the fact of increased income does not support a causal interpretation about the impact of the intervention until we know what happens to a comparable *untreated* group. Similarly, what if a group of children becomes less aggressive with their peers after their parents take a class on managing children's aggression? Again, we need to know whether children whose parents did not take such a class also became less aggressive as the children grew older in order to make the case that the declines in aggression are associated with improvements in parents' parenting strategies.

There is an additional, mostly unrecognized, problem with evaluations that provide information only from pre- and post-tests of an intervention sample. If these participants do not change over the period of the evaluation, the program providers are likely to conclude that the intervention had no effect. An untreated group followed over the same period of time, however, might show that the control participants changed in a negative direction and that the intervention was effective in preventing the decline.

I know that it is not always possible to do controlled experiments, especially experiments in which participants are randomly assigned to an intervention or to a no-treatment condition. To test the hypothesis that married parents provide a better environment for children's development, we cannot assign some single parents to the "get married" group and others to the "remain single" control group. In this case, there are responsible ways of gathering data to rule out alternative hypotheses so that we can come to a more informed decision about the impact of marriage on children. One method is to compare a sample of married and unmarried families measured on similar variables, followed over the same period of time. A second method is to measure a number of variables that could possibly influence A and B groups differently and "subtract them" from the outcome to see if any effect of the intervention remains. This method is only as powerful as the resourcefulness of the investigator in thinking about what factors outside of the intervention could have created the results.

In this chapter, I have made the assumption that decisions about what causes what, especially when considering an intervention, will be made on the basis of research data. But it is always legitimate and possible to make policy arguments based on moral or value grounds. For example, the recent decision by the Biden administration to forgive some portion of student loans was not made only on the basis of data, but rather because it was a good thing (or a politically expedient thing) to do. Many programs are funded on the basis of the funders' beliefs What I have been concerned with here are cases in which reporters or politicians buttress their beliefs with illegitimate conclusions about causality drawn from social science research. The key is for us to be explicit about when we are making arguments from a values perspective and when the conclusions are appropriately based on empirical data.

CONCLUSIONS

Both the political left and the political right have jumped to conclusions in debates about family policy based on the erroneous assumption that correlations support causal inferences. For example, from the right we hear: "Married families do better; let's get those single moms married or make it harder for couples to divorce." From the left we hear: "Unmarried mothers are poor, and poor families have difficulty; let's give them money and jobs." From the right we hear that reducing mass shootings involves increasing mental health resources. From the left we hear about limiting access to firearms.

What we need to remember is that explanations of how two facts are connected can seem simple, but they are often exceedingly complex. Unpacking the causal connection requires very thoughtful systematic research, accompanied by interventions, if possible, that test hypotheses about the direction of effects. I am aware that this kind of rigorous exploration takes time and that policy decisions must often be made in the absence of scientific proof that the proposed action will have the desired effects. What I want to convey to social service providers and policy makers is that causality is extremely difficult to nail down. We must all read accounts of research with a critical eye. The kind of complexity hidden within a "simple" correlation cannot be communicated or understood in simple sound bites.

NOTES

1. U.S. Census Bureau "Historical Living Arrangements of Children," November 29, 2021, www.census.gov/data/tables/time-series/demo/families/children.html.

2. National Fatherhood Initiative, *Father Facts* 8, 8th ed. (National Fatherhood Initiative, 2019).

3. S. Whitney, S. Prewett, Ze Wang, and C. Haigin, "Fathers' Importance in Adolescents' Academic Achievement," *International Journal of Child, Youth and Family Studies* 3, no 3–4 (2017): 101–126.

4.   R. R. Swisher and U. Shaw-Smith, "Paternal Incarceration and Adolescent Well-Being: Life Course Contingencies and Other Moderators," *Journal of Criminal Law & Criminology* 104, no. 4 (2015): 929–959.

5.   J. Peterson and J. Densley, *The Violence Project: How to Stop a Mass Shooting Epidemic* (New York: Abrams, 2021).

6.   L. J. Waite and M. Gallagher, *The Case for Marriage: Why Married People Are Happier, Healthier, and Better Off Financially* (New York: Doubleday, 2000), 260.

7.   P. A. Cowan, *The Family Context of Parenting in Children's Adaptation to Elementary School* (Mahwah, NJ: L. Erlbaum Associates, 2005).

8.   R. D. Parke, *Future Families: Diverse Forms, Rich Possibilities* (Malden, MA: John Wiley & Sons, 2013).

9.   For an example, see P. A. Cowan et al., "Promoting Fathers' Engagement with Children: Preventive Interventions for Low-Income Families," *Journal of Marriage and Family* 71, no. 3 (2009): 663–679.

10.   R. Haskins, "Evidence-Based Policy: The Movement, the Goals, the Issues, the Promise," *Annals of the American Academy of Political and Social Science* 678, no. 1 (2018): 8–37.

4

Uncovering Hidden Facts That Matter in Interpreting Individuals' Behaviors

An Ethnographic Lens

Linda M. Burton

As a social scientist who has conducted ethnographic research on low-income families for over two decades, I would argue that longitudinal ethnography moves us closer than most data collection methods to uncovering hidden facts that shape individuals' behaviors. Ethnographic research is a method of gathering data about individuals' thoughts, behaviors, and experiences in the context of their everyday lives. In ethnography, researchers engage systematically with those they are studying, participating in multiple domains of their lives and asking in-depth questions about the information they are learning.

Ethnographic research differs from surveys of human behaviors in several important ways. Surveys typically ask an individual a series of questions with fixed-option responses, usually at one point in time. Ethnographers record *over time* both what individuals say about their own behaviors and what they actually do. In the process, ethnographers build trusting relationships with those they study by listening without judgment and keeping promises of confidentiality. Ethnographers are typically able to uncover hidden data about respondents through long engagement with them and by *being there* when research participants are ready to reveal previously concealed information, on their own terms. In settings in which those studied are concerned about revealing too much of themselves, it is not until a long-term comfortable relationship has been established that research participants will share information that exposes potentially disparaging knowledge about them or important others in their social worlds.

In addition to uncovering hidden information, ethnography can also offer a check against exaggeration of such information. In the course of observing participants and doing informal yet in-depth questioning, ethnographers are able to gather many perspectives on the issue in question—and, hence, they can provide reliability checks on statements made by informants. Occasions can arise in which ethnographers experience contradictions between what people tell them and what ethnographers actually observe them doing or hear reported from others. By being there over time and participating in the social world being studied, ethnographers gain opportunities to uncover new, contradictory, and verifiable forms of data as they occur.

As a result, ethnographers' assessments of respondents usually go well beyond the "public face" and socially appropriate façades individuals tend to put on their responses to general questions. They also typically uncover patterns of behavior or experiences either that informants are ashamed to admit or that they may not even initially regard as relevant to helping ethnographers understand and interpret their lives. Such was the case in the Three-City Study ethnography of economically disadvantaged families in Boston, Chicago, and San Antonio. This multiyear team ethnography was designed to examine the impact of welfare reform in the lives of low-income African American, Latino, Hispanic, and non-Hispanic white families and revealed, beyond the ethnographers' initial estimates, that domestic violence and sexual abuse were far more central to understanding low-income women's day-to-day life experiences and vulnerability than most researchers had recognized.

More than two-thirds of the mothers who participated in the ethnography eventually disclosed that they had been sexually abused or had experienced domestic violence as children and/or as adults. Yet in most cases, it took more than six months of in-depth interviews with and participant observations of respondents for this information to come out, and in almost 20 percent of the cases, the information emerged only after ten to twenty-four months of the ethnographer "being there" with the mothers and their families. Three patterns of disclosing sexual abuse and domestic violence were identified in the ethnographic data: trigger topics disclosure, crisis or recent event disclosure, and ethnographer-prompted disclosure.

The *trigger topics* disclosure pattern occurred when mothers unexpectedly revealed sexual abuse and domestic violence histories to ethnographers when they were asked about topics such as health, intimate relationships, transportation, work history, and intergenerational caregiving. Seventy-one percent of disclosures conformed to this trigger topics pattern. For example, during an interview about her general health, a thirty-seven-year-old African American mother of three commented, "My pregnancy with Dante was hard because I was sick." The ethnographer neutrally asked for more information: "You were sick?"

> Yeah, he had been sleeping around and gave me gonorrhea. I'm still embarrassed talking about it. Sometimes I didn't want to sleep with him but he'd rape me. I told him I was gonna call the police and he said, "Go ahead. Ain't nobody gonna arrest me for wanting to be with my woman."

A different informant revealed experiences with abuse when the ethnographer asked how she had met her husband. Liza stated that this was a "funny story" and noted that she had met her husband just after ending a relationship with a man who had broken her nose. Yet another example of such unprompted disclosure was one that occurred during the twenty-third visit to the home of Delilah, a forty-year-old European American divorcée and mother of four children. The ethnographer was conducting a follow-up interview concerning Delilah's past and current work experiences, because Delilah had failed to mention particulars about her work history over the previous two years of interviews. At this point, Delilah finally told the ethnographer that she had once worked at a bank as a switchboard operator but quit when her former husband physically injured her. Delilah stated: "I went to work with a black eye. People at the bank noticed. When it happened a second time, I felt embarrassed coming to work, so I quit like cold turkey."

The second most common pattern of disclosure, accounting for almost 20 percent of the reports, was the *crisis* or *recent event* disclosure pattern. This pattern occurred when the ethnographer unexpectedly "walked in" on a domestic violence situation when she was visiting the participant, or when the participant experienced a sexual abuse or domestic violence episode a few days or weeks prior to the ethnographer's regularly scheduled visit. In both instances, the abuse situation was "fresh" in the minds of the mothers, and they chose to discuss it with their ethnographers in great detail. In most of these cases, the ethnographers had suspected abuse (as indicated in ethnographers' field notes and in discussions with their supervisors and team members), but they hadn't felt that they could directly ask the participant about it. For example, Janine, the ethnographer for Patrice, a twenty-eight-year-old European mother of two, describes the circumstances that led to Patrice's crisis-prompted disclosure:

> I arrived at Patrice's house 10 minutes before the interview only to find the streets covered with cops, patrol cars, and an ambulance. . . . Patrice was on the porch screaming, her face bloody and cut. The kids were running around everywhere

screaming and crying. . . . I feared that my worst suspicions about the prevalence of domestic violence in Patrice's life were about to be confirmed. . . . When I visited Patrice three weeks later, the flood gates opened without me asking. I listened as she told me everything about the incident and about other incidents of physical and sexual abuse that she had experienced since childhood.

The third pattern, *ethnographer-prompted* disclosure, occurred when ethnographers directly asked the mothers about their past and current experiences with sexual abuse or domestic violence. Ethnographers usually asked direct but open-ended questions about these topics in an interview if they noticed a behavioral reaction from mothers when discussing their intimate relationships with their partners. Only 10 percent of all disclosures came from such prompts.

It is also important to note that only 12 percent of the mothers who revealed sexual abuse and domestic violence experiences to the ethnographers did so during visits or participant observations that occurred in the first three months of their involvement in the study. Twenty-nine percent disclosed sexual abuse and domestic violence experiences after four to six months of visits with the ethnographers, 40 percent after seven to nine months of visits, and 19 percent after ten to twenty-four months of visits.

The prolonged wait before most informants revealed their history of sexual abuse and/or domestic violence reveals the importance of ethnographers' investing enough time and participation in the mothers' lives to reach "turning points" in their relationships. A turning point is the moment when participants trust ethnographers enough to share intimate, sensitive, and sometimes highly painful information. That such revelations often occurred almost accidentally or unintentionally suggests that ethnographic studies may capture much more of the actual incidence of violence in poor women's lives than official police reports or surveys, thus uncovering vital yet hidden facts that matter for accurately interpreting individuals' behaviors.

In Other Words

THE STUFF OF HOLIDAYS: HOW HOLIDAY OBJECTS TELL A SOCIOLOGICAL STORY ABOUT TODAY'S FAMILIES

Michelle Janning, December 10, 2018 / CCF@TSP

Holidays celebrated when it gets darker earlier—like Diwali, Hanukkah, Kwanzaa, and Christmas—can make people feel part of something larger. Maybe because people love celebrating holidays alongside those near and dear and those who may still enjoy being sentimental. Celebrating holidays reminds us that we are part of a group that shares our beliefs. But there are also the scrooges and cynics who barely tolerate the lights, songs, and other festive stuff. And there are those who feel lonely and removed from the collective support system, something that feels highly individualized; yet, perhaps paradoxically, feelings of loneliness are common during the holidays.

This time of year is when our "belonging" to something larger is paired with highly individualized stories of unique gifts, treasured mementos, and objects symbolizing good and bad things about family, past and present. Here I offer ways that seemingly individualized holiday objects tell an important collective story about roles and relationships in today's families, and about social processes that extend beyond any individual family story.

Values Associated with Materialism, Spoiled Kids, and "Good" Parenting Are Wrapped Up in Kids' Gifts

It's not hard to find buying guides for parents whose children want the latest toys and gadgets. It's also easy to find online advice columns about how best to give children gifts without spoiling them, giving in to a marketplace filled with inequalities, or damaging our natural world. But what often escapes our thinking is how social class may influence parents' gift-giving, and how kids' well-being can be affected by how they talk with classmates about the presents they received (or did not receive) after winter break.

Sociologist Allison Pugh reminds us that while it's pretty universal for parents to want to give their kids gifts, sometimes parents give in to their children's material desires and spend more than they can afford (Pugh calls this "symbolic indulgence"). Importantly, in these cases, parents are trying to give kids what they need to feel like they belong. For better or worse, consumer culture powerfully influences parents.

But if we only focus on the powerful marketplace, we miss important stories about how parents use holiday gift-giving to help their children fit into a peer culture where status is highly valued and is the currency through which children's dignity and belonging are fostered. And we may miss how parents from different economic backgrounds vary in how much they can give their kids the gift of "fitting in." This sociological finding adds complexity to claims about spoiled kids and materialistic parents.

Annually Displaying Cherished Items from Lost Loved Ones Reflects Family Role Expectations

Saving cherished items is a social act, partly because decisions to cherish something are shaped by values and experiences and by our perceptions of others' expectations surrounding those items. When giving talks about my book *The Stuff of Family Life*, the most common topic in the Q&A sessions afterward is about whether adult children will cherish objects their aging parents want to give them. Sometimes children's reluctance to be excited about antique holiday ornaments from beloved grandparents is seen as reluctance to be connected to past family. The adult child may not see the ornaments as "stand-ins" for the grandparents, but parents may see them as substitutes for grandparents rather than symbols. To preserve ornaments is to preserve memories of grandparents; to dispose of the ornaments is also to dispose of the persons. Adult children are expected to demonstrate family loyalty by desiring the ornaments. This can be hard when adult children's values about having too much stuff, or beliefs that objects are unnecessary for memories of loved ones, are stronger than their values about being dutiful to parents.

Less contentiously, sometimes adult children will save holiday objects from parents who passed away. An annual display of the holiday objects from deceased parents can honor past family influence on present family. A father's menorah may be displayed during Hanukkah to remind someone of the father; the holiday is the vehicle for that memory even if it is not explicitly celebrated.

Holiday decorations have biographies. They enter our lives, are participants in life transitions, and get lost, broken, or forgotten. They can serve as mementos. Whether old things from a grandparent or new things, they are meant to create an *imagined future nostalgia*, something I discuss in my research on the preservation of private love letters. This means they are meant to be shared with children so they know the origins of their family story.

To "hand down" a cherished holiday object entails decisions about loyalty, memory, and longevity, not to mention the object's aesthetic beauty (or lack thereof). So, when next you hear about a baby's first [insert winter holiday item here], remember it is not just about that object. It's also about expectations that it may be saved for when that "baby" leaves home and needs to figure out whether to cherish or dispose of it, which may require negotiating with others' expectations about the preservation of those memories in physical form.

Object-Centered Holiday Rituals Help Families Find Stability in a Time of Uncertainty

We live in a time of perceived uncertainty. Our everyday lives are moving fast, news headlines showcase political and economic turmoil, and our family structures are changing. Whether because of family border separations, poverty-inflicted adverse childhood experiences, or estrangement, people from varied political perspectives perceive the family and social life as more precarious than ever.

At the same time, we love rituals that offer stability. But we also live in a time that historian Elizabeth Pleck describes as post-sentimental—a reaction to the over-sentimentalization of holidays and the blues that sometimes accompany them. There is also a desire to be more inclusive about what holidays and rituals may be desirable and best represent the diversity of families who are celebrating. The rituals of gift-giving, displaying or using special objects that appear only during holidays, and expanding the repertoire of "acceptable" holiday objects and their use, all strengthen the claim that we seek rituals to clarify and stabilize our lives. This search for stability can appear via use of old objects symbolizing long-held traditions as well as new and innovative objects that create new traditions that more accurately tell the story of the varied ways that family life takes place today. In both cases, the objects serve as tools for rituals that provide glue in a climate where family life can seem fragile.

How Is This about More Than Just My Family?

Many other questions surrounding objects arise during the holidays, including whether digital gifts are as "real" as physical ones wrapped in shiny paper, whether some gifts violate norms about privacy (are underpants too personal a gift from my in-laws?), or how holiday décor, like any display in the domestic realm, calls to mind the gendered division of household labor (do women decorate indoors and men hang the lights outside?). I am sure you can think of objects in your family that carry deeper meanings this time of year.

Here I showcased a few ways to think about individualized experiences with holiday objects—dilemmas about spending and spoiling, attachment to relatives with or without retaining their possessions, and the use of objects in holiday rituals. Holding a holiday candle is never just about the candle. It also is never just about that one particular family. The candle and the person holding it are collective topics larger than any of us or our families: the marketplace where candles are made, the collective belief system that the candle represents, the light of someone no longer alive, and the tendency to value rituals as a form of social "glue" in times of uncertainty and perceived loss of social connectedness. Holidays remind us that our family stories are both private and public. Our unique gifts tell a collective story about today's families. ◼

5

Racism, Family Structure, and Black Families

Deadric T. Williams, Caroline Sanner, Todd Jensen, and Laura Simon

In April 2018, Dr. Ben Carson, the secretary of Housing and Urban Development (HUD), visited Memphis, Tennessee, to discuss the fiftieth anniversary of the Fair Housing Act of 1968, which outlawed discrimination in housing. In a conversation about the HUD program, an unwed Black mother shared the obstacles she endured living in poverty and described how the program enabled her to own a house and maintain employment. In response, Dr. Carson offered unsolicited advice for avoiding poverty, including finishing high school, getting married, and waiting until marriage to have children.[1] This argument is often referred to as the "success sequence," which highlights a series of steps whereby individuals can avoid or escape poverty and be placed on a path toward self-sufficiency.[2]

Carson's words and the success sequence continue to reflect many Americans' sentiments about unmarried mothers in the United States. For example, according to a Pew Research Center (2018) report, 66 percent of Americans believe that "more single women having children without a partner is bad for society." The statistics were more dramatic across social groups: 70 percent of White Americans, 65 percent of Black Americans, 83 percent of Republicans, and 56 percent of Democrats agree with that statement. For a similar question about "the reasons that Black people in the U.S. may have a harder time getting ahead than Whites," 57 percent of Black adults and 55 percent of White adults attributed it to family instability (Pew Research Center 2016). Even more, using data from the 2010, 2012, and 2014 General Social Surveys (GSS), researchers found that differences in life outcomes between Black and White Americans were believed to be a result of differences in "family upbringing" (Hunt et al. 2022).

The idea that family life is a "cause" of Black inequality dates to the Reconstruction Era and, despite no empirical evidence (Darity 2011), continues to permeate the American imagination. In other words, Black families are blamed for Black disadvantage.

Public opinion about why racial inequalities exist have shifted away from open endorsements of biological inferiority toward endorsements of cultural "deficiencies," such as differences in family values (Hunt 2007). Within this shift, family structure, such as whether children grow up in a two-parent family or single-parent family, rose to prominence as a key explanation for understanding inequality among Black families (Brady 2019; Darity 2011; Williams 2019). For example, in 1965, on the heels of the Civil Rights Acts of 1964 and the Voting Rights Act of 1965, a report from the U.S. Department of Labor leaked to the press wherein Assistant Secretary of Labor Daniel Patrick Moynihan (1965) argued that the next major effort in achieving equality for Black individuals was to address the instability of Black families. Originally titled *The Negro Family: The Case for National Action* but now often referred to as the Moynihan Report, the document provides a poignant example of blaming Black families for Black disadvantage. It effectively frames racial inequality as the result of personal values and choices, thereby overlooking the ways in which racism shapes our social systems and the associated systemic factors that influence both family structure and family decision-making processes. The report incited both accolades and criticism from the public and scholars (Gans 2011; Haskins 2009; Wilson 2009); nonetheless, the argument took root and would go on to shape generations of policy and scholarship.

Despite family structure continuing to persist as a popular explanation for understanding Black-White inequality, prior research shows that family structure does not fully account for the racial gap in several outcomes, including wealth, relationship quality, and education (Addo and Lichter 2013; Brown et al. 2017; Iceland 2019; Maralani 2013). In other words, being raised in a two-parent family does not create a level playing field across racialized groups; it does not give Black youth the same advantage it gives to their White peers. Said differently, when Black children are raised in two-parent households, it does not increase their chances of certain life outcomes (for example, finishing high school on time) as significantly as it does for White children. This is because living with married parents does not protect Black youth from the compounding disadvantages of structural racism (Cross 2020). And yet, scholars, laypersons, and policy makers alike maintain that the "breakdown of the two-parent family" is largely responsible for racial inequality.

The United States has a long tradition of pointing to individual or family characteristics as responsible for why people struggle or thrive. For the last several decades, social problems resulting from systemic injustices have been blamed on changes in family structure—namely, the rise in single-parent families. If more children were raised in two-parent families, the narrative goes, then children and society would fare better. Researchers have spent considerable effort exploring this premise. As family forms have diversified over the past half-century, scholars have frequently studied family structure in connection with individual and family well-being (Umberson and Thomeer 2020). Much of this research compares children in married-parent families to children in single-parent families or stepfamilies on a host of developmental outcomes, such as educational attainment, economic well-being, and physical and mental health. Consistent with the popular narrative that children in two-parent families fare best, researchers generally hypothesize that children raised outside of nuclear families will be at higher risk for negative outcomes. Prior studies generally appeal to one of four theoretical explanations as to why: economic resources, parenting, stress and instability, and selection effects (Acock and Demo 1994; Brown 2010; Cross 2020; Jensen and Sanner 2021). Although these arguments don't consider the many social forces at play and have varying levels of empirical support, they offer insight into how scholars and policy makers often view the impact of family structure on individual and children's well-being.

The purpose of this chapter is to highlight *why* family structure continues to permeate the American imagination as a "cause" of Black families' inequitable conditions. We address this question by using critical race theory to center the social construction of race and show how family structure narratives reinforce racial ideologies and racial structures that maintain racial domination and oppression. We conclude this chapter by offering a productive path forward for the study of Black family life.

CRITICAL RACE THEORY

Scholars, laypersons, and policy makers assume family structure has universal effects—that is, regardless of race, marriage has positive effects for families and children, and nonmarital childbearing has negative effects for families and children. This assumption, however, does not adequately reflect findings from a growing number of empirical studies (Baker et al. 2021; Cross 2020; Williams and Baker 2021). In this section, we draw on critical race theory to understand why marriage arguments for Black-White inequality persist and to offer a path forward for future research.

Critical race theory (CRT) focuses on *why* racial inequality persists even after the passage of important civil rights legislation (Delgado and Stefancic 2017). A group of legal scholars formed CRT as a school of thought to challenge the idea that the American legal system treated "race" neutrally in matters of law (Crenshaw et al. 1995). Over time, CRT would go on to influence many other academic disciplines, including education, philosophy, sociology, and social work. Increasingly, scholars are employing CRT to study family processes (Burton et al. 2010; Lemmons and Johnson 2019; D. Williams 2020; D. T. Williams and Baker 2021). CRT's central focus is on how structural conditions such as laws and policies, as well as institutions like the legal and education systems and the family, maintain racial inequality in the United States. CRT has several tenets. For this chapter, we focus on two: (1) race is socially constructed, and (2) racism is a permanent feature of the United States.

The Social Construction of Race

In contrast to racial essentialism—the idea that racial groups are biologically real or have innate cultural differences—race as a social construction recognizes the concept of "race," and thus "racial groups," as a *social invention* created specifically to justify domination (Bonilla-Silva 1997, 2017; Zuberi 2003; Zuberi and Bonilla-Silva 2008). These opposing perspectives differ in their understanding of the connection between race and racism. A *racial essentialist* perspective posits that the existence of biologically distinct racial groups makes racism possible. In contrast, a *social constructionist* perspective understands that racial groups were invented according to superficial physical characteristics *for the purpose of oppressing certain people*—namely, people racialized as Black. In other words, racism makes the idea of race possible.

Social constructionists understand racism as composed of both ideologies, including beliefs about the superiority and inferiority of racialized groups, and structures, including discriminatory laws, policies, and social practices (Bonilla-Silva 2017; Golash-Boza 2016). Ideologies and structures reinforce each other, and thus operate in tandem. For example, racist attitudes toward people racialized as Black (ideologies) fuel the development of racist policies and practices, including Jim Crow laws, redlining, racial profiling in policing, the war on drugs, and mass incarceration. These policies and practices destabilize Black families and create a rise in single-parent households. The rise in Black single-parent households, in turn, fuels a belief that Black families are inherently distinct from White families in their family values or family upbringings (ideologies), thus reinforcing the *racial essentialist* notion that racial groups have inherent biological, cultural, or behavioral differences between them. Consequently, ideologies and structures coalesce to both create the idea that racialized groups are biologically real and also justify and legitimize racialized hierarchies. In short, the *magnum opus* of racism (ideologies and structures) is the invention of race itself. This approach to racism moves away from thinking about racism as an individual flaw and toward understanding racism as a system (Jones 2000).

Racism Is a Permanent Feature of the United States

This CRT tenet—racism is a permanent feature of the United States—focuses on stability and change. For instance, although ideologies and structures changed from overt (for example, genocide, slavery, Jim Crow laws) to covert (color-blind racism, or an insistence that one does not "see race"), the results are the same: significant racial inequality across many categories of well-being between racial groups in the United States, including health, wealth, income, employment, and mortality. Given that racism is composed of both ideologies and structures, we can highlight how structural institutions such as marriage help preserve the hierarchical racial order. To illustrate the extent to which family structure reinforces racial ideologies and racial structures, we contextualize Black families across two historical contexts—Reconstruction and the post–Civil Rights era.

Reconstruction. Using family structure to account for racial inequality began during emancipation. Historians, legal scholars, and sociologists present marriage as a racialized institution by highlighting the unique intersection between racism and the institution of marriage (Franke 1999; Frankel 1999; Hill 2006; Hunter 2017; Lenhardt 2014, 2015, 2016). For example, marriage as a legal enterprise was co-opted by the state during Reconstruction to incorporate formerly enslaved persons into American citizens (Franke 1999; Hunter 2017). As the status of people racialized as Black shifted from enslaved persons to freepersons after the Civil War, marriage was a way to "civilize" formerly enslaved persons and to reestablish a system of control. The state encouraged African Americans to marry, in part, to relinquish responsibility for providing support for formerly enslaved persons (Franke 1999). After generations of denying enslaved persons access to legal marriage, though many married by custom if not by law, the federal government then pressed Black families to enter into legal marriage and conform to the patriarchal norm of a family, one headed by a man who was the public representative of his wife and children. However, establishing men as "head of household" was problematic for Black families, as many formerly enslaved persons were faced with new forms of exploitation and subordination that limited Black men's labor market participation (Bloome and Ang 2020; Hill 2006). Moreover, those who violated marriage policies, including men and women living together while unmarried, were incarcerated and fined (Franke 1999; Lenhardt 2014, 2015). For Black families during Reconstruction, marriage was an illusion of freedom. Many Black women viewed the institution of marriage as another form of state-sponsored oppression akin to slavery (Hill 2006; Lenhardt 2015). In response to widespread racial oppression and domination, Black Americans experienced a diverse set of family forms, including marriage, cohabitation, and "sweethearts" (Billingsley 1994; Frankel 1999; Hill 2006). (For more on marriage, gender, and reconstruction, see Franklin, Chapter 8.)

The Post–Civil Rights Era. The diverse array of family forms among Black families reflects adaptive strategies in response to omnipresent racism and patriarchy. Yet scholars, laypersons, and policy makers interpreted these strategies as deficiencies (Neubeck and Cazenave 2002; Roberts 2017; Saito 2009). Deficiency narratives were especially operative in the post–Civil Rights era, largely due to antidiscrimination laws. These laws created the idea that racism was no longer a salient explanation for understanding inequality for Black families (Kendi 2017). Specifically, if the general assumption is that racism no longer exists, then persistent inequality among Black families reflects their own lack of individual effort.

In the twentieth and twenty-first centuries, family structure narratives continued (and continue) to reinforce racial ideologies and racial structures and policies. For example, in the 1980s, the rise of neoliberal ideas of individualism—the notion that we are all personally responsible for our own well-being—reinforced Americans' notion of inequality as stemming from an individual's lack of effort. Thus, racist tropes like the "welfare queen" served the purpose of calling into question people's "deservingness" of welfare generosity.

In the 1990s and 2000s, such racial ideologies persisted, especially as marriage rates declined and nonmarital childbearing rose. This rise in single-parent households activated racist attitudes and set in motion a series of racist policies. For instance, in the mid-1990s, welfare reform focused on targeting individual behaviors, including reducing nonmarital childbearing, and restricting financial resources such as those provided by the Temporary Assistance for Needy Families (TANF) and the Welfare-to-Work (WtW) grant programs. The mid-2000s saw an explicit focus on promoting marriage as a solution to poverty via the Healthy Marriage Initiative or supporting policies that encouraged marriage and discouraged nonmarital childbearing. Marriage promotion efforts, however, do not yield demonstrably favorable outcomes (Wood et al. 2012), likely in part because studies show that low-income unmarried adults value marriage and commitment *more* than their high-income counterparts but see financial stability as an important precursor to getting married (Edin and Kefalas 2005; Gibson-Davis et al. 2005; Trail and Karney 2012). (For more on marriage promotion programs, see Heath and Randles, Chapter 21.) Despite the failure of marriage initiatives and related programs such as Building Strong Families, the idea that marriage serves as a mechanism to reduce racial inequality persists. Ben Carson's comments, with which we opened this chapter, are an example of the persistence of the family structure narrative that blames individuals for inequality.

CHARTING A PATH FORWARD: RETHINKING RACIAL INEQUALITY AND BLACK FAMILIES

Heterogeneity in Black Americans' family structure reflects a long history of racial oppression and domination in the United States. As a response to omnipresent White supremacy and patriarchy, many Black families developed adaptive family strategies (Lenhardt 2014). Presenting marriage as universally advantageous suggests that oppressed groups can thrive as much as White families do if they "just get married" and obscures how structural racism upholds Black-White inequality regardless of marital status (Bratter and Zuberi 2001; Burton et al. 2010; Few-Demo 2007, 2014; Letiecq 2019; Walsdorf et al. 2020). In this concluding section, we highlight the role of structural racism in shaping racial inequality by paying attention to historical legacies and the index of disproportionality.

Historical Legacies

When understanding contemporary racial inequality, researchers, laypersons, and policy makers must not ignore the atrocities of American racism. Instead, discussions and investigations of racial inequality must include an open and honest depiction of Black families in the United States. One way to increase our understanding of Black families is to understand the extent to which the legacy of slavery and redlining have yielded contemporary inequitable outcomes—including White advantages. For example, scholars are increasingly examining the impact of the legacy of slavery (measured as the proportion of enslaved persons relative to the total population in 1860) on racial disparities in poverty (R. Baker 2022; R. Baker and O'Connell 2022; O'Connell 2012) and racial health disparities (Kramer et al. 2017). There is more and more research that not only examines Black disadvantage but also accounts for White advantage. One recent study, for example, found that counties that relied on slave labor yielded relatively positive outcomes for White Americans (Reece 2020).

Also promising, researchers are examining how historic redlining has contributed to inequality. Redlining involves denying services that help people have a better life, like bank loans or health care, to people because of their race and ethnicity. In the 1930s, federal housing policies used redlining to keep Black people out of historically White neighborhoods. These policies standardized racial residential segregation. Recent research shows that historical redlining is associated with adverse health outcomes for Black Americans (Krieger et al. 2020; Lynch et al. 2021). These measures have the potential to help Americans understand racial inequality not as a result of the personal values and choices of Black families, but as the result of generations of socially structured oppression.

Contemporary Indicators of Structural Racism

In addition to greater understanding of the impact of historical legacies on modern families, more work is being done to understand the impact of contemporary indicators of structural racism. In this work, scholars have conceptualized structural racism as a multifaceted, interconnected, and institutionalized system of inequality that is especially harmful for Black Americans (Reskin 2012). One way to measure structural racism is to examine the extent to which there are extreme racial inequities, or larger differences across racialized groups, in education, poverty, incarceration, housing, and racial residential segregation at either the state, city, or county level. Under conditions of racial *equity*, we would not expect to see racialized patterns in outcomes of well-being. If members of racialized groups are highly concentrated into the top or bottom distribution of an outcome, racial inequities are readily apparent. Researchers use these measures, called *concentration at the extremes* or the *index of disproportionality*, as proxies for structural racism. To do this, researchers merge different data sources, such as data from the U.S. Census, with individual-level data. Studies that use these approaches demonstrate that these indicators are associated with adverse health outcomes for Black Americans (for reviews, see Braveman et al. 2022; Hardeman et al. 2022). Although these studies focus on minority health disparities, incorporating these factors into family inequality research may prove fruitful by showing the impact of these indicators on family formation.

CONCLUSION

The purpose of this chapter was to ask why family structure remains a dominant framework for understanding Black inequality. Despite the studies that consistently show marriage has greater returns for people racialized as White than people racialized as Black, the idea that marriage will "fix" the problems faced by Black families remains a popular narrative. We believe this is because this narrative reinforces individualism and personal responsibility, which, in turn, maintains racist ideologies and structures over time. Unfortunately, these ideas represent essentialist understandings of race—that is, the notion that racialized groups are biologically real and inherently distinct. Given that race is socially constructed, researchers, teachers, and students should be explicit in their conceptualization of race in their research studies and in their classrooms. A growing number of scholars are beginning to frame family structure within a racialized context (Cross, Fomby, and Letiecq 2022; Vasquez-Tokos and Yamin 2021; Walsdorf et al. 2020). We encourage people who study and talk about racial inequality to incorporate structural racism in their research and discussions. Family scholars, policy makers, and laypersons alike can make strides in our collective understandings of race and family life by being up front about race and racism in the United States, understanding how race and racism shape the narrative about family structure, paying attention to how family formation narratives shape social policy, and centering at the margins—that is, shifting the viewpoint away from the dominant group's perspective toward Black families and their social contexts.

NOTES

1.   NewsOne, "Ben Carson Tells a Black Woman to Escape Poverty She Needs to Get Married," April 11, 2018, newsone.com/3792016/ben-carson-hud-poverty-marriage/

2.   Brian Goesling, Hande Inanc, and Angela Rachidi, *Success Sequence: A Synthesis of the Literature*, OPRE Report 2020-41 (Washington, DC: Office of Planning, Research, and Evaluation, Administration for Children and Families, U.S. Department of Health and Human Services, 2020).

In Other Words

THE MOYNIHAN REPORT, THEN AND NOW

William H. Chafe, March 5, 2015

Few research documents in recent history have made as smashing an impact as Daniel Patrick Moynihan's study of the black family fifty years ago. The report, *The Negro Family: The Case for National Action*, was written by Moynihan, then assistant secretary of labor, as a fast-track shortcut to force the Johnson administration to take immediate action to improve the plight of poor black Americans through federally financed antipoverty programs. Dismayed by the fact that more than a third of African Americans lived in poverty, Moynihan intended the report to stimulate efforts to achieve economic and social equality.

Yet by framing the report as a description of the breakdown of the black family, Moynihan ended up fueling a bitter controversy about family forms and gender roles instead of contributing to a constructive discussion of how to address the need for more black jobs. He argued that "at the heart of the deterioration of the fabric of Negro society is the deterioration of the Negro family," which he described as a "tangle of pathology." Tragically, the main impact of the report was to initiate a huge debate about family life in black America, while doing little to strengthen antipoverty programs.

Moynihan made two errors of analysis. First, he traced the prevalence of single-parent households in the black community to the experience of slavery, which, he contended, resulted in the absence of strong family traditions on plantations. Not only did white masters discourage or forbid marriages; they also split up couples by selling one partner into slavery elsewhere. Their actions demeaned the status and stature of black men, creating a disorganized "matriarchal" culture of fragmented families.

In the first instance, Moynihan ignored history when he traced the prevalence of unmarried families in northern ghettoes back to the ongoing legacy of slavery. As soon as emancipation occurred, millions of black couples flocked to churches to get married. The ways that children, aunts and uncles, and husbands and wives worked to piece together a living, the collective struggle to build houses, farm the land, get an education—this has all been noted by scholars as one of the signal strengths of black life once freedom was achieved. By placing all the blame for black family issues in the 1960s on the institution of slavery, Moynihan ignored the specific conditions that created growing numbers of single-parent families in northern black neighborhoods in the mid-twentieth century.

Second, the report's claim that "broken" families were the central cause of black poverty massively oversimplified the complex relationships between socioeconomic trends and changing family forms. By attributing black poverty to the death of married-couple, male-headed families in northern ghettoes, Moynihan seemed to suggest that if blacks would only get and stay married they would cease to be poor, an absurdity that paved the way for later attempts to substitute marriage promotion for job creation.

Tragically, Moynihan's ignorance of history and confusion of cause and correlation deflected attention from the *real* issue Moynihan was concerned with—focusing federal monies on urban jobs for blacks—and fanned instead a rancorous, racially charged dispute over family values that continues to deform our discussion of poverty policy.

Since the 1960s, we have witnessed the growth of a much more sizeable black middle and professional class, largely a function of the 500 percent increase in black college graduates that occurred after the enactment of the 1964 Civil Rights Act and the 1965 Voting Rights Act. But as a huge proportion of black people remain in poverty, inequality of socioeconomic opportunity has also been rising among all racial-ethnic groups and family forms.

It is time for us to get back to the original *intent* of the Moynihan report: to answer the question of how we should act as a people and a government to address the problems of poverty and inequality. Moynihan himself answered that question in a speech he wrote for President Lyndon Johnson to deliver in June 1965 as a commencement address for Howard University:

> Jobs are part of the answer. . . . Decent homes in decent surroundings and a chance to learn—an equal chance to learn—are part of the answer. Welfare and social programs better designed to hold families together are part of the answer. Care for the sick is part of the answer. An understanding heart by all Americans is another big part of the answer.

It is a sad irony that Moynihan's report has provided so many politicians with an excuse to avoid implementing the solutions that Moynihan himself supported. ▐■

PART TWO

How Did We Get Here?

6

The Evolution of American Families

Stephanie Coontz

When most Americans think about "the traditional family," they picture a male breadwinner nuclear family where the husband earns the money needed to provide food and shelter and the wife cares for the children, cleans house, and prepares meals. But this family form is arguably the least traditional family in all of history. Among the band-level societies in which human beings spent 90 percent of our existence as a species, women were full co-providers for their families. In most traditional band-level societies in the Americas, Africa, and elsewhere, women contributed from half to almost two-thirds of the food that group members consumed. The groups that hunted big game tended to be male, but a woman was not dependent on her husband for meat protein, because no matter which individual hunter actually killed the animal, its flesh was typically divided up among all group members. And with few exceptions, such band-level societies seem to have accorded women equal autonomy with men, if not always equal prestige.[1]

A PREHISTORY OF GENDER AND LEGITIMACY

Male dominance became the rule in the socially stratified and economically unequal societies that emerged about 8,000 years ago, but that was not because women had become their husbands' economic dependents. In the patriarchal household economies of premodern England and colonial America, wives were integrally involved in producing the necessities of life. A woman in those days did not wait for her husband to "bring home the bacon." She helped butcher the pig, cure the bacon, and sell whatever the family did not use at the local market. The term *male breadwinner* did not even exist before the nineteenth century. Until then, when a man described himself as his family's "sole provider," he was not boasting but asking for sympathy because his "yoke-mate" was unable or unwilling to pull her share of the load.

In those days, married women generally delegated child care and cleaning to slightly older children or to the many single women who worked as servants in married couples' households until they and their potential mates had accumulated enough capital to start a farm or business of their own. Unlike today, women typically *increased* the time they spent producing and marketing goods when they married, rather than reducing their commitment to the workforce. Only in the nineteenth century did the White middle class of England and America develop a family system in which women withdrew from the larger economy to focus on raising their children and creating a domestic retreat from the pressures of wage labor and the competitive stresses of business.

Diverse families and marital arrangements have been the norm throughout history. In many societies, men with the greatest wealth and social status typically married more than one wife. But anthropologists have also recorded more than fifty societies where polyandry—a woman having more than one husband— was practiced. And among the Mosuo or Na of China, the family arrangements of most people traditionally did not include marriage at all. In this society, even today, brothers and sisters form the central family unit. The siblings do not have sex—indeed, the incest taboo is so strong that it even prohibits them from having intense emotional discussions. But the children the women bear by various lovers (who often only visit them at night) get more material support and socialization from their uncles than from their biological fathers.

In parts of precolonial West Africa, males who presented themselves in what their culture considered a "feminine" manner had special status as spiritual leaders. Among some patrilineal African groups, a woman could become a "female husband" by taking a wife. This was not typically based on same-sex intimacy but was one of the few ways a woman could wield the same social and economic clout as a man. The children the wife brought to the marriage or bore by various lovers were considered part of the family of the female husband, who was entitled to their labor and loyalty and from whom they derived their status and roles.

But many societies also accepted marriages based on same-sex intimacy, though typically each person in the union specialized in the kind of work and ritual activities characteristic of the "other" sex. The idea that roles in marriage and in society at large should be gender neutral is a very recent innovation.

More than one hundred different Native American societies acknowledge the existence of third gender or "two-spirit" individuals. Sometimes these people married persons of the same biological sex, sometimes not. There were many variations in attitudes and practices, but all told, there was more flexibility and fluidity among Indigenous groups than in the European societies that colonized the Americas.[2]

The historical and cross-cultural diversity of family life also extends to the emotional meanings attached to families and the psychological dynamics within them. For example, what is now considered healthy parent-child bonding in our society (see Coleman in Chapter 30 of this volume) may be viewed as selfishness, narcissism, or pathological isolation by cultures that stress child exchange and fostering as ways of cementing social ties. In Polynesia, eastern Oceania, the Caribbean, and the West Indies (and also in sixteenth-century Europe and colonial America), offering your child to friends, neighbors, or other kin for prolonged co-residence or even adoption was not considered abandonment but was rather a mark of parental responsibility, ensuring that the child developed access to support systems and social knowledge beyond what the immediate family could provide.

Other societies were more restricted in their emotional commitments. In kinship societies that trace descent exclusively through the maternal or paternal line, rather than through both parents, children are considered part of the family of only one spouse, and spouses themselves often do not count as family. In ancient China, men were often told that "you have only one family, but you can always get another wife." Among many matrilineal societies, by contrast, children gain their social status through their mother's descent lines, and children have closer ties with their uncles than with their biological fathers.

Through much of European history, a child born outside an approved marriage was a *filius nullius*—legally a child of no one, with a claim on no one. Not until 1968 did the U.S. Supreme Court rule that children born out of wedlock had the right to collect debts owed to their parents, sue for the wrongful death of a parent, and inherit family holdings. By contrast, the Indigenous societies of northeastern North America did not distinguish between "legitimate" and "illegitimate" children. When a Jesuit missionary told a Montagnais-Naskapi Indian living in what is now Canada that he should keep tighter control over his wife in order to ensure that the children she bore were "his," the native found this attitude contemptible: "You French people love only your own children," he replied, "but we love all the children of our tribe."

FAMILY SYSTEMS OF EARLY AMERICA

In sixteenth- and seventeenth-century America, three very different systems of social and personal reproduction were practiced by Native American kinship societies, the conquering Europeans, and the Africans brought as captives by the

Europeans. Each of those systems had its own sources of diversity, but overall, they had three very different patterns of organization.

Native Families

At the time of European conquest of the New World, the Native societies of North America used family ties to organize nearly all the political, military, and economic transactions that in Europe were becoming regulated by the state. Kinship rules and marital alliances regulated an individual's place in the overall social network, establishing who owed what to whom in terms of producing and sharing resources and fulfilling interpersonal obligations. Some groups were egalitarian bands with only situational leadership; others were led by elite lineages whose descendants had special authority. Some groups, such as the Cherokee, had a male governing body for times of war (and the influence of such groups grew once Native Americans became engaged in regular conflicts with settlers), but most of the time village elders, representing different kin groups and usually including women, made decisions. The Haudenosaunee, or "people of the longhouse," often called the Iroquois Confederacy, established a united confederacy of five formerly disparate and sometimes antagonistic groups (the Mohawk, Oneida, Onondaga, Cayuga, and Seneca) either right before or during their first contact with Europeans. In the 1720s, the Tuscarora joined, and the group became known as the Six Nations. But even in these more complex Native societies, kin obligations organized not just the production and distribution of goods but also the negotiation of conflicts and the administration of justice. Murder, for example, was an offense not against the state but against the kin group, and it was therefore the responsibility and right of kin to punish the perpetrator.[3]

Not all Indigenous groups were the same, and they were experiencing their own historical transformations long before European explorers arrived. Some groups were nomadic hunters and gatherers, lacking private property. Other groups constructed permanent or semipermanent settlements, sometimes surrounded with what appear to be protective or defensive structures, and these predate contact with Europeans. A few pre-contact Native groups had significant interpersonal inequality, with some families or lineages possessing special access to authority or wealth, or the population being divided into elites, commoners, and enslaved persons (usually captured from other groups). Interestingly, in many of these groups, elites maintained their social status by *giving away* much of their wealth in both small- and large-scale feasts and rituals of redistribution.

Certain Native groups held management rights to specific territories, but they did not have the concept or belief that land could be individually and permanently sold and access to it monopolized. They might, however, accept gifts in exchange for the right to use land. This led to many misunderstandings and much hostility between Native peoples and settlers. Native peoples were astonished when the Europeans they had given permission to settle somewhere fenced off traditional hunting grounds or allowed their cows and pigs to root among their clam beds and cornfields. Settlers invented the term "Indian givers" to describe what they saw as Indians reneging on deals the Native peoples never imagined they had made.

The nuclear family's lack of private property meant Native families had less economic autonomy than European households. On the other hand, the lack of a state gave Native families more political autonomy, because in most groups people were not bound to follow a leader for any longer than they cared to do so.

Contact with the European colonists was devastating to Native family systems. Having no domestic animals such as pigs, chickens, or cattle, the Native peoples had no acquired immunities to the diseases associated with such animals. Massive epidemics sometimes killed more than half a group's members, decimating kin networks and tearing apart the social fabric of life. Many Native groups were either exterminated or driven onto marginal land that did not support traditional methods of social organization and subsistence. Even where Native societies successfully defended themselves, armed conflict with settlers elevated the role of young males at the expense of elders and women. Furthermore, the fur trade and the slave trade gave some Native groups a greater incentive to raid or conquer other groups, and the introduction of firearms and horses increased their ability to do so. Meanwhile, European traders, colonial political officials, and Christian missionaries tried to undermine the authority of extended kinship and community groups and to increase the authority of men over "their" wives and children.

But Native collective traditions were surprisingly resilient, and European Americans spent the entire nineteenth century trying to extinguish them. They passed laws requiring Native peoples to hold property as individuals or nuclear families rather than as larger kinship groups. From 1819 to 1969, the U.S. government ran more than four hundred boarding schools across the country, often coercing American Indian, Alaska Native, and Native Hawaiian parents into sending their children there. The schools forcibly cut the children's hair, gave them English names, harshly punished the use of Native languages, religions, and cultural practices, and largely limited the children's education to preparation for manual labor or domestic employment. In addition, research in the 1960s revealed that almost a third of American Indian children had been placed in adoptive homes, foster homes, or institutions, with 90 percent of them being raised by non-Natives. Their Native relatives were often labeled "unfit" because of their poverty or housing conditions, not because of maltreatment.[4]

European Families in North America

The European families that came to North America were products of an older aristocratic, patriarchal order that was being challenged by a developing market economy and international mercantile system. The way their communities organized production, exchange, land ownership, and social control put Europeans on a collision course with Native patterns of existence. Europeans also operated within the framework of a centralized state whose claims to political authority and whose notion of territorial boundaries and national interests had no counterpart among American Indians.

Colonial families had far more extensive property and inheritance rights than Native families, but they were also subject to stringent controls by the state and church. Wealthy colonial families had far fewer obligations to share surpluses than Native Americans, so right from the beginning there were more substantial differences in wealth and resources among colonial families than among the Indigenous peoples.

Yet we cannot understand White colonial families if we project back onto them modern notions of individualism and nuclear family self-sufficiency. Colonial society was based on a system of agrarian household production, sustained by a patriarchal structure that greatly constrained the freedom of individual households. The property-owning family was the basis of the social hierarchy, but poor people tended to be brought into propertied households as apprentices, servants, or temporary lodgers. A household head exerted authority over all household members, and little distinction was made between a biological child and an unrelated household member of about the same age. Colonial authorities tried to ensure that everyone was a member of a family, viewing a man or woman outside a family hierarchy as a threat to the social order.

Members of the lower classes often lived in the households of their employers. A child might be removed from the child's biological family and placed in another family if the child's parents were deemed unworthy by authorities. Many families voluntarily sent their children to live in another household at a relatively young age to work as a servant or an apprentice or simply to develop wider social connections. At home, the nuclear family did not retreat into an oasis of privacy. Parents and children ate—and sometimes slept—in the same room with other household members, whether they were related or not.

Before the nineteenth century, marriage was much less sentimentalized. Men often sought a wife because they needed someone to help them on the farm or in their business, or because she came with a handsome dowry. Women married for similar economic and social reasons. It was hoped that love would develop (in moderation) after marriage, but prior to the late eighteenth century, love was not supposed to be the primary motive for marriage, and children were expected to be guided by their parents' wishes in their matches.

Africans and Families in the New World

The Africans who were captured and taken to the New World to serve the White settlers also came from kinship-based societies, although some of those societies had more complex political institutions and larger status differences than were found among the Indigenous peoples of North America. Once in America, all captive Africans had to forge new customs to cope with their involuntary relocation to America, the loss of their separate languages and religious traditions, the brutality of commercial slavery, and the gradual hardening of racial attitudes over the first two centuries of colonization.

The family arrangements of enslaved people from Africa and their descendants varied depending on whether they lived in cotton and tobacco plantations utilizing gang labor, small backwoods farms where one or two enslaved people worked under a master's close supervision, or colonial villages where there were several enslaved persons or servants. Gender imbalance on both large plantations and small farms meant that many individuals remained single, while married couples often lived on separate properties. Some slaveholders encouraged marriage, partly to increase reproduction and partly to gain leverage over individuals through their family ties. But families were often broken up, not just by routine sales but when owners died or paid off their debts. Within the constraints of the slave trade and the plantation system, enslaved people adapted African cultural traditions to their new realities, using child-centered rather than marriage-centered family systems, adoptive and fictive kin ties, ritual co-parenting or godparenting, and complex naming patterns designed to maintain or re-create extended kin.[5]

Some African captives may initially have been treated as indentured servants. White Irish children were also kidnapped and sold as indentured servants to landowners in the British colonies. In 1652, the Rhode Island General Court complained that some Englishmen were buying Africans to evade the term limits of indenture, and passed a law that "no blacke mankind or white" could be forced to serve anyone for a period longer than ten years. But that law was repealed within a few decades, and as plantation slavery in North America interacted with a spreading market economy, slavery grew into a much more extensive and brutal system than it had been in most other societies around the world.[6]

As many European and American thinkers began to challenge the autocratic rule of kings and aristocrats, an ironic contradiction developed. On the one hand, European Enlightenment ideals and the revolutionary sentiments of the American colonists gave rise to the Declaration of Independence's stirring claim that "all men are created equal" and have an "inalienable" right to liberty.

This ideal inspired a historic and radical cross-racial movement against slavery and racial discrimination—and also one in favor of equal rights for women. But it put those who profited from slavery, or tolerated its existence, on the defensive about their refusal to live up to the ideal. In response to the challenge of equal rights ideology, and to relieve their own cognitive dissonance between supporting "liberty" in the abstract and denying it to others, defenders of slavery and racial exclusion developed increasingly elaborate justifications, creating racist myths that still haunt us today. They claimed that subjugation of Blacks and Native peoples was a result of their naturally inferior mental and moral abilities. When early feminists used the ideals of the American Revolution to argue for gender equality, defenders of male dominance likewise resorted to biological justifications for inequality.

One persistent myth about the history of African American families is that their comparatively low rates of marriage and high rates of single parenthood today are a result of the cultural legacy of slavery. But after Emancipation, formerly enslaved persons rushed to take advantage of the right to marry, and separated couples made extraordinary efforts to reunite. Black and White marriage rates were actually similar until the 1950s, when Black communities were hit first by the displacement of workers from southern agriculture and then by the decline of the industrial jobs that many had moved north to find. (See Franklin, Chapter 8, for more.)

On average, Black families have long had higher rates of instability than White ones, but sociologist Frank Furstenberg points out that this is mostly accounted for by the much greater concentration of African Americans in communities of concentrated poverty, creating stresses that are magnified by ongoing racial discrimination and legal injustice. One study of African American enlistees in the army—the military being the only place in America where Blacks and Whites get equal pay, equal access to health care, and equal housing, and both groups are employed full time—found that in this setting, racial differences in the rates of marriage and divorce disappeared.

Other racial-ethnic groups have brought their own forms of family diversity to America. Hispanic and Latinx people, for example, share a Spanish or Latin American ancestry, and yet can be divided by race, especially in a color-conscious society such as the United States. Hispanic groups also differ in their cultural and political histories and in the specific historical conditions under which they immigrated to—or were incorporated by conquest into—the United States. Their different traditions and internal variations coexist and interact with and yet have often been overshadowed by the changing cultural messages about family life that have accompanied the evolution of White middle-class families. (See Sanchez-Connally, Chapter 32, on immigrant families today, and Rodriguez, Chapter 33, on immigration experiences today.)

The Rise of the White Middle-Class Domestic Family Model

During the late eighteenth and early nineteenth centuries, the spread of a market economy led to the gradual separation of home and work, of market production and household production, for growing numbers of Americans. This created new tensions between family responsibilities and "economic" ones. Free households could no longer get by as they had traditionally, consuming things they made, grew, or bartered in the community. But in the era before cheap mass production, they could not yet rely on ready-made purchased goods. Even in middle-class homes, an immense amount of labor was required to make purchased goods usable. Families no longer had to spin their own cotton and grind their own grain, but someone still had to sew factory-produced cloth into clothes and painstakingly sift store-bought flour to rid it of impurities.

Many families responded by reorganizing their division of labor by age and gender. Men (and also working-class children) began to specialize in paid work outside the home. Unmarried women also started to work outside the home, earning cash working in factories or as household help or teaching the middle-class children who were no longer obliged to work on their families' farms or small businesses. Among the impoverished lower classes in the growing cities, some women also turned to prostitution.

But White middle-class wives, who had once played a vital role in producing for the household and marketing their surpluses, now began to devote the bulk of their attention to housework and child-rearing and to processing the goods their husbands had purchased. Even in the working class, a wife could often raise the family's standard of living more by spending her days in bargain-hunting, processing, and home production than by going to work at the low wages she could normally make outside the home. Accordingly, in another reversal of current patterns, a working-class woman would typically work outside the home when her children were infants or toddlers but withdraw from work as soon as they were old enough to work for pay (in the nineteenth century, that could be as early as nine or ten).

Diverging Childhoods

As a market economy supplanted self-sufficient farms and household businesses, middle-class sons became less likely to inherit the family farm or take on their father's occupation. Parents had to prepare their male children for new kinds of employment in the wage economy and their daughters for a new form of married life. Although Black and immigrant children increasingly went out of the home to work, the middle classes began to keep their children at home longer and concentrate their resources on fewer children, often subsidizing their children's schooling or work training rather than utilizing their labor to augment family finances.

A new middle-class ideal of parenting placed mothers at the emotional center of family life and gave them the task of inculcating sexual restraint, temperance, family solidarity, and a strong work ethic in their children. This became the new "norm" for responsible motherhood, popularized in the advice books and novels that proliferated in the early nineteenth century. But many middle-class mothers were able to specialize in such activities only because so many immigrant and African American mothers had to leave their own homes to clean and do laundry for their middle-class mistresses. We see a similar pattern today. Many egalitarian dual-earner families depend on the low-paid housework and child-care services of women who do what used to be the middle-class wife's domestic tasks. Delivering these services for the middle class, though, does not provide working-class women with high enough wages to gain the kind of economic and personal independence that the middle-class women gain from paid labor.

Work and Family

As Americans adapted family life to the demands of an industrializing society during the nineteenth century, American families took on many of the characteristics we now associate with modernity. They became smaller, with fewer children. They focused more tightly on the nuclear core, putting greater distance between blood relatives and expelling servants and boarders from their midst. Parents became more emotionally involved in child-rearing and for a longer period. Marriage came to be seen as primarily about love, although the law continued to support men's legal and economic authority in the home. The distinction between home and work, both physically and conceptually, sharpened.

Average trends, however, obscure tremendous differences among and within the rapidly changing ethnic groups and classes of the industrializing United States. New professions opened up for middle-class and skilled workers. During the Gilded Age, some entrepreneurs made vast fortunes, while job insecurity became more pronounced for laborers. More than 10 million immigrants arrived from Europe between 1830 and 1882, and each wave successively filled the lowest rungs of the industrial job ladder. Their distinctive cultural and class traditions interacted with the strategies they developed to cope with the occupations they entered, along with the housing conditions and social prejudices they met, to create new variations in family life and gender relations.

After the Civil War, African Americans who moved north found it hard to get a foothold on those rungs at all. They were relegated to unskilled laboring jobs and segregated sections of the city, compelling new family adaptations. In the South, African American families eked out a tenuous living as sharecroppers, domestics, or agricultural wage workers. During the eight years of Radical Reconstruction following the Civil War, Black men were elected to public office and were making progress toward full citizenship. But that was ended by a blatantly terrorist counterrevolution marked by mob violence, voter suppression, and the passage of Jim Crow laws designed to restore White supremacy.

With such divergent family experiences, diversity in parent-child relations continued to increase even as the new ideal of the domestic middle-class family became enshrined in the dominant culture. White middle-class children were now largely exempted from the farm work and home production tasks that all children traditionally had done. But working-class youth of all racial-ethnic groups streamed out of the home into mines and mills, where they faced a much longer and more dangerous workday than in the past or roamed the streets scavenging for food or odd jobs.

THE FAMILY CONSUMER ECONOMY

In the twentieth century, a national system of mass production and mass communication replaced the decentralized production of goods and culture that had prevailed until the 1890s. The standardization of economic production and market relationships, the extension of schooling into the teenage years, the abolition of child labor, the spread of a national radio and film industry (and later television), and the growth of a consumer economy worked together to create new similarities and new differences in people's experience of family life.

In the 1920s, for the first time, a slight majority of children lived in families where the father was the breadwinner, the mother did not have paid employment outside the home, and the children were in school rather than at work. Black children in the South worked alongside their families as sharecroppers, but in the North, the lower wages paid to Black workers inspired many Black families to keep their children in school longer than the average White-identified immigrant family did. Not that this solved their economic problems. Black workers, whatever their education, continued to be last hired, first fired, and while employed paid lower wages.

The early twentieth century saw a breakdown of the nineteenth-century system of sexual segregation. Single women entered new occupations and exercised new social freedoms. Women won the right to vote in 1919. An autonomous and increasingly sexualized youth culture emerged, as young people from different class backgrounds interacted in high schools and middle-class youths adopted the new institution of "dating" Dating, which was pioneered by working-class youth and a newly visible African American urban culture, gradually spread to all youth, replacing the nineteenth-century middle-class courting system of "calling," where the girl and her family invited a young man to call and the couple socialized on the porch or in the living room under the watchful eyes of parents. By contrast, dating took place away from home, and since the man typically paid for a date, the initiative shifted to him. Young people—especially girls—gained more independence from parental oversight, but girls also incurred more responsibility for preventing their dates from going "too far."

There was a profound change at this time in the dominant ideological portrayal of family life. In the nineteenth century, ties to siblings, parents, and close same-sex friends had been as emotionally intense as the ties between spouses. Women often called their husbands "Mr. so-and-so," but wrote passionately in their diaries about their pet names and physically affectionate interactions with female friends. Men and women alike waxed as sentimental about their love for friends, siblings, and parents (especially their mothers) as they did for their intended marital partner.[7]

Now, however, especially in middle-class White families, the focus of emotional life shifted to the husband-wife bond and to the immediate nuclear family. But women became more exclusively responsible for the expression and management of those emotions. Young men were encouraged to cut "the silver cord" that bound them to their mothers and to maintain a stoic, unemotional attitude in all relationships. The same-sex female "crushes" and passionate male friendships that had been viewed as normal in the nineteenth century came to be seen as threats to the primacy of heterosexual love ties.

The growing emphasis on companionship and mutual sexual satisfaction in marriage brought new intimacy to married life but had some unintended consequences. For one thing, it encouraged premarital sexual experimentation. For the first time, a majority of boys who had sex before marriage did so with girls they dated rather than with prostitutes. The higher standards for marriage also created an unwillingness to settle for what used to be considered adequate relationships. "Great expectations," as historian Elaine Tyler May points out, could also generate great disappointments.[8] The divorce rate more than tripled in the 1920s.

All these changes created a sense of panic about "the future of the family" that was every bit as intense as the debates about unwed mothers and "family values" in the 1980s and 1990s. Commentators hearkened back to the "good old days" of the nineteenth century, bemoaning the sexual revolution, the fragility of marriage, women's "selfish" use of contraception, and the threat of the "Emancipated Woman."[9]

The challenges of the Great Depression and World War II in the 1930s and 1940s put these concerns on the back burner. But disturbing family changes continued. During the Depression, divorce rates fell, but so did marriage rates. Desertion and domestic violence rose sharply. Economic stress often led to punitive parenting that left children with emotional scars still visible to interviewers decades later. Birth rates plummeted. The outbreak of World War II led to a surge in early marriages—but also to an unprecedented spike in divorces in 1946, when the soldiers came home from the war.

The hardships and inequalities of the Depression Era sparked massive discontent that eventually led to the New Deal, a series of government measures designed to reduce the extreme economic inequality that had marked the Gilded Age of the 1890s and the Roaring Twenties. Laws were passed to curtail the viciousness with which employers and civic authorities had until that time responded to workers' attempts to organize. The new government commitment to curbing unfair labor practices, alleviating poverty, and creating living-wage jobs was the result of hard-fought and sometimes bloody battles over workers' right to organize and families' right to relief from foreclosure and hunger during the Great Depression. (See Fremstad, Chapter 10, for more history of labor and families.)

During the period from the mid-1930s to the early 1970s, America's working classes claimed a larger share of the country's economic growth than either before or since. Why? This was a result of the pro-labor reforms and government investment in jobs and social programs that began in the New Deal and were extended by the Great Society initiatives of the 1960s. By 1955 one-third of all workers were in unions, five times more than at the beginning of the 1930s (and almost three times more than today). The presence of higher-paid union jobs raised the wage floor for non-union workers. Indeed, the greatest reductions in overall wage inequality were in those regions where unions grew the most from the 1940s to the 1960s.

Racism limited the reach of many New Deal reforms. For example, southern legislators insisted that domestic and agricultural workers, who were disproportionately Black, Hispanic, and Latinx, be excluded from the Minimum Wage Act and other fair-labor standards initiated by the New Deal. The Federal Housing Authority's practice of "redlining" systematically disqualified Black and Hispanic neighborhoods from its generous new housing loans, creating a long-term racial disadvantage in wealth accumulation.

Similarly, sexism limited the options of women in this era. Women who had joined the workforce during World War II were summarily laid off when the troops came home, even though many did not want to quit their jobs. A massive cultural campaign—famously denounced in 1964 by Betty Friedan as "the feminine mystique"—urged women to find fulfillment in decorating their homes and raising their children. Psychiatrists, who had largely replaced ministers as the source of advice for families, claimed that a woman who desired anything other than marriage, motherhood, and domesticity was deeply neurotic.

On the other hand, White male workers had a degree of job security that is increasingly elusive in the modern economy, and during the 1960s Black workers also began to gain union benefits and legal protections. Between 1947 and 1973, real wages rose, on average, by 81 percent, and the gap between the rich and poor declined significantly. The income of the bottom 80 percent of the population grew faster than the income of the richest 1 percent, with the most rapid gains of all made by the poorest 20 percent of the population. Not only did economic inequality decline, but this era also had an exceptionally high rate of economic growth.

The result was a boom in family life. For the first time in sixty years, the age of marriage and parenthood fell, the proportion of marriages ending in divorce dropped, and the birth rate soared. The percentage of women remaining single reached a hundred-year low. The proportion of children who were raised by a breadwinner father and a homemaker mother and who stayed in school until graduation from high school reached an all-time high.

This is the era of family life for which so many Americans now express nostalgia. But returning to the practices of the 1950s would not solve our contemporary family dilemmas. For one thing, the prevalence and stability of marriage in that era resulted from several intertwined trends, only one of which most Americans today would like to recover. The one positive basis of the postwar family system was the availability of stable, family-wage jobs for young men, even those without a college education. From 1947 to 1973, each cohort of twenty-five- to twenty-nine-year-old men earned on average three times as much in constant dollars as their fathers had at the same age. The earnings of such a man more than doubled from age twenty-five to thirty-five, and his real wages typically rose by another 30 percent between age forty and fifty. As of 1959, the average thirty-year-old man could pay the mortgage on a median-priced home using only 18 percent of his gross monthly pay. A young man could take almost *any* job and expect his earnings to improve over time. A woman could marry almost any man and expect him to be able to support her and her children.

But an equally important reason for the postwar marriage boom was far less positive. Very few women could afford *not* to marry, or not to *stay in a bad marriage*, during that era. Female workers, whatever their education level, had much worse job prospects than males. Their real wages remained almost flat throughout the 1950s. And they were often laid off after only a few years on the job. Until 1970, the average college-educated woman who worked full-time still earned less than the average high school–educated man. Women were entirely excluded from many occupations and professional training programs.

The "family values" of that era did not protect women from physical and sexual abuse. Problems such as domestic violence, rape, and incest were swept under the rug. Psychiatrists claimed that domestic violence was usually the woman's fault. Rape was legally defined as a man's forcible sexual intercourse with a woman *other than* his wife. There was rampant discrimination against African Americans and Hispanics, Jews, Native Americans, women, older adults, gay men, lesbians, political dissidents, religious minorities, and persons with disabilities. Child abuse was not recognized as a social problem. Transgender people were invisible. Institutionalized racism was the law in the South, and in the North there was daily violence against African Americans who attempted to move into White neighborhoods or use public parks and swim areas.

Furthermore, underneath the surface stability of the era, the temporary tri- umph of nuclear-family domesticity was already being eroded by the same sys- tem that had created it. The expansion of the service and retail sectors of the economy required new workers. Employers were especially eager to hire women, who were easier to move in and out of the labor market than unionized men. But because the average age of marriage had fallen to about twenty years old, there were not enough single women to fill the demand for workers. In response, employers began to make changes in hiring practices to recruit married women.

Despite the dominance of full-time homemakers on TV sitcoms, the employ- ment of women soared in the 1950s, quickly topping its wartime peak. And the fastest-growing segment of this female labor force was married women with school-age children. Old marital norms came into conflict with new family work patterns. As early as 1957, the divorce rate started to climb again. A growing mid- dle class began to send its daughters as well as its sons to college. Even though parents often merely intended to help their daughters find a "better class" of hus- band, many young women delayed marriage to gain work and life experience— something that the invention of the birth control pill made it much easier to do.

As the "baby boom" generation grew up, there was a huge increase in the per- centage of singles in the population, accelerating the acceptance of premarital sex that had begun to spread in the 1920s. A women's liberation movement arose, helping to expose the sometimes unsavory realities that lay beneath the Ozzie and Harriet images of the time and inspiring many women to expand their per- sonal and political aspirations.[10]

There have been many changes in family arrangements since the 1960s, as detailed in Philip N. Cohen's "Family Diversity Is the New Normal for America's

Children" (6.1 in this volume). Some of these changes are a result of new opportunities, others of new constraints and insecurities. The divorce rate reached an all-time high in 1979–80 but has since declined. At the same time, rates of marriage have also fallen, and we have seen a widening class gap in the likelihood of marriage and of divorce. As courts began to protect the rights of children born out of wedlock, fewer women have felt compelled to enter a shotgun marriage if they become pregnant. College-educated men and women express more tolerance for unwed motherhood and divorce than less-educated individuals but are actually more likely to marry before having children, and once married, less likely to divorce. Cohabitation before marriage, and often as an alternative to marriage, has become much more common.

New waves of immigrants began to arrive from the 1980s onward, the majority now coming from Asia, Latin America, and the Caribbean rather than from Europe, as had been the case in the past. By the 1990s, racial and ethnic diversity had reached historic highs, creating a new acceptance of family diversity and intermarriage but also fanning racial and ethnic tensions, especially as growing socioeconomic inequality threatened the assumption that each generation of working-class Americans would live better than its parents.

The backdrop to many of the changes in family life since the early 1970s has been the interaction between growing demands for racial, gender, and sexual equality, resulting in some real gains in those arenas, and widening class inequalities, including losses for men without a college degree. An erosion of working-class security has been going on for over forty years. Many manufacturing jobs have been lost or outsourced. Most that are still around or have returned now pay lower wages and provide fewer benefits than in the past. In 1969, three-quarters of employed men age twenty-five were earning wages that could support a family of four above the poverty line. By 2004, it took until age thirty for the same percentage of men to reach this income level. And while in 1969 only 10 percent of men ages thirty to thirty-five were still low earners, by 2004 almost a quarter of men in that age range remained low earners. The trend continues.

While college-educated workers initially made big gains, sectors of them have now also begun to experience wage stagnation, job deskilling, and income insecurity. According to a 2020 study by the Pew Research Center, the share of total income going to middle-class households fell from 62 to 43 percent between 1970 and 2018, while the share going to upper-income households increased from 29 to 48 percent (with the top 5 percent making the bulk of the gains). Indeed, the wealth of the richest three individuals in America increased by almost 6,000 percent between 1982 and 2018. As of 2018, those three—Jeff Bezos, Bill Gates, Warren Buffett—were together worth more than the entire bottom 50 percent of Americans.[11]

What explains these setbacks for America's families? Ever since the passage of New Deal laws curbing the privileges of corporations and wealthy elites, and especially since the Great Society reforms, a well-funded coalition of "free enterprise" boosters and social conservatives has been working hard to roll back the restraints on private enterprise, lower taxes on the rich, and deregulate the financial industry. And they discovered early on that one of the most effective ways to gain political support for their agenda was to fan racial fears among White Americans.[12]

Until about the 1970s, race outweighed education in determining wage rates. On average, White men with only a high school degree outearned Blacks with a college degree. Today, education outweighs race, although race also affects how much access people have to education. Many working-class Whites without a college degree don't yet realize that their declining wage and job prospects are not the result of new racial preferences but of new market preferences: Studies confirm that employers still favor Whites over Blacks in labor markets where applicants have equal education. When nearly identical résumés are sent out for the same job, the candidate with a White-sounding name receives more callbacks than the applicant with a Black-sounding name. But White applicants with only a high school diploma or less are no longer favored over college-educated people of color, even if such Whites continue to receive other advantages, like being less likely to be profiled by police or discriminated against in housing markets.

Unfortunately, humans are more likely to dwell on our losses than our advantages. And savvy political strategists learned long ago that blaming the setbacks of White workers on the supposed gains of workers of color or of immigrants is a great way to divert attention from class-based attacks on workers' rights. As Heather McGhee argues in her 2021 book *The Sum of Us: What Racism Costs Everyone and How We Can Prosper Together*, "racist stereotypes and dog whistles" have for decades helped lobbyists and politicians defeat egalitarian economic reforms and family-friendly social policies that would benefit all Americans. People of color— and low-income families with children—have paid the highest price for these defeats. But, McGhee points out, the majority of White families have also lost out in the supercharged "turbo-capitalism" and billionaire-friendly political and legal system that has emerged since the 1980s.

After all, although Whites in general have more wealth than people of color, most Whites who have been falling behind have been losing ground to *other* Whites, not to Blacks or Hispanics. As of 2019, according to a report issued by the Federal Reserve System, the wealthiest 10 percent of households—fewer than 1 percent of whom identify as Black or Hispanic—owned fully three-quarters of all wealth in the United States.[13]

Concluding an Ongoing Story—for Now

The lessons from history are both positive and negative. American families have always been in flux, and many different family arrangements and values have worked for various groups at different times. We should not assume that recent changes in family forms and practices are inevitably destructive (see Rutter in Chapter 22 of this volume). But families have always been fragile, vulnerable to economic stress, and needful of practical and emotional support from beyond the nuclear family. And in every historical period, the emergence of new opportunities for individuals and families to succeed has also created new ways for them to fail. It is a mistake to ignore the trade-offs and losses that come with historical change. Doing so only makes those who feel left out even more vulnerable to misinformation and demagoguery.[14]

It's an even bigger mistake to think that restoring the family values and forms of the past will solve the challenges posed by the sweeping changes America is experiencing in gender and age relations, racial and ethnic patterns, the distribution of jobs and income, and even our experience of time and space. There are many historical precedents of families and communities successfully reorganizing themselves in response to social change. But these examples should inspire us to construct *new* family values and social support institutions rather than trying to re-create some largely mythical "traditional" family of the past.

Notes

1. Unless otherwise noted, the history here is well documented in several of my books: *Marriage, a History: How Love Conquered Marriage* (New York: Penguin Books, 2006); *The Social Origins of Private Life: A History of American Families, 1600–1900* (New York: Verso, 1988); *The Way We Never Were: American Families and the Nostalgia Trap* (New York: Basic Books, 1992), and *A Strange Stirring: The Feminine Mystique and American Woman at the Dawn of the 1960s* (New York: Basic Books, 2011). See also Stephanie Coontz, "Family Values, Social Reciprocity, and Christianity," in *Human Families: Identities, Relationships, and Responsibilities*, ed. Jacob M. Kohlhaas and Mary M. Doyle Roche, *College Theology Society Annual*, vol. 66 (Maryknoll, NY: Orbis Books, 2021); and Stephanie Coontz, Maya Parson, and Gabrielle Raley, eds., *American Families: A Multicultural Reader* (New York: Routledge, 2008). For more on band-level societies, see Frank W. Marlowe, "Hunter-Gatherers and Human Evolution," *Evolutionary Anthropology* 14, no. 2 (2005): 54; Joseph Henrich, "Human Cooperation: The Hunter-Gatherer Puzzle," *Current Biology* 28, no. 19 (October 8, 2018): R1143–R1145; Vicki Cummings, Peter Jordan, and Marek Selebi, eds., *The Oxford Handbook of Archaeology and Anthropology of Hunter-Gatherers* (Oxford: Oxford University Press, 2014); James Woodburn, "Egalitarian Societies," *Man* 17, no. 3. (1982): 431–451;

Robert Sapolsky, *Behave: The Biology of Humans at Our Best and Worst* (New York: Penguin, 2018); Brian Hayden, *Archeology: The Science of Once and Future Things* (New York: W. H. Freeman, 1993); Kim Hill, "Altruistic Cooperation during Foraging by the Ache, and the Evolved Human Predisposition to Cooperate," *Human Nature* 13, no. 1 (2002): 105–128; and Kim Hill and A. M. Hurtado, "Cooperative Breeding in South American Hunter-Gatherers," *Proceedings of the Royal Society B: Biological Sciences* 276, no. 1674 (2009): 3863–3870.

2. Kent Flannery and Joyce Marcus, *The Creation of Inequality* (Cambridge, MA: Harvard University Press 2012), 70–71, 181–183; Roger Carpenter, "Womanish Men and Manlike Women: The Native American Two-Spirit as Warrior," in *Gender and Sexuality in Indigenous North America, 1400–1850*, ed. Sandra Slater and Fay A. Yarbrough (Columbia, SC: University of South Carolina Press, 2011); Leslie Marmon Silko, *Yellow Woman and a Beauty of the Spirit* (New York: Simon and Schuster, 1996).

3. Ward Stavig, "'Living in Offense of Our Lord': Indigenous Sexual Values and Marital Life in the Colonial Crucible," *Hispanic American Historical Review* 75 (1995): 597–622; Cynthia Kennedy, *Braided Relations, Entwined Lives: The Women of Charleston's Urban Slave Society* (Bloomington: Indiana University Press, 2005); Susan Lobo, *Native American Voices: A Reader* (New York: Longman, 1998); David Wallace Adams, *Education for Extinction: American Indians and the Boarding School Experience, 1875–1928* (Lawrence: University Press of Kansas, 1988); Virginia Bergman Peters, *Women of the Earth Lodges: Tribal Life on the Plains* (New Haven, CT: Archon Books, 1995); Laura Scheiber and Mark D. Mitchell, eds., *Across a Great Divide: Continuity and Change in Native North American Societies, 1400–1900* (Tucson: University of Arizona Press, 2015); Paul Conrad, *The Apache Diaspora: Four Centuries of Displacement and Survival* (Philadelphia: University of Pennsylvania Press, 2021); Susan Sleeper-Smith, Jeffrey Ostler, and Joshua Reid, eds., *Violence and Indigenous Communities: Confront the Past and Engaging the Present* (Evanston, IL: Northwestern University Press, 2021); Andrés Reséndez, *The Other Slavery: The Uncovered Story of Indian Enslavement in America* (Boston: Houghton Mifflin Harcourt, 2016); Joshua L. Reid, *The Sea Is My Country: The Maritime World of the Makahs* (New Haven, CT: Yale University Press, 2015); Linford D. Fisher, "'Why Shall Wee Have Peace to Bee Made Slaves': Indian Surrenderers During and After King Philip's War," *Ethnohistory* 64, no. 1 (2017): 91–114; Julie Weil, "They Were Enslaved as Native Americans, then Lost to Their Tribes," *Washington Post*, December 20, 2022, www.washingtonpost.com /history/2022/12/20/native-americans-slavery-congress-new-mexico/.

4. Christie Renick, "The Nation's First Family Separation Policy," *The Imprint*, October 9, 2018, imprintnews.org/child-welfare-2/nations-first-family-separation-policy-indian -child-welfare-act/32431.

5. On African American families in slavery and freedom, see Brenda E. Stevenson, *Life in Black and White: Family and Community in the Slave South* (New York: Oxford University Press, 1996); Leith Mullings, *On Our Own Terms: Race, Class, and Gender in the Lives of African-American Women* (New York: Routledge, 1997); Stephanie McCurry, *Masters of Small Worlds: Yeoman Households, Gender Relations, and the Political Culture of the Antebellum South Carolina Low Country* (Athens: University of Georgia Press, 1995); Jennifer Ritterhouse, *Growing Up Jim Crow: How Black and White*

Southern Children Learned Race (Chapel Hill: University of North Carolina Press, 2006); David Barry Gaspar and Darlene Clark Hine, *More than Chattel: Black Women and Slavery in the Americas* (Bloomington: Indiana University Press, 1996); Tia Miles, *Ties That Bind: The Story of an Afro-Cherokee Family in Slavery and Freedom* (Berkeley: University of California Press, 2005); Harriette Pipes McAdoo, *Black Families*, 4th ed. (Thousand Oaks, CA: Sage Publications, 2007); Frank Furstenberg, "If Moynihan Had Only Known: Race, Class, and Family Change in the Late Twentieth Century," *The Annals of the American Academy of Political and Social Science* 621 (2009): 94–110; Stephanie Coontz, "The Moynihan Family Circus: How a Fifty-Year-Old Report on the Black Family and Poverty Continues to Distort American Social Policy," *Bookforum* 22, no. 2 (2015), www.bookforum.com/print/2202/how-a-fifty-year-old-report-on-the-black -family-and-poverty-continues-to-distort-american-social-policy-14579. For the study of African Americans in the military, see Jennifer Lundquist, "The Black–White Gap in Marital Dissolution among Young Adults: What Can a Counterfactual Scenario Tell Us?," *Social Problems* 53, no. 3 (2006): 421–441. For a discussion of the special stresses— and the resilient coping methods—of Black families, see Kecia Johnson and Karyn Loscocco, "Black Marriage through the Prism of Gender, Race, and Class," *Journal of Black Studies* 46, no. 2 (2015): 142–171.

6. For this and the next paragraph, see Stephanie Coontz, "Why Learning the History of Slavery in America Doesn't Have to Be Depressing," HUB pages, August 18, 2022, discover.hubpages.com/education/Why-Learning-the-History-of-Slavery-in-America -Doesnt-Have-to-Be-Depressing.

7. Donald Yacovone, "'Surpassing the Love of Women': Victorian Manhood and the Language of Fraternal Love," in Laura McCall and Donald Yacovone, eds., *A Shared Experience: Men, Women, and the History of Gender* (New York: New York University Press, 1998); Richard Godbeer, *The Overflowing of Friendship: Love Between Men and the Creation of the American Republic* (Baltimore: Johns Hopkins University Press, 2009); E. Anthony Rotundo, *American Manhood: Transformations in Masculinity from the Revolution to the Modern Era* (New York: Basic Books, 1991).

8. Elaine Tyler May, *Great Expectations: Marriage and Divorce in Post-Victorian America* (Chicago: University of Chicago Press, 1980).

9. Ruth Rosen, *The World Split Open: How the Women's Movement Changed America* (New York: Penguin Books, 2000).

10. Rosen.

11. Noah Kirsch, "The 3 Richest Americans Hold More Wealth Than Bottom 50% of the Country, Study Finds," *Forbes*, November 9, 2017, www.forbes.com/sites/noahkirsch /2017/11/09/the-3-richest-americans-hold-more-wealth-than-bottom-50-of-country -study-finds/?sh=1da30fc53cf8.

12. Ian Haney López, *Dog Whistle Politics: How Coded Racial Appeals Have Reinvented Racism and Wrecked the Middle Class* (New York: Oxford University Press, 2013); Jane Mayer, *Dark Money: The Hidden History of the Billionaires Behind the Rise of the Radical Right* (New York: Doubleday, 2016) and "The Big Money behind the Big Lie," *New Yorker*, August 9, 2021; Lee Drutman, "How Corporate Lobbyists Conquered American Democracy, *Atlantic*, April 20, 2015, www.theatlantic.com/business /archive/2015/04/how-corporate-lobbyists-conquered-american-democracy/390822/.

13. Heather McGhee, *The Sum of Us: What Racism Costs Everyone and How We Can Prosper Together* (New York: One World, 2021), xix; Ian Haney López, "Can Democracy Survive Racism as a Strategy?," Protect Democracy Project, protectdemocracy.org /project/endgame/#section-4; Jesse Bricker et al., "Wealth and Income Concentration in the SCF: 1989–2019," Federal Reserve Notes, September 28, 2020, www.federalreserve .gov/econres/notes/feds-notes/wealth-and-income-concentration-in-the-scf-20200928 .html.

14. For more on this point, see Stephanie Coontz, "The Nostalgia Trap," *Harvard Business Review*, April 10, 2018, hbr.org/2018/04/the-nostalgia-trap.

In Other Words

FAMILY DIVERSITY IS THE NEW NORMAL FOR AMERICA'S CHILDREN

Philip N. Cohen

People often think of social change in the lives of American children since the 1950s as a movement in one direction—from children being raised in married, male-breadwinner families to a new norm of children being raised by working mothers, many of them unmarried. Instead, we can better understand this transformation as an explosion of diversity, a fanning out from a compact center along many different pathways.

The Dramatic Rearrangement of Children's Living Situations since the 1950s

At the end of the 1950s, if you chose 100 children under age 15 to represent all children, 65 would have been living in a family with married parents, with the father employed and the mother out of the labor force. Only 18 would have had married parents who were both employed. As for other types of family arrangements, you would find only one child in every 350 living with a never-married mother! Today, among 100 representative children, just 22 live in a married male-breadwinner family, compared to 23 living with a single mother (only half of whom have ever been married). Seven out of every 100 live with a parent who cohabits with an unmarried partner (a category too rare for the Census Bureau to consider counting in 1960) and six with either a single father (3) or with grandparents but no parents (3). The single largest group of children—34—live with dual-earner married parents, but that largest group is only a third of the total, so it's really impossible to point to a "typi-cal" family. With two-thirds of children being raised in male-breadwinner, married-couple families, it is understandable that people from the early 1960s considered such families to be the norm.[1] Today, by contrast, there is no single family arrange-ment that encompasses the majority of children. The figure below illustrates this fanning out from a dominant category to a veritable peacock's tail of work-family arrangements.

To represent this diversity simply, we can calculate the chance that two chil-dren live in the same work-family structure (among the categories shown here). In 1960 you would have had an 80 percent chance that two children, selected at random, would share the same situation. By 2012, that chance had fallen to just

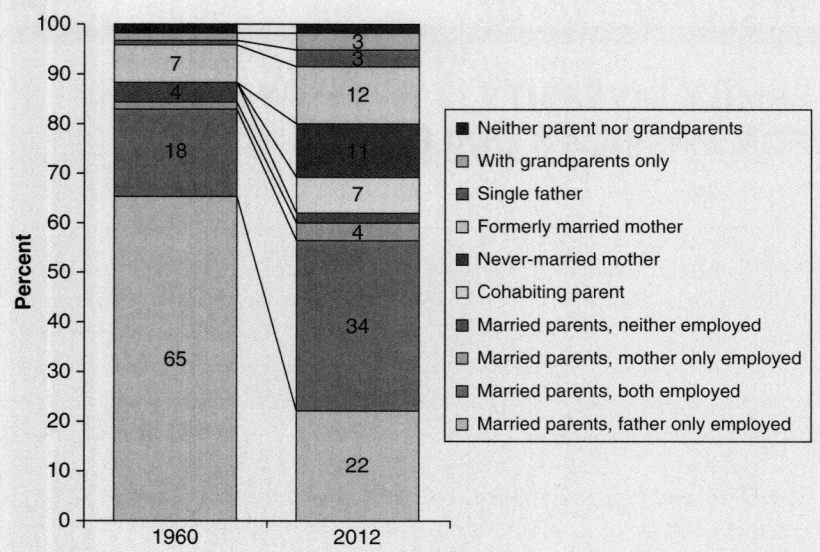

Figure 6.1 | Work-Family Living Arrangements of Children, 1960 & 2012, Ages 0–14

Source: *Author calculations from the 1960 U.S. Census and the 2012 American Community Survey, with data from IPUMS.org.*

Note: *The Census data only identify one parent per child, so married and cohabiting parent couples are identified by the relationship status of the parent (a married mother, for example, may be married to the biological, adopted, or stepfather of the child). Single fathers include never-married and formerly married fathers who are not cohabiting or married.*

a little more than 50-50. The diversity shown here masks an additional layer of differences, which come from the expanding variety of pathways in and out of these arrangements, or transitions from one to another. For example, among the children living with cohabiting parents in 2012, the resident parent is divorced or separated in about a third of cases. In those cases, the cohabiting-parent family often is a blended family with complex relationships to adults and children outside the household. Many more parents have (or raise) children with more than one partner over their lives than in the past, and many more children cycle through several *different* family arrangements as they grow up. The children in America's classrooms today come from so many distinct family arrangements that we can no longer assume they share the same experiences and have the same needs. Likewise, policy makers can no longer design family programs and regulations for a narrow range of family types and assume that they will pretty much meet the needs of all children.

The Decline of Married Couples as the Dominant Household Arrangement

The diversification of family life over time is also shown in the changing proportions of all household types, including ones without children. In the next figure, I put each household into one of five types, using Census data from 1880 to 2010. The largest category is households composed of married couples living with no one except their own children. If there was any other relative living in a household, I counted it as an extended household. The third category is individuals who live alone. Fourth are single parents (most of them mothers) living with no one besides their own children. In the final category are households made up of people who are not related (including unmarried couples). As this figure shows, the married-couple family peaked between 1950 and 1960, when this arrangement characterized two-thirds of households. This was also the peak of the nuclear family, because up until the 1940s, extended families were much more common than they became in the

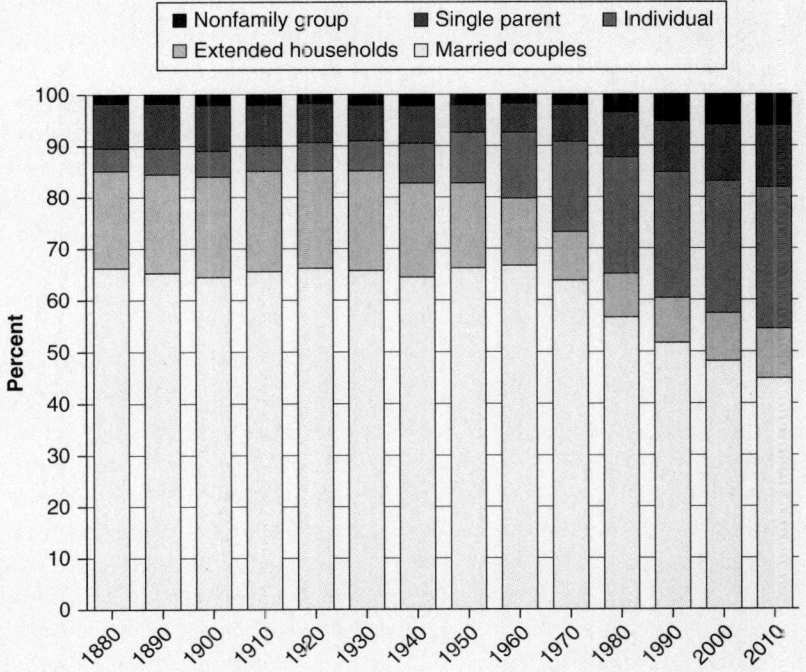

Figure 6.2 | Household Types, 1880–2010

1950s and 1960s. After that era, the pattern fans out. By 2010, the proportion of married-couple households had dropped to less than half (45 percent) of the total. The proportion of individuals living alone rose from 13 to 27 percent between 1960 and 2010, and single-parent households rose from 6 to 12 percent. The result is that households composed of lone individuals and single parents accounted for almost 40 percent of all households by 2010. Extended households are less common than they were a century ago, mostly as a result of the greater independence of older people, but their numbers have increased again in the last several decades. In sum, the dominant married-couple household of the first half of the twentieth century was replaced not by a new standard, but rather by a general increase in family diversity.

How Did We Get Here? Market Forces, Social Welfare Reform, and Family Rearrangements

As the market economy generated new products and services that could supplement or substitute for many of the core functional tasks that families had to perform in the past, people became more able to rearrange their family lives. For example, technological innovations made women's traditional household tasks, such as shopping, preserving food, house cleaning, and making clothes, far less time consuming, while better birth control technology allowed them to control the timing and number of their births. After 1960, employment rates for both married and unmarried women rocketed upward in a 30-year burst that would finally move women's work primarily from the home to the market. The shift to market work reinforced women's independence within their families, but also, in many cases, *from* their families. Women freed from family dependence could live singly, even with children; they could afford to risk divorce; and they could live with a man without the commitment of marriage.

In the aftermath of the Depression and World War II, social reformers increased their efforts to provide a social safety net for the elderly, the poor, and the disabled. The combination of pension and welfare programs that resulted also offered opportunities for more people to structure their lives independently. For older Americans, Social Security benefits were critical. They helped reduce the effective poverty rates of older people from almost 60 percent in the 1960s to 15 percent by 2010, freeing millions of Americans from the need to live with their children in old age. At the beginning of the twentieth century, the Census counted only 1 in 10 people age 55 or older living with no relative. By the end of the century, the proportion was more than 1 in 4. Most of that change occurred between 1940 and 1980.

For younger adults, the combination of expanding work opportunities for women and greater welfare support for children made marriage less of a necessity. In the 1960s and 1970s, Aid to Families with Dependent Children grew rapidly, eventually supporting millions of never-married mothers and their children. Welfare did not create single mothers—whose numbers rose partly in response to poverty, economic insecurity, and rising incarceration rates, and have continued to rise even after large cutbacks in public assistance—and it always carried a shameful stigma while providing a minimal level of monetary support. But it nevertheless allowed poor women to more easily leave abusive or dangerous relationships. Market forces were most important in increasing the ability of middle-class and more highly educated women to delay, forgo, or leave marriage. Poor women, especially African American women, had long been more likely to work for pay, but their lower earnings did not offer the same personal independence that those with better jobs enjoyed, so welfare support was a bigger factor in the growing ability of poor women to live on their own. Nevertheless, the market has contributed to the growth of single-mother families in a different way over the past 40 years, as falling real wages and increasing job insecurity for less-educated men have made them more risky as potential marriage partners. As a result of these and other social trends such as women's increasing educational attainment, diversity of family arrangements increased dramatically after the 1950s.

Changes in Women's Work-Family Situations

The work-family situations of both women and children show the same pattern of increasing diversity replacing the dominant-category system that peaked in the 1950s. The next two figures describe women ages 30 to 34. The rise in education and employment is most dramatic, while marriage and motherhood have become markedly less universal.

Rather than treating each of these as separate trends, we can create profiles by combining the four characteristics into 16 different categories—employed college graduates who are married mothers on one extreme and non-employed non-graduates who aren't married or mothers on the other. In the final figure, I show the distribution across the 10 most common of these. These clearly show the decline in a single profile—the married, non-college-educated, not-employed mother—and the diversity in statuses that have replaced that single type. In 1960, almost 80 percent of women in their early thirties had not completed college and were married with children. Now such women comprise less than a third of the total—and no category includes more than 13 percent of women. In terms of diversity, in 1960 the chance that two women picked at random would be from the same category was 40 percent. Today that chance has fallen to 11 percent.

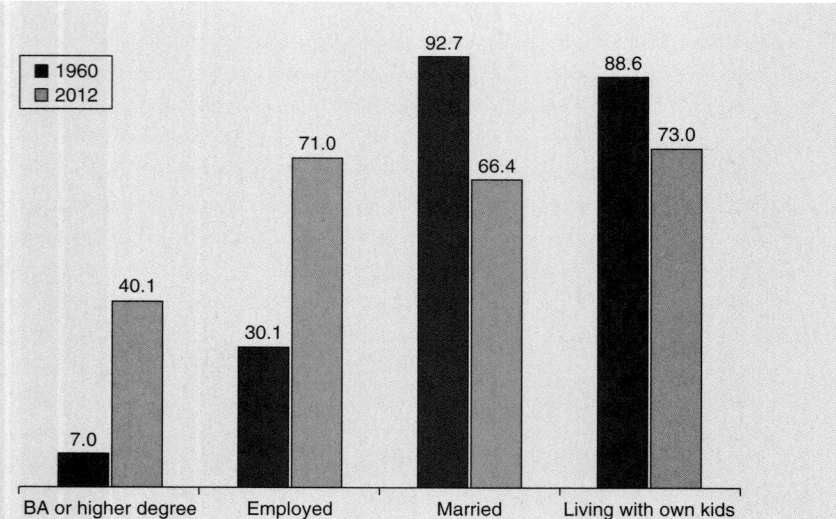

Figure 6.3 | Educational, Employment, Marital, and Parental Status: Women Ages 30–34, 1960 & 2012

Figure 6.4 | Educational, Employment, Marital, and Parental Status: Women Ages 30–34, 1960 & 2012

Source: *Author calculations from the 1960 US Census and the 2012 American Community Survey, with data from IPUMS.org.*

Diversity and Inequality

Some of the new diversity in work-family arrangements is a result of new options for individuals, especially women and older people, whose lives are less constrained than they once were. But some of the new diversity also results from economic changes that are less positive, especially the job loss and wage declines for younger, less-educated men since the late 1970s. In and of itself, however, family diversity doesn't have to lead to inequality. In the Nordic countries of Finland, Norway, and Denmark, for example, unmarried-mother families have poverty rates that barely differ from those of married-couple families—all have poverty rates less than 10 percent. Similarly, many countries do a better job of minimizing the school achievement gap between children of single mothers and children of married parents. A study of 11 wealthy countries found the gap is largest in the United States.

Different families have different child-rearing challenges and needs, which means we are no longer well served by policies that assume most children will be raised by married-couple families, especially ones where the mother stays home throughout the children's early years. As we debate social and economic policy, we need to consider the needs of children in many different family situations, and how they will be affected by policy changes, rather than privileging one particular family structure or arrangement. ▄

Note

1. Interestingly, the dominance of the male-breadwinner nuclear family was not always as great as it was at mid-century. As historian Stephanie Coontz has shown, up until the 1920s, most households contained more than one wage earner: mothers working on the family farm or business and/or children working for pay as well.

7

American Childhood as a Social and Cultural Construct

Steven Mintz

Today, Americans have a firm, although somewhat contradictory, conception of childhood. On the one hand, childhood is romanticized as a time of carefree innocence, when children should play freely, untouched by the cares of the adult world. But at the same time, many middle-class mothers and fathers engage in intensive parenting designed to stimulate their children's development. They buy their children educational toys, involve them in a host of organized enrichment activities, and intensively read and talk to their children, in hopes of cultivating their talents and skills. Schools, too, now place greater emphasis on early academic achievement, and marketers are targeting children with an intensity previously reserved for adult consumers. Notably, institutions treat some children—often boys of color—as threatening and deserving of lots of close watching and swift punishments. Some observers fear that our society is taking the playfulness out of childhood.[1]

Childhood is not an unchanging, biologically determined stage of life. Rather, childhood is a social and cultural construct that varies by region, class, and historical era.[2] Over the past four centuries, almost all aspects of childhood—including children's relationships with their parents and peers, their proportion in the population, and their paths toward adulthood—have changed dramatically. Societal views about methods of child-rearing, the nature of children's play, the ideal duration of schooling, the participation of young people in work, and the demarcation points between childhood, adolescence, and adulthood have shifted significantly. In this article, I trace the changing conceptions of childhood from early colonial America until today. I conclude by comparing the status of today's children with the status of those from the past.

Childhood in Colonial and Early United States

Two centuries ago, the experience of youth was very different from what it is today. Segregation by age was far less prevalent, and chronological age played a smaller role in determining status. Adults were also far less likely to sentimentalize children as special creatures who were more innocent and vulnerable than adults.

Language illustrates how perceptions of childhood have changed over time. Two hundred years ago, the words used to describe the stages of childhood were far less precise than those we now use. *Infancy* referred not to the first months after birth but to the whole period when children were dependent on their mother, typically until the age of five or six. The words *childhood* and *youth* could refer to someone as young as five or as old as the early twenties.

In that era, Americans did not have a category for "adolescent" or "teenager." The vagueness of the broader term *youth* reflected how fluidly the stages of life were viewed in that era. Chronological age mattered less than physical strength, size, and maturity. Young people were not automatically granted full adult status upon reaching a certain societally agreed-upon age. They became full adults only when they married and set up their own farm or entered a full-time trade or profession. In some cases, that might be as early as the mid- or late teens, but usually it did not occur until the late twenties or even the early thirties.[3]

Enslaved and Indentured Children

In the colonial era, there were important regional differences in children's experiences. In the southernmost colonies, half or more of all children were enslaved or indentured servants. In New England, that figure was far smaller, but still many children lived in other people's households as domestic servants or apprentices. In general, most seventeenth-century white American colonists regarded their own children as "adults-in-training." It was recognized that children differed from adults in their mental, moral, and physical capabilities, and the colonists distinguished among childhood, an intermediate stage they called youth, and adulthood. But in colonial America, a parent's duty was to hurry the child toward adult status. Infants, being unable to stand or speak, were thought to lack two essential attributes of full humanity, and infancy was therefore regarded as a state of deficiency to be rushed through as quickly as possible. Parents discouraged infants from crawling and placed them in "walking stools" to get them on their feet. Rods were affixed along the spines of very young children to encourage adult posture.

The goal was to get children speaking, reading, reasoning, and contributing to their family's economic well-being as quickly as possible. A key element in this process was early involvement in work, either within the parental home or outside as a servant or an apprentice. Before the mid-eighteenth century, most adults exhibited surprisingly little interest in their children's very first years of life. Children's play was commonly dismissed as trivial and insignificant. In that era, adults rarely looked back on their childhood with nostalgia or fondness.

The lives of indentured and especially enslaved children were exceedingly arduous and oppressive. Indentured servants and enslaved persons could be bought, sold, leased, and cruelly punished. Indeed, more than half of all indentured servants in Virginia and Maryland died before their term of service expired. During the colonial era, it was extremely difficult for enslaved Africans and their descendants to create and sustain families. As late as 1730, just 6 percent of enslaved persons in South Carolina lived in an individual family unit. Even in 1790 the figure was only 30 percent.

Enslaved children were extremely vulnerable to separation from their parents. Children might be separated as a result of a debt, a sale, an owner's death, or a planter's decision to move or transfer enslaved persons among his various properties. Despite the threat of sale and separation, African American parents instilled a strong sense of family identity in their children. Fathers purchased or made gifts for their children and passed down craft skills to their sons. To sustain a sense of identity over time, enslaved parents commonly named their eldest son for fathers and paternal grandfathers. Nothing better illustrates the strength of family ties than the number of runaway ads that described enslaved children running away to visit a father or a mother.

The fragility of the nuclear family gave special significance to the extended kinship group. By the mid-eighteenth century, enslaved African Americans had created dense networks of family and surrogate families. Enslaved children were encouraged to refer to older enslaved persons as "aunt" and "uncle" and to younger enslaved persons as "sister" and "brother." Kin, including aunts, uncles, nephews, nieces, cousins, and in-laws, as well as friends, served as substitute parents in the event of family separation. Together, the bonds of family and the extended kin group sustained African American children through the travails of slavery.

During the eighteenth century, a shift in parental attitudes took place. Fewer parents expected children to act like miniature adults, to bow or doff their hats in their parents' presence, or to stand during meals. Instead of addressing parents as "sir" and "madam," children began calling them "papa" and "mama."

By the end of the eighteenth century, furniture specifically designed for children was being widely produced. Painted in pastel colors and decorated with pictures of animals or figures from nursery rhymes, the new furniture reflected a growing popular notion of childhood as a time of innocence and playfulness.

Parents began to regard children not as incomplete adults but as innocent, malleable, and fragile creatures who needed to be sheltered from contamination. Childhood came to be seen not simply as a prelude to adulthood but as a separate stage of life that required special care and institutions to protect it.

MARKETS AND SHIFTING IDEAS OF CHILDHOOD

By the early nineteenth century, mothers in the rapidly expanding middle class in the Northeastern states were embracing an amalgam of child-rearing ideas. From Jean-Jacques Rousseau and the Romantic poets, middle-class parents acquired the idea that childhood was a special stage of life, intimately connected with nature, and purer and morally superior to adulthood. From the philosopher John Locke, they took the notion that children were highly malleable creatures and that a republican form of government required parents to instill a capacity for self-government in their offspring. From evangelical Protestants, the middle class adopted the idea that parents must implant proper moral character in children and insulate them from the corruptions of the adult world.

Behind these developments was a growing belief that childhood should be devoted to education and character development as well as play. Middle-class children were no longer sent out to work at an early age. Parents began to believe that their children's play should foster their moral growth. Because parents in the emerging middle class could not automatically transfer their societal status to their children through bequests of family lands, transmission of craft skills, or selection of a marriage partner, they adopted new strategies to give their children a boost by limiting the number of their offspring through birth control and prolonging the transition to adulthood through intensive maternal nurturing and extended schooling.

Over time, the concept of childhood was divided into much more precise, uniform, and prescriptive stages. Adults began to hold more rigid views about what was appropriate at each stage. By the mid-nineteenth century, informal patterns of child-rearing were being supplanted by more structured forms. Schools began to follow prescribed grade-specific curricula. Adult-sponsored and adult-organized activities began replacing activities that young people organized informally on their own.

The End of the Nineteenth Century and Dawn of the Twentieth Century

The dramatic reduction in the birth rate over the past two centuries also altered the concept of childhood. In the mid-nineteenth century, children made up fully one-half of the population. By 1900 their proportion had declined to one-third of the population. As parents had fewer children and had them over a shorter time span, families became more clearly divided into distinct generations, and parents had the opportunity to lavish more time, attention, and resources on each child.

Yet, until the early twentieth century, there was still a high degree of diversity in the experience of childhood based on social class, gender, and race, and accentuated by the rapid and uneven expansion of industrial capitalism. The children of the urban middle class, prosperous commercial farmers, and southern planters enjoyed increasingly long childhoods and were free from major household or work responsibilities until their late teens or twenties. But the offspring of urban workers, frontier farmers, and Black Americans, both enslaved and free, had briefer childhoods and became involved in work inside or outside the home before they reached their teens.

Urban working-class children often contributed to the family economy by scavenging and collecting coal, wood, and other items that could be used at home or sold, or by taking part in the street trades, selling gum, peanuts, newspapers, and the like. In industrial towns, young people under the age of fifteen contributed on average about 20 percent of their family's income. In mining areas, boys as young as ten began working in the pits as breakers, separating coal from slate and wood, and then graduated into full-fledged miners in their mid- or late teens.

On farms, children as young as five might pull weeds or keep birds and cattle away from crops. By the age of eight, many were tending the livestock, and as they grew older, they milked cows, churned butter, fed chickens, collected eggs, hauled water, scrubbed laundry, and harvested crops. A blurring of gender duties among children and youth was especially common on frontier farms.

Schooling in the nineteenth century varied as widely as did work routines. In the rural North, the Midwest, and the Far West, most mid- and late-nineteenth-century students attended one-room schools for three to six months a year. But city children spent nine months a year attending age-graded classes taught by professional teachers. In rural and urban areas, girls generally received more schooling than boys.[4]

Law and custom severely restricted educational opportunities for Black children. Despite the threat to flog or even amputate a finger of an enslaved child who learned to read or write, perhaps 5 or even 10 percent of the enslaved were literate. Even after emancipation, access to formal education was highly constrained for Black Americans. As late as 1910, just 45 percent of the Black school-aged population was enrolled. Racial disparities in educational funding were pronounced. In 1915, in the South, average state funding for education was $10.82 for a white child and just $4.01 for a Black child.

Waves and Waves of Advice for Parents

As the nineteenth century drew to an end, middle-class parents were starting to embrace the idea that child-rearing should be scientific. Through the Child Study movement, teachers and mothers, under the direction of psychologists, identified a series of stages of child development. This movement led to the "discovery"—more accurately the invention—of adolescence, a period marked by emotional and psychological turmoil tied to the biological changes associated with puberty. Within the middle class, an acceptance of scientific parenting meant that young people remained in the parental home longer and spent longer periods in formal schooling.

The attempt to apply scientific principles to the care of children produced new kinds of child-rearing manuals, now written by doctors and psychologists rather than ministers, as had previously been the case. The most influential manual was Dr. Luther Emmett Holt's *The Care and Feeding of Children*, first published in 1894. In an era when a well-adjusted adult was viewed as a creature of habit and self-control, Holt stressed the importance of imposing regular habits on infants by rigidly scheduling a child's feeding, bathing, sleeping, and bowel movements He also advised mothers to guard vigilantly against germs and to avoid undue stimulation of infants—for example, by kissing their babies. Holt also advised parents to ignore their baby's crying and to break such habits as thumb-sucking.

At about the same time, self-described "child-savers" launched a concerted campaign to universalize the middle-class model of childhood, in which childhood was defined as a period during which young people should be insulated from the stresses and corrupting influences of the adult world and free from adult-like responsibilities. Trying to universalize the modern ideal of a sheltered childhood without regard to a child's class, ethnicity, gender, and race was a highly uneven process and to this day has never encompassed all American children.

But by the early twentieth century, the middle-class conception of "modern childhood" had generally been accepted as the societal norm, although progress was slow and bitterly resisted. Child labor was not outlawed until the 1930s, and high school attendance didn't become a near-universal experience until the 1950s.

During the 1920s and 1930s, the field of child psychology exerted a growing influence on middle-class parenting. It provided a new language for describing children's emotional problems. Concepts like sibling rivalry, inferiority complexes, phobias, maladjustment, and Oedipus complexes gained wide acceptance. Child psychology also offered new insights into the effects of different styles of parenting, such as demanding and permissive forms. It categorized the stages and milestones of children's development and the characteristics of children at particular ages. This was when, for example, the phrase "terrible twos" was coined.

The growing prosperity of the 1920s made the late nineteenth-century emphasis on rigid self-control and regularity seem outmoded. The new model for a well-adjusted adult was a more easygoing figure who was capable of enjoying leisure. There was a reaction against the mechanistic and behaviorist notion that children's behavior should and could be molded by scientific control. Popular dispensers of advice now advocated a more relaxed approach to child-rearing, emphasizing the importance of meeting the emotional needs of babies. The title of a 1936 book by pediatrician C. Anderson Aldrich, *Babies Are Human Beings*, summed up the new attitude.[6]

The stresses and uncertainties of the Great Depression of the 1930s and World War II made parents much more anxious about child-rearing. In the postwar era, many psychologists asserted that faulty mothering was the cause of lasting psychological problems in children. Leading psychologists such as Theodore Lidz, Irving Bieber, and Erik Erikson linked schizophrenia, homosexuality, and identity diffusion to mothers who displaced their frustrations and their needs for independence onto their children.

Many psychologists worried that boys, being raised almost exclusively by women, might fail to develop an appropriate sex-role identity. In retrospect, these fears reflected the fact that mothers were playing a much more exclusive role in raising their children than ever before in American history.[7]

POSTMODERN CHILDHOOD IN THE TRANSITION FROM TWENTIETH TO TWENTY-FIRST CENTURY

By the 1950s, developments were already underway that would bring down the curtain on "modern childhood" and replace it with something we might call "postmodern childhood." Postmodern childhood is a product of radical changes in society that led, in the space of just over thirty years, to the breakdown of dominant norms regarding the family, gender expectations, age, and even reproduction (see Coontz in Chapter 6 of this volume).

Children today grow up under different circumstances than their immediate predecessors. They are more likely to experience their parents' divorce. They are more likely to have a working mother and to spend significant amounts of time unsupervised by adults. They are more likely to grow up without siblings.

Age norms once considered "natural" have been thrown into question. Even the bedrock biological process of sexual maturation has accelerated. Adolescent girls today, for example, enter puberty at an earlier age and are much more likely to have sexual relations during their mid-teens than their peers did a half-century ago.[8]

While society still assumes that the young are fundamentally different from adults—that they should spend their first eighteen years in the parental home and should devote their time to education in age-graded schools—it is also clear that basic aspects of the ideal of a protected childhood, in which the young are kept isolated from adult realities, have broken down.[9] Postmodern children are independent consumers and participate in a separate, semiautonomous youth culture. Adults quite rightly assume that even preadolescents know a great deal about the realities of the adult world.

Since the early 1970s, a variety of factors have contributed to a surge in the scope and intensity of parental anxieties about child-rearing. As parents had fewer children, they invested more emotional energy in each child. Greater professional expertise about children, coupled with a proliferation of research and advocacy organizations, media outlets, and government agencies responsible for children's health and safety, made parents more aware of threats to children's well-being. Many middle-class parents responded by trying to protect their children from every imaginable harm by baby-proofing their homes, using car seats, requiring bicycle helmets, and the like—things unknown a generation earlier.

Middle-class parents also worried that their offspring might underperform compared with peers and looked for ways to maximize their children's physical, social, and intellectual development. The goal of postwar parents had been to raise normal children who fit in. Middle-class parents now try to give their child a competitive advantage, a trend spurred by fears of downward mobility and anxiety that parents may not be able to pass on their status and social class to their children (see Coleman in Chapter 30 of this volume).

Today we no longer see early childhood as a stage to be rushed through. Early childhood is viewed as the formative stage for later life. Society believes that children's experiences during the first two or three years of life mold their personality, lay the foundation for future cognitive and psychological development, and leave a lasting imprint on their emotional life. We also assume that children's development proceeds through a series of physical, psychological, social, and cognitive stages. It is accepted that even very young children have a capacity to learn, that play serves valuable developmental functions, and that growing up requires children to separate emotionally and psychologically from their parents.

There are, however, significant class differences in contemporary parenting practices, as sociologist Annette Lareau has shown. Middle-class parents, she demonstrated, became invested in "intensive" child-rearing activities. These require parents to actively stimulate their children's development by organizing their leisure activities, chauffeuring them to lessons, or supervising their homework. Such intensive parenting, when taken to the extreme, has been called "helicopter parenting." Working-class and poor mothers and fathers, with unpredictable work hours and less money for expensive extracurriculars, often don't have the ability to engage in intensive parenting.

Lareau has shown that middle-class parents spend more time in conversation with their children, read to them more often, employ a larger vocabulary, and are more likely to try to reason with their children rather than simply enforce rules. Middle-class parents are also more likely to place their children in adult-supervised enrichment activities, while children in working-class and poor families spend more time in free, unstructured play and are more likely to socialize with extended family. Parents across social classes endorse the ideas of intensive parenting, but their lives produce different opportunities to practice them.[10]

Although the middle-class ideal of child-rearing has become the societal norm, social class remains a primary determinant of children's well-being.[11] In recent years, social conservatives have argued that family structure is a primary source of inequality in children's well-being, while political liberals tend to focus on ethnicity, race, and gender. But the most powerful predictor of children's welfare is, in fact, social and economic class. Economic distress contributes to family instability, inadequate health care, high degrees of mobility, and elevated levels of stress and depression.

As in the nineteenth century, contemporary American childhoods differ widely based on social class. There is a vast difference between the highly pressured, hyperorganized, fast-track childhoods of affluent children and the childhoods experienced by the one-third of all children who live in poverty at some point before the age of eighteen.

In many affluent families, the boundaries between work and family life have blurred. Parents often try to cope by tightly organizing their children's lives. But most affluent children are unsupervised by their parents for large portions of the day and have their own television, computer, and phone, which gives them unmediated access to information. Many affluent families swing back and forth between parental distance from children caused by work pressures and parental indulgence as the parents try to compensate for parenting too little.

Meanwhile, in 2023 one-sixth of children lived in poverty. And it wasn't the same by group: Black and Hispanic children are two to three times as likely as white children to be impoverished. Children who live in poverty generally experience limited adult supervision, inferior schooling, and a lack of easy access to productive diversions and activities.

During the COVID-19 pandemic, the U.S. government temporarily did more to help families with children, and these antipoverty programs reduced child poverty by nearly 50 percent in 2021. The news reports were ecstatic.[12] These programs narrowed the gap between Black, Hispanic, and white families.[13] But when the temporary pandemic support ended, so did the relief from child poverty.[14] As in the past, in these current times the conditions that children live in are a choice, not a natural outcome.

THERE IS NO "GOLDEN AGE OF CHILDHOOD"

How does the status of children today compare with that of children of the past? Are children better or worse off? This question has been of immense importance to every generation.

One of this country's oldest convictions is a belief in the decline of the younger generation. For more than three centuries, American adults have worried that children are growing ever more disobedient and disrespectful. In 1657, a Puritan minister, Ezekiel Rogers, lamented: "I find the greatest trouble and grief about the rising generation. . . . Much ado I have with my own family . . . the young breed doth much afflict me."[15]

Wistfulness about a golden age of childhood is invariably misplaced. There has never been a golden age of childhood, when the overwhelming majority of American children have been well cared for and had idyllic lives. Nostalgia typically represents a yearning not for the past as it really was but rather for a whitewashed fantasy about the past.

In 1820, children constituted about half of the workers in the early factories. As recently as the 1940s, fewer than half of all high school students graduated. In the 1950s, Alfred Kinsey's studies found rates of sexual abuse similar to those reported today. His interviews indicated that 12 percent of preadolescent girls had been the victim of exhibitionists and that 9 percent of girls had had their genitals fondled.

We also forget that the introduction of every new form of entertainment over the past century has been accompanied by dire warnings about its impact on children. The anxieties over video games and social media are only the latest in a long line of supposed threats to children that included television, movies, radio, and comic books.[16]

The danger of nostalgia is that it creates unrealistic expectations, guilt and anger.[17] If we cling to a fantasy that once upon a time childhood and youth were years of carefree adventure, we ignore the fact that for most children in the past, growing up was anything but easy. Disease, death of a parent, family disruption, and early entry into the world of work were integral parts of family life. The notion of a long childhood, devoted to education and free from adult-like responsibilities, is a very recent invention, a product of the past century and a half that only became a reality for most children after World War II.

Another problem with nostalgia about childhood in the past is that it assumes that the family home was traditionally a haven and bastion of stability in an ever-changing world. Throughout American history, family stability has been the exception, not the norm. As late as the beginning of the twentieth century, fully one-third of all American children spent at least part of their childhood in a single-parent home, and as recently as 1940, one child in ten did not live with either parent—compared with one in twenty-five today.[18]

There have been genuine gains achieved in children's lives, including the prohibition of child labor, the expansion of schooling, and the growing awareness of the evils of child abuse. But the history of childhood has not been a story of steady, linear progress. The most recent illustration—the case of the decline of child poverty in 2021 and the increase again after government support ended—is just the most recent illustration.

Each generation of children has had to wrestle with the specific social, political, and economic constraints of its own historical period. In our own time, the young have had to struggle with high rates of family insecurity and uncertainty, a growing disconnection from adults, and the expectation that all children should pursue the same academic path at the same pace, even as the attainment of full adulthood recedes ever further into the future.

Profound class differences in children's experiences persist and have even grown in salience over the past thirty years. Poor children grow up in an "ecology of poverty" characterized by substandard housing, inadequate schooling, deficient health care, unstable living arrangements, and limited access to decent child care. Many poor children are exposed to violence and have parents who suffer from depression stemming from erratic incomes and demanding work hours. In recent years, the gap between poor and working-class children and affluent children in rates of attending four-year colleges has widened.[19]

Among the most disturbing by-products of the persistence of concentrated child poverty in the United States is the so-called school-to-prison pipeline. As a result of strict zero-tolerance school discipline policies and the outsourcing of school discipline to police officers, disadvantaged children often have their first run-ins with the criminal justice system at school. Students who are suspended, in turn, are more likely to repeat a grade or drop out altogether and to find themselves enmeshed in the juvenile justice system, and they face an increased risk for arrest or incarceration as young adults.

Evolving Circumstances for Immigrant Children and Their Parents

The sharp increase in immigration since 1965, when restrictive national quotas were abolished, has had profound consequences for children. We've seen a sharp increase in the diversity of the youngest Americans. Currently, over 18 million children—one in four—are immigrants themselves or the children of immigrants Slightly more than half are of Hispanic origin; 17 percent are of Asian descent and 9 percent are non-Hispanic Black, usually from Africa or the Caribbean.[20]

Even though roughly a quarter of first- and second-generation immigrant children grow up in poverty, most experience substantial upward mobility by the time they reach adulthood. In fact, children of immigrants achieve more upward mobility than do children of U S.-born fathers. This is the case, in part, because immigrant parents are more likely to move to high-opportunity areas than their native-born counterparts.[21]

What about the approximately 1.5 million children without documentation or the 5.5 million children who live with at least one undocumented parent? Thanks to the 1982 U.S. Supreme Court ruling in *Plyler v. Doe*, undocumented children have a right to a free public K–12 education, but they face many barriers to success; many are unable to work legally, obtain a driver's license, or attend college.[22] (See Rodriguez, Chapter 33, on mixed-legal-status families.)

There is reason to think that many first- and second-generation immigrant children grow up with different expectations than native-born children. Among many immigrant families, there appears to be a greater emphasis on family interdependence than is found in the stereotypical non-Hispanic white upper-middle-class nuclear family. (See Sanchez-Connally, Chapter 32, on immigrant families and higher education.) There is a heightened stress on reciprocal family obligations and greater respect for the elderly, growing out of a strong awareness of the sacrifices made by the older generations. In addition, children and adolescents are often given more family responsibilities, including caring for siblings and family members, cleaning the home, cooking meals, and sometimes assisting in a family business.[23]

Many immigrant families attach a high value to family harmony and children's academic achievement, yet immigrant parents express it differently. They are apparently less likely to cheerlead for their children than native-born upper-middle-class non-Hispanic white parents, who exist within a culture that tends to expect mothers to boost their child's self-esteem, entertain their children, ensure that they are happy and never bored, express love frequently—physically and verbally—intervene and advocate aggressively on their behalf, and seek to insulate them from risks to their physical and emotional well-being.[24]

Even for children of the middle class and the stably employed working class, American society is not as child friendly as we might hope. Literary critic Daniel Kline persuasively suggests that contemporary American society subjects the young to three forms of psychological violence that we tend to ignore. First is the violence of expectations, in which children are pushed beyond their social, physical, and academic capabilities, largely as an expression of their parents' needs. Then there is the violence of labeling normal childish behavior (for example, childhood exuberance or interest in sex) as pathological. Third is the violence of representation, in which children and adolescents are exploited by advertisers, marketers, purveyors of popular culture, and politicians, who feed parental anxieties and take advantage of young people's desire to be stylish, independent, and defiant, and eroticize teenage and preadolescent girls.[25]

I believe there are three other forms of violence that American society inflicts on children. First is the violence of poverty, which often takes the form of hunger, insecurity, and family instability. Next, there is the violence of racism—the prejudice, antagonism, stigmatization, and suspicion directed against non-white children on the basis of their race or ethnicity. Then, there is the psychological abuse that comes from seeing children as objects to be shaped and molded for their own good. Contemporary American society is much more controlling of young people in an institutional and ideological sense than its predecessors. And as the baby boom and millennial generations age, American society has become increasingly adult-oriented, with fewer "free" spaces for the young, a society in which youth are primarily valued as service workers and consumers.

For more than three centuries, despite massive evidence to the contrary, America has considered itself to be an especially child-centered society. Yet in no other advanced country do so many young people grow up in poverty or without health care, nor does any other Western society provide so few resources for child care or restrict paid parental leave so stringently.

This paradox is not new. Since the early nineteenth century, the United States has developed a host of institutions specifically aimed at the young: the common school, the Sunday school, the orphanage, the house of refuge, the reformatory, the children's hospital, the juvenile court, and a wide variety of youth organizations. All were envisioned as caring, developmental, and educational institutions that would serve children's interests. In practice, however, they frequently end up being primarily custodial and disciplinary.

Many of the reforms that were supposed to help children were adopted in part because they served the needs, interests, and convenience of adults. The abolition of child labor removed competition from an overcrowded labor market. Separating children by age-based grades not only made it easier to handle children within schools; it also divided the young into convenient market segments.

The most important lesson that grows out of understanding the history of childhood is the simplest. While many fear that American society has changed too much, the sad fact is that it has changed too little. Americans have failed to adapt social institutions to new realities, to the fact that the young mature more rapidly than they did in the past, that most mothers of preschoolers now participate in the paid workforce, and that a near majority of children will spend substantial parts of their childhood in a single-parent, cohabitating-parent, or stepparent household.

As we navigate a new century of childhood, we need to pose new questions How can we provide better care for the young, especially the one-sixth who are growing up in poverty? How can we better connect the worlds of adults and the young? How can we give the young more ways to demonstrate their growing competence and maturity? How can we tame a violence-laced, sex-saturated popular culture without undercutting a commitment to freedom and a respect for the free-floating world of fantasy?

NOTES

1.   Annette Lareau, *Unequal Childhoods: Class, Race, and Family Life* (Berkeley: University of California Press, 2003).

2.   Colin Heywood, A *History of Childhood: Children and Childhood in the West from Medieval to Modern Times* (Cambridge: Polity, 2001); Joseph Illick, *American Childhoods* (Philadelphia: University of Pennsylvania Press, 2002); James A. Schultz, *The Knowledge of Childhood in the German Middle Ages, 1100–1350* (Philadelphia: University of Pennsylvania Press, 1995), 11.

3.   Howard P. Chudacoff, *How Old Are You? Age Consciousness in American Society* (Princeton, NJ: Princeton University Press, 1989); Joseph F. Kett, *Rites of Passage: Adolescence in America* (New York: Basic Books, 1977).

4.   Priscilla Clement, *Growing Pains: Children in the Industrial Age, 1850–1890* (New York: Twayne, 1997); David Nasaw, *Children in the City: At Work and at Play* (Garden City, NY: Anchor Press/Doubleday, 1985); Christine Stansell, *City of Women: Sex and Class in New York, 1789–1860* (New York: Knopf, 1986).

5.   Ann Hulbert, *Raising America: Experts, Parents, and a Century of Advice about Children* (New York: Knopf, 2003); Julia Grant, *Raising Baby by the Book: The Education of American Mothers* (New Haven, CT: Yale University Press, 1998).

6.   Kathleen W. Jones, *Taming the Troublesome Child* (Cambridge, MA: Harvard University Press, 1999).

7.   Steven Mintz and Susan Kellogg, *Domestic Revolutions: A Social History of American Family Life* (New York: Free Press, 1988), 189.

8. On changes in the onset of sexual maturation, see Marcia E. Herman-Giddens et al., "Secondary Sexual Characteristics and Menses in Young Girls Seen in Office Practice: A Study from the Pediatric Research in Office Settings Network," *Pediatrics* 99, no. 4 (April 1997): 505–512. In 1890, the average age of menarche in the United States was estimated to be 14.8 years; by the 1990s, the average age had fallen to 12.5 (12.1 for African American girls and 12.8 for girls of northern European ancestry). According to the study, which tracked 17,000 girls to find out when they hit different markers of puberty, 15 percent of white girls and 48 percent of African American girls showed signs of breast development or pubic hair by age eight. For conflicting views on whether the age of menarche has fallen, see Lisa Belkin, "The Making of an 8-Year-Old Woman," *New York Times*, December 24, 2000; Gina Kolata, "Doubters Fault Theory Finding Earlier Puberty," *New York Times*, February 20, 2001; Gina Kolata, "2 Endocrinology Groups Raise Doubt on Earlier Onset of Girls' Puberty," *New York Times*, March 3, 2001.

9. Stephen Robertson, "The Disappearance of Childhood," http://teaching.arts.usyd.edu.au/ history/2044/.

10. Lareau, *Unequal Childhoods*; and Patrick Ishizuka, "Social Class, Gender, and Contemporary Parenting Standards in the United States: Evidence from a National Survey Experiment," *Social Forces*, vol. 98, no. 1 (September 2019): 31–58.

11. David I. Macleod, *The Age of the Child: Children in America, 1890–1912* (New York: Twayne, 1998).

12. Kalee Burns, Liana Fox, and Danielle Wilson, "Expansions to Child Tax Credit Contributed to 46% Declines in Child Poverty Since 2020," U.S Census Bureau (2022), www.census.gov/library/stories/2022/09/record-drop-in-child-poverty.html.

13. Rebecca Charles, Sophie Collyer, and Christopher Wimer, "The Role of Government Transfers in the Black-White Child Poverty Gap," Center on Poverty and Social Policy at Columbia University (2022), static1.squarespace.com/static/610831a16c95260dbd68934a/t/622a300c46e382698827a2f1/1646932056576/Role-of-Government-Transfers-Black-White-Child-Poverty-Gap-CPSP-2022.pdf.

14. Center on Poverty and Social Policy at Columbia University, "3.7 Million More Children in Poverty Jan 2022 without Monthly Child Tax Credit" (2022), www.povertycenter.columbia.edu/news-internal/monthly-poverty-january-2022.

15. Rogers quoted in James Axtell, *The School upon a Hill: Education and Society in Colonial New England* (New Haven, CT: Yale University Press, 1974), 28.

16. Hard as it is to believe, in 1951 a leading television critic decried the quality of children's television. Jack Gould, radio and TV critic for the *New York Times* from the late 1940s to 1972, complained that there was "nothing on science, seldom anything on the country's cultural heritage, no introduction to fine books, scant emphasis on the people of other lands, and little concern over hobbies and other things for children to do themselves besides watch television." *Chicago Sun Times*, August 9, 1998, 35.

17. Phil Scraton, ed., *"Childhood" in "Crisis"?* (London: University College of London Press, 1997), 161, 164.

18. Richard Weissbourd, *The Vulnerable Child: What Really Hurts America's Children and What We Can Do about It* (Reading, MA: Addison-Wesley, 1996), 48.

19. Weissbourd, 48.

20. "Trends in Immigrant Children," *Child Trends*, December 28, 2018, www.childtrends .org/indicators/immigrant-children.

21. Ran Ambramitsky and Leah Boustan, "Why the Children of Immigrants Are the Ones Getting Ahead in America," *Time*, June 1, 2022, https://time.com/6182715 /immigrants-children-us-mobility/.

22. American Psychological Association, "Undocumented Americans," n.d., www.apa.org /topics/immigration-refugees/undocumented-video.

23. Stephen T. Russell, Lisa J. Crockett, and Ruth K. Chao, *Asian American Parenting and Parent-Adolescent Relationships* (New York: Springer, 2010); Fang Wu and Sen Qi, "Asian-American Parents: Are They Really Different?," online submission, paper presented at the Annual Conference of the Chinese American Educational Research and Development Association (San Diego, CA, April 2004), files.eric.ed.gov/fulltext /ED489960.pdf.

24. Russell et al., *Asian American Parenting and Parent-Adolescent Relationships*; Wu and Qi, "Asian-American Parents: Are They Really Different?"

25. Daniel T. Kline, "Holding Therapy," History-Child-Family Listserv. March 7, 1998, history-child-family@mailbase.ac.uk.

In Other Words

RANDOM FAMILIES: GENETIC STRANGERS, SPERM DONOR SIBLINGS, AND THE CREATION OF NEW KIN

Rosanna Hertz and Barbara Risman, December 10, 2018 / CCF@TSP

Barbara Risman: In your book Random Families, *you introduce the term "genetic strangers." Can you define it for us, and explain how the families you studied embodied the term?*

Rosanna Hertz: We use the term "genetic strangers" to describe people who share genes but who do not know one other . . . or even that the other exists. Genetic strangers are not relatives *until* a relationship is created. In fact, the core of the book is about whether and how strangers become relatives . . . and what happens to the meaning of family as a result.

In *Random Families* we refer to "donors, donor siblings and their families as 'genetic strangers' as a way to bind together something that usually connotes familiarity with something that symbolizes the opposite." In the conventional heteronormative view, there is nothing more intimate than blood ties (i.e., shared genes). As single mothers and two-mom families joined the ranks of heterosexual parents who needed gametes to create a baby, those gametes often came from commercial sperm banks. The rise in markets for sperm and eggs means that more children share half their DNA with strangers.

The donor sibling networks we discuss in *Random Families* are modern strangers in a modern world—a world in which we interact with people we do not know well and may never have met before. Think about the internet, especially Facebook groups or our own FB page, which often includes people with whom we do not share space or time. The internet extends our acceptance of strangers who we believe can provide us with a sense of connectedness or belonging, information, and perhaps even intimacy. Donor sibling networks are a special case of people who may have randomly purchased the same donor, and after finding each other they might try to turn that strangeness into some form of kinship.

BR: According to your evidence, there are distinct eras in the history of the emergence of families connected by donor siblings. Can you identify these eras and how the experience of creating familial networks differs between them?

RH: Those are important questions because they point again to the distinction between stranger and relative. The first successful pregnancy with donor sperm began nearly six decades ago. But because donors were anonymous, it didn't make sense to talk about networks, even if multiple offspring were probably created in the earliest days. It wasn't until much later that this made sense, particularly with the rise of the internet, which increased the availability of information and made it much easier for people to connect by means of Facebook and websites such as Ancestry and 23andMe, for example. That's why we distinguish different eras in donor-conceived networks based on the kind of genetic information available and by the ease of access to that information.

The first era of donor-conceived networks begins in the 1980s with lesbian couples and single mothers (straight or queer) who pioneered the formation of these families by using smaller commercial sperm banks in two important hubs: San Francisco and Boston. In contrast to the anonymous sperm marketed by the large, often national, sperm banks, these smaller banks offered identity-release donors. The parents felt that nurture—how they raised their children—would trump nature. They told their child he or she had a "father" whom they could meet when they turned 18. If at age 18 children wanted to connect, they could ask the bank to relay that desire to the donor. Surprisingly, it was usually the donor who fostered connections between their various offspring as they came forward. The child almost always expanded family to include these new relatives, and conventional terms such as father and brother/sister were also likely to be used. The donor was a good guy who kept his promise and arrived to meet his genetic offspring. The offspring met as a sort of afterthought.

The second era begins in the 1990s with parents who purchased anonymous donor sperm only to have anonymity stripped away with the growth of the internet and online networks. These nuclear families fully expected to raise their children with disclosures about the sperm donors, but they expected that family lineage would come from the parent(s) and not through paternal (donor) kin. The growth of the internet and the ease with which people could access internet sites changed all of this. Registries emerged as independent sites and then banks offered these registries as opt-in features. Parents (for the most part mothers) were started to learn about this possibility to connect with other families who shared their child's genes. Parents would register and usually they did not discuss their decision to do this with their children. They wanted to check out these strangers who lived all over the country before telling their children. Once parents were satisfied, they told their children they had "half-siblings." Children were surprised. Sometimes these relationships moved offline to a face-to-face meeting, and sometimes the children became close to these new siblings. Counting these networks as extended kin took time, as these unscripted relationships slowly developed. Parents might have orchestrated those first "reunions" when children were adolescents or teens. In the book we compare two networks from this era. Both have anonymous donors, but the donor in one network decides to reveal his identity. Moreover, the kids in these two networks react differently to meeting their donor siblings. As these networks expanded, intimacy between such a large group of children became problematic. Like other kinds of large organizations, the networks fragment into smaller groups that sometimes resemble high school cliques.

The third era of donor-conceived networks begins with children born after 2003. The distinguishing feature is that children born in this era would grow up with donor siblings as commonplace. These parents had toddlers when registries first began, and they connected early on with their child's donor siblings. Unlike the earlier era, when kids were surprised that they had donor siblings, these kids saw their half-siblings more like cousins who visited once or twice a year. Sometimes children formed close ties to one or two other children in the group. These networks are larger from the start (as more parents decide to locate a child's half-siblings). There are no large gatherings with all the members. Families are most likely to meet regionally with a smaller group.

Finally, we feature a network of younger parents whose children are under five and who knew about donor siblings when they purchased gametes. It is not the newness of the internet or registries that emerges among this group. Instead, these parents, whose children are too young to understand the idea of donors and donor siblings, question whether they can find a new kind of kinship organization. They don't want to make assumptions about the relationships within the group and how their children might feel when they are older. They hope that by creating memories of gatherings, their children will want to define those relationships with one another in the future or, at the very least, they will have one another to talk to about being donor conceived. For these parents, the donor sibling network is more like other interest groups or forums they belong to, where they can share information that they hope will benefit their child. This new period (maybe not an era) represents kinship revisited.

Since consumer demand for identity release donors increased over these eras, the people we interviewed with children born after 2000 are more likely to have this kind of donor. Yet, when the children eventually can have contact with their donor (if their child wants this), these last two networks imagine a donor who is willing to offer information. He is not the "father" who arrived in the late 1980s.

BR: In many of the narratives, you write about how individuals, and nuclear families, come to reassess the relative power of nature versus nurture in children's development. Please explain how children come to think of nature versus nurture in their experiences as they meet genetic family members.

RH: We made a point of interviewing children (ages 10 to 29) because we anticipated that at an early age they would have to puzzle through distinctions like nature versus nurture that are loaded with meaning for families as well as for children.

But to be fair to the kids, it's important to put "nature versus nurture" into context first. That is, for all the public discussion of genetics and all the information available about individual genet c makeup (e.g., from services like Ancestry and 23andMe), there is huge ambiguity about the meaning of genes for *parents*, let alone for children. Even in the scientific community, there is no consensus about the heritability of many human qualities like intelligence, musical ability, or sports. So, when we interviewed kids it was important for us to listen carefully to the way they gave meaning to genes.

In most instances, parents set the foundation for kids' understanding of nature versus nurture, usually with their first conversations about a child's origins or birth story. Donor is a hollow concept to a child. Parents fill in the concept, but always with reference to their preferred way of talking about family. A discussion about inherited traits and characteristics is how we locate children in a family system: "Your curly hair is from me, or musical ability from your grandmother." If they have a donor's profile, parents usually reference bits of information that factored into their selection of a donor (e.g., 'He is an astronaut" or "wants to become a lawyer," or he "reads a book a day" or "he likes mountain climbing"). Over time, parents and children collaborate in inventing both the donor and the child's genetic inheritance.

However, for donor-conceived children, nature versus nurture really becomes relevant—and complicated—when donor siblings are located. When half-siblings first meet, they quickly discover shared traits, starting with physical resemblances. It's important to note that children who share a donor are primed to find similarities with their half-siblings. The experience is often powerful and, not surprisingly, talk about genes and heredity takes center stage.

Donor-conceived children described a real tension between nature and nurture—if not immediately, then over time as they transformed genetic strangers into relatives. Kids who had no siblings within their nuclear family often took great delight in meeting children who were like them, especially since their parents encouraged the contact. But even with parental encouragement, some kids felt they should downplay the importance of genes because putting genes at center stage implicitly distances them from the family they've always known. This is most pronounced in families with a nongenetic parent. On the other hand, they could not deny the fact of physical resemblance and the often eerie feeling that occurred when they discovered unexpected similarities like sense of humor and musical ability.

With time and distance, a more nuanced view about nature and nurture seems to emerge. Kids assimilate the new information and arrive at workable definitions of siblinghood, for example. They make a point of preserving a central role for nongenetic parents, such as talking about deeply ingrained preferences for food, music, or esoteric matters that they share with their nongenetic parents. Talk about genes is tempered by a more sophisticated understanding that they can belong to their parents while acknowledging that they share some things with a donor and their donor siblings. ▄

8

African Americans and the Birth of the Modern Marriage

Donna L. Franklin

A long tradition of dual-career partnerships has defined most marriages among African American professionals at least since the late nineteenth century. This model, which is relatively new for whites, has been overlooked by many family historians and social scientists. This chapter will explore two fundamental questions related to these revolutionary marriages: why marriage conventions differed for professional whites and blacks, and how distinct cultural values regarding women emerged in the African American community.

We can trace the roots of dual-career marriages in the black professional community to the late nineteenth and early twentieth centuries. In an era when very few married white women worked outside the home, married black females were combining care for their families with employment responsibilities.

As industrial capitalism developed, with its low wages, obstacles to upward mobility, and poor working conditions, marriage became an attractive alternative to working for many white women. At the same time, in the culture as a whole a new ideal took hold—the image of women as fragile, delicate, and economically dependent, needing to be sheltered and supported.

The different conventions regarding work and marriage in the white and black communities were reflected in a letter that the leading women's suffragist, Susan B. Anthony, wrote to her black friend and fellow activist, Ida B. Wells-Barnett, in 1890. Anthony had never married and doubted that women could combine marriage with a career. She lamented that Wells-Barnett's activism was suffering since she married and began having children:

Women like you who have a special call for work should never marry. I know of no one in all this country better fitted to do the work you had in hand. Since you've gotten married, agitation practically seems to have ceased. Besides, you're trying to help in the formation of this league and your baby needs your attention at home

You're distracted over the thought that he's not being looked after as he would be if you were there, and that makes for divided duty.

When Ida B. Wells moved to Chicago and married Ferdinand Barnett, she was thirty-two and her antilynching campaign was in full swing. Their marriage was a union of two black professionals. He was a prominent Chicago attorney and founder and publisher of the *Conservator*, Chicago's first black newspaper. Barnett never expected Wells to stay home and be a housewife after their marriage. He employed household help, and he personally did most of the cooking for the family. Their temperaments complemented each other. Their daughter, Alfreda Duster, remembered that her "father was a very mild mannered man; he was not aggressive . . . or outspoken like my mother."[1] With the support of her husband, Ida B. Wells-Barnett remained a force to be reckoned with both inside and outside the home.

But even with such a supportive husband, Wells struggled with the conflicting demands of activism and her maternal role. She had her first child during an election year and was asked to campaign throughout Illinois for the Women's State Central Committee, a Republican political organization. She agreed on the condition that a nurse be provided to help with her six-month-old son. Wells-Barnett recalled, "I honestly believe that I am the only woman in the United States who ever traveled throughout the country with a nursing baby to make political speeches."

A year later she was pregnant again. By then her husband had been appointed assistant state's attorney. She resigned from the presidency of the Ida B. Wells Club and announced that she was retiring from public life to devote more time to her family. The "retirement" lasted five months.

Black women seemed to have an easier time juggling the role of activist with the role of mother and wife. This was reflected in the dramatic differences in the marital status of white and black women activists at the end of the nineteenth century. Historian Linda Gordon found that 85 percent of black women activists were married, compared with only 34 percent of white women activists.

Another factor in the difference between marriage rates for black and white women activists is that the pool of marriageable males was much smaller for white women during this historical period. More Americans were killed during the Civil War than during any other war the nation has fought. Hundreds of thousands of husbands, fathers, sons, and lovers were killed, and many more were disabled, resulting in a generation of white women who had limited prospects for marriage. In a culture in which women were defined by their relationship to men, many white women would for the first time be forced to discover their independence from men.[2] Black women did not suffer the same deficit of marriageable men; although black men rushed to enlist in the Union army when they were finally allowed to join, they suffered far fewer casualties because they were rarely allowed to actually bear arms.[3]

Although barely one-third of the white activists had married, Gordon reports that "the white women, with few exceptions, tended to view married women's economic dependence on men as desirable and their employment as a misfortune." Anna Julia Cooper, the fourth black woman to receive a doctorate, offered an alternative perspective. She married and was widowed at an early age and advised black women to seek egalitarian marriages. Cooper also believed that all married women should earn a livelihood because it "renders women less dependent on the marriage relationship for physical support (which, by the way, does not always accompany it)."

In Cooper's opinion, the question was not "How shall I so cramp, stunt, simplify, and nullify myself as to make me eligible to the honor of being swallowed up by some little man? But the problem rests with the man as to how he can so develop . . . to reach the ideal of a generation of women who demand the noblest, grandest, and best achievement of which he is capable."[4]

In general, black female activists were viewed more favorably within their own community than were their white counterparts because they were seen as fighting for the greater good of all black people and did not pose a threat to the political objectives of black men. Slavery, having rendered black men and women equally powerless, had leveled the gender "playing field" within the black community. In contrast, much of white women's activism, such as the fight for female suffrage, posed a direct challenge to the privileges of white men and patriarchy.

When historian Stephanie J. Shaw examined the lives of professional black women from the 1870s through the 1950s, she found that 74 percent were married at least once in their lifetime. In addition to being more likely than their white activist counterparts to be married, 51 percent of them had professional husbands. Among the more affluent black women who emerged as leaders, marriage to prominent black men often gave them a distinct advantage in that it gave them greater access to the network of powerful black men. Shaw notes that many of the women in her study had been socialized in such a way that "the model of womanhood held before [them] was one of achievement in *both* the public and private spheres. Parents cast domesticity as a complement rather than a contradiction to success in public arenas."

Ida B. Wells made a similar point when speaking about balancing motherhood with her activism. Although she did not have the "longing for children that so many women have," she was glad that she had them nonetheless, adding that not having children robbed women "of one of the most glorious advantages in the development of their own womanhood."[5]

The lives of white activists Alice Freeman Palmer and Antoinette Louisa Brown Blackwell are indicative of a different convention. In 1881, twenty-six-year-old Alice Freeman became president of Wellesley College, the first female to head a nationally known institution of higher education. During her tenure as president, she met George Palmer, a Harvard professor, and in 1887, upon announcing her engagement to him, she resigned as Wellesley's president.

Antoinette Louisa Brown Blackwell, a women's rights activist and social reformer, was the first American woman to become an ordained minister. She married Samuel Charles Blackwell, an abolitionist businessman. After her marriage, even though she had a sympathetic husband, she struggled to combine marriage and her "intellectual work." They had seven children, two of whom died in infancy. While she was raising her children, Brown Blackwell for the most part gave up public speaking. She continued, however, to study; and as her children got older, she wrote and published many books on science and philosophy. Although she was more in favor of marriage than Susan B. Anthony, she had doubts about a woman's ability to juggle marriage, a family, and a career. She advocated part-time work for married women, with their husbands helping out with child care and housework.[6]

FREE AT LAST

The defeat of the Confederacy in the Civil War and the abolition of slavery brought profound changes to black family life, altering the economic, social, and legal arrangements within which the formerly enslaved persons lived. Formerly enslaved persons began creating communities, establishing networks of institutions, churches, schools, and mutual aid societies. When they were enslaved, blacks had established secret churches and families, and after emancipation these institutions provided an important sense of community. With their newfound freedom, black men and women shared a common dream of living as free people.

The formerly enslaved persons particularly welcomed the opportunity to marry, a right that had been denied to them. In 1850, Henry Bibb, who had escaped slavery, had written that "there are no class of people in the United States who so highly appreciate the legality of marriage as those persons who have been held and treated as property." When laws were passed requiring marriages among formerly enslaved persons to be registered, some whites were "astonished by the eagerness with which former slaves legalized their marriage bonds."[7]

THE CLUB WOMEN'S MOVEMENT

The efforts of Ida B. Wells-Barnett to build a broad campaign against lynching by lecturing to groups in the United States and internationally, despite her increasing family responsibilities, had the side effect of fostering the growth of black women's clubs.

In response to a letter from an Englishwoman who had become interested in the issue of lynching after hearing Wells-Barnett give a speech in Britain,[8] John W. Jacks, president of the Missouri Press Association, published an open letter asserting,

> Out of some 200 [Negroes] in this vicinity it is doubtful if there are a dozen virtuous women or that number who are not daily thieving from white people. To illustrate how they regard virtue in a woman, one of them, a negro woman, who asked who a certain negro woman who had lately moved into the neighborhood was. She turned up her nose and said, "The negroes will have nothing to do with 'dat nigger,' she won't let any man except her husband sleep with her, and we don't 'sociate with her."[9]

Josephine St. Pierre Ruffin, editor of *The Woman's Era*, the first American magazine owned and managed by black women, widely circulated Jacks's letter to prominent black women around the country, and the ensuing indignation led to organizing the first national conference to discuss black women's social concerns. In July 1895, a hundred women from ten states convened to formulate plans for a national federation of black women.

The following year, Ruffin, who was president of the Women's Club of Boston, called the first Conference of Negro Women, which launched the National Association of Colored Women (NACW) under the motto "lifting as we climb."

These club women, primarily northerners, were reformers and activists who subscribed to the class values of Victorian America. The NACW's goal was to uplift poor women by emphasizing respectable behavior and introducing alternate images of black females. Ruffin saw it as "fitting" for the women of the race to take the lead in the movement, while recognizing "the necessity of the

sympathy of our husbands, brothers, and fathers." She emphasized that the movement "is led and directed by women for the good of women and men, for the
benefit of all humanity."

The club women's movement enabled black women to take a leadership role
in their communities and to participate with black men in "uplifting" the race.
African American studies professor Paula Giddings notes that at a time when
patriarchal notions of men's roles were dominant, "there was a greater acceptance among black men of women in activist roles than there was in the broader
society."[10]

A BLACK WOMAN'S ERA

Although black women faced many challenges, the emergence of black female
leaders and the conscious efforts to improve the education of black women bore
significant fruit around the turn of the century. Novelist Frances Harper, whose
writings focused on the political struggles of African American people, characterized this period as a "woman's era." Chicago activist Fannie Barrier Williams
declared that although "the colored man and the colored woman started even,
the achievements of black women during this period eclipsed black men."[11]

From 1890 to 1910, the number of professional black women increased by
219 percent, compared with a 51 percent rise for black men. In 1890, about
25 percent of all black professionals were women. By 1910, that number had risen
to 43 percent. The growing achievement of women was reflected in the fact that
in 1910 female graduates outnumbered male graduates by two to one at Dunbar
High School, the leading black high school in Washington, D.C.[12]

In her study of black women's education, Jeanne Noble argued that black
women had higher levels of educational achievement than men because the

> social system of the Negro rewarded the enterprising, clever, ambitious woman.
> Later, when attitudes that challenged the women's right to college education
> emerged, missionaries and earlier college founders were able to overcome these
> attitudes partly because of the need for teachers to educate the masses of ignorant
> Negroes.[13]

The perceived limitations in job opportunities for black men also contributed to the disparity between male and female academic achievement. Benjamin
Mays, who received a PhD from the University of Chicago and became president
of Morehouse College, faced great opposition to his education from his father,
who believed the only occupations for black men were preaching and farming.

Two additional factors encouraged black women's academic achievements. The first was the high probability that even married black women would need to find employment outside the home. In addition, many black women sought to avoid the degradation of domestic service, seen as a continuation of the oppression they had experienced during slavery.

The growth in black women's quest for education during this period can be seen in the enrollment trends at the thirteen schools of higher education run by the Baptist Home Mission. In 1880, male enrollment in these schools was twice as high as female enrollment. But by 1892, female students outnumbered males nearly three to two, and 120 of the 202 teachers were women. Most of the female students specialized in teacher training.

Not only were black women going to school in increasing numbers; they were also providing leadership by founding new schools specifically to train black women. Lucy C. Laney, Nannie Helen Burroughs, Charlotte Hawkins Brown, and Mary McLeod Bethune all founded training institutions.

In addition, black women actively challenged the authority of black men. Charlotte Hawkins Brown, for example, declared that her own work and writings were just as important as those of Booker T. Washington. Nannie Burroughs defied the male-dominated leadership so forcibly that she nearly lost church financial support for the National Training School for Women. Burroughs also canceled a speech before the National Christian Mission when administrators insisted on censoring her remarks.

THE COMMITMENT TO MARRIAGE

When studying black middle- and upper-income women in Illinois at the turn of the century, the historian Shirley Carlson found that

> the black community did not regard intelligence and femininity as conflicting values, as the larger society did. That society often expressed the fear that intelligent women would develop masculine characteristics. . . . Blacks seemed to have no such trepidations, or at least they were willing to have their women take these risks.[14]

Many prominent black women were married to professional black men. In addition to Wells and Barnett, there were figures like Shirley Graham Du Bois, an author, composer, playwright, and activist, who was married to W. E. B. Du Bois, a scholar, visionary, activist, and author. Teacher and social worker Sadie Grey Mays was the wife of Benjamin Mays, mentor to Martin Luther King Jr.

and president of Morehouse College. Eslanda Goode Robeson was a writer and social anthropologist and was business manager for her husband, Paul Robeson, the athlete, lawyer, author, activist, actor, and singer.

Margaret Murray Washington was president of the National Federation of Afro-American Women and was the wife of Booker T. Washington, president of Tuskegee Institute. Lugenia Hope Burns had a distinguished career as a social work reformer and was married to John Hope, the first black president of Atlanta University. Josephine Wilson Bruce, the first African American principal of a Cleveland public school, was married to Blanche K. Bruce, the first African American to serve a full term in the United States Senate.

Josephine St. Pierre Ruffin, the editor and publisher of *The Women's Era*, was married to George L. Ruffin, a member of the Boston City Council and Boston's first black judge. Madam C. J. Walker, owner of a beauty products company, was the first self-made female millionaire (black or white) and was married to a newspaperman, Charles J. Walker. Mary Terrell was a distinguished educator, suffragette, and civil rights activist, whose husband, Robert Terrell, was a Harvard graduate and principal of the M Street High School and the first African American judge on the D.C. Municipal Court.

In that era, prominent black women tended to have experienced greater upward mobility than their white counterparts. About 90 percent of the black women who were classified as middle to upper class had been born into working-class families, compared with 35 percent of white women. The difference arose in part because blacks had been emancipated for only a relatively short time, and higher education was the vehicle for social mobility for African Americans. Surveys conducted during that period found that black women were going to college for two primary reasons: to train for a vocation and to prepare for marriage and family life.[15]

Many educated black males were also enthusiastic about marriage and family life with an educated woman. Lugenia Burns and John Hope were both University of Chicago graduate students during their courtship. John, eager to marry and start a family, proposed after Lugenia received her degree. But she had been looking forward to a life of service and declined John's first proposal. Lugenia had four other men also vying for her hand in marriage. But John had an advantage over her other suitors because of his commitment to marital equality. He wrote her a letter saying that when they marry "neither of us [is] to be the servant, yet both of us gladly serve each other in love and patience."[16]

In writing about these marriages, Dr. Marion Cuthbert described them as a "deference of comradeship" by the men to their wives.[17] Anna Julia Cooper described the wives as having a "partnership with husbands on a plane of intellectual equality."[18]

CHANGES IN AFRICAN AMERICAN MARRIAGE

The strong tradition of black women's education and professional employment that began during the club women's movement continued through the twentieth century. Jessie Bernard documented the higher levels of professional achievement found among black women, noting that in 1960 black women constituted 60.8 percent of black professionals, while white women constituted only 37.2 percent of the white professional class.[19]

One reason for the lower professional involvement of white women was the persistence of the nineteenth-century ethos that a woman's place was in the home. When Adlai Stevenson addressed the graduating class of Smith College (ironically the alma mater of both Gloria Steinem and Betty Friedan) in 1955, he told the students that their role in life was to "restore valid, meaningful purpose to life in your home."[20]

Three decades after Jessie Bernard's study of black and white females in the professions, Andrew Hacker found that black women made up 65.1 percent of black professionals, a rise of less than 5 percent, while white women had increased 15 points to 52.6 percent of white professionals.[21] The women's movement had been a catalyst for white women to move into the professional arena. An analysis conducted since Hacker's has found that despite gains in educational attainment and occupational status between 1975 and 2000, the median earnings of white women grew by 32 percent, while the median earnings of black women grew by only 22 percent. In addition, although the proportion of black women with college degrees increased, a racial gap in education has endured. In 2007, a study found that 19 percent of black women twenty-five and older had college degrees compared with over 30 percent of white and non-Hispanic women.[22] This gap is even wider between white and black men.

In the three decades between the Bernard and Hacker studies, the black community underwent what demographers describe as a "marriage squeeze," where a decrease in the availability of eligible partners leads to lower marriage rates, especially among women.

Using the College and Beyond (C&B) database, which contains the records of more than 80,000 undergraduate students who matriculated at twenty-eight academically selective colleges and universities in 1951, 1976, and 1989, we can compare the marriage and divorce patterns of black and white college-educated men and women. The "marriage squeeze" is reflected in the marriage rates of black graduates of these academically selective institutions roughly twenty years after they entered these schools. Black graduates in the database were less likely to be married and more likely to be divorced or separated than their white counterparts. Whereas 77 percent of white women were married, 51 percent of black women were. For male graduates, these figures were 79 percent and 61 percent, respectively. Some 14 percent of the black women were divorced or separated, compared with 6 percent of the white female graduates. For males, the differences in divorce and separation rates were minuscule: 5 percent for black men and 5 percent for white men. Of the four groups, black women had by far the highest rates of marital breakups.[23]

Although the marriage squeeze and/or the mate availability perspectives were first used to explain trends among blacks in lower economic strata, they also affect educated black women in that fewer black men with equivalent education are available for them to marry. Social scientists and policy analysts have not paid enough attention to the challenges faced by professional black women in this regard.

For African American women, the marriage squeeze has been exacerbated by the marriage of some of the most eligible black men to either white or Hispanic women. The C&B database didn't indicate the race of a graduate's spouse, but there is reason to believe that many of the black male graduates are not married to black women. In the three decades since the *Loving v. Virginia* decision was declared unconstitutional, ending all race-based legal restrictions on marriage, mixed couples tripled from 2 percent to 6 percent of all marriages. Black/white interracial married couples have increased from 51,000 in 1950 to 363,000 in 2000, a sevenfold increase. Most of these marriages were of professional black men to white or Hispanic women. In view of this, it is not surprising that well-educated black women have fewer marriage options than their black male counterparts.

Black women are also more likely to be married to men who earn less money than they do. Data from the C&B studies show that white married women's *household* incomes were higher than those of black married female graduates, even though the *personal* incomes of the black women were 6 percent higher. This is because the husbands of white women graduates made substantially more money than the husbands of the black women. In fact, black women graduates also earned considerably *more* money than their husbands—exactly the opposite of the pattern for the white women graduates. This was because many of the black women graduates were married to men with less education than they had.

My analysis of the data indicates that the black women graduates, on average, contributed 63 percent of the household income, while white women graduates earned 40 percent of the total household income. Not surprisingly, the income of both black and white male graduates was substantially higher than it was for female graduates. What is more interesting is that the white and black male graduates, on average, earned 78 and 75 percent of the household income, respectively.[24] This suggests that the male graduates may have entered more traditional marriages, in terms of gender, than either the white or black female graduates.

In classic exchange theory, traditional marriage has been described as an exchange of a male's economic resources for a female's social and domestic services. As American couples make the transition from more traditional to modern marriages, these marital exchanges are changing, which can be a source of tension and conflict. A wealth of research suggests that when couples get married, they bring with them a mixture of the "good things" and "bad things" from earlier generations, making the transition from traditional to modern marriages a challenging one. On the whole, both black and white male graduates, with substantially higher incomes than those of their wives, are in more traditional marriages than female graduates. This may help explain their lower divorce rates and the fact that differences between the divorce rates of black and white males were infinitesimal.

The tensions and pressures in college-educated professional black women's marriages, however, are reflected in their much higher rates of divorce and separation. As noted earlier, household income for white women graduates was higher than for black women even though their own earnings were, on average, 6 percent lower than those of the black women and considerably lower than their husbands' earnings. This seems to indicate that white women graduates may "downsize" their careers as they perform more family functions than their husbands, who focus on increasing their incomes. Black women had less opportunity or pressure to downsize their careers.

Some black wives may harbor anger and resentment that they earn more than their husbands, and some husbands may be resentful that they do not earn enough money to have wives who can downsize their careers, and that anger may be displaced or misdirected at spouses. This may help explain the higher divorce and separation rates of African American female graduates.

Bart Landry analyzed data from the National Survey of Families and Households (NSFH), which was first conducted in 1987–88, and he found that black husbands contributed somewhat more to household chores than white husbands. According to Landry, black husbands spent on average 22.2 hours on household tasks, whereas white husbands spent 18.4 hours.[25] Other studies have supported Landry's findings and suggest that the greater involvement of black husbands in household chores may be one way of compensating for their smaller incomes relative to their wives.

The late C. Wright Mills, in *The Sociological Imagination*, distinguished between an individual's personal troubles, such as being unable to find a job or experiencing a divorce, and public issues, such as patterns of widespread joblessness or high rates of marital disruption. Mills argued that the "sociological imagination" allows us to see the interconnection between an individual's troubles and broader patterns in society.[26]

Marriage in the African American community is a case in point. The historical analysis of black marriage over the past 100 years demonstrates that African Americans were in the vanguard of creating the modern egalitarian marriage. Marriage has both public and private domains, and the evolution of the institution is determined by the individual emotions, cultural ideals, and practices that couples bring to their unions as well as the values and constraints of any given historical moment. African Americans have helped shape modern marriage, and now they must adapt to economic circumstances where wives not only are equal partners but often outearn their husbands. The complex reality that couples must pave new paths but also feel pressure to adapt to current conditions must be addressed as we create public policy to support marriage as an institution.

NOTES

1. Wells (1970), 101.
2. Gordon (1991), 583.
3. Wells (1970), 244.
4. Cooper in Loewenberg and Bogin (1976), 325.
5. Wells (1970), 251.
6. Harris (1978).
7. Foner (1988), 84.
8. See Giddings (2008).
9. Jacks in Moses (1978), 115.
10. Giddings (1985), 59.
11. Williams (1904), 544.
12. Higginbotham (1993), 41.
13. Noble (1956), 45.
14. Carlson (1992), 24.
15. Higginbotham (1993), 24.
16. Hope in Rouse (1989), 23–24.

17. Cuthbert (1936), 48.
18. Cooper in Carby (1987), 100.
19. Bernard (1966), 68–70.
20. Stevenson in Mintz and Kellogg (1988), 181.
21. Hacker (1992), 120.
22. Bowen and Bok (1998), 175–176.
23. Bowen and Bok (1998), 175–176.
24. Bowen and Bok (1998), 176–178.
25. Landry (2000), 158–159.
26. Mills (1959).

In Other Words

PEOPLE ARE NOT AS CONSISTENT IN THEIR SOCIAL IDEOLOGIES AS WE THINK: CHANGING VIEWS ON GENDER AND RACE, 1977-2018

William J. Scarborough and Joanna R. Pepin, August 16, 2021 / CCF

As people come to oppose one type of inequality, are they more likely to also begin to oppose other types? To find out, we analyzed nationally representative data from the General Social Survey (1977-2018), documenting whether shifting gender atti-tudes over that period coincided with changing racial attitudes. In this brief report prepared for the Council on Contemporary Families, we summarize the key find-ings of our article in the *American Sociological Review*.

Racist and sexist attitudes were extremely widespread in the early 1970s. Two-thirds of Americans believed that women should devote themselves to homemaking and that they could only raise children successfully by forgoing paid employment. And among the White population, there was a widespread belief that disparities between Black people and White people resulted from individual deficiencies rather than dis-crimination, with only 40 percent attributing these disparities to discrimination.

Interestingly, these views changed at very different rates in the ensuing years. In 1977 only a third of Americans rejected the notion that wives should stay home while husbands worked for pay, but opposition rose steadily after that point. By 2018, three-quarters rebuffed that notion. By contrast, the percentage of Americans attributing inequalities between Black and White people to racial discrimination, as opposed to in-born racial differences, actually declined for several decades, reach-ing a low of 32 percent in 2004, substantially below the 40 percent figure of 1977. By 2012, however, some new patterns emerged.

We identified four configurations of racial and gender attitudes over this period. We measured racial attitudes with a set of survey questions designed to capture whether individuals felt racial inequality was due to structural factors like discrimi-nation and unfair educational opportunities, or whether it was due to individuals' deficient motivation. We inferred people's views on gender by using questions that measured their opinion on whether women were as suited as men for politics and whether they thought women should primarily focus on raising families while men focused on their careers. We assigned people to one of four distinct groups describ-ing their combination of beliefs about race and gender inequality. One group held universally progressive attitudes that supported gender equality in politics and in the home, while also attributing racial inequality to discrimination rather than individual deficiencies. Another group held universally conservative attitudes that endorsed conventional gender arrangements based on male breadwinning and female home-making alongside beliefs that racial inequality was due to individual flaws. Two remaining groups held contradictory opinions. One held progressive gender atti-tudes but conservative racial attitudes. The other was the converse.

The bad news: For most of the past forty years, Americans' growing under-standing of gender inequality as a social problem was not matched by the same growth in their understanding of racial inequality. Although one might think recognizing inequality in one area would open people's eyes to other inequali-ties, that did not happen for several decades. A very large proportion of people

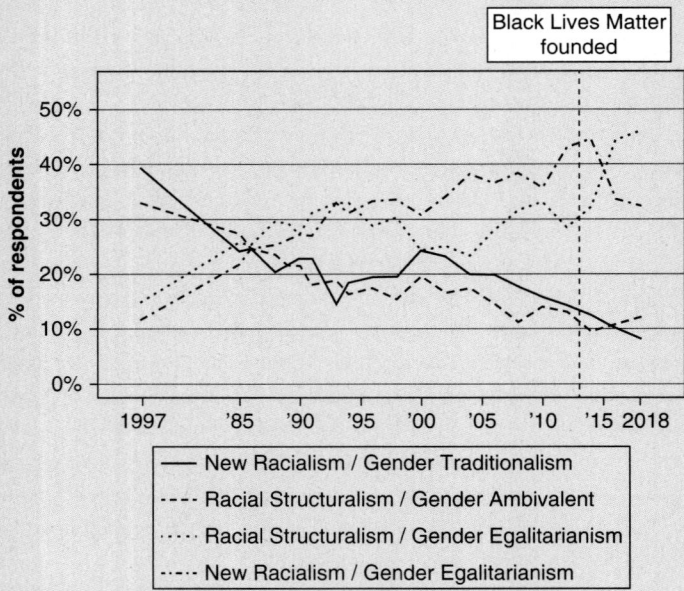

Figure 8.1 | Combinations of Race and Gender Attitudes

Source: *General Social Survey data (1977-2018); Scarborough et al. 2021.*

Notes: *Racial Structuralism/Gender Egalitarian attitudes are those who support gender equality and attribute racial inequality to discrimination. New Racialism/Gender Egalitar-ians support gender equality but do not agree racial inequality is mainly due to discrimina-tion. Racial Structuralism/Gender Ambivalent perspectives hold conventional attitudes about gender in the family while also acknowledging racial discrimination. New Racialism/ Gender Traditionalist attitudes are conservative across race and gender, opposing gender equality and denying racial discrimination.*

discarded their old prejudices about gender without shedding their prejudices about race.

Compared with people who endorsed conventional gender arrangements, people who supported women's leadership and gender-equal divisions of household labor back in 1977 (27 percent of the population), were also quite likely to attribute racial inequality to discrimination. Of these gender egalitarians, 56 percent agreed that racial inequties were due to discrimination and educational disparities. But as gender equality became more mainstream, the proportion of people recognizing gender inequality and racial inequality fell. By 2004, the proportion of Americans supporting gender equality in politics and the home had grown to 62 percent, but only 38 percent of these gender egalitarians thought racial disparities were mainly due to discrimination, though, of course, the total numbers had increased. As of 2012, nearly three-fourths of survey responders endorsed gender equality in public leadership and in the home, but six out of ten gender egalitarians continued to blame racial inequality on personal flaws rather than discrimination. We refer to this combination of attitudes as *New Racialism / Gender Egalitarianism*.

These findings show how people can oppose inequality in one area of life but be blind to it in another.

The good news: From 2012 to 2018 there was a growing alignment of gender and racial attitudes. After 2012, the view that racial inequality is due to discrimination and educational access became increasingly common, especially among people who supported gender equality. From 2012 through 2018 the percentage of responders supporting gender equality and also believing that racial inequality stems from discrimination and unequal access to education rose from less than 30 percent to

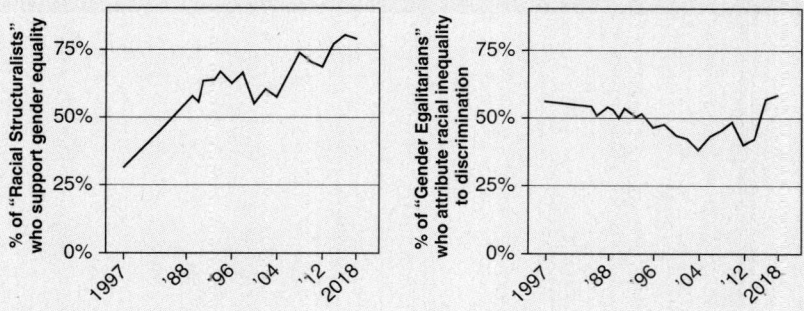

Figure 8.2 | Combinations of Race and Gender Attitudes

Source: *General Social Survey data (1977-2018); Scarborough et al. 2021.*

almost half (47 percent). Starting in 2014, and especially since 2016, people who support gender equality have increasingly adopted more progressive racial attitudes, perhaps reflecting growing overlap between anti-racism and anti-sexism. In 2018, nearly 60 percent of gender egalitarians also identified discrimination and access to education as main sources of racial inequality.

The rebound in this combination of race and gender attitudes, which we call *Racial Structuralism / Gender Egalitarianism*, may reflect the influence of social movements such as Black Lives Matter (BLM). It seems likely that BLM and other social movements have had a substantial effect on individuals' perceptions of racial discrimination, particularly among people who had already come to support gender equality.

Conclusion: When people reject one type of inequality, they do not automatically reject others. Over most of the period under review, people who adopted liberal perspectives on gender were slow to see the need for policies aimed at addressing structural racism. From 1996 to 2014, the most commonly held combination of gender and race attitudes was anti-sexist but not anti-racist. Yet, since 2016, the proportion of Americans who support gender equality and also feel that racial inequality stems from structural factors like discrimination has risen to almost half. This coincides with the rise of contemporary social activism, such as the Black Lives Matter movement, that advocates for racial equity along with gender equity. It is very likely that the recent increase in anti-racist attitudes among people who hold anti-sexist attitudes is related to the visibility of this movement. Our findings suggest that while individuals who hold some progressive ideals may be open to understanding parallels with other dimensions of inequality, this does not occur automatically but in response to social activism and debate. ◤

9

_____

Change That Counts

The Evolution of Americans' Definitions of Family

Claudia Geist, Catherine Bolzendahl, Lala Carr Steelman, and Brian Powell[1]

Who counts as family as seen through the eyes of the American public? It is a much trickier and consequential question than what one might think of at first glance. Imagine your own family: what living arrangements describe them? Or, to turn the question around, what living arrangements do you have now: are you living as part of a "family"? These questions motivate our work and serve as the basis of this chapter. Starting in 2003, perhaps before some of you were even born, we asked Americans which living arrangements count and do not count as family. We followed up with similar questions in 2006 and 2010. The responses reveal a great deal about what matters to most people in the United States when they define family and how this has changed in such a brief time period. Understanding these recent changes will help you consider how society will define "family" in the future.

Consistently our data show three patterns:

1. Large differences in how Americans see certain living arrangements: nearly everyone sees a husband and wife with children as family, and very few (less than 10 percent) consider housemates as family.

2. A great deal of disagreement about whether gay and lesbian couples (both with and without children) count as family.

3. Finally, we identified three broad groups of Americans: exclusionists, moderates, and inclusionists. These groups differ not only in which living arrangements they "count" as family but also in how they speak and think differently about what family means to them.

Yet, looking at responses over time, we also see a significant change in these views over a short span of time, namely, an increasing number of Americans are counting same-sex[2] couples in their definition of family. This change parallels the movement toward greater approval of same-sex marriage, as we show in more detail later in this chapter. The factors behind these changes—such as generational changes and increased contact with lesbians, gay men, and their families—suggest that Americans will continue to move toward a more inclusive vision of family, even while pockets of resistance remain and there are signs of a backlash against LGBTQ people and their rights.

As our opening questions alluded to, defining family is complicated! The term *family* is ubiquitous: we hear of family values, family meals, family vacations, family-friendly policies, family visitation hours in hospitals, and pro-family advocacy groups. These terms imply that everyone agrees on what *family* means. But there is no universally accepted definition of family. People disagree about what makes a family: Is it marriage, parenthood, length of commitment? Does sexuality matter?

It's not just a difference of opinion, though. Where people draw the lines around what "counts" as family can sway legal rights, economic well-being, social ties, and even citizenship status. Living arrangements accepted as "family" enjoy many rights and privileges, ranging from family discounts to inheritance rights, that are not available to others. Imagine, for example, finding out your partner whom you have been living with for over a decade was seriously hurt in a car accident, but you were not allowed to visit your partner in the hospital because you were not counted as a "legal" family member. Imagine that after spending forty years together and building a life with a partner, you find that all your joint possessions were taken away upon your partner's death because the two of you were not recognized as a family. Imagine being informed that your child was going to be removed from a school because the school officials did not consider you and your partner to be a family.

While some of these rights can be achieved by completing complex legal paperwork, recognition as "family" allows people to bypass time-consuming and complicated forms. Knowing where most people stand in our definitions of family tells us who is seen as deserving of the rights and privileges of family. Understanding how our definitions have changed over time also provides insight into how law, culture, and society may be transforming overall.

These issues drove us to dig deeper, and for nearly two decades we have focused on a simple question: What living arrangements do Americans count in their definition of family and what living arrangements are counted out of the definition of family? Our answers come from our interviews with more than two thousand Americans in 2003, 2006, and 2010.[3] Many different living arrangements could fall under the category of family. For this project, we asked about eleven of these arrangements:

- A husband and a wife living together with one or more of their children
- A man and a woman living together as an unmarried couple with one or more of their children
- A man living alone with one or more of his children
- A woman living alone with one or more of her children
- Two women living together as a couple with one or more of their children
- Two men living together as a couple with one or more of their children
- A husband and a wife living together with no children
- A man and a woman living together as an unmarried couple who have no children
- Two people living together as housemates who are not living as a couple and have no children
- Two women living together as a couple who have no children
- Two men living together as a couple who have no children

These living arrangements vary along three key dimensions: whether they are married, cohabiting, or single; whether they are a couple; and whether they have children.

WHICH LIVING ARRANGEMENTS COUNT AS FAMILY?

Figure 9.1 displays the percentage of Americans in the 2010 survey who viewed each living arrangement as a family. Looking at these responses, we see a great deal of agreement about some living arrangements and a great deal of disagreement about others. Everyone (100 percent) counted a husband, a wife, and their children as a family. Closely following were a single mother and her children (96 percent), a single father and his children (95 percent), and a married heterosexual couple without children (92 percent).

There also was a great deal of agreement regarding housemates, but in this case nearly everyone (90 percent) agreed that housemates did not count as a family. This was even true among young adults, including college-aged adults who recently may have lived with roommates and presumably should be the most open-minded regarding this living arrangement. In fact, the group most likely to say that housemates count as family ironically consisted of people from the other

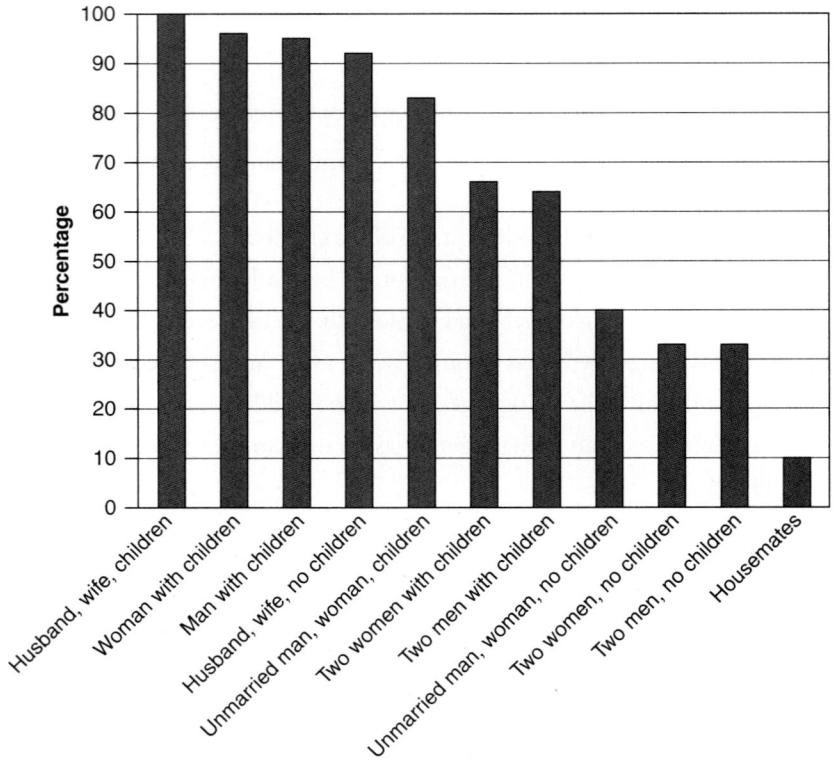

Figure 9.1 | Which Living Arrangements Count as Family?

Source: *Constructing the Family Survey (Powell 2010).*

end of the spectrum: adults over the age of sixty-four. Their greater receptive-
ness to what some refer to as "chosen family" or "fictive kin" may be due to their
recognition of the increasing number of people from their generation who share
living facilities with non-relatives and the decreasing number who live near their
extended kin.[4] Though their definition of family included this arrangement, the
oldest participants were otherwise among the most narrow in their definition of
families, as discussed below.

Americans clearly confer a lot of family legitimacy to marriage. But for household arrangements outside of heterosexual marriage, the agreement starts to
unravel. Regarding a man and a woman living together as an unmarried couple,
approximately five-sixths of Americans (83 percent) conferred family status to this

couple if they had children, but only two-fifths (40 percent) counted this couple as a family if it was childless. The numbers for same-sex couples are even lower almost two-thirds defined a lesbian couple (66 percent) or a gay male couple (64 percent) with children as a family, while only one-third (33 percent) counted either couple as a family if the couple was childless.

PATTERNS IN FAMILY DEFINITIONS

These percentages provide just one very broad picture of how Americans define family. But there is a different way of looking at Americans' responses: by examining how these responses cluster together.[5] The people we interviewed fell into three unique categories:

- **Exclusionists:** Exclusionists believe in the most "traditional" definition of family, which strongly emphasizes heterosexual, married households that include children and in which women and men assume traditional gender roles.[6] Exclusionists may accept other family forms under certain conditions; for example, counting single-parent households as family by assuming that the single parenthood was involuntary (for example, being a widow or widower). Exclusionists are divided about whether cohabiting heterosexual couples count as family but unequivocally exclude same-sex couples with or without children in their definition of family. This group of responders is the least flexible in their viewpoints of who counts as family.

- **Inclusionists:** As the term implies, inclusionists embrace a very broad, all-encompassing definition of family. This group makes little or no distinction between households with and without children, between married and unmarried households, or between gay and lesbian and heterosexual households. This group accepts the widest range of alternative definitions of family.

- **Moderates:** Moderates are positioned somewhere in between the restrictive views of exclusionists and the "all-in" views of inclusionists. That is, they are partially open to a more expansive definition of family, especially if, as we discuss later, the people in the household tangibly signal commitment to each other. These signals can include marriage or the presence of children. For moderates, married cross-sex couples and all living arrangements that involve children, including same-sex couples with children, count as family. For moderates, caring for children seems decisive to bestowing family status on various living arrangements.

How Americans Talk about Family

To better understand exclusionists, moderates, and inclusionists, we asked people to explain why they counted certain living arrangements but not others as family and to describe what they thought determined whether a living arrangement could be construed as a family. Exclusionists, moderates, and inclusionists relied on starkly different frames and emphasized different words in their explanations.

To summarize these differences, Figure 9.2 identifies some of the most frequently used words in the interviews from 2010. As you can see, exclusionists most frequently brought up comments regarding the Bible: for example, "It's the rules, the Bible," "What the Bible tells me," and "The Bible is very specific about it as well as religion and God." In fact, nearly four-fifths (79 percent) of all references to the word *Bible* were made by exclusionists; to this group, the definition of family is firmly rooted in religious tradition and the Bible. The remaining

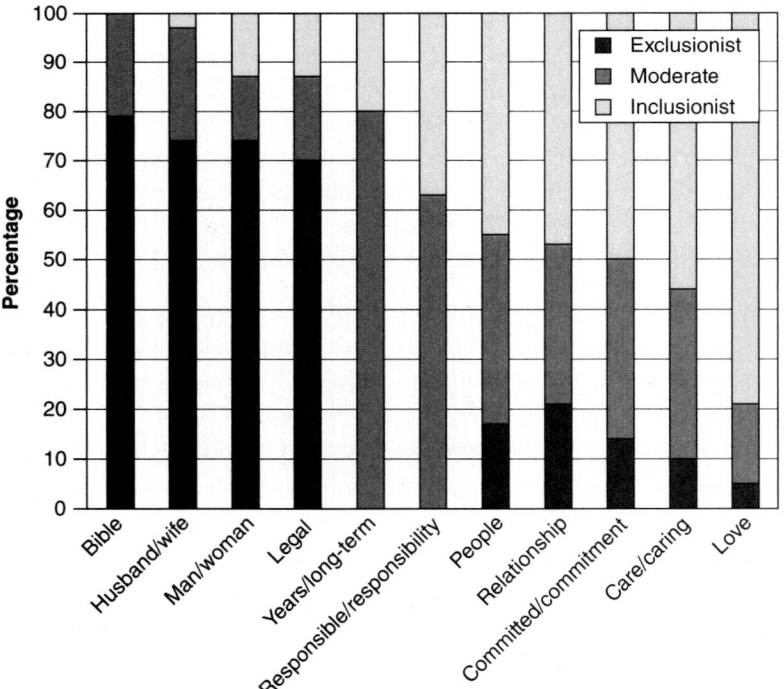

Figure 9.2 | Words Frequently Used by Exclusionists, Moderates, or Inclusionists

Source: *Constructing the Family Survey (Powell 2010).*

one-fifth (21 percent) were made by moderates. Conspicuously absent were inclusionists, none of whom explicitly referred to the Bible.

Exclusionists also were much more likely to discuss family in gender-specific terms: for example, "husband and wife," "a biblical reference to a man and a woman," and "a relationship between a man and a woman." These comments often were accompanied by a discussion of legal institutions, especially marriage. To exclusionists, the legal status of marriage was fundamental to the definition of family—for example, "It's a legal relationship. You need to make it legal when living together," "As long as they're a legally constituted couple, they're a family: legally married, it's husband and wife," and "It's a legal, lawful relationship." In other words, exclusionists were most likely to focus on the structure of family—a structure consecrated by either law or religion.

If exclusionists emphasized structure, inclusionists emphasized function. That is, inclusionists focused on how families act and what families actually do. To inclusionists, if a living arrangement acted like a family and felt like a family, it was a family. In many ways, inclusionists were the most romantic of the three groups. Their frequent discussions of love signaled their romantic view of families—for example, "People who love each other, that's all," "A group of people that live together and love each other are a family," and "It's two souls together who love each other and have a commitment to each other."

Approximately four-fifths (79 percent) of the references to love were made by inclusionists, in contrast to the very few mentions of this word (5 percent) by exclusionists. To inclusionists, it did not matter if the living arrangement was man/woman, two women, or two men as long as they were "living together, sharing love, and sharing their lives with one another." In fact, because most inclusionists did not distinguish between heterosexual and same-sex couples, they were much more likely than exclusionists to refer to relationships or people (as opposed to gender-specific or legal terms like *husband* and *wife*), for example:

> People living together are the unit, no matter what their marital status and what their sexual preference is. If they're living together with the same goals, to me, that constitutes a family.

Not only were inclusionists the most romantic; they also were the most pragmatic. For example, they were over five times more likely than exclusionists to mention the word *care* (or the phrase *taking care of*), often at the same time they referred to love or commitment:

> People committed to one another wanting the best for each other with a mutual love and respect. They take care of each other and make sure their needs are met, everyone's needs are met.

Moderates also often used the term *commitment* but in a different way than inclusionists. Inclusionists started with the assumption that if a couple defined itself as a family, it automatically should be seen as committed and as a family. Moderates required a more clear-cut sign that the couple was committed. This signal could take the form of marriage or parenthood because both suggested a permanent relationship, or at least a relationship that would be hard to dissolve. As one respondent explained,

> A family is a group of people who have responsibility for each other and who you cannot get away from. For example, maybe two people live together, even have a relationship. But they can leave anytime, you know. But with children, they will carry these things for life.

The absence of marriage rights for most same-sex couples was problematic for our survey purposes. Same-sex marriage was illegal in every state during our first set of interviews in 2003 and was legal in very few states (Iowa, Massachusetts, New Hampshire, and Vermont, along with Washington, D.C.) during our third wave of interviews in 2010. This situation made it difficult for moderates to see a same-sex couple without children as sufficiently committed to be considered a family, as seen in the following comments:

> Oh, God! Okay to me, it's like people that are planning on being together for a long period of time. Like being together forever. I've heard of best friends moving in together, and they're kind of like family. So, to me, it's two people that are going to be committed to each other for the long haul, not just . . . I don't know, no, I mean, I'm not saying that two men and two women can't be in it for the long haul, but there's nothing binding them together.

The legal landscape has changed dramatically since then. In 2015, the Supreme Court ruled in the case of *Obergefell v. Hodges* that the fundamental right to marry is guaranteed to same-sex couples by both the Due Process Clause and the Equal Protection Clause of the Fourteenth Amendment to the U.S. Constitution. This ruling meant that gay and lesbian couples have more opportunity in the eyes of moderates to "be in it for the long haul" because there's something (that is, marriage) binding them together.

But even before the Supreme Court decision, moderates were nevertheless willing to look for other markers of commitment. Among these was the duration of the relationship, in particular, the presence of a long-term relationship, regardless of marital status or parenthood:

> I think it's a long-term couple, whether you're a man and woman, woman and woman, or man and man. Whether you have children or not. If you're a long-term couple, I think that's a family.

The frequent references to relationship length led us to ask a series of supplementary questions that spoke to this issue. Recall that moderates considered a same-sex couple a family only if the couple had children. We decided to provide additional information about childless same-sex couples. We asked whether moderates (as well as inclusionists and exclusionists) considered a childless, same-sex couple a family "from the moment they move in together" and, if not then, "if they have lived together as a couple for ten years." This information dramatically changed moderates' views. Almost three-fifths (58 percent) counted a childless same-sex couple as a family if the couple had lived together for a decade (versus 33 percent if no information about time together was provided). In other words, time together is such a compelling indicator of commitment that it can budge many otherwise moderates toward a more inclusive vision of family.

Evidence of responsibility and interdependency was another proxy for commitment. This responsibility could be emotional, personal, or financial, or some combination of these:

> My definition of a family? I guess one or more people that live together under one roof with or without children where there is some semblance of responsibility toward each other. More than just monetarily but also romantically if they have a mutual dependence on each other.

When we asked more detailed questions, we discovered that moderates' willingness to consider other indicators of commitment beyond parenthood and marriage also provided an opening for moderates to move further away from the views of exclusionists and closer to those of inclusionists. We suspect that the more that moderates become aware of people in other living arrangements who are committed to each other and who are responsible for each other, the more receptive they will become to a more inclusive definition of family.

CHANGES IN FAMILY DEFINITIONS OVER TIME

On most issues, public opinion changes incredibly slowly and only over long stretches of time. Views regarding the definition of family are an important exception, as can be seen in Figure 9.3. In 2003, almost half (45 percent) of

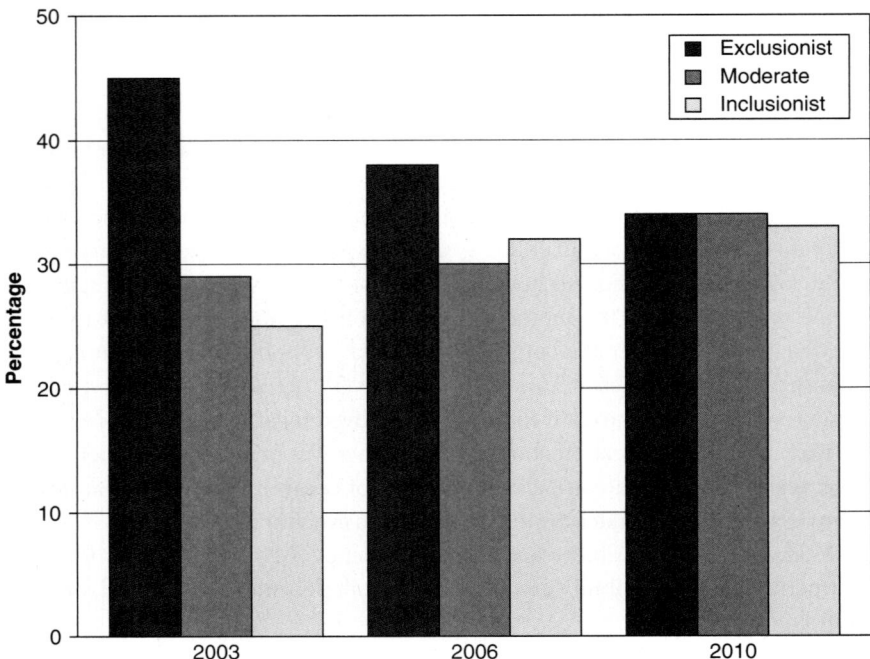

Figure 9.3 | Family Definition Clusters: Changes between 2003, 2006, and 2010

Source: *Constructing the Family Survey (Powell 2003, 2006, 2010).*

Americans were exclusionists. Far more Americans were exclusionists than either moderates (29 percent) or inclusionists (25 percent).[7]

In a short period of time, however, the number of exclusionists declined while the number of both moderates and inclusionists increased. By 2010, the country was evenly divided among exclusionists (34 percent), moderates (34 percent), and inclusionists (33 percent). To put it another way, in 2003, approximately half of all Americans counted at least some type of same-sex couple (for example, a lesbian couple with children) as a family; but by 2010, two-thirds of Americans were willing to do so. This is a remarkable and rapid change in public opinion.

The Future of Queer Families

The landscape is clearly evolving, which is why social scientists, including us, continue to study and collect data on the changing opinions on family. What do we know about gay and lesbian families post-2010? One of the most helpful

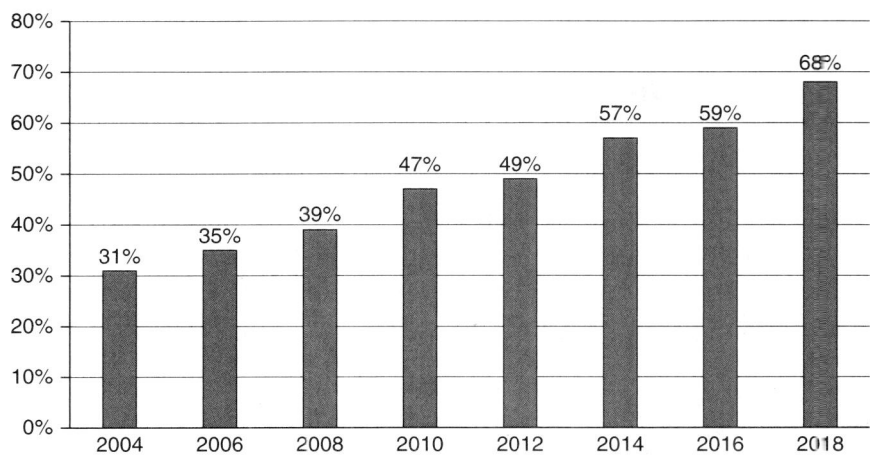

Figure 9.4 | Percent of Americans Who Agree That Gay Men and Lesbians Should Have the Right to Marry

Source: *General Social Survey (2004-2018).*

insights comes from trends in answers to a question asked in the U.S. General Social Survey (GSS) on support for same-sex marriage, which mirrors our findings on changing attitudes toward family definitions. Figure 9.4 illustrates changes in responses to the GSS question asking respondents how much they agree or disagree that gay men and lesbians should have the right to marry.[*]

Nearly twenty years ago, a minority of Americans supported the right of same-sex couples to marry. This steadily increased over the years, in step with the several states that legalized it within their borders. Even prior to the 2015 Supreme Court ruling that legalized same-sex marriage nationally, the majority of Americans were already supportive. However, it is particularly notable that within three years of the ruling, overall support increased by more than 10 percent.

In our own research, we also sought to better understand support for same-sex marriage. Perhaps not surprisingly, nearly every exclusionist staunchly opposed same-sex marriage, while nearly every inclusionist favored it. Moderates fell in between; at least half were in favor of same-sex marriage. Given the decrease in the number of exclusionists and corresponding increase in the number of inclusionists and moderates since 2003, it is not surprising that support for same-sex marriage increased profoundly. We found that, echoing the 2004 GSS data, in 2003 approximately three-fifths of the Americans we interviewed opposed same-sex marriage. Americans' views on this topic shifted so quickly that by 2010, more Americans were in favor of same-sex marriage than opposed to it. Yet, it is important to note that even in 2018, 22 percent of Americans polled by the GSS disagreed with the statement that same-sex marriage should be a right, suggesting that there remains a robust exclusionist class that resists the broad changes in public opinion and legal context.

Several factors help explain the large, rapid changes in the acceptance of same-sex marriage and the families of gay and lesbian couples. One is "cohort replacement": as societies age, younger generations who grew up in different times become the older generations. The oldest participants in our survey were the most likely to be exclusionist and the least likely to count any type of same-sex couples in their definition of family. Conservative views of adults over the age of sixty-four were a mirror image of the more liberal views of adults under the age of thirty, who were the most likely to be inclusionists. It is true that sometimes people become more conservative as they age. But with cohort replacement, change is not just about aging. Instead, we observed that the shift to more inclusionists and fewer exclusionists is about generations—members of the younger generation are likely to continue to hold their inclusionist views as they age. This means that as the younger generation replaces the older one, the number of inclusionists and moderates will rise and the number of exclusionists will decline. As this happens, support for same-sex marriage will continue to increase—even if no one changes their mind about these topics.[9]

People, however, are not stuck with the same views their entire lives; they sometimes change their minds! Because the change in opinion has been fast and vast, we know that the greater acceptance of broader definitions of family is not solely due to cohort replacement. It also reflects what is called a "period effect." In other words, people exposed to the same ideas in the same period of time can be affected quite broadly. The past few decades have brought a much greater social, political, and cultural openness to same-sex relationships. Thanks to increased openness around gay and lesbian identities, more Americans have contact with—or increased recognition that they know—gay men, lesbian women, and same-sex couples. For decades, social psychologists have posited and confirmed that increased intergroup contact reduces prejudice toward and discrimination against minority group members.[10] This insight applies to attitudes about sexuality and views regarding who counts as a family.

From our interviews, we find that a growing number of Americans realize that some of their relatives, friends, co-workers, and neighbors are gay or lesbian. Our interviews also show that Americans who know someone who is gay or lesbian, especially Americans who are close to someone who is gay or lesbian, are much more inclusive in their definitions of family. Interestingly, even "knowing" a gay or lesbian fictional character from a television show (for example, *Gossip*

Girl, Grey's Anatomy, Modern Family, and *Riverdale*) or an openly gay, lesbian, or bisexual media or public figure (for example, Pete Buttigieg, Anderson Cooper, Kristen Stewart, and RuPaul) can trigger similarly favorable reactions to those elicited by direct interpersonal contact. In other words, contact—both real and mediated—is a driving force behind Americans' greater openness toward a broad range of family forms.

These factors, along with others (for example, the rising number of people who do not see sexuality as a "choice"), give us great confidence that Americans will continue to move toward a more inclusive definition of family that recognizes families as they really are: people who love each other, who care for each other, and who are committed to and are responsible for each other. There may be pushback from some exclusionists, perhaps emboldened by recent Supreme Court decisions regarding gender and privacy. We encourage you to notice and learn and return to these questions as our policies about families evolve. That said, our research shows a strong movement toward accepting same-sex couples' households as family, and shows that today, for most Americans, these families are counted in.

NOTES

1. The authors thank the many graduate and undergraduate students who served on the research team that conducted these interviews. Special thanks are owed to Oren Pizmony-Levy and Christina Ek, who offered valuable feedback on this manuscript.

2. The phrase *same-sex* doesn't fully capture complexities of sex, gender, and biological and social constructions, but serves as a convenient shorthand term. It substitutes here as a catchall term for gay, lesbian, men with men, and women with women couples. We did not study attitudes toward the living arrangement of the full spectrum of the LGBTQ community. We also did not explore attitudes toward the living arrangements of people who hold gender identities outside of the gender binary.

3. More information about the project and a more detailed discussion of the patterns can be found in Powell, Bolzendahl, Geist, and Steelman (2010).

4. For a discussion of the various conceptualizations of chosen family, see Weston (1997).

5. We used a method called Latent Class Analysis that allowed us to identify the way people's views clustered together. For more information on latent class analysis, see McCutcheon (1987).

6. This has been termed the Standard North American Family. A more detailed description and critique of the Standard North American Family can be found in Smith (1993).

7. Some percentages in Figure 9.3 do not add to 100 because of rounding errors: 45.3 percent of Americans were exclusionists, but this number was rounded to its closest whole number (45 percent).

8. When this survey question was originally created the phrasing was "homosexual," and it was meant to refer to lesbian couples, gay couples, and sexual minorities. In order to make sure that changes in public attitudes are carefully measured, the General Social Survey typically keeps the phrasing of questions the same over time. For the labels we use in this chapter, we shifted the language.

9. For a fuller exploration and explanation of this process, we recommend Peter Hart-Brinson's *The Gay Marriage Generation* (2018).

10. For a discussion of the contact hypothesis, which was introduced by psychologist Gordon Allport (1954), see Pettigrew and Tropp (2006).

10

Labor Unions and Families, a Very Brief History

Shawn Fremstad

Being part of a union is about so much more than just the individual benefits. It's about being part of a collective movement creating a good society with shared prosperity, security and fairness for all.

—Frances O'Grady, General Secretary of the Trades Union Congress (2014)[1]

Families and households have always been sites of labor and production. With the rise of industrial capitalism, various types of production that had long taken place in the household shifted into factories and other workplaces. In response, workers increasingly banded together to ensure fair treatment by their employers, change public understanding of labor issues, and push elected officials to set labor standards, like the minimum wage and the eight-hour workday. Since the very beginnings of the labor movement, workers and labor unions have framed their demands in ways that went beyond individual wage earners and included working-class families as a whole. For much of labor's history, this included calling for a male family wage, one that allowed a male wage earner to support a wife and children at a decent level without these "dependents" having to work outside the home. Especially at its peak in the early 1900s, this idea became explicitly exclusionary—working women, and especially mothers, were openly viewed as an obstacle to fair and just wages for working men. The labor movement has been a source of progress for families but not without missteps and limits.

Increasingly over the course of the twentieth century and on through today, the labor movement has been a force for gender and racial justice. In addition to calling for equal pay for women, labor expanded its demands to include benefits that made it easier for mothers of young children to work outside the home, including paid leave and universal child care. That popular work-family policies like these have yet to be adopted nationally is due in part to federal and state policy decisions that reduced labor's membership and power since its peak in the 1950s. Looking forward, a revitalized and powerful labor movement would reduce inequality and improve the well-being of today's diverse working class.

Labor Beginnings

In 1790, some nine out of ten people counted in the U.S. Census lived on farms.[2] This figure included about 700,000 enslaved people but recorded very few of the Indigenous people being displaced by settler colonialists.[3] (Under the newly adopted Constitution, "Indians not taxed" were excluded from the Census.) During this preindustrial period, "the modern distinction between producers and consumers did not exist."[4] Male "household heads owned and controlled the means of production, and their wives and children were obliged to provide the unpaid labor needed to sustain family enterprises."[5]

Worker associations in the late eighteenth and early nineteenth centuries were largely limited to local societies restricted to a single trade, particularly printing and shoemaking in New York City, Philadelphia, and a few other major cities. There were occasional walkouts and strikes but no mass national unions. As work shifted out from the family labor system into a waged labor system, male workers increasingly argued that their wages should be set at a level sufficient to support a wife and children—what became known as a family wage—rather than by what employers argued were market forces. An early articulation is seen in 1806 when journeymen shoemakers in Philadelphia argued—after being indicted for going on strike—that they were being "torn from our fireside for endeavoring to obtain a fair and just support for our families."[6]

The rise of industry led to changes in family life and worker organizations. In the last decade of the 1700s and the first decades of the 1800s, textile mills in New England began employing adults and children, both boys and girls. Child labor was viewed by many as a social good. As a Pawtucket mill owner in 1801 put it, employment "kept children out of mischief" and allowed them to serve God and their families.[7] The introduction of the power loom in the United States in 1813 enabled the large-scale manufacturing of cotton in New England. In Lowell, Massachusetts, young, unmarried women were recruited from farm families to work in the mills. The Lowell mill girls lived in company boarding houses overseen by "respectable" female keepers, often widows, who required them to attend church and follow other rules.

Poor working conditions in the mills led to worker unrest and strikes. In 1824 women participated in the first strike of factory workers.[8] Between then and 1837, at least twelve more textile factory strikes involved women as key participants or leaders.[9] In 1828, child workers, with the support of their parents, walked out of their jobs in cotton mills in Paterson, New Jersey, after mill owners tried to push their lunch hour from noon to 1:00 p.m. The children worked thirteen hours a day in the mills and feared if they gave in, "the next thing would be to deprive them of eating at all."[10] Child workers in the Paterson mills went on strike again on the Fourth of July in 1835. To support the children's strike, their parents formed the Paterson Association for the Protection of the Working Classes. The strike ended two months later when the owners agreed to cut the children's work week to twelve hours on Mondays to Fridays and nine hours on Saturday.

THE RISE OF A MASS NATIONAL LABOR MOVEMENT

After the end of the Civil War, the first mass national labor organizations emerged. Before the establishment of the American Federation of Labor, the Knights of Labor was the most important of these organizations. Founded by local garment cutters in 1869, the Knights started as a secret society that aimed to eventually unify all wage earners—"regardless of sex, race, creed, or color"—and replace capitalism with a co-operative system.[11] They supported an eight-hour workday, gender equal pay for equal work, the abolition of child labor, and women's suffrage, while also bringing "large numbers of skilled and unskilled black workers into the predominately white labor movement for the first time."[12]

At the same time, their commitment to unifying the working class had limits. In an organization that was notable at the time for being open to nearly all male workers, Chinese workers were excluded. The Knights supported the infamous Chinese Exclusion Act of 1882—absolutely prohibiting the immigration of all Chinese laborers to the United States—and other restrictions on immigration from Asia and Europe. The Knights were almost exclusively male workers, but eventually the organization opened to women. Leonora Barry, an Irish immigrant and the first woman to be a paid labor investigator in the United States, was employed by the Knights. Near the height of Knights' membership in the 1880s, Barry estimated that one in ten members of the Knights were women, just below their share of overall employment at the time. Women's involvement in the Knights was not limited to wage-earning women. By addressing housewives as well as wage earners, the Knights opened important options for working-class women. "Ladies' locals" encompassed both housewives and employed women— sometimes together, sometimes in distinct assemblies—and women possessed full rights and privileges within the organization. Defining productive toil by a moral rather than a strictly economic yardstick, the Knights thus offered women a role in the movement not directly dependent upon their status in the labor market.[13]

After the 1886 Haymarket Square Riot, where seven policemen and four workers were killed, the Knights' membership declined and rival labor organizations became more prominent. That same year, just before Haymarket, leaders of the Cigar Makers Union and the United Brotherhood of Carpenters and Joiners issued a call to all national trade unions to attend a conference that would lead to the creation of the American Federation of Labor (AFL) in December 1886.

The AFL was dominated by men in the skilled trades and craft unions. It emphasized what AFL founder Samuel Gompers called "pure-and-simple" unionism: membership was limited to workers and the focus was on defending the interests of members in the collective bargaining process. By contrast, the Knights had organized community-based organizations that were not limited to employees and included both employed women and homemakers. Especially in their early decades, the AFL's interest in legislative advocacy for better labor standards was limited. Still the AFL consistently supported legislative efforts to restrict child labor, although not very successfully until it started working with nonlabor groups at the federal level in 1906.[14] In 1906, Samuel Gompers "only slightly exaggerated the facts when he declared: 'There is not a child labor law on the statute books of the United States but has been put there by the efforts of the trade-union movement.'"[15]

While the AFL supported equal pay for equal work and eventually women's suffrage, the group's efforts to organize women workers were limited and "genuine ambivalence tempered its efforts."[16] Among women working in industrial jobs in 1900, only about 3 percent were organized.[17] Many male workers in the AFL viewed women laborers as competition that reduced bargaining power with employers. Union workers, legislatures, and class reformers rallied together to restrict women's hours and regulate their work. The idea of home-and-motherhood was the pretext for promoting protective legislation.[18] Writing in 1900, an AFL columnist argued that women should be classed as children "because it is to the interest of all of us that female labor should be limited so as not to injure the motherhood and family life of a nation."[19]

MOTHER JONES, THE NATIONAL CONSUMER LEAGUE, AND THE FIGHT FOR "PROTECTIVE LEGISLATION"

Although views like this were commonplace at the time, women were also emerging as key organizers and movement leaders. Not long after its founding in 1890, the United Mine Workers of America (UMWA) hired Mary Harris, later known as Mother Jones. Born in Ireland, Harris immigrated to Canada with her parents as a teen during the Great Famine. After losing her husband and children to yellow fever and her home and dressmaking shop to the Great Chicago Fire she joined the Knights and became an organizer. Her efforts at the UMWA to organize coal miners quickly became legendary. "In June 1897, after Mary addressed the railway union convention, she began to be referred to as 'Mother' by the men of the union."[20] Just after the turn of the century, she developed her signature tactic—men and women were organized to take the union pledge with the wives rising "before the men, with babes in their arms, and pledged themselves to see that no one went to work."[21] When the company responded by trying to bring in nonunion workers, Jones "persuaded the men to stay at home with the children while the women attended to the scabs" by dressing in a "wild assortment of rags," letting "their hair loose," and then "marching to the mine entrance banging pots and pans."[22]

In 1902, Jones helped found the Social Democratic Party with Eugene Debs and others. She later joined the Socialist Party and helped found the Industrial Workers of the World, or IWW. In 1903, she organized the March of the Mill Children from Kensington, Pennsylvania, to President Theodore Roosevelt's summer White House in Long Island. The marchers demanded a reduction in the work week, increased wages, and an end to child labor. Speaking to a class at Princeton University, she arrived accompanied by a "stooped, ten-year-old boy, and said: 'Here's a text book on economics. He gets three dollars a week, and his sister, who is fourteen, gets six dollars. They work in a carpet factory ten hours a day, while the children of the rich are getting their higher education.'"[23]

While Roosevelt never met with Jones or the mill children, the march and the crowds it attracted arguably helped pass child labor laws in Pennsylvania and the surrounding states. In 1907, Congress passed legislation requiring the then–Department of Commerce and Labor to investigate and report on both children's and women's labor. The resulting nineteen-volume *Report on the Condition of Woman and Child Wage-Earners in the United States* set the stage for subsequent legislation and ultimately the passage of child labor regulation in the Fair Labor Standards Act of 1938.[24] As the title of this report demonstrates, women and children were often grouped together as subjects of labor reforms during this period

Along with unions, the National Consumer League—founded by Jane Addams, Florence Kelly, and other social reformers in 1899—and other progressive organizations played crucial roles in pushing states to adopt maximum hours, minimum wage, and other labor laws limited to women workers. The National Women's Trade Union, founded at the annual convention of the AFL in 1903, viewed unionization of women workers and the passage of protective laws as complementary. But ultimately, they "found that it was easier for working-class women to articulate and win entitlements from an expanding state than from male colleagues in their own unions."[25]

In 1905, the Supreme Court ruled in *Lochner v. New York* that a New York law limiting the number of hours people employed as bakers could work violated a liberty-to-contract that the Court said was in the Fourteenth Amendment's Due Process Clause. A few years later, in *Muller v. Oregon* (1908), the Court declined to overrule a gender-specific law that limited women to ten hours of work a day. The Court justified its decision based on "differences between the sexes," explaining that because "healthy mothers are essential to vigorous offspring, the physical well-being of women becomes an object of public interest and care in order to preserve the strength and vigor of the race." By 1915, most states had enacted minimum wage, maximum hours, or other employment protections that were specific to working women. The Court backed away from *Lochner* in 1937 and began upholding minimum wage and other labor laws that applied to all workers.

THE NEW DEAL AND WORLD WAR II

In 1933, FDR nominated Frances Perkins to be secretary of labor. Perkins was highly educated and had been the head of the New York office of the National Consumers League and industrial commissioner of New York. But she was viewed with suspicion by labor leaders, including the head of the AFL who said labor was "profoundly disappointed" by her selection and could "never become reconciled" to it.[26] Perkins served as labor secretary for twelve years and played a key role in the New Deal, including the passage of the National Labor Relations Act (NLRA; 1935), the Social Security Act (1935), and the Fair Labor Standards Act (1938). The NLRA, or Wagner Act, recognized and promoted private-sector workers' right to join a union and bargain collectively. Between 1935 and 1945, the number of union members tripled from 3.8 million to 12.6 million.[27]

At this point, little by little, women were making inroads into the labor movement. In 1935, a group of industrial unions established the Committee of Industrial Organizations within the AFL and eventually broke away to create the Congress of Industrial Organizations (CIO) in 1938. The CIO did not talk about women directly in any statements, but women were obviously necessary for the work of unionizing along industrial lines.[28]

Indeed, it was the inevitability of the necessity of women to the movement on the ground that kept helping bring women into organized labor. At a strike in Akron, Ohio, involving 14,000 rubber workers at Goodyear, the International Ladies Garment Workers Union's (ILGWU) Rose Pesotta was sent in to help other CIO organizers and quickly saw that women, as family members of the striking (male) workers, were crucial activists and supporters.[29] The Goodyear workers eventually won and the strike "demonstrated how much a women's auxiliary could contribute to winning a strike" although "many male members were still unwilling to accept this truth."[30]

In another famous strike, at General Motors in Flint, Michigan, in early 1937, the Women's Emergency Brigade, a "vanguard detachment of the Women's Auxiliary," played a crucial role and led to the creation of similar groups in Detroit and other automaking cities. The brigades could mobilize thousands of women on short notice to form protective picket lines around striking workers outside plants.[31] The strike ended when GM recognized the United Auto Workers and agreed to begin collective bargaining on workers' demands for "an American standard of living" and other rights. The brigades' founder later explained that wives joined the brigades to help their husbands but also themselves and their children: "The man was so driven by the speedup . . . that he came home unable to be a decent companion to either his wife or his children. And some wives had to take an awful lot of bad treatment from their husbands."[32]

By 1940, the CIO had 800,000 women members, which represented about 7.3 percent of employed women in the United States; the number grew to 1.5 million by 1945.[33] Despite women's essential role in war production during World War II, their efforts didn't "erase the old fears and suspicions that unions harbored about women workers. . . . Unions often thought of women as merely 'until' workers"—until marriage, until children.[34] Women workers themselves were often less supportive of unionization than men—"unions, they felt, were either insensitive or indifferent to the needs and aspirations of women workers, especially those who were married, and over 75 percent of the women entering the wartime labor force were married."[35]

In 1943, the CIO's Congress of Women's Auxiliaries proposed a wide-ranging program of infant care, nursery care, elementary care, youth programs, and programs to feed children at all child care centers. They declared that "the care and protection of our children in wartime is a definite duty and responsibility of labor, the community and government" and that "[a]n adequate child program must be made available to every child of working mothers, regardless of race, creed or color."[36] At a 1944 Conference on Full Employment sponsored by the CIO, women labor leaders called for child care, equal pay, and continued employment for women after the war, including training and retraining for reconversion from war to civil production.[37] In 1944, the Women's Bureau, after consulting with the CIO and AFL, recommended that collective bargaining agreements include clauses prohibiting discrimination based on sex and marital status; establishing wage rates by job, not sex; and granting job-protected pregnancy leave at least six weeks before delivery and two months after.

The Rise of the Dual-Earner Family and the Decline of the Male Family Wage

After men returned from World War II, the AFL, CIO, and other unions did little to prevent massive layoffs of women. The family-wage ideal became a reality for many white working-class men in the decades immediately following World War II, especially if they were members of powerful unions, like steelworkers and auto workers. While benefits like maternity leave, family and medical leave, and child-care services were viewed by women as "centrally related to health, child neglect, juvenile delinquency, and family relationships," they were viewed as "frills" to male unionists.[38] At the same time, women's employment continued to grow after the war, particularly in clerical and sales occupations, and more modestly in skilled and operative occupations and professional and managerial ones.

Over the last half-century, the dual-earner household became dominant among couple families. In 2021, among different-sex parent couples with children, both the father and mother worked in about 60 percent of the couples (only the father worked in about 29 percent, only the mother worked in about 6 percent, and neither in the remaining small percentage).[39] As other chapters in this book have documented, there is no longer a single, hegemonic family ideal. Solo parents (mostly solo mothers), same-sex couples, and different-sex couple families in which women outearn men all became more numerous and visible during this period. Yet unpaid household labor remains substantial, and conflict between employer demands and household demands, particularly the care needs of children and elderly parents, has become increasingly acute.

When it comes to family policies that unions have long supported—including universal child care and paid family and medical leave—little progress has been made at the federal level despite the rise in women's employment. In 1967, the National Education Association—a union chartered by Congress in 1906 that today is the largest union in the United States—called for universal public pre-K starting at age four. In the early 1970s, unions joined other children's, women's, and civil rights' groups to support the Comprehensive Child Development Act (CCDA), federal legislation that "both supporters and opponents viewed as a step toward a permanent national framework for the universal provision of preschool services" and child care.[40]

While Congress passed the CCDA in 1971, it was vetoed by President Nixon, who issued a sharply worded veto message claiming it would put "the vast moral authority of the national Government to the side of communal approaches to childrearing over against the family centered approach."[41] Coming a year after he had signed both the Occupational Health and Safety Act and the Environmental

Protection Acts, Nixon's child care veto was one of the strongest public signs of the ascent of neoliberalism combined with a resurgent social conservatism, which together aimed to "reestablish the private family as the primary source of economic security and a comprehensive alternative to the welfare state."[42] (For examples of neoliberal family policy, see Williams et al., Chapter 5, and Heath and Randles, Chapter 21.)

CONCLUSION: UNIONS TODAY

In 2021, about 14 million U.S. workers—just over one in ten workers—were union members and another 1.8 million workers were covered by a union contract.[43] After peaking in the first half of the 1950s—when about one-third of households included a union member—the union share of households began to decline.[44] In 2022, only about 16 percent of adults resided in a union household.[45] Over the last century, income inequality has narrowed as union membership rates increased and widened as rates decreased. There is now a large body of research finding that unions, especially in the mid-twentieth century, have been a "powerful force for equalizing the income distribution," including in ways that go beyond their direct effect on the wages of union members.[46]

Inequality is higher in the United States than other wealthy countries in part because union membership rates in the United States are so low. In the nearest English-speaking countries (Canada, Ireland, and the United Kingdom), about one in four workers are union members. In the Nordic countries (Denmark, Finland, Iceland, Norway, and Sweden), between 50 percent (Norway) and 92 percent (Iceland) of workers are union members. In the most populous Nordic countries, Denmark and Sweden, about two-thirds of workers are unionized.[47] Some countries have much higher coverage rates than membership rates: in France, for example, the union membership rate is not that different from in the United States, but because French labor law is so different from U.S. labor law, 98 percent of workers are covered by collective bargaining agreements.

In many of these countries, especially the Nordic social democracies and France, unions have played a key role in the development of universal welfare states that make it possible for primary caretakers of children to work outside the home; as a result, women in their prime working years (ages twenty-five to fifty-four) in these countries have much higher employment rates than prime-age women in the United States.[48] By contrast, labor in the United States has made only modest progress when it comes to work-family policies like universal child care and pre-K and paid family leave. Still, unions have played a key role in the increasingly successful movement to pass laws like these at the state and local levels, and in 2021, Congress came within one vote in the Senate of passing President Biden's Build Back Better proposal, which included all three major work-family policies.

With unions serving the needs of families, and so tied to supporting families, is there a public cry for more unions? In August 2022, 71 percent of Americans told Gallup that they approved of labor unions. This is the highest level of union approval in a Gallup poll since 1965 and within the margin of error of union approval in 1936 (72 percent), a year after the passage of the National Labor Relations Act.[49] Support for unions is especially strong among Black and Latino Americans and young adults. In a 2021 Pew poll, 69 percent of eighteen- to twenty-nine-year-olds said unions have a positive effect, compared with 44 percent of adults over age sixty-four.[50]

The disparity between the share of workers who are union members and the share who approve of unions, especially among younger workers, and other recent trends suggest that union membership could grow over the next decade. At tech firms, which have traditionally been hostile to unions, there has been an "unprecedented rise in labor organizing," including the first-ever successful efforts to unionize Amazon workers and large video-game firm workers as well as a growing number of unionized Apple Stores.[51] At the same time, it remains very difficult for workers to unionize in the face of employer opposition, in part because of laws and court decisions that have tipped the balance too far in favor of employers and also conservative opposition to pro-worker labor law reforms like the Protecting the Right to Organize (PRO) Act.[52] It's too early to say if today's favorable signs of a labor resurgence will turn into real gains in union membership and worker power in the years ahead. But it is clear that today's diverse working class would benefit from such a resurgence and that the story of the labor movement supports families as they really are.

Notes

1. Trades Union Congress (TUC) (2014).

2. U.S. Department of Agriculture (2018).

3. U.S. Census Bureau (1909), 132.

4. U.S. Department of Agriculture (2018).

5. Ruggles (2015).

6. May, p. 3 in Milkman (1987).

7. Foner (1979), 21.

8.   Foner, 19.

9.   Foner, 28.

10. Foner, 29.

11. Foner (1947), 437.

12. Foner (1982), 47.

13. Levine (1983), 328.

14. Walker (1970).

15. Bremner (1956), 218.

16. Kessler-Harris (1975), 95.

17. Kessler-Harris, 92.

18. Kessler-Harris, 100.

19. Kessler-Harris, 101.

20. AFL-CIO, n.d.

21. Foner (1979), 282.

22. Foner, 282.

23. Foner, 286.

24. Neill (1916).

25. Woloch (2015), 10.

26. Associated Press, March 1933.

27. Troy (1965).

28. Foner (1982), 320.

29. Foner, 322.

30. Foner, 323.

31. Foner, 325–326.

32. Foner, 329.

33. Foner, 337.

34. Foner, 387.

35. Foner, 388.

36. UE News (2021).

37. Foner (1982) at 392.

38. Foner, 388.

39. U.S. Bureau of Labor Statistics (2022).

40. Karch (2013), 60.

41. Nixon (1971).

42. Cooper (2017), 9.

43. Brown (2022).

44. Farber et al. (2021).

45. McCarthy (2022).

46. Farber et al. (2021).

47. International Labour Organisation (2022).

48. Organization for Economic Co-operation and Development (2023).

49. McCarthy (2022).

50. Gramlich (2021).

51. Clark (2022).

52. Gonyea (2021).

In Other Words

FROM THE FOLKS WHO BROUGHT YOU THE WEEKEND: WHAT UNIONS DO FOR WOMEN

Ruth Milkman, June 7, 2013 / CCF

The Equal Pay Act is often presumed to be an accomplishment of the feminist movement of the 1960s. In fact, it was spearheaded by female trade unionists, who first introduced the bill in 1945 as an amendment to the 1938 Fair Labor Standards Act. The bill was defeated, largely because of staunch opposition from business interests, but a coalition of labor activists reintroduced it every year until it finally passed in 1963.

The bill originally required "equal wage rates for work of comparable character on jobs the performance of which requires comparable skills," wording that would have forced employers to pay women in traditionally sex-segregated jobs as much as men with comparable skills in traditionally male occupations. The 1963 act that finally passed was a compromise that instead required equal pay for "equal work." Given the pervasiveness of job segregation by gender, this weakened requirement for equity ensured that the law had a far more limited impact.

Had the unionists gotten their way, the gains for women workers since 1963 would have been more everly distributed along class lines. Whereas for elite professionals and many other college-educated workers, job segregation by gender has been substantially reduced in the past half-century, the extent of segregation in working-class jobs is just as high as it was in 1963.

Most non-college-educated women remain trapped in the pink-collar ghetto, working as waitresses, child care and eldercare workers, or as clerical and retail sales workers. In such jobs, women are typically paid at or near the minimum wage, often without even basic benefits like paid sick days, and with few opportunities for advancement. If the Equal Pay Act required equal pay for comparable work, child care workers, a traditionally female-dominated job, could not be paid less than zookeepers, for example.

Although female unionists led the campaign for the act, they were woefully underrepresented in the organized labor movement at the time. In 1960, 24 percent of U.S. workers were unionized, but women made up only 18.3 percent of union members. Half a century later, in 2012, women make up nearly half (48.3 percent) of the U.S. workforce and nearly as large a proportion (45.0 percent) of all union members. At the same time, the power and reach of unions have declined dramatically. Today, only 11 percent of American workers are union members, and in the private sector, the figure is below 7 percent.

The simultaneous decline in union power and rise in female representation among unions reflect the massive expansion—starting in the 1960s and 1970s—of public-sector unionism, alongside the massive contraction of private-sector unionism over the same period. Women are overrepresented in public-sector employment, making up a large majority of workers in fields like education, health care, and government administration—all now highly unionized sectors. In contrast, private-sector union membership is far more male-dominated, with strongholds in sectors like construction, utilities, transportation, and manufacturing.

Employers have successfully attacked private-sector unionism in the past few decades, and unionization rates have fallen apace. By contrast, until very recently, public-sector unions remained largely intact. But starting in 2011, a wave of state-level legislation weakening collective bargaining rights for public sector workers has directly targeted teachers and other unionized female-dominated occupations. These attacks will roll back many of the gains women have made since the 1960s. In 2012, the average hourly earnings of unionized women stood at $24.18, compared to $18.74 for nonunionized women workers. Unionized workers also are much more likely than their nonunion counterparts to have access to benefits like employer-sponsored health insurance, paid sick days, and pensions. And union workers have more job security as well.

The labor movement has fought to improve women workers' situation throughout American history. And today, women have a bigger stake than ever before in the survival of unions, which now face unprecedented attacks and are virtually threatened with extinction. As we commemorate the 50th anniversary of the Equal Pay Act, we should not only recall the history of women in unions but also consider the potential impact of ongoing union decline on women working today. ◾

PART THREE

What Do We Talk about When We Talk about Diversity of Family Forms?

11

Childfree Families

Amy Blackstone, Brittany Stahnke, and Amy Greenleaf

Family is your supportive community. It's the people you feel a sense of responsibility to that you don't simply give up on and you don't simply throw away.

—Bill, a married man in his late thirties

Family is comfort. It is a feeling of belonging.

—Brittany, a married woman in her late forties

Family is my partnership with Emily.

—Bruce, a married man in his thirties

Family is the idea of people bonding together and taking care of each other and becoming a unit.

—Kim, a married woman in her forties

Family is me and Tim and our little kids [nods toward pet dogs lounging on the floor].

—Mandy, a married woman in her thirties

What does family mean to you? For many people, family includes parents and children, but not every adult chooses to have kids of their own, as is the case for those quoted on the previous page. What do we call the bonds and household arrangements created by people who don't have children? Are adults without kids also without family? How do we know what counts as family and what does not?

It would be easy to say that family can be whatever we want it to be, and in many ways, that is true. But leaving the definition at that does not help us understand what families are, why they matter, and what purpose they serve. This chapter considers how adults without children "do" family. Just as gender scholars note that gender is something that is accomplished through our interactions with others,[1] family, too, is something we create, something we *do* rather than something we simply *have* or *are*.[2] By examining families in this way, we shift our focus from simply defining family to understanding how the notion of family is constructed, changed, and maintained.[3]

We've learned from the struggles of gay and lesbian couples that expectations for what families should be persist, even as they evolve (see Chapter 9 by Geist et al.). We've learned from work on *queering* families (see Chapter 34 by Guadalupe-Diaz as well as Chapter 40 by Whalley) that recognizing diversity and the links between larger systems and intimate lives can foster more humanity for us all. But for same-sex couples, cross-sex couples, and other intimate partnerships, the status of childfree shows us ways to do family that support more of us.

Across time and cultures, families facilitate their own survival and prosperity in many ways; these ways are often grounded in the presumption that all families include children. However, we work to examine childfree families as one way that families in different regions, classes, and ethnicities meet their social, emotional, physical, and psychological needs.

Families help societies meet many of the needs of their members.[4] In particular, families provide emotional and sexual companionship, facilitate economic provision, provide a home, and facilitate biological and social reproduction.[5] As you can see, the list typically involves children. In a previous publication, one of this chapter's coauthors, Amy Blackstone, presented findings from prior research to examine how childfree families might fulfill similar functions as families that include children. Here, we extend that work by presenting findings from interviews with forty-five childfree adults (thirty-one women, fourteen men) to understand how the childfree "do" family. We use the term "childfree" to refer to individuals who have made the explicit and intentional choice not to have or rear children. Two of the functions in particular—companionship and reproduction—are relevant, as they reveal how childfree families are both similar to and different from families that include children. In 2020, one of the chapter's other coauthors, Brittany Stahnke, conducted an interview study with the fourteen older (65+) childfree women that found very high rates of life satisfaction.[6] Further, while studies over the last four decades have failed to find an association between being parents and higher life satisfaction, there is support that partnership[7] (versus being single) and childlessness[8] (versus being a parent) are associated with higher life satisfaction.

EMOTIONAL AND SEXUAL COMPANIONSHIP

A key function of families is to serve as a source of emotional support and sexual intimacy for members.[9] Just as families with children provide intimacy and companionship for members, so do childfree families. In fact, some research shows that childfree families may offer greater emotional rewards to their adult members than families with children. Several studies have found that marital satisfaction among nonparents is much higher than that of parents.[10] These studies also show that parents experience depression more often than nonparents and that they are generally less happy than nonparents, suggesting that emotional well-being for adult members may be a unique strength of childfree families. When asked why they do not want children, one of the most common responses is that the childfree prefer to focus their time and energy on nurturing their relationship with their partner.[11]

In our interviews with childfree adults, the freedom to nurture sexual companionship with their partner came up as one reason these individuals prefer not to form households that include children. Janet, a woman in her thirties who lives with her male partner, shared: "One of my favorite things [about my child-free life] is my healthy sex life. One thing I've seen with people who have kids is how horrible their sex life is. I don't want to lose that [with my partner]." Jan, a married woman in her forties, shared that not having to worry about getting pregnant and enjoying her sexual freedom enhanced her sense of sexual connection with her partner, Fred, noting that the pressure to have children "is simply a way to control women's sexuality."

Others described their perception that the emotional intimacy they felt with their partners differed from the emotional intimacy of their friends with kids. In reflecting on how his life might differ if he and his wife had kids, Jack, a man in his early forties, stated:

Everything would be different! (Laughing) So much different. I guess we could go on for a while but our marriage is very independent. We're very fluid and with a child, you need to have built-in routines and times and stuff like that. We're very flexible with everything that we do.

Jack's wife, Kim, nodded throughout Jack's remarks, adding that their current arrangement, in which they are both independent but also a couple, makes their relationship strong.

Mandy and Tim, a married couple in their late thirties, suggested that not having kids enabled them to take the time to nurture their relationship in ways that would not be possible if they had kids. Mandy said, "Last year, we went on vacation for seventeen days. That's a long time to be hauling kids around. It would never have been possible with kids because of the nature of it." Both Tim and Mandy went on to reminisce about that trip along with others they have taken together, saying the trips were essential to their connection as a couple. They said their travels helped them understand each other, learn one another's quirks, and enjoy each other's company.

Robin and Joel, a married couple in their late thirties, felt similarly. When asked what they most appreciate about being childfree, Robin said it was being able to spend time with Joel. Joel said, "The freedom, the ability to do anything with each other spontaneously. . . . It's mostly the freedom of our schedule. Being with each other and being able to do as we wish together." Robin and Joel went on to recount some of their favorite spontaneous outings—movies, lunches out, road trips—all activities that they felt brought them closer as a couple and that they said would not have been possible had they chosen to have kids. The notion that they are closer to each other than couples who are parents came up in nearly all the interviews with childfree adults who were in long-term relationships. This is one area where childfree families felt they *differed* from parent-child families.

An area where the childfree said they share something in common with parents is in the nurturing roles they play for dependent others in their household. Nurturing is one way of attaining the emotional intimacy humans need. In the case of the childfree, such nurturing was directed at pets. Relationships of attachment, bonding, and affection that mimic relationships between parents and children are built between some pets and their owners.[12] Most interviewees noted that pets and children are vastly different beings with vastly different needs. Others noted and appreciated the bond they share with their pets. However, some interviewees spoke of pets *as* their children or as surrogate children. For them, pets were able to provide similar companionship as children do; however, most people get pets knowing the animals will not outlive them. For some people with pets, the grief and activities around loss are similar to that of human loss.[13] Childfree families with pets sometimes fulfill the need for emotional intimacy not just through their relationships with significant other humans but also through their relationships with their pets.

As noted in Mandy's description of family provided at the outset of this chapter, some childfree include their pets in their definitions of family, suggesting that these nonhuman companions play an exceedingly important role in their lives. In describing the role that her pets play in her family, Nicole said simply, "Pets have always been members of the family." Others used similar language to describe their pets, some going so far, as noted earlier, as to describe their pets as their children. Most acknowledged that caring for pets and caring for children differ dramatically, but at the same time, they emphasized the importance of their pets to their own emotional fulfillment. As Tanya said, "My ex-husband and I both view our cats as our children. He refers to them as 'the boys.' And for me, my cats really are a big part of my life."

For Tanya, a woman in her forties who had recently divorced her husband of ten years, the postdivorce arrangement around her pet cats obliged her to maintain a relationship with her ex-husband much in the way that children serve as a compulsory link between divorced parents. She shared that her ex-husband "still has contact with me because of the cats." Tanya went on to say,

> Honestly, our whole divorce went very smoothly except for the cats. The only thing that we ever argued about as we went through the process was the cats. I got to keep the cats, but he wanted to still have the keys to the house and come visit them when I'm not here. I had interesting conversations with people about, you know, should we be doing this and there are many people who firmly believe no way he shouldn't have access to your cats, they're not children so he shouldn't and then there are a couple of people who have gone through divorce situations, guys especially, who've said to me I wasn't able to see my children the way I wanted to and he certainly should be able to see the cats because he treats them as his children.

In the end, Tanya and her ex came up with an arrangement that worked for them where he would visit only at times that she told him she would not be at home, but she did note that if it weren't for their "shared custody" of the cats, they may not have contact at all anymore.

Pets may be able to fulfill the emotional needs of families when other people cannot.[14] In a study conducted during the COVID-19 pandemic, companion animals diminished stress and isolation. In the context of social isolation, pets can provide focused attachments. Since the COVID-19 pandemic, pets have been increasingly viewed as members of families.

In sum, childfree families serve to meet the emotional and sexual companionship needs of their members in ways that are both similar to and different from families with kids. Childfree couples note that they may have more time, energy, and financial resources available to dedicate to nurturing their partnerships than do parents. At the same time, they speculate that in at least some ways, their emotional and other connections to their pets may resemble parents' connections to their children. In other words, while the couple relationship is central to childfree families, other beings also play a role in facilitating their emotional well-being and providing companionship.

Biological and Social Reproduction

Another way that families help meet the needs of societies is through reproduction. Biological reproduction or adoption is perhaps the first thing that comes to mind when one thinks about the purpose of families. Clearly, childfree families do not participate in this aspect of reproduction. But producing and rearing more humans is only one aspect of bringing new members into a culture. When a new person enters our culture, someone must engage in "various kinds of work—mental, physical, and emotional—aimed at providing the historically and socially, as well as biologically, defined care necessary to maintain existing life and to reproduce the next generation."[15] Social reproduction includes all the roles, actions, and responsibilities needed to help individuals become participating and contributing members of society. As childfree individuals note, this role is not limited to those who participate in biological reproduction or legal adoption

One myth of the childfree is that they do not like children.[16] The reality is that not only do many childfree like children, but children play significant roles in their lives. As Jack put it, "There are a lot of kids in our lives. Just look at our fridge [nods to refrigerator covered in artwork by nieces, nephews, and the children of their friends]." The childfree we have interviewed include people engaged in professional roles that place them in the position of helping to rear the next generation. Others, like Tanya and Allison, worked as babysitters and nannies when they were younger and enjoyed the experience. Tanya described becoming "quite attached" to the children she cared for, while Allison noted, "I have really enjoyed being around kids my whole life." Bob, a man in his thirties who was engaged to the woman who is his partner, noted, "When I go over to people's houses who have kids, I like playing with the kids. I enjoy it. In fact, it's often easier to hang out with some people's kids than with the parents." In other words, for most childfree, the choice not to have kids is not rooted in a dislike of children. Many of them are involved in the lives of the children they know.

Notably, over 25 percent of the childfree in our sample have relationships with children because of their professions. The sample includes therapists, social workers, counselors, pediatricians, elementary and high school teachers, and others with education degrees seeking work in the field. Kate, a young woman in her twenties with an education degree, summed up what was echoed in several of the interviews when she said, "I am able to relate to kids in a certain way. I have the ability to be really patient and I want to make sure that children have access to advocacy and to adults who aren't parents."

Indeed, one of the strongest themes to emerge from the analysis of our interviews was that participants emphasized how they are able to have unique and important relationships with children *because* they are childfree. The 2020 study by Stahnke found that all its childfree women fulfill "surrogate parent" roles in their relationships with nieces, nephews, children of friends, and other individuals of younger generations.[17]

As Kim said when she described her relationship with the daughter of one of her close friends, "I get to be her playmate." Kim noted that her friend's child sees her as a peer—a much different role than that which the child's parents play. Participants' friendships with children came up frequently in the interviews. Kim, married to Jack who was quoted earlier, went on to say, "We're good with little kids. We try to invite the kids [of our friends] over and we all have this sort of joke that our house is called summer camp."

Jack followed up on what Kim shared:

> As the couple without kids, we have more of an ability to play with kids than other couples. When we come to [friends'] houses [who have kids], we actually really do that role with their kids, like an aunt and uncle thing. We just get in there and hang out. It's really funny because the kids see us as a bigger, older friend. We have a lot of really good relationships with a bunch of kids because we have the time to do that. I have two nephews who I see a lot and I mean we can really focus on them. There's a lot of attention we can give them.

Aside from their unique friendships with children, participants also described how not having kids themselves made them more available to take on special responsibilities for the kids in their lives, such as through legal guardianship or as godparents. Tanya described the relationship she and her ex-husband shared with their nephew:

> My ex-husband and I had an opportunity with his nephew, who is college-aged, to take him in. He comes from a family where there's a lot of mental illness and the parents have not, cannot, achieve much in life. So when our nephew was struggling in college, he got kicked out and we took him in. He lived with us for five or six months because we wanted to help care for him. We wanted to provide someone who had so much potential with the opportunity to see a different way of living. . . .

I think it really did make a difference for our nephew. . . . We took him to different places; we took him to wonderful restaurants, to concerts, to New York City and gallery openings. . . . We introduced him to our friends, and it was just a world so far from what he had grown up with.

Allison and her husband, a couple in their mid-thirties, believe they are in a unique position to offer their nine-year-old niece a broader view of the world than she may receive without their involvement:

We really, really, really enjoy spending time with our niece. Last Christmas we suggested to have her come stay with us for a few days, for long weekends especially in the summers. She's always so sad when we leave her house to go home and we thought it would be nice for the parents but mostly really a nice change of environment for our niece. I just feel like I get some of her issues [including OCD and anxiety] on a different level than her mom and grandma do. I just feel like it would be good for her to maybe have a connection with someone else who sees her in a different way than the people who interact with her on a regular basis.

Jan and Fred, a married couple in their forties, also described significant relationships with nieces, nephews, and their friends' kids. Noting that some of their friends had questioned their choice to marry given their decision not to have kids, Jan shared her emphatic disagreement with the notion that the purpose of marriage was to produce children: "The idea that the whole purpose in life is to create babies is pretty ugly. The expectation that every woman is gonna have children is a way of controlling women's bodies; it's a lack of control over reproduction." While childfree families control their own reproduction by opting out of parenthood in a biological or legal sense, they contribute in significant ways to the social reproduction function of families. As the adage goes, it takes a village to raise a child. Childfree families are one example of where and how that happens.

WHAT IS FAMILY? EXPANDING THE BOUNDARIES

Childfree families fulfill similar functional purposes as families that include children. They also help us think differently about why individuals form bonds with others, what roles families serve in our lives, and the diversity of ways that individuals "do" family. This chapter has demonstrated that the childfree form bonds with others that help to meet their human need for emotional and sexual companionship and our cultural need for producing new members of society who have been socialized according to our cultural values and norms.

Today, 20 percent of women in the United States do not have children, a number that has increased steadily and doubled since the 1970s.[18] Data demonstrating a rising childfree population aged 55+ were released in August 2021: 15 percent of women and 18 percent of men who are 55+ are without children.[19] Further, following the childbearing dip during the heart of the COVID-19 pandemic, more than one in five adults reported that it is highly unlikely they will ever have children. The most common reason reported was that "they just don't want to have children."[20] Thanks to the efforts of the feminist movement in increasing opportunities for women and to the increasing availability of reliable methods of birth control, more and more adults are creating families of their choosing. Examining the lives of the childfree reveals that these individuals form bonds to create family in much the same way that parents do. At the same time, the childfree demonstrate that having children is not a prerequisite to forming families that fulfill emotional needs and that support social reproduction in our society.

Notes

1. C. West and D. Zimmerman, "Doing Gender," *Gender & Society* 1 (1987): 125–151.

2. R. F. Oswald, L. Balter Blume, and S. R. Marks, "Decentering Heteronormativity: A Model for Family Studies," in *Sourcebook of Family Theory and Research*, ed. V. L. Bengtson, A. C. Acock, K. R. Allen, P. Dilworth-Anderson, and D. M. Klein, 143–155 (essay, SAGE Publications, 2005).

3. Oswald, Blume, and Marks, "Decentering Heteronormativity: A Model for Family Studies," 143–155; J. F. Gubrium and J. A. Holstein, *What Is Family?* (Mountain View, CA: Mayfield, 1990); R. F. Oswald and E. A. Suter, "Heterosexist Inclusion and Exclusion during Ritual: A 'Straight versus Gay' Comparison," *Journal of Family Issues* 25, no. 7 (2004): 881–889.

4. D. Knox, *M & F* (Belmont, CA: Wadsworth, Cengage Learning, 2011).

5. A. Blackstone, "Doing Family without Having Kids," *Sociology Compass* 8, no. 1 (2014): 52–62; K. Bogenschneider, *Family Policy Matters: How Policymaking Affects Families and What Professionals Can Do* (Mahwah, NJ: Lawrence Erlbaum Associates, 2006); J. M. Henslin, *Sociology: A Down-to-Earth Approach, Core Concepts*, 4th ed. (Boston: Pearson, 2010); S. Horwitz, "The Functions of the Family in the Great Society," *Cambridge Journal of Economics* 29 (2005): 669–684; L. Kramer, *The Sociology of Gender: A Brief Introduction* (Oxford University Press, 2011).

6. B. Stahnke, A. Blackstone, and H. Howard, "Lived Experiences and Life Satisfaction of Childfree Women in Late Life," *Family Journal* 28, no. 2 (2020): 159–167.

7. B. Stahnke and M. Cooley, "A Systematic Review of the Association between Partnership and Life Satisfaction," *Family Journal* 29, no. 2 (2021): 182–189.

8. B. Stahnke, M. Cooley, and A. Blackstone, "A Systematic Review of Life Satisfaction Experiences among Childfree Adults," *Family Journal* 31, no. 1 (2023): 60–68.

9.   Kramer, *Sociology of Gender*; L. Angeles, "Children and Life Satisfaction," *Journal of Happiness Studies* 11 (2010): 523–538.

10. Stahnke, Blackstone, and Howard, "Lived Experiences and Life Satisfaction"; Stahnke, Cooley, and Blackstone, "Systematic Review of Life Satisfaction Experiences"; Kramer, *Sociology of Gender*; Angeles, "Children and Life Satisfaction"; B. Burman and D. de Anda, "Parenthood and Non-parenthood: A Comparison of Intentional Families," *Life-styles* 8 (1986): 69–84; T. Hansen, "Parenthood and Happiness: A Review of Folk Theories versus Empirical Evidence," *Social Indicators Research* 108 (2012): 29–64; M. D. Somers, "A Comparison of Voluntarily Childfree Adults and Parents," *Journal of Marriage and the Family* 55 (1993): 643–650; J. M. Twenge, W. K. Campbell, and C. A. Foster, "Parenthood and Marital Satisfaction: A Meta-analytic Review," *Journal of Marriage and Family* 65 (2003): 574–583; M. Zagura, "Parental Status, Spousal Behaviors and Marital Satisfaction" (master's thesis; ProQuest, 2012).

11. I. Y. DeOllos and C. A. Kapinus, "Aging Childless Individuals and Couples: Suggestions for New Directions in Research," *Sociological Inquiry* 72 (2002): 72–80; S. K. House-knecht, "Voluntary Childlessness," in *Handbook of Marriage and the Family*, ed. M. B. Sussman and S. K. Steinmetz (New York: Plenum, 1987); L. M. Tomczak, "Childfree or Voluntarily Childless? The Lived Experience of Women Choosing Non-motherhood" (master's thesis; ProQuest, 2012); Jean E. Veevers, *Childless by Choice* (Toronto: Butterworths, 1980).

12. S. Volsche and P. Gray, "'Dog Moms' Use Authoritative Parenting Styles," *Human-Animal Interaction Bulletin* 4, no. 2 (2016): 1–16.

13. S. Volsche, "Pet Parents and the Loss of Attachment," in *Pet Loss, Grief, and Therapeutic Interventions: Practitioners Navigating the Human-Animal Bond Book*, ed. L. Kogan and P. Erdman: 55–69 (Routledge, 2020).

14. E. Johnson and S. Volsche, "COVID-19: Companion Animals Help People Cope during Government-Imposed Social Isolation," *Society & Animals* 29, no. 2 (2021): 1–18.

15. Volsche and Gray, "'Dog Moms' Use Authoritative Parenting Styles."

16. A. Blackstone, "Setting the Record Straight on 6 Myths about Childless Adults," *Bangor Daily News*, September 17, 2013.

17. Stahnke, Blackstone, and Howard, "Lived Experiences and Life Satisfaction."

18. Lindsay M. Monte and Renee R. Ellis, *Fertility of Women in the United States: 2012* (U.S. Census Bureau, July 2014), www.census.gov/content/dam/Census/library/publications/2014/demo/p20-575.pdf; R. S. Osborne, *Percentage of Childless Women 40 to 44 Years Old Increases since 1976, Census Bureau Reports* (U.S. Census Bureau Press Release, 2003).

19. T. Valerio, B. Knop, R. M. Kreider, and W. He, *Childless Older Americans: 2018* (U.S. Census Bureau Current Population Reports, 2021).

20. A. Brown, *Growing Share of Childless Adults in U.S. Don't Expect to Ever Have Children* (Pew Research Center, November 19, 2021), www.pewresearch.org/fact-tank/2021/11/19/growing-share-of-childless-adults-in-u-s-dont-expect-to-ever-have-children/.

12

Stepfamilies as They Really Are

Lawrence Ganong, Marilyn Coleman, and Caroline Sanner

S tepfamilies, defined as families in which at least one adult has children from a prior relationship, are not new. In fact, stepfamilies likely have been around since people first formed family households. For most of human history, the creation of stepfamilies was a common way of managing challenges parents faced when they were widowed. Until one hundred years ago or so, life spans were relatively short—the global average life expectancy in 1900 was just thirty-two years, due in part to high infant mortality rates. Even so, parents of young children often died while children were still in the home. Women died in childbirth, men were killed in work accidents and wars, and diseases were not well understood or effectively treated. Parents who lost a spouse were motivated to re-partner quickly because it was necessary for family survival. Widowers had no time to care for infants or young children. They needed to earn a living and immediate child-rearing help was necessary. Widows with young children often ended up poverty stricken after their spouses died, with no viable options other than remarriage. These postbereavement stepfamilies—made famous through folktales about wicked stepmothers, evil stepfathers, and neglected stepchildren like "Snow White," "Cinderella," and "Hansel and Gretel"—were quite common. For example, most U.S. presidents were members of postbereavement stepfamilies, and many First Ladies have been stepmothers to the presidents' children.

WHO LIVES IN STEPFAMILIES?

Look to your left, look to your right, look at yourself. Nearly everyone is in a stepfamily or is close to someone who is. As it was in the past, so it is now! The question of *who* is in stepfamilies, though, gives us more information about how this family fixture has evolved over time.

Americans have the highest rates of marriage, divorce, and remarriage in the industrialized world, even though our rates are declining. Cohabitation, or unmarried partners living together, also commonly results in stepfamily formation if one or both partners bring children into the household. Demographic statistics about remarried and cohabiting stepfamilies are hard to obtain, especially for cohabiting stepfamilies, so we must rely on multiple surveys to get a complete picture. In 2008 and 2018, data from the American Community Survey (ACS) indicated that among all U.S. adults who were currently married, 23 percent were in a remarriage and 77 percent in first marriages. Between 1990 and 2019, however, the remarriage rate dropped 50 percent in the ACS data. Likely these rates dropped because many formerly married adults opted to cohabit with subsequent partners rather than remarry. The remarriage rate in 2019, the most recent year statistics are available, was much higher for men than for women. Men tend to be older than women at the time of remarriage, and ages for both have been increasing. Women under fifty are more likely than men to create stepfamilies through either remarriage or cohabitation because women often have physical custody of children after divorce or separation.

Of course, not all stepfamilies are formed from remarriage or cohabitation. According to data from the 2015–2019 National Survey of Family Growth (NSFG), 15 percent of first marriages in the United States formed stepfamilies. The March 2019 and 2021 Current Population Survey showed that 11 percent of minor-aged children lived in married or cohabiting stepfamily households, a rate slightly higher than previous years. NSFG data from 2017 showed that a third of all unions for women under age forty-five were in stepfamilies, with 49 percent of cohabitations and 27 percent of marriages forming stepfamilies. Over a decade ago, a national survey reported that 42 percent of respondents had step-kin. These percentages were higher for Black Americans (60 percent), Hispanic Americans (46 percent), and younger adults (52 percent) and were lower for college-educated Americans (33 percent) and older adults (34 percent for adults age sixty-five and older). The takeaway message from all these statistics is that there are a lot of stepfamilies in the United States.

Some individuals live in more than one stepfamily over the course of their lives because remarried and cohabiting couples in stepfamilies are more likely to divorce or separate than couples in first unions. The greater likelihood of financial problems, issues involving raising children from prior unions, and what are called "selection factors" contribute to this more frequent partnering. Selection factors mean that people who have already separated or divorced—they've "selected in" to this group—may be more likely to do so again in the future because they may have different attitudes about divorce and separation as solutions to couple problems. They know they can cope with a breakup because they've already survived one, so dissolution may hold less fear for them. It is feasible that a sizable minority of those in stepfamilies are in their third (or higher) union. Children in these higher-order stepfamilies are more likely to have half-siblings and stepsiblings than other stepchildren. Needless to say, stepfamilies can be very structurally complex.

Stepfamilies are formed by people from every social class, from diverse racial and ethnic backgrounds, and across the life span. However, the chances of being in a stepfamily are somewhat greater for Americans who are young, are Black, and do not have a college degree because stressors from historic and contemporary structural racism, including poverty and unequal access to education, strain relationships in ways that contribute to separation, divorce, and multiple partnerships. As in the past, families today make adaptations to help one another when living in distress. Curiously, stepfamilies in a wide range of communities continue to be poorly understood. Younger adults have more step-relatives than older adults do because younger adults' parents had higher divorce rates and because increasing numbers of never-married parents later partnered with someone other than the parent of their child.

GAY AND LESBIAN STEPFAMILIES

Stepfamilies may be headed by gay and lesbian parents as well as heterosexual couples. Most stepfamilies headed by gay men were formed similarly to heterosexual stepfamilies, in that children were born to a married different-gender couple, the father came out as gay, then separated or divorced from the child's mother, and formed a new union with a man. In the past, most lesbian stepfamilies also were formed when one partner brought children from previous heterosexual unions to the family. Recently, growing numbers of lesbian couples have used assisted reproductive technologies so that one partner bears a child, although they usually consider these children as belonging to both partners. The nonbiological parent, like a stepparent in a heterosexual union, however, lacks legal recognition as a parent in most states. If a lesbian stepfamily dissolves, the partner who did not give birth usually has no legal access to the child. This is true of couples who used assisted reproductive techniques as well as those who brought children from prior relationships to the union. Gay and lesbian stepfamilies face many of the same issues as heterosexual stepfamilies, such as establishing stepparent roles, renegotiating co-parenting relationships, and "becoming a family," but they often do so in the context of added stress from heterosexism.

Lesbian stepfamilies have described the process of reclaiming and affirming their sense of family legitimacy when navigating institutions and communities that marginalize their experiences.

LATER-LIFE STEPFAMILIES

Stepfamilies do not always include young children and child-rearing. Increasingly, as older adults live longer and divorce at higher rates than in the past, more step-families are forming later in life. In fact, the later-life divorce rate in the United States is at an all-time high: in 2015, more than one in four people who divorced were over age fifty, compared with just one in ten in 1990. The greater number of single older adults has led to higher levels of dating and cohabiting in later life; in just the past decade, the number of cohabiting adults age fifty-plus surged 85 percent, from 2.3 to 4 million. Although remarriage rates have declined among older adults due to increases in cohabitation, many do remarry. Some older stepfamilies are long-term unions of couples that re-partnered when they were much younger. Consequently, the number of older stepfamilies is the largest it has ever been.

Men remarry in old age more often than do women, and older women with adequate finances are the least likely to remarry. Older women who were previously in marriages where they did more of the household work and caregiving of other family members may be unwilling to take on those responsibilities again. Although often interested in a partner to spend time with, they do not want the gendered obligations associated with marriage. Re-partnering in old age has some significant benefits, especially for older men. Older divorced or widowed men who don't re-partner are more likely to become isolated and depressed.

STEPFAMILY DIVERSITY

Within our definition of stepfamilies as families in which at least one adult has either biological or adopted children from a prior relationship lies a huge amount of diversity and complexity. Some of this diversity is structural: social scientists have identified as many as thirty different structural configurations of stepfami-lies based on which adult has children from prior relationships and where those children reside. This complexity has created challenges for scholars, policy mak-ers, and stepfamily members. For example, people often refer to the concepts of a "stepfamily" and a "stepfamily household" as if they are interchangeable, but they are not always the same. The membership of many stepfamilies extends beyond a single household, which means many stepfamily members do not live in the

Simple Stepfamily

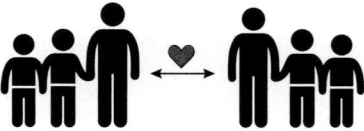

Blended or **Complex** Stepfamily

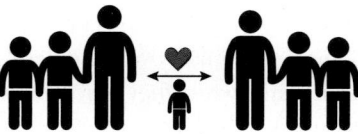

Blended or Complex Stepfamily
with a **Shared Child**

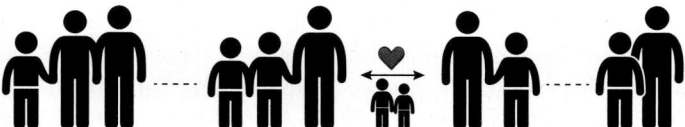

Stepfamilies across Households

same household, at least not all the time. "Simple" stepfamilies are households consisting of a stepparent (usually a stepfather), a parent (usually a mother), and the parent's children from earlier unions. Researchers consider a stepfamily household to be "blended" or "complex" when each adult brings children to the household from previous relationships. Some simple and complex stepfamily households also include children born to the remarried (or cohabiting) union, so there truly are children who are his, hers, and "theirs." Some stepchildren end up with full, half-, and stepsiblings spread across several households. See the accompanying illustrations of different stepfamily structures.

STEPFAMILIES AS THEY REALLY ARE?

One of the challenges in addressing how stepfamilies "really are" is to manage the divergent perspectives through which they have been viewed. Over the past fifty years, four broad perspectives may be found in how researchers, clinicians, and, to some degree, the general public have thought about stepfamilies. These perspectives, listed in the order in which they first emerged, are stepfamilies as (1) reconstituted nuclear families, (2) incomplete institutions, (3) deviant and dysfunctional, and (4) adaptive and resilient. All four perspectives have adherents. Supportive evidence may be found for each, and to understand stepfamilies we must consider all the evidence. Over the past half-century, stepfamily research has grown from about a dozen studies in the United States to thousands of studies conducted all over the world.

Stepfamilies as Reconstituted (or Reconstructed) Nuclear Families

For most of human history, stepfamilies were formed after the death of a parent. It was not uncommon for parents to die when children were young, and finding a new spouse or partner was a necessity for the widowed parent. These postbereavement stepfamilies were seen as re-forming or "reconstituting" a nuclear family (two married parents with shared biological or adopted children), and stepparents generally were seen as replacements or substitutes for deceased parents. We have no data to tell us how effective or satisfying these stepfamilies were—folktales like "Cinderella" and "Hansel and Gretel" suggest that the stepparent-stepchild relationship was a concern—but stepfamilies were necessary for survival.

It was not until the early 1970s that more stepfamilies were created after the divorce of parents than after parental death. The combination of more divorces and longer life spans led to this shift. This change in the most common precursor to stepfamily life was not sudden, but to social observers, social scientists, policy makers, and stepfamily members themselves, these postdivorce stepfamilies seemed like a new family form that introduced many challenges for individuals, families, and society. The fact that divorced, nonresidential parents were not only alive but were often actively involved in child-rearing resulted in much confusion about the roles and responsibilities of parents and stepparents. If stepparents were not replacements for absent parents, then what were they?

Although clinicians generally discourage postdivorce stepfamilies from trying to re-create themselves as nuclear families, the first-marriage nuclear family was the model most familiar to people, so many people continued to think of stepparents as replacements for absent parents and of stepfamilies as re-created nuclear families; for example, a newly remarried mother might tell her child that "you have a new daddy now" while a newly remarried father, referring to his new wife, might tell his child to "call her Mommy." Researchers have found that a portion of stepfamilies (the prevalence is not clear) have embraced this model for themselves. For example, in the United States most single-parent adoptions are by stepparents who adopt their spouse's children, thus moving from having little or no legal rights and responsibilities to becoming a legal parent holding all rights and responsibilities of a parent. Children's last names are changed, and families present themselves to the outside world as a nuclear family. Not all stepfamilies employing this nuclear family model adopt stepchildren, due to practical reasons (for example, the nonresidential parent has to relinquish their parental rights, which many refuse to do), but even non-adopting stepfamilies interact with one another and with outsiders as if they are nuclear families.

There are many reasons for this: (1) this is a widely known model of family life, so family members generally know their roles and how to interact with one another, (2) they can avoid the stigma of divorce or being in step-relationships by reframing who they are, and (3) stepfamily members often want to feel "normal" after transitioning through separations, and they may assume this model helps them do that. For some stepfamilies, it may be easier to enact nuclear family identities than to negotiate and create new ways of being a family.

We do not know what percentage of these "reconstituted nuclear" stepfamilies are successful in adapting to stepfamily life, but we know from research that some are. To succeed, all family members have to agree on the nuclear family model, which means that anyone who rejects this dynamic may risk losing family membership. This model appears to be more effective when children acquire stepparents at an early age, and when nonresidential parents are completely uninvolved. This model is generally not effective if a nonresidential parent wants to be involved, one or more children refuse to accept a stepparent as a replacement parent (this could include children of the stepparent who live elsewhere), or grandparents (and stepgrandparents) protest at being excluded from extended family interactions.

It should be noted that stepfamilies re-creating the nuclear family model are often hard for researchers to find because they don't self-identify as being part of a stepfamily. For this reason, they are often excluded from stepfamily research. If a stepdaughter thinks of her stepfather as "dad," she will not readily identify herself as a stepchild or a stepfamily member. Consequently, stepfamilies who relate as nuclear families may be underrepresented in studies. Nonetheless, there is sufficient research evidence to conclude that this is a common model used by stepfamilies.

Stepfamilies as Incomplete Institutions

The shift for stepfamilies from mostly postbereavement to mostly postdivorce was gradual, but to stepfamily members and to individuals who worked with them, the prevalence of postdivorce stepfamilies seemed to create considerable confusion and ambiguity. If stepfamilies were not re-created nuclear families, then what were they? If stepparents did not replace an absent parent, then who were they and what were they supposed to do? Sociologist Andrew Cherlin wrote in 1978 that stepfamilies formed after remarriage were *incomplete institutions*, meaning they were family units that lacked formal societal supports and clear guidelines for family roles and behaviors. Cherlin noted that there were no English words to describe some stepfamily relationships (for example, what are stepfathers and fathers to each other?), suggesting that the lack of terms made it difficult for stepfamily members to even imagine the existence of such relationships. Social institutions such as schools, legal systems, faith-based organizations, and youth organizations were unprepared for dealing with children who had three or four individuals in "parental" positions, leaving stepfamily members to sort out their roles and responsibilities with little societal help. The absence of formal institutional support meant that stepfamily members experienced greater stress because they lacked aids to help them figure out how to be a family with multiple parental figures and with family members living in two or more households. The absence of clear norms for how to "be a stepfamily" was one explanation for why stepfamilies attempted to function as if they were first-marriage nuclear families.

Although postdivorce stepfamilies are more common and more visible than when Cherlin wrote about them as incomplete institutions, parts of his argument still ring true today. On the one hand, almost everyone knows people who are members of stepfamilies, and social systems have gradually adopted new policies and procedures for accounting for stepfamilies. There certainly is more awareness and greater understanding of stepfamilies now than in the past. On the other hand, social customs still largely support and celebrate parent-child relationships and first-marriage nuclear families, and the legal system has been unwilling to grant many new rights and responsibilities to stepparents. In the United States, children can have up to two legal parents, but no more; there is no room for stepparents legally. Although the United Kingdom and other countries have made laws that grant stepparents some rights and responsibilities while still honoring parental roles and responsibilities, the United States has not. Legal barriers serve as practical limitations to how stepparents may interact with stepchildren's teachers, youth leaders, and health care providers. In short, there is still evidence that stepfamilies are incompletely institutionalized. The fact that many new stepfamily members report being unsure of what to do when they are forming a stepfamily household or unclear about how to enact their roles (for example, stepmothers feeling pressure to be "mother-like" without usurping the role of mothers) suggests that widespread norms do not exist.

Stepfamilies as Deviant and Dysfunctional

Postdivorce stepfamilies have been perceived as deviant or dysfunctional in comparison to first-marriage nuclear families for a very long time. Just as in the folktales of abusive stepfathers, wicked stepmothers, and neglected and abused stepchildren, modern stepparent-stepchild relationships often are seen as negative, unloving, and damaging to family members. This *stepfamily as deviant or dysfunctional* perspective is common in media portrayals and public and professional discourse.

Therapists and counselors started focusing their work on postdivorce stepfamilies before researchers did. Because clinicians focused mainly on family problems, much of the early scholarly writing framed stepfamily relationships from a social problems perspective, which perhaps contributed further to the views that stepfamilies were deviant and dysfunctional. Researchers followed suit, and most studies on stepfamilies over the past fifty years have implicitly or explicitly been framed under the expectations that stepfamilies and stepfamily members would be at a deficit to nuclear families.

Researchers previously conducted and often still conduct studies in which stepfamilies are compared with first-marriage nuclear families. Early studies often were unsophisticated. For instance, data were collected from anyone who lived in a stepfamily—parents, stepchildren, stepparents, stepsiblings—and then analyzed together as though everyone experienced stepfamilies similarly. Structural variability of stepfamilies usually was ignored, and samples often comprised White, middle-class people only.

Finding small but consistent differences in favor of nuclear families has often led researchers to conclude that stepfamilies are deviant and dysfunctional, a perspective we have referred to as a *deficit-comparison* approach. Deficit-comparison studies compare children in stepfamilies with children in first-marriage nuclear families on various indicators of well-being (sometimes, children in single-parent families also are included in these comparisons). The prevailing assumption in these deficit-comparison studies is that stepchildren will fare worse on outcomes when compared with children living with both their parents.

These investigations consist mostly of cross-sectional study designs, meaning they are snapshots of family life at a single point in time, with little consideration of the personal histories of the individuals that precluded them living in stepfamilies, or single-parent households, or first-marriage families. A variety of topics have been studied with this deficit approach, including children's behavioral and psychological problems, academic achievement, interpersonal relationship quality, and emotional well-being. Although not all studies find differences, researchers consistently have found that, on average, stepchildren fare worse than children in first-marriage families but are similar to children living with never-married or divorced single parents. Although the developmental and behavioral differences generally have been small between these groups of children, there has been a tendency for some researchers and for the general public to perceive these findings as large and absolute. It is simply not true that *all* stepchildren do less well on all measures of well-being than do children whose parents are still married. What gets lost is that most stepchildren function well, and their development is not damaged permanently by their parents' re-partnering. These reports also generally leave out the extent to which children in stepfamilies and nuclear families overlap on outcome measures; careful analysis shows that there is far more similarity than difference. The nuclear family, however, as the standard to match, remains a compelling framework for researchers. Similarly, remarriages are often compared with first marriages and are consistently found to be less stable, or more prone to divorce, and, less often, not as satisfying as first marriages.

Many theories have been proposed to explain these average differences between stepfamilies and nuclear families. Theories purport the differences are due to greater stress, fewer resources, evolutionary preferences to support genetic kin, stepfamily deficits in attachment styles, communication skills, mental health, substance abuse, and other psychological and interpersonal problems. Differences also are attributed in some studies to "selection effects," which refers to characteristics of stepfamily members that the researcher did not measure but that make individuals more likely to be in stepfamilies in the first place, making them different from members of nuclear families in ways that affect the study's findings. It should be noted that when researchers control for the effects of variables such as socioeconomic status, number of family transitions experienced, number of children in the household, and other possible ways in which stepfamilies demographically differ from other family structures, differences between stepfamilies and other families often disappear or are greatly reduced in magnitude. Social problems, not family structure, are the source of troubles, yet, as you have read in many other chapters, family structure—in this case stepfamilies—still gets named as an explanation.

Stepfamilies as Adaptive and Resilient

Eventually, clinicians began to write about ways in which stepfamilies could be effective, satisfying, and capable of meeting the needs of family members. Researchers also began to study stepfamily dynamics from a resilience framework that examined adaptive behaviors of stepfamily members rather than looking only at problems. After a slow start, this *normative-adaptive* perspective, with its resilience lens, has led to clinically and empirically documented ways in which stepfamilies could interact and were interacting to serve family members well.

Studies from a normative-adaptive approach assume that separation/divorce and remarriage are often normal and healthy choices rather than the result of personal psychopathology or maladaptive interpersonal or social problems. Using a normative-adaptive approach, some researchers conduct longitudinal studies that follow individuals and their families over time and across family transitions, yielding a more complete picture of the contexts within which stepfamilies live; conducting research this way is like taking videos rather than still photos of stepfamily interactions. In addition, normative-adaptive researchers often use qualitative methods that involve in-depth conversations with stepfamily members to understand their experiences living in stepfamilies more holistically than is possible from questionnaires in anonymous surveys.

Normative-adaptive perspectives include the study of resilience processes. For instance, researchers have investigated stepchildren who are doing well in stepfamilies to see how they and their families differ from those who are struggling, to determine what factors contribute to successful adaptations at the individual level (for example, inclusive definitions of family), interpersonal level (parent-child communication), and community or societal level (neighborhood environment). These studies also examine the context of successful stepfamily relationships as well as how stepfamily members build and maintain positive relationships.

So, Stepfamilies as They Really Are

Thus far, we have reviewed how (1) some stepfamilies try to re-create themselves as nuclear families, (2) most stepfamilies lack societal norms as guides, (3) stepfamilies differ from first-marriage families on several individual and family outcomes, and (4) many stepfamilies adapt in healthy ways to stepfamily life. Now, we describe evidence-based information about stepfamilies that links and even transcends these four perspectives.

Structural Characteristics

In addition to diverse arrays of stepfamily structural complexity, there are other structural characteristics of stepfamilies that distinguish them from other families. These characteristics make it hard for stepfamilies to function as reconstituted nuclear families and stimulate many stepfamilies to create new ways of doing family life.

Multiple Family Transitions. Stepfamilies are usually preceded by several family transitions, including parental death, divorce, and separation. Change is hard, and family transitions tend to be no exception. Of course, people vary in how well they respond or adapt to change; even siblings can vary tremendously in how easily they adjust to family transitions. How transitions are managed individually and as a family has implications for stepfamily success. Validating the loss that children (and adults) feel as their family evolves tends to be an important step in family adjustment. No matter how the family has changed, family transitions tend to involve grieving: for the loss of the family as it had been known, for the loss of family rituals and roles, and for time lost with family members. Children often are unaware of parents' relationship troubles and thus have less time to acclimate to parental separations and divorce and to grieve losses. Stepfamily members thus vary in how they have adjusted to family transitions and in their readiness to begin new relationships.

Asynchronous Family Histories. In stepfamilies, parent-child relationships predate adult romantic relationships. Therefore, stepfamilies begin with the parent-child ties being the closest emotional bonds. For step-couples who are thrust into an ongoing system of child-rearing, they tend to have little or no time to adjust to living together, develop rituals, and settle into life rhythms without children present, at least some of the time. The children may have different ideas than the stepparent about family rituals, rules, and roles. Because of these different family histories, family life often must be negotiated, which can be stressful. Stepfamily therapist Patricia Papernow calls this negotiating process *establishing a middle ground*, a necessary step in stepfamily development. The middle ground is where everyone in the family can agree. Papernow says that too much middle ground leads to boredom (seldom a problem in stepfamilies). While effortful to get there, finding middle ground makes life easier. Having to negotiate everyday activities, such as when dinner is eaten, what is eaten, where dinner is eaten, and who must be present at dinner, can be exhausting. As family and household behaviors become more routinized—more middle ground—there is more emotional space for stepfamily members to bond and more energy to do so.

Stepchildren Often Belong to Two Households. Children in stepfamilies often are members of two households because of legal preferences for joint physical custody. Consequently, some children go back and forth between parental households. These *accordion* households involve frequent transitions and changes in household routines. Shared custody also means that the adults in both households are linked as they share co-parenting responsibilities. Co-parenting across stepfamily households often involves one or more stepparents as well as the parents. Shared custody is so common in fact that there are 'best of' lists of co-parenting apps that help coordinate between households, and they include roles for stepparents or other partners.

Stepchildren and adults fare better when co-parents, including ex-partners, new partners, and all adults across households, work collaboratively, minimize conflicts around children, and act "businesslike." Keeping children out of the middle of parental disputes can reduce loyalty conflicts for children (feeling like they have to "choose sides") and lower their stress and anxiety. Co-parents can make decisions more easily when conflict is minimized, but perhaps the main benefit of reduced co-parental conflicts is that children feel closer to parents and stepparents, do not feel they have to choose between them, and generally feel more secure.

Stepfamily Dynamics

There is no universal way for stepfamilies to interact any more than there is no universal way for any kind of family to interact. Factors such as the age of children when step-relationships begin, amount of stepparent-stepchild contact, the presence of half- and stepsiblings, genders of stepchildren and stepparents, and previous family experiences affect how stepfamily dynamics unfold. Amid the diversity, researchers have identified some consistent findings with regard to "what works" in stepfamilies.

Parent-Child Relationships. The closeness and continuity of parent-child relationships appears to be especially predictive of stepchildren's well-being. Children are sensitive to changes in relationships with parents after parents re-partner, often rating them as more distant and less involved. Parents who set aside one-on-one time with children and regularly display warmth, affection, and interest in children's lives are more likely to maintain close ties with them. For example, when parents talk openly with children about what is going on in their lives—about grades, school, friends, dating—children in stepfamilies experience more positive outcomes. Additionally beneficial is the spillover effect between parent-child closeness and stepparent-stepchild closeness; parents who nurture their relationships with children also may be supporting the development of positive stepparent-stepchild ties. There is growing evidence that stepchildren's emotional, cognitive, and behavioral development is better when they have close bonds with stepparents and parents.

In addition, stepchildren tend to adjust better, and stepparent-stepchild relationships develop more positively, when parents take the lead in discipline and rule-setting early in stepfamily formation. Stepchildren face many changes when parents re-partner, and maintaining household rules with parents as rule setters and enforcers helps sustain some continuity amid these changes. Even as stepparents gradually become more active co-parents over time, stepfamilies appear to operate best when parents are ultimately supported by stepparents in their disciplinary decisions.

Stepparent-Stepchild Relationships. Stepparents and stepchildren are related because of their mutual tie to a third person—the child's parent who is the romantic partner of a stepparent. Rather than being a relationship that is entered into freely by both participants, stepparent-stepchild relationships are often formed involuntarily. Children don't choose their parents either, but this new relationship emerges later in life. Part of the success of a stepfamily hinges on the quality of the stepparent-stepchild relationships; negative, hostile, or distant bonds can create stress that reverberates throughout the entire stepfamily system, whereas close and affectionate bonds can be a major resource for stepfamilies that indirectly strengthens other family relationships. How stepparents develop close bonds with stepchildren is a major task of stepfamily life.

As simple as it sounds, stepparents have to try to be likable and build bridges Stepparents are more successful in establishing close relationships with stepchildren when they focus on building close emotional bonds, or building friendships with stepchildren, as opposed to establishing authority. Stepchildren generally expect the adults to initiate relationship-building activities. Stepparents who pay attention to children's wants and needs when initiating these activities generally have an easier time bonding with them. Efforts to bond are generally more successful when stepchildren have input into what is being done, activities move at a pace comfortable for children, and there is a genuine give-and-take between stepparent and stepchild. Observing, listening, being open to stepchildren's disclosures, and being willing to disclose to stepchildren themselves are among the identified ways of attending to stepchildren's internal states and adapting efforts to build affinity to stepchildren's comfort levels. Parents help by interpreting stepchildren's behaviors for stepparents and adding informed observations about the children.

Stepfamily activities based on having fun in low-stress situations also can be effective at promoting stepfamily cohesion and positive child outcomes. Effective stepfamily couples plan whole-group activities prior to moving in together to facilitate familiarity and bonding, and they continue these activities once they create a stepfamily household. Just hanging out together or talking daily also develop step-relationships by letting step-kin get to know each other gradually Eventually, stepfamilies might create new rituals. Rituals range from daily routines to major events marked by ceremony and symbolism. Both new rituals and the retention of rituals from their prior family households aid bonding and adjustment. Effective stepfamilies merge prior family rituals and routines in ways that help stepfamily members feel they belong. Rituals are valued in part because of the meaning they give to events. Therefore, managing rituals is critical because new or altered rituals have the potential to damage relationships, just as they can heal relationship wounds and bring family members closer.

Step-Couples. Unlike nuclear families, stepfamilies are unique in that couple relationships are developed amid efforts to both develop bonds with new stepchildren and extended kin as well as maintain ties with children and children's nonresidential parents. Additionally, the parent-child dyad has more shared history than the couple dyad, which can present challenges, particularly when stepfamily formation occurs following a period when parent-child boundaries have become enmeshed from residing in a single-parent household. Stepparents entering the family system may feel like "outsiders" to the parent-child pair, while parents who are trying to maintain ties to their children may experience guilt from having to divide time and attention between children and their new spouse or partner. Establishing boundaries around the couple that are closed enough to protect the relationship while permeable enough to promote cohesion as a stepfamily unit is complex, and disagreements may form around issues regarding negotiating and adapting to these boundaries.

Two major tasks for step-couples include explicitly discussing expectations—particularly regarding parenting and stepparenting roles—prior to re-partnering and maintaining realistic expectations across the transition to stepfamily. Remarried couples have been found to disagree the most about issues related to children from previous relationships, such as rules for children's behavior and disciplinary practices. Stepfamilies function better, and step-couples are more satisfied in their relationships, when parents and stepparents explicitly discuss and reach consensus on rules, including household responsibilities, and roles played by stepparents. Agreement on rules and roles within co-parenting relationships also contributes to children's well-being and stepfamily adjustment.

Given the lack of clear norms for how to establish stepfamily roles and relationships, stepfamily adjustment is more positive when stepparents and parents maintain realistic expectations. For example, expecting stepparents and stepchildren to experience immediate love for each other is a common unrealistic belief that clinicians observe. Consequently, reasonable expectations help stepfamily members adjust, including (a) anticipating that new relationships take time to form, (b) assuming new household and family dynamics develop in nonlinear ways, and (c) presuming that it takes effort, compromise, and clear communications for the stepfamily to "feel like a family."

Stepsibling Relationships. Stepsibling relationships are formed when both adults bring children from prior unions into the stepfamily. Just under half of complex stepfamilies bring two sets of children from prior unions together. Only a handful of studies have explored the nature of stepsibling ties, generally finding that stepsiblings have less close and less supportive relationships than full siblings, though they also exhibit less conflict and aggression in their relationships than full siblings. Adult stepchildren report that they see their stepsiblings significantly less than their full siblings, though stepsiblings who shared a household as children and who lived geographically close as adults were more likely to keep in touch. Although stepsiblings are nonvoluntary kin who are asked to bond with individuals with whom they may have little in common, some do develop sibling-like bonds or close friendships. Others describe themselves as distant acquaintances because of having few opportunities to interact, a lack of contact, or large age differences.

Half-siblings. Children who genetically share one parent are half-siblings. Like stepsiblings, half-siblings vary in the nature and quality of their relationships. Some half-siblings have large age differences, live far apart, and never share a residence. Under these conditions, half-siblings often are emotionally disengaged from each other and may have little contact. Other half-siblings spend much of their childhood together, identify as brothers and sisters, and interact as if they were "full" siblings. Younger half-siblings in stepfamilies may even be unaware that their older half-sibling is not fully biologically or legally related to them until they get older. Half-sibling relationship quality generally depends on the extent to which parents and stepparents draw inclusive boundaries of family membership that bring everyone into the fold, or "into the family."

Grandparents and Stepgrandparents. Given longer life spans and greater relationship instability and re-partnering, there are more multigenerational stepfamilies than ever before. Individuals become stepgrandparents when their stepchildren reproduce, when they remarry or re-partner with a grandparent, or when a child remarries or re-partners with someone with children from earlier unions. Studies in recent years have found that stepchildren's relationships with grandparents and stepgrandparents are often important to them. For example, close relationships with stepgrandparents are found to promote family ties with other extended stepfamily members. As the matriarchs and patriarchs of the stepfamily, stepgrandparents' acceptance of stepgrandchildren into the family sets a precedent for how other stepfamily members should behave toward stepgrandchildren. Grandparents in stepfamilies also serve as valuable resources of love, care, and support. There is growing evidence that grandparents and stepgrandparents are helpful to parents and stepparents in raising children by providing tangible and intangible support to younger generations.

LOOKING AHEAD

What will stepfamilies be like twenty or thirty years from now? That is hard to say, but we anticipate that social scientists will know much more than they do now. For one thing, we expect research to better attend to racial and ethnic diversity in stepfamilies and further explore other marginalized or underrepresented stepfamily forms, such as those headed by same-sex couples. As with all other domains of family research, stepfamily research will continue to improve when we stop centering whiteness and heteronormativity in framing what we see and what is knowable. As society changes, investigations can advance that examine stepfamilies within multiple social, cultural, and physical contexts. Because we can safely conclude that stepfamilies are here to stay.

In Other Words

FROM COUNTERCULTURAL TREND TO STRATEGY FOR THE FINANCIALLY INSECURE: PREMARITAL COHABITATION AND PREMARITAL COHABITORS, 1956–2015

Arielle Kuperberg, October 9, 2018 / CCF

In the early 1960s, fewer than 3 percent of women who married for the first time had lived with their husband before the wedding. As late as 1968, news of a college student living with her boyfriend touched off a national scandal. As you can see in Figure 12.1, even by the end of the 1970s, fewer than one-third of first marriages began after premarital cohabitation. Since the mid-1990s, however, cohabiting before marriage has become the norm. Between 2011 and 2015, around 70 percent of women marrying for the first time had lived with their husband before marriage, and a 2015 national poll of U.S. adults found that only 17 percent believed living together outside of marriage was not an acceptable way of life.

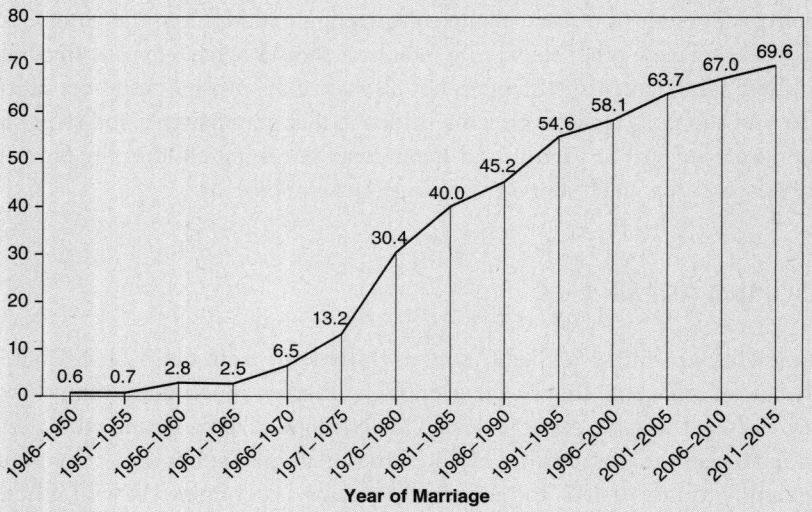

Figure 12.1 | Percent of First Marriages Preceded by Cohabitation with Husband, by Year of Marriage (Women <36 at First Marriage)

Note: *Numbers calculated from the 1988 National Survey of Families and Households (1946–1985, N = 4,356) and National Survey of Family Growth (1986–2015, N = 9,480) and based on women <36 at first marriage.*

As I show in my article in the journal *Marriage & Family Review* based on an analysis of national data on more than 13,000 women who married between 1956 and 2015, the characteristics of couples who live together before marriage have changed over time. Despite the widespread acceptance of premarital cohabitation, its practice has changed in ways that reflect a growing divide between Americans with a college degree and those with some or no college education. This change has interacted with differences in premarital cohabitation between more and less religiously observant Americans in some surprising ways.

Early cohabitation rates: only small differences between more- and less-educated Americans

Throughout the earliest period, from 1956 to 1985 (see Figure 12.1), when premarital cohabitation was still practiced by a minority of couples, the few couples who lived together before marriage generally belonged to one of two distinct groups. One was composed largely of couples with the lowest level of education: 27 percent of premarital cohabitors had less than a high school education when they moved in together. But an even larger group of early cohabitors had higher levels of education: 31 percent of cohabitors had at least some college education when they moved in together.

Whether college grads or people without a high school degree, cohabitors transgressed powerful social norms when they decided to live together before marriage. This is likely for different reasons: the least educated women may have delayed marriage until they were more financially stable or to save money for a wedding, while more highly educated women were more likely participating in a new countercultural trend that stemmed from the sexual revolution of the 1960s. Still, overall, there were no significant differences between rates of premarital cohabitation among couples with different levels of education during the period from 1956 to 1986.

When rates of cohabitation began to change by education

Beginning in the late 1980s, however, premarital cohabitation began to grow *most* rapidly among the *least* educated Americans. Between 1986 and 2000, premarital cohabitation rates grew more quickly among couples who had not completed high school than among any other group. At the next levels of education, differences in cohabitation rates remained small. Their rates grew more slowly, and there wasn't a big difference among couples with at least a high school degree over this time period.

All that growth meant that, starting in 1995, a majority of first marriages began with premarital cohabitation. Here's where a new educational divergence occurred: Since 2000, cohabitation rates of the most educated couples have grown markedly *more slowly* than those of all other educational groups—people with high school diplomas and even ones with some college. By 2011-2015, women who married directly, without first cohabiting, were a minority in every educational group. Even so, marrying directly was twice as common among women with a college degree as among women who had a high school diploma or less. More than 40 percent of women with a bachelor's degree married in the so-called traditional way, without having first cohabited. But fewer than 20 percent of women who had never attended college did so.

In other words, although acceptance of premarital cohabitation is equally high among highly educated as among less-educated Americans, the actual rates of cohabitation among couples with a bachelor's degree or higher are much lower than those of any other educational category. College-educated couples, often considered the group most likely to challenge traditional relationship and sexual norms, are now the group *most likely* to practice the traditionally "respectable" route to marriage—with women moving in with their husbands only after the wedding.

Religion, Education, and Cohabitation

Direct marriers became an increasingly select group in another way as well, as you can see in Figure 12.2. Not only did they tend to be more educated than average, but they were also more religious. In 2011-2015, 73 percent of women who married without first cohabiting attended religious services at least once a month, compared

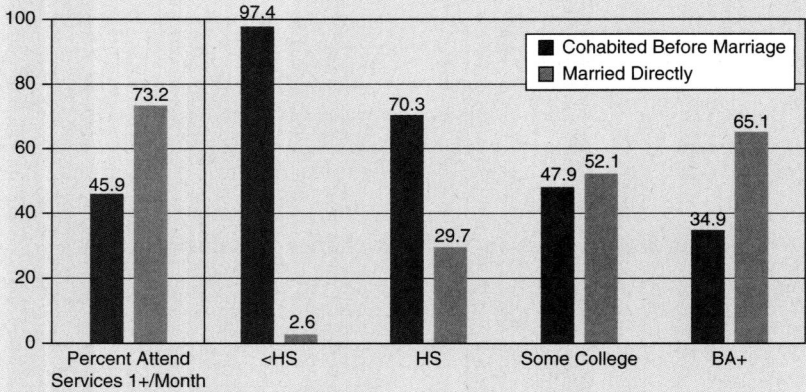

Percent Frequent Attenders Cohabited or Directly Married by Education

Figure 12.2 | Cohabitation, Direct Marriage, and Education among Religious Service Attenders (1+/Month) who Married in 2011-2015

Note: *Numbers calculated from the National Survey of Family Growth and based on women <36 at first marriage (N = 553; Frequent Religious Service Attenders, N = 315).*

to only 46 percent of premarital cohabitors. While almost a third (29 percent) of women who cohabited before marriage never attended religious services, this was true of only 10 percent of women who married directly.

In a new analysis for this report, I found that the education gap in premarital cohabitation was even larger among women who attended religious services at least once a month than among women as a whole (see Figure 12.2). Among women who had a college degree and regularly attended religious services, only 35 percent cohabited before marriage. By contrast, among women who did not attend college but attended religious services regularly, a full 86 percent cohabited before marriage. The difference is even greater when we look only at equally religiously observant women with no high school degree, 97 percent of whom cohabited before marriage!

These figures suggest that in today's social and economic environment, it has become harder to act on one's personal values in the absence of the good economic prospects conferred by a college education. The majority of young adults today believe that living together before marriage is okay, and research from the early 2000s found that these rates do not differ by education. But among those who do *not* share this acceptance of cohabitation yet lack the high levels of education associated with stronger labor markets and greater financial stability, contemporary economic circumstances make it harder to live up to their values. The highly religious may sometimes marry even without that financial stability due to the strong social disapproval of their peers and a belief that "God will provide." But others facing financial insecurity resulting from their low levels of education are more reluctant to make that leap, even when they would *prefer* to marry directly.

Even More Evidence That Resources Influence Romantic Decisions

Recent research finds that, in addition to being more likely to cohabit before marriage, working-class couples move in together *earlier* in their relationships than college-educated couples, often because of financial difficulties or housing needs. Among college-educated couples, financial difficulties seldom play a part in the decision to cohabit. Increasingly, then, the ability of couples to make decisions about cohabitation and marriage based on their values seems to depend on their financial circumstances. And this can have consequences for relationship stability. As I show in Figure 12.3, premarital cohabitation no longer predicts divorce, but moving in together rapidly does increase the possibility that a relationship will dissolve without moving on to marriage.

The Relationship of Cohabitation and Divorce Reversed over Time

In a new analysis prepared for this report and shown in Figure 12.3, I find that the relationship between premarital cohabitation and divorce has also changed over

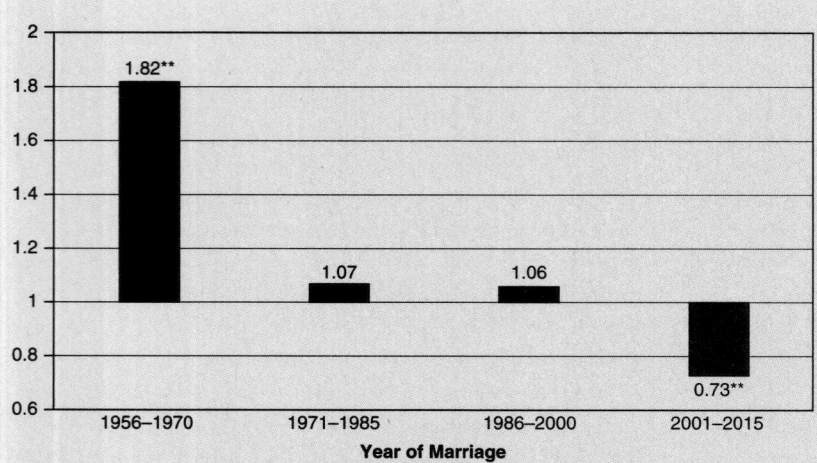

Figure 12.3 | Odds Ratios for Relationship between Premarital Cohabitation and Divorce in First Marriage

Note: *Numbers calculated from the 1988 National Survey of Families and Households (1956-1985, N=3,594) and National Survey of Family Growth (1986-2015, N = 9,420) using Cox regressions and based on women <36 at first marriage. Controls for age at co-residence, age at co-residence squared, raised not religious, religious attendance, race, education at marriage, mother's education, prior cohabitations, lived with both biological parents at age 14, birth prior to co-residence, began co-residence while pregnant. **p < 0.01.*

time. Not surprisingly, those who were willing to transgress strong social norms to cohabit from the 1950s to 1970 were also more likely to transgress similar social norms about divorce. Indeed, in that earlier period, people who lived together before marriage were 82 percent more likely to divorce than people who moved in together only after marriage. But as cohabitation became more widespread, its association with divorce faded. In fact, since 2000 premarital cohabitation has actually been associated with a *lower* rate of divorce, once factors such as religiosity, education, and age at co-residence are accounted for.

But the likelihood of divorce, other research shows, also varies by education level and economic stability. Regardless of whether people live together before marriage or not, college-educated couples have far lower rates of divorce than couples with a high school diploma or less. On average, women with a high school diploma or less have a 60 percent chance of a marriage ending in divorce within twenty years. The chance that a woman with a college degree will divorce within the same time period is nearly three times lower—about 22 percent. ▬

13

When LGBTQ People Become Parents

Abbie E. Goldberg

ecoming a parent is a life-changing transition. It is often a time of great excitement, marking the welcome beginning of a very different stage of one's life journey. It is also characterized by disequilibrium, adjustment, and renegotiation of one's identity, roles, and relationships. Many studies have examined the transition to parenthood, but these tend to focus on heterosexual parents of genetically related children.[1] This chapter describes LGBTQ people and their experience of transitioning to parenthood, a topic that is far less researched. This chapter acquaints you with the available research, and it centers on data— quantitative and qualitative—from my LGBTQ Family Building Project. In this study, over the course of a decade, I surveyed 543 LGBTQ parents who took diverse routes to parenthood.[2]

Regardless of gender, sexual orientation, and parenthood route (for example, heteronormative sex, donor insemination, or adoption), all parents must incorporate "parent" into their repertoire of roles and identities, which creates shifts in other identities and roles, such as partner, daughter, and employee. All parents must also navigate the demands of child care, and the increased workload that accompanies parenthood—work that is likely to be greater under certain circumstances, including twins, adopting siblings, or a medically challenged child. This extra work typically means a (re)negotiation of the division of unpaid and paid labor with one's partner(s) and may prompt consideration of whether and how to engage outside help, such as paid child care, a decision that is especially salient for single parents.

Managing a changed relationship with partner(s), job/career roles and responsibilities, and a new role as parent is inevitably made more complex against the backdrop of personal, family, friend, community, religious, societal, and cultural expectations. To breastfeed/chestfeed or not, and for how long? To use day care or not, and when? To take the maximum amount of parental leave allotted, or not? If fortunate to be able to make these decisions, LGBTQ folks may struggle with what is the "right" thing to do for themselves and their families without being unduly influenced by the expectations and judgment of those around them. This can be a challenge for all parents, but especially LGBTQ parents, who navigate parenthood against a predominantly heterosexual backdrop of parenting arrangements and decisions.

A number of other significant changes may also occur during the transition to parenthood. These include adjusting to less sleep, managing feelings of loneliness, balancing increased financial obligations, and dealing with feelings of not quite measuring up in multiple domains, including parenting, relationships, and work. Some new parents also feel overwhelmed or not in control, which may be especially intense among certain groups, such as single parents and parents experiencing significant financial pressures.

MENTAL HEALTH AND RELATIONSHIP QUALITY

Given all these changes, it should come as no huge surprise that most new parents experience changes to their mental health across the transition to parenthood, including increases in symptoms of anxiety, such as fearfulness and restlessness, and increases in symptoms of depression, such as sleep or appetite disturbances, lack of motivation, and feelings of helplessness. These changes are more pronounced for parents who lack sufficient emotional support, such as people to talk to, and practical support, including help with child care from one's partner. They are also more pronounced for parents who are experiencing conflict, strain, or violence in their intimate partner relationships.[3] New parents who perceive their children as especially challenging also tend to experience worse mental health.[4] Financial stress, unemployment, and a history of mental health difficulties are also associated with greater mental health struggles across the transition to parenthood.[5]

Likewise, many new parents report declines in intimate relationship quality, including less satisfaction with the relationship and increased conflict. Lower income, financial worries, unplanned pregnancy, dissatisfaction with the division of labor, and poor communication and conflict management skills are often associated with poorer relationship quality.[6]

The limited research that has explored the transition to parenthood for people in same-gender relationships has found that, like people in different-gender relationships, they experience declines in their mental health and relationship quality across the transition.[7] Some predictors of LGBQ people's mental health and relationship quality are similar to predictors for heterosexual people. Higher levels of support from one's family, friends, and workplace have been linked to better mental health among LGBQ women during the transition to parenthood.[8] Healthier and more adaptive coping skills are also associated with better relationship quality among LGBQ people across the transition.[9] Better mental health and greater preparation for parenthood have also been linked to relationship quality among LGBQ people during the transition to parenthood.[10]

But the process of becoming a parent and navigating the transition to parenthood is indeed different for LGBTQ folks. It can be complicated by societal obstacles to parenthood (for example, prejudice encountered in the family-building process), nuances of their particular family-building route (adoption, foster care, donor insemination, surrogacy), lack of LGBTQ parent role models and support, lack of support from friends and family, and stigma within one's neighborhood, community, workplace, or place of religious worship. For many LGBTQ parents, becoming a parent is a lengthy and highly intentional process that may involve months and years of work and waiting. In turn, when the highly anticipated goal of parenthood is reached, the reality may be more challenging than expected, which may lead to sadness, guilt, or ambivalence.

In some cases, too, parents differ in their genetic relationship to the child and, in turn, in their social recognition as a parent; genetic/gestational parenthood is generally given more weight, or seen as more "real," than social parenthood.[11] Historically, many LGBTQ parents have faced barriers in terms of their legal relationship to their child, such that in many families only one parent was legally recognized as the child's parent—the genetic parent, in families formed with the use of reproductive technologies, or, in families built through adoption, the parent who legally adopted. Differences in genetic, legal, and social recognition within couples can create friction, especially if the nongenetic/non-gestational or nonlegal parent feels less recognized as a parent, or the genetic/gestational or legal parent feels entitled to more recognition or rights as a parent. For LGBTQ parents in more complex arrangements, such as those in consensually non-monogamous relationships, lack of recognition for one or more partners may be especially significant.

Notably, laws and policies surrounding coparent or joint adoption by same-gender couples have changed drastically in many states over the past decade. Prior to 2017, states varied widely in their adoption laws, with some granting full adoption rights to same-gender couples, allowing couples to jointly adopt their children. Others allowed only second-parent adoptions, meaning a non-gestational mother could adopt the child her partner birthed. Still others banned adoption by LGBTQ folks entirely. Same-gender couples who adopted from abroad almost uniformly had one parent adopt as a single parent, since co-parent adoptions by same-gender couples were generally not permitted. In 2016, a Federal District Court struck down the last of the gay adoption bans—one that was in Mississippi. In 2017, the Supreme Court ruled that all states must treat same-gender couples equally to heterosexual couples in the issuing of birth certificates. These court rulings, taken together, have made adoption by same-gender couples legal in all fifty states. We continue to watch as new policies emerge that influence the daily lives of new LGBTQ parents and their children.

Couples who adopt have also been found to experience declines in mental health (due to unique stressors) and relationship quality.[12] Parents who become foster parents with the intention to adopt may face a lengthy period during which they are not yet legal parents—and may never be, depending on the outcome of the placement, for example, if the children return to their birth parents. Parenting in legal limbo can be uniquely stressful, as parents anxiously await confirmation that they can fully embrace the identity and title of "parent."[13] Parents who adopt via domestic private adoption may be navigating early relationships with their children's birth parents and anticipating what these relationships might look like in the future. Adoptive parents, including LGBTQ parents, may also be dealing with lingering feelings of loss, disappointment, and anger regarding their inability to conceive or have a biological child.[14] The transition to adoptive parenthood is also unique in that the timing of it is often uncertain; there is no predictable timetable (for example, nine months) during which to prepare for impending parenthood.[15] In turn, it is possible to become parents "overnight" with little warning; for example, a birth parent might deliver a child in the hospital and make an adoption plan.[16] Finally, LGBTQ folks who adopt—who are often more open to adopting children with special needs, older children, and siblings than cisgender heterosexual folks—may face a variety of both expected and unexpected stressors during the early months of parenthood related to their children's abuse, neglect, or trauma history, attachment or behavioral challenges, or health care needs. All these issues—legal uncertainty, new relationships with birth family, loss surrounding infertility, unexpected timing of parenthood, and child-specific challenges—may affect new adoptive parents' mental health, amplifying stress, uncertainty, and feelings of parenting incompetence. If not offset by access to support and services, these issues could contribute to depression and anxiety.

Couples who adopt may experience unique stressors to their intimate relationships as well. One study of eighty-four individuals in same- and different-gender relationships who were placed with a child via foster care three months earlier found that, just like heterosexual biological parents, some participants described the loss of their partner's undivided attention as stressful to the relationship.[17] Adoption-specific stressors were also identified, including the need to find state-approved child care to facilitate "couple time" and the legal insecurity of foster-to-adopt placements. And some members of same-gender couples cited experiences with stigma, including homophobic birth parents or social workers, as a stressor affecting their relationships.

Other research suggests that a history of infertility may have lingering effects on adoptive couples' relationships.[18] Couples who adopt older children, or siblings in particular, describe additional strains to their intimate partner relationships, often related to differing approaches to children's adjustment or behavioral issues.[19] Significantly, couples who make it through the challenging and complex process of adoption (and sometimes infertility) often show significant relationship strengths and resilience and may even experience increased closeness across the transition to parenthood.[20]

NOT ALL PARENTS . . .

Not all parents experience mental health and relationship declines—and there are things that individuals and couples can do to mitigate these declines. Early researchers of the transition to parenthood pointed out, quite rightly, that we generally tend to focus on averages: on average, parents' mental health declines.[21] But in fact, there are subgroups of parents whose mental health declines and then improves, or whose mental health improves overall, or who show no change at all. For example, in the LGBTQ Family Building Project, just 37 percent of parents said that their mental health declined across the first year of parenthood, with another 12 percent reporting decline followed by improvement. Another 24 percent reported no change, 26 percent reported improvement, and just 1 percent reported improvement followed by decline.

Similarly, just over half—52 percent—of parents said that their intimate relationship quality declined during the first year of parenthood, with another 7 percent saying it declined and then improved. Sexual intimacy, however, declined for almost three quarters (71 percent) of parents.

New parenthood can be a challenge in many ways. But communication can go a long way in enabling LGBTQ folks to remain committed to each other amid the stresses of parenthood. As one participant in the LGBTQ Family Building Project said,

Like every couple who becomes a parent, there are learning curves. With each stage our child passes through, we have new things to learn. As a couple, we have had times where intimacy and time as a couple is hard because jobs and child raising take front and center. But we are always big on checking in. Expressing feelings. And listening. So we always seem to work through and find the balance. When it comes to child care, we are very much in it together. . . . It's more the other household stuff. Sometimes the day-to-day chores become one-sided. But again, we talk it out. . . . We have always had good mechanisms for discussing it, communicating, and rebalancing.

SEEKING HELP, GETTING SUPPORT

There are numerous obstacles to LGBTQ parents receiving mental health and relationship support during the transition to parenthood and beyond. LGBTQ parents may be fearful of disclosing mental health symptoms to health care providers out of fear of being judged—for example, confirming stereotypes that queer people are mentally unfit to raise children, and even having their children removed from their homes.[22] These fears are rooted in historical data: Lesbian mothers in the 1970s and 1980s were known to lose custody of their children in the context of ending heterosexual marriages, wherein their ex-husbands would argue that women's sexual orientation (often a reason for the marriage ending) rendered them unfit to parent.[23] LGBTQ parents may also lack access to LGBTQ-competent providers, particularly if they are living in politically conservative regions or have limited financial resources.

LGBTQ parents may find support from friends as well as online.[24] They may search out other LGBTQ parents, especially those with similar parenting philosophies and those who share certain key characteristics, including family-building route and child age, via online support forums.[25] Such online resources can be helpful in providing support and validation. But like all new parents, they may need—and certainly deserve—affirming, knowledgeable providers who are aware of the societal pressures that impinge on LGBTQ parents as well as the varied and often complex paths that they take to parenthood, which shape the challenges they may face during their parenthood journeys. Finding an LGBTQ-friendly and affirming therapist is made easier by online sources, such as *Psychology Today*, which offer searchable directories of therapists by location, insurance, and key areas of expertise such as sexual orientation, gender identity, and the like. Teletherapy—therapy via videoconferencing or phone—is often available and may be more accessible, and more affordable, for some LGBTQ folks, such as those with disabilities or in rural areas.

Couples Therapy Can Help Too ...

Couples therapy, or relationship-focused counseling, may also help during the transition to parenthood. Such counseling can aid new parents in anticipating and coping with various challenges, including unexpected disagreements and communication difficulties; grief and loss issues, including those related to infertility; and problem-solving around the division of parenting responsibilities. Even couples who feel that their relationships are relatively strong may benefit from relationship counseling during the transition to parenthood and beyond, as parenthood can amplify issues that were previously manageable but now take on new meaning or urgency, including different ways of spending money and challenging relationships with in-laws.

Regardless of whether couples seek out relationship-focused counseling, research suggests a couple of key practices that can support couples' relationships during the transition to parenthood:[26]

- Check in regularly. New parents can check in with their partner(s) about how they are, including how they feel about parenthood and their relationship.

- One thing at a time. New parenthood involves new issues and challenges, including negotiating "who does what," financial obligations, and so on, often on little sleep and with little alone time. It helps to address one issue at a time, focusing on solutions and remaining flexible.

- Make time. New parents often don't have time to get away for long periods of alone time together. Making time for each other daily or weekly can help partners to maintain connection—even if it's just snuggling on the couch or drinking tea on the porch for fifteen to thirty minutes.

- Get support. New parents should develop a roster of individuals they can count on for regular and occasional child care. If family/friend support is not available, try asking for child care referrals from friends or enlist a babysitting or child care service.

- Be flexible. It may be necessary to try out new ways of handling conflict, finding time together, getting time alone, and connecting. Partners should remain open to the possibility of shifting their outlook or approach.

- Prioritize intimacy. It is easy to become overwhelmed with fatigue and stress and ignore intimacy and sex. Physical changes, including those associated with pregnancy, may be a barrier. New parents should seek opportunities to touch, cuddle, and communicate, keeping in mind that one's sexual life may change but should not be put on the back burner indefinitely.

- Value each other. Partners need to acknowledge each other's contributions and express appreciation, reminding themselves that they chose to be on this journey together and have each other for support.

Worth noting here is that in the LGBTQ Family Building Project, partnered participants who had children of varying ages were asked about sources of tension in their relationship with their partner. The top five issues identified were sexual intimacy issues (45 percent), parenting disagreements (36 percent), communication issues (34 percent), division of labor (32 percent), and financial issues (25 percent). This gives a sense of the kind of issues that are likely to be salient not just during the transition to parenthood but possibly beyond.

THE DIVISION OF LABOR: DISHES, DUSTING, AND DIAPERS

One area that emerges as salient for many same-gender couples during the transition to parenthood is the division of labor. Overall, same-gender couples tend to share paid and unpaid labor (child care, housework) more equally than heterosexual couples, both in general and when they become parents specifically.[27] But when differences in contributions to paid and unpaid labor do occur, they can cause tension, in part because same-gender couples may have higher expectations for equality—or at least equity—in the division of labor. Women and trans folks in particular seem sensitive to inequities in the division of labor, even when it favors them, perhaps in part reflecting their socialization as individuals on the lower rungs of gender and power hierarchies.[28] In fact, large discrepancies between the actual division of labor and ideal or preferred division of labor are related to poorer mental health and relationship quality among parents.[29]

Discrepancies in the division of labor may occur along the lines of biology: Among female couples who became parents via donor insemination, gestational mothers tend to perform more unpaid work and non-gestational mothers tend to perform more paid work, in part due to the early demands of breastfeeding and greater access to parental leave for the gestational mother.[30] Likewise, research on lesbian stepparent families has found that biological mothers perform more housework than stepmothers, which was associated with greater power over other aspects of the household, such as household decision making.[31] Beyond biological and genetic factors, relative work hours and financial contributions also affect the division of labor, such that with same-gender couples who are parents, the partners who work fewer hours or earn less of the household income tend to do more housework and child care.[32] Having more income often enables couples to divide chores more equally—and may minimize conflict related to the division of labor. When couples can "buy out" of certain tasks through the use of house-cleaners, nannies, laundry services, car washes, and restaurant takeout, it reduces their overall workload and makes it easier to share.[33]

Differences in contributions to unpaid and paid labor do not *necessarily* lead to tension or conflict. Although the dominant mantras are that (a) same-gender couples divide labor more equally than heterosexual couples and (b) equality (or equity) is desired by and ideal for all,[34] some people in queer relationships have work-family arrangements that do not conform to a perfect fifty-fifty split but are still working well for them. If one partner loves their career, and one partner wants to stay home, then this is probably a better arrangement than having both partners work outside the home and contribute equally to child care. As one participant in the LGBTQ Family Building Project said,

> I am happy with the way we arranged our division of labor. I chose to work half time because I wanted to spend more time with the boys and be very involved with their schools and activities. . . . I appreciate her sacrifices in commuting and working full time. She appreciates my contributions.

Beyond personal preferences, work- and income-related constraints may affect how unpaid labor is divided. One partner may have a more flexible work schedule or lower pay than the other, which exerts pressure on the couple to divide up labor unevenly.[35] Lengthy commutes and working nontraditional hours may also affect the division of unpaid labor.

Regardless of exactly how unpaid and paid labor is divided, it is important to consider the following:

- Child care isn't housework. Housework isn't child care. One partner may prefer to do more of the child care, which involves humans and relationships, but not housework, which is often repetitive, dull, and unappreciated.

- Certain household tasks—often those that are the most time consuming and least valued, such as doing dishes—have been "feminized" through their historical association with women. Likewise, certain tasks have historically been associated with and thus relegated to men, such as home repairs. Couple discussions focused on finding long-term strategies that work for both partners can help disentangle chores from their gendered associations.

- The division of housework and child care may need to be renegotiated. The birth or adoption of additional children, employment changes, and other life changes may prompt a renegotiation of tasks. Alternatively, it may be important to revisit the division of tasks if one or both partners would like a break from chores that they are taking primary responsibility for.
- Showing one's partner(s) grace, compassion, and appreciation goes a long way. Each partner's load may wax and wane a bit depending on a variety of factors, including work stress, mental health, and physical health. Picking up each other's slack is a way to show care to each other and can become a mutual dynamic if regularly enacted by both parties over time.

All in all, it is important to communicate about household and child care chores. Couples can even use a chore chart that includes a comprehensive list of chores that need to be done on a daily, weekly, monthly, and less frequent basis to anchor conversation. Constructing a chore chart can be helpful in developing a shared sense of "who does what." Evaluating who does the most frequently performed chores, for example, may reveal inequities that might go unnoticed if everyone continued on autopilot. It might prompt important and useful discussions about the most disliked tasks in the house and whether it is possible to make a more appealing—or less unappealing—plan for who gets what tasks done.

It is also generally a good idea to talk about "standards." How often should certain chores such as laundry, dishes, and deep cleaning be done? What does a "clean bathroom" look like to each partner? It can be useful to openly acknowledge the existence of different standards for housework, cleanliness, and order, thus enabling partners to adjust expectations and behaviors in order to reach some common ground.

ATTACHMENT AND BONDING

Another significant area related to the transition to parenthood is one's relationship to one's child. Despite the pressures to immediately bond with one's child, the reality is that not all new parents experience an immediate attachment. Non-gestational LGBQ mothers in particular have described challenges associated with forming an attachment to the child that their partner is carrying or has carried for nine months.[36] Some women, in turn, purposefully engage in activities that can help foster attachment even during the prenatal period, such as reading books about pregnancy, attending prenatal appointments, and calling their future child by a special name. Once the baby is born, non-gestational mothers describe engaging in a variety of activities and strategies to both promote bonding and counterbalance the "leg up" that their partner has via genetic connection, pregnancy, birth, or nursing.[37] These behavioral strategies, ranging from being primary caregiver, to bottle feeding, to taking parental leave at a different time than one's partner, may help enhance parental confidence and competence, and support closeness to the child. (They may also be valuable strategies for adoptive parents.)

Gestational parents who wish to facilitate their partner's equivalent role can actively support them as they seek to engage with the child, possibly "backing off" or doing other household chores during times of one-to-one contact. They can also consider alternating breastfeeding or chestfeeding with bottle feeding as a way of enabling their partner's participation in the intimate experience of feeding.

A variety of symbolic, linguistic, legal, and reproductive strategies may also help promote the non-gestational parent's role:

- Giving the child the non-gestational parent's last name or using a family hyphenated name

- Having the non-gestational parent choose what they wish to be called (for example, Mama)

- Ensuring that the non-gestational parent completes a second-parent adoption[38]

- Using reciprocal in vitro fertilization (IVF): one partner carries the child using the other partner's egg

Sometimes parents want to know: What types of relationships do children have with their genetic/gestational and nongenetic/non-gestational parents? How equivalent or different are these relationships? In a longitudinal study of lesbian-parent families formed via donor insemination, researchers found that when children were three and a half to four years old, women described a range of patterns of parental preferences on the part of their children.[39] Many described an initial preference for the genetic/gestational parent, which they often attributed to pregnancy, breastfeeding, or the "biological bond," followed by an "evening out" of such preferences, such that children preferred their moms equally, or for different things (for example, roughhousing/play or security/comfort), or their preferences changed day to day or week to week. More rarely, parents described a stable preference for the gestational mother. When parents had multiple children, these children were sometimes described as having different preferred parents. Other work suggests that non-gestational mothers may experience jealousy, at least early on, surrounding their partner's ability to be pregnant, give birth, and breastfeed, or their initially closer relationship with the child.[40] Such dynamics often dissipate over time but may become activated under certain circumstances, such as when a nongenetic/non-gestational parent's role or parental legitimacy is questioned or ignored.[41]

For new adoptive parents—and especially those who adopt older children who have experiences, memories, and attachments to prior caregivers—a delayed or gradual attachment may be especially common. In turn, it is useful for prospective adoptive parents to be aware of the diversity in initial attachment experiences. In a study of ninety LGBQ and heterosexual parents who were interviewed two years postadoption, more than half of parents described a strong and stable bond to their child beginning at the time of placement, which they attributed to a variety of factors, such as the child's young age at placement, as well as their own personality and strong desire to parent. Many parents, however, detailed a slow initial bond to their child, which they attributed to the shock of becoming parents overnight, not feeling entitled to parent, and legal insecurities. This initially tentative bond gradually strengthened over time.

In turn, it is important for parents, such as nongenetic/adoptive parents, to know that they may not immediately bond to their children. It may help to talk with a therapist prior to adopting about feelings of insecurity or a lack of a sense of entitlement to parent, as well as any legal concerns and how to address them.

Beyond the Immediate Family: Changes in Social Support Networks

So far, this chapter has predominantly addressed what happens within the immediate family in terms of mental health, relationship issues, the division of labor, and the parent-child relationship. Changes may also occur in new parents' relationships with people outside their immediate family during the transition to parenthood. Research suggests that overall, LGBTQ parents often perceive less support from members of their family of origin than do heterosexual parents. At the same time, they tend to *report* greater support from family members than LGBTQ nonparents.[42]

Family members may become more supportive once a child enters the picture:[43] One study of lesbian new moms found that women's perceptions of support from their own and their partners' families increased across the transition to parenthood.[44] Thus, some family members may push their feelings about non-heterosexuality and same-gender relationships aside and seek to repair problematic or damaged relationships in the interest of developing a relationship with a new grandchild, niece, or nephew.[45] In some cases, family ties may be strengthened by the arrival of a child, such that, for example, LGBTQ parents feel closer to their parents after becoming parents themselves.[46] Also, there is evidence that regardless of parenthood status, LGBTQ people may experience increasing support from their families over time, as families come to accept their identities and relationship.[47] As one parent in the LGBTQ Family Building Project said, "Initially my mother-in-law didn't support me being an equal parent. This is 100 percent resolved now."

Not all family members become more supportive and involved across the transition to parenthood. Some LGBTQ parents confront reduced support from their families upon announcing their intention to parent. For example, family members may express opposition to this decision to parent on moral or religious grounds, or because they believe that life as a member of an LGBTQ parent family will be too difficult—particularly for children. They may also oppose the LGBTQ person's route to parenthood (adoption in general or transracial adoption specifically) or feel less invested in children's lives if they are not genetically related to them.[48] In LGBTQ couples in which one partner gives birth, this decision may have implications for family of origin support, such that family members who lack a genetic relationship to the child may be less excited about the child's arrival and ultimately less involved in that child's life.[45]

Relationships with friends may also shift across the transition to parenthood. LGBTQ parents may find that they drift apart from nonparent LGBTQ friends, while becoming closer to cis heterosexual parents in their circle and community, based on the shared experience of raising children. For many, "parent" or "queer parent" becomes one of their most salient identities.[50] Gay and bisexual men in particular have reported a lack of support and even outright rejection from childless gay friends and the LGBTQ community at large, sometimes noting that they are cast as assimilating to heteronormative ideals—the "package deal" of marriage, parenthood, et cetera—and conformist values.[51] LGBTQ parents may also lose touch with their LGBTQ friends because children are not welcome in certain spaces or their friends do not want to spend time with children. Some LGBTQ parents do maintain friendships with nonparent LGBTQ friends but may also spend less time socializing together, or broaden their networks to include other parents.[52] Feelings of exclusion or nonsupport from the broader LGBTQ community may be more salient or significant for bisexual parents, parents of color, and working-class parents due to additional issues of biphobia, racism, and classism, respectively.[53] Trans people in particular may find that becoming a parent drives a wedge between themselves and nonparent trans people; and trans parents may feel excluded from queer communities of parents due to transphobia within the queer community.[54]

Support from family and friends is important for LGBTQ parents insomuch as it is linked to better well-being. For some LGBTQ parents, maintaining a relationship to the LGBTQ community at large may also be of great value; a sustained sense of connectedness and "sense of belonging" to the community may enhance their well-being.[55]

OTHER CONTEXTS: COMMUNITIES, NEIGHBORHOODS, DAY CARE, AND BEYOND

LGBTQ parents interface with a variety of important and interrelated contexts during the transition to parenthood and beyond. Where LGBTQ folks live has a significant impact on the ease or difficulty of navigating day-to-day interactions, as well as access to resources that reflect and meet their family's needs. LGBTQ parent families where one or both partners are men, trans, of color, or disabled will face extra scrutiny because of the ways in which these identities do not figure into dominant ideas about "ideal" parenthood.

Living in an LGBTQ-unfriendly area can have negative health consequences. Specifically, living in a state or community with anti-LGBTQ laws or policies has been linked to poorer mental health among LGBTQ parents.[56] LGBTQ parents who live in less gay-friendly areas, likewise, have been found to *perceive* more discrimination from their children's day cares and preschools than those in gay-friendly areas; perception of discrimination, in turn, creates stress.[57] Although moving might seem to be a reasonable solution, geographic mobility is not an option—or desirable—for many LGBTQ parents. Financial constraints, job commitments, family obligations, or a love of and connection to rural life or a particular region may keep LGBTQ parent families rooted in regions that are hostile to their sexual, gender, and family identities.[58] Thus, it is essential that families do what they can to protect their families, such as by obtaining wills, powers of attorney, legal adoptions, and other legal safeguards.[59]

OTHER IDENTITIES

There are a variety of other identities that can intersect with one's LGBTQ status to shape and add nuance to their experience of the transition to parenthood. Here, just a few are identified:

- **Male parents.** Gay, bisexual, and queer cis men may experience additional scrutiny of their parenting abilities since women are often assumed to possess superior and more "natural" abilities as parents, and GBQ men parenting with other men presumably "lack" some fundamental ingredient in the parenting equation. In fact, like most parents, GBQ men do not parent in a vacuum: their children have access to birth mothers, female teachers and doctors, aunts and grandmothers, family friends, babysitters, and a variety of other female caregivers and role models. The assumption that children "need" a caregiver of a particular gender is problematic, and research suggests that the quality of caregiving is far more important than the caregiver's assigned sex or gender. Nevertheless, all LGBTQ parents are vulnerable to scrutiny regarding their children's gender identity and gender expression and may therefore experience gender anxieties related to their children having "normative" gendered interests, behaviors, expression, and so on.[60]

- **Trans/gender-nonconforming parents.** Many LGBTQ people will experience pregnancy, birth, and new parenthood in ways that differ from the dominant cis/heteronormative model that is so often assumed by parenting resources such as books and blogs, therapists, and health care providers. Trans, nonbinary, and gender-nonconforming people may experience scrutiny of their parenting identities and behaviors because they challenge cis/heteronormative assumptions. They may carve out parental identities for themselves that differ from the gendered stereotypes of mother/father that are so frequently highlighted as the "only" way to be. In turn, they may meet resistance in trying to get outsiders to see, refer to, and accept them simply as a *parent*, for example, as opposed to a mother or father. Fortunately, an increasing number and range of parenting resources have emerged, especially online, that are explicitly encompassing of parents with a range of gender identities.

- **Consensually non-monogamous (CNM) parents.** Some LGBTQ parents are in CNM relationships or arrangements, which in many ways defy central assumptions around families and parenthood: namely, that people (and especially parents) don't have relationships with more than one person and that children have no more than two parents. LGBTQ parents in CNM relationships may have casual or more serious relationships with multiple individuals and may reside with more than one partner. Transitioning to parenthood often means a "pause" on one's engagement in consensual non-monogamy, related to a lack of time, new roles, and new responsibilities.[61] Closing relationships temporarily early on during the transition to parenthood is one strategy for maintaining one's sanity during a stressful time.[62] It may be helpful for parents to anticipate such changes and to discuss them with partners or develop a plan for whether, when, and how to see partners upon the transition to parenthood and beyond.

- **Bisexual parents.** Bisexual, pansexual, and queer parents may experience erasure during the transition to parenthood. As a coparent, their sexual identity is interpreted through their gender in relation to the gender of the other parent. Bisexual parents, at least women, may not feel welcomed or included in either dominant heteronormative parenting communities or LGBTQ communities, which can cause loneliness and strain.[63] It may be helpful to identify other bisexual or queer parents in online groups or forums to find connection and support, which may help reduce feelings of invisibility.

- **Stepparents.** This chapter focuses largely on LGBTQ folks who are intentionally becoming parents. Stepparents become (step)parents through partnering with someone who already has children. This transition is different from the transition to intended parenthood because of the lack of shared experience with one's partner, the often older age of the children involved, and, often, the existence of a nonresidential parent who has legal and emotional claim to the children. These differences lead to unique dynamics that intersect with one's LGBTQ status. LGBTQ stepparents may face particularly heightened levels of invisibility and stigma in society due to both their sexuality/gender identity and stepparent role, particularly when interfacing with schools and health care professionals. They may also face unique challenges in bonding with children and interacting with their partners' former partners.[64]

- **Parents of color.** LGBTQ parents of color inevitably face unique issues as a result of their own, and their children's, intersecting family and racial identities. LGBTQ parents of color and their children are more likely to be poor and to lack health insurance than white LGBTQ parents and their children. In turn, they may face greater challenges accessing high-quality family child support and services as well as LGBTQ-friendly providers, not to mention racially conscious providers. Furthermore, LGBTQ-affirming communities are not necessarily racially diverse; in turn, LGBTQ parents of color may face difficult decisions about where to live, balancing various competing considerations related to racial diversity and LGBTQ friendliness as well as cost of living, proximity to job and extended family, school quality, etc. Finally, LGBTQ parents of color may face stigma related to their race as well as their gender, sexual orientation, and family identities, such that their parenting is doubly scrutinized by outsiders, including health care providers and school officials. They may also encounter racial discrimination within the larger LGBTQ community.[65]

CONCLUSIONS

The transition to parenthood is a monumental life transition. LGBTQ parents face a variety of potentially unique stressors related to their family-building route, stigma in the outside world, and other intersecting identities—but they may also bring certain resources to parenthood, such as an orientation toward equity and a connection to the larger LGBTQ community, which can serve a source of strength and support. It is important for LGBTQ people who are transitioning to parenthood to seek support and advice—from the internet, family and friends, and possibly therapists and other support professionals.

NOTES

1. Kohn et al. (2012); McKenzie and Carter (2013); Mitnick et al. (2009).

2. In this study, just over two-thirds of participants were cisgender women, 17.5 percent were cisgender men, and 14.5 percent were trans or nonbinary. A total of 82 percent were white, and 18 percent were of color, including biracial and multiracial. Among the 88 percent of participants with partners, 72 percent of their partners were white and 28 percent were of color. A total of 42 percent of participants identified as lesbians, 20 percent as queer, 19 percent as gay, 14 percent as bisexual, 3 percent as pansexual, 1 percent as asexual, and the remainder as something else. More than three-quarters of participants worked full-time, and 90 percent had at least a college education. They lived in forty-four U.S. states, with a small number (<5 percent) living outside the United States. Participants had between one and six children, with most having one (47.5 percent) or two (40.5 percent). Regarding child age, 42.5 percent had at least one child age five and under, 35 percent had at least one child between six and ten years old, 35 percent had at least one child eleven to fifteen years old, 10.5 percent had at least one child sixteen to eighteen years old, and 9 percent had at least one child over age eighteen. Sixty percent of participants used donor insemination (DI) or surrogacy to become parents, 32 percent used adoption or foster care, 6 percent used cis/heteronormative sex, and 5 percent were stepparents.

3. Faisal-Cury, Tabb, and Matijasevich (2021); Logsdon and McBride (1994); Parfitt and Ayers (2014).

4. Goldberg and Smith (2008).

5. Katon, Russo, and Gavin (2014).

6. Adamson (2013); Doss et al. (2009); Lawrence et al. (2010).

7. Goldberg, Smith, and Kashy (2010); Goldberg and Smith (2011).

8. Goldberg and Smith (2008); Goldberg and Smith (2011).

9. Goldberg et al. (2010).

10. Goldberg et al. (2010).

11. Cao et al. (2016); Goldberg and Perry-Jenkins (2007).

12. Goldberg et al. (2010); Goldberg and Smith (2011); South, Jarnecke, and Foli (2019).

13. Goldberg, Kinkler, Richardson, and Downing (2011); Goldberg, Moyer, Kinkler, and Richardson (2012).

14. Goldberg, Downing, and Richardson (2009); Goldberg (2010b).

15. Goldberg (2010b).

16. Goldberg (2019).

17. Goldberg, Moyer, Kinkler, and Richardson (2012); Goldberg, Kinkler, Moyer, and Weber (2014).

18. Goldberg (2010b); Ward (1998).

19. Frost and Goldberg (2020); Ward (1998).

20. Timm, Mooradian, and Hock (2011).

21. Belsky (1990); Belsky and Rovine (1984).

22. Alang and Fomotar (2015).

23. Tasker and Lavender-Stott (2020).

24. Alang and Fomotar (2015).

25. Blackwell et al. (2016).

26. Belsky and Kelly (1995); Price Askeland, Bush, and Price (2016).

27. Chan, Brooks, Raboy, and Patterson (1998); Goldberg, Smith, and Perry-Jenkins (2012); Patterson, Sutfin, and Fulcher (2004); Prickett, Martin-Storey, and Crosnoe (2015).

28. Goldberg (2013).

29. Tornello, Sonnenberg, and Patterson (2015).

30. Goldberg and Perry-Jenkins (2007).

31. Moore (2008).

32. Goldberg, Smith, and Perry-Jenkins (2012).

33. Goldberg (2013); Goldberg, Smith, and Perry-Jenkins (2012).

34. Goldberg (2013).

35. Downing and Goldberg (2011); Goldberg (2012); Goldberg, Smith, and Perry-Jenkins (2012).

36. Wojnar and Katzenmeyer (2014).

37. Goldberg and Perry-Jenkins (2007); Wojnar and Katzenmeyer (2014).

38. Second-parent or "stepparent" adoptions are, in the legal sense, a means of "confirming" parental rights. Adoption is usually defined as creating a legal parental relationship where there was none before. In turn, these terms can feel inappropriate; as such, these adoptions can also be referred to as "confirmatory adoptions," which more adequately captures the process by which a nongenetic or non-gestational parent can confirm parental rights to their child. This will involve paperwork and typically a court hearing, and possibly a home study, depending on the state. Married same-gender couples can pursue these adoptions in every state, but not all do, in part because many assume that having both the gestational and non-gestational parent on a child's birth certificate establishes their parental rights. However, birth certificates are a form of record, not a determinant of legal parentage. Additionally, some parents believe (for example, based on where they live) that their parental rights will never be questioned. Finally, the time and cost of confirmatory adoptions may discourage some people from pursuing them. Yet, these adoptions are important because they protect parents' rights, specifically the nongenetic or non-gestational parents' rights, in the event of a custody dispute, or if their parental rights are challenged, and can help ensure that their children have access to important benefits and resources such as inheritance rights. Of note, too, is that in

some states a judgment of parentage is available to confirm parental rights by court order without the need for an adoption. This is a suitable alternative when it is available. See www.familyequality.org/resources/confirmatory-adoption/ for more.

39. Goldberg, Downing, and Sauck (2008).

40. Pelka (2009).

41. Goldberg, Downing, and Sauck (2008).

42. DeMino, Appleby, and Fisk (2007); Goldberg (2012).

43. Gartrell et al. (1999); Goldberg (2006).

44. Goldberg (2006).

45. Gartrell et al. (1999); Goldberg (2012).

46. Gartrell et al. (1999); Gartrell et al. (2006); Goldberg (2012); Titlestad and Robinson (2019).

47. Greif, Leitch, and Wooley (2019).

48. Gartrell et al. (1996); Goldberg (2012); Patterson, Hurt, and Mason (1998).

49. Nordqvist (2015); Patterson et al. (1998).

50. Forenza, Dashew, and Bergeson (2019).

51. Goldberg (2012); Lewin (2009).

52. Bergman et al. (2010); Goldberg (2012).

53. Goldberg (2012); Carroll (2018); Goldberg, Frost, Manley, and Black (2018).

54. Ellis, Wojnar, and Pettinato (2014); Ryan (2009).

55. Manley, Goldberg, and Ross (2018).

56. Goldberg, Smith, McCormick, and Overstreet (2019); Goldberg and Smith (2011).

57. Goldberg and Smith (2013).

58. Goldberg, Moyer, Weber, and Shapiro (2013); Goldberg, Weber, Moyer, and Shapiro (2014).

59. See Elizabeth Schwartz's (2016) book *Before I Do: A Legal Guide to Marriage, Gay or Otherwise*; see Movement Advancement Project (www.lgbtmap.org) and the American Civil Liberties Union (www.aclu.org) for more information about the necessity of and ways of obtaining legal safeguards.

60. Averett (2016); Goldberg (2009).

61. Manley, Legge, et al. (2018).

62. Manley, Legge, et al. (2018).

63. Manley, Goldberg, and Ross (2018); Ross, Dobinson, and Eady (2010).

64. Lynch (2004a, 2004b); Tasker and Lavender-Stott (2020).

65. Brainer, Moore, and Banerjee (2020).

14

Reflections on Race, Family, and Identity

Is There Anything New about Multiracialism Today?

Jenifer L. Bratter

Some years ago, I learned information that would cause me to question my understanding of how my background informed my identity. Since my mother's death, my aunt became the keeper of the family history and caretaker of my grandmother, who was then in her late nineties. While visiting, I found myself staring at the family photographs—this time with special curiosity.

I had never considered that there was another mixed-race person in the family besides myself.

After the release of 2020 U.S. census figures, a stunning trend captured headlines. The *Washington Post* ran a story titled "'We're Talking a Big, Powerful Phenomenon': Multiracial Americans Drive Change" (Foster-Frau, Melink, and Blanco 2021). Many articles like this one focused on the growth and substantial share of the population that identifies with multiple racial categories. According to the newly released data, one in ten American residents reported their race with multiple categories, a massive increase from 2010, where a little more than 2 percent, or one in fifty Americans, selected multiple racial boxes (see also U.S. Census Bureau 2021).

This demographic shift highlights changes in the meaning and significance attached to race and racial identity (Herman and Campbell 2012; McCarthy 2021) as well as the ways race operates within the American family (Alba 2020; Osuji 2019). The family is a space that houses the formation of interracial unions, the production of mixed-race offspring, and the socialization of identities. All of this sets the tone for whether race is experienced as a rigid or flexible social boundary and how distant minoritized groups are from the majority. Frequent intermarriage and mixed-race offspring that combine Whites and non-White groups theoretically indicates "closeness" and weaker boundaries between these groups (Alba 2020; Lee and Bean 2010). An expanding number of couples cross a race/ethnic line. Nearly 20 percent of newly married couples are interracial as of 2019, compared with only 3 percent in 1970 (Parker and Barroso 2021). Meanwhile, the percent of all families, marital or otherwise, with multiracial children also increased across this timeframe (Alba et al. 2018; Bratter et al. 2022). We seemed to be witnessing the product of both a rise in multiracial families and a social context where embracing one's racial mixture is normalized.

While these are certainly substantial changes, did they necessarily herald a new era as the *Post* article asserted? Were these changes reflecting a "big, powerful phenomenon"? Is this moment of expanding racial mixture—this intersection of race, ethnicity, and culture—new? And if so, what is actually new about it? Indeed, the growth in multiracial populations and interracial couples reflects a range of social transformations—a greater social openness to interracial relationships of many types, including friendships and romantic pairings (Kao, Joyner, and Balistreri 2019), as well as declining stigmas attached to interracial romance and marriage; fully 94 percent of adults express approval of marriages between Blacks and Whites (McCarthy 2021). All of this has happened within a context of a rapidly diversifying nation, fueled by increases in international migration as well as racial intermarriage and multiracial identification (Lee and Bean 2010). Taken together, such relationships facilitate and normalize greater exposure of various cultural groups to one another, with more and more people hailing from a range of backgrounds and interacting with groups that are not like their own.

The mainstreaming of multiculturalism is reflected in various realms, from the election of mixed-race political candidates such as former president Barack Obama and Vice President Kamala Harris (who is also in an interracial union), to Hollywood celebrities such as Zendaya, Dwayne "The Rock" Johnson, and Halle Berry. We even see racial mixture within British royalty with the marriage of Prince Harry to Meghan Markle as well as the presence of racially mixed characters and families in television commercials, stories, and films (Childs 2009) While the appearance of interracial families has drawn public attention, such as the controversy surrounding the use of an interracial family in the Cheerios commercial in 2013 (Elliot 2014), many instances occur without notice. All of this points to a social environment where crossing racial lines and embracing multiracial ancestries are increasingly understood as part of the social fabric.

MY STORY

Determining whether and how race and family have actually changed requires asking the question, what exactly has shifted? Examining expanding possibilities for racial mixture requires a reckoning with our past, which I began thinking about while exploring my own family history. I am a mixed-race person with an African American mother and a Jewish father who identifies as White. They met in New York City in 1969, married soon after, and had me. We were, by most accounts, a close family. Both my parents were embraced by their in-laws, and we visited them often. In the midst of this closeness, I understood that my dual racial heritage provided me with a unique experience, navigating and negotiating race in ways my relatives or parents did not.

Some years ago, I learned information that would cause me to question my understanding of how my background informed my identity. I learned something that made me think my experience in my family might not be unique. Since my mother's death, my aunt has become the keeper of the family history and caretaker of my grandmother, who was then in her late nineties. While visiting, I found myself staring at the family photographs—this time with special curiosity. I focused on the pictures of my grandmother's family taken during the early 1900s when she was a baby. She was seated in her mother's lap while her siblings sat and stood around her parents. The photograph was deeply sepia toned—everyone's skin was a reddish-brown color that typified the photographs of that era. Beside this photograph was another one. It was a black-and-white picture of my grandmother's father, William, taken years later. He sat in profile in a dark, seemingly black, suit that was in sharp contrast to his white hair and mustache, which almost matched his nearly white skin. I had seen both these photos for years and had never reconciled the differences in my great-grandfather's appearance—brown-skinned in one, nearly white in the other. Without asking, I had always assumed that both pictures were colored by time and older photographic technology that made some Black people appear brown-skinned in some pictures and White in others.

But on this day, I decided to ask my aunt, his granddaughter, why her grandfather looked so fair-skinned in the photo. She replied simply that this was the way he looked. After all, he was half-White himself.

I was stunned—*half-White*? My great-grandfather was mixed-race? I had never considered that there was another mixed-race person in the family besides myself. I learned that his father was a White man, a person of prestige in their local town in Arkansas, and his mother was a Black woman, likely enslaved. William had been raised with relatives; however, the nature of these ties was never clear. Despite not growing up with his parents, he was known in the local town of his origin as the son of a prominent person, perhaps carrying his father's last name. This afforded him some social advantages. However, William was also acutely aware of the anti-Blackness that surrounded him and his family. To evade the dangers of living in a southern town, the family moved to the urban Midwest to cities with neighborhoods and opportunities for Black families to grow and thrive.

My understanding of my mother's and grandmother's solidly African American identity had never wavered; they were "Black" people unquestionably, despite roots extending to a White person that could be identified on a branch of the family tree. Vague stories of non-Black roots, particularly Native American or European roots, were common, but these were ultimately swept into an understanding of singular Blackness. While there was likely racial mixture in our ancestry, there were never any ancestors whom we named or whose stories of living as a racially mixed person, whatever that meant, we pointed to.

As I wrestled with this information, I realized that I had always understood my own racial mixture as solely located in a single generation. While part of this reflected my own way of "constructing" my racial history, selectively setting aside the possibility of a racially complex heritage, I was also puzzling through a tie between my great-grandfather and myself.

Mixed Race a Century Ago and Today

In many ways, his life as a mixed-race person was lived in a world far away from mine. I, like many mixed-race people in the contemporary era, had spent a lifetime questioning how I might fit into racial categories (Khanna 2010; Rockquemore and Brunsma 2002) while surrounded by a tight-knit family that openly encouraged me to explore my racial identity. He, on the other hand, lived in an era where ties between parents and children, intimate partners, and extended family operated alongside mandates to maintain clear distinctions between racial groups as well as racial hierarchies. There are numerous examples of multiracial communities and families as well as mixed-race romantic pairings occurring pre– and post–Civil War across the Americas (Nash 1995; Hollinger 1998; Hodges 1999). However, policies, practices, and cultural norms of a racially segregated era mandated racially separate social spaces while disenfranchising communities of color and upholding privileges for Whites (Baradaran 2017; Feagin 2006; Oliver and Shapiro 2006). Such a system relied on sharply drawn racial distinctions that were supported by state laws banning interracial unions. The combined forces supporting segregation limited, if not outright removed, social or legal obligations of White family members to their mixed offspring (Curington et al. 2021; Pascoe

2010). Meanwhile, court decisions literally set racial definitions depending on the proportion of Black relatives to White "blood" kin (Gross 2003); such legal standards existed alongside negative framing of racial mixing as signaling degeneracy, rebellion, or treason to one's group (Romano 2003; Doering 2014) and notions that mixed people were doomed to lives as "marginal" or "tragic" people (Gardner and Hughey 2019; Stonequist 1935). These pessimistic images of racial mixture emerged in various forms during the pre–Civil War era (Gross 2003) and continued, in some ways becoming more prominent, following slavery's end (Pascoe 2010) and into the early to mid-twentieth century (Romano 2003). Black and White racially mixed people were ascribed (and largely embraced) the social category of Black following the policy of segregation dating back to the *Plessy v. Ferguson* ruling in 1896 that declared the constitutionality of "separate but equal" spaces. Meanwhile, the notion of a validated racially mixed family or mixed-race identity during this time was rare if not impossible. Therefore, while instances of racial mixture are deeply intertwined with the nation's history, so, too, is the goal of erasing it (Hollinger 1998; Nash 1995; Pascoe 2010).

MY GREAT-GRANDFATHER AND I NAVIGATING RACIAL CATEGORIES

My great-grandfather and I did have some experiences in common. His story offered some parallels to my own journey with navigating racial categories that did not exactly fit who I am. My aunt showed me my great-grandfather's census records for different years. In one year he was identified as "Black," and in another he had the designation of "Mulatto"—a term in common use a century ago for a Black/White mixed person but now considered offensive. These records were taken when interviewers, called census enumerators, would have perceived him differently at different times. While it's impossible to know the circumstances surrounding the shift in categories, the use of different designations for the same person resonates with dynamics of race today. The racial designation of multiracial people often provides windows into the multitude of ways that race can be appraised—either because racial identities can, and often do, change over time (Doyle and Kao 2007; Hitlin et al. 2006; Tabb 2016), or because available official categories often shift depending on the year the data are collected (Perez and Hirschman 2008), or because racial perceptions often depend on other factors beyond just skin color such as clothing or hairstyle (Good et al. 2010). All of this has bearing on how individuals are captured in official records. On a population scale, studies of linked census records reveal that millions of people changed their race responses between 2000 and 2010, often between selecting a single race in one year and then multiple categories in the next, or vice versa (Liebler et al. 2017).

When I learned about my great-grandfather William's mixed-race heritage after a lifetime of thinking I was the only one, I puzzled over what this era of multiracialism means for the ways family and race intersect. The distinction between my time of more openness and my great-grandfather's submerged experience tells us that race organized social life *and* the family. It did it then in one way and in another way today. In his time, ensuring clear racial boundaries, particularly around Whiteness, went hand-in-hand with limiting opportunities for people of color (Gullickson 2006; Saperstein and Gullickson 2013; Onwuachi-Willig 2013; Pascoe 2010). Keeping these distinctions in place, thus limiting the possibility of validating racial mixture, however, required employing rigid racial boundaries within the realm of families—influencing both the selection of spouses and partners; the ties between parents, children, and extended family members; and the identities those children carry. In the contemporary era, race continues to matter to social life, shaping interactions, identities, and access to opportunities, but the role of families in maintaining clear racial distinction is less strictly governed directly by policies and thus less institutionalized. By the 1950s and 1960s, there was a movement (slowly) away from racialized policies, an enactment of civil rights legislation, the conscious integration of social spaces, and the social and economic mobility of an African American middle class. In addition, policies that governed the race of one's spouse and the definition of race in terms of "blood" and specific ancestral ties were either removed or ceased to be enforced. Finally, international migration from Asia, Latin America, and Africa, which followed the removal of ethnic quotas and other institutionalized efforts to control the race/ethnic mix of immigrant streams (Lee and Bean 2010), provided massive opportunities for interracial interactions and fewer means to control them. Socially legitimized racial mixture undoubtedly became more frequent; this shift in social circumstances meant families had more ways to engage in racial mixing. However, in the absence of policies, norms that dictate idealized notions of a family as including members of one race or identities that emphasized one cultural background persisted. From my experience and my review of the research, racial mixture within these spaces still constitutes an exception, one that is welcome in some spaces but not in others. The very fact that these types of interactions and identities are incidences of "racial boundaries" being "traversed" or "crossed," tells us that race is still significant. Mixed race in this context highlights the relevance of race in ways that are sharp but increasingly subtle. I turn to how this unfolds in the contemporary era in the next section.

Does Multiracial Matter Today?

In an earlier era, ongoing racial mixture occurred but did very little to disrupt the ways racial boundaries operated. Today, however, there is a question: Do increases in racially mixed populations and interracial coupling translate into race becoming less consequential or less defining of one's identity or the selection of who one loves? Despite how alluring that question is, race continues to structure day-to-day lives, translating into broad and persisting disparities in access to quality neighborhoods (Krysan and Crowder 2017), wealth (Oliver and Shapiro 2019), and health (Williams et al. 2019), among other social outcomes. Calls for racial justice raise political controversy (Ray and Gibbons 2021) even as racial mixing continues to be part of the same social landscape. It turns out that the rise in recognizing racial mixture may remind us of how race is fluid. But a more pressing question it raises is, what do we learn about the ongoing persistence of race's relevance? I now turn to the site where the realities of racial interactions and their impact are clearest: the family.

Capturing Multiracial in a Time of Expanded Options

One of the clearest markers of difference between today and an earlier era is our enumeration of the multiracial population through the U.S. census by allowing people to select one or more racial categories. Even so, the number of self-identified multiracial people gives an incomplete picture of the full range of individuals whose family histories contain known interracial contact. According to the Pew Research Center, approximately 10 percent of adults can locate interracial contact beyond their grandparents' generation, while only 2.5 percent of adults have parents of different races (Morning and Saperstein 2018). Who *identifies* as multiracial is another matter. Only 1 percent of the adult population described their race with two or more races, and they come largely from those directly descended from interracial couples (Parker, Horowitz, Morin, and Lopez 2015). Exploring the connection between ancestry and identity in an era of DNA testing adds another layer of complication. The advent of 23andMe and the like has provided information that is interpreted as evidence of a person's "real" ancestral ties, with some interpreting the results as "hard evidence" of their racial past with implications for their present (Roth and Ivemark 2018; Roth 2018). Embracing this information corresponds with seeing race (Roth 2018). Such recognition, validated by "science," influences how many people view themselves as multiracial.

Let's take it to the next stage: We have new possibilities for identifying with racially complex parentage. But do such histories, if known, shape identities?

Do people come to speak up from a mixed-race identity and behave in ways that reflect a mixture? And what does that mean? Finally, is this mixture its own unique identity that is not simply additive? Does the claiming of multiple racial heritages correspond with experiences that produce a shared sense of people-hood? Do those claiming Asian and White see commonality with those of Black and Hispanic backgrounds, for example?

Multiracial advocates who argued fiercely for the addition of a multiracial race category in the census aimed to use these figures to identify what they hoped was an emerging multiracial community (Bernstein and Olsen 2009; Da Costa 2007 Jones 2011). As Da Costa (2020) writes, is multiracial a category or a community? Today's racial mixture is indeed far more self-conscious, with individuals embracing labels such as "multiracial" or "biracial" as well as organizations that support and focus on mixed-race people and their shared concerns (Da Costa 2010; Malaney and Danowski 2015). Some of this community-building occurs within single-race political movements, where mixed-race people are often members (Loblack 2020). For example, the Netflix series *Colin in Black and White*, based on Colin Kaepernick's life, examines the emergence of Kaepernick's stance against police brutality targeting Black people. He explores this, however, through the lens of his racially mixed biography. This very distinction illustrates this point: within the "new" era, multiracial identity matters in multiple ways and demonstrates the continued salience that race carries.

Race's Enduring Impact on Whom We Love and the Families We Make

While racial mixture is more visible than it was in an earlier era, race continues to operate as a social boundary. The social and cultural context, in some ways, seems eminently welcoming of such partnerships. As Curington et al. (2021) argue, attitudinal biases against interracial marriage are at all-time lows (McCarthy 2021), and ample opportunities exist for people of different races to meet and partner (Lee and Bean 2010). Despite all this opportunity, only 10 percent of currently married adults are married to people of different racial/ethnic backgrounds (Livingston and Brown 2017). How is it that adults match their spouses' race more so than any other characteristic—including ethnicity, religion, or education (Rosenfeld 2008; Schwartz 2013)? While people may claim "broad acceptance," their actions point in another direction. Support by Whites is largely voiced as endorsing the principle that such unions should be allowed, yet there is significantly less comfort in engaging in such relationships (Herman and Campbell 2012). For non-White groups, approval is generally higher, but this may depend on social context. Field et al. (2013) explore this possibility for students across colleges, finding that those at historically Black colleges and universities (HBCUs) express the lowest approval. They assert that this pattern "may represent a conscious effort to preserve African American history, culture, and relationships" (p. 771). Ultimately, the cultural atmosphere around racial mixture may be one where we celebrate it in public but have private reservations or even biases against the practice.

This understanding has clear effects on the lived experiences of intermarried couples. Interracial partnering continues to be more common among those who live together than it is among the married (Choi and Goldberg 2020; Fu 2008), suggesting some reluctance to enter marriages, or a lack of community support, when a couple is interracial. Some work on Black-White couples points to experiences of exclusion or isolation (Steinbugler 2012). The availability of "crossing the racial line" is also structured by race and gender. The majority of interracial coupling today involves White partnerships with Asians, Hispanics, and American Indians (Qian and Lichter 2007; Livingston and Brown 2017). Approximately 30 percent of newlywed Asian adults have White spouses, and the majority of those marriages involve Asian women married to White men. Gender also patterns Black-White relationships, as Black men are persistently more likely than Black women to have non-Black spouses (Livingston and Brown 2017). While we know that some of these patterns are linked to the opportunities that individuals have to meet each other, the evidence points strongly to racialized preferences driving these patterns (Curington et al. 2021; Lin and Lundquist 2013). Even on the open and boundless spaces of the internet, gendered and racial stereotypes that exoticize, fetishize, or demean groups affect whom one is inclined to or avoids dating (Curington et al. 2021). In our era of heightened mixing, dating and marriage patterns drawn on racialized beliefs serve to perpetuate social hierarchies that rank people higher or lower depending on their race.

Once couples form and have children, the status of being a racially mixed family can distinguish the availability of support and resources. While we know a good deal about married families, who are generally more resourced, understanding contemporary multiracial families requires a closer look beyond marriage. A substantial share of multiracial children live outside of marital circumstances. For example, Choi and Goldberg (2020) reveal that a substantial share of multiracial children experience multiple transitions from one family structural arrangement, such as living with a married parents, to another, such as a parent cohabiting with another partner. Bratter et al. (2022) estimate that close to 15 percent of all single-mother families include a multiracial child.

Crossing racial lines continues to shape families, including the connections with our extended kin. Grandparents and other extended relatives are often a source of support for families. Grandparents remain an important source for ethnic and racial socialization (Jackson et al. 2020). However, families may not always perceive extended relatives as supportive (Bratter and Whitehead 2018), raising some real questions about how crossing racial lines may correspond with less support.

How Does Race (Still) Shape the Lives of Multiracial People?

The impact of race on the lives of multiracial people is undeniable—but how it matters is complex. There is no one way that multiracial people slate themselves or navigate around racial designations. Rather, attachments to racial communities come in many forms: solidly embracing one identity, embracing multiple identities or a "mixed" identity, code switching depending on the context, and even letting go of race altogether (Khanna 2010; Mills 2021; Rockquemore and Brunsma 2002). For example, partially Black multiracial people are more likely to identify as Black and least likely to embrace their non-Black origins. Relative to other partially White multiracial children or adolescents, Black/White adolescents and adults are least likely to embrace a "White" identity and among the most likely to identify as biracial or solely as Black (Davenport 2016; Liebler 2016; and Roth 2005). This reflects the desire among Black/White multiracial adolescents and adults to fully engage their Black identities, deeming it the "best race" that describes then (Bratter and Gorman 2011) and engaging in strategies signaling Blackness (Khanna 2010). The priority of Black identity for multiracial people also mirrors the ways this group is racialized and thus exposed to anti-Black racism (see Long and Joseph-Salisbury 2019). Other partially White multiracial people have different experiences that are generally interpreted as being less dictated by a mandate to identify with communities of color. These groups are both more likely to be classified as White by their parents (Alba 2021) and more often embrace a "White" identity on their college applications compared with their partially Black peers (Davenport 2016). They are also more likely to indicate "White" as the race that "best describes them" as adults (Bratter and Gorman 2011). Additionally, many partially White multiracial people (who are not partially Black) occupy relatively higher-income neighborhoods, come from high-income families, and live in spaces that are dominated by other White families (Alba 2021; see also Campbell 2009). Again and again, the fact of difference depending on the kind of racial mixture a family has brings home the point: multiracial experiences demonstrate a persistence of racial boundaries, with some suggesting that the boundaries around Whiteness are changing (Alba 2021).

The family experience of multiracial people provides pertinent clues for understanding how racial complexity is experienced. We learn from multiracial people's experiences that identity is negotiated in relationships, with peers, partners, even parents and other family members, who may or may not validate a person's identity (Mills 2021). The appeal of a multiracial or blended identity for mixed-race people can vary but is structured by more than one's racial background; gender and religion are strongly tied to whether one sees a multiracial identity as available to them (Davenport 2016). A growing body of work explores multiracial people as parents and partners (Mills 2021; Song 2016; Buggs 2019; Bratter 2007), rather than solely as offspring of interracial couples. This work reveals that race remains consequential but requires new ways of thinking to understand it. For example, Buggs (2019) reveals a range of ways multiracial women think through racial distinctions between themselves and their partners (see also Song 2020). Some women describe racial differences between themselves and their partner in terms of skin color. Meanwhile others, particularly those who had lighter skin tones, understood relationships with men with similar skin tones as interracial due to their partners' "culture" being distinctive from theirs, most often for "White"-appearing multiracial women who dated White partners (Buggs 2019). These reveal how merely being "mixed" does not minimize the importance of racial differences for assessing partners but rather affords the possibility of seeing established forms of difference (for example, White vs. non-White) in new ways.

Additionally, as parents endeavor to pass along or transmit knowledge of their cultural background to their children, how does this happen when one parent is mixed race (Bratter 2007)? Song's 2016 analysis of multiracial parenting reveals, among other insights, that partially White mixed-race respondents worry about dilution of their cultural heritage when they are parenting alongside a White partner. This fear of losing the ability to transmit one's cultural heritage counters a narrative that the rise of multiracial populations is a sign that race is of diminishing personal consequence. Experts writing about rearing multiracial children emphasize the need to talk about the realities of a racialized world where they may be read or perceived in multiple ways, experience discrimination or privileges that their peers do not share, or confront exclusion from communities they endeavor to identify with (Chang 2015; Nayani et al. 2020; Rockquemore and Laszloffy 2005). This underscores the ways participating in one's identity does not happen naturally but rather requires "identity work," or adopting strategies that allow a person to present their authentic self (racial self or otherwise) to the world (Khanna 2010). Multiracial adults and their partners are called to engage in creative and varied strategies to help children learn how their unique race and ethnicity matter. This includes navigating a racialized world.

CONCLUSION

What is new about racial mixture in today's era? Comparing my great-grandfather's era with my own reveals a lot of change—and some significant continuity too. My great-grandfather, separated from me by a century, had a mixed background similar to mine. But, as the details of demographic and legal changes have indicated, he was in a world apart, with boundaries that do not exist today. Understanding how multiracial lives were lived then versus how they are lived now underscores the fact that race as a category keeps changing (see Williams et al., Chapter 5), and therefore the meaning of multiracial changes as well. So, though I have been a demographer for over twenty years, I find myself continually surprised. That fateful conversation with my aunt about those old photographs taught me some new demography. I have a reminder for you: the realities of family and race and how they intersect, are all around us, if we are ready to see them. While often believed to be stagnant, these realities are ever-changing. In order to build a future that truly embraces differences, we must first reckon with the aspects of our social context that defined "difference" in the first place and what conditions kept it (or keep it) in place. The realities of racial mixture within families is built on centuries of circumstances that ensured that race was defined in narrow ways. Keep observing how race and family operate in your own lives and question how it became that way and if it's truly working for all of us.

In Other Words

DATING PARTNERS DON'T ALWAYS PREFER "THEIR OWN KIND": SOME MULTIRACIAL DATERS GET BONUS POINTS IN THE DATING GAME

Celeste Curington, Ken-Hou Lin, and Jennifer Lundquist, July 1, 2015 / CCF

Despite growing approval of interracial dating, researchers have long documented the existence of a racial hierarchy within the dating world, with white women and men the most preferred partners, blacks the least preferred, and Asians and Hispanics in between. But where do the growing numbers of biracial and multiracial individuals fit into this hierarchy? Do they, too, get ranked by descending shades of lightness?

It's clear that individuals already have a lot of preferences when it comes to dating, excluding race. There are sites for BBW dating, BDSM dating, and even sites for people who wear a uniform. Aside from the color of someone's skin, people can choose their partners based on their hair color, height, and hobbies and that is shown by the vast amount of unique dating sites available.

Between 2000 and 2010, the number of individuals who identified themselves to census takers as being of two or more races increased by a third. These 9 million individuals still represent less than 3 percent of the population, but studies predict that by the year 2050, nearly one in five Americans may claim a multiracial background. How will this affect dating and marriage patterns in the United States?

We recently completed a study of how multiracial daters fare in a mainstream online dating website. Using data from 2003–2010 from one of the largest dating websites in the United States, we examined nearly 6.7 million initial messages sent between heterosexual women and men. Specifically, we looked into how often Asian-white, black-white, and Hispanic-white daters received a response to their messages compared to their monoracial counterparts.

The most surprising finding from our study is that some white-minority multiracial daters are, in fact, preferred over white daters. We call this the multiracial "dividend effect," something that has never before been reported in the existing literature on dating and mate preferences. This finding suggests that the treatment of multiracial people may in certain circumstances be more complex than is commonly recognized in research on racial hierarchies.

We found that three multiracial groups received a "dividend effect." Asian-white women were viewed more favorably than any other group of women by white and

Asian men, beating out women of the same race or ethnic group. Asian-white and Hispanic-white men were also afforded "dividend" status by Asian and Hispanic women, respectively. Asian and Hispanic women responded more frequently to the multiracial men than to either their co-ethnic men or to whites.

Although white women did not prefer Asian-white men to white men, they did respond to this group as frequently as to white men. This is in practice a multiracial dividend, because white women responded to monoracial Asian men as infrequently as they did to black men.

Much scholarly discussion of multiraciality in America has been dominated by the concept of the "one-drop rule" that was long enforced in the Jim Crow South, meaning that white-minority multiracial people are treated as minorities. But our study finds no support for this dynamic in the online dating world.

That is not to say that the color line has been erased. For example, white men and women are still less likely to respond to an individual who identifies as part black and part white than they are to a fellow white. But the color line has certainly been blurred, with white daters responding more favorably to such individuals than to black daters. And white women actually prefer black-white men to Asian and Hispanic men, a phenomenon that explicitly contradicts what the one-drop rule would predict.

When we look at the preferences of black daters, we find that both men and women are slightly more likely to respond to white daters than to same-race daters. They are also more likely to respond to black-white daters than black daters who contact them. In earlier research we found that while black women are reluctant to send messages to out-group daters, they are extremely willing to respond to messages from daters of other racial groups. Taken together with our current findings, this behavior is likely driven by an expectation of rejection by men of other racial backgrounds, not by an inherent preference for black men over other men.

There are several possible explanations for the multiraciality dividends we found, and they may represent different dynamics in each case. In some cases, they seem to be closely linked to a continuing partiality for lightness or whiteness. In the case of the preference that white and Asian men show for white-Asian women, we may be seeing the influence of long-standing cultural representations of multiracial women as unique and sexually exotic. Likewise, Asian and Hispanic women may have been influenced by the media's increasing portrayal of multiracial men as attractive, chic, and trendy.

Some research also suggests that Asian American women may perceive Asian men with a more recent immigration history to the United States as more patriarchal and gender conservative than white American men. Thus, Asian and Hispanic women may perceive multiraciality as a marker of Americanization or gender progressiveness. At the same time, multiracial co-ethnics may be more appealing than monoracial white men in the sense that they bring a shared cultural heritage and may be accorded greater acceptance by family members.

These findings provide us with potential insight into the social meaning of multiraciality in the United States in the post-Civil Rights era and how demographic changes in racial identification operate at the level of everyday interactions. The growing multiracial population in the United States is likely to change not just the overall racial landscape but the most intimate arenas of personal life. ▄▄

15

Queer Bat Signals

*Families of Origin and Choice under
Social Distancing and Lockdown*

Amy Brainer

Content warning: This article discusses joyous forms of connection as well as forms of disconnection, abuse, and death, including one instance of suicide. These things may be close to home and to your heart. Take care of yourself as you read and know that you are not alone.

Time stamp: September 2021

I am in a classroom—a feeling at once familiar and strange, eighteen months after our ejection from campus in March 2020. I ask the students how they are doing. It's not an easy question to answer. Some hold back; others exhale (but carefully, masked). Members of our LGBTQ+ studies class are Arab, Black, Indigenous, mixed, South Asian, and White; devoutly, nominally, and formerly religious, with significant numbers of us Muslim and Christian in our roots; diverse in our ages, genders, and the other constellations of identities we bring to the classroom.[1] This is a commuter campus, and most students work; a large number have caregiving responsibilities. The LGBTQ+ students are no exception.

Under social distancing and lockdown mandates, many risked their lives daily in service industry jobs, dealing with an increasingly hostile public; meanwhile, every "safe" or safer space available to them closed. A majority were not out at home. They took LGBTQ- studies classes online with their headphones on and mics and cameras off; they ended therapy or dialed in to therapy from parked cars; they picked up extra shifts; they lost their jobs; they homeschooled their children or younger siblings; they fell sick; they dropped their classes; they attended the funeral of an aunt, a cousin, a friend; there was no funeral and so they grieved alone; they met other queers online; they made sure their phones were always locked; they snuck out to meet their partners; they didn't see their partners at all. "They," of course, does not refer to all the students; the total number of students in each circumstance is unknown. But at least *some* students in my classes experienced each of these things, and a good number experienced more than one.

Time stamp: April 2020

Detroit, where I currently live, has one of the highest death rates in the United States. Within my local friend group, everyone has someone hospitalized; recoveries at this stage are rare. In the laundry room of my apartment building, I pass another tenant at a respectful distance; we ask after each other's families. "My nephew died," he says. One friend loses multiple members of her family in a span of six weeks. Gradually, evidence will emerge of the inequities that shaped these outcomes: collapsed health care systems in Black neighborhoods, lack of protection for frontline workers who are disproportionately women of color and also caregivers, a stratified safety net in which salaried professionals retreat to their homes while using underemployed people for their shopping and other public-facing needs.

Some students fall silent and stop turning in work; I worry about their health, their families, their spirits. Others stay active in online classes and on WhatsApp, where I parse together the conditions of their lives from blocks of text—a huge departure from tea in my office, Pride meetings, and conversations in class twice a week. Their sleep schedules morph, and some communicate with me mainly between the hours of 12:00 a.m. and 4:00 a.m.—in part for privacy and in part because they are anxious, depressed, restless, sad, bored.

Time stamp: April 2021

Four hundred thousand new cases per day in India and, of course, that is only what is reported. There are not enough beds, vaccines, oxygen. A photo shows a health care worker walking past funeral pyres. On each pyre, a whole life, around which other lives revolve. Another photo shows a health care worker collapsed, their body seemingly boneless, while a coworker tries to lift them up. I think of what I said to my sister, a COVID nurse in Arkansas, about the agonies heaped on her profession during a recent surge: "Where is the line—when you lie screaming in the middle of the floor? There has to be a line before that."

One of my closest friends, a member of my own "chosen family," tells me she is up all night navigating hospitalization and oxygen for people in India, where she is from and where her mother and family live. In the daytime she still tries to teach her classes and attend faculty meetings by Zoom. I text an Indian trans woman student: "How are your loved ones?" Three little dots rise and fall, a digital pulse.

"Honestly, terrible," she writes. "Everyone is terrible."

Time stamp: Today—that is, the day you find yourself reading this chapter, arriving at this page

Maybe some of this resonates with you. COVID did not strike all of us in the same ways. But it did touch each of our lives in one way or another. I think it is important for us to write and talk about these things, not to let them disappear They are part of us. This is true for everyone, regardless of their sexuality or gender, and I hope that every reader finds a point of connection to this chapter. The chapter also has a specific focus on LGBTQ+ people and families. More precisely, it tries to answer the question, how did LGBTQ+ people experience "family" under social distancing and lockdown?

This question matters to me professionally and personally. I have spent the last decade researching and writing about LGBTQ+ families; I am also a queer person in a family. From my research and research by my colleagues, I know that material conditions such as living arrangements, care responsibilities, and physical proximity to family members can significantly shape the family dynamics surrounding sexuality and gender. The pandemic touched all of these and more.

There is no single answer to the question I have posed, and the stories I share in this chapter will take many different shapes. Like the pandemic itself, these stories are global in scope. I draw from scholarly articles and media reports (in English, so that is a limitation), each speaking in a unique way to the question.[2] I can only dive into a small number of them here. I have tried to pick out important themes and cases that illustrate those themes. At the same time, I encourage you to dive deeper by exploring and building on the list of sources at the end of this chapter. New work is coming out all the time, and there is much to learn.

The rest of the chapter is organized into two parts. In the first part, I describe ways that people drew on queer histories and innovated in the present to nurture their communities and chosen families during the COVID-19 pandemic. In the second part, I highlight families of origin as sites of care, conflict, love, and violence. Under social distancing and lockdown, many people were forced into family living arrangements that they did not choose. I will propose some implications of this and places to go from here. I also invite you, the reader, to bring your expertise and experience to this chapter and to raise implications of your own. Learning how to care for one another through crisis is a collective process and one that is ongoing.

Part 1: Chosen Families and Community Care

In her book *Families We Choose: Lesbians, Gays, Kinship*, anthropologist Kath Weston defines *chosen family* not as derivative of biological and adoptive family, nor as "like" family,[3] but as a transformation of family life in which people began to name for themselves who their family members were. The timing of Weston's book is important. Published in 1991, with data collected in the 1980s, the book captured lesbian and gay ideas about family that were forming during the height of the AIDS crisis in the United States. During this period, many LGBTQ+ people fell sick and died without being cared for by their families of origin or by the government. Even health care workers were at times unwilling to touch or interact with LGBTQ+ patients. Chosen families stepped up to provide the care that others withheld. (For an intimate portrait of chosen family in this period, I recommend the episode "Among the Oak Trees" with Ruth Coker Burks on the podcast *This Is Love*.)

There are, of course, many examples of chosen family bonds that predate HIV/AIDS and exist independently of this crisis. But the HIV/AIDS pandemic brought chosen families to the foreground in new ways. It necessitated new forms of caregiving and made the role and urgency of chosen families more visible. You can probably see where I am going with this. The COVID-19 pandemic, similarly, did not create chosen families and community care out of thin air. People built on bonds and networks that already existed. This history is important. At the same time, COVID-19 necessitated new forms of connection as the world around us changed very quickly. This pandemic spotlighted, once again, the ways that LGBTQ+ people care for one another and where traditional care structures continue to fail.

Networks of Care / Care for Whom?

Most often, it was not people who were economically secure but those coping with the starkest poverty and loss that organized responses to the COVID-19 pandemic in LGBTQ+ communities. Transfeminine people led many of these efforts. In Lima, Peru, trans women pooled resources and cooked communal meals as a way to feed one another through pandemic-induced periods of unemployment (Garcia-Rabines and Bencich 2021). In Yogyakarta, Indonesia, *waria* (an Indonesian term that combines "man" and "woman" and described by some in the community as having the heart and soul of a woman within a male-assigned body)[4] set up community kitchens, distributed food, and sewed masks; they extended this care both to *waria* and to other residents suffering from a lack of income and support (Mallay et al. 2021). In Rio de Janeiro, Brazil, a collective of LGBTQIA+ people and sex workers took in unhoused people and animals and distributed hygiene kits and food to vulnerable residents, including food for animals who also suffered during the pandemic (Santos et al. 2021). (The longer acronym used by this group stands for lesbian, gay, bisexual, transgender, queer, intersex, asexual, and a plus sign recognizing other genders and sexualities that defy social norms.)

In each case described, preexisting networks of trans women, *waria*, LGBTQIA+ people, and sex workers made it possible to quickly organize at the community level. Many lived together in shared households and cared for one another as kin. They already recognized and looked after their unhoused, unemployed and underemployed, HIV-positive, and food-insecure members; in Brazil, care for animals was a core value predating the pandemic. The bonds they shared, built up through experiences of shared trauma, became important tools when social distancing, lockdowns, sickness, and death increased the human and nonhuman vulnerability around them.

Members of these groups are routinely met with hostility and violence from the general public. They nevertheless opened their hands and shared what they had, even when they had very little. This social and spiritual leadership is surely something to acknowledge and respect. It is also important not to make a person's value contingent on their willingness to sacrifice, as Adnan Hossain (2022) reminds us in an essay on the impact of COVID-19 on *hijras* in Bangladesh. (*Hijras* have a long history, predating the term *transgender women* with which they are at times associated, as well as their own kinship structures outside the heteronormative family;[5] in some places, including Bangladesh, *hijra* is an institutionalized third gender.) Hossain describes how *hijras* were extolled as heroes in the media when they put their lives on the line to provide emergency services, such as taking sick people to and from the hospital. At the same time, *hijras* continued to face severe discrimination and to be associated with impurity and social contagion (HIV/AIDS and now COVID-19) in ways that kept them on the margins of society. Gratitude for *hijras*' care work is warranted; protection and care for *hijras* who are not sacrificing themselves but merely living are also warranted.

Readers who have been treated as if they need to justify their own lives may understand this last point deeply. Readers for whom this is a new concept may be absorbing and digesting it. We can all, in light of this, consider the moral systems we have inherited, the scope of them and their limits. We can also consider the forms of care they produce—by families, by the government, by aid organizations—and for whom. That is, whose lives have we been taught to care about? Whose lives are treated as expendable?

Care Online

During surges of COVID-19 infection and hospitalization, gathering in person became extremely difficult, if not impossible. Community care in many cases moved online. This created new forms of togetherness as well as new vulnerabilities and inequalities for LGBTQ+ chosen families and communities.

As physical venues closed, people lost not only sources of connection and pleasure but also, in many cases, employment and income linked to those places. Drag communities were especially hard hit. Under these conditions of hardship and loss, drag artists and other community leaders continued to pool and share their labor. Adrian Shanker's (2022) edited volume *Crisis and Care: Queer Activist Responses to a Global Pandemic* documents this labor across the United States and transnationally. For instance, drawing from the diverse chapters in Shanker's volume, virtual drag shows invited viewers to decompress and also to process their stress and grief through pandemic-themed art. Queer youth centers set up gathering spaces on Discord. A roundtable led by chronically ill and disabled people educated the community on COVID-19 preparedness; this aired in March 2020 before any federal guidance on the matter. Community organizers and groups shared best practices for having sex and sustaining intimacy during the pandemic. Others launched online campaigns and legal battles against COVID-era inequalities. These are just a few of the many queer initiatives and activities that took place online.

Tunay Altay (2022) describes such online spaces as "digital publics" where both socializing and organizing work happen. Anchored in Turkey, Altay's work explores LGBTQ+ digital clubs, performances, storytelling, and other activities and events that served as lifelines for isolated queers as well as acts of resistance to political homophobia. In Nepal, the Queer Rights Collective (2022) checked in continuously with its members and hosted numerous online gatherings, prioritizing fostering personal connections and friendships that could sustain them through the pandemic. For some, online activities like these were easier and safer to access compared with events in person. As an activist in Lebanon shared, "COVID-19 means I can join Pride [online] and not get arrested" (Cheded and Skandalis 2021).

Of course, care online is not free from challenges. Nepalese activists experienced hacking of their online Pride event; this in turn inspired more community care and organizing around ways to protect themselves from ongoing hacking, trolling, and doxing (Queer Rights Collective 2022). Olakunle Ayokunmi Oginni and colleagues (2021), writing about queer experiences of COVID-19 in Nigeria, point out the limits of online connection due to both suboptimal internet and close quarters with unsupportive family. The authors identify data protection and data privacy as critical issues for LGBTQ+ Nigerians. Megan Paceley and colleagues (2021) echo this writing about queer youth in the United States. Some youth in their study had difficulty accessing support due to high degrees of parental surveillance and control. In some cases, parents checked even their texts, making queer-affirming connections, including phone and text-based therapies, out of the question.

Data security and privacy, infrastructure such as internet access, and degrees of state and family control over digital life have long been queer issues. The COVID-19 pandemic exposed and amplified these issues. The concerns raised by Oginni and colleagues, Paceley and colleagues, and other scholars are ones we must address if we are to build more equitable care structures going forward.

"Queer Bat Signals"

Along with housing, food, and other material needs, the need *to be with other queer people* emerged over and over again in the literature I reviewed. This came up perhaps more than any other theme. It came up for LGBTQ+ people of all ages, living under different political regimes, in small-town, rural, urban, and suburban areas. People quarantined with heterosexuals only (and this was a majority of the queers in quarantine or lockdown) expressed this need strongly. This lets us know that even as digital life flourishes for some, the physical presence of other queers remains essential to well-being for many LGBTQ+ people. As with care online, this became a dance between creativity and limits.

At the University of Michigan–Dearborn, some socially distanced classes resumed before other kinds of gatherings were permitted on campus. In the absence of places to gather, my students devised what they called "queer bat signals." Someone would share (via group chat) that they were in the library, or at alcove in a certain building, and people in the vicinity would find them there. For the duration of the year, Pride was officially virtual, but pop-up Pride gatherings were happening at random.

The bat signals metaphor is layered with meaning. We might think, for instance, of bats in the wild using echolocation to determine the shape and proximity of otherwise invisible objects—in this case, a queer community materializing in the mostly deserted landscape of the campus. In the Batman comic series, the bat signal projected over Gotham City is fundamentally a sign of hope. "That's the funny thing about the signal. People think it's an alarm, a warning that danger is coming, a call for help," says Commissioner Gordon in the short story "Always." He explains that, instead, "it's to let them know we'll make it to morning, even if we make our own damn light." This is why he leaves the signal on all night during especially chaotic times.[6] Continuing the metaphor, even if someone who sees the bat signal cannot gather in that place, on that day, the knowledge that queer people are still gathering somewhere becomes soul-sustaining in and of itself.

Actually, queer bat signals had been going on all along—though not yet named as such—in the larger radius of southeast Michigan, where most students lived. Early in the pandemic, before any of us were back on campus, two students shared a joyous photo of their unexpected meeting in Target; a third student bemoaned that they had just left that very store. Inexplicably, people seemed to be able to recognize specific Targets (for example, "the Dearborn Target" versus "the Westland Target") from photos alone—a skill that, along with queer bat signals, intensified during the pandemic. Watching this unfold, I was reminded of Mary Gray's (2009) fieldwork with queer youth in Kentucky, who performed drag in the aisles of Walmart in the absence of more fixed spaces to gather. Gray wrote this book eleven years before the COVID-19 pandemic, focusing on rural queer life. But her analysis of how queer young people claimed space within a space—a sort of roaming home base—feels relevant here. Displacement and isolation remain a part of many queer stories. Thus, LGBTQ+ young people have continued to cultivate homemaking abilities on the fly. Finding other queers is not a luxury; it's a life skill. Some of this is inherited, a part of the intergenerational transfer of queer survival strategies, as the rug of family and home can be pulled so quickly from under us. But it is also undeniably theirs, or *yours*, if you are a queer young person reading this book—a new generation of queer homemaking in the COVID-era landscape.

When we think of queer home and family in this way, examples begin to flicker into view all around us. *AfroQueer Podcast* throws a signal: *How are you doing?* And answers stream back, (echo)locating the community: A queer shelter, serving as home for its residents, is violently disbanded by Ugandan police under the guise of stopping the spread of infectious disease. Ugandan human rights lawyers and activists fight to release the now jailed residents, to protect their right to a home. A gay couple discusses married life under lockdown. A woman shares that she is "figuring out dating and love in the period of prolonged quarantine." From the traumas of police violence to the mundane, steady drip of isolation exhausting the spirit, the stories people tell are about queer homemaking; they are also a kind of homemaking in and of themselves, since the act of telling them connects queer people across the African continent and its diaspora. People fighting, figuring out love, making their own damn light.

PART 2: FAMILIES OF ORIGIN AS SITES OF CARE, CONFLICT, LOVE, AND VIOLENCE

On the same episode of *AfroQueer* just described, a West African activist voiced her concerns for the many queer people who were forced to return to their childhood homes to avoid starvation during the pandemic. Often this meant living with homophobic parents and navigating complex relationships with their families of origin. By families of origin, I mean the families that we were raised in; these may be our biological relations or not. They include what in North America at times are called "extended families"—aunts, uncles, cousins, grandparents, and others that for many cultures and people throughout the world are not so much "extended" as a part of the core family and everyday life.

Throughout the pandemic, LGBTQ+ people exchanged care, love, and support with their families of origin. Some were also abused and terrorized by their families during this period. Larger numbers of people than usual were "outed" (having their identities exposed without their consent) with at times deadly results. This happened as many people went back into their family homes after losing employment and housing in other places. Those who had always lived at home but left for some period of each day were suddenly home 24-7. A majority of elder care happens in homes, and as elders are more vulnerable to severe disease and death from COVID-19, families took on the responsibility of protecting them. Elders who do not have family care (and LGBTQ+ people are overrepresented in this group) were even more vulnerable, whether living alone or in long-term-care facilities (on LGBTQ– elders and COVID-19, a topic that is generating an important body of scholarship not covered by this chapter, see Banerjee and Rao 2021; Johnson 2022; and Perone et al. 2020).

Drawing on decades of family violence scholarship, Caroline Bettinger-Lopez and Alexandra Bro predicted in 2020 a "double pandemic" of domestic violence and COVID-19. This prediction tracked with the stories that began to emerge globally, including in LGBTQ+ populations. I will begin this part of the chapter with a discussion of family conflict and violence, before shifting focus to the love and care work that also happens within queer family of origin relationships

Conflict and Violence

"I used to spend as much time out of the house as I could. With the lockdown, everything has changed. . . . I'm not allowed to eat the food my mum and her partner buy. My mum's partner talks about me as if I can't hear him. He says I'm disgusting, and he hopes he doesn't catch what I have. . . . As bad as it is at home, I just can't afford to move out. I'm using the deposit I saved up just to get by. I need to wait for all of this virus stuff to be over before I start trying again."

—Nicky, UK, March 2020 (Hunte for *BBC News*)

"For years [Sasha] coped with the tension and rows by staying with friends or changing how they presented themselves around their parents. But since the start of a lockdown aimed at curbing the spread of the coronavirus in Moscow two months ago, they have been forced to stay at home 24/7, existing in a constant state of anxiety and helplessness. 'Every time I walk through the door to the apartment it brings back painful memories. . . . I have to suppress myself at home, change the way I walk, talk, my mannerisms.'"

—Sasha, Russia, June 2020 (Berkhead for the *Moscow Times*)

"Since being in quarantine, my dad has had very serious quarrels with me almost every day about my girlfriend or marriage." As a result of these arguments, Fang broke up with her girlfriend to search for a male partner. "If the pandemic had never happened and we hadn't broken up, we would be celebrating our three-year anniversary," Fang said at the end of our interview.

—Tianyu Fang, China, September 2020 (Iyengar and Yu for the *Diplomat*)

When these media interviews appeared in March, June, and September 2020, very little research had been published on queer experiences of the pandemic. Journalism offered a critical window into LGBTQ+ lives. We now have a growing body of peer-reviewed research on LGBTQ+ family relationships and family violence during the pandemic. This research lets us know that the experiences of Nicky, Sasha, and Tianyu are not isolated or rare but shared by many LGBTQ+ people around the world (see, for example, Barrientosa et al. 2021 on Chile; Gato et al. 2020 on Portugal; and Gonzales et al. 2020 on the United States, among numerous others). Azwihangwisi Mavhandu-Mudzusi and colleagues (2021) interviewed transgender women in South Africa about COVID-era online education; challenges to their education included stigmatization by parents, name-calling by family members, and physical and sexual violence perpetrated by family members. In Niharika Banerjea and colleagues' (2022) edited volume *COVID-19 Assemblages: Queer and Feminist Ethnographies from South Asia*, researchers and community workers reported LGBTQ+ people beaten at home, thrown out of their homes and refused reentry, and forcibly broken up (from same-sex partners) and married (to different-sex partners). In one such heart-wrenching case, a trans man, Riad, and cis woman, Rumi, were discovered to be a couple due to their phone calls during lockdown (Ara 2022). They were separated by their families, and Rumi was married off without her consent. Soon after, Riad died by suicide.

Riad's death is a casualty of the pandemic, of homophobia and transphobia, of family violence. It is also a powerful statement about and against the unlivable conditions that some families create for their sexually and gender-diverse members. The surge in anti-LGBTQ+ family violence during the pandemic is something many scholars and community activists warned about, the scope of which we have yet to fully grasp.

It is important to remember that this violence does not stem from a specific culture, religion, or region of the world; the "global north" (more wealthy and powerful countries, often countries that have colonized others) is certainly not exempt from it. It is also important to remember that "the family" is not a monolith. Within a family experiencing anti-LGBTQ+ violence, there are often heterosexual individuals who support their LGBTQ+ siblings, cousins, children, and grandchildren; they also suffer deep harm and loss when their LGBTQ+ loved ones are driven away. Responding to this violence and healing from it will be a lifelong task. Lifting pandemic restrictions and the decreasing risks of infection and death change people's life circumstances but do not reverse or erase the traumas they have endured or the ways their family relationships have changed as a result.

Care and Love

Stories of pandemic-era support and closeness between LGBTQ+ people and families of origin were harder to come by. Whether that is because these stories were less notable to journalists and researchers or because they were actually less common is not something I can say. But I did find them, and they point to a different path—one in which families treasure their LGBTQ+ members.

An early United Nations report on LGBTQ+ life in the pandemic centered Min Min, a young trans man volunteering at a quarantine center in small-town Myanmar. As a volunteer, Min Min helped distribute food and clean the repurposed school that housed locals and returning migrant workers needing to quarantine. He initially worried about how his gender would be received by others; however, his worries were quickly eased:

> "I was fortunate that everyone knew me in town, and they accepted me for what I am and accepted the support I gave. I mingled freely with the occupants at the center and even hung my sarong with the laundry of other men." In Myanmar society, families often separate their laundry not by color but by the sex of the wearer. . . . For Min Min's sarong to be left undisturbed among those of other men was an unusual show of acceptance.
> —Min Min, Myanmar, July 2020 (UNIC Yangon report)

In a small town, where in Min Min's words "everyone knew me," this, too, is a family and community of origin story—that is, a young person in the community in which he was born, raised as a girl, transitioned, and now lives as a man, exchanging support with his relations and neighbors. This story and others like it remind us that family disruption and rejection are not inevitable. LGBTQ+ people can remain embedded in families and communities of origin and exchange care and support with them in times of crisis.

Periods of lockdown and social distancing at times sparked reflection and conversation among couples and families about how to live together. In one study, Filipino gay couples separated by the pandemic communicated often about their family lives, showing care and concern for one another's family members as a way to preserve intimacy from afar. Some discussed the pros and cons of coming out to their families and strategized ways to do so (Labor and Latosa 2022). In another study, Mayle, a young queer woman in Turkey, found herself doing drag from the confines of her family's three-room apartment. The close physical quarters prompted Mayle to open this part of her life to her parents: "After days of putting on make-up for the events behind closed doors, I decided to show my mother the make-up I had put on. . . . I can see how this experience changed their ideas [positively] about the LGBTQ community and drag" (Altay 2022, p. 70S).

(Please note: This paragraph includes a story of sexual violence.) Mayle's story is one of many showing the porous boundaries between different kinds of spaces under social distancing and lockdown. Mayle's drag community, by moving online, also moved into her home; hence, her mother met her nonbinary drag persona for the first time.[7] The two parts of this chapter—chosen families and community care, and families of origin as sites of care, conflict, love, and violence—coexist and may converge in people's everyday lives. For some, this convergence is devastating. For others, it brings greater peace and wholeness. The family of origin can even be a place of protection and healing. As Grey, a queer woman in Zimbabwe, shared, "This lockdown has been traumatising. I was raped by my friend's boyfriend because he wanted to turn me straight. I'm still recovering physically and emotionally. Some days are better because I have my family around. They make me laugh and make sure I have eaten" (Maenzanise 2021). Grey was outed to her mother and aunt but did not experience rejection from them. As a result, the family was a refuge—a place of laughter and sustenance and a place to recover—and not a source of added suffering.

WHERE DO WE GO FROM HERE?

We, author and reader, might stop here to take an emotional temperature, to assess our respective journeys through this chapter. Each story offered to us by a queer person somewhere in the world is precious in its own right. The remembering itself matters. There may be one story or a handful of stories that will stick with you long after you close this book. These stories also reveal themes and patterns in how people have lived and cared for one another through the COVID-19 pandemic.

Emerging evidence makes it clear that queer chosen families remain important. These relationships continue to sustain health and life in periods of crisis. When the pandemic struck, trans and other gender-diverse people drew on preexisting networks of support—often queer kinship and family networks—to quickly mobilize community care. LGBTQ+ people expressed a deep need to be with other queers and found creative ways to do this, on- and offline.

These strategies also had limits. Many people were locked down in unsupportive homes; they could not gather on- or offline easily or at all. Some people experienced great suffering at the hands of their families. Others felt affirmed by their families in ways they hadn't before. Overall, the boundaries between queer communities, chosen families, and families of origin became more porous. That is, as people lost access to jobs, schools, and other spaces and were confined to their homes, it became harder to compartmentalize these relationships.

As a family scholar, one of my biggest takeaways is the continued power of families of origin in queer lives. Political and legal struggles to mitigate this power are crucial, including those that free people to prioritize other relationships (see Mano 2021 for an insightful analysis of this grounded in Singapore) At the same time, these struggles alone will not ensure LGBTQ+ well-being, particularly for youth, elders, and others in situations of dependence. The hearts and minds of family members must be changed as well. This requires different tools from those used in activism and advocacy external to the family. For example, the uncompromising position of a human rights activist in a legal battle is unlikely to work in her relationship with her own mother or grandmother. We cannot neglect these more personal negotiations and relationships in our visions for change.

Time stamp: October 2022

I have a long to-do list; finishing this chapter is near the top. In my LGBTQ+ studies classroom, we discuss the relationship between trauma and the kinds of demands activists make on the state. A student critiques the impulse to go back, to restore life to what it was before the trauma occurred. This impulse cannot heal us, he explains, because it ignores what has happened and who we are because of it. I pause, then venture away from my outline for the class. "Are we doing this with COVID?" I ask. "Is this hurting us?"

"Yes and yes," says a student in the front row.

As students and as experts in areas other than mine, you likely have takeaways of your own based on what you have read. I hope this chapter has deepened and broadened your thinking about LGBTQ+ family life under social distancing and lockdown. There are, of course, many points of view left out of the chapter, and I hope you feel empowered to add them. Finally, I hope this chapter has opened a door, whether in your classroom or internally, to acknowledge the COVID-19 pandemic; to honor grief and sit with loss; and to think about who we are and want to be—individually, in our relationships, as a society—given all that has happened and what we now know.

Acknowledgments: I thank the Anthropology of Children and Youth Interest Group for inviting me to give a talk in April 2021 that precipitated this chapter. I thank the Pride student organization at the University of Michigan–Dearborn for coining the phrase that became its title. Your ingenuity kept us, and me, going through isolated times.

NOTES

1. Positioning myself in the class just described: I am White, raised Christian, and identify as queer and femme. In September 2021, I was thirty-nine; at UM–Dearborn, I nearly always have students my age or older than me, in addition to much younger students.

2. In total, I collected and reviewed fifty research articles, two edited volumes, and twenty-four interviews with queer and trans people appearing in the media between 2020 and 2022. Adding up the total number of survey respondents and interviewees, these comprise a check-in with nearly 4,000 sexually and gender-diverse people in more than thirty countries on five continents. The larger-scale check-ins were brief, as in surveys or one-time interviews; smaller-scale, deeper check-ins also occurred through repeated interviews or ethnographic studies. The works I have reviewed are the tip of the iceberg as far as knowledge about LGBTQ+ people and COVID-19 is concerned.

3. If you think about it, the phrase "like family" still suggests that there is an original family against which other relationships are measured. Weston was very clear that chosen families are not copies of or secondary to the families we were raised in.

4. See Toomistu (2022) for more on *waria* identity.

5. See Saria (2021) for more on *hijra* identity.

6. See Bacon (2020) for the meaning of the bat signal according to various writers. For the original comic cited here, see www.dc.com/comics/detective-comics-2016/detective-comics-1027 (last accessed October 2022).

7. At the time of this interview, Mayle used she/her pronouns and identified as a woman in her everyday life while performing nonbinary drag.

In Other Words

STILL BEING LEFT BEHIND: THE INTIMATE LIVES OF QUEER DISABLED PEOPLE

Alan Martino, July 19, 2022 / CCF@TSP

There have been growing calls for heightened attention to intersectionality in queer spaces and for greater mobilizing. Yet, many queer disabled people still feel like they are being left behind and remain invisible within the queer movement. This is what I found in my recent study focused on the romantic and sexual experiences of thirty-one queer people labeled/with developmental and intellectual disabilities in Alberta, Canada.

Disabled people, especially those labeled/with intellectual disabilities, are so commonly desexualized in their everyday lives that it is often believed that conversations about sex and sexuality are irrelevant to this social group. Not only that, but it is also the case that some non-disabled people assume that disabled people simply cannot identify as queer. Sometimes, talking about sexualities (in the plural) among disabled people is seen as "going too far." I have personally encountered service providers who referred to the intersection of disability and queerness as being "too much" or "too nuanced" to be addressed. Many service providers struggle to find resources to support queer disabled people when they come out. The needs of queer people with disabilities are rarely considered in service provision and community supports. In fact, none of the participants had access to sexuality education in their schools and communities that addressed questions of sexual orientation in ways that would be relevant to disabled people.

By living at this intersection, queer disabled people often have to navigate experiences of both ableism and queerphobia. As one bisexual autistic participant shared, "Being on the spectrum, in my mind, was already bad enough. If people knew I was bisexual, too, I feel like that made me just even more of an outcast. So, I just followed what everyone else did. And I tried to keep my head down low." In addition, many must decide whether to "come out" as queer and/or disabled at different times. For those receiving direct care from family members and care workers, the fear of potentially losing those relationships and supports can discourage them from being open about their sexual identities. Some disabled people are even ridiculed, criticized, or punished for expressing their sexual desires. This might mean, for instance, increased surveillance from family members and direct care workers.

The current pandemic has had devastating impacts across various marginalized communities, including among queer people. From a lack of access to queer-friendly spaces and communities to access to (already few) supports and resources, the pandemic hit the community hard. The pandemic proved to be as harsh, if not harsher, for many disabled people in the community. Activists from People First of Canada, a national organization representing people labeled/with developmental and intellectual disabilities, pointed out how this social group was the "left behind of the left behind." For some, the experiences with social distancing, for example, reminded them of times living in institutions.

More and more disabled people now live in the community rather than in segregated care, and it is important to ensure that people with disabilities can be active participants in the community. Yet, queer spaces, and even some Pride-related events, can be inaccessible to disabled people. It is worth mentioning that accessibility is more than merely building ramps at the back of the club. What participants have pointed out is that accessibility is also about being meaningfully invited into queer spaces and offered spaces that are not overly sensory stimulating. For instance, for some queer disabled people, queer spaces, especially those involving loud music and other forms of sensory stimulation, can be inaccessible: "I have to be like in a headspace where I can deal with the sensory stuff with it." Instead, people shared their desire for "sensory friendly place[s] where there's like, good lighting, um not really too much noise. And you can just kind of hang out."

Many participants also commented on the lack of representation of queer disabled people, which led some to feel like "outsiders" in their own communities. As one participant put it, "I didn't really want to participate in queer spaces because I felt like an interloper. I felt like I did not belong." According to many participants, it is hard navigating queer spaces that do not consider disability and accessibility while they are attempting to find disabled spaces that are thinking about questions of gender identity and sexualities. Not having a community that fully embraces both their queer and disabled existence, many participants feel stuck in the middle, an outsider in both communities.

In the face of these challenges, queer disabled activists and scholars are taking matters into their own hands and are using a variety of platforms, such as blogs, podcasts, and YouTube channels, to raise awareness about experiences at this often-disregarded intersection and to challenge the invisibility of queer disabled people. Also, recent TV shows, like *Special* and the reboot of *Queer as Folk*, are trying to increase the visibility of queer disabled people. In these ways, queer disabled people are showing that disabled people are "also here and queer." ∎

PART FOUR

Intimacy in the Twenty-First Century

16

Why Is Everyone (Still) Afraid of Sex?

Nicholas Velotta and Pepper Schwartz

Americans are often portrayed as sex obsessed. And even if studies on the exact frequencies of how often people speak, or even think, about sex are few and varied in their methods and findings (Fisher et al. 2012; Hofmann et al. 2012; Wellings 1995), *most* American adults think about sex frequently. As sociologists, we recognize that the salience of sex varies by age, religiosity, social class, gender, and race. In the past two decades we've seen greater acceptance of an increasingly wide range of sexual expression and intimate arrangements. But in this change, a puzzle persists: Despite the universality of sexual thoughts and imagery, and in spite of diverse sexual behaviors and identities, we believe sex is something many people, and certainly many Americans, still deeply fear. *Why is this so?*

In this chapter we answer this question. We believe that much of our collective fear comes from the fact that Americans practice *cultural dissonance* toward sex. By that we mean, because our culture is both prohibitive and permissive about sexuality, stigma and shame continue to shade our sexuality. Therefore, it is no surprise that people will hold, at best, conflicting feelings about sex and, at worst, self-loathing and fear, even as they yearn for more sexual contact. For instance, a person could enjoy oral sex but since it conflicts with religious teachings or fears about hygiene, they may regret having oral sex or even avoid seeking it out entirely.

In the United States, familiarity with sexual materials and imagery in popular books, in movies, and certainly on the internet may make us seem like we are now sexually sophisticated and uninhibited. But even while endorsing these "liberal" sexualities, many Americans remain somewhat to deeply fearful of their implications. Cultural dissonance toward sex is widespread: We have contradicting ideas about who should be having sex and with whom, what sexual behaviors are "good" and what kinds of behaviors are "bad" or "risky," when sex is appropriate to have in a given situation (for example, after a wedding versus after a funeral), and from a life-course perspective (for example, casual sex among the residents at nursing homes versus hook-up culture at college campuses). In many cases, it can feel like we are not even sure what *sex* means anymore. American media may celebrate the idea that we're *finally* sexually liberated, but this ignores just how anxiety-ridden, ignorant, and sometimes unsatisfied Americans are when it comes to sex.

This is not, we hope, a controversial starting point for our discussion. After all, it makes sense for humans to worry over sex quite a bit given its (usually) crucial role in forming satisfying intimate relationships and its evolutionary function in reproduction. This is exacerbated, to say the least, by how much television shows, advertisements, and social media sexualize the world we live in. Even if you never watch a TV show or go on the internet (which is unlikely), everyday life will force you into a sexualized event. For example, even certain local coffee drive-thru windows known as "Bikini Baristas" ask you to access your erotic imagination. Our claim, then, is that while sex is everywhere, the penetration of sexual themes into everyday life has not ameliorated our cultural dissonance—we remain worried about sex.

CULTURAL DISSONANCE

Popular Culture

Any American with an internet connection, cable subscription, or smartphone has access to an immeasurable cache of sexual content. Not just pornography, which we will discuss shortly, but also extremely popular television shows centered on sexual intrigues (consider Netflix's *Sex Education*, *Bridgerton*, and *Big Mouth*; HBO's *The Sex Lives of College Girls* and *Euphoria*; and Showtime's *Masters of Sex*, *Queer as Folk*, and *Gigolos*—to only mention a handful). Celebrities' sex lives are posted in mass media, and video games sexualize female characters and gravitate toward sexually explicit (and oft-violent) story lines. There have always been books with sexual content, but pornographic potboilers have become more mainstream. All three of the top-grossing books of the last decade were installments in the *Fifty Shades* sexually explicit trilogy, which introduced millions of readers to the eroticism of BDSM—bondage, dominance/discipline, submission/sadism, masochism (Aviles 2019). "Sex," as they say, "sells," and the drumbeat of sexual imagery continues, with ads selling erectile dysfunction (ED) medications like Viagra and Cialis appearing during prime-time hours on major cable networks.

Yet these examples do not tell the whole story of how sex is policed by mass media. As Michel Foucault instructed readers in his magnum opus, *The History of Sexuality, Volume 1*, the absence of certain sexualities in popular discourse is integral to the regulation of sex in society (1980). For example, advisory panels rarely permit images or explicit discussions of sexual anatomy or show non-heterosexual sex scenes. It is easy to find shows that feature the breasts, body, face, and moans of women in sex scenes with men but intentionally obscure the male participant's body and sounds during sex. Masturbation is especially rare on film. Even when sexually explicit content is shown on screen, it is undoubtedly accompanied by a TV-MA, an NC-17, or an R rating.

Tabloids and blogs forgo these advisory rating systems but still maintain oddly righteous moral policies toward the celebrities they cover. For example, magazines publicize celebrities' bodies and star couples in the throes of passionate make-outs, only to cast criticisms about them ("50 Best & Worst Beach Bods," "Shocking Weight Gain!" "Skinny, Bony, & Haggard Post-Break-up!") and their sexual behaviors ("We See Your Undies . . . Oh Wait You're Not Wearing Any!" "Caught with His Pants Down!" "Is There Another Woman?!!"). Sexist and denigrating headlines, like these from mainstream tabloids, are common.

No sector of society is immune from a double-edged approach to sexuality. In 2014, tensions erupted in the gaming landscape between the emerging market of diverse, feminist gamers and the industry's predominantly white heterosexual male gamers. An explosive debate occurred over representations of female sexuality in the video game world. Known as Gamergate, this culture war was kicked off by a spurned ex-boyfriend who posted accusations of his ex-girlfriend's infidelity (she happened to be an indie game developer) that snowballed into a months-long barrage of violent threats and online sexual harassment aimed at female gamers and their supporters (Hanson 2016; Jane 2016; Mantilla 2015). Since Gamergate, sociologists have provided empirical analyses of video games and have found a lack of nonmale, nonheterosexual subjects in them (Geena Davis Institute on Gender in Media 2021).

It is hard to find many places in our culture where sex and pleasure are put together in a straightforward way that is inclusive of diverse populations. Even medical ads seem queasy about sexuality when they promote sexual aids. For example, pharmaceutical ads for ED medications usually eschew discussing sex explicitly or even through imagery. Most of the ads for ED medications are innocuous, with actors gardening, working out, or doing pottery. Older people, who are most likely to need their product, are generally pictured in nonsexy ways. It is easy to conclude that pharmaceutical companies are ambivalent about the sexual lives of older people even while promoting their sex-enhancing medications.

While at first glance popular culture seems "sex positive," a critical examination of the media landscape begs to differ. We may be seeing more sexual imagery and behavior in our movies, apps, video games, and on TV, but only within guidelines that presume highly normative acts and only certain populations. This is our cultural dissonance: there is real attraction to sexual content, but even producers of sexual content know that if they go "too far" they'll provoke a conservative backlash. For example, in 2013, the nearly twenty-one-year-old pop star Miley Cyrus performed at the MTV Video Music Awards (VMAs) alongside singer Robin Thicke to a medley of her song "We Can't Stop" and his controversial song "Blurred Lines." Having matured out of her child-friendly Disney Channel role of "Hannah Montana," Cyrus danced and made sexy gestures while donning a nude two-piece bodysuit. The coverage of the event was brutal and sexist. Cyrus was shamed for everything from looking too skinny to dancing too sexually. But most of all, Cyrus faced backlash for renouncing the pure (and puerile) image that Disney manufactured for her six years earlier. This debacle sent Cyrus into a new phase of her career marked by constant coverage about her "rebellious" (often coded as sexual) behavior. More recently, the pop star revealed that the public shaming from her VMA performance pushed her to stop wearing revealing clothing out of embarrassment and body dysmorphia (Singh 2020). Singer Robin Thicke, who'd been dancing alongside Cyrus on the stage and singing lines that implied nonconsensual sexual behavior, did not, at the time, face a similar controversy . . . that is, until years later when he was accused of sexually assaulting actress and model Emily Ratajkowski on the set of the "Blurred Lines" music video (Carras 2021). Thicke initially avoided censure because sexuality in men, particularly heteronormative men, fits into our culturally approved versions of sex. The same cannot be said for sexuality in women.

Because we accept the sheer volume of sexual content around us as proof that we are liberated, the limits that are actually at play in the portrayal of sex persist with little examination. This is true at both the societal and the individual level. We'll look closer at these constraints in the following sections.

Hookup Culture and Casual Sex

What about the actual behaviors of young people? There has been all kinds of hand-wringing over premarital sex, presuming that young people are having sex often and indiscriminately. Multiple studies discuss the "decoupling of relationship status and sex" and the rise of casual dating apps and hookup culture (HUC) for (mostly) college-aged people. *Hooking up*, or a *hookup*, is vaguely defined as a transient or unplanned interaction between uncommitted sexual partners that can encompass anything from just hanging out to intercourse (England et al. 2008; Thorpe and Kuperberg 2021). *Does this mean that American youth have conquered prejudice about premarital sex and are enjoying sex unencumbered by moralistic judgment and shaming?* While this is undoubtedly a more liberal sexual culture than seen in previous generations, research indicates that young people do not enjoy hooking up as much as dating apps, media outlets, or young people themselves claim.

For one thing, women have long reported their experience with hookup culture as male dominated and filled with double standards for the sexual behavior of (heterosexual) men versus women (England et al. 2008; Orenstein 2016). Multiple studies suggest that HUC caters to men's sexual pleasure and tends to neglect women's desire for pleasure and orgasm during sex (Andrejek et al. 2022; Armstrong et al. 2012; England et al. 2008; England and Bearak 2014). Sexist tropes are deployed against women who want a relationship rather than a hookup. In fact, due in part to the higher number of women than men attending college and the increased pressure to see casual sex as an inevitable part of higher education, competition among women for men's sexual attention is as intense as it has been for previous cohorts (Wade 2017). Furthermore, there are additional risks depending on one's race, gender, and sexuality. Black men report being fearful of false sexual assault accusations coming out of a hookup (Orenstein 2020), while nonwhite women and Asian men also report barriers to their participation in HUC (Spell 2017). Nonbinary and trans people also have concerns for their physical and psychological safety while hooking up; rather than participate in HUC per se, queer people regularly form their own niche sexual subcultures outside of HUC (Wade 2017).

That said, there are contradictions within hooking up for *all* participants. In her book *American Hookup*, Wade (2017) notes how the use of alcohol in hookups reveals ambivalence and alienation rather than sexual freedom:

> Being drunk . . . is useful to students, not only because alcohol is liquid courage; it also frames the sexual activity, boxing it into the realm of meaninglessness. It's how students show that they are being careless in both senses of the word: they aren't being careful, and they don't care. (p. 45)

While the symbolic function of alcohol allows participants to signal the unserious, no-strings-attached nature of their trysts, the "meaninglessness" assigned to hookups also has negative psychological effects. Wade's sample of college students reported feeling ambivalent about their sexual encounters at best and used, depleted, or ashamed about their encounters at worst. Taking this one step further, we would like to propose that one explanation for the heavy alcohol use in HUC is to numb anxieties and fears about what sex means to us as individuals, especially in situations where our individual meanings surrounding sex are a breach of social norms. In effect, this is another site of cultural *and* cognitive dissonance toward sex. For those within hookup culture, alcohol can be an acceptable coping mechanism for the internal discomfort of simultaneously desiring and fearing meaningful sex.

What we have described is no secret to participants. Many young people admit hookups aren't satisfying, and over time, many opt out of hooking up or customize the way they hook up so that it works better for them. For one thing, average sexual frequencies are dropping significantly among millennials and Gen Z (Centers for Disease Control and Prevention 2015; Herbenick et al. 2021), indicating the value of casual sex is being debated by younger generations. Another portent of change comes from an annual survey of over six thousand singles conducted by Match (2021), the online dating company, which found that more singles prefer emotional maturity in a partner (83 percent) over physical attractiveness (78 percent). Additionally, the number of Match users who prefer physical attractiveness in a partner (78 percent) is down from 90 percent in 2020. Match claims only 11 percent of their users want to date casually, while 62 percent say they are more interested in finding a meaningful, committed relationship. Two out of three singles want to wait until after the third date to have sex. Other findings from this survey that may affect HUC's racial and gender inequalities include a 22 percent increase in the number of singles open to dating someone of a different race or ethnicity and a large increase in the number of male users looking for long-term relationships (rather than casual sex). A big takeaway so far is that people desire more connection than what hookup culture has traditionally afforded its participants.

Porn

There are few, if any, articulations of America's cultural dissonance toward sex that are as eye-catching as our use of pornography. Online options run an almost unimaginable spectrum of pornographic possibilities. The range is from "classic" films of heterosexual oral and vaginal sex to exotic porn produced for people with specific fetishes and kinks, organized for every conceivable sexual orientation. While this pornography is supposedly available only to adults, the fact is that very young children and adolescents have smartphones and tablets that make it relatively easy to find sexually explicit content. Studies indicate that the normal age range for one's first exposure to pornographic material can be as young as nine to eleven years old (American Psychological Association 2017; Orenstein

2020; Wolak et al. 2007). Given that exposure to porn is often an individual's first exposure to sexually explicit information, the variety of information and misinformation becomes a de facto form of sex education for the entire world. Porn simultaneously makes observers believe "everyone is doing everything," which can make them feel inadequate, and that sex has strange and often violent elements that are repulsive and to be feared. Without understanding these nuances to pornographic content and building a relationship with a consenting partner, the imagery easily becomes a confusing mix of arousal, shame, and guilt.

... The Sex We Aren't Having

Online porn's variety, accessibility, and discretion are what has attracted tens of millions of daily viewers and built a multibillion-dollar porn industry. Yet we believe that the ubiquity of porn in the United States is one symptom of a sexually conflicted society, with the pornographic universe showing a much wilder sexual landscape than what people say they want or even what they do. Normative sexuality is always supposed to be relational and monogamous, but porn depicts sexual desire as more complicated than normative mandates.

While the images are wild, people's accounts of their sex lives are not. To add to the story of dissonance, recent research finds that young Americans are having less sex and watching more porn—and more aggressive porn—than previous generations (Herbenick et al. 2020, 2021; Orenstein 2020). What is more, a large share of couples consistently report they want more sexual variety, novelty, excitement, and adventure in their sex lives (Northrup et al. 2012). This raises the controversial question: *Could online porn use be a more accurate depiction of some Americans' sexual desires and identities than the sex they're having in real life?* We believe it might be. And while we would not argue that watching a particular genre of porn is the same as desiring to act out the behaviors portrayed in the videos, we do not find it unreasonable to assume most viewers at least like to imagine a variety of the behaviors they see on screen. So the next question is, why don't they?

Perhaps it is because at least some of their sexual desires and identities lie outside of our gendered heterosexual standard and so they are considered inappropriate to discuss with anyone but a therapist or in an online chatroom. For example, after analyzing the top searches on PornHub, a pornographic video-streaming website, Stephens-Davidowitz (2017) found many of the top 110 terms searched for by men looking for "straight porn" videos were anything but heteronormative.

More troubling to many people's sensibilities are porn destinations that cross boundaries of consent, show internalized victimization, and violate women's safety. For example, incest porn is also a popular genre for men on PornHub.

Stephens-Davidowitz's review of women's PornHub use may seem especially shocking to some: "Fully 25 percent of female searches for straight porn emphasize the pain and/or humiliation of the woman" (Stephens-Davidowitz 2017, p. 121). Terms associated with sexual violence against women such as *rape, forced sex, public disgrace,* and *extreme brutal gangbanging* are searched at least twice as frequently by female users than they are by male users. Then there are users with desires surrounding "race play" and those that search for videos showing performers acting out racist stereotypes during sex. Examples of subversive content online could fill another chapter, and this is exactly why so many Americans don't disclose their sexual desires outside the safety of an internet search.

Some readers will say, but the porn industry is changing with the popularization of webcamming and self-employed sex workers on subscription sites like OnlyFans that offer more personal access between performer and subscriber. Will viewer behavior change as well? Will subscribers care more about the performer's sexual pleasure and well-being if subscribers also message with that performer one-on-one? More research is needed to understand how the porn industry and the sex work industry writ large are and are not changing viewers' behaviors. But, at the time of this writing, a large share of Americans who watch porn want to watch porn that eroticizes breaks with deeply held cultural beliefs surrounding sex.

SOURCES OF FEAR

Cultural dissonance applies to the way that some groups—and the individual members of those groups—consider our mainstream versions of sex liberating, while others feel fear, and still others feel repression. It does not, however, explain *why* there's so much cultural dissonance to begin with. In this section, we will begin to tackle the question that inspired the title of this chapter: *Why is everyone still afraid of sex?*

Religious Indoctrination and Tradition

Whatever the Bible says, and scholars differ in their interpretations, the teachings of most religious institutions vary from conservative to extremely conservative when it comes to sexual behavior. Sex outside of a (monogamous) marriage is often condemned, even if it is now almost universal. Masturbation is seldom mentioned, and when it is, self-pleasure is usually presented as a sign of weakness or moral corruption. Even in many "new wave" churches, the best that parishioners can hope for vis-à-vis homosexuality is a policy of tolerance and compassion. The result of this generally negative or hushed approach toward sexuality is widespread guilt, shame, blame, horror, and ire over various populations' sexual behaviors. At the individual level, many people trace their inhibitions and inability to enjoy sexuality to their religious training or background.

Patriarchal Norms

Over time our society has watched women's sexuality change to mirror men's sexuality. Most women have premarital sex, many women embrace overtly sexual self-presentations, and the sex toy market—which is dominated by female customers—is worth an estimated $35.1 billion (Global Industry Analysts 2022). These changes have provoked fear and anger in some organized groups as well as individual moral outrage. Conservative religious leaders give sermons on resisting these changes in modern sexual behavior and offer dire prognoses for American families and our nation overall. While we pay millions of dollars to watch explicit sexual moves in popular music videos and sexual availability is expected after very short periods of dating, the fact is that when women do not want to be sexual with a particular man, the very act of female agency over their consent can ignite dangerous reactions from men. Individual women can be vulnerable to sexual expectations that can erupt in aggression if male desire is not reciprocated. Sexual frustration in a climate of potential sexual availability has caused men who believe in patriarchal privilege to pressure women for sexual access and to sometimes forcefully and violently demand it.

In 2017 this tension over expected sexual access exploded in an unexpected space: the workplace. Over the course of the movement, which quickly became known as #MeToo (a term coined back in 2006 by activist Tarana Burke), an extraordinary group of powerful men were accused of sexual misconduct ranging from reputational slander, to inappropriate touching, to serial rape. Their victims, who were mostly but not exclusively women, took to social media and exposed their perpetrators using the hashtag "MeToo" as a sign of solidarity with the movement. Years later, Americans are still grappling with the ramifications of #MeToo. The process of listening to alleged offenders' apologies (or denials) while deciding whose trespasses should be forgiven without letting egregious offenders off the hook is complex and challenging. One thing is for certain: we have begun seeing sex as more consequential for men than it has been in the past. Since #MeToo, the urgency of seeing the difference between negative but consensual sex and nonconsensual sex has grown. Even with the growing support for women's voices, women are still threatened with words like *slut* or the amorphous "bad" reputation. And so, the double standard, though greatly changed, still exists.

... Queer and Trans Sex

The social critic Michael Warner (1999) once wrote,

> The received wisdom in straight culture is that all of its different norms line up, that one is synonymous with the others. If you are born with male genitalia, the logic goes, you will behave in masculine ways, desire women, desire feminine women, desire them exclusively, have sex in what are thought to be normally active and insertive ways and within officially sanctioned contexts, think of yourself as hetero-sexual, identify with other heterosexuals no matter how tolerant you might wish to be, and never change any part of this package from childhood to senescence. Het-erosexuality is often a name for this entire package, even though attachment to the other sex is only one element. If you deviate at any point from this program, you do so at your own cost. And one of the things straight culture hates most is a sign that the different parts of the package might be recombined in an infinite number of ways. But experience shows that this is just what tends to happen. If heterosexuality requires the entire sequence, then it is very fragile. No wonder it needs so much terror to induce compliance. (pp. 37–38)

Warner correctly observes that we remain deeply fearful of sexualities that do not confirm the primacy of heteronormative sexuality. American patriarchal norms have especially violent consequences for people outside the male-female binary. Notably, trans women (and particularly trans women of color) have their bodies fetishized by the media and porn sites. Unsurprisingly, sex work has become one way these women can survive financially, lay claim to their sexuality, and pay for expensive gender-affirming procedures. And while individual trans women may find this a viable situation, a considerable number of trans women[1] encounter violent victimization within the context of sex, dating, and intimate relationships (Peitzmeier et al. 2020). So-called panic defenses, which make it legal for perpe-trators to "react violently to discovering the victim's sexual orientation or gender identity," are still legal in most states and allow the assaulters and murderers of trans women to evade legal repercussions or incarceration (Mallory et al. 2021, p. 21). In 2021, only ten states and the District of Columbia had laws that banned such a defense (Movement Advancement Project n.d.).

Queer sexuality, especially when it includes traits associated with femininity, is policed by groups such as churches, schools, law enforcement, and political parties; by individuals in particular moments, such as when a parent or friend chastises a child for acting like a "sissy"; and by legal rulings such as panic defenses, anti-trans bathroom bills, and bills that prohibit LGBTQIA+ mate-rial from being taught in classrooms. There has been some progress in reducing damaging stereotypes and proscriptions around sex in America, but LGBTQIA+ people, and especially trans women, continue to face higher levels of victimization and discrimination because of their sexuality (see Guadalupe-Diaz's chapter in this volume).

Sex, Death, and Disease

Fears about sex can also be rooted in vulnerability to contracting sexually transmitted infections (STIs). Without prophylactic measures that could prevent transmission, centuries of sexually active people have suffered from debilitating and often fatal infections after the exchange of fluids during sex acts. Even when those prophylactic measures became more effective, availability, promotion, and consistent use of them has been limited. HIV, the virus that causes AIDS, is transmitted through blood and semen. Infections in the United States grew first in communities where people had reused needles and where people had anal sex, but infections quickly ballooned to impact tens of thousands of queer people—especially gay men. When HIV/AIDS first emerged as a modern-day plague in the early 1980s, all the fears and hysteria of earlier periods of contagion reemerged. Leading conservatives and policy makers reacted by blaming sex, gay men, and modern immorality for the deaths. During other pandemics such as influenza and the COVID-19 pandemic, which killed millions of people globally, we have seen similar society-wide panics. But when sexual transmission is added to a contagion, sex itself becomes the villain. Contrast this with the COVID-19 pandemic, where certain public health agencies provided suggestions on how to reduce the risk of COVID-19 transmission on dates and during sex (Parker-Pope 2020); sex wasn't villainized.

Instead of concentrating on good public health initiatives that would reduce transmission in sexually active populations, policy makers, some religious leaders, and various moral entrepreneurs go on the attack, using the medical crisis to create a moral one. Sex is not restricted to the monogamously married anymore (if it ever was), yet many moral and political leaders refuse to accept the fact that teenagers, single adults, and LGBTQIA+ individuals are having sex, will continue to have sex, and need the best health protections they can get.

"Am I Normal? Am I a Good Lover?"

More and more, sex is framed as a self-expansive act rather than an immoral and reproduction-oriented impulse. Americans are seeking partners who can contribute sky-high levels of pleasure and intimacy during sex. Certainly, fear also arises out of our worry that we are sexually incompetent or sexually ineffective.

As a society, we pretend that because sexual activity is in part biological, it is easy to do. At the same time, we advertise products that undergird fears of not being thin enough, hard enough, busty enough, or athletic enough in bed. We aspire to be gifted in the bedroom, afraid that we are not, yet we can also be inhibited because we don't want to cross the line into feeling that our sexuality is somehow abnormal. While some lucky people get comprehensive—or even sex positive— sex education and, at a deeper level, advice and information about their own sexual quandaries and challenges, most of us learn through trial and error how to be what we hope is a good lover.

Namely, it is our attractiveness and acceptability that we worry about. Each period of recorded history has normative evocations of what is beautiful and sexy and what is not. This imagery is idealized rather than representative, and it is hard for the average person to fit the media and model standard for sexual attractiveness and competency. As a result, there are often anger and anxiety associated with the mainstream images of sexuality—anger at the standards we are held to and anxiety about whether we are sexually desirable, or even legible, to others if we stray from those standards. It is therefore no surprise that many Americans condemn sex-saturated media while trying desperately to conform to their standards.

Conclusion

For all the sexual imagery in American society, it seems clear that we are not at ease with our sexuality at either the policy or personal level. There are mixed signals in every realm. On television, we sell everything from cars to hamburgers with sexual innuendo, but we cannot sell vibrators or condoms during these same timeslots. Women are now having almost as much premarital sex as men, yet there is still a sexual double standard. It is normative to have sex before marriage, yet there are still guilt and shame and inadequate preparation for physical or emotional safety. We still have more trouble talking about sex than we do having it. Policies that fund abstinence-only sex education remain in place even though nearly all men and women in the United States have intercourse by the time they're twenty-one, and most parents are in favor of comprehensive sex education regardless of political affiliation (Finer 2007; Kantor and Levitz 2017). Fear, not comfort, lies only a few centimeters under our bravado because ours is a culture of dissonance toward sexuality.

The answer to this confusion and irrationality is clear but still oddly out of reach. We need to reduce sexual anxiety and ignorance through comprehensive, wholistic sex education. We can do that by using well-trained sex educators, activists, researchers, and teachers to distribute scientific data and reassuring counsel to both children and their parents. This does not mean a sexual free-for-all. Far from it. It means giving valid sexual information and help in sexual decision-making throughout the life cycle that allows people to respect and care for themselves and each other. It also means recognizing that sexual desire is natural and that people of all ages and identities need information and support to remain healthy and feel secure about themselves, their bodies, and their sexual behavior. It means legitimizing pleasure and giving people information about how to give it to themselves and others in honorable, honest, and safe ways. It means we need to make sex part of our mental and social health curriculum from early childhood to late adulthood. This education would not be relegated to the classroom, university, or doctor's office. We need media and public figures to include diverse sexualities in their discourses on sex. We need representation and appreciation of nonheteronormative sexuality in our education and media. This is not a new or brilliant idea; it is merely a rational one. Our culture is (still) afraid of sex, and it is in our individual interest, the interests of our families, and the interests of public health to quash the toxic tactics that are aimed at creating sexual fears and instead to make sexuality a source of happiness in our own lives and in our intimate relationships.

NOTE

1.   The number was enough for the trend to be addressed as an epidemic of violence by news and human rights organizations as well as by President Biden when he was the Democratic nominee (Garcia 2020; Human Rights Campaign Foundation 2021; Taylor 2020).

In Other Words

HOW YOU TALK WITH YOUR CHILD ABOUT SEX MATTERS

Shelby Astle, October 4, 2022 / CCF@TSP

Talking with your children about sex is important for setting them up for healthy sexual development, but it's also really hard work! It can be difficult to know what information your children need from you if you're not sure where they are at with their own sexual feelings, behaviors, and concerns. You may wonder: "Is my child sexually active or just spending romantic time with her girlfriend?" or "Does my child have questions or insecurities about their body I'm not aware of?" or "Is the information I've provided my child enough for where he's at in his development?"

This is where our research comes in! We wanted to know if the frequency with which parents talked with teens about sex, and how open the parents were during these conversations, was related to how much the child would open up to parents about their sexual feelings, concerns, and behaviors. We wanted to know so we could provide tips for parents on how to potentially help their child feel like they can open up about these topics.

Our Study

We surveyed 603 pairs of mothers and their teenage children ages twelve to seventeen. We asked each of them questions about how often they talk about sex-related topics together (frequency) and the level of communication openness of these conversations (openness). More open conversations were more comfortable, interactive, honest, and involved the mother actively listening to the teenage child. We also asked about how often the teenager deliberately told their mom about their sexual feelings, concerns, and behaviors (disclosure) and how often they kept secrets related to sex from their mom (secret keeping).

Our analysis showed that:

- teens who talked with moms more often about sex-related topics were more likely to disclose to mothers about sex BUT were also more likely to keep secrets from moms about sex;

- teens who talked with moms with a more open communication style were more likely to disclose to mothers about sex AND were also less likely to keep secrets from moms about sex; and

- when communication about sex-related topics was BOTH frequent AND open, teens were more likely to disclose to mothers about sex AND were also less likely to keep secrets from moms about sex.

What Does It Mean?

Our findings show that how often you talk with teens about sex and how open you are during these talks are both important.

Talking frequently in a way that is not open (for example, lecturing, not respecting the child's point of view) may create more conversational opportunities for a child to answer questions, but it may also send negative messages to the child. If parents are constantly lecturing their children or sending messages that children don't agree with, children will likely feel unable to disclose certain information about their beliefs, identity, or experiences to parents. For example, a child who is constantly lectured that sex is only okay in marriage may be unlikely to tell their parents if they are sexually active or if they've experienced sexual violence, even when they need support.

This is why openness during parent-child talks about sex-related topics is so important! As shown in our analysis, if these conversations were frequent AND open, children shared more with their mothers. Even if parents are talking with their child about sexuality regularly, if these conversations are one-sided, parent-dominated, and discouraging or dismissive of child input or perspectives, which is typical of most parent-child conversations about sex, this may further cement the message that parents do not want to hear about the child's true experiences and feelings. Children may not feel safe, comfortable, or able to share secrets related to sexuality.

Start Having Open Conversations with Your Child Today!

If you want to lay the foundation for an open and honest dialogue with your child about their sexual concerns, feelings, and behaviors, you can start today by having open conversations about sex-related topics with your child—no matter what age! Visit my favorite resource, Sex Positive Families, for tips on how to get started. Parents can be extremely influential in positively influencing their child's sexual development, so I encourage you to start today! ▰

In Other Words

WOMEN WHO CHEAT ON THEIR ROMANTIC PARTNERS: AN INTERVIEW WITH ALICIA WALKER

Arielle Kuperberg, October 31, 2017 / CCF@TSP

In her book *The Secret Life of the Cheating Wife: Power, Pragmatism, and Pleasure in Women's Infidelity* (2018), Alicia Walker, associate professor of sociology at Missouri State University, reports on the results of interviews with forty-six heterosexual married or partnered women who used the website Ashley Madison to intentionally seek out and form affairs with other men. The book develops a sociology of infidelity, examining issues related to the meaning of marriage, power, social norms in affairs, and why women have them.

AK: You found that the women in your book often had affairs because they were trying to preserve their marriage. How could an affair help preserve a marriage?

AW: For the women of the study, these outside partnerships served as a release valve for the resentment, hurt feelings, and deprivation they experienced in their primary partnerships (marriages or preexisting long-term relationships). The women talked about being able to better overlook the challenges in their relationships, as well as the daily irritants of shared living quarters, because they had this secret source of pleasure in their lives. Additionally, for women whose primary partnerships were sexless and/or orgasmless, these outside partnerships function as a space of sexual freedom and sexual pleasure, which is sorely missing in their "real lives." These women reported that without the relief these outside partnerships provide, they would be forced to exit their primary partnerships. For most of the women I interviewed, remaining in their primary partnerships was a chief goal. Thus, the relief provided by these outside partnerships proved crucial for these women to stay in primary partnerships. where their own sexual pleasure and needs were not being addressed.

AK: One of the things I find fascinating about the book is how social norms (informal social rules) are completely upended in affairs compared to other romantic or sexual relationships. Women avoided forming emotional ties with their partners and were not seeking to form long-term romantic partnerships,

which counteracts narratives we normally hear about gender and relationships. What were some of the ways you found the norms about affairs differ from other relationships?

AW: What is really fascinating about these outside partnerships is that there are no established expectations for how the women are supposed to behave. As a result, women could step out of typical expectations of gender around dating and sex. Even in traditional online dating, we take those expectations with us online. Without established norms and procedures, the participants in these outside partnerships make them up as they go along.

The women of this sample reported an extensive vetting process designed to protect themselves—and their families by extension—and to find a suitable partner without wasting a lot of time and energy. The amount of care and calculation applied stood out as different from partnering initiated face-to-face, where we often walk blindly into relationships under the magical influence of chemistry.

The freedom the women felt to set boundaries struck me as interesting as well. Frank discussions of preferred sexual acts, stamina, and scheduling take place as soon as the initial exchange. If those details do not match up, the conversation does not continue. There is none of the "oh, we have so much in common, I should overlook the other stuff" because these women don't get that far with men who don't fit the bill. The women had the freedom to create outside partnerships where the sole focus was their own pleasure. That's very different than the other relationships in their lives. Overall, the amount of power and freedom the women exercise in their outside partnerships is much more than what we often see them employ in their marriages.

AK: Your sample—women who used Ashley Madison—allowed you to explore some behaviors that may be common to any sexual relationship formed with partners met online. What are some of the things women in your study did specifically because they met their partners through a website? How might this experience differ from people who have affairs but don't actively seek them out on the internet?

AW: Women specifically vetted for sexual preferences and skills, which we do not typically do in relationships initiated face-to-face. We rarely see this among folks who meet at work, through friends, or in social settings. We do not habitually ask new suitors about their genital size before we have invested a lot of time in the relationship. We simply find out in the moment, at which point we may already be so invested in that relationship that we are unwilling to walk away.

But these women dismissed any potential partners whose sexual desires, stamina, scheduling, or physical traits did not mesh with the women's preferences. Compatibility in all areas drove the associations.

While an outside partnership formed with a coworker, neighbor, or family friend may be heady and exciting to the point that we set aside our good sense, outside partnerships formed online are based solely on the man's potential to bring the pleasure the women sought. ▄■

17

Love (and Lust) in the Age of Viruses

Sexual Health and Relationships

Adina Nack

S hame. Stigma. Silence. Every year, millions of Americans find out they have contracted sexually transmitted infections (STIs). Beyond the clinic walls, the U.S. public remains undereducated, underdiagnosed, and largely ignorant of the cumulative harm STIs cause to individuals' bodies as well as their social and psychological well-being. The impacts of STIs on a patient's self-image and on their relationships are also often overlooked. This chapter charts the paths by which highly contagious and chronic infections, like genital HSV (herpes simplex virus) and HPV (human papillomavirus), affect not only intimate relationships but also U.S. families. From casual sex to dating to marriage and from pregnancy to parenting, sexual health shapes the way we live and love. Using interviews and contemporary health policy debates, readers will learn why the destigmatization of STIs is key for supporting healthy sexual relationships and supportive familial relationships in the twenty-first century.

A PERSONAL INTRODUCTION

For readers who have contracted an STI, allow me to welcome you to the club! After being diagnosed with a cervical HPV infection when I was twenty, I focused my first research project on understanding adults' experiences with medically incurable STIs.[1] The topic of sexually transmitted viruses continues to be timely, especially with the 2022 outbreak of monkeypox inspiring a new conversation about how old viruses can become a global threat when they start to spread via sexual contact.[2] The U.S. Centers for Disease Control and Prevention (CDC) estimates that there were 26 million new STIs in 2018, and those of ages fifteen to twenty-four account for about half of all new STIs.[3] These infections range from curable to treatable (but incurable) to potentially fatal. So statistically speaking, those of us who are infected are the norm, but most of us have felt deviant or socially stigmatized for having an infection that spreads through sexual contact. STI stigma and overall lack of education about sexual health in the United States often result in psychological and social experiences that affect our relationships.

Medically incurable, or chronic, infections make up a significant portion of the STI epidemic in the United States. The CDC identifies HPV as the most common STI: with 13 million new infections per year and a prevalence of 42.5 million, most sexually active Americans are likely to contract HPV during their lifetimes.[4] The American Sexual Health Association (ASHA) estimates that more than half of American adults have been infected with HSV, though up to 90 percent may not have a diagnosis: at least 50 percent have oral infections and 12 percent have genital infections because herpes simplex virus type 1 and type 2 can be transmitted by skin-to-skin contact of mucous membrane tissue.[5] High incidence rates result from these viruses having the ability to remain asymptomatic for long periods of time and a lack of health education campaigns to inform the sexually active public about the risk of skin-to-skin transmission: risks are reduced—but not eliminated—by the correct and consistent use of "safer" sex barrier methods such as condoms and dental dams. In addition, there are no definitive tests for oral or genital HPV or HSV infections,[6] and public understanding of both have been distorted by popular euphemisms (for example, 'cold sores" rather than "herpes lesions," and "abnormal Pap smear" rather than "cervical HPV infection"), myths about risks of transmission such as believing you're contagious only if you see a herpes sore or genital wart, myths about modes of transmission (both HSV and HPV can be transmitted via kissing), and purposefully misleading marketing of HPV vaccines (more on this later).

Sexually transmitted HSV and HPV infections, while medically treatable, often have lasting health consequences. Therefore, these STIs have greater likelihoods of long-term effects on the sexual aspects of STI-positive[7] individuals' lives: on their approaches to and experiences of (1) intimate relationships, (2) reproductive plans, and (3) parenting. However, these effects are not necessarily negative. As medical sociologist Arthur Frank noted, "Illness takes away parts of your life, but in doing so, it gives you the opportunity to choose the life you will lead, as opposed to living out the one you have simply accumulated over the years."[8]

When other scholars[9] and I[10] have interviewed and surveyed people about STIs, our many studies confirm that gendered double standards of sexual morality serve to stigmatize infected women more than infected men and also that

STI stigma negatively influences individuals' sexual selves,[11] often resulting in social-psychological damage and serving as a barrier to testing, contact tracing, and treatment.[12] In this chapter, I draw on a multidisciplinary body of scholarship focused on STIs, as well as on formal, in-depth interviews I conducted with over fifty men and women living with genital HSV or genital HPV infections. I also reflect on additional informal, unstructured interviews I have had with over one hundred HSV- and HPV-infected adults. I found that formal and informal sex education had taught both men and women to see these infections as "symbols of impurity, antithetical to feminine ideals."[13] In sum, a *good* man can be infected, but any STI-positive woman is assumed to be *bad*. Not surprisingly, all but one of the women from the in-depth interview study experienced their STI diagnoses as highly stigmatizing to their moral characters, denigrating their social statuses and also making them feel negatively about their sexual body parts such as genitals. By contrast, only about half of the men described their STI as being more than mildly stigmatizing.

STIs were experienced differently by my interviewees, depending not only on their sex and gender but also on their age/generation, racial/ethnic identity, socioeconomic status, sexual orientation, and religious background. Individuals' sex lives are more accurately understood when examined within relevant socio-historical contexts. For example, Americans born before 1946 came of age during a time of sexual silence—strong taboos against talking about sexual health. Then, baby boomers, born between 1946 and 1964, mostly grew up when herpes was a growing threat but before HIV and HPV were widely discussed. Though pop culture narratives of the late 1960s and 1970s, when many boomers were teenagers, described "free love" clashing with traditional values, the advent of accessible and effective birth control better explains why many chose not to use condoms. In contrast, Gen X, born between 1965 and 1980, came of age during the highly publicized and publicly tragic early years of the HIV/AIDS pandemic. Condoms regained popularity, though mainstream America was slow to rally behind preventing a disease that had been wrongly stereotyped as a gay man's issue and instead remained focused on teen pregnancy as the top sexual risk.

More recently, most of Gen Y (also called millennials), born between 1981 and around 1995, completed high school when U.S. federal funding supported abstinence-until-marriage (rather than comprehensive) sex education, leaving them undereducated about STIs. The most recent cohort to come of age is Gen Z, born between the late 1990s and early 2010s. Going through puberty in the 2010s and 2020s, Gen Z has experienced inconsistent formal sex education—highly dependent on the political climate of the state in which they live and on whether they attended public or private schools. When it comes to informal sex education, the COVID-19 pandemic ensured internet access for most of

Gen Z. Online, they have been able to explore a diverse range of online information about sexual health, though many do not know how to assess the medical accuracy of what they find on websites and what they learn from social media influencers.

While specific socio-historical contexts vary, overall, STI-positive individuals across generations consistently note the ways in which stigma management becomes key to sex-related interactions (with potential or current sexual partners, family, and friends). Similar to sociologists Rutter and Schwartz,[14] I argue that these interactions are socially constructed in relation to sexual norms and stereotypes, often reflecting cisgender and heterosexist social scripts about sexual health.

STI DISCLOSURES AND INTIMATE RELATIONSHIPS: HAVING "THE TALK" (PART I)

Just because you have tested positive for a STI doesn't mean you stop wanting to find love, desiring sex, and craving intimacy. It does, however, mean that you likely have new concerns, worries, or even fears. Medically, psychologically and socially, STIs have the potential to alter the way individuals imagine sexual scenarios at the cultural level and how they experience sexual interactions at both the interpersonal and intrapersonal levels. Those I interviewed represented a variety of relationship statuses. When it comes to dating, their experiences reflect a spectrum of experiences throughout the different stages in seeking STI "positively" great sexual relationships.

Because skin-to-skin contact is a relatively easy mode of transmission for both HSV and HPV, many STI-positive individuals believe it is ethical to tell others about their STI statuses before they put those others at risk for contracting their infections. Research on individuals living with stigmatizing illnesses confirms that they often worry about what "others think of them and 'their kind' and about how these others might react to disclosure."[15] Given the negative connotations of STI infection—promiscuity, immorality, "dirtiness," irresponsibility—they understandingly worry: *How will this person view me once they know about my STI status?*

Many STI-positive individuals feel relief from cathartic disclosure.[16] Unfortunately, sometimes these disclosures may be received poorly: Dismissive reactions range from a potential romantic partner opting to "remain friends," to ending the relationship altogether, to clear rejection (verbal or physical expressions of disgust and condemnation). The COVID-19 pandemic inspired many to try virtual/Zoom dating and, in theory, created a new space in which to build trust and rapport with a potential new sexual partner before the physical intimacy that comes with dating "in real life." It will be interesting to see if "e-disclosures" become the norm, even now that in-person dating has resumed.

As a sexual health educator, I have advised STI-positive people to view their disclosures as a sort of "litmus test": if a person rejects you, then they were not "the one." Some people may at first be surprised, confused, or somewhat distressed to find out about your STI. But a good partner will be open to (1) learning more about your medical condition, (2) getting themselves tested for STIs/HIV (and being open about their own STI status), and (3) learning how to practice safer sex in ways that allow you to experience physical intimacy and to give and receive sexual pleasure. My hope is that the pandemic's normalization of seeking testing and then disclosing one's COVID-19 status will reset the ways in which we manage our relationships when one person contracts a contagious infection.

STI "Positively" Great Sex

In the best cases, STI disclosure and safer-sex negotiations lead to (potentially uncomfortable) dialogues that open channels of communication about topics beyond sexual health: building trust, respect, and strengthening nonsexual intimacy. When you enter into an intimate relationship with a partner who is interested in understanding your health, you'll both likely want to find out more about the practical and sensual aspects of safer sex. If only one of you is infected, or if you are each infected with different STIs, then the first question is usually one of prevention: How do you have a sexual relationship without putting your partner or yourself at risk? With HPV and HSV, you have to reconcile the odds of your chosen treatment options' effectiveness with the types of sexual contact you wish to have with each other. STI vaccines, including those for HPV[17] and hepatitis B,[18] have been found to substantially reduce risk.

Sexual health educators talk about ways to practice safer sex, acknowledging the limitations of sexual health techniques as well as human error that can reduce the effectiveness of attempts to prevent STI transmission, HIV transmission, and unintended pregnancy. We're now living and loving in an age where research has found that chronic and sometimes fatal STIs are being transmitted via kissing, including HPV-related oral/throat cancers that result in thousands of deaths each year in the United States. "Open-mouth" kissing is a documented—though likely rare—mode of transmitting potentially cancer-causing types of HPV.[19]

Given what we know about transmission routes for HPV and HSV, clothes-on hugging and holding hands are very safe expressions of physical affection. Non-mouth kissing (kissing of earlobes, necks, backs, etc.) is also low risk, as is manual-genital stimulation, or "hand jobs." Still among low-risk behaviors is safer oral sex (entailing the use of barriers, such as condoms on a male receiving partner and dental dams on a female receiving partner) because the partner giving the oral stimulation can hopefully avoid any mouth-to-skin contact around the edges of the protective barrier. Higher-risk-level behaviors include oral-vaginal and oral-anal sex with the use of condoms: the risk increases because not all skin-to-skin contact can be eliminated during penetrative sex (risk depends on exact location of infection and whether the barrier device completely covers that area). Then, the highest-risk behaviors include kissing, unprotected oral sex, unprotected penile-vaginal sex, and unprotected penile-anal sex. With any of these behaviors, healthy immune systems and appropriate medical treatment(s) can reduce the likelihood of transmission. In addition, the particular risk is shaped by the presence or absence of viral shedding/infected cells in the areas of skin-to-skin contact. Even those who are well educated about STI transmission may make context-specific decisions, deciding they are comfortable taking lower to higher degrees of risk in order to enjoy different types of sexual contact with particular partners.

As a sexual health researcher and educator, I encourage people to (1) get tested for STIs (acknowledging that not all STIs have definitive tests), (2) disclose their STI status to any partner before engaging in behavior(s) that could put the partner as risk, (3) ask the partner to get tested and share their results, (4) educate yourself about the particular risks, (5) and then decide which risk(s) you are each willing to take to enjoy the types of sexual contact that you desire. COVID-19 and monkeypox have further raised awareness that kissing and close physical/nonsexual contact comes with risks, so it will be interesting to see how growing awareness of infectious viruses shapes how we approach safer sex in the late 2020s.

Recent CDC publications illustrate how global health emergencies are changing today's public health education campaigns about sexually transmitted viral infections. The CDC directed readers wondering about "sex and COVID-19" to an August 2020 publication from the National Coalition of STD Directors, which explicitly advises to "avoid kissing; wear a face mask . . . and ask your partner to do the same; always use condoms to reduce your contact with saliva, semen and feces during anal and oral sex"[20] as ways to practice safer sex during the COVID-19 pandemic. Then, in July 2022, the CDC published "Social Gatherings, Safer Sex and Monkeypox,"[21] which actually recommended partners "have virtual sex with no in-person contact" or "masturbate together at a distance of at least 6 feet, without touching each other" in addition to avoiding kissing and avoiding touching your own rash to avoid spreading it to other parts of your own body. As education and conversations about safer sex become integrated into daily news and social media posts, we may finally see a significant reduction in STI stigma.

Single, Again?

Whether it's the end of a long-term committed relationship or the death of a partner, many find themselves back in the dating pool at a later stage of life, not sure if the "old" rules still apply. Often apprehensive, adults who find themselves dating and having new sexual partners after a long stretch of being "off the market" can benefit from education that emphasizes not only how to prevent contracting a STI but also how to live and love after becoming STI positive. In recent years, better sources of sexual relationship advice have become available for older people.[22] Over time, sexual health education that serves to destigmatize STIs and HIV will inform new generations on how to better navigate sexual relationships at any age.

Reproduction

As chronic viral infections, HSV and HPV tend to become more symptomatic in individuals with compromised/weakened immune systems, such as those who are pregnant. In my interviews and conversations, all who hoped for future pregnancies also had concerns about their STIs being transmitted to their newborns. In the case of herpes, medical experts agree that neonatal herpes transmission is rare but potentially fatal:

> If a woman with genital herpes has virus present in the birth canal during delivery, herpes simplex virus (HSV) can be spread to an infant, causing neonatal herpes, a serious and sometimes fatal condition. . . . Babies are most at risk for neonatal herpes if the mother contracts genital herpes late in pregnancy. . . . Herpes can also be spread to the baby in the first weeks of life if he or she is kissed by someone with an active cold sore (oral herpes). In rare instances, herpes may be spread by touch, if someone touches an active cold sore and then immediately touches the baby.[23]

With genital HPV infections, the concerns are somewhat different. In cases of HPV 6 and HPV 11, the two types causally linked to about 90 percent of genital warts cases,

> neonatal transmission can occur in the absence of clinically evident lesions. HPV 6 or 11 may lead to Juvenile Onset Recurrent Respiratory Papillomatosis (JORRP). TCA, liquid nitrogen, laser ablation or electrocautery can be used to treat external

genital HPV lesions at any time during pregnancy. Caesarean section is recommended only if the lesions are obstructing the birth canal.[24]

For the types of HPV that cause cervical HPV infections (including those that
progress to cervical cancer), several of the medical treatments can cause scar-
ring and other types of damage to the cervix that some researchers have linked
to fertility problems and preterm delivery.[25] Primarily on the basis of this evidence, medical practitioners have become more hesitant to recommend medical
treatments for women who hope to become pregnant and have mild to moderate *cervical dysplasia* (abnormal/precancerous cellular changes), in hopes that
their immune systems will naturally resolve the HPV infection. However, a 2012
study found that "no clear evidence emerged of adverse effects resulting from the
[cervical dysplasia] treatment itself," and the researchers "did not discover any
reduced incidence of pregnancy or livebirths both after treatment for [cervical
dysplasia]."[26]

Finding an obstetrician or a midwife with expertise in genital herpes or HPV
can reduce risks of transmission, and they can discuss the potential benefits of
having a Caesarean section if the woman has an active outbreak at the time of
delivery. For example, I interviewed a woman living with both genital herpes
and genital HPV infections who planned ahead to holistically strengthen her
immune system[27] before becoming pregnant. She "really wanted to have a vaginal birth," so she interviewed different OB-GYNs and was happy to find one who
would support her with additional checkups to detect any outbreaks: she was able
to have an outbreak-free pregnancy and deliver a healthy baby vaginally without
any complications.

PARENTING: HAVING "THE TALK" (PART II)

Having "the talk" with kids used to mean telling them about how babies are
made. In a world where STIs can be spread via kissing, I join many sexual
health researchers in recommending that sex education focus more on defining
abstinence to specify abstaining not only from behaviors that can result in
pregnancy but also from behaviors that can transmit a STI.

In addition to talking about which partnered sexual behaviors may be safer
than others, today's parents face new challenges. For instance, if you're one of
the millions of STI-positive parents, if/when/how do you disclose your own STI
status to your children? To date, research on parental disclosure has not been
done on parents living with HPV and HSV infections. But questions like this
are starting to arise in pediatricians' offices, where it is becoming more common

for parents to be asked if they want their child to be vaccinated against HPV. It's interesting to note that HPV vaccination of tweens/teens was initially plagued by similar misinformation campaigns about vaccine risks that slowed U.S. uptake of COVID-19 vaccines for children.

From about 2006 to 2009, U.S. ads promoted a "cervical cancer" vaccine. While it was initially FDA approved and CDC recommended only for girls and women (ages nine to twenty-six), many of us HPV researchers knew that you didn't need a cervix to benefit from Merck's vaccine, trademarked as Gardasil. It also works for males. The original vaccine was designed to protect against four types of HPV: types 16 and 18 (estimated to cause about 70 percent of cervical cancers) and types 6 and 11 (estimated to cause about 90 percent of genital warts).[28] Then, the FDA approved Gardasil 9 in 2014, which expanded protection to a total of nine types of HPV.

Several health organizations were concerned that the American public's acceptance of the vaccine would depend on whether it was viewed as a cancer vaccine or as an STI vaccine. Given the strong, negative STI stigma specifically directed at girls and women, it wasn't surprising that their concerns became reality: Initial press coverage of the vaccine trials inspired protests from some conservative organizations. For example, the conservative Family Research Council (FRC) equated it to a "license" for young people to have premarital sex. However, recent research has concluded that there is no association between HPV vaccination and increases in sexual activity among vaccinated girls.[29]

About three years after seeking FDA approval for use in girls and women, Merck sought approval for Gardasil in boys and men (ages nine to twenty-six), meaning Gardasil could no longer be exclusively marketed as a cervical cancer vaccine. Initially approved only for prevention of genital warts in boys and men, FDA approval and CDC recommendations have increased as information has mounted: In addition to causing cervical cancer, HPV 16 and HPV 18 can also cause penile, anal, and oral cancers—all of which affect boys and men. In fact, the 2021 U.S. Cancer Statistics Data Brief showed that, by 2018, HPV was causing more oropharyngeal (throat) cancers than cervical cancers in the United States.[30] With low public awareness of the risks, types, and severities of HPV-related cancers, U.S. acceptance of HPV vaccination remains fairly low: "The percentage of adolescents who were up to date with HPV vaccination increased from 54.2 percent in 2019 to 58.6 percent in 2020."[31] With regard to the ongoing development of HSV vaccines, the mRNA technology that has rapidly developed during the COVID-19 pandemic may lead to new HSV vaccine candidates.[32] Researchers of infectious pediatric diseases have noted, "Once an efficacious herpes vaccine is available, its effectiveness will depend ultimately on vaccine acceptance by professional organizations, healthcare professionals, and parents."[33]

Conclusion

Sexual attitudes and behaviors are shaped by our experiences—both the advantageous and disadvantageous ones—that accumulate over time. And those experiences reflect the contexts of relationships with partners—past, current, and future—and with family members, including children, whose STI-positive parents may question how much is too much to share. Many of those I have spoken with have come to view their STI as a catalyst for positive change in sexual health attitudes as well as behaviors. When an STI diagnosis comes with inclusive and accurate health education as well as social-psychological support, then patients are more likely to learn new techniques for safer sex and also to employ more effective sexual negotiation skills. Though a medical cure for HSV and HPV remains a hope for the future, the lessons we're learning from COVID-19 and monkeypox signal that now is the time to correct our social values and norms so that all STIs are destigmatized. By doing so, we can free millions of infected adults and adolescents from unwarranted guilt, shame, and self-loathing.

Notes

1. See my 2008 book, *Damaged Goods*, for more details.
2. See CDC (2022).
3. See CDC (2021d).
4. See CDC (2021d).
5. See American Sexual Health Association (n.d.).
6. "CDC does not recommend herpes testing for people without symptoms in most situations. This is because of the limits of a herpes blood test and the possibility of a wrong test result. The chances of wrong test results are higher for people who are at low risk of infection" (see CDC 2013a). "No HPV test for men has been approved by the FDA, nor has any test been approved for detection of the virus in areas other than the cervix" (see Vives et al. 2020).
7. In this chapter, I use the shorthand term *STI positive* to refer to someone who has been diagnosed with an oral or genital infection of HSV or HPV.
8. See Frank (1991, p. 1).
9. For example, see East et al. (2010).
10. See Nack (2002, 2008).
11. See Nack (2000).
12. For example, see Lichtenstein (2003) and Melville et al. (2003).
13. See Nack (2002, p. 463).
14. See Rutter and Schwartz (2011).

15. See Schneider and Conrad (1981, p. 35).
16. See Adler and Adler (2006).
17. See CDC (2021b).
18. See WHO (2022).
19. See D'Souza et al. (2009) and Kreimer (2009).
20. See CDC (2020).
21. See CDC (2022).
22. For example, see Schwartz (2008).
23. See American Sexual Health Association (n.d.).
24. See Singhal, Naswa, and Marfatia (2009, p. 71).
25. For examples, see Kyrgiou et al. (2006), Albrechsten et al. (2008), and Jakobsson et al. (2009).
26. See Bednarczyk et al. (2012).
27. While there are three FDA-approved antiviral medications for treating genital herpes, many medical experts do not consider these to be safe during pregnancy. Many individuals successfully manage outbreaks of herpes and HPV via immune-boosting behaviors, for example, "effective stress management and getting adequate rest, nutrition, and exercise" (see American Sexual Health Association 2022).
28. See National Cancer Institute (2013).
29. See Brouwer et al. (2019).
30. See CDC (2021a).
31. See CDC (2021c).
32. See Awasthi and Friedman (2022).
33. See Rupp et al. (2005).

18

Orgasm in College Hookups and Relationships

Elizabeth A. Armstrong, Paula England, and Alison Ash

I s the sex in college hookups good? How does hookup sex compare with relationship sex? How often do men and women have orgasms in hookups and in relationships? Is the sex in some situations good for men but not so good for women, or the other way around?

We describe college student sexual experiences in hookups and relationships, with a focus on gender differences. We define hookups as sexual events that occur outside of an exclusive relationship, often without a prearranged date, involving varying degrees of interest in a relationship. Hookups sometimes involve just making out, or they may involve oral sex or intercourse.[1]

This report uses data from an online survey of 12,925 undergraduates at seventeen universities and qualitative in-depth interviews at two universities. Students taking the online survey were asked fixed-response questions about their experiences with hooking up, dating, and relationships.[2] We share statistics from survey responses from students at the seventeen universities between 2005 and 2008. Quotations in the paper are from approximately fifty in-depth qualitative interviews conducted at Stanford University and Indiana University between 2006 and 2008. In this article, we discuss only heterosexual sex and relationships. If you are interested in the experiences of queer women in the hookup scene, you can read one of our other articles.[3]

While most students hook up, few know what others are doing in their hookups. Thus, we begin with an overview of college student sexual behavior to provide background for a closer investigation of sexual pleasure in hookups and relationships. Using orgasm as an indicator of good sex, we then describe how rates of orgasm differ for men and women in hookups and relationships. We find a gender gap in orgasm across both hookups and relationships, with men experiencing more orgasm in both. This gender gap is not constant, however. It is largest in first hookups, smaller in repeat hookups with the same person, and the smallest in relationships. A big question we studied is, how does sexual reciprocity—and how it varies—contribute to the orgasm gap for different groups? To foreshadow some of our findings, women are more likely to receive oral sex in relationships than in hookups, and this is associated with women reaching orgasm. These findings suggest that both women and men have absorbed a notion that women are entitled to sexual pleasure in relationships. Women and men are, however, more ambivalent about the importance of women's sexual pleasure outside of relationships. This ambivalence, supported by a stubborn double standard that stigmatizes women who have sex outside of relationships, lets men off the hook in terms of responsibility for sexually pleasuring hookup partners and makes it more difficult for women to actively pursue sexual satisfaction in hookups.

These empirical findings inform debates about the rise of hookup culture. Sexual conservatives often argue that hooking up is damaging, particularly for women—counseling that it is better to limit sex to serious relationships (and in extreme versions of the argument, to marriage).[4] They see changes in gender and sexuality as having gone too far, and they advocate a return to more traditional arrangements. Their position is expressed in the "Take Back the Date" movement.[5] Like sexual conservatives, a number of feminist sociologists and activists have focused on the negative aspects of sexual culture on campus—particularly on sexual assault and sexual harassment.[6] In contrast to sexual conservatives, though, feminists tend to see gender and sexual change as having not gone far enough. This position is expressed in the annual "Take Back the Night" marches organized on many campuses in protest of sexual violence. Our focus on sexual pleasure—and our finding that college women enjoy sex, albeit not as much as men, and not equally in all contexts—leads us to see the situation as less dire than these two groups. Most college students—both men and women—see women as entitled to sexual pleasure in relationships and the reciprocity required to achieve it. This is a meaningful change from prior generations where women were seen as entitled to sexual pleasure only within marriage.[7] That these norms of reciprocity and entitlement to pleasure have not fully diffused beyond relationships leads us to sympathize with both the conservative distaste for hookups—after all, sex is better in relationships, particularly for women—and with the feminist insistence on tackling sexual double standards. Hookup sex is not usually great for women. It could be a lot better. Further extension of egalitarian norms and practices would improve women's experience of hookup sex.

Sexual Activity in Hookups and Relationships

Seventy-four percent of respondents—both men and women—reported at least one hookup by their senior year in college. Of these, 40 percent had hooked up three times or less, 40 percent had hooked up between four and nine times, and 20 percent had hooked up ten or more times.

In addition to asking students about how many hookups they had overall, we also asked them for details about their most recent hookup, including a question on the number of times the student had previously hooked up with this same partner. From these questions, we learned that multiple hookups with the same person were common. About half of the hookups reported were first hookups with that partner. Eighteen percent were cases where the student had hooked up with this same person once or twice before, and in 33 percent of the cases the couple had hooked up at least three times before. Sixteen percent of these hookups involved someone the student had hooked up with ten or more times. The media often refer to higher-order hookups as "friends with benefits" or "fuck buddies."[8] Students know and occasionally use these terms, but they are more likely to refer to them as "repeat," "regular," or "continuing" hookups, or to not label them at all.[9] When we report below on what happened in these different kinds of hookups, we'll use the term *repeat hookup* when the hookup was with someone the individual had hooked up with three or more times before.

The rise of hookups has not meant the demise of relationships among college students. By their senior year, 69 percent of heterosexual students reported that they had been in a relationship that lasted at least six months while they were in college.[10] In interviews, we learned that many more have had shorter relationships. Our interviewees told us that, to them, relationships involved sexual exclusivity, spending time together, and frequently a talk to clarify that they had become girlfriend-boyfriend.[11] While college students still form relationships, the rise of the hookup has changed how relationships begin. Traditional dating has been largely replaced by hookups as the main pathway to relationships.[12]

The online survey asked students who had hooked up while in college to tell us about what happened on their most recent hookup. Students who had been in a relationship were asked to report on the most recent time they did something more sexual than kissing in that relationship. We classify events into four contexts: first hookups, second or third hookups (one or two previous hookups), repeat hookups (three or more previous hookups), and relationships. Figure 18.1 shows what happened sexually in these different contexts, categorized by the behavior that entailed going farthest, as students generally view it. For example, if a couple had oral sex and intercourse, it is classified as an intercourse event. Students did

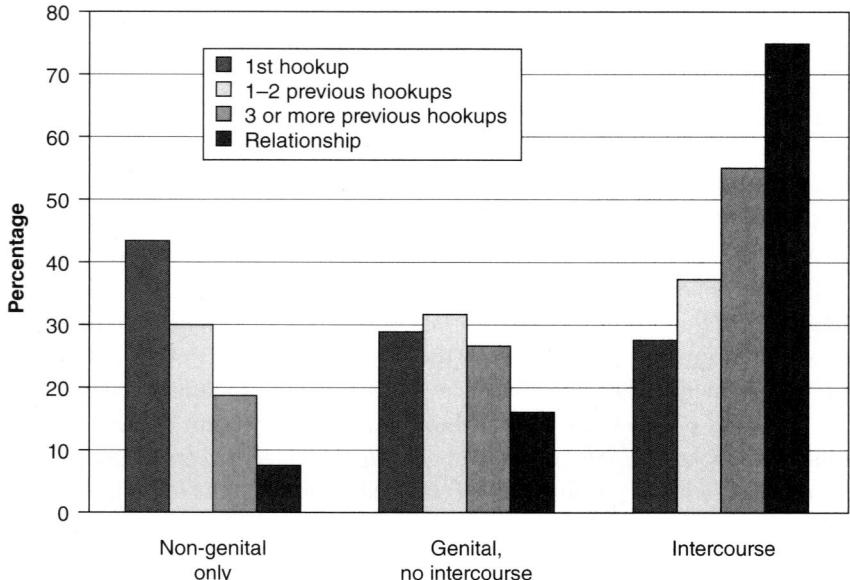

Figure 18.1 | Percentage Engaging in Various Sexual Behaviors* in Four Sexual Contexts

*Respondents are classified in "Non-genital only" if they did not engage in oral sex, hand-genital stimulation, or intercourse; in "Genital, no intercourse" if they did not engage in intercourse but engaged in oral sex or hand-genital stimulation (irrespective of who gave or who received it); in "Intercourse" if they had intercourse. Percentages for three behaviors within one context may not add up to 100 percent because of rounding error.

not go as far on first hookups as on higher-order hookups, and they went farther in relationships. In first hookups, 44 percent of students reported kissing and touching but no genital contact (stimulation of one partner's genitals with the other's hand, no oral sex, and no intercourse).[13] In contrast, the percentage that only had non-genital activity was 30 percent among those who had hooked up one or two times before, 19 percent in repeat hookups, and 7 percent of those in relationships. The percentage having intercourse was 27 percent on the first hookup, 37 percent when they had hooked up once or twice before, 54 percent in repeat hookups, and 76 percent of those in relationships.[14] In sum, most relationship events involve intercourse, while most hookups don't; but the more times people have hooked up before, the more likely they are to have intercourse.

We also asked students what sexual acts they had ever done. Eighty percent reported intercourse by senior year of college, so 20 percent graduated from college as virgins—a bit of information that some may find surprising. Of those who engaged in intercourse by their senior year, students reported a median of four partners and 67 percent reported having intercourse outside of a relationship.

WHO HAS ORGASMS IN HOOKUPS AND RELATIONSHIPS?

The survey asked students whether they had an orgasm in their most recent hookup and in their most recent relationship sexual event.[15] While orgasm is certainly not the only indicator of sexual pleasure, most who have experienced it find it to be extremely pleasurable.[16]

Figure 18.2 shows what percentage of men and women had an orgasm in first hookups, higher-order hookups, and relationship sexual events. Both men and women experience orgasm more in repeat hookups than with a new hookup partner, and relationship sex is most likely to lead to orgasm for both men and women. This is partly a function of the fact that couples go farther sexually the

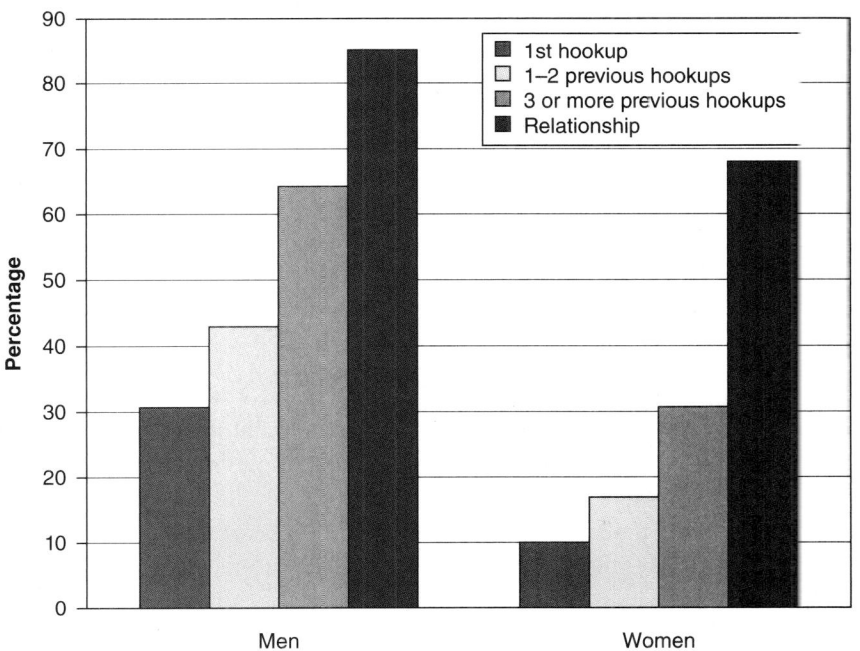

Figure 18.2 | Percentage of Men and Women Having an Orgasm in Four Sexual Contexts

more times they have hooked up, and they go the farthest in relationships. But this effect is not only driven by behavior. For both men and women, the same behaviors yield higher rates of orgasm in relationships than in hookups and in higher-order hookups than in first hookups. Sex in relationships tends to be better in part because, in any encounter, one has a greater incentive to treat one's partner well if a repeat is likely.[17] Also, good sex takes practice, as, over time, partners learn what turns each other on. The importance of partner-specific sexual skills was mentioned by numerous men and women in the qualitative interviews. For example, a man, when discussing why he believed women would be more likely to orgasm in relationships, explained, "Because a guy will already know how she likes it, where she likes it and how much she likes it." Similarly, a woman noted that in a relationship you are accustomed to communicating with your partner about everything, which means that "you're more open to talking about different things that you want out of the sex or if you want to experiment. You could explore more because you have knowledge about the other person. You trust the other person." Context matters for both men and women.

But, in an odd echo of the gender gap in pay, there is a gender gap in orgasm as well. This gap exists in all contexts, but it is less severe in repeat hookups than in first hookups and least severe in relationships. If we take the percentage of women having an orgasm as a ratio of the male percentage, the ratios are 0.32 for first hookups, 0.39 if they've hooked up one to two previous times with this person, 0.49 on repeat hookups with the same person, and 0.79 in relationships. Comparing the two extremes, this means that women orgasm only 32 percent as often as men in first hookups but 79 percent as often as men in relationships.

WHY IS SEXUAL PLEASURE MORE EQUAL IN RELATIONSHIPS THAN IN HOOKUPS?

Why is sexual pleasure more equal between men and women in relationships than in hookups, particularly first hookups? Some might find this a ridiculous question—viewing men's greater enjoyment of uncommitted sex as simply obvious. Others might explain this difference by applying evolutionary psychology—arguing that women need commitment to enjoy sex because of a "hard-wired" need to secure male resources for any offspring produced.[18] Some might argue that gender socialization leads women to be more relationally oriented than men, in sex as well as other arenas.[19] Others might argue that partner-specific experience matters more for women than for men because women's orgasm is more difficult to achieve. Still others might attribute the difference to a sexual double standard: women may feel guilty about casual sex and thus enjoy it less. These explanations are not mutually exclusive, but our data don't allow us to judge their relative merits. We can, however, demonstrate more immediate, proximate causes of some of the gap: behaviors especially conducive to female orgasm are more likely to occur in repeat hookups and relationships. Below we document variation in rates of cunnilingus and women's genital self-simulation across contexts and their role in boosting rates of orgasm.

WHAT MEN AND WOMEN GIVE: ORAL SEX IN HOOKUPS AND RELATIONSHIPS

Cunnilingus (a woman receiving oral sex) is more likely to produce a female orgasm than is fellatio (a man receiving oral sex). Additionally, many women need direct clitoral stimulation along with intercourse to reach orgasm. This point, sensationalized by *The Hite Report* in the 1970s, has since become well-documented in sex research.[20]

Cunnilingus, effective as it is for women's orgasm, is less well-represented in college students' sexual repertoires than fellatio. Figure 18.3 illustrates the percentage of men and women receiving oral sex in sexual events without intercourse. If only one person received oral sex, it was more likely to be the man. But this disparity was shown less in repeat hookups and least in relationships. Men received oral sex roughly 80 percent of the time in all contexts (combining when men alone received oral sex and when both men and women mutually received it), while women received it (combining when women alone received oral sex and when both men and women mutually received it) 46 percent of the time in first hookups, 55 percent in second or third hookups, 59 percent in repeat hookups, and 68 percent in relationships.[21] Men gave oral sex to their female partners more in repeat hookups and especially in relationships. Women gave oral sex to their male partners in all contexts at higher rates than women received it in any context.

What about when the couple had intercourse? Our survey showed that when they also had intercourse, men received oral sex in 77 percent of first hookups, 82 percent of second or third hookups, 88 percent of repeat hookups, and 91 percent of relationship events. Women, on the other hand, received oral sex between 60 percent and 68 percent of the time in hookups but in 84 percent of relationship events. And, sure enough, women's orgasm rates reflect the difference. In events that included intercourse and oral sex for the woman, she was generally more likely to report an orgasm than when intercourse was not combined with oral sex.[22] In repeat hookups with intercourse, women had an orgasm 40 percent of the time if there was no oral sex but 55 percent of the time when

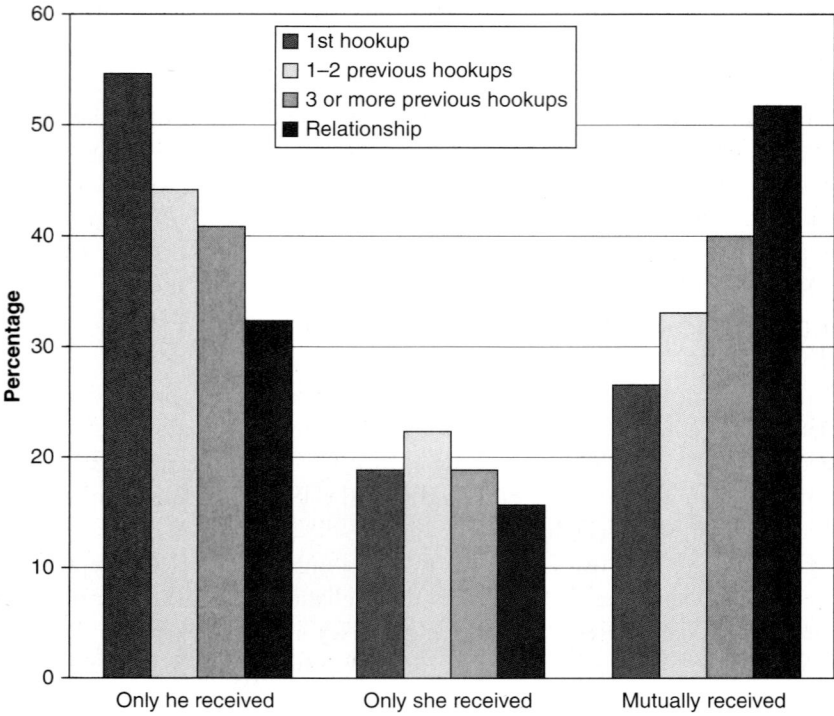

Figure 18.3 | Percentage of Men and Women Receiving Oral Sex in Events Where at Least One Received Oral Sex and Intercourse Did Not Occur, in Four Sexual Contexts

intercourse was accompanied by oral sex. In relationships, orgasms in women increased from 55 percent when there was intercourse but no oral sex to 80 percent when oral sex was combined with intercourse. Oral sex is important for some women to have orgasms, so the fact that women are much more likely to receive it in repeat hookups and relationships is part of why they have orgasms more often in those contexts.[23]

LET'S TALK ABOUT THE SEXUAL DOUBLE STANDARD

These findings suggest that women treat hookup partners with sexual generosity—often giving oral sex even in first hookups. Men, on the other hand, appear to be comparatively sexually selfish in hookups, particularly first hookups, and more sexually generous as they become more committed. This pattern is built into gendered sexual scripts: men feel entitled to fellatio on a first or second hookup and women feel obligated to provide it, while women do not similarly feel enti- tled to cunnilingus, nor do men feel obligated to give it.[24]

This brings us to a good news/bad news story about gender equality in sex. Our culture continues to have a double standard that judges women's and men's sexual practices differently. In the past, women were expected to be virgins before marriage, while men were not.[25] Women were evaluated negatively for premarital sex, and they were certainly not viewed as entitled to sexual satisfac- tion in premarital sexual relationships. Over the course of the past forty years or so, among most groups the stigma associated with premarital sex within relation- ships for women has almost entirely disappeared. The removal of this stigma has the added bonus of making it not just acceptable for women to have sex in premarital relationships but acceptable for women to enjoy it. Men and women agree that it is normal for women to expect sexual satisfaction in relationships, to ask for what they need to get it, and to be disappointed, and perhaps even end relationships, if they do not get it. Relationships have become defined as an appropriate space for unmarried women to express sexual desire and to engage in sexual exploration. Men and women also agree that it is expected that men in a relationship attend to a partner's sexual needs as well as their own. This is the good news, and it accounts for the greater reciprocity of oral sex in relationships as many men now care about women's pleasure in relationships.

The bad news is that sexual double standards have not disappeared. Instead, what we see now is a new double standard in which women who seek sexual plea- sure outside of committed relationships are judged more harshly than men who do. Men and women at both universities told us that women perceived as hook- ing up too much, or going too far on hookups, are called "sluts" by both men and women.[26] Along with ambivalence about women's participation in sex outside of relationships comes ambivalence about women's pleasure in these contexts. The survival of a sexual double standard may be an important reason why men tend to treat hookup and relationship partners differently—in short, some men think that it is acceptable to be sexually selfish with hookup partners, especially first-time partners. Men's lack of respect for women who will have sex outside of a relationship seems to translate into a sense that hookup partners are not owed the same level of sexual reciprocity as girlfriends—both in terms of what sex acts are engaged in (for example, giving her oral sex) and in the care and attention to her sexual pleasure.

In interviews, men were upfront about expressing different levels of concern for hookup and relationship partners. For example, one man explained that with his girlfriend, "definitely oral is really important [for her to orgasm], you can do it for pretty much as long as needed." He then said that in a hookup, "I don't give a shit." Another noted, "I mean like if you're just like hooking up with someone, I guess it's more of a selfish thing." A third man explained:

> Now that I'm in a relationship, I think [her orgasm is] actually pretty important. More important than [in a] hookup. Because you have more invested in that person. You know, when you have sex, it's more a reciprocal thing. When it's a hookup you feel less investment. You still want [her to orgasm] in that, sort of, "I'm a guy who's the greatest lover in the world and I want to, you should orgasm."

This man suggested that his interest in a hookup partner having an orgasm was primarily selfish, as her pleasure reflected on his sexual performance and sense of masculinity. A number of others noted that in hookups, her orgasm just did not matter. In contrast, men's comments revealed universal endorsement of the notion of women's entitlement to sexual pleasure in relationships. For example, one man explained, with pride,

> [In my relationship] she comes every time and that's because I know what she likes and I make sure she does. And if I have to go down on her for a longer period of time, I'll do that. I've a pretty good idea of what she likes and it's been partly through trial and error, partly through explicit instruction. She definitely likes for me to go down on her and usually it goes both ways before we have sex.

This passage suggests—and this is reflected throughout the interviews—that college men understand the importance of oral sex to women's orgasm.

Some women complained about the lack of mutuality in oral sex, particularly in early hookups. One woman said, "When I . . . meet somebody and I'm gonna have a random hookup . . . from what I have seen, they're not even trying to, you know, make it a mutual thing." Another complained, "He did that thing where . . . they put their hand on the top of your head . . . and I hate that! . . . Especially 'cause there was no effort made to, like, return that favor."

A third woman complained of a recent encounter,

> I just was with some stupid guy at a frat party and we were in his room and I gave head. And I was kind of waiting and he fell asleep. And I was like, "Fuck this," and I just left. It's degrading.

This woman did not consider hooking up to be degrading. What she felt was degrading was the one-sided nature of the encounter. Some women reported learning to turn the tables. For example, one assertive woman said,

In my first relationship . . . it was very one way . . . and that just didn't do much for me in terms of making me feel good about myself . . . so . . . I hate it when a guy is like take your head and try and push it down, because I then just switch it around to make them go down first usually. And some guys say no and then I just say no if they say no.

Women provided descriptions of sexually attentive boyfriends, confirming men's self-reports. For example, in describing her boyfriend, one woman told us,

I know that he wants to make me happy. I know that he wants me to orgasm. I know that, and like just me knowing that we are connected and like we're going for the same thing and that like he cares.

In general, students reported that their relationships were characterized by much greater mutuality than their hookups.[27]

WOMEN'S AGENCY: GENITAL SELF-STIMULATION AND ENTITLEMENT TO PLEASURE

It is not just men whose sexual practices may be affected by the new version of the sexual double standard. The double standard may also lead women to feel ambivalent about enjoying hookup sex or not entitled to pleasure within it. While we typically think of the double standard as involving how men and women are differently judged for participating in sex, double standards also often involve gendered notions about appropriate degrees of enthusiasm, pleasure, or initiative. In interviews with adolescent girls, Deborah Tolman found that the expectation that it is girls' job to play the role of the "gatekeeper" interfered with girls' experience of bodily desire because they had to monitor and suppress their own physical responses in order to keep the sexual activity from going "too far."[28]

We found both quantitative and qualitative evidence that women feel less entitled to pleasure in hookup contexts than in relationships. In the survey data, the practice of women stimulating their own genitals with a hand as part of partnered sex, much as one would in masturbation, proved to be particularly interesting. Engaging in this practice clearly shows one's interest in one's own pleasure and reveals to a sex partner one's familiarity and competence with masturbatory technique. We asked students if they had done this and learned that only 4 percent of women did this in a first hookup, 6 percent in second or third hookups, 10 percent in a repeat hookup, and 24 percent in a relationship. Examining only events where the partners had intercourse, it was also true that women were least likely to self-stimulate in first hookups and most likely in relationships. Like oral sex, self-stimulation helps women to orgasm. We found that among women having intercourse and receiving oral sex, there was still a big boost to orgasm from the addition of self-stimulation. In first hookups, 37 percent of women had orgasms without any self-stimulation; with it, it was 63 percent. For those in relationships, the difference was 80 percent versus 92 percent (see Figure 18.4). In every context, the addition of self-stimulation made a difference to orgasm. But women were more likely to feel comfortable enough to self-stimulate in repeat hookups, and most likely in relationships. Women's reticence about self-stimulation in hookups is another part of the reason that women orgasm less in these contexts.

Evidence that women feel more entitled to sexual pleasure in relationships was also present in interviews. This attitude was reflected in general discussions of rights and obligations. For example, one woman explained that, for her, "being

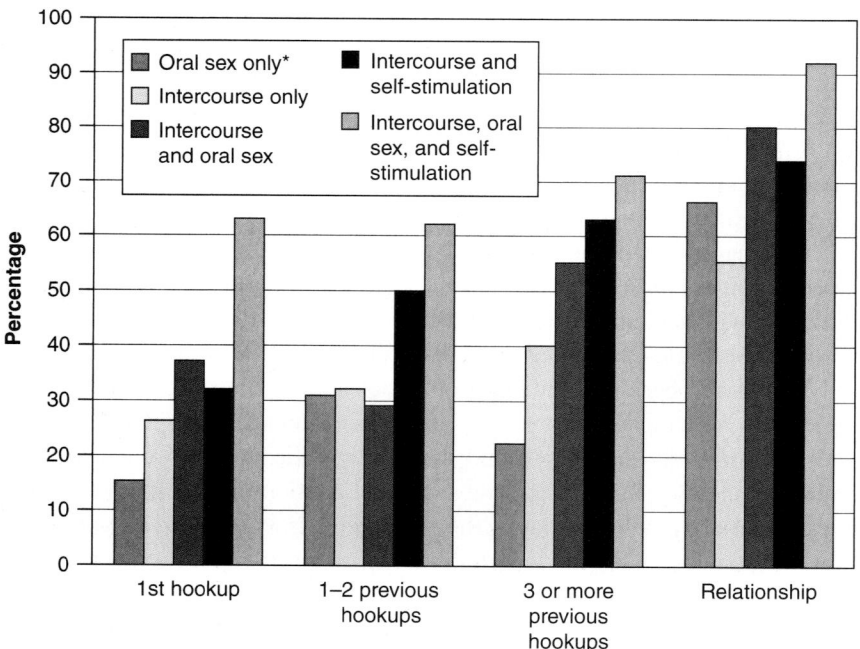

Figure 18.4 | Percentage of Women Having an Orgasm in Four Sexual Contexts, by Occurrence of Selected Sexual Behaviors

*Oral sex refers to receiving of oral sex.

able to communicate" about what she wanted and needed was important for good sex. But, she added,

> I feel like when it's just a hookup, I just feel like I almost like don't have the right. Or not that I don't have the right but it's just not comfortable enough to be like, "You know, hey, this isn't doing [it] for me."

In contrast, a number of women stated their sense of entitlement to good sex within a relationship:

> I think that I'm assertive enough of a person to know what it takes for me to orgasm and like be able to communicate that. I probably would try to work it out, try to give him more practice, more lessons, before I would ultimately break off the relationship. But I'm gonna say this very hesitatingly, I probably would end the relationship after having tried many, many things to fix it so that it's sexually pleasurable.

While she was willing to work hard with a boyfriend to improve sex to make sure she had orgasms, she viewed lack of success in this department as grounds to end the relationship. This sense of entitlement to sexual satisfaction was less evident in women's discussions of hookup sex—although there was variation on this issue. A number of women noted that they had gotten better over time about insisting on getting their needs met in hookups.

One woman, implicitly contrasting relationships with hookups, pointed to the more egalitarian nature of relationship sex:

> I think also just because in a relationship, there's much more expected as far as like equality wise, like give and take sexually. If you're gonna be in a relationship, it's expected, like more equality. . . . You can explore more, be more fun and goofy and stuff like that, which I think is always fun too.

Her reference to exploring in a relationship hints at the way that relationships, by creating a zone in which sex is viewed as acceptable for women, give women license to relax (be "goofy") and experiment. One woman noted that she could imagine the conditions for good sex to be present outside of a relationship:

> But for me, I feel that to have good sex there's a few qualities that need to be present. Like the desirability and that confidence in being able to ask for what you want or what you don't want. And if you can find that outside of a relationship, I think that's good. But I feel that [it] would be a lot more difficult to find those qualities with someone that you're not in a relationship with.

And some women did find the conditions necessary for good sex outside of relationships. The more times couples hooked up, the greater the degree of comfort and familiarity, and, consequently, the higher the rates of orgasm.

It is important, however, to emphasize that differences in rates of orgasm in hookups and relationships are not driven solely by the behaviors we were able to measure, such as whether the woman received oral sex or engaged in self-stimulation. We suspect that a sense of entitlement led to other behavioral changes by women in repeat hookups and relationships that our survey didn't measure—such as initiating changes in position. But as Figure 18.4 shows, at every level of sexual activity, relationship sex yields orgasm for women at higher rates than hookup sex (and repeat hookups at higher rates than first hookups). This pattern is true for men as well as for women, although both context and behavior seem to matter more for women than for men. Women's rates of orgasm become nearly universal and almost converge with men's (92 percent compared with men's 96 percent) only in one situation: in relationships when couples engaged in intercourse and the women received oral sex and engaged in self-stimulation. This convergence suggests that a gender gap in orgasm is not inevitable, but it is largely a consequence of the *social organization of sexuality.*

Overall, our findings suggest that women's orgasm is strongly affected by how comfortable women are seeking their own sexual pleasure, how motivated men are to provide stimulation of the sort that a particular woman finds pleasurable, and the extent to which either partner engages in behaviors that provide plentiful clitoral stimulation for women. We strongly suspect that the sexual double standard is an important factor behind why women feel less entitled to sexual pleasure in hookups. The sexual double standard also permits men not to care about their partner's pleasure in hookups. Women would orgasm more in hookups if their sexual satisfaction were considered as important as that of their male partners.[29]

CONCLUSION: THE SOCIAL ORGANIZATION OF SEXUALITY

If you want to understand what we mean by *the social organization of sexuality,* you need look no further than the story of the gender gap in orgasms. As measured by orgasm, relationship sex is better than hookup sex for both men and women, but especially for women. Similarly, sex is better in repeat hookups than in first hookups, particularly for women. The gender gap in orgasm is the lowest in relationships, in part because men are more likely to engage in cunnilingus—a practice strongly associated with women's orgasm—in relationships than in hookups. In contrast, women engage in fellatio at high rates across all contexts.

The skewed nature of sexual reciprocity is in part a consequence of a new version of the old sexual double standard. In relationships, today's norms support women's right to sexual pleasure, whereas in hookups, especially first hookups the double standard means that the man does not feel obligated to provide oral sex or to ensure his partner's sexual satisfaction. Women's behavior varies across these contexts too. In early hookups, women may feel they have to focus on limiting how far things go because of concerns about negative judgments if they go too far. Many don't feel comfortable enough to focus on their own pleasure through self-stimulation of their genitals, or to communicate what they want. In relationships, women are freer of the effects of the double standard, and this decreases the orgasm gap between men and women.

Curious readers can look even further into the social organization of sexuality: others who study this topic find similar patterns. Researchers continue to ponder the gender gap in orgasm, and a 2022 interview and survey study, for example, found that both men and women engaged in "gender labor" to justify the persistent gender gap in orgasm.[30]

If we think the current hookup culture doesn't foster gender equality or good sex for all women, what would be better? According to sexual conservatives, the sexual revolution has led men to have more access to sex, but it has also led women to be exploited by men who don't respect the women they have sex with and don't concern themselves with women's pleasure. In this view, women would be better off refusing to hook up and instead holding out for relationships before they have sex.

In one sense our research supports this strategy. If college women want good sex without stigma, relationships make sense. This may help explain why college women report a stronger desire for relationships than college men.[31] Men, who are less stigmatized for having sex outside of relationships, may prefer hookups because they provide sex with orgasms while not limiting their options to hook up with other people. Thus, one way to view gender inequality in college sex is as a gender struggle over hookups versus relationships as contexts for having sex. From this perspective, women try to form relationships, while men try to avoid them. Some research suggests that women participate in lower-quality hookup sex because they can't get men to commit to relationships and in hopes that a series of hookups will turn into a relationship.[32] If this is the main reason why so much of the sex college women engage in does not lead to orgasm, perhaps a campaign to move all sex back into relationships could be seen as a move toward gender equality.

But moving college sex back into relationships would have drawbacks. First, not all women want relationships with their hookup partners. We found that although more women than men reported an interest in a relationship with their most recent hookup partner, fewer than half of the women reported any such interest. At the same time, after a hookup, women reported high levels of enjoyment (even without orgasm) and low levels of regret.[33] These findings are inconsistent with the view that college women would prefer relationships as a context for all their sexual activity. Second, focusing exclusively on getting sex back into relationships would not improve the treatment of those women who choose to hook up. The woman who was annoyed with her partner who fell asleep after getting fellatio did not want a relationship with this man—she just wanted him to be considerate enough to return the favor. And third, while relationships are better contexts for sex than hookups, relationships involve a lot more than sex. Sometimes relationships lead women to withdraw from college or scale back their career ambitions; even worse, they sometimes involve physical or emotional abuse.[34]

Our research suggests a second, complementary response to the poor quality of hookup sex for women. In addition to creating conditions that facilitate college relationships, we advocate addressing the factors that degrade the quality of hookup sex for women: sexual double standards and lack of reciprocity. Subverting the contemporary sexual double standard would involve defending the position that young women and men are equally entitled to sexual pleasure and sexual respect in hookups as well as relationships. To achieve this, the attitudes and practices of both men and women need to be confronted. Men should be challenged to treat even first hookup partners generously and with the respect and consideration that they treat their girlfriends. (They might find that if they did so, more women would want to hook up with them and that the hookups would be more fun!) Women should grow into adulthood with a sense of entitlement to sex and sexual pleasure. For women, a first condition is understanding their own sexual response (for example, learning how to masturbate). A second condition is the confidence to ask for what they want in all contexts. This means assertiveness to say no as well as to say yes.[35] If this seems utopian at present, then it is evidence of how far we still have to go to achieve gender equality in premarital sexual relations.

NOTES

1. Paul, McManus, and Hayes (2000); Glenn and Marquardt (2001); and Bogle (2007).
2. Participating universities include University of Arizona, Indiana University, Stanford University, University of California at Santa Barbara, State University of New York at Stony Brook, Ithaca College, Evergreen College, University of Massachusetts at Amherst, Ohio State University, Whitman College, Foothill College, Harvard University, University of Illinois at Chicago, Framingham State University, Radford University,

Beloit College, and the University of California at Riverside. In almost all cases, respondents were recruited through classes. We did not employ probability sampling, so our sample is not strictly representative of college students at these institutions.

3. Rupp, Taylor, Regev-Messalem. Fogarty, and England (2013).

4. This paper uses the June 2008 version of the OCSL data. Anonymous, M.D., *Unprotected: A Campus Psychiatrist Reveals How Political Correctness in Her Profession Endangers Every Student* (New York: Sentinel HC, 2006); Glenn and Marquardt (2001); Kass (1997); Popenoe and Defce Whitehead (2000): *The State of Our Unions, 2000: The Social Health of Marriage in America* (2000); Sessions Stepp (2007); and Waite and Gallagher (2000).

5. Kasic (2008).

6. Boswell and Spade (1996); Yancey, Martin, and Hummer (1989); and Stombler (1994).

7. Evangelical Christians have not moved in this direction. See Freitas (2008) for a discussion of the ideal of purity among conservative Christian college students. Immigrant groups may also retain ideas of premarital chastity. See González-López (2005) for a discussion of sexual ethics among Mexicans immigrating to the United States.

8. Denizet-Lewis (2004).

9. See also Bogle (2008); Freitas (2008); and Hamilton and Armstrong (2009) for more discussion of repeat hookups.

10. Glenn and Marquardt (2001) also find high participation in relationships.

11. England, Fitzgibbons Shafer, and Fogarty (2007).

12. For discussions of the rise and fall of dating as a social form, see Bailey (1988); and Bogle (2008).

13. Men and women's reports of what happened in their most recent hookup differ slightly; men report a bit more action. This may be a result of men's overreporting or women's underreporting of sexual activity and/or of women more often than men classifying "making out" as a hookup. We combine male and female respondents' reports here.

14. While 76 percent reported intercourse in the last relationship sexual event, 84 percent reported intercourse ever in this relationship.

15. If a couple had never gone beyond kissing, they were not asked the question, but only 3 percent of those in a relationship of at least six months had not.

16. Orgasm is correlated with a subjective measure of sexual satisfaction for our respondents—and, contrary to common lore, more so for women than for men.

17. See Laumann et al. (1994); and Waite and Joyner (2001) for more detailed discussions of this perspective. Laumann and his colleagues found that married people reported higher levels of sexual satisfaction than single people. Waite and Joyner found that how long women thought their relationship would last and sexual exclusivity were associated with emotional and physical satisfaction with sex.

18. Buss (1994); and Townsend (1995).

19. Chodorow (1978).

20. Hite (1976); Darling, Davidson Sr., and Jennings (1991); Fisher (1973); and Mah and Binik (2001).

21. These percentages and those in the next paragraph use both men's and women's reports.

22. In these percentages, we excluded intercourse events that also included the woman self-stimulating her own genitals with her hand. Figure 18.4 shows that, in events with intercourse, when oral sex also occurred, it helped women's orgasm in three of the four contexts, but not in intercourse events in hookups where the couple had previously hooked up one to two times.

23. Richters et al. (2006) similarly found that the addition of oral or manual stimulation to vaginal intercourse provided a big boost to women's experience of orgasms.

24. See Gagnon and Simon (1974) for a discussion of the ways in which sexual scripts organize sexual behavior.

25. See Schwartz and Rutter (2000); and Crawford and Popp (2003) on sexual double standards.

26. See Bogle (2008); Freitas (2008); and Hamilton and Armstrong (2009) for discussions of the double standard among today's students. See Tanenbaum (1999); and White (2001) for discussions of how girls and young women get labeled as sluts, and the consequences of such labeling for their lives.

27. See Braun, Gavey, and McPhillips (2003) for a more critical view of the consequences for gender equality of the discourse of sexual reciprocity among heterosexuals.

28. Tolman (2002).

29. Our argument echoes that of Richters et al. (2006), who found that "the proximal cause—the sexual stimulation delivered to women in the typical, rigidly scripted hetero-sexual interaction—has more to do with whether they reach orgasm (and, we suspect, enjoy sex) than with more obscure and distant causes" (p. 252).

30. Andrejek et al. (2022).

31. See England et al. (2007); and Bogle (2008).

32. Bogle (2008).

33. England et al. (2007).

34. Hamilton and Armstrong (2009); Holland and Eisenhart (1990); and Gilmartin (2005).

35. Feminist scholars often use the term *sexual subjectivity* to refer to women's feelings of ownership of their sexuality and feelings of entitlement to pleasure. See Martin (1996); Schalet (2004); Schalet (2009); and Tolman (2002).

In Other Words

MAINTAINING THE GENDER GAP IN ORGASMS TAKES WORK

Nicole Andrejek, June 21, 2022 / CCF@TSP

Why is there a gender gap in orgasms in heterosexual sex? Research has long shown a gender gap in orgasms between men and women in heterosexual sexual encounters. They have also shown that sexual practices that focus on clitoral stimulation reduce the gap. Since we know this, why are couples not engaging in the types of sexual activities that might reduce the orgasm gap?

In my research with Tina Fetner and Melanie Heath in *Gender & Society*, we examine data from the nationally representative Sex in Canada survey and find that 86 percent of men had an orgasm in their most recent heterosexual sexual encounter compared to 62 percent of women. We found that women whose most recent encounter included receiving clitoral stimulation via oral sex were more likely to have had an orgasm than those who did not. Other recent studies have documented similar gender discrepancies in orgasm rates, but since many focus on a particular group, such as undergraduate students, it has been unclear until now whether this was a problem across heterosexual couples more generally. Our study shows that it is.

To better understand why the gender gap in orgasms persists despite all we know about what increases women's likelihood of reaching orgasm during heterosexual partnered sex, we conducted in-depth interviews with women and men across Canada. Our interview participants drew on traditional beliefs about gender to justify men's orgasms as natural and expected and women's orgasms as time-consuming work.

Three different perspectives stood out. Our participants voiced essentialist views of gender and sexuality that naturalized differences between men and women to explain why men prioritize physical pleasure, while women are expected to prioritize emotional intimacy during sex. Another theme was that many of the people we interviewed defined "regular" sex as penile-vaginal intercourse. Through this narrow, phallocentric understanding of sex, stimulation of the penis (and consequently men's pleasure) inherently becomes a part of "regular sex." Alternatively, sexual behaviors focused on clitoral stimulation, like oral sex, were considered "special," "separate" from the main event, and "extra work." Finally, some of those we talked to relied on the sexual double standard to justify why women self-regulate their sexual expression. In these instances, women's sexual desire and sexual practices focused on women's pleasure were understood as dirty or wrong, and their bodies were considered simply too difficult to please. These narratives were produced by both men and women, revealing how heterosexual couples reinforce traditional, essentialist gender norms during sex.

Our participants' explanations for the orgasm gap made men's orgasms appear natural and expected and women's orgasms as extra, more work, and more difficult. Their understandings contribute to the normalization of penile-vaginal intercourse as "regular sex" and this itself privileges men's pleasure and orgasms. Although women's lack of orgasms compared to men may feel like an individual, intimate problem, we demonstrate that the gender gap in orgasms takes work. It is enabled by the gender essentialist beliefs embedded in the institution of heterosexuality. These findings help us move beyond essentialist "men are from Mars, women are from Venus" justifications that women simply do not care about orgasm to how gender beliefs deprive women of an equal opportunity to orgasm in heterosexual sex. ▬

In Other Words

THE DATE'S NOT DEAD AFTER ALL: NEW FINDINGS ON HOOKING UP, DATING, AND FORMING ROMANTIC RELATIONSHIPS IN COLLEGE

Arielle Kuperberg and Joseph E. Padgett, February 11, 2016 / CCF

For more than one hundred years, Valentine's Day has been a time for romantic candlelit dinner dates. But today, many observers worry, romance and courtship are falling out of favor. According to the *New York Times*, "Traditional dating in college has mostly gone the way of the landline, replaced by 'hooking up.'" With women outnumbering men on most college campuses, we are told, women can't attain the long-term relationships they *really* want; there aren't enough men to go around. Men, "as the minority, hold more power in the sexual marketplace," and they use it to promote a culture of casual sex on campus. Instead of going out on dates, young adults are supposedly meeting up at their homes to "Netflix and chill" or hooking up at big parties, then moving on to the next in a long series of casual sex partners. This is said to harm their chances of entering long-term romantic partnerships.

How accurate is this picture? We analyzed a survey of over twenty-four thousand college students from twenty-two colleges and universities around the United States between 2005 and 2011 and found that reports of the death of dating are greatly exaggerated. College students have essentially equal rates of hooking up and dating. Since beginning college, approximately 62 percent of students reported having hooked up, while 61 percent said they had gone out on a date. Only 8 percent of all students had hooked up without ever going on a date or being in a long-term relationship. More than three times as many students—26.5 percent—had never hooked up at all but instead had dated or formed a long-term relationship. So while it is clear that hookups are widespread, they have certainly not replaced the traditional date.

Men's rate of hooking up was 3.5 percentage points higher than women's—a difference that is statistically significant but very small. However, this was not necessarily because men preferred more casual relationships. In fact 71 percent of the men, compared to just 67 percent of the women, said they wished they had more opportunities to find a long-term romantic relationship. And almost two-thirds of the men expressed the desire for more chances to date, compared to less than half who reported wishing they had more chances to hook up.

The idea that men are leveraging their scarce presence on campus to avoid long-term relationships and force women to settle for unsatisfactory hookups is also called into question by a number of other findings in the survey. Women were not substantially more likely than men to regret their last hookup; only 14.5 percent of women, versus 12.5 percent of men, regretted their last hookup. Overall, a similar number of men (48 percent) and women (45 percent) instead reported being glad about their most recent hookup encounter (the rest were neither glad nor regretful). Other recent research finds that even though men are more likely than women to have an orgasm during hookup sex, men and women are almost equally likely to report enjoying their most recent hookup. Our research also revealed that on campuses with a higher proportion of women, women were not more likely to hook up with men or less likely to form long-term relationships with them. They were instead more likely to have dated other women.

While hookups certainly do not carry the expectation of a lasting commitment, many do in fact lead to one. A recent report found that one-third of recent marriages that they studied began in a hookup context. And despite the prevalence of hookups during their college years, female college graduates are in the long run *more likely to marry* than women with less education. Since women now earn more degrees than men, this means that many marriages are between a woman and a less educated husband; contrary to widespread concerns, recent research finds this is no longer a risk factor for divorce.

Our survey did find some problematic behaviors associated with many college hookups. Fully half of all men and 46.5 percent of women reported engaging in binge drinking (defined as four or more drinks for women and five or more for men) during or right before the hookup. Students who were binge drinking (male as well as female) faced a higher risk of sexual assault. And even when sex was consensual, each additional drink during or right before a hookup was associated with lower sexual enjoyment from the hookup for both men and women. Other recent research confirms that women in particular are more likely to feel discontented with their hookups when they drink beforehand. In fact, 31 percent of women and 28 percent of men reported that they would not have hooked up with the partner at all had they not been drinking.

Most students who described themselves as having "hooked up" either didn't have sex during their last hookup or used a condom when they did. Overall, 42 percent of hookups included vaginal or anal sex. Of these, only 13.3 percent included *unprotected* vaginal or anal sex. In other words, a majority of hookups did not end with sex, and more than two-thirds of students who did have sex during hookups used a condom. Students who had sex on dates also used condoms two-thirds of the time, but since only 22 percent of dates included sex, that meant that only 7 percent of all dates included unprotected sex. So the chance of having unprotected sex was almost twice as high in a hookup as on a date.

Students who were intoxicated were more likely to have unprotected sex during a hookup. Binge drinking increased the likelihood that students would have unprotected sex during their hookup by around one-third; using marijuana during a hookup (which 11 percent of students reported) was associated with nearly double the risk of unprotected sex.

Surprisingly, truly casual hookups tended to be safer than others. Despite not having an exclusive relationship with that partner, women who reported knowing their partner "very well" were almost 60 percent more likely to have unprotected sex during a hookup than women who only knew their partner "somewhat." When students had repeat hookups with the same nonexclusive partner, they were more likely to have unprotected sex in later hookups; each additional hookup with the same partner increased the risk of unprotected sex by 17 percent. These students may feel a false sense of security with that partner, leading them to take unnecessary risks. Also, women may worry that asking their partner to use a condom would be seen as mistrustful and, as a result, avoid the issue when hooking up with a friend or otherwise well-known partner.

Hookups were most common among fraternity and sorority members, who were more than twice as likely as non-members to have hooked up. Fraternity and sorority members were no more likely to form a long-term relationship while in college, despite the fact that sorority members were about 50 percent more likely than non-members to want more opportunities to form long-term relationships in college, and *not* more likely to want hookup opportunities. Fraternity and sorority members were also both about 50 percent more likely to binge drink while hooking up compared to non-members. On the other hand, sorority members were less likely than other college women to report unprotected sex during their last hookup.

Religious service attendance was also related to whether students hooked up, but in distinct ways for men and women. Women who attended religious services at least once a month were significantly less likely than women who attended services less frequently or never attended services to have ever hooked up in college. When women who attended religious services did hook up, they were less likely to have unprotected sex, or any sex.

For men, a different pattern emerged. Men who attended services a few times per year but less than once per month were the *most* likely to have either hooked up or dated in college—more likely than men who never attended services. And college men who attended services most frequently—at least once a month—had hookup rates similar to those who never attended. Religious service attendance also had no impact on the likelihood of a man engaging in unprotected sex during hookups. Religious standards of sexual morality seem to constrain the behavior of very religious women; men, on the other hand, may be using religious social networks to find casual sex partners, counteracting any suppressing effect religious doctrine may have on casual sex.

Three groups stood out as having significantly lower rates of unprotected sex during hookups compared to other students: men hooking up with men, women who were members of sororities, and students who met hookup partners in dormitories. What do these groups have in common? Each has been the target of accurate, nonjudgmental public health and sexual education campaigns.

Spreading accurate information about risks related to binge drinking during hookups and emphasizing clear, honest communication with partners about condom use, even with trusted partners, could mitigate the many risk factors found in our research. In the absence of these risk factors, hooking up does not appear to have the bad results that are often attributed to it. Rather than panicking about the death of romance on campus, accepting hooking up as part of the normal campus scene while educating college students about the specific behaviors that make it risky or unpleasant can more effectively protect college youth. ▄▄

19

Independent Women

Equality in African American Lesbian Relationships

Mignon R. Moore

Researchers on lesbian and gay populations have tended to generalize the experiences of lesbian practice and gay sexuality from past research on white, middle-class, feminist women. But alternative histories and experiences of women from other racial and socioeconomic groups offer new information on the relationship among race, class, gender, and homosexual relationships. The present study covers three years in the lives of a population of gay women who are not often visible in public life—lesbians of color who are creating families. In this article, I offer an examination of the ways black gay women evaluate the concept of equality or egalitarianism in same-sex unions.

This research is drawn from my book *Invisible Families: Gay Identities, Relationships, and Motherhood among Black Women*, which argues that previously formed identification statuses, such as those based on race or class, influence how individuals perceive and enact later group memberships, like those based on sexuality. It does this by analyzing a group of women who, because of year of birth, geographic location, socioeconomic status, and other characteristics, came of age during periods of heavy racial segregation and entered into their gay identities with firmly entrenched black racial identities. The larger project from which this essay is drawn suggests there is value in analyzing the ways past experiences in families of origin influence the expectations individuals have for their own relationships, regardless of sexual preference.

In this essay, I examine the concept of equality in lesbian relationships by looking closely at the two primary aspects of egalitarianism: equal responsibility for paid work and housework. Past studies of lesbian households have emphasized the egalitarian nature of these couples vis-à-vis their division of family labor, which includes household chores such as cooking and cleaning as well as child care and supervision. This body of literature has had little to say about the other aspect of egalitarianism: how lesbian couples distribute paid work, evaluate its importance in their relationship, and construct ideologies about economic independence. These studies have also tended to understate the experiences of women of color and working-class and poor women.[1]

In this work, I examine the relative importance of both components of egalitarianism for black lesbians, looking at differences across socioeconomic background as one explanation for how women come to make decisions about what they value in their relationships.

EGALITARIANISM: ECONOMIC INDEPENDENCE AND AN EQUITABLE DIVISION OF HOUSEHOLD LABOR

Since the 1970s, feminist research on the division of household labor has conceptualized the gender specialization model of husband as primary wage earner and wife as primary caretaker as an indicator of gender stratification. This research generally defines egalitarianism as "joint responsibility for paid work, housework, and child rearing."[2] From 1989 onward, the social science literature on household decision-making in lesbian-led families has tended to measure egalitarianism and equality in relationships by focusing on the ways couples distribute household chores and child care. It has not paid close attention to how much lesbian partners value, or the extent to which they enact, the other component of egalitarianism—economic independence and financial contributions from both partners in the relationship.[3]

Part of the problem has been the way research on lesbian-headed households has been conducted. Scholars who study lesbian families have been interested in addressing the literature on heterosexual couples that measured the distribution of and time spent on household chores by husbands and wives. Studies of gender in the heterosexual division of labor sought and revealed explanations for the greater responsibility of wives for household chores.[4] Studies of the division of labor among lesbian and gay couples sought to illuminate how these same issues played out in the absence of sex differences between partners.[5] After 1989, the emphasis in the family literature focused heavily on the domestic realm, and researchers of lesbian-headed households tended to follow suit.

Lesbian subjects have also persisted in emphasizing the egalitarian nature of their unions because of deep-rooted concerns about the public image of gay communities. Carrington's 1999 study of the ways gay couples assign various aspects of domesticity revealed this tendency. Even though the subjects of more recent scholarship on lesbian families may not take on a dominant identity as feminist, they hold significant ideological commitment to egalitarianism and form unions with the principles of egalitarian feminism in mind.

Recent studies show evidence that lesbian couples tend to distribute housework, paid work, and child care duties across the couple using an "ethic of equality" that is drawn from lesbian-feminist ideologies.[6] Much of the research has focused on one component of this notion of equality—the distribution of housework. But as far back as 1983, Blumstein and Schwartz revealed that for lesbian couples, equal responsibility for household financial responsibilities was also a very important measure of equality. Partners' interest in each individual's economic independence was linked to an effort to avoid the breadwinner/homemaker patriarchy found in some heterosexual relationships.[7] In drawing attention toward domestic matters and away from the economic sphere, contemporary lesbian family scholars may have inadvertently shifted the definition of egalitarian ideologies too far in the other direction. I draw from a sample of women who do not use a lesbian-feminist framework to measure equality in their same-sex relationships, and I examine how experiences in the families they were reared in influence the expectations they have for their same-sex partners.

AFRICAN AMERICAN GAY WOMEN AND EQUALITY IN LESBIAN RELATIONSHIPS

There are several reasons why African American women are the focus of this inquiry. First, the family studies literature identifies several household patterns that are more common among black than white heterosexual couples, such as the greater importance black women place on their partner's economic contributions when they choose and evaluate a mate, more traditional gender ideologies among black wives and husbands relative to white wives and husbands, and a greater tendency for separate rather than joint financial bank accounts in black heterosexual unions.[8] It is instructive to see if these patterns of family life are also more likely to occur in a population where sexuality is experienced differently.

Black lesbians are also a useful population for studying the division of household labor, because historically as a group they developed a gay culture outside the ideology of lesbian feminism. While middle-class white women largely came to understand lesbian sexuality in the context of consciousness-raising meetings in the women's movement or women's studies classes on college campuses,[9] racial segregation in housing, education, and occupations as well as the very fabric of social life limited black women's involvement in these groups. Instead, black women were entering the lesbian world through parties and social events taking place in informal environments that were more distant from lesbian-feminist ideals. The racial segregation of these social and political environments influenced whether and in what form egalitarian ideologies would be incorporated into their self-images.[10]

A final benefit in analyzing household organization and feminist ideologies among black women in same-sex unions is that it grants us the opportunity to examine how past experiences connected to race and class background relate to the patterns of social organization lesbians use in the families they form. Analyses of unmarried partner households in the 2000 Census suggest significant differences between black and white female same-sex couples, including lower median household incomes, lower rates of homeownership, and lower rates of employment for black women. Black female same-sex couples are also significantly more likely to have children living with them in the home.[11]

INVISIBLE FAMILIES STUDY AND ASSESSING EGALITARIAN ATTITUDES

The Invisible Family data consist of one hundred women who identify as lesbian, gay, bisexual, in the Life, or women-loving-women. It includes women in committed relationships with other women as well as unpartnered mothers. To be eligible for the study, one person in the relationship had to identify as black. There are four types of data: participant-observation field notes collected over approximately thirty months, four focus groups, fifty-eight in-depth interviews, and a mail-in survey.

I used participant-observation methods at predominantly black lesbian social events to recruit women. Sixty percent of survey respondents were recruited directly through my attendance and participation in these social activities, 11 percent were recruited through announcements and presentations made at these events, 25 percent were obtained through referrals from those who were in the study (using a snowball sampling method of data collection), and 4 percent were recruited through referrals from nongay people. In total, 131 surveys were mailed and 100 were returned, giving the study a response rate of 76 percent.

The mean age of the sample in 2004 was 36.7 years, with a range of twenty-four to sixty-one years of age. Sixty-four percent of the sample identified as black American, 21 percent as West Indian or African, 10 percent as Latina, and 5 percent as white. Thirty-four percent completed high school and 62 percent received a four-year college degree or advanced degree. At the time of the interview, 45 percent were in working-class occupations, including construction worker, security guard, and administrative assistant.[12] Forty-two percent were considered middle class, in jobs that included teacher and human resources administrator. Thirteen percent of the sample were upper middle class, in occupations such as attorney and physician.[13]

The survey asked respondents to evaluate three statements that measured the strength of egalitarian attitudes: "Both mates in a relationship should divide evenly the household tasks (washing dishes, preparing meals, doing laundry, etc.)," "If both mates work full time, both of their career plans should be considered equally in determining where they will live," and "It is better if one person in the relationship takes the major financial responsibility and the other person takes the major responsibility of caring for the home." Responses to all three of these statements show that most of the respondents profess views that are consistent with feminist measures of equality or egalitarianism in relationships. Eighty-four percent agreed or strongly agreed that both mates should divide household tasks evenly, 89 percent agreed or strongly agreed that both partners' career plans should be equally considered when making decisions about where to live, and 84 percent disagreed or strongly disagreed with the specialization model of one person taking on the major financial responsibility and the other person primarily caring for the home.

Despite their ideological agreement with feminist egalitarian principles, however, survey, participant-observation, focus group, and in-depth interview data all suggest that respondents tend not to behave in egalitarian ways. In most households, one person spends much more time performing household chores. But while this is sometimes a source of frustration for the partner who does more housework, it is not the primary source of conflict in their relationships, it is not the primary measure of whether respondents believe their relationships are fair, and it is not related to the balance of power in the home.[14] Instead, the focus group, participant-observation, and in-depth interviews reveal that self-sufficiency and autonomy are highly valued, and respondents place a premium on economic independence rather than the division of family labor as a value and a behavior that is critical for relationship satisfaction. This importance is expressed through the belief that each partner should contribute her own financial resources to the relationship.

Class backgrounds and experiences growing up provide different explanations for why self-sufficiency is so important. Many of these background experiences relate to the socioeconomic status of respondents' families and their experiences around race and gender. These analyses focus on how the family backgrounds of black women who grew up poor, working class, or middle class influence their ideologies regarding the importance of women's economic independence in relationships. Thirty-two percent of these women grew up in poverty, 33 percent were raised in working-class families, and 35 percent lived in middle-class or upper-middle-class households during their childhoods.

POOR AND WORKING-CLASS FAMILY BACKGROUND: ECONOMIC INDEPENDENCE TIED TO PERSONAL SURVIVAL AND ABILITY TO MOVE OUT OF BAD RELATIONSHIPS

Karen Jabar[15] is a forty-two-year-old African American woman and mother of three who left her husband of twenty-one years when she came out as gay. Karen is also a child of two alcoholic parents whose addictions resulted in traumatic consequences for everyone in her family of origin. Under conditions of extreme poverty, homelessness, and constant instability, she and her ten brothers and sisters banded together to protect one another from the taunting and bullying they received from other children in their neighborhood. She says,

> My life was rough. We struggled. I would probably say that we were a poor family because I could remember eating sugar sandwiches, things like that. I remember mice and roaches being in the house, taking care of my brothers and sisters and not having electricity or the fact that we would plug in the TV cord or the extension cord into the hallway socket to get light into our apartment; having the door cracked and not really knowing who is coming into the building.

In 1974, when Karen was thirteen, her mother killed her father in self-defense during a fight that began after heavy drinking. After that incident, Karen and her siblings were separated from one another and placed in different homes. At that time, the New York child welfare services agency had not designed policies to keep siblings together after a family removal, so Karen found herself having to survive in a group home for girls without the security of her brothers and sisters. She describes her teenage years as a life of loneliness, vulnerability, and uncertainty about her day-to-day future.

Despite the dire circumstances of her childhood, Karen has been able to rise above some of the challenges she has faced. After several starts and stops, she received a four-year college degree and is the only one of her siblings to have achieved this level of education. Karen avoids drugs and is able to provide for herself economically. Nevertheless, she does not maintain close relationships with her family members, battles with depression and low self-esteem, and has a difficult time staying employed. She has held and lost positions in the U.S. military, New York State Department of Correctional Services, various security positions for private firms, and several civil service jobs in New York City.

While a snapshot of Karen Jabar at the time of her interview might have indicated a middle-class status (college education and a job as a supervisor for the Administration for Children's Services city agency), her family background of extreme poverty, her struggle to complete her education, and other factors in her personal life make her experience quite different from that of many of the middle-class lesbians usually studied by researchers. These background experiences have influenced several areas of her adult life, including the things she finds important in her intimate relationships. For Karen, economic independence, even through a succession of short-term jobs, allows her to maintain some type of control over her own life. She has had a series of negative, temporary relationships with women who have taken advantage of her financially and emotionally. Regardless of the status of the women she dates, she stays employed so that she will be able to care for herself and have the resources to leave unhealthy relationships when she is ready to move on. While she has taken on more than her share of the financial responsibilities with the women she has dated, she expects "equal sharing of all of the family responsibilities" with a partner in a serious relationship, and this includes paid work. For Karen, economic self-sufficiency rather than strict equality in the division of household chores carries the most weight in her satisfaction with her mate.

WORKING-CLASS FAMILY BACKGROUND: ECONOMIC INDEPENDENCE TIED TO CHILDHOOD EXPERIENCE OF WORK AND TO INDIVIDUAL SURVIVAL DURING TIMES OF MARITAL DISTRESS

Roberta "Ro" Gaul is a licensed electrician who was born in Jamaica, West Indies, in 1966. Throughout her adult life, her intimate relationships have only been with women. Ro was raised by her mother with her siblings in Flatbush, a working-class, largely West Indian community in Brooklyn, New York. When Ro was growing up, her mother worked as a nurse's aide and her father did not live with the family. Currently, Ro lives with her partner, Sifa Erody, and in separate interviews they both said that Sifa does most of the housework and that Ro does not do enough of it. But in their interviews, they each reported being very satisfied with their relationship. On separate surveys they both reported spending equal amounts of time on the relationship and having equal power in it.

Ro's feelings on the importance of each partner's financial independence stem from her own experiences with work as an adolescent. When asked about the qualities she looks for in a partner, she said,

> They have to be working because I'm extremely independent and I believe people, everybody should work. I grew up as a young child working, and I am still working. So I believe that you must have a job. If it means that the job is paying you enough for you to maintain yourself or your own independence, you have to be working.

While Ro links her opinions about work to her experiences in her family of origin and the necessity of each person's income to the well-being of the household, other working-class women draw on an ideology of independence as a means of self-empowerment and protection against poverty. They believe in economic independence for themselves and their mates, and they have created a life that assures their own survival when a partner is not able to fulfill her or his own financial responsibilities.

Shelly Jackson is a thirty-eight-year-old bus driver. She was raised by her black American parents, grandparents, and great-grandparents, who have all shared a two-family house in Crown Heights, Brooklyn, since her parents married in 1962. She says her father took care of the family financially while her mother was "the homemaker." Before entering into a gay relationship, Shelly had been heterosexually married twice. At the time of the interview, she was legally separated but not divorced from her second husband, and she was living with her children and her female partner, Shaunte Austin, in an East New York housing project. She is emphatic that regardless of sexuality, each partner should bring her own resources to a relationship, saying, "I don't give a damn who you're with, you always need . . . to be independent and take care of yourself." She told us she learned the importance of financial independence by watching her father provide for the family, and knew she wanted to always be able to do that for herself and her children. When asked about some of the positive aspects of her life while growing up, she said,

> That my father was always there to take care and provide for us, and that's what made me who I am today. 'Cause even when I was married, I always took that role of being the provider. I was always the one to go out there and work and pay the rent and pay the bills and do this and do that. And not look for him to take care of me—I've seen what my mother went through and that's not what I wanted to go through growing up, being an adult.

Shelly's first marriage was tumultuous largely because of an abusive husband. After five years of kicking him out of the house and then letting him back in, she ended the relationship. Her second marriage was characterized by significant drug use that involved herself and her husband. Although her own illicit drug use ended once she was pregnant, her husband continued to use, and that eventually caused their relationship to end. Throughout both of these marriages, Shelly continued to work. Had she not remained financially independent, she would certainly have slipped into poverty. She defines a "provider" as someone who has the ability to take care of herself without the help of others.

Schwartz, in her 1994 study of egalitarian heterosexual marriages, defines the provider role or provider complex as a combination of roles that give one person the responsibility for financially supporting the family, and the other person responsibility for all the auxiliary duties that allow the first person to devote himself or herself to his or her work.[16] Schwartz's definition is different from the way Shelly Jackson uses the term *provider*, and this becomes clear as Shelly continues in her description of the financial contributions she expects from her mate. On separate surveys, Shelly and her partner, Shaunte Austin, each report that Shaunte spends more time on household chores and takes on much of the child care responsibilities. Shelly often works the night shift or double shifts, and relies on Shaunte to feed and bathe the children, help them with their homework, and keep the house tidy. But when asked how happy she is with the way she and her mate divide household responsibilities, Shelly says she became much happier once Shaunte found a job:

> Don't get me wrong. She [Shaunte] has always been so good to me as far as helping me out with the kids, 'cause my hours [at work] is crazy and Shaunte is somebody I could depend on. But it was hard when she wasn't working. She wasn't having no income coming in, and I was like, "I'm not your sugar mama!"

Shelly's comment draws on negative images of a woman's dependence on a male "sugar daddy" and simultaneously emphasizes her expectation that her partner will contribute economically to the family. But she has also prepared to provide for herself and her children in the event that her mate cannot or will not contribute her share, or if their relationship comes to an end. For working-class lesbians raising families, economic independence provides a financial and psychological barrier against a step backward into poverty.[17]

MIDDLE-CLASS FAMILY BACKGROUND: ECONOMIC INDEPENDENCE TIED TO UPWARD MOBILITY AND LEADERSHIP IN SOCIETY

Dr. Renee Martin is a physician. Born in 1967, Renee grew up in New Orleans with her parents and younger sister in a middle-class neighborhood that bordered two racially segregated areas of the community. One might characterize Renee's family background as upper middle class. Her father was one of the first African Americans in Louisiana to receive a doctorate in mechanical engineering. After having two children, Renee's mother continued to work as a college professor until her retirement. Although Renee's father earned more than her mother, throughout Renee's childhood she witnessed her mother thrive in a respectable, middle-class occupation that she found personally fulfilling. Both of her parents were active members of their church and other volunteer organizations, and they played important leadership roles in their African American community.

Renee currently lives in New York City, where she owns her own home, has considerable authority at work, and is advancing steadily in her career. Renee's partner, Naja Rhodes, has a master's degree in education. They report spending similar amounts of time on household chores, though Naja believes she spends about two additional hours per week taking care of the home. Renee also tends to perform more of the stereotypically male tasks like yard work, household repairs, and taking out the trash. Both say they are satisfied with the way they organize their household responsibilities and invest equal amounts of time and have equal power in the relationship. Renee's discussion of economic independence does not mention economic survival or a worry about being able to provide for herself in the absence of an employed partner. These issues are not part of her current life, nor are they part of her past experiences. Coming from a socioeconomically secure background and having a high status and economically lucrative occupation preclude Renee from experiencing many of the worries expressed by the working-class respondents in this study. She could easily take on the traditional provider role in her relationship, relieving Naja from any obligation to contribute financially to the household.

Instead, Renee's discussion of egalitarianism in her relationship involves ways of helping her partner achieve greater independence and fulfillment in her own career. Renee encourages Naja to build her finances and to own her own property, and she has shown Naja how to build wealth. When talking about Naja, Renee makes reference to the independence her mother has always had from her father's income. She is proud of the fact that her mother has always maintained her own financial accounts and used her income to create a mutual interdependence in her relationship with Renee's father. In turn, Renee wants to help her own partner achieve these things.

The structure and functioning of Renee and Naja's relationship have their parallel in the way Renee's parents organized their marriage, as described by Landry (2000) in his historical research on black working wives. Landry argues that for the black middle class, women's paid work was not simply a response to economic circumstances but the fulfillment of women's rights to self-actualization. His evidence lies in the experience of black women who married men who could support them yet continued to pursue careers throughout their marital lives.[18] For couples like Renee and Naja, egalitarianism is expressed not merely through each person's ability to contribute economic resources, but in the desire of each person to pursue a life of self-fulfillment in the economic sphere. It is reminiscent of the argument in Betty Friedan's *The Feminine Mystique* about middle-class white women in the 1950s. But Donna Franklin (Chapter 8 of this volume) shows how these beliefs were championed much earlier than the 1950s in African American middle-class families.[19]

Katrice Webster is a thirty-six-year-old attorney. She attended Ivy League institutions for college and law school and is employed at one of the top three law firms in Manhattan. Katrice was born and raised in Romulus, Michigan, a lower-middle-class, racially integrated small city just outside Detroit. Her parents divorced when she was six, and she and her siblings were raised by her mother who worked her way up from administrative assistant to office manager at her place of employment. After the divorce, the children lived with their mother, but they spent holidays and vacations with their father, who remained nearby. He was a business executive with a much higher income than Katrice's mother had, and he continued to contribute financially to their household throughout her childhood. An extensive extended family also lived in the area and served as an important source of support for the family. Katrice describes her childhood as happy.

When asked about the qualities she looks for in a mate, Katrice does not emphasize a college background or particular socioeconomic status. Because she is a corporate attorney, her salary is higher than the salaries of women she has dated, and it is higher than what her current partner earns. Her interest in economic independence is not to ensure her own survival. She has obtained the education and occupational opportunities to secure that part of her life, and she is not reliant on her partner's income for her own upward mobility. Instead, she wants a partner who is ambitious, and Katrice is willing to help that person move toward the type of financial independence she has obtained for herself. When asked what she looks for in a mate, she says, "They just have to have a drive and want to be successful at something. If they own their own house-cleaning business, they just have to run it well."

Her partner, Caroline Tate, is a self-employed makeup artist. Caroline and Katrice each pay their own bills, but Katrice pays for a greater portion of their expenses and is the sole owner of the home where they live. Caroline is the mother of a seventeen-year-old daughter who was born in a prior heterosexual union. Caroline not only spends more time parenting, but she also takes on much more of the household chores like cooking and laundry. They hire a person to come in and clean. They report some disagreement over parenting and discipline, but they do not raise the issue of housework as a problem in the relationship. Katrice would like her partner to become more financially stable and to learn about different methods of building assets. She says, "I try to encourage her to save because I always like to think everybody needs to have a nest egg for a rainy day." For her, promoting self-sufficiency in her partner will not improve Katrice's economic standing, but it is a way to uplift her mate and help her become more stable for her own personal gain.

Among black women born before 1970, it was uncommon to have parents whose lives represented the traditional patriarchal relationship that feminist egalitarian ideologies attempt to dismantle. Mothers and fathers both worked to provide (when they could find employment), and many households did not contain two married biological parents for a person's entire childhood. When looking at the family structures of the women in the study, we see that Katrice's single-mother household, though different because of its middle-class status, was quite similar to the family backgrounds of most women in the study. Just 36 percent of respondents were raised with two married biological parents, and only two of the black women reported having a stay-at-home mother. Forty-four percent grew up in single-mother households, and 42 percent of these single-parent families were multigenerational and included a grandparent or other adult female relative. Fourteen percent of the respondents were not raised with any biological parents, and they grew up in households with their grandparents or nonrelatives. In regard to community context, more than 90 percent were raised in predominantly black or well-integrated neighborhoods. These experiences suggest that the black heterosexual family, in all of its varied forms, has been the dominant model for expectations that African American lesbian women have for their families.

LINKING THE EXPERIENCES OF AFRICAN AMERICAN WOMEN TO FEMINIST PRINCIPLES OF EQUALITY

I find that the way lesbians think about partner responsibilities in their relationships is influenced by the social contexts in which they were raised. The women in this study ideologically support the equal division of paid work and housework like lesbians in previous studies, but in practice they more closely emphasize economic independence in their relationships. Unlike the respondents in other research, they do not necessarily draw from egalitarian feminist ideologies in their relationships. Insights from the literature on black feminist thought can shed light on why this is so. Historical documents outlining the tenets of black feminism reveal that the equal division of housework and market labor in male/female relationships was never a dominant component of black feminist frameworks.[20] Egalitarian relationships were certainly important to black feminists, but unlike white feminists, who saw inequality as rooted in relationships between men and women in home life and in economic life, black women concentrated their platform on how to reduce the gender inequality they believed was connected to inequalities based on race and socioeconomic disadvantage.[21]

Patricia Hill Collins and Bonnie Thornton Dill both argue that, relative to whites, black family structures have historically been more varied.[22] Comparatively fewer blacks have spent time in nuclear family units where there is one male primary or solitary earner. Black women have had comparatively greater labor force participation, and their male partners have had less earnings advantage relative to white men.[23] Historically, black women have experienced competing sources of oppression, based not only on gender but also on race, socioeconomic status, and blocked occupational mobility.[24] These factors combine to focus the attention of black women on other problems and issues outside of the platforms white lesbian feminists were fighting for.

The poor, working-class, and middle-class family backgrounds of the respondents in this study shape the values they bring to their lesbian relationships. Their values are consistent with egalitarian ideologies, but they also add other dimensions to our analyses of equality and fairness in relationships. These women create families using their understanding of role expectations that were learned through their socialization in black family structures. While patriarchy is something they find oppressive, it is not often directly related to how and why they organize same-sex partnerships in a particular way. Instead, economic independence, survival, and mobility are most important to them. The economic contribution of partners does not have to be equal—they grant their partners some leeway to complete their education, to recover from illness, or to deal with various other extenuating circumstances. However, what is paramount is that both partners can contribute as well as take away their own financial resources.

NOTES

1. Examples include work by Patterson (1995), Kurdek (1993), Carrington (1999), Gartrell et al. (2000), and Mezey (2008). But Maureen Sullivan's 2004 study is one exception. Although her sample is almost all white and middle class, the family backgrounds of her respondents include both working- and middle-class experiences, which are reflected in the way they conceptualize their lesbian relationships.

2. Walby (1990).

3. For example, in Sullivan's 2004 study of lesbian-headed families, economic independence is not a direct concern for her respondents because they are largely middle-class, dual-earner couples with relatively secure jobs and financial resources. A portion of her sample is working class, but the author's analysis of egalitarianism in these families concerns how the partners divide housework and child care and does not focus on the

association between economic independence and relationship satisfaction. Sullivan finds that self-sufficiency is a trait some women from working-class families were raised to value in their relationships, but it is not a deciding factor in their decision-making about family and work responsibilities (p. 108). Nelson's 1996 study of lesbian-headed households finds conflict around parenting authority among partners in blended families, but it does not provide an analysis of the way respondents feel about economic independence and self-sufficiency in their unions.

4. See, for example, Ferree (1991); Hochschild (1989); Tichenor (2005).

5. See, for example, Carrington (1999); Sullivan (2004); Kurdek (1993); Moore (2008).

6. See Kurdek (1993); Patterson (1995); Nelson (1996); Sullivan (2004).

7. Blumstein and Schwartz (1983), 60.

8. For differences between black and white heterosexual couples in the relative importance of economic contributions of partners, see Bulcroft and Bulcroft (1993). For the relationship between race and gender ideologies among women and men, see Ransford and Miller (1983); Hunter and Sellers (1998); Kamo and Cohen (1998). For understandings of married and cohabiting couples and their financial accounts, see Kenney (2006).

9. Wolf (1979).

10. I make this argument in my 2006 article, "Lipstick or Timberlands? Meanings of Gender Presentation in Black Lesbian Communities." Even many college-educated black lesbians first came into their gay sexualities in predominantly black social circles and predominantly black college settings. See Cornwell (1983); Abdulahad et al. (1983).

11. See Dang and Frazer (2004); Gates (2008).

12. Four percent of women in the sample might be considered "working poor" because they were single mothers and their income-to-needs ratio at the time of the interview put them below the poverty line for their family size. These women have been included in the working-class socioeconomic category in this study.

13. For details on the sample recruitment and other aspects of these data, see Moore (2008).

14. See Moore (2008) for an analysis of the division of household labor and the importance of economic independence in the Invisible Families data.

15. All names are pseudonyms. The ages given for the respondents are their ages in the year 2004.

16. See Schwartz (1994), 111.

17. Sullivan (2004) reports something similar among the portion of her sample that was working class. She found that women from working-class backgrounds were taught "not to depend on anyone for material or other support but to survive and make a life for oneself, by oneself, because no one would be there to help" (p. 107).

18. Landry (2000), 79.

19. Landry (2000) also makes this argument in his work.

20. See Combahee River Collective (1983).

21. See King (1988) and Combahee River Collective (1983).

22. See Collins (2004); Dill (1979).

23. See Kessler-Harris (2003).

24. See Crenshaw (1995); Collins (2004).

In Other Words

WHAT IS FRIENDSHIP? LEARNING FROM ASEXUAL AND AROMANTIC PERSPECTIVES

Emily Fox and Canton Winer, October 25, 2022 / CCF@TSP

Imagine a world where everyone searches for their one true Friend, someone they hope to spend the rest of their life with. You can have as many lovers as you'd like, as long as those extra relationships don't interfere with or detract from this central Friendship. Esther Rothblum, a psychologist whose work centers lesbian relationships and LGBTQ+ life, proposes this thought experiment to highlight how our culture privileges romantic relationships over friendships in all areas of life.

Defining "friend" is surprisingly difficult, and friendships are often conceptualized in contrast to other types of relationships. A friend is likely someone you know, like, and trust more than someone you consider an acquaintance. You might think of a friend as someone you love but don't want to have sex with. Or a friend may be someone you like to hang out with, but who you wouldn't want to hang out with over an expensive candlelit dinner surrounded by other romantic couples.

We usually treat friendships like "extra" relationships that add a little fun to our everyday lives, but we don't organize our lives around them. For instance, most people wouldn't turn down a dream job because their best friend didn't want to move to another city with them. If you noticed that someone brought their best friend to a wedding as their plus-one, rather than their romantic partner, you might wonder if they broke up. Spending too much time with a friend or appearing "too close" may solicit inquiries and rumors questioning if you really are "just friends." These examples reveal the cultural assumption that everyone wants sexual and romantic relationships, but this isn't the case. What is friendship when romantic and sexual relationships are not a relevant point of comparison?

First, we can turn to *asexuality*, which commonly refers to the experience of little or no sexual attraction. Although asexual people often do not experience sexual attraction, many report experiencing other forms of attraction, including romantic and platonic attraction. Based on this framework of multiple forms of attraction, many asexual people combine their romantic and sexual attractions to form identities like heteroromantic asexual, homoromantic asexual, panromantic asexual, etc.

But what *is* romantic attraction in the absence of sexual attraction? Without sexual attraction, how can you tell if you are drawn to someone as a friend or as a lover? Put plainly, when you can't define a friend as someone you like but do not want to have sex with, the line between friend and lover becomes much fuzzier.

Because of this, asexual folks often think of relationships as a spectrum rather than as either friendships or romantic relationships.

Further complicating all of this, some individuals (and not just those under the asexuality umbrella) experience little or no romantic attraction, often described as *aromanticism*. Whereas asexuality blurs the line between friendships and romantic relationships, aromanticism challenges the idea that romance is the pinnacle of emotional intimacy. People who are aromantic ask us to question why, exactly, romantic relationships are privileged over all other relationships, and why sex and romance are so tightly linked.

Other sexual and romantic relationship lifestyles challenge similar assumptions. For example, people who have sex with friends or are in consensual nonmonogamous relationships also challenge the idea that sexual experiences should be limited to romantic relationships. Polyamorous folks and those who practice relationship anarchy do not restrict emotional intimacy to one central relationship, opposing the idea that romantic love should be exclusive and scarce. Queer folks have contested the boundaries between friend and family, creating chosen families that are accepting and loving.

The privileging of romantic and sexual relationships creates barriers for anyone who does not follow the "traditional" trajectory of heterosexual, monogamous marriage. Relationships that are not family or marital relationships don't receive institutional or legal recognition. There is no ceremony to solidify and celebrate your status as friends. Many benefits and rights allotted under family law cannot be extended to friends, such as insurance coverage, the ability to file joint taxes, visitation rights for someone in the hospital, and the release of deceased to next-of-kin for burial or cremation.

In other words, challenging the privileging of sexual and romantic relationships involves coming up against various cultural, legal, and economic institutions. How would our world look different if all types of connection and closeness were recognized and celebrated? The perspectives of asexual, aromantic, queer, and nonmonogamous folks raise perhaps more questions than current research has answers to, but they point toward the cultural assumptions that underlie dominant understandings of "friendship." ■

PART FIVE

How Does Policy Link to Personal Lives?

20

Beyond Family Structure

Family Process Studies Help to Reframe Debates about What's Good for Children

Philip A. Cowan and Carolyn Pape Cowan

Ever since 1992, when Republican vice president Dan Quayle criticized Murphy Brown, a television character, for having a baby without being married, family values and family policies have assumed an important role in political debates between those with a liberal or conservative bent. Should single parenthood be discouraged and marriage encouraged? Should abortion be restricted? Should divorces be made more difficult or easier to obtain? Should poor families receive income supplements or tax breaks? These questions frame the discussion of family issues in terms of categories or typologies. Most often, the focus is on family structure—are the biological parents married, divorced, cohabiting, separated, or single? In this chapter, we argue that what is left out of too many contemporary family policy discussions is a concern with family process—the quality or pattern of the interactions among family members.

We are concerned with family policy debates, not only because government regulations affect the lives of many families but also because the debates in themselves have the power to influence what ordinary families actually do. Conclusions about the presumed negative consequences of single parenthood and divorce, for example, propel at least some toward marriage and others to preserve their marriage despite misery or domestic violence. It would be well, then, to make sure that both the logic and the evidence cited by conflicting policy advocates actually support their positions.

We see some difficulties with the evidence cited by both liberals and conservatives who describe families in terms of categories or types. Both sides typically justify their policy positions by pointing to social science research that purports to show that their view would lead to children's enhanced development and well-being, whereas the opposing view would fail to help children and might place them in harm's way. Some examples:

- Those who advocate policies to encourage marriage note that single mothers are more likely to be poor, and their children more likely to be at risk for academic difficulties and behavior problems.[1] Marriage, they argue, could bring the family out of poverty, with resulting benefits to children. Those who advocate policies to support family diversity point to research showing that a large majority of children in every type of family arrangement do well, and that poor mothers who marry do not tend to achieve new levels of income.[2]

- Opponents of same-sex marriage often claim that children will suffer from the absence of both male and female role models in their household. Supporters of same-sex marriage point out that, contrary to stereotype, children of lesbian parents are not significantly different from children of heterosexual parents on a number of key developmental measures.[3]

- In *The Case for Marriage: Why Married People Are Happier, Healthier, and Better Off Financially*, Waite and Gallagher summarize large numbers of studies showing that, on average, in comparison with nonmarried couples, married couples are better off.[4] Although the authors mention that many of these advantages accrue primarily to happily married couples, they continue to minimize that distinction throughout the book. This is an important omission, because they do not cite a good deal of evidence that couples in high-conflict marriages are less healthy than couples who can regulate negative emotion in the course of an argument, and that the children of unhappily married couples suffer from their parents' heated or unresolved conflicts.[5]

We live in a time when polarized public discussions are the norm. The proponents of a particular view assume that they can be right only if they prove the other side wrong. In our attempt to highlight the importance of family process, we will not argue that categorical descriptions of families in terms of structure or demographics are irrelevant to discussions of family policy. There are often important differences in outcomes for children whose parents are married, divorced, or single, and these facts can help us fashion appropriate policies or interventions. But, as clinical psychologists, we intend to add a relatively neglected perspective to those of family sociologists and demographers by focusing on the *quality* of relationships within the family. Our own view is that (1) both ways of describing families are important in understanding children's well-being, and (2) a consideration of information about family processes will lead to more nuanced policy recommendations for governments, social service agencies, and families themselves that differ from typical conservative and liberal approaches to American family policy.

Due to the constraints of chapter length, we have chosen to focus our discussion of family process and children's well-being primarily on issues concerning the involvement of fathers in family life, and the quality of the relationship between the parents. This choice leads us to ignore other equally important family decision-making and policy questions such as whether both partners should work outside the home and use local child care facilities, whether the government should regulate workplace practices to provide support for workers' family lives (e.g., through family leave), or whether it is the government's responsibility to provide high-quality child care.

We begin by briefly summarizing the voluminous data on the association between categories of family structure and children's well-being. We then summarize the research on family process guided by a family systems model, which demonstrates that a combination of data regarding five family risk or protective factors provides the best explanations of children's level of development, adaptation, and problematic behavior. This model has guided a new set of interventions designed to encourage fathers' involvement in the daily lives of their children. We then explore the implications of this family systems model for parents, family intervention providers, and family policy makers. We conclude that, in contrast with conservative thinkers who advocate inducements to poor single parents to marry and liberal thinkers who advocate family income supplements to poor families, the data suggest that interventions to strengthen couple relationships and support fathers in a more central role in family life—regardless of whether the co-parents are married or intimate partners—have the potential to provide important benefits for children's social, emotional, and academic development.

FAMILY STRUCTURE, FAMILY DEMOGRAPHICS, FAMILY VALUES, AND CHILDREN'S WELL-BEING

As Stephanie Coontz points out in Chapter 6 of this volume, a great many changes in family structure and demographics have occurred over the past century, although the amount of change depends in part on the beginning and end points of our historical search. We focus here on the fact that beginning in the 1960s there have been marked increases in the rates of single parenthood and divorce and a decline in marriage rates and birth rates. The central question for family policy is how to interpret these changes. If they are interpreted as evidence of a decline in the quality of family life, then we should consider what kinds of family arrangements, social services, and government policies might alleviate the negative impact or reverse the negative effects. If the changes are interpreted as evidence of family variety, resilience, and an adaptive response to historical and economic shifts, then proposals that would affect marriage and divorce *rates* through government regulation or the provision of social services may not be necessary.

Controversies about the Impact of Divorce

The question of how divorce affects children remains one of the most contested areas of family research. There is not room for details here, but the issue has been well described elsewhere in both U.S. and U.K. publications.[6] There is no doubt that, at least in the short term, both parents and children are affected when parents separate. Most children of any age are extremely upset by the divorce of their parents, and a substantial number suffer at least temporary setbacks in social and emotional development and academic achievement. In the long term, however, the negative effects often dissipate, so that "only" about 20 percent of children suffer in lasting ways.[7] This means that although some children may be suffering some negative consequences of their parents' divorce, it is also true that the vast majority will go on to develop healthy and productive lives. In our view, the sociologist Paul Amato has a sensible perspective on the issues surrounding divorce.[8] He suggests that the usual framing of the question "Does divorce hurt children: yes or no?" is misleading. He suggests a more differentiated approach:

> Divorce benefits some individuals, leads others to experience temporary decrements in well-being, and forces others on a downward trajectory from which they might never recover fully. Understanding the contingencies under which divorce leads to these diverse outcomes is a priority for future research.

As we will see later in this chapter, some important contingencies can be found in the research on family processes, especially based on how conflict between parents before and after divorce is handled.

Controversies about the Impact of Single Parenthood: Problems with the Definition

There is no doubt that if you are an actuary interested in predicting outcomes for single-parent and two-parent families, you can rely on the myriad of studies showing that, on average, a large list of behavioral and school problems appear more frequently in children living with only one parent.[9] Again, the question is how to interpret the correlational finding. Some senior policy makers treat the correlational data as causal; if single parenthood increases poverty and produces risks for children, then provide incentives for single parents to get married and the lives of children will improve.[10] Of course, it is impossible to do a randomized clinical trial of this hypothesis by assigning some women randomly to a "get married group" and others to a "stay single" group. But we lack even correlational data to show that when poverty declines and single parents marry, their children's well-being increases.

Some researchers argue that the association between single parenthood and negative outcomes for children reflects a selection effect—parents with more financial, intellectual, and social resources are more likely to marry and less likely to divorce. In a careful summary of the literature, Cherlin concludes that even after selection effects are considered, there is a small but statistically significant effect of family structure (married vs. single) on children.[11] That is, family structure plays some role in determining outcomes for children, but most of the children raised in single-parent homes fare quite well. It is necessary, then, to examine other factors to explain the finding that children of single parents are more likely to have cognitive, social, or emotional difficulties.

Beyond the controversies about whether single parenthood represents a risk factor for children, there lies a serious flaw in the way single parenthood is conceptualized and whether the term is adequate to describe the heterogeneous array of family arrangements that exist in modern nuclear family cultures.[12] There certainly are parents who are raising children on their own, but most are collaborating with at least one other person actively involved in raising their child.[13] The co-parent may be an intimate partner such as a boyfriend or girlfriend, or a non-intimate partner such as the child's grandparent, the parent's uncle or aunt, brother or sister, or close friend. The fact that all these possibilities have been lumped together in the category of "single parent" means that it is impossible to determine whether the discrepancies in child outcomes between two-parent and single-parent families found by researchers is actually due to the number of parents in the child's life.

Controversies about the Negative Impact of Historical Changes in Family Values

Many social observers who assert that families are in decline place the blame for this decline on an erosion of family values.[14] They argue that changes in single-parent, divorced, and dual-worker families result from individual decisions about family life that reflect a lack of investment in the importance of becoming "responsible" parents devoted to the care of their children. It follows from this analysis that to protect children, we need interventions that will remind parents of these important family values and convince them to reinvest in them.

There are two puzzling aspects of this argument. First, the idea that a change in family values triggered the social trends we have been discussing is not based on any data we know of that (1) assess changes in family values over time and (2) show that values held by individual men and women are in fact correlated with the family arrangements they have constructed. One counterexample can be seen in an interview study of low-income unmarried women[15] suggesting that they hold rather traditional family values concerning the importance and desirability of marriage and the need to be on a stable footing financially before marrying or becoming parents, and that these ideals lead them to be wary of entering into marriages they believe are doomed to fail.

A second response to the focus on family values as explaining negative family trends comes from newly emerging studies using quantitative data. One of the major sources of stress for contemporary families is financial.[16] Financial circumstances often affect family decisions about marriage, divorce, and whether both partners need to work outside the home. Not only do families feel external stress from lack of adequate earnings and little workplace flexibility, but social service resources for families in difficulty are limited. Even fewer resources are available for preventive services to offer assistance to families before their dysfunction reaches a level that is difficult to treat. From this perspective, what is needed to protect children is not an exhortation to parents to adopt more positive family values (a relatively inexpensive approach valued by many politicians) but rather serious governmental commitment to change the economic circumstances that play havoc with the lives of mothers, fathers, and children.

These brief accounts of research on family values, divorce, and single parenthood serve to make our main point. "Family decline" proponents who pay attention only to family categories overstate the magnitude of the effects; their presentations make it appear as if nontraditional family structures account for the major proportion of social problems and psychopathology in children and youth. These overstatements are then used to justify recommendations to parents, social service providers, and policy makers. To protect children, they say, we should encourage married parents to stay together, make divorces harder to obtain, and encourage single parents to marry. We will use the same data and additional studies to come to a different conclusion: to protect children and prevent parents' divorce, we could profitably provide services to strengthen couple relationships before they become so problematic and painful that separation and divorce become reasonable options.

FAMILY PROCESS AND CHILDREN'S WELL-BEING: A FRAMEWORK BASED ON FIVE FAMILY RISK AND PROTECTIVE FACTORS

The family structure and demographic approach represents an outsider perspective on family life. One can categorize a family as, for example, low income or high income, married or not married, on the basis of the kind of information gathered in the census. By contrast, the family process approach pays attention to the characteristics of each family member and especially to how the members behave with each other. What are the central factors in a family process approach? Elsewhere, we have summarized our own research and many other studies that support a five-domain family systems risk model of children's adaptation.[17] This model demonstrates that a child's cognitive, social, and emotional development can be explained by information concerning five kinds of risk or protective factors that affect children's development:

1. The level of adaptation of each family member, their self-perceptions, and indicators of mental health and psychological distress
2. The quality of both mother-child and father-child relationships
3. The quality of the relationship between the parents, including communication styles, conflict resolution, problem-solving styles, and emotion regulation
4. The patterns of both couple and parent-child relationships transmitted across the generations from grandparents to parents to children
5. The balance between life stressors and social supports outside the immediate family

Each Parent's Level of Adaptation

Beyond the questions of whether parents are married or poor, a family process approach looks at either or both parents' well-being and whether they are suffering from depression, anxiety, personality disorders, or serious mental illness. The task here is not to place parents in a particular diagnostic category, but to discover whether their difficulties interfere with or affect the quality of their relationships with each other and their children. Not surprisingly, evidence suggests that parents who are depressed, antisocial, or schizophrenic are less effective at solving their problems as a couple and function less effectively to provide nurturance, guidance, and limit setting appropriate to the age of their children.[18]

Mother-Child and Father-Child Relationships

People have many different ideas about what constitutes effective parenting. It is noteworthy that the proliferation of self-help books on parenting presents widely different prescriptions for parenting behavior, most without systematic evidence to support the author's recommendations.[19] The picture brightens somewhat when we turn to systematic studies of parenting styles. There is reasonable agreement in the research literature on children's development that authoritative parenting—a combination of parental warmth, structure, limit setting and appropriate demands for maturity—provides a context in which children are more likely to develop effective cognitive skills, better relationships with peers, and fewer behavior problems.[20] Other parenting styles are less effective. Authoritarian parenting is harsh and highly structured. Permissive parenting is warm but laissez-faire, with few if any limits. Neglectful or uninvolved parenting is neither warm nor structured and demanding. It is probably obvious that parental harshness and neglect are not good for children. The lesson here for modern parents who both work and tend to see their children for shorter times during their waking hours is that warmth without some limits and maturity demands is not helpful in stimulating children's growth or the development of social and cognitive skills and self-regulation.

A serious limitation of both the popular and social science literatures is that *parent* has generally meant "mother." Only in the past few decades have there been systematic studies of father-child relationships,[21] and an even smaller body of information examines how the combination of two parents' parenting styles affects children's development. Yet it should be no surprise that systematic studies find that when fathers are more positively engaged with their children's daily lives, the children, the mothers, and the fathers themselves are more likely to be competent, form more positive relationships with peers, and show fewer signs of emotional distress. Furthermore, when we add information about the *quality* of the father-child relationship, it enhances our ability to account for children's adaptation, over and above what we know about the quality of the mother-child relationship.

We should make clear what we are not saying here. We do not mean to imply that fathers should be encouraged to be involved with their children when they are abusive to the child or the mother. And we are not arguing, as some do,[22] that having a father is essential to raising a well-adjusted child. We are simply stating that a second, positively engaged parent or parent figure can make an additional and unique contribution to children's cognitive, social, and emotional development.

The Couple Relationship

Another conspicuous omission from popular books on raising children is the conclusion from a growing body of recent research based on family systems principles about the effect of the parents' relationship on their children. With few exceptions,[23] the popular books focus almost entirely on how mothers relate to their children. What recent family systems research studies reveal is that the quality of the relationship *between* the parents—whether they are married, separated, or divorced—is consistently correlated with how children fare. When couples are unable to resolve their disagreements and either escalate their anger or withdraw into freezing silence, their children are at risk for difficulties in every developmental domain.[24]

We describe later in this chapter some intervention studies that help answer the question of whether conflict or withdrawal in the relationship between parents plays a *causal* role in children's development. Here we briefly summarize two speculations to explain the correlations. First, parents' behavior can have a direct, anxiety-provoking effect on children. When parents' anger toward each other is out of control or they fail to talk with each other for hours or days, many children become increasingly frightened, anxious, and vulnerable. Second, when parents fail to provide a nurturing environment for each other, it is difficult to provide a caring environment for their child; the metaphor of "spillover"—anger or resentment that overflows from the relationship between the parents to one or both parent-child relationships—is used to explain the link between couple conflict and children's problematic outcomes.[25]

Intergenerational Transmission of Family Patterns

Substantial evidence exists to support the widespread belief that family patterns tend to be repeated from one generation to the next.[26] We are not suggesting that difficulties in our family of origin doom us to repeat the maladaptive patterns of our forebears. We are simply reporting the finding that mental illness in individuals, harsh or neglectful treatment of children, and dysfunctional couple relationships in one generation increase the risks of similar negative outcomes in the next generation.[27] Fortunately, although positive patterns do not guarantee good outcomes, they function as protective factors that increase the likelihood of good outcomes.

During the transition to first-time parenthood, patterns from the parents' relationships in their families of origin become particularly salient. Each parent has some patterns they wish to repeat and some they wish to change in this new family. Coordinating these potentially different dreams is a challenge faced by many new parents. If neither parent has positive models, the challenge is even greater Attempts to change current family relationship quality almost inevitably involve increasing the consciousness of both parents about the patterns they wish to carry over or avoid from the families in which they grew up.

Life Stress and Social Support Outside the Family

What happens inside the nuclear family is affected by the external environment and the family's relationship to it. Families tend to fare better when outside stressors are few or at least balanced by adequate support from kin, friends, and social institutions. Evidence from McLoyd and colleagues' summary of research on African American families[23] and Conger and colleagues' research on white farm families during a recession[29] indicate that poverty affects children through its corrosive effects on the quality of both couple and parent-child relationships Stress in the workplace has a similarly disruptive spillover effect on family relationships.[30]

The Full Model

Most studies of children's development focus on one or at most two of these five family risk and protective domains. Elsewhere we have shown that each of these domains contributes uniquely to predicting children's academic and social competence as well as their internalizing and externalizing problem behaviors in early elementary school.[31] Child-rearing is not simply a matter of "good parenting." Children are also affected by their parents' psychological adjustment and their ability as a couple to resolve problems and disagreements between them, by the repetition of cycles across generations, and by the availability of people and institutions to provide support when the culture, country, and neighborhood impose pressures that are difficult to avoid. Data from studies based on this model imply that when family interventions focus on only one of these aspects of families' lives, they may have limited effectiveness.

For example, there is currently a large public and private industry devoted to "parenting classes." For a long while, the news was disappointing; the few evaluated programs amassed very little evidence that the classes had direct positive effects on children's behavior, but more recently, parenting classes embedded in university-based research programs have shown some signs of success.[32] The importance of thinking in terms of more than one domain during a parenting intervention is supported by studies showing that therapeutic treatment for mothers of aggressive children often fails to work until fathers become involved and the relationship between the parents is addressed directly.[33]

We have only begun to test the hypothesis that family processes play a causal role in children's well-being. It can be argued that some of the links between family process and children's well-being are genetic and that genetic transmission is not subject to interventions that can change family relationships, but newer formulations of the interaction of genes and the environment indicate that even when personality characteristics are highly heritable, changes in the family relationship environment can affect how and whether heritability leads to negative outcomes in the children.[34]

The correlations between marital conflict and children's outcomes suggest that interventions focusing on the relationship between the parents will be helpful to children,[35] but we cannot use correlational studies as proof of our claim. We need to provide some data from intervention studies that have used randomized control designs to demonstrate that when the interventions were followed by more effective and satisfying couple relationships, parenting effectiveness and the children's behavior were affected in positive ways.

Some Examples of Preventive Intervention Studies Based on Our Multi-Domain Model

The reason for our emphasis on couple relationships when we consider children's well-being lies in an unfortunate fact. In addition to marital dissatisfaction leading to a high divorce rate (around 50 percent of marriages), more than fifty studies in Western industrialized societies[36] find that, on average, men's and women's satisfaction with their relationship declines over at least the first fifteen years of marriage (we know of no longitudinal studies beyond that point). This trend is significant not only for the well-being of couples but also for the well-being of their children, because other studies show consistent connections between marital dissatisfaction and unresolved couple conflict, and children's and adolescents' achievement, aggressive behavior, and depression.[37] Given these links, interventions that help couples maintain satisfaction with their relationship would be an important goal.

Over the past forty-five years, we and our colleagues have conducted and evaluated interventions in the form of couples groups led by clinically trained co-leaders.[38] Of eight evaluations of this approach, five used a randomized clinical trial in which some couples were randomly chosen to participate in the intervention while comparable others were not. The co-leaders met with the couples weekly over at least four months, and assessments of the family factors were made before and after the group interventions to evaluate the groups' effectiveness. The couples were not seeking family treatment but responding to an invitation to meet with our staff around a key family transition or during their children's early development; for example, the transition to parenthood or the children's transition to school. Our goal was to create a preventive intervention to enhance family relationships when the children were early in their development and prevent small problems and strains from becoming more serious. We did not attempt to teach couples specific skills but to help them become the kind of couples and parents they were hoping to be. We aimed to do this by providing a safe environment in which they could consider issues concerning their needs as individuals, as a couple, and as parents. Our interventions and assessments also focused on their ties with their parents and children and on how to cope with stress and distress and enlist supports inside and outside the family.

Working with Couples during the Transition to Parenthood

In the Becoming a Family Project,[39] we followed ninety-six couples regularly over a period of five years: seventy-two entered the study when pregnant with their first child, and twenty-four were not yet parents and not pregnant.[40] All ninety-six couples completed regular interviews and questionnaires until their first child had completed kindergarten. Some of the expectant couples, randomly chosen, were offered the opportunity to participate in a couples group that met weekly with their co-leaders for twenty-four weeks (six months). Each group session included some open time to discuss personal events and concerns in their lives and a topic that addressed one of the five aspects of family life in our model.

Relevant to the focus of this chapter, we found that the new parents who were not offered the intervention experienced a decline in satisfaction as a couple. The new parent couples who took part in an ongoing couples group maintained their level of satisfaction over the next five years until their children finished kindergarten. Although expectant couples in both conditions were initially quite happy, five years later, the average scores of couples in the control group had descended into the range in which half of them resembled couples already seeking therapy. Five years after the groups for the parents ended, the quality of the couple relationships and the parent-child relationships in all the families during the preschool period predicted the children's adaptation to kindergarten as their teachers rated it—academically, socially, and in terms of problematic behaviors. This finding seemed especially strong since the teachers who were in many different schools did not know which children in their class were participants in the study.

Couple Relationships and Children's Transition to School

A second intervention study, the Schoolchildren and Their Families Project, followed a new set of 100 couples from the year before their first child entered kindergarten until the children were in eleventh grade.[41] There were three randomly assigned conditions—an offer to use our staff as consultants once a year (the control group), a couples group that emphasized parent-child relationships, and a couples group that focused more on the relationship between the parents during the open-ended part of each evening. That is, we were comparing the effects of a more traditional parenting intervention (although it is unusual to have fathers attending with mothers) with a group in which leaders focused more on the relationship between the parents. The study followed up with the families when their children were in kindergarten and first grade. Parents who had been in a group emphasizing parent-child relationships had indeed improved in aspects of effective parenting that we observed in our project playroom, whereas the parenting style of parents in the control group showed no change. By contrast, parents who had participated in a group in which the leaders focused more on couple relationships showed significantly less conflict as we observed them, *and* their parenting became more effective.

In this study, both variations of the ongoing intervention groups had an effect on parent-child relationships and the children's behavior. Notably, parents in the couples groups became less disengaged, more likely to be warm and responsive, less harsh, and more likely to provide structure and appropriate limits when their children disobeyed them. The children of parents who received the parenting-focused intervention improved in positive self-image, and they were less likely to exhibit shy, withdrawn, and depressed behavior at school. Children of parents in the couples-focused groups earned higher scores on individually administered achievement tests and showed lower levels of aggressive behavior at school. The interventions continued to have a significant impact on the families over the next ten years—in terms of both self-reported and observed couple relationship quality and low levels of behavior problems in the high school students. The impact of the couples-focused groups was always equal to or greater than the impact of the parenting-focused groups.

Enhancing Father Involvement in Low-Income Families

Based on the results of the first two studies, the California Department of Social Services Office of Child Abuse Prevention asked us to design and evaluate an intervention intended to enhance and maintain the positive involvement of low-income fathers with their children. Along with Marsha Kline Pruett from Smith College and Kyle Pruett from Yale University Medical School, we completed the first phase of the Supporting Father Involvement Project, in which ninety-six couples in four counties attended a single-session workshop that presented material about the importance of fathers in children's lives (the control group), ninety-two fathers attended a sixteen-week fathers group, and ninety-five fathers and their partners attended a sixteen-week couples group.[42] Again, the assignment was random, the groups were led by clinically trained male/female co-leaders, and the curriculum for both fathers and couples groups focused on the five family risk and protective factors we have been describing.

At the beginning of the study, children ranged in age from in utero to seven years old. The project was mounted in Family Resource Centers in four California counties; two-thirds of the participants were Mexican American and one-third were European American; 75 percent were married, and 20 percent were cohabiting; and two-thirds of the households in both ethnic groups had incomes below twice the federal poverty line. Assessments (in English or Spanish) at baseline, two months after the groups ended, and again one year after the groups ended, revealed the positive impact of participation in one of the intervention groups: compared with participants in the control condition, participants in both the fathers group and the couples group showed improvement. Fathers' involvement in the day-to-day activities of their children (feeding, playing, taking to the doctor) increased significantly, and the children's level of aggressive and depressed behaviors remained stable. In comparison, the parents of the children in the control group described their children as increasingly aggressive or depressed over the same period of time. Participants in the couples group showed additional important benefits. Both fathers and mothers showed a significant decline in parenting stress, and they maintained their satisfaction as couples, in contrast with parents in the control group and those assigned to the fathers-only group, whose parenting stress rose and relationship satisfaction declined.

A second trial of the Supporting Father Involvement study was conducted with a new cohort of 236 Mexican American, African American, and European American families in five California counties.[43] This time, because the participants in the earlier single-session meeting had changed negatively, we did not include a control group with no intervention. And, because the couples group had stronger effects than the fathers-only group, fathers and mothers were enrolled in a couples intervention trial. The positive changes over the eighteen months of the study were very similar to those we observed in the earlier study. A third replication of the Supporting Father Involvement study with 239 low-income participants in five California counties recruited community couples and couples who had been referred by the child welfare system in California.[44] Some couples were randomly invited to participate in couples groups immediately, while others were placed on a waitlist and offered a chance to participate in couples groups six months later (the control condition). Compared with the results of those in the control group, the intervention produced a significant reduction in couple conflict, which, in turn, was related to reductions in harsh parenting and in children's aggressive behaviors and depressed symptoms eighteen months after their parents entered the study. Outcomes were as positive for the families referred by child welfare as for the families recruited from the community. A surprising outcome was that the couples who received the intervention also showed a statistically significant gain in yearly income.

Service centers in other locales have evaluated the Supporting Father Involvement intervention. New studies have been conducted in Alberta, Canada, funded by a private foundation;[45] in England, funded by the British government;[46] and in Malta, funded by an international bank.

In sum, we have shown that the preventive intervention groups, especially the groups for both mothers and fathers, had positive effects on fathers' involvement, parenting styles, parenting stress, couple relationship satisfaction, and children's problematic behavior. All these aspects of life are related to children's well-being, and all function as either risk or protective factors for child abuse and neglect.

WHAT FAMILY PROCESS RESEARCH CONTRIBUTES TO DISCUSSIONS OF CURRENT FAMILY ISSUES

Implications for Parents

Men and women who make the transition to parenthood together become wrapped up in the mysteries and wonders of raising a baby. They devote most of their non-worktime to nurturing the baby; feeding, soothing, and playing with the baby; and looking after the baby's physical needs. They often report feeling guilty about taking time for themselves or each other. The research we have described in this chapter suggests that maintaining the connection between the parents is actually a gift to their child that is likely to improve the quality of the parent-child relationship.

Authors of a number of books and articles that draw heavily on social science research conclude that, except for situations of domestic violence or abuse, parents in unhappy marriages should attempt to stay together to avoid the negative impact of divorce on their children. Almost all the research they refer to adopts a family structure perspective, simply following children of divorce over time or comparing them with similar samples of children whose parents did not divorce. What is usually missing is a second comparison group—children of high-conflict parents or low-conflict but unhappy parents who stay together and are similarly followed over time.[47] Studies of families in which the parents are unhappy indicate that keeping the family structure intact without regard to the quality of the key family relationships does not guarantee children's well-being.

Implications of Family Process Findings for Family Interventions

In earlier sections of this chapter, we pointed to the fact that although various domains of family life are correlated, that does not mean that they are *causally* related to each other—or that we could expect change in one domain to produce change in other domains, as family systems theory suggests. However, our couples group intervention data, especially when the intervention participants were compared with randomly assigned control group participants, provide strong evidence that changes in the quality of the relationship between parents causally affects the quality of parent-child relationships and children's problematic behavior. This fact should help service providers to design their family-strengthening interventions more effectively.

We have stated that one of the best predictors of whether a father will become and stay involved with his child is the quality of the father's relationship with the mother. The few existing systematic evaluations of fathers groups composed only of low-income men show disappointing outcomes.[48] Most of the fathers groups attempting to increase father involvement have occurred long after the parents have separated or divorced and after the fathers have lost contact with their children. Not surprisingly, the mothers of the children were not supportive of their ex-spouse or ex-partner's attempts to take an active role in their child's life. Our own family intervention studies show stronger effects for couples groups than for fathers groups. Father involvement, then, emerges not simply from men's decisions to be involved in the family but from the ways in which the quality of family relationships enhances or interferes with men's relationships with their children.

Both correlational studies and the intervention studies we have cited suggest that the many classes for parents offered in community colleges and social service agencies require some rethinking. First, the classes need to make stronger efforts to recruit *both* parents or co-parenting figures and provide experiences that will help them want to continue attending the classes. Second, the curriculum should pay much more attention to how the partners work together— or fail to work together—to deal with co-parenting and other challenges or disagreements.

Implications for Government Policy Makers

In its growing concern over the erosion of marriage and the problems of children whose parents dissolved their marriage, the U.S. Federal Administration for Children and Families (ACF) used research-based findings from the Fragile Families Study[49] as a rationale for government intervention. The finding that many unmarried biological fathers have an ongoing romantic relationship with the mother when their child is born but fade from their child's life over the next few years[50] was used as a justification for promoting marriage, especially among low-income populations. Starting in 2005, this policy objective was supported by more than $150 million per year for five years with money from the Deficit Reduction ("welfare reform") Act.

While some of this money has been used in direct efforts to encourage marriage, a substantial amount was allocated to two very large research projects funded by the ACF to test the effectiveness of "marriage education." One large intervention project involving more than four thousand couples—Building Strong Families, conducted by Mathematica—focused on unmarried low-income couples having babies.[51] Although the results of this study were disappointing, indicating no overall effects of the intervention when contrasted with a randomly assigned no-treatment control group, there were significant effects for African American couples. A flaw in the implementation of this project was a very low attendance rate of around 35 percent. Another equally large random-assignment study, Supporting Healthy Marriage, conducted by the nonprofit organization MDRC, focused on married low-income couples, most of whom were already parents.[52] This study, with attendance rates around 70 percent, did find small but statistically significant effects on both self-reported and observed couple relationship quality and on child outcomes for the youngest participants.

The effects of these interventions are not large, and we have yet to determine whether achieving small effects yields benefits that are worth the costs. Some argue that if one goal of the enterprise is to improve conditions for low-income families, why not supplement their incomes directly or at least provide job training, since unemployment is directly linked to low income? Because we are not aware of evidence that income interventions improve distressed couple relationships or parent-child relationships, we suggest that it seems reasonable to give relationship approaches that have shown benefits a chance.[53] Anecdotal reports from the staff conducting these large national projects, along with our own results with both middle- and low-income couples, give some hope that this approach to preventive intervention—strengthening couple and parent-child relationships—holds promise for strengthening families and boosting children's development.

Finally, family process research argues against the currently siloed approach in government policy and service delivery.[54] If, as systematic research has shown, domains of family life are interconnected so that, for example, the extent of fathers' positive involvement with their children is influenced by the fathers' mental health, the state of their relationship with their co-parent, the trajectory of family practices across generations, their financial stresses, and the availability of supports outside the nuclear family, what sense does it make to have separate administrative departments of maternal and child health, mental health, child support, and employment, each providing separate programs in an attempt to strengthen families?

Conclusions

It is too simplistic to think that our evidence about the causal connection among couple relationships, parenting quality, and children's adaptation will be heard by politicians and family agency staff and quickly lead to changes in fatherhood and parenting programs. Haskins,[55] a passionate advocate of using evidence in policy decisions, estimates that only about 1 percent of family-based programs use evidence as a main determinant of their choices, although this state of affairs may be changing.

Researchers and policy makers speak in different languages. Researchers are cautious and talk about probabilities and the need for replication. Policy makers are more concerned with evidence-based programs, as are government and service delivery staff. All are very concerned about costs. But researchers have not provided data on the benefits of programs, with convincing evidence that these benefits actually result in reduced expenditures.

Nevertheless, there are some encouraging signs of a rapprochement. Policy makers are reaching out to researchers. Currently, there is an almost universal demand by funders that the intervention proposals be "evidence-based." Researchers are reaching out to policy makers. In a collaboration between the Princeton Center for Research on Child Wellbeing and the Brookings Institution, the journal *The Future of Children* publishes research on various topics, including child health, couple relationships, and postsecondary education, with a view to promoting effective policies and programs to foster children's development and well-being. In another example, *The Annals of the American Academy of Political and Social Science* recently published a special issue, "Evidence-Based Social Policy: The Promises and Challenges of a Movement." Edited by Haskins (2018), this issue of the journal includes articles from seventeen experts from a variety of settings: various academic disciplines, foundations, nongovernmental organizations, and two U.S. senators. This volume is an exciting illustration of the kind of integration we have been advocating for in this chapter. And the *Journal of Family Theory and Review* (2020) published a special issue on family policy, with contributions from a number of family scientists.[56]

Our goal in this chapter has been to show that systematic research on family processes can add new dimensions to current discussions about how to foster the well-being of parents and children. We have shown that in addition to considering the structure of the family, what fosters children's healthy development and adaptation is having (at least) two parents who are positively involved in the children's lives and in maintaining a satisfying relationship with each other that can approach differences, conflicts, and challenges effectively. We believe that while children can grow up healthy in a one-parent household, they can also benefit from positive relationships with an additional co-parent or co-parenting figures.

In particular, we have highlighted how positively involved fathers and parents who nurture the quality of their relationship as a couple and as co-parents contribute to their children's emotional, social, and academic competence. Furthermore, studies of family process provide important messages for parents, family service agencies, and government policy makers about the need to go beyond attempting to persuade parents to "be responsible." If the policy makers are truly concerned with making a difference in children's well-being, they will need to provide more support for individual mothers and fathers and for the relationship between the parents or parenting figures. Rather than starting family policy discussions with attempts to influence family structure and hoping that children will benefit, we recommend starting with programs that enhance the quality of family relationships, with the expectation that improved family relationships will ultimately make family structures more stable and supportive of the development of all family members.

NOTES

1. Brookings Working Group on Poverty and Opportunity (2015).
2. See summary by L. Lippman (2014).
3. Stacey and Biblarz (2001).
4. Waite and Gallagher (2000).
5. Davies, Cummings, and Winter (2004).
6. For reviews of the research, see Ahrons (2004); Amato (2001); Hetherington and Kelly (2002); Pruett and Barker (2009); Wallerstein, Lewis, and Blakeslee (2000).
7. Hetherington and Kelly (2002).
8. Amato (2000).
9. Dush (2009).
10. Haskins (2018a).
11. Cherlin (2009).
12. Parke (2013); Golombok (2015).
13. Carlson and McLanahan (2002).
14. Wilcox and Lerman (2014).
15. Edin and Reed (2005).
16. Wikle et al. (2021)
17. P. A. Cowan and C. P. Cowan (2014).
18. Perrone et al. (2021).
19. Even very good ones, e.g., Brazelton and Sparrow (2006).

20. Larzelere, Morris, and Harrist (2013).

21. Lamb and Lewis (2013); Cabrera and Tamis-LeMonda (2013); Parke (2002).

22. Blankenhorn (1995); Popenoe (1993).

23. Parke and Cookston (2019); Gannon and Lawrence (2019).

24. Harold et al. (2016).

25. Cowan et al. (2019).

26. Pickreign Stronach et al. (2011).

27. Caspi and Elder (1988).

28. McLoyd et al. (2006).

29. Conger et al. (2011).

30. Schulz et al. (2004).

31. Cowan and Heming (2005).

32. Sheffield et al. (2021).

33. An example can be seen in Dadds, Schwartz, and Sanders (1987).

34. Harold et al. (2013).

35. Harold and Sellers (2018).

36. Twenge, Campbell, and Foster (2003).

37. Harold et al. (2016).

38. Cowan and Cowan (2020).

39. Cowan and Cowan (2000).

40. Cowan and Cowan (2000).

41. Cowan and Heming (2005).

42. Cowan et al. (2009).

43. Cowan et al. (2014).

44. Pruett et al. (2019).

45. Pruett, Gillette, and Pruett (2016).

46. Casey et al. (2017).

47. Booth and Amato (1994).

48. Mincy and Pouncy (2002).

49. Harknett et al. (2001).

50. Carlson and McLanahan (2006).

51. Wood et al. (2014).

52. Lundquist et al. (2014).

53. Cowan and Cowan (2014).

54. Cowan and Cowan (2020).

55. Haskins (2018b).

56. Cowan and Cowan (2020).

In Other Words

RAISING A VILLAGE: IDENTIFYING SOCIAL SUPPORTS FOR ALL KINDS OF FAMILIES

Caitlyn Collins, October 15, 2019 / CCF@TSP

Today, two-thirds of mothers in wealthy Western countries work outside the home. But mothers' experiences managing their work and family commitments vary a lot from country to country. It's easier to be a working mother in some nations than others. Why? One main reason is that countries offer very different public policies to support families.

National governments offer different kinds and levels of policy supports because societies have diverse beliefs about who should work for pay and provide care to others. Such policies give us a glimpse into national culture: Policies are powerful symbols about what a nation thinks women and men are capable of, good at, and deserve. These policies matter. My research shows how.

I conducted interviews with 135 middle-class working mothers in Sweden, Germany, Italy, and the United States for my book *Making Motherhood Work: How Women Manage Careers and Caregiving.* I wanted to understand what working mothers themselves say helps and hinders their work–family balance. It was immediately clear that moms in the United States were more stressed, guilty, overwhelmed, and fatigued than the mothers I spoke to in Europe. In the United States, managing family and paid work is seen as a personal struggle. In Sweden, Germany, and Italy, citizens think of child-rearing and work–family reconciliation as matters of public concern. In these European countries, public policies help ensure that people have the time and resources needed to care for their loved ones. These policies vary in their effectiveness, but they exist. In the United States, adults are encouraged to find solely private solutions for child-rearing and housework.

The United States has no national work–family policy to support caregiving. We are the only wealthy nation on the planet with no paid parental leave. No universal health care. No universal social insurance entitlement. No guaranteed income. No universal child care. And no minimum standard for vacation and sick days.

To be clear, mothers didn't say it was a breeze to work and raise kids in Europe. But it was far easier because of the various work–family policies available to women and their families in Sweden, Germany, and Italy. Let's take a close look at these policies. This can help give a sense of what could be possible here in the United States.

Parental Leave (Job-Protected Paid Leave Available to Both Parents)

After the addition of a new child to the family, parents' jobs are protected in the three European countries, and they are entitled to paid leave. The length of leave and wage replacement rate varies. In Sweden, couples have an entitlement to sixteen months (480 days) paid at 80 percent of previous wages, up to a ceiling. This time is meant to be divided between parents, and it can be used flexibly until children are eight years old. Each parent has an exclusive right to three of the sixteen months. This "use it or lose it" model is meant to incentivize both parents to take time off. It means that unless fathers take at least three months off, the family is entitled to only thirteen months. In Germany, couples can take up to twelve months of paid parental leave total, paid at roughly two-thirds of their net earnings, also up to a ceiling. If moms and dads share parental leave, they get two bonus months, for a maximum of fourteen months. As in Sweden, parents can take leave flexibly anytime until the child is eight years old. In Italy, parents are each entitled to six months of parental leave at 30 percent pay. Parental leave is an individual, nontransferable entitlement, and families can take ten months total. Again, parents can use these days flexibly at their discretion until their child is eight. If the dad takes at least three months' leave, the family gets an additional month for a total of eleven months. Of course, that means in Sweden and Germany, more families can afford to spend more time with newborns, whereas in Italy, only those who can afford to live on 30 percent pay can use the time allotted them. Although Italy may not be as generous as the other European countries I studied, it is far better than what we have here in the United States, which is no paid leave. The Family and Medical Leave Act (FMLA) gives eligible employees up to twelve weeks unpaid, job-protected leave to care for a new child or an ill family member, or to recover from an illness. Even that protection applies only to businesses with more than fifty employees, and workers must have worked for at least twelve months and a minimum of 1,250 hours to qualify.

Maternity Leave (Job-Protected Paid Leave for Mothers Surrounding Childbirth)

In Sweden, mothers have the exclusive right to three of the sixteen months' parental leave at 80 percent pay. Employed women in Germany may take maternity leave for up to six weeks before childbirth and are required to stay home for eight weeks afterward, receiving full pay. Mothers in Italy are required to take five months of maternity leave at 80 percent pay. Although requiring women to remain home may seem paternal, it is surely more appreciated by families than no statutory entitlement at all, which is what we have in the United States: no right to paid maternity leave after the birth of a baby.

Paternity Leave (Job-Protected Paid Leave for Fathers during or Following Childbirth)

Fathers in Sweden have the exclusive right to three of the sixteen months' parental leave at 80 percent pay. In Germany, fathers have no entitlement to paternity leave. If both parents take at least two months' parental leave, they earn two extra months' paid leave, for a total of fourteen months. In Italy, as of 2018, fathers have four days mandatory paternity leave at 100 percent pay. They are required to take these days within the first five months of birth while mothers are also on leave. Before 2013, there was no designated paternity leave whatsoever. Five days may not seem like much, but that's five more days than fathers have a right to in the United States.

Paid Vacation and Holidays

In Sweden all workers have twenty-five days per year of paid vacation days. Many receive more as a result of union agreements. If a person falls ill while on vacation, those days aren't counted against the vacation allowance. Swedes also get eleven paid holidays per year. In Germany, workers have a right to a minimum of twenty vacation days per year. As a result of collective agreements, most receive thirty days. Those working less than full time get proportionally fewer days. Depending on the state, Germans also enjoy between nine and thirteen paid holidays a year. In Italy, workers are entitled to a minimum of twenty vacation days per year. As in Sweden and Germany, because of collective bargaining agreements, most receive at least twenty-five days. Italians also have ten paid holidays annually. Once again, the United States has no minimum federal standard. The U.S. government designates ten federal holidays per year, but paid holidays are at employers' discretion.

Paid Sick Days

In Sweden, if you have been employed for at least one month, an employee gets roughly 80 percent of income for the first fourteen days of illness. After that, the employer contacts the state, which works with the person's doctor to determine eligibility for extended sickness benefits. Unemployed or self-employed people get a sickness benefit from the government. And parents may stay home with a sick child for up to 120 days a year until children reach twelve years old (paid at 80 percent of wages, up to a limit). For seriously ill children, there is no limit to the number of days parents can take off work. Workers in Germany may take as many personal sick days as needed over the course of a year at full wages. All employees get ten days per year to tend to a sick child, at 70 percent pay. In Italy, parents can take unlimited unpaid days off work to care for ill children under three, and five days unpaid annually for kids ages three to eight. For seriously ill family members, workers can take two years at full pay (with a cap) total. Here, too, the United States is the outlier, with no minimum federal standard. Eligible workers may use FMLA for their own serious illness, or to take care of a seriously ill family member, for up to twelve weeks, without pay.

Child Care

Sweden provides universal child care for children ages one to twelve years old. The cost for parents is income-related up to a low ceiling, and it's free for low-income families. The maximum rate for even the wealthiest families is about $160 per month in U.S. dollars. In Germany, universal care is available for children ages three to six. As of August 2013, all children older than one are legally entitled to a child care space (although these are still difficult to come by in some places). A recent nationwide study found that in Germany, day care costs families on average $172 per month in U.S. dollars. In Italy, child care is universally available for children three and up, but is difficult to attain for children under three. A recent survey found that child care costs families $343 monthly, on average, in U.S. dollars. The United States has no state or federal child care systems. The limited federal child care provisions are means-tested for only the poorest families. The average cost of private child care is $799 per month ($9,589 a year)—more than the average cost of tuition at many in-state colleges.

What Do U.S. Policies Imply about American Values?

Given all this, what message do you think the U.S. government sends to residents with these policies—or should I say, the lack of policies? You are on your own. You are owed nothing. Yet, regardless of marital or parental status, wealth, race, region, or religion, every single person needs care throughout their lives. No one is an island. Society would collapse without care. Other countries came to this realization a long time ago. The United States lags way behind: it is exceptional for its *lack* of policy support for caregiving and families. That's not a title we should be proud of.

The United States was founded on the belief that citizens have inalienable rights to life, liberty, and the pursuit of happiness, and that government is meant to protect these rights. If we believe this nation should be at the forefront of human rights—a country where residents can truly lead free and happy lives alongside those they care for and care about—then the path ahead is obvious. We don't need to start from scratch in envisioning better policy supports. The benefits already available in other countries are models from which to choose.

We need to pass robust, egalitarian work–family policies at a federal level. I suggest we start with paid family leave and affordable, high-quality child care and health care for all. We can do far more and far better for U.S. families. Our future depends on it. ▆

21

The Marriage Movement

Melanie Heath and Jennifer Randles[1]

Marriage today is less likely to anchor family life in many poor and working-class communities. . . . [C]hildren from these families are markedly less likely to live under the same roof as their biological parents than their peers from better-off backgrounds are.

—Wilcox and Boyd (2020)

S ociologist W. Bradford Wilcox and family scholar Hal Boyd refute the narrative that the nuclear family and marriage are endangered. Against such accounts, they state that "the nuclear family is still indispensable."[2] According to them, "the quintessential nuclear family consists of a married couple raising their children." They argue for the superiority of married parents over what political scientist Daniel Burns calls "forged families," or chosen families whose members may or may not be related by blood or marriage but become "fictive kin" who support each other no matter what.[3] The problem for Wilcox and Boyd: the children who, according to them, do best when raised in a nuclear family. A gap exists, they argue, between children being raised by college-educated, married parents and those raised by unmarried, poor or working-class parents—predominantly mothers—with worse outcomes for the latter. They caution against the idea that society can "successfully replace families headed by married parents with models oriented more around kith and kin," especially for extended families and communities seeking upward mobility in places where "marriage has broken down in their midst."[4]

The arguments of Wilcox and Boyd represent some of the fundamental tenets of what is known as the "marriage movement" in the United States. Emerging in the late twentieth century, its aim has been to revitalize marriage and reverse the trends in family formation of the past few decades that have seen fewer people start lifelong marriages before having children. Americans are generally familiar with the controversy over marriage equality that led to *Obergefell v. Hodges* in 2015, the U.S. Supreme Court decision that struck down all state bans on same-sex marriage and legalized it in all fifty states. Less known is that the marriage equality debate was part of broader political and cultural conversations about the implications of changing families for sustaining a successful society. Marriage advocates seek to promote and strengthen marriage in society against broader trends of divorce, single parenthood, and blended families. While they disagree over whether to support the legalization of same-sex marriage—with religious conservatives most prominently against—most agree on the implications of lower marriage rates and the rise of cohabitation and single motherhood, especially for poor and working-class Americans and their children. For them, marriage "breakdown" impedes upward mobility. To counter these trends, marriage advocates have instituted marriage and relationship education programs and policies, often with the specific goal of helping unmarried, poor and working-class populations with children get married.

This chapter provides an overview of the marriage debates in the late twentieth and early twenty-first centuries, focusing particularly on the marriage education component that involves efforts by a variety of faith-based, community, and government-funded organizations to promote marriage and educate American heterosexual couples about the benefits of marriage and healthy relationship dynamics. We have each studied marriage promotion policy and the marriage education movement. Heath traveled to Oklahoma to do eleven months of ethnographic research on a statewide initiative that sought to promote and strengthen marriage. Randles studied twenty government-funded marriage education programs and spent eighteen months studying one program she calls "Thriving Families" that targeted low-income, unmarried couples who were expecting or just had a new baby. Both of us participated in and observed numerous marriage education classes, interviewed participants and instructors, and examined how marriage education unfolds on the ground.

We were struck by two similar puzzles. First, most sociologists, demographers, and historians agree that character-based explanations—such as individuals' failure to marry before having children—do injustice to persistent patterns of social and economic inequalities surrounding family formation. Yet the marriage education movement has largely ignored the patterns underlying inequality at the heart of shifting family forms. Second, while marriage education and promotion policies were billed as antipoverty measures, they have had limited effect on poverty. Instead, our fieldwork pointed to a different likely explanation for the embrace of these policies: a moral battle against changing family forms in favor of the married, two-parent family. In what follows, we describe the emergence and growth of the marriage movement to explain these puzzles, trace the debates and controversies over its philosophy and policies, and provide an overview of the research assessing the success of these programs and efforts to promote marriage.

EMPIRICAL REALITIES: THE MARRIAGE GAP

When scholars and activists refer to the marriage debates, they typically mean debates over marriage equality: the question of whether same-sex couples should have the right to legally marry. The political battle over same-sex marriage rights was an issue of equality and citizenship because marriage is associated with a variety of legal, social, and economic benefits, including rights to inheritance, hospital visitation, insurance coverage, and social recognition of one's intimate relationship, among numerous others. This important issue of marriage equality once garnered the most public attention concerning what sociologists call "intimate inequalities."

Intimate inequalities was coined by sociologist Ken Plummer to describe how social and economic inequalities shape the most personal aspects of our lives.[5] The term provides a useful analytic lens to assess other trends in contemporary American family life because it emphasizes that our access to economic resources, social recognition, and political rights is affected by and reflective of our marital status. This is one of the main reasons legal battles over marriage equality were so significant, culminating in the hard-won 2015 *Obergefell v. Hodges* Supreme Court decision that secured marriage rights for all U.S. couples.

However, other changes in the structure of family life in the United States have also contributed to intimate inequalities. Changing patterns in family life accelerated in the second half of the twentieth century and contributed to class inequalities. Americans still almost universally aspire to marry, but their social class largely predicts whether they will marry. Sociologists find that Americans who live below or near the poverty line are more likely to delay or avoid marriage indefinitely compared with the more economically advantaged or those who have more education, make more money, and struggle less with finding consistent, well-paying employment. Poor and low-income Americans are also significantly more likely to cohabit before marriage, have children outside of marriage, and have children with more than one partner.[6]

Social scientists refer to this social class disparity in marriage rates as the *mar-riage gap*. This gap is important because children who grow up in always-married families with resident fathers tend to benefit from the economic and relational stability that is often associated with marriage and the involvement and resources of two parents.[7] There is evidence that, on average, children raised in two-parent families do better on a number of outcomes than children who grow up with one parent, including a lower likelihood of being poor, better educational achieve-ment, and fewer substance abuse and behavioral problems, among others.[8] Put another way, the family as a social institution is a primary mechanism of inequal-ity that perpetuates class divisions from one generation to the next, a cycle that sociologists refer to as *social reproduction*. The higher one sits on the socioeco-nomic ladder, the more likely one is to get married, stay married, and have chil-dren *after* getting married.[9] As we turn to consider the marriage movement's goals and strategies, it is important to keep in mind that social trends of concern to the marriage movement—cohabitation, nonmarital childbearing, divorce, and nonresidential fathering—are significantly more common among socially and economically disadvantaged groups.

THE IDEOLOGICAL DEBATE:
WHAT IS THE SIGNIFICANCE OF MARRIAGE?

Social commentators of all ideological stripes agree on the demographics of the marriage gap. However, they vary widely in their analyses of the causes of these gaps and their implications for individuals and American society as a whole. Soci-ologists such as W. Bradford Wilcox, cited in the epigraph at the beginning of this chapter, focus on individual *choices*—like the failure to follow what has been termed the "success sequence"—getting at least a high school degree, then work-ing, and finally marrying before having children.[10] Others, like historian Stephanie Coontz and sociologist Andrew Cherlin, focus on demographic and cultural shifts that demonstrate that the marriage gap, like other changes in marriage and family life over the past half-century, is intimately linked to broader changes in American society. According to Coontz, in America and throughout much of the world, the social norms that once regulated decisions about heterosexual marriage have relaxed in favor of norms that privilege the emotional component of marriage.[11] Love, personal choice, and self-fulfillment compete with laws, religious sanctions, and economic constraints as the social glue of marriage and family.

Transformations in family and sexual mores have been centuries in the mak-ing, but they began to accelerate in the 1960s in tandem with other social and economic developments. Over a twenty-year period, between the 1960s and mid-1980s, the divorce rate more than doubled. By the early 1980s, one out of six births occurred outside marriage, and by the twenty-first century, this figure had grown to one out of three. Yet not all children are similarly affected by these changes. Most of the children born to unmarried parents are born into poverty or low-income homes, and African American and Hispanic children are more likely to be born to unmarried, low-income parents.[12]

Scholars disagree about the social and cultural meanings of these changes. Some argue that we are witnessing a family crisis because most people now deviate from traditional family-formation patterns that put lifelong marriage at the center of family and social life. They argue that excessive individualism is undermining the institution of marriage, as indicated by high divorce rates and the growing number of individuals who cohabit and have children outside of marriage. In other words, these changes reflect pervasive moral failures. Others claim that family life is not deteriorating but simply changing to accommodate more egalitarian gender dynamics, economic restructuring, and growing social acceptance of diverse family forms. Cherlin argues that we have a unique marriage culture in the United States, one in which marriage as a cultural ideal is stronger than elsewhere in the developed world. Americans have among the highest marriage and divorce rates of all Western industrialized countries, trends that can be explained in large part by the simultaneous and often contradictory commitments of Americans to stable and secure lifelong marriage and to individual fulfillment and self-expression that justify ending marriages when they cease to be happy.[13]

These empirical realities, competing interpretations of the meanings of marriage in the United States, and divergent assessments of the implications had social activists, politicians, and academics scratching their heads about the best ways to respond. In the late 1990s a potential solution emerged in the form of a marriage movement that sought to encourage marriage, discourage divorce, and improve the relationships of American couples. The movement brought together an unlikely coalition of therapists, clergy and other religious leaders, community activists, politicians, think tank experts, welfare agency workers, and government officials. Its goal was lofty: to implement a renaissance of marriage in the United States.[14] Some in the movement were motivated primarily by the moral implications of what they viewed as the decline of the "natural" nuclear family; the "marriage decline" camp also tended to support legislation to define marriage as a union of one man and one woman. Others were more concerned about the empirical outcomes of changing family forms; they focused on structural patterns, such as unemployment and poverty, rather than so-called individual failures. Though their ideological convictions varied widely—for example, the conservative Heritage Foundation and the centrist Brookings Institution were on board—movement participants were united by their belief that a reinvigorated marriage culture could address the range of social problems associated with single motherhood, prolonged cohabitation, high divorce rates, and lack of father involvement. Mirroring the diversity of actors, the marriage movement promoted a variety of initiatives, including introducing divorce reform (undoing no-fault divorce and expanding covenant marriage through which couples agree to limited grounds for and restrictions on divorce, such as mandatory marital counseling), rejuvenating marriage culture, developing fatherhood initiatives, and opposing same-sex marriage.

MAKING A MARRIAGE MOVEMENT: PROMOTION AND EDUCATION

The marriage movement seeks to expand the role of government, schools, and social service agencies in reinstitutionalizing marriage—that is, revitalizing marriage as a key institution in American society. It was officially set in motion in 2000 with the release of "A Statement of Principles." The 113 signatories included many prominent conservatives and a few self-identified liberals. The marriage movement sought to implement these principles through promotion of policies in state and federal legislatures and services such as relationship skills training and parenting classes.

The marriage movement ideologically and practically privileges marriage as the ideal way to shape one's intimate life and create a family. It intersected with several other national conversations and policy changes, in particular the growing debate about marriage equality and the enactment of the Defense of Marriage Act—subsequently declared unconstitutional by the Supreme Court in June 2013 as a violation of personal liberty protected by the Fifth Amendment—which explicitly defined marriage as between one man and one woman; President George W. Bush's Faith Based Initiative, which allowed federal funding of faith-based organizations;[15] the rewriting of welfare under President Clinton, which included provisions to directly promote marriage and two-parent families using public money; and the emergence of a range of state and community marriage initiatives, including those in Oklahoma and California that we describe later.

While the debate over marriage equality produced legislation and constitutional amendments to ban same-sex marriage, debates over changing family structures led to policies to promote heterosexual marriage and "responsible" fatherhood. Public funding for marriage and fatherhood programs can be traced to the 1996 Personal Responsibility and Work Opportunity Reconciliation Act

(PRWORA). The law was a major change in the U.S. welfare system, and it claimed that "marriage is the foundation of a successful society" and "promotion of responsible fatherhood and motherhood is integral to successful child-rearing and the well-being of children."[16] Ever since, the federal government has devoted well over $1 billion to fund healthy marriage and relationship and responsible fatherhood programming as companion policies in a dual effort to promote two-parent married families.[17]

The 2002 federal Healthy Marriage Initiative (HMI) paved the way for a patchwork of funding that added up to about $200 million for marriage promotion activities. The 2005 welfare renewal legislation included $500 million for marriage programs through 2011. Federal funding for healthy marriage and responsible fatherhood (HMRF) programming has been renewed ever since, most recently through five-year (2020–2025) HMRF grants administered by the federal Office of Family Assistance to support 111 marriage, relationship, and fatherhood programs across the United States. Individual states have also used portions of their federal Temporary Assistance for Needy Families (TANF) grants for marriage promotion activities.

The idea was simple: state and federal funds would be used both to promote marriage as the best family context in which to raise children and to provide couples with skills for succeeding at their relationships. This, in turn, would address high rates of divorce, cohabitation, and single motherhood, leading to reduced poverty rates. Oklahoma, which launched a statewide marriage initiative in 1999, provided a blueprint for the national movement while community organizations, including welfare agencies and faith-based organizations, provided the boots on the ground to test out these new initiatives around the country. Yet, as we discuss later, over time, much of the federal and state funding has gone to programs that provide marriage and relationship education with the goal of preventing marital distress and divorce and strengthening marriages but without paying much attention to the specific needs of individuals living in poverty.

Marriage education involves classes and workshops based on the premise that marital success is rooted in couple dynamics and individual skills—such as how spouses divide household chores, fight, and spend their leisure time—and that such dynamics and skills can be taught and developed. Therapists, clinical psychologists, and other students of human relationship dynamics have amassed knowledge about how relationships work. Studies of such dynamics have coalesced into relationship science—a multidisciplinary endeavor that draws on empirical work from psychology, sociology, communication studies, and economics to theorize the basic laws that shape satisfying interpersonal interactions. As evidence mounted that marriage failure or success hinges on predictable patterns of interpersonal interaction, relationship experts began to translate this knowledge into teachable skills. Marriage education is an applied extension of this work.

The logic, repeated by marriage educators we have interviewed and observed across the country, is deceptively simple: having a healthy marriage is something one can *learn*. People who receive the information, practice the skills, and develop the attributes known to be linked to healthy marriages will be able to achieve marital bliss—or at least transcend the marital blah, or the everyday rut. Unlike couples therapy, which involves a single couple and a trained psychologist or counselor, marriage education is delivered to several—sometimes dozens—of couples at a time, typically by a team consisting of a man and woman educator pair (often a married couple). There are numerous programs on the market, though some industry favorites enjoy particular financial success and visibility. Programs typically include units that address communication and conflict resolution skills, goal setting, benefits of marriage, and financial management techniques such as budgeting. They deliver this content through alternating periods of instructor presentations, group discussion, and couple exercises. Educators typically need to be certified to teach a certain curriculum, but these requirements vary widely across programs.

Government-funded marriage promotion programs extend the basic premise of helping couples build better marriages into a new realm: these better marriages, the proponents hold, can alleviate poverty. The philosophy sees single parenthood as a *cause* of poverty, and supporters argue that strengthening marriage represents a plausible poverty-reduction strategy. For example, author Kay Hymowitz of the Manhattan Institute, a longtime proponent of and key actor in the marriage movement, argues that "marriage remains a defining landmark in the lives of more well-to-do, college-educated Americans. But it is well on the path to obsolescence only among the less educated, poor, and working class. Marriage is, in other words, another dimension of the nation's inequality, one that both explains and perpetuates America's divisions."[18] Although Hymowitz acknowledges how economic factors, such as unpredictable work schedules and financial worries, contribute to couple conflict, she claims that middle-class families' tendencies to plan and deliberate in interpersonal relationships helps advantaged couples negotiate and organize important family decisions in ways that support happiness, stability, and longevity. Hymowitz believes that those in poverty who delay marriage neither value the institution nor make major life decisions with the goal of creating a stable married family life. Others in the marriage movement share Hymowitz's logic: put simply, marriage makes you a better, happier, and healthier person, and marriage reduces poverty; therefore, marriage is good for people and society.

The real picture, however, is much more complicated. Sociologists Kathryn Edin and Maria Kefalas found that poor and low-income women highly value marriage but view it as a luxury they may never achieve given their difficulty reaching the high economic bar for marriage.[19] Like many Americans, they believe that to be ready for marriage, they and their future spouse must be financially secure first and need to accomplish certain economic and social milestones such as finishing school; getting a secure, well-paying job; and being able to afford a nice wedding. In other words, poor and low-income women are well aware of the "success sequence," but these pre-marriage milestones are significantly harder for them to reach because of economic and social hardships that have little to do with marriage. As for poor fathers, sociologists Kathryn Edin and Timothy Nelson found that they embrace a "new package deal" not anchored in marriage but focused on primary relationships with their children, who become conduits to secondary relationships with their children's mothers.[20]

Here's the catch: marriage advocates view low-income people's lower rates of marriage as a failure that can and should be fixed by educating them about the importance of marriage. Yet advocates largely neglect the economic and job market realities that underpin people's choices about marriage and family. Meanwhile, marriage promotion policy represents an unprecedented attempt to intervene in the marriage and childbearing decisions of Americans, especially low-income women. While it was heralded as a solution for a range of social problems such as teenage pregnancy, high crime rates, and low high school graduation rates, the policy has failed to achieve its goals of increasing marriage rates, reducing poverty, and significantly improving the relationships of couples attending government-funded programs. In 2012, researchers released final results from a federal healthy marriage evaluation project. Building Strong Families (BSF) was a relationship-strengthening program for low-income, unmarried parents.[21] Of the eight BSF sites that participated in the study, only one—a BSF program in Oklahoma—had a positive impact on couples' relationship quality and stability. None of the programs affected the marriage rates of unmarried, poor couples. There is also no evidence that marriage education programs have had an impact on rates of cohabitation, divorce, or single motherhood.

In response to these findings, recent federally funded marriage, relationship, and fatherhood programs have focused more on providing services intended to improve individuals' and families' economic situations. Of the 111 current HMRF programs, thirty are Family, Relationship, and Marriage Education-Works (FRAMEWorks) projects that combine marriage and relationship education services with "efforts to address participation barriers and the economic stability needs of adult participants"; fifty-eight projects are funded through the

Fatherhood Family-focused, Interconnected, Resilient, and Essential (Father-hood FIRE) grants that integrate healthy marriage and responsible parenting education with "robust economic stability services."[22]

Local evaluations of HMRF programs find that many improve self-reported communication skills, conflict, and relationship satisfaction, but programs tend to have fewer positive effects on labor market outcomes and family financial stability. A federal evaluation of the Empowering Families program, which integrated marriage and relationship education with economic stability services, including employment services and financial education, had mixed results. Program participation among low-income couples raising children together was associated with a greater likelihood of marriage among unmarried couples and fewer economic hardships after one year (measured in terms of borrowing money from family or friends and going without medical care due to lack of money). Yet, taking all the results together, the program had no overall impact on couples' relationship status, employment, or earnings. These mixed results raise questions about if and how HMRF programs meaningfully improve families' material well-being; couples felt better equipped to communicate about and manage their money but did not have more of it to manage.[23]

Findings also urge us to consider whether these outcomes justify program costs. Empowering Families—including an eight-session couples workshop, case management, employment counseling, and monthly financial coaching—costs $10,844 per couple, equal to almost six months of the average income for men and seventeen months of the average income for women enrolled in the program. Thus, although newer programs include services that acknowledge and try to address how poverty undermines relationship stability, rigorous evaluation raises the fundamental question: would providing couples with equivalent cash or basic needs assistance be a better use of public funding than teaching people how to better manage their limited means?

Our collective work provides insight into these questions and why marriage promotion policies have not delivered on their antipoverty goals. As we unravel this puzzle, we also highlight the tensions, successes, and implementation challenges the larger marriage movement faces.

GOOD COMMUNICATION, NOT MARRIAGE

Since 2002, the federal government has funded hundreds of relationship and marriage education programs across the country, many targeting poor and low-income, unmarried couples who are expecting or just had a new baby. The logic of targeting this particular social group is that couples might consider the time around a child's birth as a "magic moment" or unique window of opportunity to get married and create a more stable married family.

Yet, in her research on Thriving Families, Randles found that, in line with previous sociological research on the marriage gap between low-income and more affluent Americans, couples in this program delayed marriage because of a phenomenon she calls *curtailed commitment*—the belief that if a couple cannot live up to middle-class norms of family life, including meeting a specific economic threshold, they are not equipped for marriage.[24] Randles also found that parents responded positively to instruction in co-parenting and communication skills because they felt empowered and better equipped as partners and parents.[25] Couples viewed the classes as a rare opportunity to learn communication skills in an environment free of the material constraints that overwhelmingly characterized their daily lives and their intimate relationships. The classes offered parents in poverty a free and safe collective space to discuss romantic and parenting challenges, and this helped normalize the relationship conflicts that they experienced. Furthermore, the classes helped couples recognize that others shared their struggles and that their relationship challenges were not necessarily the result of personal or psychological shortcomings but rather were related to the challenges of trying to raise a family and keep a relationship intact while living in poverty. Mason, a twenty-four-year-old white father, told Randles during an interview that he really appreciated the relationship skills classes because

> you figure out what your problems were. You have to know what your issues are before you can address them together. . . . And with everyone else in the classes, you're not the only one going through it. Everyone has the same problems. . . . Everybody was all in the same boat. They were all not married, having a baby, whether it was their first, second, or fourth kid. They were all there wanting to work on their relationship and help build a family.

While couples benefited from learning to communicate better and understand their situation in context, Randles also found that economic challenges significantly impeded the usefulness of the classes. Practicing the skills they learned in class required parents to have control over their time, living space, and finances. The couples did not always have access to these advantages given their frequent need to work multiple low-wage jobs to make financial ends meet and live with others in small, crowded apartments. Thus, although Thriving Families staff and instructors effectively devised strategies that appealed to low-income parents, the parents were not always able to enact the strategies outside the classroom, largely because of the same material constraints that prevented them from realizing their marital aspirations.

Overall, the classes were unsuccessful at convincing parents of two of the main ideas behind marriage promotion policy: that married families are healthier and that marriage is a precursor to economic self-sufficiency. Nor, significantly, did parents find helpful the financial management tips that are often part of marriage education for poor couples. Most parents told Randles that either they did not have money to manage, or they already knew how to manage the little money they did have to the best extent possible by prioritizing necessary expenses. As Joshua, eighteen and white, told Randles, "Money's easy to manage when you have some." Similarly, one mother, Marcy, twenty-one and white, told her, "We already know how to manage our money to a 'T.' As soon as we get paid, [our son] comes first. His diapers, his wipes, soap, if he runs out, we get him more. Then we buy what we can from there."

The Empowering Families evaluation found more positive results regarding the financial skills training of marriage education. Women reported better money management and being better off financially after one year despite no improvement in employment or earnings. What could explain this seeming paradox? Evaluators speculated that the program's financial literacy services and communication skills training helped participating couples avoid financial hardship by teaching them to communicate more effectively about how to manage their money.[26] A lot may come down to how "financial hardship" is measured in such evaluations. Participation in Empowering Families was associated with a lower likelihood of borrowing money from friends and family and having to forgo health care for financial reasons; however, participants were no less likely to skip meals, move in with others, go without a phone, or sell or pawn belongings. Participants may have objectively felt better, but the program seemed to have no impact on their access to food and housing, which are basic needs that are foundational to healthy relationships and families no matter how you define them.

Policy responses to the COVID-19 pandemic, notably the Coronavirus Aid, Relief, and Economic Security (CARES) Act, which provided government cash payments, extra unemployment benefits, additional food assistance, and an eviction moratorium, are helpful for understanding how public programs can mitigate economic relationship stressors that undermine couple communication and relationship functioning. Ensuring that partners' basic needs are met, in addition to any relational services, is likely the best approach to creating a context in which all families can flourish. Rather than helping couples communicate more effectively about financial hardships, policies can directly prevent those hardships through tangible assistance and benefits.[27] In contrast, policies focused on behavioral interventions that promote marriage to escape and avoid poverty prop up the ideology of marital self-sufficiency that links marriage to the socioeconomic opportunities of the shrinking American middle class.

In the end, marriage education programs that are based on the "individual failure" logic (promoted by commentators such as Wilcox and Hymowitz) have the potential to *exacerbate* rather than alleviate the intimate inequalities that often lead to curtailed commitments among couples in poverty. While the federal government has funded many programs targeting low-income couples like the one that Randles studied, many of the government-funded programs have a different focus: providing marriage education to as many people as possible. Our research found that this strategy has the unintended consequence of diverting money away from needy families, another important piece in the puzzle of perpetuating intimate inequalities.

PROMOTING MARRIAGE AMONG THE MASSES

A number of individual states have used TANF (welfare) funds for the purpose of strengthening marriage. In 1999, Oklahoma became the pioneer of a statewide effort to do just that. Former governor Frank Keating declared his state's divorce and unwed childbearing rates to be social problems and committed an initial $10 million out of its TANF funds for the initiative. It ran until 2016 when the state ended it due to budget cuts. Heath, in her research on this controversial policy, asked, What do state policies to promote marriage look like on the ground? Her findings were surprising. For months, she attended marriage education classes for the general population that focused on strengthening communication skills. Unlike the classes studied by Randles, which specifically targeted low-income couples, Heath discovered that most of the classes offered by the Oklahoma Marriage Initiative recruited white, middle-class couples. Interviews with leaders and staff of the marriage initiative confirmed that although they viewed low-income families as an important target for relationship programs, privileged families were more likely to benefit from the services. During an interview with a staff member who described the new BSF program that would target unmarried, low-income couples at the "magic moment" around the birth of their child, Heath responded enthusiastically that this seemed a positive direction because it appeared that many of the current services were going to . . . Before Heath could complete her sentence, a staff member finished it: "the middle class."

While the state initiative provided marriage education to more privileged families, these classes were funded with money specifically meant to help needy families. This finding led Heath in search of an answer to what she called the *marriage initiative puzzle*: What is the logic behind using TANF funds that are meant for needy families to offer marriage workshops to people who can afford to pay? The answer to this question offers a window into the complex debates over government policies to promote and strengthen marriage. The logic behind marriage promotion can seem compelling. In her award-winning 2003 *New Yorker* story, Katherine Boo, a journalist who traveled to Oklahoma to study what is often called the "marriage cure" for poverty, described marriage as "probably the most cost-efficient antipoverty instrument a society possesses."[28] For what Boo characterizes as a very small investment—but one that diverts direct payments away from those in need—the government can offer marriage education classes to poor, single mothers. If these classes help them to marry, a combined income of husband and wife might presumably "remove both of them, in one fell act, from America's poverty rolls." Yet, as Randles discovered in her research (and as the 2012 BSF study confirmed), these classes missed the mark in convincing unmarried couples to marry.

Heath's finding that most of the classes were not serving the population for which the funding was targeted raises an important question concerning the goal of marriage promotion. It also points to a second tension that characterizes the marriage promotion goal of the marriage movement and the policy response it has helped generate: marriage advocates worry about the problem of unwed motherhood and poverty, but they also worry about ensuring that marriage is upheld by law and public policy as the best institution for raising children. In other words, they are motivated by a moral belief that marriage is the best kind of family for society. This focus on strengthening marriage throughout society helps explain why the marriage initiative in Oklahoma would redistribute resources meant for needy families to offer marriage education to the general population. Ultimately, the goal of many participants of the marriage movement is to reinstitutionalize marriage among *all* populations and not just the needy. Yet the redistribution has its own moral consequences—siphoning money away from poor women and their children. A director of one program in Oklahoma had this concern:

> I tell you that the amount of money that is spent on [the marriage initiative] really, really bothers me. I think it was $2 million this year! So, it was money that was taken away from poor women, and it hasn't been targeting poor women. In February on Valentine's weekend, there's a Sweethearts Getaway, and all these people come, and then you have the PREP [Prevention and Relationship Enhancement Program] spin-off for [adoptive] couples and high school kids. Not that those things are not important, but they are being paid for with funds that were set aside for poor families.

The lack of a social safety net and the low monthly payments for women on TANF (in 2003 when the marriage program was newly underway, an Oklahoma family of three could receive a maximum benefit of $292 a month) underscores the punitive nature of redistributing welfare money, whether intentional or not.[29] The monthly maximum TANF benefit for a single parent with two children remained $292 a month in 2021, representing a 43 percent decrease in benefits from 1996 to 2021 when adjusted for inflation.[30] As the state's cash assistance welfare program has declined in participation, there has been a buildup of more than $25 million. Still, the maximum benefit remains the same in 2022.[31] While Oklahoma is no longer using TANF money to fund its marriage initiative, one must wonder about the justification for not putting more money into direct benefits.

While marriage workshops have been ineffective at reducing poverty, there have been no real efforts to devise any other antipoverty programs at the state level. Like the general marriage movement of which it is a product, the marriage education movement prides itself on taking a "big tent" approach to the range of stakeholders who constitute it. The movement was emboldened by its ability to draw into its ranks a variety of stakeholders and sought to straddle the welfare and cultural goals of marriage education. Over the past decade and a half, it has generated organizations that have professionalized the field, streamlined delivery of services, provided legitimacy through certification programs, and ensured its longevity through lobbying. The movement has also given rise to movement leaders and a reliable pool of industry experts who help set its tone and chart its directions. Despite the marriage education movement's emphasis on its big-tent approach, it ultimately remains focused on the cultural implications of changing family forms and on helping individual couples change their behavior—rather than on eradicating poverty. While the rhetoric of the marriage education movement focuses on antipoverty, the actual strategies and practices do not.

THE "AHA" MOMENT: THE MARRIAGE EDUCATION INDUSTRY

A key player in the marriage movement was family therapist Diane Sollee, a self-described liberal, who in 1996 founded the Coalition for Marriage, Family, and Couples Education (CMFCE). The CMFCE served as a clearinghouse for the movement and sponsored the annual Smart Marriages conference from 1996 to 2010. These conferences drew thousands of therapists, educators, clergy and other religious leaders, researchers, and couples to a yearly gathering where they could catch up on the latest research, train to become marriage educators, learn about new programs and curricula, network with other marriage educators, and collaborate on legislative initiatives.

The Smart Marriages organization and its yearly conferences in particular were crucial to the marriage education movement. With the addition of

$100 million in federal support for marriage education programs starting in 2006, the conference became an important site for curricula developers to market their products. Some of them, along with several other industry experts, became movement stars who were featured regularly in the conference's listings and keynote addresses.

Leaders of successful marriage education organizations across the country launched a new group at the 2010 Smart Marriages conference: the National Association for Relationship and Marriage Educators (NARME). While its initial key mission focused on ensuring the movement's success through legislative action, it soon also took over the reins from Smart Marriages and started organizing its own annual summits, which have continued as of 2022. The organization bills itself as "equipping those leading the way for healthy relationship development, family formation, and poverty prevention, with the knowledge and strategies to be most effective in the workplace and in the community."

NARME's membership includes marriage educators from a variety of local, regional, and national organizations and marriage and relationship researchers. Based on more than 200 hours of ethnographic observation at two Smart Marriages conferences and three NARME annual summits, along with site visits and interviews with marriage educators across the country, sociologist Orit Avishai found that poverty prevention through relationship enhancement is a key goal of the movement.[32] At the 2013 NARME summit, a session titled "The Case for Relationship and Marriage Education" featured Patty Howell, then president of Healthy Relationships California, a statewide marriage initiative. She asked audience members, "What if I told you that I had a perfect solution for poverty? For teenage pregnancy? For high dropout rates? What if I told you that by investing in marriage education, you can save a whole lot of money?" A common refrain among NARME leaders like Howell is that interpersonal relationship skills can solve deeply entrenched structural inequalities. The logic that marital decline, especially among poor, lower-income families and families of color, is responsible for unequal life chances was a prevalent theme across speeches given by marriage and relationship education (MRE) advocates and marriage education curricula analyzed by Avishai and Randles. Kay Hymowitz explained in her 2013 NARME summit keynote address that educated and uneducated women pursue distinct life scripts. Citing data from the Pew Research Center, she explained: "By the time they turn 30, about two-thirds of women have had a baby, typically out of wedlock. This is not an equal opportunity phenomenon. . . . College-educated women don't have their children outside of marriage. . . . We have two very different scripts for how young women are spending their lives. . . . There is a great deal of instability when they have children during cohabitation. Those children pay the price." Marriage and relationship education, Hymowitz noted in a typical refrain of marriage educators, can teach women to follow the "success sequence" of waiting to have children until one first secures a high school diploma, a job, and a husband.

Despite these earnest aspirations, it is difficult to escape the perception that the movement is ultimately invested more in the cultural and moral, rather than the antipoverty, aspects of marriage education. The term *marriage* in the movement remains unqualified; it is taken for granted that the term applies to heterosexual marriages only and does not account for how children can thrive in various kinds of families—even single-parent families—especially if they are stable. In the wake of the Obama administration's restructuring of marriage education funding to include a job-training component, many marriage educators Avishai interviewed were at a loss as to why "the one program that focuses on marriage should spend some of its measly dollars on jobs training. Aren't there enough programs that already do that?" This logic was on full display at the conferences of the movement. Although the welfare imperative was the one that persuaded lawmakers to fund marriage education, Smart Marriages and NARME conferences have featured only a handful of speakers who addressed the economic and structural aspects of the changing nature of family dynamics in the United States. Most keynote speakers at these conferences have been industry insiders who promote marriage education for the sake of helping individual couples overcome their marital woes.

The rare speakers who have emphasized the structural aspects of family formation received a lukewarm reception from their audience. For example, the 2012 NARME conference featured a speaker from the Annie E. Casey Foundation, a private nonprofit organization invested in building better futures for marginalized children. The speaker walked the audience through well-known facts: children from single-family homes and disadvantaged backgrounds were much more likely to drop out of school, be incarcerated, and get pregnant; and they were less likely to attend college. Yet the narrative this speaker offered strayed from the much-rehearsed narrative in these gatherings: rather than emphasizing the "breakdown" of the family as the key culprit, the speaker surveyed the range of cultural, historical, and economic shifts (discussed earlier in this chapter), and suggested policy solutions that de-emphasized marriage education. Not surprisingly, the speaker's departure was not accompanied by thunderous applause, and many conference attendees Avishai later spoke to said they were "disappointed" with this speaker.

Perhaps most telling is the marriage education movement's flat refusal to accept the outcomes of research clearly showing that marriage education is not delivering on the poverty-prevention front. Although organization leaders Avishai interviewed were very familiar with social science research about the correlation between family structure and the range of social outcomes they hoped to address through marriage education, they routinely dismissed lack of evidence for the efficacy of marriage education. Instead, they cited anecdotal evidence, testimonies from individual couples who were supported by the programs and research generated by industry insiders (most prominently the Prevention and Relationship Enhancement Program [PREP] Lab) about program efficacy. Although research consistently finds that many couples, including low-income families, enjoy and benefit from MRE through improved communication and greater social support for their relationships,[33] such programs simply don't move the needle on poverty and other social problems rooted in inequitable access to resources and opportunities for upward mobility.

Ultimately, the best indicator of where the movement's deepest concerns lie goes back to the original "aha" moment that prompted Diane Sollee to found Smart Marriages in her kitchen. The "origin story," as she tells it, was her rude awakening that marriage therapy just wasn't addressing marital crises. She had this realization when a reporter asked her why divorce rates have not plummeted despite the growing circle of trained family therapists.[34] Marriage therapy, like marriage education, does not account for structural aspects of family formation. It seems as if marriage education as an antipoverty measure was doomed from the start—or perhaps it was never really intended for that purpose.

This is not to say that the marriage education movement and marriage education organizations are not doing good work or helping some couples achieve happier and more stable relationships. They are—to a degree—as indicated by studies that measure outcomes such as relationship quality and satisfaction.[35] But when we try to understand why marriage education has failed as an antipoverty measure, the movement's own logic, founding documents, and directing rationales provide excellent clues.

CONCLUSION

Is it a surprise that marriage education has failed to deliver on its antipoverty goals? Not to social scientists or, for that matter, to anyone who has taken an introductory course in sociology. The philosophy behind marriage education and the policies of marriage promotion ignore the demographics of marriage and divorce. While marriage advocates like Wilcox and Boyd, with whom we started this chapter, point to the problem of the marriage gap, their solutions have focused on so-called individual failings and character traits. Relationship experts see individual skills, psyches, experiences, and relationship dynamics as important to marital success and failure. In contrast, sociologists, demographers, and economists have looked to social factors, such as class and education. From them, we know that the United States is characterized by a class-based marriage (and divorce) gap: highly educated and middle-class women and men are more likely than poor and struggling Americans to get married, stay married, and enjoy a stable relationship. In other words, at the macro level, the most important predictors of marriage and divorce (and the range of outcomes associated with marriage) are not whether an individual has mastered good communication skills but whether one has a stable job and a college degree. This is not because more privileged Americans understand the "success sequence" or because less privileged Americans choose to ignore this sequence, but rather because race, class, and education differences make the success sequence plausible, rational, and accessible to some but not others.

This failure to account for macro dynamics of family formation is central to why marriage educators miss the mark in offering marriage education to low-income couples whose relationships will remain precarious in the face of severe economic insecurities. It also explains why it is so easy for the marriage education movement to obscure antipoverty goals. It is much easier to strengthen relationships and marriages among couples who are not struggling to make ends meet. Behind the goals of the marriage movement is a moral agenda to promote the nuclear family over other family forms, making sure that it remains "indispensable," as Wilcox and Boyd argue, rather than seeking structural and policy solutions that would offer better support to poor and working-class families.

The important question from a policy perspective is whether the government should fund these programs even in the face of growing evidence that the policy has little value as an antipoverty measure. Given the research of sociologists Kathryn Edin and Maria Kefalas showing that low-income women do value marriage but find it a difficult institution to enter,[36] we argue for the need to provide low-income couples with the economic supports that could give them a shot at a future of marital stability.

Marriage promotion policies do not recognize and support diverse family forms and practices. Our research points to the need to direct our attention away from the idea of promoting marriage and toward policies that can alleviate the intimate inequalities that persist in American society.

Notes

1. Authors are listed alphabetically and made equal contributions to the chapter. We are grateful to Orit Avishai, who contributed as an equal co-author to the original version of this chapter and whose research we reference throughout.

2. Wilcox and Boyd (2020).

3. Quoted in Brooks (2020).
4. Wilcox and Boyd (2020).
5. Plummer (2003).
6. Fry and Parker (2021).
7. McLanahan, Tach, and Schneider (2013).
8. Brown (2010).
9. Conger, Conger, and Martin (2010).
10. Wang and Wilcox (2017).
11. Coontz (2005).
12. Livingston (2018).
13. Cherlin (2009).
14. Brotherson and Duncan (2004); Heath (2012).
15. Sager (2010).
16. United States Congress (1996).
17. Randles (2020).
18. Hymowitz (2021).
19. Edin and Kefalas (2005).
20. Edin and Nelson (2013).
21. Wood, Moore, Clarkwest, Killewald, and Monahan (2012).
22. Office of Family Assistance (2021).
23. Wu, Moore, and Wood (2021).
24. Randles (2017).
25. Randles (2017).
26. Wu et al. (2021).
27. Kanter, Williams, and Rauer (2021).
28. Boo (2003).
29. Heath (2012).
30. Safawi and Reyes (2021).
31. Felder (2022).
32. Randles and Avishai (2018).
33. Halpern-Meekin (2019).
34. Waters (2004).
35. Hawkins and Fackrell (2010).
36. Edin and Kefalas (2005).

In Other Words

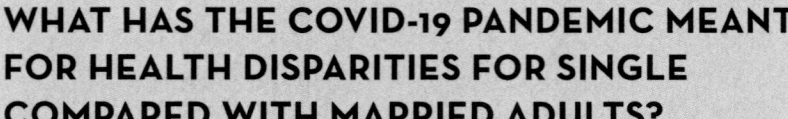

WHAT HAS THE COVID-19 PANDEMIC MEANT FOR HEALTH DISPARITIES FOR SINGLE COMPARED WITH MARRIED ADULTS?

Mieke Beth Thomeer, August 30, 2022 / CCF@TSP

At wedding showers, guests are often asked to provide advice to the newlyweds. As someone who values my alone time, one of my favorites has always been "The key to a happy marriage is spending lots of time apart." But for many married couples in the United States in March 2020, "spending lots of time apart" became unattainable due to workplaces, schools, churches, restaurants, gyms, and other public or semi-public spaces closing their doors. Other couples—in which one or both spouses worked "essential" jobs with a high risk of COVID-19 infection—contended with very little time together. At the same time, although shutting down public gathering spaces and avoiding social interactions outside of households was clearly beneficial to reducing the spread of COVID-19, it also likely posed unique risks for the mental health and social well-being of single adults, especially those who lived alone or provided care to children and other family members.

These complex dynamics point to a likely reality: families have been especially salient for our health and well-being during the pandemic period. Family scientists have long shown that family status—including relationship status—is linked to health, with most studies finding (broadly speaking) that married adults have better health outcomes than never married, divorced, and widowed adults. Yet these patterns, like all social science patterns, are context-specific, and studies are only beginning to consider how this may have shifted during the COVID-19 pandemic.

To address this, I analyzed survey data from April to December 2020. I found that never-married respondents had increased probabilities of fair or poor health, depression, and anxiety relative to married adults as the pandemic progressed. The dominant ideology within the United States even before the pandemic privileged marriages and legal families, as reflected in public policies such as people having access to their spouse's employer-based health insurance and "greedy marriage" norms, which encourage married couples to prioritize their spouse above other relationships. The pandemic may have amplified this social advantage for the married, as the pandemic period was generally characterized by increased reliance on families—giving adults with a spouse a potential health-related benefit. Spouses likely provided important financial and practical support for each other in the context of unstable employment and child care and emotional support while navigating the death and illness of loved ones and uncertain social times. Given limited opportunities to gather and socialize outside of the household, single adults who lived alone may have had less access to these supports. These dynamics perhaps underlie the patterns I found in my survey analysis of widening health disparities between never-married adults and married adults.

Yet I also found a narrowing of the difference in health outcomes for married compared to previously married adults over these same months, demonstrating the need to disentangle groups of nonmarried adults and not treat the "marital advantage" as universal. Although these survey data did not allow me to examine marital quality, other studies have shown that relationship strain increased as the pandemic progressed. Being isolated together as a couple—alongside new financial and health stressors—may have increased tension within relationships. Additionally, many couples experienced conflict around discordant views on masks, social distancing, and (in later months) vaccines. As an additional caution against seeing marriage as universally beneficial for health during the pandemic, my analysis further showed that marriage was more meaningful for men's mental health than women's, in line

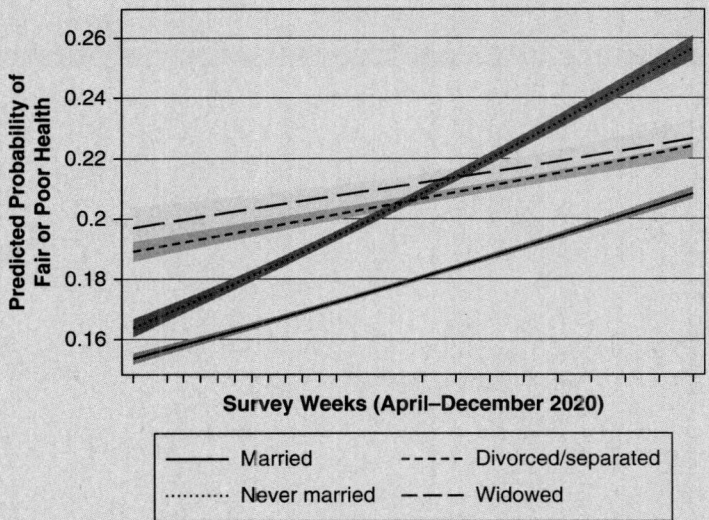

Figure 21.1 | Estimated Trends in Reporting Fair or Poor Health by Relationship Status

Source: Pulse Survey, April–December 2020.

Note: N = 1,422,733. Weighted. Models adjust for gender, race/ethnicity, age, educational attainment, household income, coresidential children, and pandemic-related stressors (lost income, food insufficiency, delayed medical care, and issues with paying for housing).

with feminist understandings of his and hers heterosexual marriages where men and women in the same marriage experience starkly different dynamics and benefits.

The patterns are not inevitable but rather reflect the public policies and organizational decisions across the pandemic months. Health disparities, including family-based health disparities, are not static but dynamic, shifting alongside changes within society. During the first few months of the COVID-19 pandemic, public policies were enacted to specifically strengthen the social safety net, including changes to unemployment benefits, stimulus payments from the federal government, and protections against evictions and debt repayment. Yet rather than extending these policies, many expired after a short period of time, likely to the detriment of the most vulnerable within society and resulting in strains on families and individuals. Within the current environment, married couples are generally at an advantage because society privileges marriage above friendships, siblings, cohabiting and dating relationships, and other social arrangements. We should aim to create policies that support multiple types of family arrangements beyond marriage, recognizing the multiple forms and functions that families and communities take, and in turn reduce disparities across these diverse family types—not broaden them. ▄

22

![black bar]

The Case for Divorce

Virginia E. Rutter

D o you know the answer to this question: "Is the divorce rate increasing in the U.S.?" Try googling it.

I asked one of my top students to do this in a meeting with me. Before googling, the student guessed, "I think it is going up?"

Spoiler (as my student was reminded): the divorce rate has not increased in the United States since 1980. That was more than forty years ago. In the past twenty, it has declined overall, though rates vary by group. Even so, we keep hearing the story of increasing divorce rates. Stephanie Coontz (see Chapter 6) has called this type of thinking a nostalgia trap. How are thoughtful, studious people—like my student, and maybe you—left with the impression that a myth that is roundly false is a commonsense fact?

For the record, here are some divorce statistics:

In 2020 the overall divorce rate was 36.7 percent.[1]

There was an unexpected 12 percent decline in divorces during the pandemic. The rate remained the same in 2021.[2]

The states with the highest divorce rates were Arkansas, Mississippi, Idaho, Oklahoma, and Louisiana—states you might think of as ranking higher on old-time "family values."

The states with the lowest divorce rates were New Hampshire, New Jersey, Massachusetts, Connecticut, and Rhode Island.

Even though they have a lower divorce rate than other age groups, people over fifty are getting divorced more and more than in the past, while younger people are getting divorced less and less often.[3]

Finally, as couple researcher Neil Jacobson used to quip, "The best divorce prevention is marriage prevention." And indeed, the rate of marriage has declined since the beginning of this century by 25 percent; in 2019 there were 300,000 fewer existing marriages than in 2000.[4] But the myths of marriage and divorce continue apace, and putting the facts in context helps us to understand marriage and divorce, as well as how we think about families as they really are.

SOME CONTEXT

When I discuss divorce with my college students, the topic brings up a lot of personal stories. Our stories point us to how complicated the topics we study in this book are. There are stories of relief, stories of community, stories of loss, and stories of disappointment. Like my students, my story of divorce—my parents' divorce—made me curious about what the statistics really say about divorce and also gave me a deeper curiosity about why there is still, in 2023, so much misunderstanding about divorce.

My own story is this: As a child, my parents fought all the time, and when they weren't fighting they treated each other with contempt. I longed for an end to this from an early age. They finally divorced when I was fifteen and when my three older brothers had already left home. That was around 1978, which, as you will see in this chapter, was around the peak of the divorce rate in the United States. There was a lot of shame and secrecy but also a lot of resiliency, especially as my mom pushed forward working a professional job in our school and then other jobs at night.

People continue to cite outdated or miscalculated evidence about how marriage makes you healthier or wealthier. Meanwhile, much valuable research demonstrates the problems with claims about "one true family structure." In this book, you can read Deadric Williams and colleagues (Chapter 5) explain how claims that family structure (like whether parents are married, divorced, single, or cohabiting) explains the Black-white inequality gap are used to minimize the impact of larger social systems that generate that inequality. You can read Melanie Heath and Jennifer Randles describe a marriage movement (Chapter 21) that ignores the gender politics of insisting on marriage as the solution to economic ills and reinforces a backward-looking way of addressing human needs, including the need to connect within families.

At the beginning of the twenty-first century, the book *The Case for Marriage* was the scholarly set piece for claims against divorce—and led me to respond with "The Case for Divorce." As this chapter demonstrates, there are times when divorce leads to greater well-being. In fact, there are negative health consequences to remaining in a distressed marriage.

How have we ended up having a lot of quasi-science make folks believe that marriage is a cure-all and divorce is a disaster? Part of the story is about research methods! As you read this chapter, you will learn how to weigh claims about marriage and divorce. In short, there are three things any reader of marriage and divorce research should look out for when assessing information. Ask whether marital quality has been considered—and how it has been measured. Ask if domestic violence and other pathologies have been examined. And look for whether "selection effects," or situations that occurred prior to marriage and that don't have anything to do with the marriage or the divorce itself but that make people more likely to divorce, have been tested.

A Little History on Divorce in the United States

Starting in 1880, when U.S. divorce statistics first started to be recorded, the rate of divorce increased steadily for eighty years and then increased dramatically from 1960 to 1980.[5] By 1980, about half of all marriages ended in divorce. In the next twenty years, our 50 percent divorce rate leveled off. Since the turn of the twenty-first century, divorce rates, like marriage rates, have declined, and now the divorce rate is below 40 percent.

Divorce policy in the United States has changed over time. In the 1970s, divorce laws shifted to allow unilateral divorce ("no-fault divorce"). Since that time, rates of wife's suicide, domestic violence, and spousal homicide have declined.[6] Meanwhile, the number of children involved in any given divorce has gone from 1.34 children to less than 1 child per divorce[7] because of the declining birth rate.

The increases in divorce from the 1960s to the 1980s made divorce a fixture in family life—and a "problem" to be understood, interpreted, analyzed, and fixed.[3] But what exactly is the problem? A better understanding of divorce—and divorce research—clarifies the case for divorce, and by extension informs us about life as it really is in contemporary families.

The Case for Divorce

The case for divorce asks, are there some cases where divorce is a *better* outcome than remaining married? Three decades of research on the impact on adults and children points to yes. The case for divorce also asks you to consider, why is this topic still so poorly understood?

While discussion of research methods leaves some people sleepy, the consistent hallmark of reliable research on the impact of divorce is that it makes a logical and reasonable comparison. Some studies do this. Some don't. It is as simple as this: if my now-divorced parents had been happily married, life would have been different, and a divorce would have been a big loss to them, me, my brothers, and the community. But that wasn't the case. They treated each other with contempt, led parallel lives, lived through their children (and also did a lot of good things). Then they were divorced.

The logical comparison for divorce versus not divorce in my own biography is a comparison between having unhappily married parents or divorced parents who moved on. My parents' postdivorce lives were up and down (as were their pre-divorce lives that included spells of unemployment and sudden, unexpected moves) but ultimately a lot more sensible for all involved and (crucially) better than the life that preceded the divorce. Research that asks "Compared to what?" is designed to do a what-if exercise—not just with one person's story, but with the stories of many.

When researchers carefully examine "Divorce compared to what?," they are sometimes searching for *selection bias*—a particular kind of problem that shows there is something about the people who get divorced that happened before they got into their current situation that makes them more likely to divorce. Situations from before the marriage may affect who divorces. So when we compare divorced people to people who stayed married, the question is whether selection bias has influenced how people ended up in one group or the other. There is selection bias if the divorced group was already different from the stably married group. For example, getting married at a younger age, experiencing poverty, and not having a college degree are all associated with divorce. Already we see that selection bias plays a role in divorce.

But how have researchers answered the question about how or whether divorce *causes* problems for adults or their children? Selection bias may explain some, but not all, of today's divorces. Things like age or poverty don't explain away divorce. Instead, they point to the need for more help for people transitioning to adulthood, the need to reduce poverty, and the importance of a social safety net that doesn't privilege people with a particular level of education.

Some of our case for divorce is about children, and some is about adults. In the first section below, "Resilient Children of Divorce," we learn two lessons from research on the impact of divorce on children. First, most children of divorce do well. And second, children who remain in high-conflict families, where the parents have a distressed marriage, are at greater risk for problems. When parents divorce, children have already been subject to their parents' distressed marriages, and that is what puts these children at greater risk for problems. The second section—"Does Divorce Make You Happy?"—discusses how research on the impact of divorce on adults follows a similar pattern: the negative consequences of a harsh or conflictual marriage exceed the consequences of divorce. In the fourth section, "Measuring Divorce's Impact with and without a Comparison

Group," you will read about the neutral impact of divorce on children. At the same time, this section shows you, again, the problems of research that fails to have a logical comparison group.

The case for divorce is straightforward. The consequences—for both children and adults—of remaining in a distressed marriage are myriad and long-lasting. In those cases, perhaps the saying shouldn't be "Stay together for the kids," but "Get divorced for the kids," not to mention for the health and well-being of the parents on whom the children depend. Families experience challenges before marriage, during marriage, and following any marriage. The sources of challenges for parents and children—when we look at context—are ones that merit care and concern in the form of resources, not blaming or shaming.

RESILIENT CHILDREN OF DIVORCE

In 1989, psychologist Mavis Hetherington presented her research to thousands of members of the American Association for Marriage and Family Therapy, which showed that most children of divorce fare just as well as children from intact families. She had established a comparative rate of distress among children: while 10 percent of children in the general population have behavioral or school-related problems, 20–25 percent of children from divorced families have these problems (but about 80 percent of the children of divorce do not have such problems). Numerous research papers provided more detail and supported these findings.

Hetherington reported on specific kinds of distress that parents and children experience with divorce. She found a "crisis period" of about two years surrounding the divorce. She learned that, depending on the timing of divorce, boys and girls have different responses: when boys have problems, they tend to "act out"; when girls have problems, they are more likely to become depressed. But what Hetherington saw overall was the *resilience* of children of divorce.[9] Most children did fine. They were able to use personal resources and social networks in their family and community to cope.

Another study came out that year that refuted these findings, but it also differed in terms of how the research was conducted. Psychologist Judith Wallerstein reported her research finding that children of divorce experienced more mental health problems than children of nondivorced, married couples. She found that children of divorce sometimes suffered a "sleeper effect"; their difficulty emerged as adults—hence the phrase "adult children of divorce" came into common use—suggesting people must be ever vigilant for some lurking form of damage that could pop up like a dormant cancer.

Remarkable as it is, the conflicts between these two studies, both several decades old, continue to plague our understanding of divorce and children. To judge between these two pieces of research, we need to look at how these psychologists collected their information.

Wallerstein's methods: she studied a *clinical* sample of young, white, upper-middle-class teenagers whose parents had been divorced and who sought treatment at a mental health center in Northern California.[10] A clinical sample involves people who want help. They are a sample of folks who are, by definition, troubled. While a clinical sample can teach us much about the course of mental disturbances or adjustment problems, it cannot inform us about the prevalence or origins of a problem in the population or reveal why some people end up doing well in the face of adversity while others do not. Wallerstein provided cases full of rich detail, but they were not *representative*. Her study has the strength of being *longitudinal* (that is, she tracked her subjects over time), but her evidence couldn't tell us whether these problems occur consistently in the population or if they were due to selection bias. Children of divorce who are troubled are, by definition, the ones who seek therapy.

Hetherington's methods: Researchers obtained a population-based sample of stably married families with a four-year-old and followed them over time. It was a *prospective* longitudinal study. *Prospective* means that the study started before any divorces happened. Using a series of observations, parental reports, and teacher reports, Hetherington tracked these children in their everyday lives. Some children's parents went on to divorce; others remained together. We can't do experiments where we randomly assign some children to divorced parents and others to married parents, but Hetherington's study gives us a quasi-experimental design that helps us evaluate the impact of divorce compared to no divorce. In the comparison, all the children started off the same in the sense that they weren't part of the study because they already had "problems." Not only did this design allow researchers to compare children whose parents divorced with children whose parents stayed together, it also enabled the researchers to see how children fared before the divorce versus how they were doing after the divorce. Hetherington had built-in comparisons.[11]

As research progressed, Hetherington learned more about divorce and children. Because she had detailed information about both kinds of families, she was able to compare married families with divorced families. Sometimes the married families were extremely distressed; sometimes they were civil. Hetherington was able to analyze the well-being of children in extremely distressed married families versus children of divorce and children in harmoniously married families. By adding comparisons about the level of distress in all the families, she observed that children in harmonious married families fared better than children in divorced families *and* in distressed married families. Here's the takeaway: the worst kind of family for a child to be raised in, in terms of mental health and behavior, was a *distressed married* family.[12]

Several key pieces of research extended Hetherington's results by using comparison groups and a prospective design. In 1991, demographer Andrew Cherlin and his colleagues wrote about longitudinal studies in Great Britain and the United States in the journal *Science*. The studies included data from parents, children, and teachers over time. At the first time point, age seven, all the children's parents were married. Over the study period, some went on to divorce, and some did not. Cherlin confirmed Hetherington's findings: While about 10 percent of children overall are at risk for adjustment and mental health problems, children of divorce are about 20–25 percent at risk for problems. Seventy-five to 80 percent of the children are fine.[13]

Cherlin also found that the difference between the children of divorce and the children in stable marriages existed *prior* to the divorce. These were *predisruption effects*, and here's what that means: parents who end up divorcing are different from parents who don't end up divorcing. They relate to each other differently; they relate to their children differently; and their children relate to them differently. Cherlin had identified selection bias, or a case of selection for who divorces.

In 1998, Cherlin and his colleagues offered an update on their continuing research.[14] Respondents analyzed in the 1991 study had gotten older, so he had more information. While the 1991 paper highlighted predisruption effects, this one reported that there were *postdisruption* effects (negative effects after the divorce) that accumulated and made life more difficult for children of divorce. Financial hardship and the loss of paternal involvement were key culprits. He called this phenomenon the "cascade of negative life events" and emphasized, as he had back in 1991, the importance of social and institutional supports for children in disrupted and remarried families.

A similar longitudinal study by Paul Amato and Juliana Sobolewski replicated these results in 2001.[15] They studied stably married families, distressed but married families, and divorced families over the course of seventeen years. They observed that grown children whose parents had divorced during their childhood had more adjustment problems. Although these adjustment problems were associated with predisruption effects—in other words, trouble in the family that preceded the divorce—postdisruption effects accumulated, too. Finally, the researchers found that children who grew up with married parents in distressed unions were more likely to experience psychological distress in later life, in contrast to their counterparts with nondistressed, stably married parents.

Starting with Hetherington in the 1980s, and following through Cherlin's parallel work later, research designs that included comparison groups helped bring to light three points. First, using a population-based rather than a clinical sample provided a rate of distress among children of divorce that exemplified their *resilience*: approximately 80 percent were doing well versus 90 percent of children in the general population who were doing well. Second, difficulties—predisruption effects—found in prospective longitudinal studies indicated that children in families where their parents were headed for divorce were having trouble prior to the breakup. Postdisruption effects—and the cascade of negative life events—also played a role. Third, distressed marriages were harder on children than divorces. As you'll read in the next section, parents' subsequent relationships have come to be understood as having potential as resources (see Chapter 12)—or challenges.

DOES DIVORCE MAKE YOU HAPPY?

People who divorce do not go through it just to "feel good" or in some casual way to be happy. As you'll see, research shows us just how difficult living in a distressed marriage is. The research shows us that divorce makes people feel better in the same way that the cessation of pain or illness makes people feel better.

In 2002, Linda Waite, a demographer at the University of Chicago, and several of her colleagues released a study titled "Does Divorce Make People Happy?" At the same time, I was completing research at the University of Washington for a study titled "The Case for Divorce: Under What Conditions Is Divorce Beneficial and for Whom?"[16]

We both asked, how does people's level of well-being change when they divorce (versus when they stay married)? Both projects relied on the same data set; they both used a longitudinal design where all the people were married at the first time point, and some of them went on to divorce by the second time point. I found that adults who exited unhappy marriages were less depressed than those who stayed. According to Waite, there were no differences in happiness between those who stayed in their marriages and those who divorced. Our results were completely divergent.

What is the point? Should we throw up our hands and claim that research is merely a Rorschach test, a projective test that displays and reveals our deep-seated values and biases? For goodness' sake, no!

Instead, ask, "Divorce compared to what?" Were people who divorced compared to those who stayed in a happy marriage, or compared to those who stayed in a stressed-out marriage? One difference between Waite's study and mine was that I used a high-intensity measure of marital distress—I was able to detect the people who were in seriously distressed marriages that would be likely to put them in the situation of considering divorce. I also took severe domestic violence into account, and I measured depression rather than "happiness." The contrast makes all the difference. When comparing how unhappily married people fare compared to people who divorced, divorcing people were less depressed, and unhappily married people were more depressed. My additional statistical tests ("fixed effects," discussed below) confirmed that marital distress, not other factors, accounted for the differences between the unhappily married and divorced groups. In other words, what made the married people in distressed marriages more depressed was *being in a distressed marriage*, not their risk of depression.

Other longitudinal studies, including a study by Daniel Hawkins and Alan Booth,[17] found similar results regarding marital distress: the more carefully marital distress was measured, the more pronounced were the psychological advantages of leaving over staying. Again, using a thoughtful measurement of marital quality led to a better comparison. A study by Pamela Smock and her colleagues assessed the economic costs of divorce and also used methods that took into account selection bias. Smock and her colleagues found that divorced women experience economic disadvantages but that some of that economic disadvantage would have existed even if they had remained married.[18] With psychological distress, as with economic distress, people who divorced were different for reasons *other* than divorcing, not *because* of divorcing.

More recent research has examined how the accumulation of marital transitions—a divorce, a cohabitation, a breakup, perhaps a remarriage—may be an additional, important way to examine the impact of divorce. This approach examines "relationship trajectories." Sarah Meadows and her colleagues examined the consequences of these multiple transitions for women who started as single mothers.[19] They found that the health of women who face continuous instability—rather than a single transition—was negatively affected. Such research allows for even more complexity and requires that we compare higher levels of disruption with lower levels of disruption, including divorce.

These relationship transitions also have an effect on children. After the breakup, when children are exposed to multiple transitions—a divorce, then a cohabitation and breakup, then perhaps another marriage—they may be at elevated risk of behavioral or emotional problems relative to children who just experience one transition, such as a divorce. In a 2007 study that focused on single parents, Osborne and McLanahan[20] found that the accumulation of a mother's relationship transitions leads to hardship for her children.

WHY MARITAL QUALITY MATTERS

Marital quality makes a difference when we ask whether divorce is better than staying married. The benefits of marriage accrue only to people in happy and well-functioning marriages; the benefits of happy marriages are, indeed, robust. The same is not true for people in distressed marriages, and we save those marriages at our—and our partners'—peril. For example, studies on the psychophysiology of marriage—ones that measure how your body responds to social stress—show that when men and women are in distressed marriages in which they may experience contempt, criticism, defensiveness, and stonewalling, their immune systems decline over time.[21] These people are less healthy and less happy. Troubled marriages have immediate costs; they also have downstream health costs as the years of distress accumulate.

Research has demonstrated how high those costs are. Public health researcher Myrna Weissman used community mental health samples to assess the impact of marital distress on rates of major depression.[22] While the study found that depression was reduced for people in happy marriages, depression for men *and* women in unhappy marriages was *twenty-five* times more likely than for people in happy marriages. Another study found that women who experienced marital dissatisfaction in the past year had a 2.7 times greater risk of depression. Men with marital distress in the past year also had an elevated rate of depression. Even more alarming is a study that showed that among married women who were more depressed than average, by far the most common explanation was domestic violence.

In my research, women who were victims of domestic violence—severe enough to have been injured in the past year—responded differently to distress and divorce than did women in nonviolent distressed marriages. These differences are likely because the problems that domestic violence victims have to solve are different from the problems of those who are in distressed but nonviolent marriages. Research on divorce should always seek to identify victims of abuse because these cases follow a different story line.[23] The COVID-19 pandemic provides another reminder of the importance of exit strategies. During the lockdown phase, in the United States and internationally, rates of intimate partner violence and threats increased.[24]

When researchers measure marital distress in terms of level of conflict, or they use multiple measures of distress, and find high conflict and distress, they discover that divorce is a relief to those couples. This is like what Hetherington found for children—that divorce is better than living in a high-conflict family. It is easy enough to ask, "How was marital distress measured?" in order to learn whether researchers used a measure of general happiness that merely captures transient feelings of satisfaction or whether they used a measure of serious distress or conflict, which tends to identify which couples are "candidates" for divorce.

MEASURING DIVORCE'S IMPACT WITH AND WITHOUT A COMPARISON GROUP

In April 2008, the questions about the impact of divorce and its costs were still alive and well. Two studies were released the very same week on the topic. A release from the Council on Contemporary Families was based on demographer Allen Li's research. The other paper, by economist Ben Scafidi, was released by the Institute for American Values. Li's paper focused on the emotional impact of divorce on children, while Scafidi's paper addressed the economic impact of divorce across America.[25]

The papers pointed in opposite directions. Li's asked, what is the impact of divorce on children? He found that divorce itself does not explain the differences between children with divorced parents and children with married parents. He found differences between the two groups (on average)—just as researchers have been finding since the 1980s. With increasingly refined analysis, however, Li was able to show that *selection bias*—or a case of improper comparisons—accounted for the differences.

Li's technique included testing for "fixed effects"—a statistical tool used in economics and biomedical research with longitudinal data. Fixed-effects models tell us if there are aspects of the individuals that are not measured explicitly but that account for results. The children in Li's study whose parents ended up divorcing were getting a different kind of parenting all along when compared with the children whose parents stayed married.

Meanwhile, Scafidi's paper asked, what does divorce cost the general public? Hold on to your hats. By his calculations, divorce—plus single parenthood— costs taxpayers $112 billion a year. To calculate this, he assumed that divorce and single parenthood *cause* poverty (not allowing for the possibility that it is the other way around, for example). In a 2002 report, historian Stephanie Coontz and economist Nancy Folbre examined the problems with assuming that divorce and single parenthood cause poverty by taking into account selection bias.[26] While there is a correlation between single parenthood and poverty, the correlation does not mean that single parenthood *causes* poverty. *Causation* is complex and challenging to establish, but the evidence that causality flows in the other direction—that poverty often *causes* or precedes single parenthood—is to many analysts a lot stronger. As Stevenson and Wolfers point out, Scafidi neglected comparisons in another way as well: while some women end up losing financially following divorce, others actually gain.[27] Scafidi did not include these economic gains in his equations.

The results were divergent because of fundamental differences in thinking about "what causes what?" While Li's article asks, "Divorce *compared to what?*" Scafidi's does not assess the costs of divorce relative to, for example, remaining in a distressed, tumultuous, or violent family situation. Scafidi didn't test the premise that divorce (and single parenthood) causes economic problems. He assumed it. By neglecting the causality question, Scafidi—like many others—focused on family structure and paid no attention to the original causes of poverty. By posing his message as "This costs taxpayers money," he suggests that personal moral failings lead to burdens on the other "good" people who pay into the system. It is another form of blaming and scapegoating. There continues to be plenty of good information about how to reduce poverty, and stopping divorce isn't on the list. For example, the pandemic gave us a test of how to reduce poverty, and the answer had nothing to do with family structure. From 2020 to 2022, low- and moderate-income families were given the kind of financial support and housing protections that families in other rich countries get to help them raise their children. In this case, support for families with children helped us reduce the percentage of people in poverty by nearly 6 percent.[28]

The effects of divorce result not only from what happened prior to the divorce but also after. In 2007, Fomby and Cherlin found that the characteristics of the mother from before the divorce helped explain the reduced cognitive outcomes for some children of divorce.[29] But they also found that *postdisruption* effects of the divorce, rather than just selection bias or pre-disruption effects, contributed to behavioral problems sometimes seen in children of divorce.

LESSONS LEARNED

Divorce researchers who use comparison groups and control for selection bias, who measure marital quality carefully, and who take domestic violence into account may still disagree about just how different children of divorce are from children of married parents. (Are 20 percent affected? Are 25 percent affected?) But they recognize the resilience of children over time after divorce. Researchers may disagree about whether the impact of divorce is neutral, as Allen Li argues, or how much of the impact of divorce is due to preexisting factors like high conflict, or whether some of the impact of divorce is due to postdisruption factors related to the resources available in that family as well as to families in general.

More recently, some research has noted that subsequent new relationships are an important piece of the puzzle.

Scientists agree, however, that comparing married families to divorced families without taking selection bias into account is a case of comparing apples to oranges and will get us nowhere in terms of helping families. As Hawkins, Hetherington, and I show in studies you've read about here, failing to take the quality of the marriages seriously is like ignoring the elephant in the room! The distressed marriage is where most people considering divorce start. And this distress is costly to the health and mental health of parents and their children. In those cases, there is no time machine that helps people go back and have a do-over. Furthermore, scholars in this book, like Williams et al. (Chapter 5), Heath and Randles (Chapter 21), and Cross (Chapter 23), remind us that claims about family structure—including marriage and divorce—are often a way to ignore gender inequality and a history of racism as explanations for how different groups of people struggle. When you hear a family structure argument, look out for this kind of bias!

When reading research on marriage and divorce—or listening to someone's conclusions about it—be sure to ask, "Did this study include a comparison group and take selection bias into account?" and "Did the researchers measure things—especially marital distress—carefully?"

When I ask these questions—and when I look at the role of divorce in U.S. history—I see a complicated story. Above all, I have discovered that there is a case for divorce. There are times and situations when divorce is beneficial to the people who divorce and to their children.

Notes

1. This is calculated by the number of divorces (630,505) divided by the number of marriages (1,676,911) in 2020.
2. Marino (2022).
3. Carlson (2021).
4. CDC (2023).
5. Ruggles (1997).
6. Discussed by Stevenson and Wolfers (2006).
7. Reported by Cowen (2007).
8. Coltrane and Adams (2003).
9. Hetherington and Stanley-Hagan (1997).
10. Wallerstein and Blakeslee (1988).

11. A complete, accessible review of Hetherington's longitudinal research is in Hetherington and Kelly (2002).

12. Hetherington (1999).

13. Cherlin et al. (1991).

14. Cherlin et al. (1998).

15. Amato and Sobolewski (2001).

16. Waite et al. (2002); Rutter (2004).

17. Hawkins and Booth (2005).

18. Smock, Manning, and Gupta (1999).

19. Meadows, McLanahan, and Brooks-Gunn (2008).

20. Osborne and McLanahan (2007).

21. Gottman (1994); Kiecolt-Glaser et al. (1988); Robles and Kiecolt-Glaser (2003).

22. Choi and Marks (2008).

23. See Whisman (1999) on depression; and Campbell (1998) on domestic violence.

24. UN Women, n.d.

25. Li (2008); Li (2007); Scafidi (2008).

26. Coontz and Folbre (2002).

27. See Stevenson and Wolfers's note in Li (2007); and Ananat and Michaels (2008).

28. CBPP (2022).

29. Fomby and Cherlin (2007).

In Other Words

DIVORCE ANXIETY? FOR SEXUAL MINORITY YOUNG ADULTS, NOT SO MUCH

Aaron Hoy, Jori Adrianna Nkwenti, and Sachita Pokhrel, May 17, 2022 / CCF@TSP

Many young adults today say that they are anxious or afraid of divorce. In many cases, they saw their own parents' divorce up close and want to avoid a similar fate. In other cases, they saw divorce play out from a distance, in their broader social networks, and eventually reached the same conclusion. Whatever the reason, many young adults say that although they generally approve of divorce they are worried that they may one day go through a divorce themselves. Indeed, research shows that divorce haunts cohabiting young adults like a "specter," and many choose to cohabit first as a way of "divorce-proofing" their eventual marriage.

Still, when it comes to how young adults think about divorce, few have paid attention to sexual minorities. Thanks to the Supreme Court's 2015 decision in *Obergefell v. Hodges*, sexual minorities can now think about marriage, and divorce, with respect to their own lives. That is why we looked at written responses to open-ended survey questions about sexual minority young adults' thoughts on divorce. All 257 of our respondents were unmarried individuals between the ages of eighteen and thirty-five who identify as lesbian, gay, bisexual, and/or queer.

In stark contrast to the divorce anxiety so commonly reported by heterosexual young adults, the sexual minority young adults in our sample made clear that if they ever do get married, they would have no trouble divorcing. In fact, in response to the statement "There are some circumstances under which I would consider getting a divorce," approximately 81 percent said that they strongly agree, and another 19 percent said that they agree. To be clear, our respondents also indicated that they would try to avoid divorce by engaging in active communication and seeking out marriage counseling if necessary. However, they consistently emphasized that they are not afraid of divorce, and in many cases, do not see divorce as a negative outcome. As one thirty-year-old bisexual woman wrote, "I would absolutely get a divorce, and I don't see it as a last resort, 'Break glass in case of emergency' type of thing. If it's not working and two people are no longer in love or simply don't want to be married anymore, then they should split."

In general, our respondents tended to explain their willingness to divorce in one or more of the following ways. First, many said that they value their individual happiness and well-being more than they would value being married. Although most (60 percent) did express a desire to get married someday, many also explained

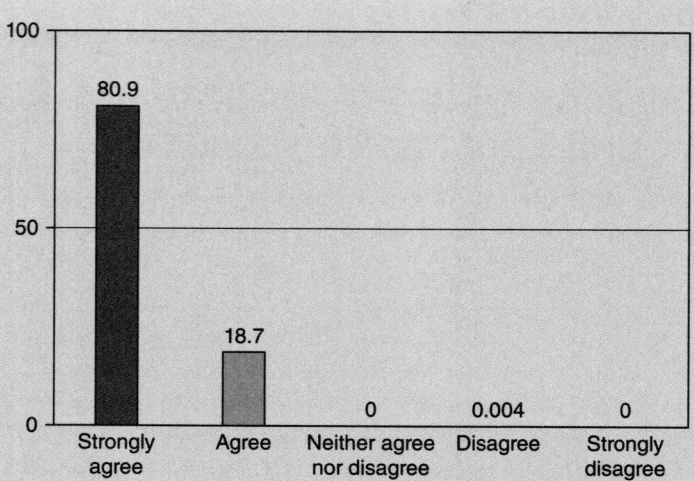

Figure 22.1 | Percent of sexual minority young adults saying they agree/disagree with the statement "There are some circumstances under which I would get a divorce."

that leading a happy, healthy life is simply a bigger priority for them. Second, some respondents said that they would be willing to divorce because they see being "stuck" or "trapped" in a bad marriage as a far worse outcome. Flipping the divorce anxiety script, these respondents are more worried about the possibility of an unsatisfying or troubled marriage than they are about divorce. Finally, a few said that they reject the idea that marriage is a lifelong commitment. As one thirty-two-year-old lesbian woman put it, "The possibility of divorce is part of marriage. . . . It's not failure, just time to change the structure and expectations of a relationship."

Given that worries or concerns about divorce are so well documented among heterosexual young adults, our findings raise the question of how and why sexual identities might matter so much here. Our study cannot address this question directly, but we suspect that a significant factor is how sexual minorities are, as research suggests, socialized in *both* the dominant, heteronormative culture, which continues to celebrate marriage as a lifelong relationship, and in a distinctive queer culture, where individual autonomy is considered paramount, even in committed relationships. Perhaps participation in queer culture offers a kind of license to pursue divorce and thus helps alleviate some of the divorce anxiety that heterosexual young adults so often report? Although not all our respondents connected their willingness to divorce to their sexual identities, those who did tended to be the most willing.

It is important to note that some legal observers see warning signs that the *Obergefell* decision might be challenged and possibly overturned by the Supreme Court. But for now at least, national marriage equality is a settled matter, and as a result, we have a lot to learn about marriage and divorce in the lives of sexual minorities. Our study, like others, suggests that sexual identity does play a key role in shaping how people think about and approach marital relationships, and future research should continue this line of inquiry.

In Other Words

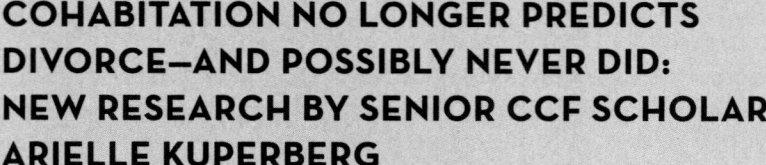

COHABITATION NO LONGER PREDICTS DIVORCE—AND POSSIBLY NEVER DID: NEW RESEARCH BY SENIOR CCF SCHOLAR ARIELLE KUPERBERG

Virginia E. Rutter, March 3, 2014 / CCF

Want to Know What Predicts Divorce? Let's Start with What Does Not

For more than twenty years, researchers have reported that premarital cohabitation is associated with an elevated risk of divorce. Yet these findings have failed to deter young people from "shacking up." According to a briefing report presented today to the Council on Contemporary Families, cohabitation has increased by more than 900 percent in the past fifty years. Author Arielle Kuperberg, a sociologist at the University of North Carolina at Greensboro, notes that "today 70 percent of women aged thirty to thirty-four have cohabited with a male partner, and two-thirds of new marriages take place between couples who have already lived together for an average of thirty-one months."

In "Does Premarital Cohabitation Increase Your Risk for Divorce?" Kuperberg sees no need for panic. Her new research finds that previous studies have overstated the divorce risk from premarital cohabitation by ignoring how old the individuals are when they move in together. It turns out that the age at which people move in together is a much more important factor than whether or not they have taken out a marriage license.

On average, she reports, cohabitors begin living together at an earlier age than couples who marry directly. But "when couples are compared by the age at which they move in together and start taking on the roles associated with marriage, there is no difference in divorce rates between couples that lived together before marriage and those that didn't."

Kuperberg states that premarital cohabitation has very little, if any, impact on a couple's chance of divorce. Rather, "early entry into marriage or cohabitation, especially prior to age twenty-three, is the critical risk factor."

CCF Commentators: Delay, Protect, and Look for More Change in the Future

Cornell University sociologist Sharon Sassler agrees that it is wrong to claim that premarital cohabitation causes divorce, but she suggests that "perhaps more important is how long one is involved with a romantic partner before moving in together." Sassler's research demonstrates that individuals without a college degree tend to move in together in less than half the time that college-educated couples take to make such a decision, probably because of their greater financial need to split living expenses. But this gives them less time to get to know their partner, making it more possible that they will end up in a bad match that will not stand the test of time.

Sociologist Kristi Williams (The Ohio State University) notes that an unintended pregnancy may lead a couple to move in together or to marry. Either way, such relationships are much more likely to dissolve than relationships that are not formed under the pressure of an unplanned pregnancy. For that reason, she suggests that the best way to lay the groundwork for healthy marriages is to make sure that couples do not end up dealing with an unintended pregnancy: "Given that premarital sex has been nearly universal in the U.S. for more than forty years and that early marriage poses divorce risks, it is vital to provide teens and young adults with access to effective contraceptives and family planning services." Yet nine states currently restrict abortion providers or affiliated organizations like Planned Parenthood from receiving public funds, Williams finds, while "thirteen states restrict access to emergency contraception. Challenges to the contraceptive mandate in the Affordable Care Act are currently pending in eighty cases." Williams's research suggests that such restrictions may promote more divorce in the long run.

Economist Evelyn Lehrer (University of Illinois–Chicago) argues that when it comes to marriage, there are benefits to waiting quite a while past age twenty-three, the age at which Kuperberg suggests moving in or marrying may become less risky. Lehrer's analysis of longitudinal data shows that every year a woman delays marriage, right up until her early thirties, decreases her chance of divorce. And contrary to earlier research, she finds that even delaying marriage well past the average age does not raise the risk of divorce. People who marry later than average are more likely to enter "unconventional" matches, which have long been known to pose challenges to partners, but these challenges are outweighed by the couple's greater maturity.

Historian Stephanie Coontz (Evergreen State College) notes that all the studies mentioned in the report and the commentaries reveal how rapidly the dynamics of relationships are changing. She points out that what Sassler found to be a dangerously "short" transition between when less-educated couples meet and when they move in together was once the norm for all couples: in the 1950s, the average length of time a couple dated before marrying was just six months.

Coontz suggests that as cohabitation becomes more common and marriage is less bound by predetermined gender roles, "the United States may well follow the same pattern that researchers found in Australia. In that country, in the 1940s and 1950s, premarital cohabitation significantly increased the risk of divorce. But the added divorce risk declined each year for marriages up to 1988 and then it reversed, so that since then, premarital cohabitation has *reduced* the risk of separation." One rule that has already been reversed in the past forty years, Coontz notes, is the relationship between a woman's educational level and her chance of being married. "Who knows what other old rules may be shattered in the next few years?" ∎

23

Family Structure, Race, and Child Well-Being

Christina J. Cross

As a rapper, cultural icon, and billionaire entrepreneur, Shawn Corey Carter—professionally known as Jay-Z—is no stranger to controversy. But in 2019, just months before a Minneapolis police officer brutally murdered an African American man by the name of George Floyd, Jay-Z found himself at the center of a likely unexpected social media storm. During a panel discussing social justice issues, Jay-Z made comments that appeared to blame single-mother families for police brutality. In reflecting on his own experiences growing up apart from his biological father, Jay-Z said that this family situation causes people to have "an adverse feeling for authority. So, you're like 'I hate my dad, nobody tell me what to do, I'm the man of the house,'" which leads them to tell police "f**k you," resulting in a set of interactions that "causes people to lose lives."[1]

While Jay-Z's assessment of single parenthood as the root cause of deadly interactions between police and civilians is troubling, it is not unique. His words reflect a sentiment held by many Americans, including local Jersey City news reporter Sean Bergin, who, four years earlier, made a similar connection between single parenthood, police mistrust, and lethal violence. After the killing of a police officer in 2015, Bergin stated on air that "the underlying cause" of the "anti-cop mentality that has so contaminated America's inner cities" was "of course, young black men growing up without fathers."[2]

LAW, POLICY, AND THE TWO-PARENT FAMILY

Both Jay-Z's and Bergin's comments reflect a long-held belief by many Americans that living in a married, two-biological-parent family (hitherto referred to as "two-parent family") offers children the best chance of success and that devia-tion from this family structure is to blame for a multitude of social ills, including poverty, police brutality, racial inequality, and reduced child well-being. Indeed, this line of thinking is upheld by some of the highest-ranking leaders of America's political and legal system. Historians and family scholars estimate that there are over one thousand laws, policies, and practices that endorse, protect, and advan-tage the two-parent family over all others as part of a federal strategy to promote child and family well-being and reduce poverty and racial inequality.[3]

An exemplary case of this can be found in Temporary Assistance for Needy Families (TANF)—commonly referred to as "welfare"—the United States pri-mary program for providing cash assistance to low-income families with chil-dren. Created in 1996 through bipartisan congressional legislation, this program provides funds to states to assist families living at or near the poverty line achieve self-sufficiency.[4] It is clear from TANF's program goals that lawmakers view fam-ily structure, specifically the two-parent family, as essential to poverty reduction and improved child well-being. The U.S. Department of Health and Human Services Office of Family Assistance describes the goals of TANF as follows:

1. To provide assistance to needy families so that children may be cared for in their own homes or in the homes of relatives;

2. To end the dependency of needy parents on government benefits by promot-ing job preparation, work, and *marriage*;

3. To prevent and *reduce the incidence of out-of-wedlock pregnancies* and establish annual numerical goals for preventing and reducing the incidence of these pregnancies; and

4. To encourage the formation and maintenance of *two-parent families*.[5]

Three of the four goals of TANF explicitly identify marriage, the two-parent family, and the reduction of nonmarital births as key components of a federal plan to support families. While the goals do not explicitly identify the two-parent family as an important tool for reducing racial inequality, program practices might lead a reasonable person to infer that this logic undergirds its efforts. States are allowed significant discretion with respect to how TANF dollars are spent, and research has shown that a state's racial makeup is the strongest predictor of how it allocates TANF funds.[5] States with the highest percentages of African American families (i.e., southern states) are more likely to direct TANF dollars toward activities that promote two-parent families than to provide cash assis-tance.[7] As a consequence of such practices across the United States, compared with a poor white family, a poor African American family seeking financial assis-tance is more likely to be offered "support" via family-structure-related efforts like marital counseling than cash assistance.[8] The race-specific nature of these practices suggests that program administrators believe that living in a two-parent family will do more to help low-income African American families than simply giving them money.[9]

THE CONSEQUENCES OF FAMILY STRUCTURE FOR CHILDREN

At first blush, this valorization of the two-parent family appears justified. It has been the most common family structure in the United States for decades, and an abundance of scholarly studies has found positive effects of living in this arrangement. Since at least the 1960s, researchers have sought to understand how family structure affects individuals' early life outcomes and future life chances. Commonly investigated family structures include two-parent families, single-parent families, stepparent families, cohabiting families (households that include at least one biological parent who is partnered but unmarried to their significant other), and extended families (where at least one relative who is not a child's biological parent lives in the household).

One of the most consistent findings in this literature is that, in general, children who grow up in two-parent families tend to fare better academically, behaviorally, and emotionally compared with children who live outside this arrangement.[10] On average, they earn higher grades in school and are more likely to enroll in and complete college. They also tend to exhibit fewer behavioral problems and are less likely to report symptoms of psychological disorders than children who do not live in a two-parent family.[11] Differences in outcomes across other family structures like cohabiting, single-parent, and stepparent families are generally small and often negligible.[12]

KEY THEORETICAL PERSPECTIVES

While it may be tempting to attribute the worse outcomes of children who grow up outside two-parent families to the fact that their living arrangements diverge from this model, we must be careful to not confuse *correlation* with *causation* (see Cowan, Chapter 3). That is, just because two things occur at the same time—like living in a single-mother family and having a deadly police encounter—does not mean that one causes the other. Furthermore, another factor, one that has not yet been considered, might be the underlying cause—a concept that statisticians refer to as *confounding*. Confounding occurs when something that potentially affects an outcome goes unaccounted for. Consider the classic example of ice cream sales and shark attacks. In the United States, shark attacks are at their highest at the same time that ice cream sales peak.[13] This does not mean that eating ice cream *causes* shark attacks. It is more likely the case that people eat more ice cream and also swim in the ocean more frequently when it is warmer outside. Thus, warm weather may serve as a confounder.

Might confounding be at play when it comes to the positive relationship between living in a two-parent family and children's well-being? In recent years, researchers have attempted to answer this very question. A number of studies have sought to understand whether it is this family structure per se that leads to better outcomes for children or whether there are other unobserved factors that help explain the correlation between the two. Over time, researchers have developed a framework known as the *family resource perspective* that helps us see inside the black box of family structure and address this issue.

On the whole, key tenets of the family resource perspective suggest that there is no inherent primacy of the two-parent family.[14] This framework focuses on how the resources required for children's growth and development differ by family type. Scholars have found that when parents live together, they are better able to pool and leverage the resources needed to help children thrive.[15] However, living outside this family structure does not, in and of itself, prevent parents from providing the resources needed to promote positive outcomes for children. What is more, there can be significant variation in the resources available to children even when they live in the same family structure, an issue that I will return to later in this chapter.

Scholars have identified two sets of resources that are essential to helping children flourish: economic resources and parenting resources. High levels of economic resources, particularly income and wealth, enable parents to purchase access to an array of social goods such as access to high-quality child care and schools, safe neighborhoods, and desirable amenities and public services. Financial precarity, on the other hand, impedes parents' ability to provide the material goods and services that children need to excel.[16] Children living in two-parent families typically benefit from their parents' ability to pool financial resources, resulting in greater access to income and wealth than children raised in other families, especially single-parent families.

Parenting resources, especially parents' time and mental health, are integral to parents' ability to provide good, consistent parenting, which leads to better outcomes for children. Studies show that on average, children who live apart from a parent receive less monitoring and supervision than children who grow up with both biological parents; this is especially the case among youth raised in single-parent families, who often have fewer adults present in their homes to care for them.[17] Research also suggests that single-, step-, and cohabiting families tend to have weaker and more ambiguous parental authority structures compared with two-parent families, which can lead to inconsistent parenting.[18] Moreover, divorce and single parenthood may compromise the mental health of parents by inducing short-term stress and engendering the conditions for chronic stress, which may reduce parenting quality.[19] What is more, good parenting is determined, in part, by parents' economic resources. As previously mentioned, economic precarity reduces the level of material resources and services that parents can provide to children; it can also be an acute stressor for parents, both of which may undermine parenting quality.

Because children in two-parent families tend to enjoy greater access to economic and parenting resources than their peers in other types of families, they generally experience better outcomes. In fact, researchers have found that differences in household income between two-parent and single-parent families explain up to nearly 70 percent of the gap in outcomes between groups.[20] When it comes to parenting resources, studies show that differences in parental involvement between two-parent and single-parent families account for 10 to 15 percent of the gap in child well-being.[21]

In addition to these explanations, researchers have noted that *selection* may also account for the association between family structure and children's well-being (see Rutter, Chapter 22, on selection and divorce). *Selection* refers to the idea that characteristics of parents that are present prior to their own family formation may be related to both their family structure and to their children's outcomes. Put differently, children may perform better in two-parent families because adults who form and maintain such households may be more well-adjusted and economically advantaged in the first place.[22] Is it living in a two-parent family that causes better outcomes for children, or are these children and families simply more advantaged, which leads to better outcomes? It would be unethical to randomly assign children to various family structures to answer this question. Therefore, studies rely on observational data rather than randomized experiments, which makes it impossible to fully address this question. Nonetheless, results indicating that economic and parenting resources explain much of the association between family structure and child outcomes lend support to the notion that selection plays a role in understanding family structure effects.

Thus, the literature on family structure and child well-being suggests that growing up in a two-parent family can offer advantages to children, but this is contingent on the degree to which living in this family structure leads to greater access to resources. That is, family structure is not the fundamental cause of children's outcomes.[23] *Absent important economic and parenting resources— like money and time—family structure has little to no direct effect on children.* This point is underscored by a recent study indicating that children raised in low-income, two-parent families tend to have similar educational outcomes as those raised in single-parent families that are also struggling financially.[24] They are no more likely to earn good grades in school, and their odds of being suspended or repeating a grade were virtually the same.[25] Moreover, children raised in low-income, two-parent families had worse academic outcomes than children raised in high-income, two-parent households.[26]

RACIAL DIFFERENCES IN THE EFFECTS OF FAMILY STRUCTURE

Results from this study are part of a growing body of research that has shown that the effects of family structure are not the same for all children (see Williams et al., Chapter 5). Much of this research has focused on single-parent families, and it has found that living in this family structure is often less negatively impactful for African American children's educational and behavioral outcomes compared with their white peers who grow up in this family structure. While some work has shown that the negative effects of living in a single-parent family are smaller for this group, others show virtually no effect of single parenthood on African American children's academic success or engagement in risky behaviors.[27]

What explains the differential effects of single parenthood on child outcomes? Recall the importance of economic resources in shaping the relationship between family structure and child well-being. Owing to America's legacy of structural racism, African American children are, on average, raised in environments that are more economically deprived than the environments of white children—even when they live in the same family structure as white children.[28] They are more likely to live in poverty and have less household wealth, and their parents are less likely to be bachelor's degree holders. These disparities in access to economic resources between African American and white children are an important piece of the puzzle. Differences in access to economic resources, such as mother's education, accounted for nearly 50 percent of the gap in children's educational outcomes between groups.[29] Scholars suspect that because African American children are already facing many social and economic disadvantages, the negative effect of parental absence from the home may be less independently impactful, above and beyond existing disadvantages.

Studies suggest that another important factor may also be at work: embeddedness in extended family networks. Research on the extended family networks of African Americans shows that this group is engaged in ongoing and reciprocal exchanges of support with extended relatives, and that African Americans are more likely to be involved in practical support like child care assistance and help with household chores and transportation than white families.[30] African

Americans also tend to live in closer proximity to extended relatives than white Americans do, making these forms of support more easily accessible.[31] Scholars believe that greater involvement in extended family networks for African American children may reduce some of the negative psychosocial effects associated with parental conflict or separation.[32] In this way, embeddedness in extended family networks may protect African American youth from some of the adverse effects of parental absence from the home. Indeed, research suggests that receipt of support from extended family members and more frequent contact with these relatives is positively associated with children's educational outcomes. African American children's deeper embeddedness in extended family life helps reduce the negative impact of single motherhood, which results in fewer consequences for this group relative to their white peers who live in this same family structure.[33]

CONCLUSION

Many Americans view the two-parent family as the ideal family structure within which to raise children. Although research has shown that youth who grow up in this arrangement tend to fare better than their peers who are raised in other types of families, these findings do not establish causation. Economic and parenting resources like household income and parents' mental health play a critical role in shaping the relationship between family structure and children's well-being. In the absence of these resources, children face significant challenges that often undermine their growth and development. Thus, in and of itself, the two-parent family is insufficient to ensure children's long-term success.

Studies also indicate that the link between family structure and child outcomes differs by racial group membership. In particular, the impact of single parenthood tends to be less negatively consequential for African American youths' educational and behavioral outcomes than for their white counterparts. Scholarship has shown that group disparities in access to economic resources help explain much of the differential effect of living with a single parent. African American children's deeper embeddedness in their extended family networks may also serve as a buffer against some of the negative consequences typically associated with living away from a parent.

Despite a large body of research showing a small—and sometimes nonexistent—direct effect of family structure on individuals' outcomes, numerous laws and public policies encourage the formation and maintenance of the two-parent family as a key strategy for promoting family and child well-being and reducing poverty and racial inequality. This discrepancy in legislation raises a critical question for researchers, policy makers, and other key stakeholders:

How can our society craft policies and programs that better align with scientific evidence and the needs of our most vulnerable members? If disparities in access to resources largely explain the relationship between family structure and individuals' outcomes, as well as effects of racial differences in family structure, then focusing on reducing social and economic hardships for disadvantaged groups will likely be more effective than promoting any particular family form.[34]

NOTES

1. "Jay-Z Blames Single Parent Households for Police Brutality," September 2, 2019, You-Tube, retrieved August 2, 2022, youtu.be/ByTkbZTYZaU.

2. Fox News, "Reporter Who Commented on 'Black Men Growing Up without Fathers' Suspended," January 8, 2015, www.foxnews.com/us/reporter-who-commented-on-black-men-growing-up-without-fathers-suspended.

3. Stephanie Coontz, *Marriage: A History* (New York: Penguin Books, 2006); Shawn Fremstad, Sarah Jane Glynn, and Angelo Williams, *The Case against Marriage Fundamentalism: Embracing Family Justice for All* (Washington, DC: Family Story, 2019), familystoryproject.org/case-against-marriage-fundamentalism; Bethany L. Letiecq, "Surfacing Family Privilege and Supremacy in Family Science: Toward Justice for All," *Journal of Family Theory and Review* 11 (2019): 398–411.

4. U.S. Department of Health and Human Services Office of Family Assistance, "About TANF," July 19, 2019, www.acf.hhs.gov/ofa/programs/tanf/about.

5. U.S. Department of Health and Human Services Office of Family Assistance, "About TANF."

6. Zachary Parolin, "Temporary Assistance for Needy Families and the Black-White Child Poverty Gap in the United States," *Socio-Economic Review* 19, no. 3 (2021): 1005–1035.

7. Parolin, "Temporary Assistance for Needy Families."

8. Zachary Parolin, "Welfare Money Is Paying for a Lot of Things Besides Welfare," *The Atlantic*, June 13, 2019, www.theatlantic.com/ideas/archive/2019/06/through-welfare-states-are-widening-racial-divide/591559/.

9. Parolin, "Welfare Money."

10. Susan L. Brown, "Marriage and Child Well-Being: Research and Policy Perspectives," *Journal of Marriage and Family* 72 (2010): 1059–1077; Donna K. Ginther and Robert A. Pollak, "Family Structure and Children's Educational Outcomes: Blended Families, Stylized Facts, and Descriptive Regressions," *Demography* 41, no. 4 (2004): 671–696; Sara McLanahan and Gary Sandefur, *Growing Up with a Single-Parent: What Hurts, What Helps* (Cambridge, MA: Harvard University Press, 1994); Sara McLanahan and Christine Percheski, "Family Structure and the Reproduction of Inequalities," *Annual Review of Sociology* 34 (2008): 257–276.

11. Brown, "Marriage and Child Well-Being"; McLanahan and Percheski, "Family Structure."

12. W. D. Manning and K. A. Lamb, "Adolescent Well-Being in Cohabiting, Married, and Single Parent Families," *Journal of Marriage and Family* 65, no. 4 (2003): 876–893.

13. Z. Bobbitt, "Correlation Does Not Imply Causation: 5 Real-World Examples," Statology, August 18, 2021, www.statology.org/correlation-does-not-imply-causation-examples/.

14. C. J. Cross, F. Fomby, and B. Letiecq, "Interlinking Structural Racism and Heteropatriarchy: Rethinking Family Structure's Effects on Child Outcomes in a Racialized, Unequal Society," *Journal of Family Theory and Review* 14, no. 3 (2022): 482–501.

15. McLanahan, and Percheski, "Family Structure."

16. P. R. Amato, "The Impact of Family Formation Change on the Cognitive, Social, and Emotional Well-Being of the Next Generation," *The Future of Children* 15, no. 2 (2005): 75–96; Jeong-Kyun Choi, Megan S. Kelley, and Dan Wang, "Neighborhood Characteristics, Maternal Parenting, and Health and Development of Children from Socioeconomically Disadvantaged Families," *American Journal of Community Psychology* 62 (2018): 476–491; McLanahan and Percheski, "Family Structure."

17. A. Kalil, R. Ryan, and E. Chor, "Time Investments in Children across Family Structures," *The ANNALS of the American Academy of Political and Social Science* 654, no. 1 (2014): 150–168; McLanahan, and Percheski, "Family Structure."

18. Andrew Cherlin and Frank Furstenberg, "Stepfamilies in the United States—a Reconsideration," *Annual Review of Sociology* 20 (1994): 359–381; Kalil, Ryan, and Chor, "Time Investments in Children"; McLanahan and Percheski, "Family Structure."

19. McLanahan and Percheski, "Family Structure."

20. Jennie E. Brand, Ravaris Moore, Xi Song, and Yu Xie, "Why Does Parental Divorce Lower Children's Educational Attainment? A Causal Mediation Analysis," *Sociological Science* 6 (2019): 264–292.

21. Marcia J. Carlson, "Family Structure, Father Involvement, and Adolescent Behavioral Outcomes," *Journal of Marriage and Family* 68, no. 1 (2006): 137–154.

22. Brown, "Marriage and Child Well-Being"; S. Hofferth, "Residential Father Family Type and Child Well-Being: Investment versus Selection," *Demography* 43, no. 1 (2006): 53–77; Cross, Fomby, and Letiecq, "Interlinking Structural Racism and Heteropatriarchy."

23. Melissa S. Kearney and Phillip B. Levine, "The Economics of Nonmarital Childbearing and the Marriage Premium for Children," *Annual Review of Economics* 9 (2017): 327–352.

24. Christina J. Cross, "Beyond the Binary: Intraracial Diversity in Family Organization and Black Adolescents' Educational Performance," *Social Problems* 70, no. 2 (2023): 511–532.

25. Cross, "Beyond the Binary."

26. Cross, "Beyond the Binary."

27. P. R. Amato and B. Keith, "Parental Divorce and Adult Well-Being: A Meta-Analysis," *Journal of Marriage and the Family* 53 (1991): 43–58; Christina J. Cross, "Racial/Ethnic Differences in the Association between Family Structure and Children's Education," *Journal of Marriage and Family* 81, no. 2 (2020): 691–712; R. Dunifon and L. Kowaleski-Jones, "The Influence of Grandparents in Single-Mother Families," *Journal of Marriage*

and Family 69 (2007): 465–481; P. Fomby, S. Mollborn, and C. Sennott, "Race/Ethnic Differences in Effects of Family Instability on Adolescents' Risk Behavior," *Journal of Marriage and Family* 72 (2010): 234–253.

28. National Center for Education Statistics, "Characteristics of Children's Families," *Condition of Education* (Washington, DC: U.S. Department of Education, Institute of Education Sciences, 2022), nces.ed.gov/programs/coe/indicator/cce.

29. Cross, "Racial/Ethnic Differences."

30. N. Sarkisian and N. Gerstel, "Kin Support among Blacks and Whites: Race and Family Organization," *American Sociological Review* 69 (2004): 812–837; C. B. Stack, *All Our Kin: Strategies for Survival in a Black Community* (New York: Harper & Row, 1974); C. B. Stack and L. M. Burton, "Kinscripts," *Journal of Comparative Family Studies* 24 (1993): 157–170; R. J. Taylor, A. D. Skipper, C. J. Cross, H. O. Taylor, and L. M. Chatters, "Racial/Ethnic Variation in Family Support: African Americans, Black Caribbeans, and Non-Latino Whites," *Journal of Marriage and Family* 84, no. 4 (2022): 1002–1023.

31. N. Farber, J. Miller-Cribbs, and M. Reitmeier, "Kin Networks in the South: A Comparison of Low-Income, Rural African-American and White Women," *Rural Social Work and Community Practice* 10 (2005): 52–63.

32. V. C. McLoyd, A. M. Cauce, D. Takeuchi, and L. Wilson, "Marital Processes and Parental Socialization in Families of Color: A Decade Review of Research," *Journal of Marriage and the Family* 62 (2000): 1070–1093; L. D. Pittman, "Grandmothers' Involvement among Young Adolescents Growing Up in Poverty," *Journal of Research on Adolescence* 17 (2007): 89–115.

33. Cross, "Racial/Ethnic Differences."

34. Kristi Williams, "Promoting Marriage among Single Mothers: An Ineffective Weapon in the War on Poverty?," in *Families as They Really Are*, 2nd ed., ed. B. J. Risman and V. Rutter (New York: Norton, 2016): 324–326.

24

The New (Post-COVID) Normal?

Workplace Flexibility Matters

Marni Fritz, Sejin Um, and Barbara Risman

How was it during the pandemic?

Yes, there are some days I would cry because it would just be so overwhelming some days, you know, I have people crying to me about their situation. And then I have my eight-year-old who is not listening, getting up and walking around. I'm trying to get him to pay attention, or while I'm working, he's getting up trying to talk to me. And it was just some days I really couldn't take it.

—Denise (thirty-four, intake specialist and mother of two)

Cutting out the commutes has led to a lot more just being around each other a lot more. Yeah. And like I said, like we almost, almost never only on weekends, did we get a family meal together and now we're sitting down to three family meals a day, most days if I don't have a meeting over the top of breakfast.

—Tommy (thirty-nine, state employee, father of one)

THE PANDEMIC CHANGED US

The COVID-19 pandemic changed the way many people work. In the United States, measures to curb the spread of the virus, such as lockdowns and stay-at-home orders, led many people to work from home. The proportion of the U.S. workforce working from home at least occasionally rose from about

25 percent prior to the pandemic (U.S. Bureau of Labor Statistics 2019) to about 42 percent in May 2020 (Bloom 2020). Most of those who worked from home were white-collar workers; those who could not, newly labeled as "essential workers," braved infection at their workplaces. However, for many parents, whether working at home or outside of it, life changed dramatically as schools and daycare centers closed. They were now responsible for earning a living for their families and taking care of their children or supervising their online learning at the same time. Work-life balance, already fragile in the United States, went into complete disarray as work and child care responsibilities collided.

We set out to understand how parents were experiencing a crisis that seemed to never end. While much research on the COVID-19 pandemic began soon after it started, our research began after July 4, 2021, the date President Joe Biden had hoped we would be celebrating our independence from the virus. That was before the new and more virulent Delta and Omicron variations emerged. We asked our respondents to talk about their experiences before the pandemic began and after more than a year had passed. We also asked about their expectations and hopes for the future.

Most parents reported disruption in their caregiving routines due to daycare centers and preschools shutting down for at least some time during the pandemic. What we found, however, was that a care infrastructure, while important, was not the entire story in determining parents' experiences of child care during the pandemic. It was *workplace flexibility* that shaped how families experienced and coped with the disruption of formal care infrastructure. For some, workplace flexibility enabled them to create their own work schedule. For others, this meant blocking off "no call, no meeting" times in their schedule that their workplace honored. While the situations were variable, the outcomes were nearly identical. Having flexibility over when, where, and how they could work—all facilitated by the option to work from home—was central to minimizing the challenges that come from competing demands of work and caregiving.

Moreover, we found that while mothers were often the default primary parent picking up the new family care work required by the pandemic, this was more common in dual-earning couples without access to flexible work schedules or flexible remote work options. We found that flexible work schedules provided couples with the ability to be more gender-equitable and negotiate care when formal infrastructures like daycare and aftercare shut down. We also found that flexible on-site work environments were mentioned by essential workers, especially single mothers, who appreciated workplaces where they could sometimes bring their children or at least set their schedules to accommodate their children's needs. Those without flexible schedules reported being burned out and overwhelmed. We conclude with some lessons from our respondents for how our society could move forward to ensure parents have the ability to manage family caregiving and paid work. Only when that happens will we be able to assure the well-being of families in the United States.

STUDYING THE PANDEMIC

The data for this study came from in-depth interviews that were conducted between July 2021 and January 2022. All were conducted via Zoom. We recruited our sample from two waves of a nationally represented online survey conducted by the National Opinion Research Center. We added questions to their survey about whether those people who had been caregivers would be willing to have a Zoom or phone interview about their experiences during the COVID pandemic. About 20 percent agreed. We also added a few more respondents based on those original respondents' referrals.

Interviews ranged from forty minutes to two hours and thirty minutes, averaging about ninety minutes each. They were audio-recorded, transcribed, and coded by the researchers. Table 24.1 provides an overview of the demographics of our respondents. We analyzed fifty-five in-depth, open-ended interviews with a wide range of adult women and men with child care responsibilities across the United States. The selection of these fifty-five respondents from our pool of 118 interviews was guided by our attempt to represent the diversity of family contexts. We analyzed roughly equal numbers of women and men from varied race and

Table 24.1 | Sample profile

	Age	23–63 (mean = 36.6)	N
Women (N = 27)	Marital Status	Unpartnered	7
		Married	14
		Cohabiting	5
		Divorced/Separated	1
Men (N = 28)	Age	29–57 (mean = 39.1)	N
	Marital Status	Unpartnered	0
		Married	25
		Cohabiting	1
		Divorced/Separated	2
Total			55

class backgrounds. Our sample consists of people who identify as White, Black, Asian, Hispanic,[1] or some other race, from social class backgrounds ranging from working class to upper-middle class, covering various occupations. Pseudonyms were used in this study to protect confidentiality.

What We Know about Caregiving during the COVID-19 Pandemic

The initial studies of COVID-19 and families showed how hard it was on women at work and at home. Some called it the "women's employment crisis" (Hinchliffe 2022) because it was largely women who picked up the extra caregiving and homemaking, at the expense of paid work. In the first few months of the pandemic (February to April 2020), researchers observed that mothers with young children experienced a reduction in paid work hours "four to five times more than fathers," widening the gender gap in work hours (Collins et al. 2021). Not only were women working for less pay, but in heterosexual couples, their child care responsibilities increased when compared with their husbands' (Carreo et al. 2021). As a result, married mothers became the default caregivers, and more gender-equitable divisions of household labor fell by the wayside. The overwhelming burden of caregiving carried by mothers took a toll on their careers as well as their relationships and overall well-being (Calarco et al. 2021).

These discoveries were from the first year of the pandemic. We know very little about how families negotiated behavior once the pandemic was no longer a short-term crisis but transitioned into an ongoing *new normal*, after a year and half of ongoing adjustments. By then, most schools were going back into session and daycare centers had reopened. We talked to these caregivers about what they had learned from their experiences during the pandemic and what they hoped their post-pandemic trajectories would look like.

The Haves and the Have Nots: The Impact of Flexibility on Our Pandemic Lives

While our interviewees shared the loss of access to an infrastructure of care during the pandemic, how they experienced and coped with this disruption varied substantially. Their post-pandemic trajectories largely depended on the degree of *workplace flexibility* available to the individual and their partner. In the absence of public schooling or daycare, the option to work from home was essential for parents to balance paid work with care work, regardless of whether they had access to informal support such as help from extended family members.

We found three household contexts among respondents: gender-traditional households, dual-earner households, and single-parent households. In each of these contexts, we saw how flexibility shaped their coping strategies during the absence of infrastructure for child care. Dual-earner households have varied patterns of flexibility and gender ideology. The dual-earner households diverge into more egalitarian—and happier—households or those with rigid ways of doing things, which often led to resentment and burnout. We also learned about the needs of those who had no access to flexibility.

Gender-Traditional Households

Women and men in gender-traditional homes did not experience significant changes in the structure of their day-to-day lives during the pandemic. Having one parent—the mother—already dedicated to unpaid care labor provided the couple with continuity in their arrangement of work and caregiving in the household. The stay-at-home mother absorbed the schooling and other basic needs of the children, and the breadwinning father kept his work routines. Such stability was particularly clear in cases where the male breadwinner continued to work outside the home rather than working remotely.

For Beth (thirty-nine, White), a stay-at-home mother of six children, the pandemic made taking care of her children even easier because she had less planning and logistics for her children's activities outside the home: "My job description didn't change. . . . Caring for the kids became a little less complicated because we were home." Similarly, for Jesse (forty-seven, White), the way he and his partner arranged tasks for maintaining their household did not change. His partner had been homeschooling the younger children and taking care of all kinds of housework before the pandemic: "It was not a dramatic change for our younger kids because we were homeschooling them anyway. . . . Having worked from home, there are aspects of the relationship of being able to see my kids through the day to have brief interactions with my wife while I'm working that I'm going to miss."

Though the gendered division of labor between the partners remained largely intact, as in the cases of Beth and Jesse, a large number of male respondents pointed out that the pandemic opened their eyes to how much work it took for their partners to run the household, which previously went unseen when he was at work. Gabriel (forty-three, Latinx), a father of four children who worked from home briefly during the pandemic but was now back on-site, recounted,

> We learned a lot about my wife and how dependent this family is on her, really, because she does run a lot of errands, takes my kids to all their appointments.

While many men discussed their newfound appreciation for their partner's care labor, very few men actually made tangible changes in their work situations in line with their new lessons. One man who did change was Jamie (thirty-three, White). He remarked that he observed, for the first time, just how much his stay-at-home wife was struggling to raise their four-year-old son alone while taking care of all domestic tasks. He embraced a pay cut and took a new job that required fewer work hours and provided better family-friendly policies so that he could share household labor with his partner. He noted,

> I love my wife and I want the best for her. I don't want her to feel like a slave in her own home. But that's what I made her feel like [before the pandemic]. . . . That's when I started trying to make the changes that we needed. The job change itself wasn't like a marriage-saving job change or anything like that; it was so that I could be home more.

Dual-Earner Households

Unlike single-earner families, families where both parents worked for pay experienced substantial changes in their work and family life. Prior to the pandemic, most of these two-job families had some paid child care beyond parents, such as daycare, babysitters, learning co-ops, early preschool programs, and public school for children ages five and older. Child care allowed both parents to work for income outside of the house during the day and attend to their children's needs at night and on the weekends. Some parents had more flexibility to attend to sick children or take children to various events during working hours before the pandemic. When the pandemic hit, however, these support structures disappeared, increasing the stresses of parenting for many. Others enjoyed having more family time overall despite these challenges. The flexibility they had in their paid work played a major role in how couples managed the new challenge of integrating child care into their work lives. In this section we present the broad patterns we observed within these dual-earner couples.

One-Sided Flexibility

When only one parent had work flexibility, that parent absorbed care work. In many families, it was the mother who had a more flexible work schedule and thus absorbed more of the extra care work the pandemic introduced than the father.

Jeff (thirty-four, White) and his partner Rachel's experience is a powerful example that illustrates how work flexibility can radically change family life. Prior to the pandemic, Jeff had zero work flexibility. His work schedule was at the whim of his employer; he often worked over twelve-hour days with no oppor-tunity to take time off. Rachel, on the other hand, worked as a nanny, a job that allowed her to bring their son to work with her on a regular basis. This offset the need for paid child care while allowing the family to maintain two incomes.

Before the pandemic, Jeff believed both he and Rachel maintained gendered outlooks on care work responsibilities. Referring to his partner, Jeff said, "She's the backbone that keeps, I mean, with me working so much, someone's got to hold down the home front and kind of make sure everything else is managed and she's taken that on. No questions asked and just handles everything. It's unbeliev-able." The lack of flexibility on Jeff's part required his wife to both work and "hold down the home front." The flexibility of her nannying job before the pandemic allowed her to absorb these responsibilities. Once the pandemic hit, however, Jeff was furloughed, so he became a full-time caregiver for their son. Even though his job loss put a strain on their finances, Jeff reported higher overall life satisfaction during this time. Before the pandemic, Jeff felt like his life was consumed with work, and he would have liked to have spent more time at home: "I did feel like I didn't spend enough time at home. I kind of took it for granted, especially having a newborn, right." Jeff reported that his priorities re-centered on family when he took a step back from his hectic work life: "I think now I'm more emphasized on family morals where I think before the pandemic, I was kind of just work, work, work all the time. Yeah. So I think with the pandemic and being home and being able to create those bonds, I think that kind of the family aspect of it kind of definitely changed and improved, I believe." While respondents recounted their many struggles during this time, we also heard about positive twists of fate, like Jeff's discovery.

This is not how their story ended. About halfway through the pandemic, Rachel also lost her job just as Jeff began training for a new job that would require the family to move across the country. Since Rachel remained unemployed and without an income, Jeff went off to train for his new job in a different city, while Rachel and their son moved in with her family to save money until they could afford for the family to reunite. The multiple changes in this family's life illus-trate how paid work dramatically shapes families at home.

Denise (thirty-four, Black), a mother of two children, ages eight and fourteen, experienced even more significant problems. Since the pandemic hit, Denise had been working from home while also attending school full time, and she was solely responsible for monitoring the children's remote school. Her eight-year-old required a lot of attention during his online schooling. She reported having a lit-tle flexibility to shift her schedule as an intake specialist for a nonprofit. Denise's partner, Ron, a maintenance technician, did not have any flexibility or control over his schedule and was on call after normal working hours for emergency repairs. Although Denise was juggling being a full-time mom and a full-time student, because she was working from home and had flexibility in her schedule, she absorbed the extra burden of child care and at-home education. This arrangement caused her great stress. She wished that she had more time off. She felt a lack of support both from her employer and the government.

Denise made a wide variety of excuses as to why her husband didn't help more, ranging from lack of skills to forgetfulness to his lack of organization. At first when she asked her husband to step up and share more of the household chores and the child care, he declined. Only when she reported that "she couldn't take it anymore" did her husband step in, showing that he was fully capable of doing so. But he refused to commit to ongoing support. And yet, Denise saw this as an equitable relationship even though she admitted that because she is the mother, the responsibility of such tasks falls on her: "And, you know, I'm mom. So I'm, you know, the ultimate, you know, the main caregiver of the family." This arrangement, although buttressed by traditional gender beliefs, still had an adverse effect on Denise:

> Yes, there are some days I would cry because it would just be so overwhelming some days, you know, I have people crying to me about their situation. And then I have my eight-year-old who is not listening, getting up and walking around. I'm trying to get him to pay attention, or while I'm working, he's getting up trying to talk to me. . . . Some days I really couldn't take it.

Denise and Ron illustrate what we found in other couples: when only one partner has flexibility in dual-earner couples, this often leads that partner to accept full responsibility for child care while working. As a result, they can experience serious adverse consequences.

Like Denise, other parents in this situation reported exhaustion, burnout, and negativity. For one father, this inequitable distribution of labor created resentment toward his partner. Brandon (thirty-four, Asian) became the primary caregiver for his son when his partner, Tracy, was deployed as a National Guard's emergency COVID response team member. Before the pandemic, daycare was the couple's primary source of care. Once the pandemic hit, their daycare shut down and their son was home full-time. This meant that Tracy was gone Monday through Friday for five months while Brandon had to take time off work to accommodate child care. Tracy would come back on weekends to help, but the bulk of the responsibility fell to Brandon. This created resentment toward Tracy, especially because this meant Brandon had to stop working as a volunteer paramedic, something that brought him a lot of joy.

> So there became a point where it was no longer fun and easy to balance Simon [their son] and work and all that. And honestly, you do start to become a little

resentful of your partner when they're out doing the thing that you would like to be doing. And you just get that you are forced to stay home because her job is a non-negotiable and me going and doing paramedic stuff is absolutely a part-time volunteer thing.

Even when stay-at-home orders began to ease up, daycare was not open reliably, as they were low on staff and closed when illness struck. When daycare was not available, Brandon still had to do the child care. After Tracy returned home from her deployment, the couple's division of household chores and child care went back to what it had been before, and they both felt they shared the work equitably. This situation represented a twist on typical gender stories, but with similar feelings: when the daycare couldn't accommodate their son, Brandon continued to miss work because of his more flexible schedule. This increased Brandon's feelings of resentment and put a strain on their marriage.

I was a little resentful towards the whole fact of like, hey, you've been gone for five months now. Like it's my turn to do something cool. . . . She knew that I needed a break because I was just completely burnt out with child care, home care, not sleeping, and school.

Another dilemma, even for couples who share the family work more equitably, is when they continue to maintain essentialist gender beliefs that mothers are *naturally* better at care work. These beliefs were centered when women in inequitable partnerships expressed extreme burnout and dissatisfaction with life itself. Emily (twenty-nine, White), a mother of two in Pennsylvania, worked two highly demanding jobs with long commutes. She lost a long-term job she loved two months after the pandemic hit and took on two jobs to make up for the loss of income. She worked in the medical industry and often was required to work sixteen hours a day for one job and twelve-hour shifts for her other job with no days off. She was then fired from one job because of transportation; she later quit her second job because, she explained, "they weren't flexible with my schedule" for her child care needs. She was burned out. Her fiancé and partner, Dan, was a part-time custodian when the pandemic began. Dan quit his job to do the child care, since Emily was the main breadwinner, and they could not afford child care after schools shut down. It was more financially viable for them as a couple for Dan to quit his job and become the primary caregiver. At first glance this seems like a gender-progressive couple. Emily claimed their division of labor was equitable. Even so, she reported that Dan, the stay-at-home dad, would often leave home as soon as she returned from work. His escape from the kids created a "second shift" for Emily after she got off work. She would get home from work and be expected to perform the same amount of housework as her fiancé, who was home all day.

Even more stressful, however, was the invisible mental labor Emily did when planning and tracking tasks, doctors' appointments, and teacher meetings (Daminger 2019). She didn't give herself credit for this invisible work but acknowledged her partner's maintenance and handiwork. She seemed to devalue her own labor and contribution to the home despite being the main breadwinner. She reported feeling like "it was all put on me." Her perception of her contributions to the family is based on her own gendered expectations of being a "good mother." For Emily, the pandemic experience took a major toll on her relationship with her partner. Emily reported heightened stress in the home, more fights, and a more negative evaluation of the relationship. She consistently blamed herself for this:

> It kind of got worse. We were drifting apart. We didn't really care to spend a whole lot of time together. So I pretty much became controlling. I didn't like it on myself. But I was doing that. So it kind of made him drift. Like separate from me as well. We weren't as close and united like we were.

Flexibility All Around

When both partners had access to flexible remote work options, we found quite a different set of experiences. Partners who both had flexible working conditions reported feeling closer to each other and grateful for the newfound time to spend with their family. Tommy (thirty-nine, White), a father of one child, reported feeling very anxious at the beginning of the pandemic. However, once he settled into his new at-home routine, he said he loved it and never wanted to go back to the way his work was arranged prior to the pandemic. Specifically, Tommy loved the extra time with his family and enjoyed helping his son with kindergarten: "I made the decision to be the one who can basically sit with him and make sure he's doing school and his computer is working. So, I chose to take on a larger role. I was willing to basically dedicate my time to be the one to do it."

His flexible work schedule allowed him to do so. For him, flexibility means that he has control over when people are allowed to contact him and when he is doing solo work. His partner, Trish, is also telecommuting and changed positions throughout the pandemic, increasing her level of flexibility. Taking out the commute time gave both partners about two hours a day back into their lives. As a result, they spent more time together. They started eating family meals regularly, which is not something they did prior to the pandemic. As Tommy explained,

> Cutting out the commutes has led to a lot more just being around each other. . . .
> Only on weekends did we get a family meal together and now we're sitting down to
> three family meals a day.

Due to their high anxiety around COVID and a lack of vaccine mandates where they lived, they opted to have their son participate in completely remote schooling even when in-person was an option again. Both parents had to take on extra care work, but good benefits and flexible working conditions made this possible. This experience also inspired Tommy to reprioritize family over work going forward:

> I want to try and make more time for my family. The telework and being home and
> being together made me realize that I could probably have found a way to do better,
> but I [didn't] know exactly how [to prioritize] for that. I would very much like to be
> able to have more time together moving forward, post-pandemic, and not just go
> back into such a split-up schedule.

In interview after interview, workplace flexibility encouraged a more gender-equitable distribution of care. More flexibility also increased well-being and reduced burnout.

Gender Ideology and Family Strategies in Dual-Income Families

Flexible work taught some couples to be more equitable. This took place without active or explicit verbal discussion or negotiation between the couple but rather unfolded organically as the pandemic unfolded. In many cases, this involved the man noticing the woman's unseen labor while he worked from home. This led to happier couples and healthier families.

One example is Joanna (thirty-five, White), a mother of a four-year-old and a six-month-old. Before the pandemic, Joanna and her husband worked outside the home, with Joanna taking primary responsibility for caregiving. However, during the pandemic, as her husband's work went remote, he began to see things he was not able to before as he spent time at home. As Joanna described,

> He didn't realize like how much I was doing until he started like helping out and
> doing those things and he's like, *oh my gosh*. You know because before with his

previous job he was really working long hours and really just not available to pitch in as much, but with this new job, he has more flexibility and more time. . . . So I don't know if it's because of the new job or the pandemic, but he has admitted to me, *I didn't realize how much you were doing.* So now he pitches in and I feel like he gets more stressed, or like the things that used to stress me out are also stressing him out, so it helps me feel less stressed.

Joanna believes that she and her husband are a "better team" than before the pandemic and reported higher marital satisfaction. She explained that it is due to the increase in communication and a mutual effort to coordinate various types of tasks around the home:

> [There had to be] more collaboration. And just figuring out like the day-to-day things, and just who's doing this. I have a work call at ten, I have this call at eight, like how we gonna shuffle that. . . . I think we are a better team.

Similarly, for Miranda (forty-two, White) and her husband, Oscar, parents of twelve-year-old twin boys, work flexibility allowed them to become more egalitarian and more engaged as parents. They are both architects, but Oscar earns most of the household income working on large projects. Before the pandemic, after returning from her part-time job in the afternoon, Miranda trained in martial arts along with her sons, prepared for dinner, and took care of other tasks around the home. When the pandemic hit, however, Oscar's large-scale project was canceled, and he lost his job. This compelled him to stay home and find another job. Pre-pandemic, when asked how she felt about working part-time and doing more housework than her husband, Miranda answered: "Fine. It just worked out that way. . . . If I were working full-time and still doing all that I would probably have resentment [laughs]. But it wasn't like that, so it was just responsibilities that I assumed and wanted to because they're part of working part-time and being there with the boys. Those are things that I would do because I was here, you know."

After the pandemic, Miranda increased her work hours to full-time because she no longer needed to drive her children to school at a set time. This, together with Oscar being home, led to a change in how the couple shared housework.

> I think we would share more equally now, because we're both at home and we both work from home and we're both full-time because we, *we can be.* So I think it's an equalized mark, because I would do everything, just because that's how we set it up, because his income is so much higher than mine, but even with the income disparity, *we're both home, we just can share those responsibilities more.*

For a subset of dual-earner couples, the dad's physical presence at home enabled or nudged him to pick up more household labor, which he had previously neglected by virtue of working outside the home. This often happened in the absence of any explicit conversation between the couple.

When Work Flexibility Doesn't Exist

When the pandemic first hit, 42 percent of the population pivoted to remote work (Bloom 2020). But not everyone could shift to at-home remote work: Nurses, grocery store workers, and eventually teachers had to go to work in-person. These "essential workers," representing 45 percent of the labor force, were required to work on-site throughout the pandemic. They had the added stress of having to be physically at work while children were sent home due to school and daycare closures. This created serious dilemmas for parents. Those with family nearby leaned on their support, but those without family to help suffered financially and mentally. Essential workers desperately needed access to flexible work schedules too.

Victoria (twenty-three, Latinx) was one such essential worker. As a pharmacy technician, she was required to work fully in-person during the pandemic. She was hoping for limited windows where customers could pick up their prescriptions, but her employer made few accommodations for the pandemic. Instead, Victoria was pressured to work even more hours than normal due to low staffing. This meant finding child care for her three-year-old and five-year-old children. One of her bosses was understanding, but the other was not. Eventually, Victoria had to reduce her working time by ten hours per week to care for her children once school shut down. When we interviewed her, with her children back at school in-person, she still needed the flexibility to pick them up at 3:00 p.m. "I really don't have a chance to get all the hours that I want, because I have to pick them up from school or find somebody that can help me pick them up from school."

Victoria contracted coronavirus twice and felt vulnerable at her job. Her illness forced her to take time off to quarantine. As the work stress increased, so did the home stress. Even though there was a period where Antonio, her cohabiting partner and father of her younger child, was out of work during the pandemic, Victoria still handled the bulk of the household tasks. This inequitable division of labor put a strain on their relationship: "I was kind of mad because I had all the responsibility, and now he's just at home. . . . He's just at home watching kids, and I was working, so I was kind of mad and upset." Overall, Victoria reported wanting more child care support throughout the pandemic. A lack of flexibility from both her job and her partner burdened this essential worker during a time of heightened stress and anxiety.

For Sarah (thirty-six, White), a schoolteacher and single mother of two children under five, work shifted from in-person to remote at multiple points during the pandemic. She was a classroom teacher who transitioned to a more administrative position within her school during the pandemic. As a classroom teacher she had to shift to remote teaching, but her new administrative job required her to be in-person more. When she was working from home, Sarah felt as though she had more flexibility, and she preferred it: "Being at home, it was more flexible. They didn't pile on the work as much as they would here in the building. So I liked the flexibility in that."

Child care was provided by a babysitter before the pandemic, but that changed once things went remote. When Sarah was back in-person, she sent her children back to the babysitter, but shortly thereafter the sitter quit. On occasion, she brought her children to work, and this alleviated some stress. "When the students weren't there for the summer months, I was able to bring them with me some, and then I had to get help from family members, [but] I don't have many family members near me. So I had to either drive and drop them off a long distance or take them with me." Bringing her children to work allowed her to maintain her hours and reduce child care costs. Once eligible, she signed her youngest child up for a free early preschool program in-person. Even then, when school was over, her child would get dropped off at her workplace, and she watched him there.

Sarah reported being stressed having to manage everything herself and even more stressed out about having to take on extra work at her job. Since there were no vaccine mandates for teachers in her district, teachers who were not vaccinated and were exposed to COVID had to work remotely. This meant someone else had to be in the classroom with the children, which placed extra burdens on the teachers who were vaccinated. In her school district, if you were vaccinated, you were expected to work even when exposed to COVID unless you showed symptoms. This policy added extra work for Sarah because, since she was vaccinated, she was required to take on that extra work.

Tanya (thirty-two, White) was a grocery store cashier on weekends as well as a full-time student during the week. Her partner, Charlie, worked out of the house full-time in a high-stress job. When COVID first hit, working as an essential worker was scary for Tanya. She reported harassment on the job and fear of getting COVID and even experienced violence that required calling the cops when belligerent customers refused to wear masks or take precautions. Tanya had to take on many extra hours for the store when the pandemic first hit because panic shopping cleared the shelves, requiring extra shipments to be unloaded frequently. While she earned extra hazard pay, that only lasted for six months and ended before the arrival of vaccines.

Tanya's job was structured around her child care needs. She was responsible for child care during the week, and Charlie was responsible on weekends while she was at work. They had a son in kindergarten, but during the pandemic he was in and out of in-person schooling depending on virus caseloads. During the week, Tanya supervised her son's remote schooling, leaving her little time for her own schoolwork. She did most of the child care because of her husband's schedule. She had a gendered outlook of care: "Occasionally he will do things. But like I said, he's usually at work. So most of it falls on me, and, honestly, he's a very messy person. If it was mostly on him, we would probably live in shambles."

As with other couples without work flexibility, Tanya shouldered most of the load yet reported that the household labor was equitable. She described Charlie as absent, messy, and stressed, with his work validating his inability to take time for his family. This took a toll on their relationship: "I feel like it would help so much overall with our family life if he was a little bit more involved and not to say that he's not involved, but I mean like mentally, if he was there, cause sometimes he does stuff and you could tell mentally he's checked out. And it's not as fun kind of building your life together when one of you is mentally checked out most of the time."

Ways Forward to a New Normal

The COVID-19 pandemic created crises for many families. Working parents depend on assistance with child care from daycare centers, nannies, babysitters, and schools. During the pandemic, this patchwork infrastructure of care fell apart. Parents were left to earn income and care for their children, on their own, at the same time. We wanted to know what happened to these families, how they coped, and what lessons they learned from this experience.

We found that *workplace flexibility* led to higher satisfaction in relationships. Many of our respondents with workplace flexibility reported being grateful to have more time to spend with their families. Many people with flexible schedules reported shifting their priorities to center their families. Importantly, we found that flexibility only helped partnered mothers if both members of the couple shared the extra work created by the pandemic. When male partners ignored the need to do their share, female partners were overburdened and sometimes resentments arose. For heterosexual married or cohabiting women to benefit from work flexibility, they needed partners who would step up to the plate and do their fair share. Even though essential workers couldn't work remotely during the pandemic, we found that they also benefited from workplace flexibility, including the option to change their hours and, if necessary, bring their children to work with them.

What are the implications of our findings for post-pandemic families? Many respondents told us they enjoyed prioritizing their families more. Until now, postindustrial workplaces were organized the same way they were in the twentieth century, presuming workers have wives and mothers to take care of their families. Until the pandemic, the structure of work in American society had stayed rigid for over a century, with at least eight-hour days and little flexibility. You were lucky if your job came with sick leave and a few weeks of paid vacation. The pandemic challenged that model. What will happen with paid work now that schools and daycares have reopened? Will employers try to take us back to the twentieth century where paid work is done outside the home all the time? Or will some people always work at home? Perhaps a hybrid model, with a few days in-person and the rest at home, will become the new normal. Since that new normal won't be possible for all workers, workplaces must recognize the need for other kinds of flexibility and a more robust social safety net.

Our study suggests that parents want and need flexibility in their paid work—flexibility both about *where* to work and about *when* and *how* to do so. While working from home gave some parents the ability to juggle child care more effectively than they did in the past, remote work is not a solution to child care needs in the United States. We still need a strong child care program to support working families and encourage gender equity nationwide. Given that most children live with parents who work for pay, we hope that this major disruption to workplace culture can be a silver lining to the COVID-19 pandemic. Our data suggest that for women partnered with men, workplace flexibility will be a positive development only if we make sure not only that it is women's jobs that are flexible but that both mothers and fathers retain flexible options and that both parents use those options.

Flexibility brings couples closer if they hold feminist beliefs and integrate equality into their relationships; without that, flexibility only lightens women's loads but does not overcome their greater burden of family labor. We hope that going forward, fathers retain their new respect for the need to share the family labor. Children will benefit if employers allow parents to prioritize their families' well-being. A flexible work culture can be used to promote a more gender-equitable future so that couples who want egalitarian marriages are able to create them.

Notes

1. *Hispanic* is used here as the way that the National Opinion Research Center (NORC) asked survey respondents to identify themselves. It refers to Spanish language. Note that *Latino* refers to a geographic region that includes non-Spanish-speaking people. We use *Latinx* to describe participants in our interviews; it is a gender-neutral word.

In Other Words

CCF RESEARCH BRIEF: REALLY? WORK LOWERS PEOPLE'S STRESS LEVELS

Sarah Damaske, May 22, 2014 / CCF

National surveys and other studies continuously tell us that work is a major source of stress for Americans, and there have been plenty of reports of people turning to a personal injury lawyer when workplace stress reaches such a point that it causes a breakdown. Stress can be a lot for anyone to deal with, so it's no wonder that some people going through it choose to use alternative methods like space cookies to help manage their stress levels.

A 2005 Work and Families Institute study found that almost 90 percent of workers felt they either never had enough time in the day to do their job or that their job required them to work very hard. A Pew Research Center report from 2013 found that more than half of all working moms and working dads experience work-family conflict. One-third of working moms and dads feel rushed on workdays, and almost 50 percent of working dads (and 25 percent of working moms) say they don't have enough time with their children. And in a research project I helped conduct, we found that people report feeling less stressed out on non-workdays than on workdays. Stress often negatively affects sexual health, but rather than buy drugs for impotence, first try to deal with stress. If you're feeling stressed at work from things such as workload or even conflict with colleagues, there are things you can do to combat it. You can let your boss know that your workload is too much, or if it's conflict getting you down, then you can embark on a conflict management training course with other employees. There are numerous work stresses to contend with, so it would be fair to say that most of us believe that home is where we recover from the stress of the workday.

But actually, when my fellow Penn State researchers, Joshua Smyth and Matthew Zawadzki, and I measured people's cortisol levels, a major biological marker of stress, we found that *people have significantly lower levels of stress at work than at home.* These low levels of cortisol may help explain a long-standing finding that has always been hard to reconcile with the idea that work is a major source of stress: people who work have better mental and physical health than their nonworking peers, according to research published in the *Journal of Health and Social Behavior*, *Social Science Research*, the *American Sociological Review*, and the *Handbook of the Sociology of Mental Health*. Mothers who work full-time and steadily across their twenties and thirties report better mental and physical health at age forty-five than mothers who work part-time, who stay at home, or who experience repeated bouts of unemployment.

Further contradicting conventional wisdom, we found that *women as well as men have lower levels of stress at work than at home.* In fact, women may get more renewal from work than men do, because unlike men, they report themselves happier at work than at home. It is men, not women, who report being happier at home than at work.

We were surprised to find that even parents—both mothers and fathers—had lower stress at work than at home. However, parents did not experience as big a decrease in their stress levels as nonparents.

Our findings suggest that telling people to quit or cut back on work in order to resolve their work-family conflicts may not be the best long-run advice. Rather, companies should consider adopting family-friendly policies that allow workers to continue getting the health benefits of employment while still being able to meet their family responsibilities One model is the "results-only work environments," a policy adopted by Gap, Inc., which allows workers more flexibility in the time and place of their schedules, as long as they are getting their work done. Remote work, paid sick days, and paternity and maternity leave are all policies that make it easier for workers to retain the health benefits of employment and for companies to retain the financial benefits of having loyal employees rather than having to deal with constant job turnover. ◾

PART SIX

How Parents and Kids Relate

25

"This Is Your Job Now"

Latina Mothers and Daughters and Family Work

Lorena Garcia

Olivia slips off the padded shoulder straps of her backpack and sets it on the table with a loud sigh. Smiling at her mentor, she pulls out two heavy textbooks—trigonometry and U.S. history—along with a worn notebook and a couple of pencils. Within a few minutes, the seventeen-year-old high school junior is already at work trying to solve trigonometry problems with the assistance of her mentor, a thirtysomething Latina professional who is there at the community organization through an employer-run volunteer program.[1] Many of Olivia's peers are still settling down, chit-chatting with each other or with mentors about compliments on outfits, school-related gossip, or just complaints about homework—small talk that most often draws in any person, including myself and other mentors. But Olivia remains focused on her work, occasionally looking up as she thinks about a trigonometry problem. Often described by Hogar del Pueblo youth program staff as a "good student" and "smart," the slender, young Puerto Rican woman does not join any of these conversations until she has completed her homework, which isn't usually until the remaining ten to fifteen minutes of the two-hour tutoring session.

It is not until my interviews with Olivia that I am able to fully appreciate her ability to be so disciplined during the weekly tutoring program. With both her parents working full-time jobs—her mother as a downtown hotel housekeeper and her father as a factory worker in a nearby suburb—Olivia, the eldest of three children, is "in charge of helping at home." She walks me through her typical weekday: When she leaves school around 2:30 p.m., she picks up her eight-year-old sister from an after-school program. At home, Olivia gives her sister a snack;

while her sister watches cartoons, Olivia handles some cleaning, since her parents do not arrive home until around 6:00 p.m. Counting off each task on her fingers, she explains:

> I wash the dishes, sweep and do [make] the beds, but only my parents' bed and my bed [which she shares with her sister]. I don't do it for my brother [who is fifteen years old] anymore 'cause he can do that himself. And if I don't have to clean anything else, like the bathroom, maybe I'll try to do a little bit of homework.

She's unable to begin her homework until around 8:00 p.m., after her family has a quick dinner together that her mother usually prepares. Olivia works at the kitchen table as her mother cleans up after dinner and watches *telenovelas* (soap operas) on a small portable television. The tutoring session is the one weekday she can have an uninterrupted block of time to do homework, and Olivia takes advantage of it. "I don't have time to mess around when I get there, especially when I have questions about trigonometry or need help with other stuff. I only socialize after I finish, if I have time," she explains to me.

Olivia's experience, like that of other young women in my study, suggests that our discussions about who cleans the home and cares for family members and the time spent doing such work often fail to consider how children are incorporated into this central aspect of family life. Generally, the division of household labor is regarded as relevant only to couples. White heterosexual married couples' experiences receive the most attention, though we are witnessing more consideration of how a wider range of couples, such as same-sex and immigrant couples, sort out the work that needs to be done in the home.[2] One key pattern that interests many of us and generates heated debates about men's and women's "roles" in their families is that work to maintain the home and meet the various needs of family members is organized by gender. For instance, we know that women tend to do more of the repetitive labor necessary to their family's day-to-day functioning, such as washing dishes, doing laundry, and cooking, whereas men's work is likely to be more infrequent, such as mowing the lawn and taking out the trash.[3] And we are also intrigued by how and under what conditions families move away from relying on gender expectations to determine the division of household labor.[4] But we really do not know much about how this plays out between parents and their children. What are parents' and children's experiences of the work they do for their families? And how do parents and their children negotiate and make sense of this work?

This chapter draws on interviews and ethnographic fieldwork with second-generation Latina girls and a subset of their mothers to consider these questions. The findings presented here are from my research for my book *Respect Yourself,*

Protect Yourself: Latina Girls and Sexual Identity, in which I explore how Latina girls experience their emerging sexuality and their approaches to safe sex.[5] Though I did not ask about it, girls and their mothers often discussed how they contributed to their family. Mothers focused on what their paid labor allowed them to do for their families, and daughters talked of the unpaid labor they did for their families. Most mothers worked full- or part-time jobs outside the home, which they deemed to be relevant to their parenting practices and identities as good mothers. They saw their employment as necessitating that other family members do more family work, and it was particularly young women who were expected to take on this responsibility.

The young Latinas I got to know encountered a "second shift," a term introduced by sociologist Arlie Hochschild to describe the unpaid additional labor done by some family members when they arrive home from work, such as grocery shopping, cooking, and caring for children. Generally, it is women who do a disproportionate share of such work, even among heterosexual couples in which both individuals work outside the home. I found that Latina girls also grappled with juggling the demands of the family work assigned to them with that of their schoolwork, and sometimes they brought their own ideas to their families' division of labor.

The narratives of this group of mothers and daughters provide us with further insight into how they make sense of what family work is and how this relates to the formation of their identities. Following what I learned from these interviews, I explore three major themes in this chapter: women's paid work as part of their mothering identity, daughters' contributions to family work, and generational change in gendered expectations for boys and men.

IT'S WHAT MOTHERS DO

Most mothers were initially noticeably self-conscious about their daughters' sexual behavior and how it reflected on them as mothers. Forty-six-year-old Lilia, for instance, stated at least two times within thirty minutes of our first interview that most people would think she had insufficiently supervised her sixteen-year-old daughter, Eva, because Eva was no longer a virgin. But as the interview progressed, Lilia asserted, "I am still a good mother, even if people don't think so!" Lilia's initial embarrassed demeanor, like that of other mothers, gave way to an unapologetic determination to continue to provide guidance to her daughter. Refusing to be classified as "bad mothers" on the basis of what were deemed to be daughters' sexual transgressions, they highlighted how they fulfilled what was expected of them. One theme that emerged in these conversations was how their employment outside the home fit into their assessments of their parenting.

Nearly all mothers believed that working outside the home was not incompatible with their identities as mothers.

Rather, as conveyed to me by Julia, this was understood as integral to what it meant to be a "good mother." The busy Mexican mother of three invited me to her home one early afternoon for our second interview. Sitting in her small kitchen, I watched as Julia washed dishes and checked on a pot of beans simmering on the stove. A full-time laundry attendant, she was already in her uniform and would be heading to work in about an hour. She explained that she would leave the beans on very low heat and her sixteen-year-old daughter, Inés, would then monitor the beans until they were fully cooked when she arrived home from school—about thirty minutes after Julia left for work. According to Julia, her daughter would finish making dinner for her two younger siblings and herself by preparing some rice and quesadillas to serve with the beans. Sitting down on the kitchen chair across from me, she told me, "I wish I could be here to do that for them more when they get home from school. And I think they would like that, too. But there is a necessity to pay bills and the rent. As their mother, I want to give them everything they need." Julia then went on to list the things she worked hard to procure for her children, such as food, clothing, and school supplies.

As a single mother, Julia was the only wage earner and believed that her ability to financially provide for her children made her a good mother. But talk of the necessity of employment due to family economic struggles was not just confined to single mothers. Most mothers, whether single, married, or cohabiting, described their families as barely making ends meet. Women who were married or cohabiting sought to avoid relying on only their partners' income. They saw their employment as a safety net in the event their partners lost their jobs, recognizing the instability of some work, such as in landscaping and construction. They also wanted to meet particular financial goals, such as buying a home, paying off a debt, sending money to relatives in Mexico or Puerto Rico, and being economically self-sufficient women. The last reason—economic independence—was particularly relevant to their parenting, because they also viewed their employment as a teaching tool for financially educating their children.

Mothers believed their employment made them good role models for their children because it allowed them to teach their children two important lessons about work. The first was about one's approach to labor, namely, that one works for the things one wants or needs. Elsa recounted a conversation she had with her daughter when she stole a small toy from the store:

> Arely was eight years old. . . . I walked her back to the store and made her return it. It was a good thing the owner knew us and did not get mad. At home, I asked her if she ever saw me or her father take anything from the store without paying for it.

She said no. And then I told her that I wanted a lot of things, but if I didn't have the money then I can't get them. I said to her, "That is why we work, to pay for things. And sometimes we still can't get what we want, but the things we do have are paid for with the money we worked for."

When Martina's teenage son wanted an expensive pair of Nike basketball shoes, she told him, "That is too expensive! We aren't rich. I wish we could buy them for you, but we're unable to. We have to work hard to earn the little money we have! You will see what it is like when you have to work and pay for the things you want."

And while they were proud of the economic subsistence they provided for their families, another message for their children was that they should strive for better jobs than those held by their parents. As they were (im)migrant women with low levels of education, their opportunities for employment were generally confined to factory or service work. Working at physically demanding jobs, they stressed to their children the importance of an education to avoid such work.

Emma attributed her chronic back pain to the repetitive bending and heavy lifting she did for her factory job. She often remarked to her children that what she did for a living was drudgery and that she did not want that for them.

> When I think they aren't focusing on their studies, I say to them, "Do you want to end up like me?! You think I like to work like a donkey every day?! I don't have a choice. I can't find too many jobs. But you do have opportunities. *Preparanse para una carrera* [prepare yourself for a profession]!"

And as a way to further promote the lesson about the value of an education, Lilia took her sixteen-year-old daughter, Eva, to work with her at her factory. On her spring break, Eva spent the week working on an assembly line in a packaging factory.

> She hated it! But I wanted her to see how hard my job was so she stays in school. I told her, "That's why you need to go to school and study so that when you work, you will get paid for using your head and not have to do what I do."

Though they did not point their children down particular career paths, this group of mothers made it very clear what their children should endeavor to avoid in their future employment.

These lessons about economic self-sufficiency were for all their children. But for their daughters, it was also layered with a message about how to navigate gender inequality.[6] As they did with their sexual education of their daughters, in which they advised them to respect themselves and take care of themselves, they communicated to them the importance of personal responsibility for their finances in the near future. Although nearly every mother expected marriage for their daughters and assumed their daughters wanted this in the future, they did not want them to be economically dependent within the marriage. Gina expressed this when she considered the experiences of her cousin at the hands of her abusive man.

> She doesn't work so she really can't leave him because he has all of the money. My daughter says she should just leave him, as if it is just that easy! I tell her, "That is why it is important for a woman to have her own money, so she is not stuck with a man who thinks he can mistreat her whenever he feels like it."

Jasmine stated that she often told her daughter,

> You have to go to school to get a career so that you can always take care of yourself. That way no matter what happens with your husband, you won't need to depend on him or other people for money.

She spoke from her experience of moving in with her sister's family in an already overcrowded apartment after her children's father broke up with her and moved out of state, very rarely communicating with them ever since. Jasmine's children were seven and ten years old at the time. Jasmine initially struggled to find a job, and it took her almost two years to save enough money to move out of her sister's place. She used her experience to illustrate to her daughters the importance of a woman's economic independence.

These Latina mothers did not describe their employment as a "temporary" situation or themselves as "helping" their husbands or partners or "supplementing" their earnings. Prior to their arrival in the United States, the mothers explained that as young girls, they and their own mothers had contributed to their family's ability to economically and reproductively maintain itself by handwashing clothes, making and selling different types of food, or caring for younger siblings. As with their families of origin, mothers expected that they would participate in economic activities for their own families and understood employment outside the home and family work as connected to each other and relevant to their roles as mothers rather than as two separate spheres.[7] Seeing themselves as legitimate economic providers for their working-class families, this group of Latina mothers drew on this role to further validate their perceptions of themselves as good mothers and as a valuable resource in socializing their children on the advantages of an education and economic independence. Thus, their employment outside the home was not at odds with their identities as mothers.

Everyone Has to Make Sacrifices

Aracelia, who worked full-time as a cashier at a local grocery store, talked of want-ing to "dedicate more time to her children" and her children's frustration when she was required to work a double shift. Speaking of what was required of every-one in the family, including children, she said matter-of-factly, "But we all have to make an effort and sacrifice a little to get ahead." Aracelia and other mothers reasoned that they and their children might need to forgo time with each other in the interest of meeting their family's financial needs. And for daughters, this might necessitate relinquishing some of their own interests and time to do more in the home—as was the case for Inés, whose mother relied on her to head home right after school to finish prepping and later serving dinner to her younger sib-lings. Like their mothers, Latina girls were initiated into "women's work" in the home at a young age and were expected to assume more responsibility for it as they grew into young women.

Proudly claiming that her enchiladas were better than her mother's enchila-das, seventeen-year-old Isela shared with me the secret ingredients in the dinner she had prepared for her family the evening before. When I inquired as to how she learned her enchilada-making skills, she rolled her eyes and explained,

> My mom's been having me help her make them since I was like eleven or twelve. When she first started showing me how to make them, she said I should know how to make them 'cause I'm a girl and I could make them for my husband and stuff.

Similarly, sixteen-year-old Yvette recounted how her father and her uncle communicated this to her at the age of ten:

> I was outside playing tag with my friends and they [her father and her uncle] were hanging out in front of our house, too. After a while they told me to go inside and help my mom finish cooking and cleaning. I was like, "Why?" They told me because I was a girl and that I needed to start knowing how to do stuff like that and help her more. I ignored them and kept on playing. Later that night, I guess my dad told my mom that I didn't listen to him about helping her and she whooped [spanked] my ass!

Like Isela and Yvette, young Latinas spoke of being enlisted into family work at a young age. The primary explanation was that they "needed" to learn how to do tasks such as cleaning, cooking, and caring for young or older family members because of their gender.[8]

And when mothers described how they introduced their daughters to house-hold work, they also framed it as something that they "needed" to do because of the gender identities they claimed for themselves and their daughters that intersected especially with their racial/ethnic identities. It was a way they assisted their daughters in learning to be women, but more concretely, Mexican or Puerto Rican women. And it was also another practice that affirmed their presentations of themselves as good Mexican or Puerto Rican mothers. Take, for example, Carmen's interaction with her seventeen-year-old daughter while at her niece's birthday party:

> Minerva was just sitting in the living room, and I told her to go in the kitchen and offer to help. She responded that the boys didn't have to do it. I told her not to worry about that, to just worry about what she has to do. Later on at home, I told her that she should always offer to help with stuff like serving food, cooking, or washing dishes. I told her it didn't look right if a woman doesn't do that. That is how we were taught in Mexico and that is what you should be accustomed to doing. And I didn't want anyone to think she was *mal educada* [not well-mannered].

Carmen's vigilance over her respectability as a good mother reminds us of the pressures felt by mothers in general in a larger culture of mother blaming in our society. Assumed and expected to be the primary caretakers of children, they are primarily the ones we blame when something goes "wrong" with their children. And since mothers are expected to model normative gender behavior for their daughters (as fathers do for their sons), the misbehavior or failure of a daughter is read as a shortcoming of her mother's own femininity. In talking to me about what they wanted for their daughters, mothers acknowledged that their daughters were not growing up in Mexico or Puerto Rico, as they had done. But they still believed their daughters shared their gendered racial/ethnic identity. They wanted and insisted that their daughters maintain a gendered identity that was grounded in their identities as Mexican and Puerto Rican women.

Even before becoming aware of their daughters' sexual behavior, mothers warned them not to behave like white young women, whom they described as having too much freedom. Mothers sometimes accused their daughters of acting like white young women when the mothers disapproved of their daughters' behavior, a characterization that daughters adamantly rejected because they viewed themselves as Mexican or Puerto Rican despite growing up in the United States. One key site where they negotiated this identity was within their families. As U.S.-born daughters of Mexican immigrants or Puerto Rican migrants from poor and working-class backgrounds, they were expected to contribute to their families' economic efforts, most often in the form of reproductive labor. But unlike their mothers, the young Latinas I spoke with never used the word *sacrifice* to talk of their work in the home. Instead, they tended to describe themselves as "helping" their family.

For those with younger siblings, "helping out" often required that they forgo some extracurricular activities. Such was the experience of Minerva, who felt unable to attend a campus visit to a university about one hour from Chicago that was organized by Hogar del Pueblo. This trip would require one overnight stay—something that Minerva felt was out of the question for her. Assuming she would be joining the group of students leaving for the campus visit the next day, I asked her if she had already packed for the trip. Giving me a half-hearted smile, she shook her head, stating, "What for? They [her parents] ain't going to let me go." She added,

> They never let me sleep over anywhere—not even my cousin's house. Anyways, I can't go 'cause they need me to help out with my brother and sister 'cause there's no one else to watch them after school. It would just be too hard for them to deal with all that right now.

Minerva shared with me that she had not even asked her parents for permission to go on the trip. Resigning herself to the situation, she stated that she would still apply to the school, but just "check it out on the website." I later found out from some of the youth program staff that they had strongly encouraged Minerva to go and even offered to speak to her parents about it, but she insisted that they not approach her parents out of her concern that it would "cause a fight or something."

However, my interviews with Minerva's mom, Carmen, led me to think that she would have tried to make it work so that her daughter could go on the trip. Carmen, like most other mothers I spoke with, did describe restricting her daughter's time outside the home to sexually "protect" her as well as to have her "help out" at home. But mothers were flexible about their daughters being outside the home if it was for educational activities.

As discussed earlier, mothers stressed educational success as a way for their daughters to gain more independence and avoid economic reliance on men. One way they promoted this message was by encouraging daughters to seek additional educational opportunities such as tutoring or summer enrichment programs at community centers, even when they encountered opposition to daughters' participation in these types of activities from other family members or were criticized for allowing their daughters *demasiado libertad* (too much freedom) outside the home. Some mothers, for example, stated that their daughters' fathers were worried that their daughters would not be properly supervised in such contexts.

Young Latinas expressed awareness of these tensions in their interviews and spoke of how they wanted to do well academically, especially so as not to disappoint their mothers. They also commented on their family's limited finances and child-care resources and their parents' efforts to economically provide for their family, as Minerva did when she conveyed her concern over how her parents would manage child care for her siblings if she went on the college tour. Their mindfulness of the pressures facing their family and their concerns about family relations and their efforts to minimize some of their family's stress through their labor in the home suggest that these Latina girls were also doing emotion work.[9] In other words, they sought to sustain their family's emotional well-being through their emotional support of family members, particularly their parents. Therefore, their family work also encompassed emotion work.[10]

Reflected in these Latinas' accounts of their labor for their family are their understandings of what it means to "do gender" appropriately.[11] A key component of this for them was their willingness to "give up" something to better their family's circumstances—for mothers, it was especially the "sacrifice" of more time with their children; for their daughters, it was forgoing extracurricular activities to "help out" at home. Informing their commitment to their family's ability to sustain itself in the midst of economic struggles was their integration of their gender and racial/ethnic identities.[12] Mothers took primary responsibility for recruiting their daughters into family work at a young age, seeking to demonstrate their competency as "good" Mexican or Puerto Rican mothers but also to provide their daughters with lessons about what femininity required of them.

Evident in my interviews with Latina girls was their attentiveness to the needs of their families in relation to what they wanted or needed for themselves as young women coming of age. Their awareness of their family's financial circumstances and their attempts to minimize or not add tension may be why they approached their labor within the home as providing support to their families. Not a single young Latina I spoke with described her work within the home as "chores," nor did she mention expecting some type of financial compensation for it (i.e., allowance). As their mothers articulated what their employment outside the home meant for their identities within their families, their daughters also negotiated what their participation in family work meant for their sense of themselves as young Mexican or Puerto Rican women. At this point in their lives, their development of gender identities and practices was closely linked to their racial/ethnic identities as well as to their family's needs.

Changing It Up

Latina girls' contribution to the work of family life did not mean that they uncritically assumed their "place" in the gendered division of household labor. Their enactment of the work expected of them was also about protecting the little freedom they had outside the home. Seventeen-year-old Carla conveyed this to me when she described the various household tasks she handled: "It's annoying to do some of it, but I just do it 'cause if I don't, she would never let me go anywhere! Man, I can't really go anywhere now, so *imagínate* [imagine]!" And sixteen-year-old Asuzena explained that her parents allowed her to go to the Centro Adelante youth program so long as she "behaved," which included "not getting in trouble, like cutting school or hanging around with boys all crazy, and like cleaning and stuff like that in the house."

One crucial way this group of Latina girls carved out some freedom for themselves was through youth activities at community organizations. For more than half of them, this was the only after-school activity they were permitted to join. Feeling that their parents restricted their time outside their home as their bodies began to develop, these young women were cautious about jeopardizing what little autonomy they did have away from their families. They believed it was already limited by household work that was required of them because their mothers worked outside the home. Thus, through their family work, they also sought to demonstrate that they were "good girls" deserving of permission to at least hang out with other youth at community organizations.

Some young women also attempted to reduce the uneven distribution of family work, particularly between themselves and their brothers. For those with younger brothers, this was done purposefully by incorporating them more into family work routines. This is how sixteen-year-old Gloria introduced her ten-year-old brother to his cleaning responsibilities:

> He would leave everything lying around. Toys, shoes, clothes, dishes, whatever! One day I was starting to pick up his toys that were on the floor and I was like, "Hold up, uh-uh, this ain't my mess. He is big enough to take care of this himself." I made him clean it up. Then I was like, and he should start doing more around here. So I was like, this is how you sweep the floor and this is how you clean the table. This is your job now when you get home from school. If you don't do it, you ain't watch TV or play your stupid little video games.

That Gloria and some of the young women were able to obtain the cooperation of their younger brothers was most likely related to their age—they were older and had probably garnered some respect from their brothers because of the care they provided for them. It is difficult to ascertain whether their parents supported them in this effort because I did not have an opportunity to ask mothers about it (given the focus of my research), though some girls' narratives suggest that mothers were comfortable with it. And studies on parents' gender socialization of their children indicate that these young women's mothers and fathers might have agreed that developing sons' household-related knowledge and skills was a good idea.[13]

Latina girls' interactions with older brothers on household work were a more trying experience. Some reported that when they criticized their brothers for failing to clean up after themselves or help out, their older brothers would claim their male privilege by replying that it was not required of them. Declaring, "My brother gets on my nerves!" Sara shared that her brother often "left a mess on purpose" for her to clean up. Sometimes he taunted her by telling her, "I'm not a woman; that's what you're supposed to do, so just shut up and do it!" These brother-sister interactions often led to very heated arguments that mothers or both parents intervened in and tried to resolve.

Such was the experience of eighteen-year-old Alicia, who told me that although she often did the family laundry, she folded everyone's clothes except those of her brother (who was nineteen). Without my asking why this was, she explained, "He can fold his own clothes. He's a big boy." When Alicia's brother complained about it, her mother scolded her, but Alicia still refused to fold his clothes. "I told her, 'Just 'cause he's a guy, don't mean he don't gotta do anything up in this house!'" After this "fight," Alicia was no longer obliged to handle that task for her brother. And although he was now expected to assume responsibility for his own clothes, she noted,

> He usually doesn't do it anyway, just once in a while. He just leaves his clothes on the bed or throws it on the floor. But they don't say anything to him for that. But if it's me, they'll be like, "Why is your room like that?"

Like Alicia, other girls took up these frustrations primarily with their mothers. These types of interactions, in which daughters justified their efforts to get brothers to do more household work or their refusal to do certain things for them, also led some mothers to revisit their approaches to teaching sons and daughters about their roles in the work of family life. Emma recalled how her daughter, sixteen-year-old Miriam, recently challenged her expectations of her eighteen-year-old son when Miriam asserted that her brother should iron his own shirt and refused to do it for him:

> I reminded her that he didn't know how to iron, so she should help him. She said, 'Well, isn't it time for him to learn how to do it?" I started giving some thought to this and decided that she was right. Arturo [her son] should know how to do something like that for himself. I guess I just thought she should do it for him because that is the way my mom taught me. We get used to doing certain things, but sometimes we need to ask why we do them, you know?

As reflected in Emma's narrative, these kinds of mother-daughter interactions sometimes presented opportunities for mothers to reflect upon their beliefs about household work and to consider alternative ways of teaching their children to engage with family work.

These young Latinas' strategies to address the inequality in their family's gendered division of labor entailed interactions with brothers and mothers. Even though these were the interactions that they spoke of with me, it is likely that they were not just limited to those family members. The exchanges with brothers and mothers they described highlight how lessons about "doing gender" in the context of family work are not just passed down from older generations to the younger generations but are also sometimes transmitted in the other direction and across generations. These exchanges hopefully can invite collaboration across various generations to "undo gender" in the organization of family work.[14]

Conclusion

Culture is almost always the starting point for popular and academic discussions of gender and sexuality among Latinas/os. *Familismo, machismo,* and *marianismo* are three concepts that tend to consistently surface in attempts to make sense of some of their "attitudes and behaviors" as well as some of their "outcomes." Described as placing a strong emphasis on the family, Latinas/os are generally understood as having a deep sense of loyalty to their families that requires their appropriate embodiment and practice of gender to demonstrate the centeredness of their families in their lives. For Latinas, *familismo* is explained as requiring a self-sacrificing femininity and a mindfulness to avoid behavior that could be shameful to one's family, which as some argue, is in line with their *marianismo.*[15] This "cultural trait" is also seen as complementing and sustaining Latinos' *machismo,* which is commonly conceptualized as a strong and exaggerated sense of masculinity specific to Latinos. There are certainly aspects of Latinas' cultural backgrounds that privilege men, but this is not unique to Latinas/os. Therefore, we should be cautious in interpreting the behaviors, attitudes, and outcomes of Latinas/os as if they solely originate from a "Latino culture," which is already contested as homogenizing of a diverse group.

Though it is clear from my interviews with Latina girls and their mothers that their families were indeed important to them, their narratives of how they made sense of the work they did for their families and how it related to their identities tell us that simply attributing this to culture is insufficient. We have a very limited view of their worlds if we just start and end with culture as *the* explanation for how their family lives unfold. In my in-depth interviews with this group of women and ethnographic fieldwork, I specifically concentrated on how they assigned meaning to their work to move beyond and complicate cultural frameworks as they relate to Latinas/os.[16] In doing so, I was able to uncover some of the ways in which their families' socioeconomic positioning, their work in the labor market, their educational barriers and opportunities, and their generational status informed their perspectives and approaches to their labor for their families as well as how this connected to their formation of their intersecting identities.

NOTES

1. The Chicago nonprofit community organization Hogar del Pueblo provides comprehensive services to Chicago's low-income families. Most clients of the organization are predominantly Latina/o immigrants. One of the youth-focused services is a mentoring and tutoring program that connects high school students with Chicago-area professionals for weekly one-on-one sessions centered on academics, college preparation, and life skills.

2. See, for example, Carrington (1999); George (2005); Hondagneu-Sotelo (1994); Moore (2011); Nelson (1996); Sullivan (2004).

3. See, for example, Coltrane (2000); Hochschild (1989); Shelton (1992).

4. See, for example, Risman (1998); Gerson (2010); Sullivan (2006).

5. Garcia (2012).

6. Messages about the importance of women's economic independence have also been found in other studies on Latinas that consider lessons that mothers transmit to their daughters (Ayala 2006; Fine, Weis, and Roberts 2000; Hurtado 2003; Lopez 2003; Villeñas and Moreno 2001).

7. This is relevant particularly to working-class women of color in the United States (Collins 1987; Collins 1994; Dill 1988; Glenn 1994; Hondagneu-Sotelo 1997; Segura 1994).

8. Other studies have also found this; see, for example, Ayala (2006); Hurtado (2003); Lopez (2003); Souza (2002).

9. Emotion work, also referred to as emotional labor, most often is discussed in relation to paid employment with a significant amount of interaction with customers, such as that of teachers, health care workers, sales clerks, and flight attendants. Such workers often perform emotion work such as smiling, thanking, and providing undivided attention. This is work that is invisible and can be taxing for workers (Hochschild 1983).

10. Erickson (1993, 2005) points out that emotion work within families has been understudied and that family work should be reconceptualized to include emotion work (and not just thought of as household work and child care).

11. Rather than conceptualize gender as traits and behaviors that individuals possess, the "doing gender" framework concentrates on gender as a situated accomplishment that is influenced by accountability. That is, social interactions are viewed as central to how gender differences are created and come to be seen as natural rather than socially constructed (West and Zimmerman 1987).

12. Segura and Pierce (1993) argue that it is necessary to account for how unique social contexts may produce particular family configurations of various groups, which may also mean different gender identity development processes for girls. In their article, they specifically focus on working-class Chicanas to illustrate how their family relationships and dynamics inform their intertwining of gender and race/ethnic identities. One such way this occurs is through their commitment to improving their families' and communities' circumstances.

13. See Berridge and Romich (2011); Hill (1999); Kane (2006); Penha-Lopes (2006).

14. While research on how gender is "done" has been critical to understanding how gender inequality is created and maintained, we must also focus on how it is challenged, from the level of individuals' gender identities to broader institutional practices (Chafetz 1990; Deutsch 2007; Lorber 2005; Ridgeway 2011; Risman 1998).

15. This is a gender ideology that refers to women's passiveness, submissiveness, and self-sacrificing. It is assumed to be unique to Latinas' gender identities and practices.

16. For more on scholars' concerns of an overreliance on cultural frameworks as it relates to Latinas/os' gender and sexual lives, see Cantú (2000); Carrillo (2002); González-López and Vidal-Ortiz (2008). And for further discussion of meaning-making as it relates to cultural perspectives and practices, see Lamont (2002); Swidler (1986); Young (2004).

In Other Words

MOTHERING IN SANCTUARY

Sarah Bruhn, January 31, 2023 / CCF@TSP

On a bright day last spring, a group of Latina immigrant mothers gathered in a park in Somerville, Massachusetts, a small, densely populated city north of Boston. They were there to participate in a weekly arts and conversation group for immigrant parents in the city's public schools, a collaboration between a local nonprofit and the city. Snacks and craft materials were strewn across the long table, all of us sipping coffee from Styrofoam mugs, when the conversation turned to death. Losing a family member is always painful. But for the women around the table, immigration policy seeps into their decisions. One mother, a vivacious El Salvadoran with a green card, explained how she had been the one to go home when her father had died. Her brother, living without authorization in another state, could not travel without risking permanent displacement from the United States. "It isn't fair," she murmured, as the other women nodded in agreement.

In some places, where restrictive policies and racialized immigration enforcement leave families in fear, talking about immigration status so openly and in a city-sponsored space would be unthinkable. But in Somerville, which has declared itself a sanctuary for immigrants since 1987, women frequently and openly discuss the constraints of immigrant motherhood, including but not limited to undocumented immigration status. Somerville is not alone in its self-proclaimed sanctuary identity. In the wake of the 2016 election, sanctuary cities proliferated across the United States, drawing the ire of the forty-fifth president, who threatened to withdraw funds and raid immigrant families' homes if cities did not cooperate with federal immigration authorities.

Despite this public attention, we actually know quite little about how sanctuary ordinances shape the lives of the immigrant families they purport to help. Refusing to enact a 287(g) agreement, which enables cooperation between local law enforcement and federal immigration agents, is an important step in creating safe living conditions for immigrants and their families. Beyond this, though, what are the consequences of sanctuary policies on immigrant families, especially women, who, through motherhood, are fulfilling gendered family and social roles? And what role do local institutions, especially schools, as legally accessible institutions for all immigrant children and their families, regardless of immigration status, play in enacting sanctuary in meaningful ways?

My research tackles these questions through an ethnography of Latina immigrant mothers' lives in Somerville (where I also live and raise my children). I have observed and interviewed immigrant mothers, educators, and community leaders. I argue that welcoming school districts, in the context of a sanctuary city, become central sites of belonging and inclusion for Latina immigrant mothers. The city offers programs for immigrant parents across the district, including parent English classes, an advocacy committee, and the arts and conversation group. While the mothers in my study (and it was almost always mothers who participated) use these programs to learn English, advocate, and develop new artistic skills, they also transform these spaces into sites of what I term *intersectional recognition*. I define *intersectional recognition* as the process through which individuals and institutions affirm the intersections between multiple marginalized identities. By acknowledging their mutual social positions as Latinas, immigrants, and mothers, the women position themselves and their families as worthy members of a community, even as xenophobic national discourses situate them as outsiders.

Yet as women offer one another this recognition, they bear witness to the ways immigration laws shape their individual experiences of motherhood. One morning, for instance, a meeting of the parent advocacy group had come to an end, and most of the women had left to fetch children from school or get to work. A few of us lingered behind, and Carolina, an El Salvadoran mother and leader of the group, leaned across the long table, telling the stragglers that she had something to say. She reminded us that some of the mothers were paid for their work, hired by the school district as parent leaders. But undocumented mothers could not be hired, and Carolina was unsettled by this inequality. She continued advocating until gift cards to a local grocery store were distributed to mothers who could not be legally hired.

The gift cards were helpful to the undocumented mothers, and Carolina's organizing was rooted in her intersectional recognition of how immigranthood, motherhood, and being Latina were intertwined in women's caregiving and relationships with their children's schools. But the cards were also inadequate in the face of two broader barriers that shape immigrant mothers' familial roles and responsibilities: restrictive immigration policies at the national level and extraordinarily high costs of housing locally. While sanctuary cities can refuse to cooperate with Immigration and Customs Enforcement (ICE), the federal government still holds jurisdiction on immigration and pathways to citizenship. So, despite Somerville's welcoming stance, and a school district that strives to support immigrant families, gentrification threatens the community ties that women foster through participating in city and district programs. Eva, a gifted painter who revealed her talents one day at the arts and conversation group to the surprise and delight of the other mothers, relocated to another, less expensive state. Nadia, a skilled seamstress who crafted beautifully designed children's clothes from donated scraps, was evicted and homeless for months; she could not secure housing in Somerville and left for a nearby city. Even as women felt a sense of belonging, worthiness, and inclusion in the city, immigration policy and rising housing costs remained critical, intertwined obstacles.

Although these obstacles may feel insurmountable, cities and schools should not acquiesce. They can and should enact welcoming programs and ensure resources are accessible to immigrants with and without authorized immigration status. The symbolism of sanctuary is important, but my research points out that it is how sanctuary is enacted that really matters. To keep spaces of belonging thriving as gentrification threatens the social and cultural fabric of immigrant neighborhoods, sanctuary cities must respond proactively and creatively to the exorbitant housing costs that are reshaping our cities. Otherwise, the women who gathered at the park, making art and recognizing the intersectional aspects of who they are—as mothers, immigrants, and Latinas—will not be able to stay in the very city that claims to offer sanctuary. ▬

26

Trans Kids and Their Families

From the Kitchen Table to the Culture Wars

Tey Meadow

N oah was immediately warm and present when we met, even over Zoom. He smiled at me, talked easily, told me he was on his way to the zoo with friends. Noah is used to talking with strangers. At sixteen years old, Noah and his mom, Katie, have become reluctant activists. They've been in an NBC documentary, testified before legislative hearings, and written op-eds for newspapers. They've also been the targets of violent threats. They've been forced to move from their home in Texas across state lines so that Noah might be assured a safe school environment and access to medical care. Noah is transgender, which means that he was assigned female at birth but identifies and lives his life as a boy. And this is a really complicated time to be a transgender young person in the United States.

In 2018, I published a book called *Trans Kids: Being Gendered in the Twenty-First Century.*[1] The book profiled dozens of families with transgender and gender-nonconforming children as they moved through their lives right at a moment when American culture changed dramatically in two ways: First, the internet offered broad access to both information on trans lives and connections to other families. And second, popular media began covering the lives of transgender youth with eager interest, bringing those stories into the minds and homes of people with absolutely no experiences with transgender people at all. These changes have produced predictable effects in the years that followed. Young people and their families have a rapidly expanding range of words to use to describe their experiences and identities. And adults who cling to the outdated notion that trans identities are undesirable, unethical, or pathological have more information to use in their efforts to restrict the freedoms of these youth and their families.

In the last few years, conservative politicians have proposed dozens of bills, in states across the country, limiting access to trans-related medical care, prohibiting participation in gendered sports, even banning the mention of transgender identities in elementary and middle schools. In 2021 alone, more than 100 anti-trans bills were introduced into state legislatures;[2] many of the most restrictive came from Texas,[3] where Katie and Noah were then living. "It felt very violent," Katie told me. Katie went to the state legislature to testify against the bill. As she walked back to her car, she passed hundreds of protesters lining the sidewalk. While many came to support trans youth and their families, what Katie remembers most were the anti-trans protesters. Many wore pro-life shirts or NRA pins. They screamed at Katie, calling her a child abuser, a genital mutilator. One of them stepped forward and spit on her. Katie teared up as she recounted the experience. "I hadn't ever experienced that . . . that physical presence of malice."

Noah wasn't with her that day. But the idea that he might have been shook Katie deeply. She said, "I just couldn't stop thinking, 'What if Noah had been there? What if he had been under attack like that?'" And then, she said, "It just occurred to me, like, he *is* under attack. This is the reality." Within a few months, Katie and Noah were living in a different state. Noah enrolled in a new school. They have needed to find a new community, new friends, new doctors and counselors. Noah's stepfather, father, and younger brother still live in Texas. The family is unsure when they will all live together again. It has been a financially devastating, emotionally draining, logistically impossible time for everyone.

What could be so important, so essential to someone's being, that it would be worth all this turmoil? In what follows, I'm going to introduce you to some kids and their families and show you what it really looks like to be a transgender youth in a "cisgender" (or gender-normative) world. Most transgender children have cisgender parents, who must themselves learn new lessons about gender to support their children. The time I spent watching parents struggle to understand their child's evolving identity taught me that gender is fundamentally relational, which is to say, it is something we feel subjectively, but we create it with, and in relation to, the people in our lives.[4] Transgender kids signaled their identities in all kinds of ways, from clothing choices to interests to ways of interacting with others. Parents struggled to make sense of those surprising behaviors, to disentangle them from concepts like sexuality, and to find supportive professionals and institutions. And even before the recent surge of violent anti-trans laws restricted medical care and social access for trans youth, states across the country regulated the lives of trans youth through administrators at Children's Services, in courts, and in institutions like schools.

Epiphany Day

Katie told me Noah had always been masculine. From the age of four or five, Noah insisted on dressing and being treated like a boy. But it took Katie and Noah's father many years to realize he was transgender. She told me that even as Noah asserted his identity to her in small ways, she didn't get it. She would tell him. "It's okay. You're just a tomboy. You don't like to be dressy, and that's okay." Coming to understand that he was trans took the family many years. This was not unusual.

Charlotte Lopez was a forty-nine-year-old white mother living in a small Midwestern town she described as "very conservative." She had been married to her husband, Damian, for twenty years. They had six children, all of whom were assigned male at birth. Charlotte's description of her very male-dominated household suggested it would be an ideal breeding ground for hegemonic masculinity. Yet, at the age of two and a half, her youngest child began asking for girl's toys. At first, Charlotte didn't pay much attention.

> I remember being in Wal-Mart and she asked me for her very first Barbie doll. And my first thought was, well, there's nothing wrong with playing with Barbie. In my opinion. However, I had better call my husband and ask him first because my husband is a Latino. He is extremely manly, and we have five very manly boys. They are all very athletic, very daredevil, very rough and tumble, very manly.

Damian told her he thought buying a Barbie doll was okay. At that point, neither parent considered occasional gender-deviant behavior to be any big deal. Indeed, many families with whom I spoke tolerated (and even ignored) a fairly substantial amount of transgressive behavior, before confronting the question of why it was happening and whether and how to respond. Over the next year or so, Ashley (who was nine and living full-time as a girl) began engaging in other forms of cross-gender play. Since Damian cut all the boys' hair into military-style fades, Ashley took to wrapping towels around her head, walking around in Charlotte's shoes, and periodically asserting to her parents and siblings that she was a girl. Charlotte recalled exchanging concerned glances with Damian from time to time, but said she mostly assumed this was a developmental phase.

While Damian and Charlotte felt comfortable giving Ashley space to explore these parts of herself, their surrounding community was not as supportive. At four and a half, Ashley, then still using a male name and pronouns, began attending a local Christian preschool affiliated with the family's church. At mid-year, Charlotte and Damian went into school to discuss Ashley's progress with her teacher, and they were informed that the pastor, school director, and teachers had

had a special administrative meeting in which they discussed Ashley and decided she would no longer be allowed to play in the dress-up corner of her classroom— her favorite activity. They had already been enforcing the rule for some time. Charlotte remembered Damian's entire body tensing up.

> My husband was horrified. He was so embarrassed. He was not angry that they had said that to our child. He was angry that it needed to be said. He was embarrassed. His manhood was threatened. He was being told that his son was a sissy and he did not like it.

This was a catalytic moment for the family. What previously felt to them like "no big deal," something Ashley would outgrow, became something disruptive that upset adults who played significant roles in her care and that called into question Ashley's ability to assimilate in her school environment. Charlotte and Damian realized they had a gender problem on their hands.

Many children engage in gender-atypical behaviors during childhood. For these children, those incidental behaviors coalesced into a pattern that was difficult to ignore. Whether because of emotional distress on their child's part, the disapproving glances of others, or simply because the wish to be differently gendered seemed too ardent, at a critical tipping point, parents concluded that they needed support to manage the negative assessments of others. Once they reached out, they came into contact with affirmative communities, with labels for what they saw happening at home, and with a marketplace of advice on how to reorient their parenting to fit this new reality.

When Charlotte and Damian left Ashley's school, they began to argue about whether her gender transgressions were a behavioral pattern that they could minimize through socialization. They began a process of trying to make meaning of the jumble of Ashley's desires, their beliefs, and the actions of the school administrators. Like many parents, Charlotte and Damian moved back and forth between attempts to prevent and facilitate Ashley's gender-nonconforming expression. Whereas before their encounter with the school, both parents tolerated and even participated in facilitating Ashley's cross-gender play, after the meeting, Damian became anxious and began displaying the regulating behaviors commonly associated with men. Instead of giving Ashley a hug, he'd pick her up and roughhouse. He invited her to play baseball. When she refused, he became angry. Charlotte sensed that his efforts were having an entirely different outcome than the one he intended.

> Obviously she didn't want to do any of the things that he was proposing. And the more she was reluctant, or refused, or the more she complained, the more he

pushed. And the angrier he got. And what ended up happening is she hated him. I don't mean she disliked him. I mean she hated him. Every fiber of her being displayed her hatred for him. She wanted nothing to do with him.

Around the same time, Charlotte and Ashley began having what she calls "secret girl time." They would get together and Ashley would ask Charlotte to call her girls' names, to tell her she was pretty, to help her dress up, and Charlotte would. But, Charlotte says, she felt deeply conflicted about doing so.

Parents decided in small daily interactions whether they had sons or daughters (or, on rare occasions, something else). They did this in language, in play, in the ways they touched their children, in the emotional closeness or distance they cultivated in the face of their child's behavior or distress. Jane Ward calls this "giving gender," the interpersonal, affective labor we undertake to assist others in shoring up their identities.[6] Charlotte made attempts to give Ashley the gender she wanted. Damian, at that point, was attempting to give Ashley the masculinity she lacked. They were in an ongoing process of negotiation, with Ashley and with one another. This was typical, as parents and children negotiated an interpersonal relationship in which the child's evolving gender was first recognized, then facilitated and reinforced. This was done through "calculated and intentional shifts" in interactional work,[7] re-naming, creation of fantasy narratives, and consumerism—including purchasing clothes and toys and decorating bedrooms. Charlotte said,

> I saw how much she enjoyed it and how happy it made her to hear those things. And how her behavior evolved. She was so confident when she was that person being told those things, which I was happy for her, but yet I was also quite honestly a little sick to my stomach because [this was] my son.

On what Charlotte called her "epiphany day," Ashley asked Charlotte for an advance on her allowance so that she could stop at a wishing well and wish to be a girl. Charlotte explained, "I felt like . . . here's a five-year-old who conjured up this wish that seems so far out there, but yet so poignantly real." She paused, then added, "This was something about *who she is*." Most parents recounted an epiphany day story, one in which they understood their child's gender not as behavior or convention, but as a core identity. That day was the catalytic event that convinced both Charlotte and Damian that Ashley saw herself and demanded to be understood as a girl. They reached out to a support group and began attending meetings.

Both Noah and Ashley, as young children, did and said things their parents struggled to understand. It took their families years to piece together that conflicts over clothes and toys, together with things their children said and did, indicated that each child had a core gender identity that differed from the one they were assigned at birth.

GENDER IS NOT SEXUALITY

The relationship between the two was often confusing, as gender deviance can be one of the primary signals of homosexuality to others.[8] Thus, a young child displaying atypical gender traits may, in fact, grow up to be either a gay or transgender adult.[9] For parents whose children asserted a strong gender prior to puberty, these distinctions seemed more crisp; for pubescent children, however, parents thought carefully about how to disaggregate the two.

Noah first came out to Katie as gay in the third grade. At the time, Katie said, imagining that Noah was a lesbian made sense. His masculine demeanor, friendships with boys, emerging attractions to girls, all cohered. But over the following five years, Katie began to feel that "lesbian" didn't quite explain Noah's experience.

Bess, a forty-six-year-old mother of two from a northeastern suburb, remembered thinking long and hard about how to understand her daughter's masculinity. Always a staunch tomboy, Benjamin, then an eighteen-year-old transboy, played with boys and favored Pokémon cards and hockey games over other forms of recreation. But he was solitary, often preferring to hang out alone in his room. Bess remembered vividly sitting on the family's sofa one day, when Ben was a preteen.

> I was sitting on the couch and going, "What is going on with this kid?" I don't think she's a lesbian. . . . She just wasn't like other kids. . . . I remember, as I was sitting on the couch, thinking, If I had to peg this child, I would say it's a gay boy, but that's ridiculous because this is a girl. That doesn't make sense.

Bess understood that Benjamin was masculine, but she couldn't comfortably situate him in any of the cultural categories she had at her disposal. He didn't seem gay. She said, in retrospect, he didn't seem entirely male, either. So, what was he? Was his behavior about gender or sexual identity? Were these the same thing, or were they different?

When I first met Rafe, I asked myself the very same question. I first met him at a conference for transgender teens, in the sitting area of a large hotel suite. He was dressed in skinny women's jeans, a tight tank top, scarf, and slouchy boots. When I entered the room, he was commanding the attention of a handful of kids, demonstrating dance moves from a recent Britney Spears video. His presentation of self was campy, hyperbolic, like something one might find among the gay men of musical theater. He held his body like a dancer, moved fluidly and expressively. His speech was loud and brash. I walked over and perched on the arm of a sofa. He immediately turned on his heel, put his hands on his hips, interrupted the conversation and firmly demanded, "And who are you?"

Rafe was asking me the very question that was so often, and by so many adults, directed at him. Rafe's parents, Claudia and Rick, told me they had assumed Rafe would grow up to be gay for much of his childhood. Like Ashley's family, at first they tried to socialize the feminine behaviors out of him. Rafe became increasingly withdrawn, taciturn, and volatile. It appeared, for a time, that they had been correct. In eighth grade, at the age of thirteen, Rafe came out to his mother as bisexual. But Claudia continued to struggle with a sense that something wasn't quite right. She remembered feeling uncertain about how Rafe's identity would mature, and conflicted about his feminine clothing choices and mannerisms. "This didn't feel like 'bisexual' to me," she told me, making scare quotes with her hands. Rafe claimed a sexual identity, but there was something in the tone of his struggles that Claudia felt to be distinctly about gender.

Part of the process of understanding a child to be transgender required parents to stake out a territory of gender that existed apart from sexuality. Because we often recognize gender nonconformity as a signal of homo- and bisexuality, and since people mark parts of their sexualities through the ways they present their gender,[10] parents had to determine that their child's gender transgression was, in some sense, "not sexuality."

CONSULTING THE EXPERTS

Once Katie, Claudia, Rick, Bess, and many other parents of teenage children understood that their children had gender-nonconforming identities, each reached out to experts for support. For transgender children who made full social transitions, "gender confirming" medical care was a common consideration. Parents researched the hormonal and surgical interventions from which they might choose when their child reached the appropriate age. For gender-nonconforming children, the approaches varied. Some would never undergo medical transitions, and that choice seemed straightforward. For others whose gender felt unclear or emergent, parents and physicians alike weighed the possible costs and benefits of different medical interventions, hoping to give those children the best chances for normative adulthoods. These decision-making processes reflected the fundamental role the body plays in social gender, even as gender identity becomes less contingent on the body.

Though Jade was only eight years old when I met her parents, David and Lynn, they planned to take her to a pediatric endocrinologist at the onset of puberty. Since Jade had already been living as a girl for several years, and felt comfortably situated and certain of her identity, putting Jade on puberty blockers didn't feel like a fraught decision. "It wouldn't make any sense to make her go through a painful male puberty, when we all know where this is going to end up," David said. "As a father, you want to place your child on the easiest path, the one that seems most in line with the self you see emerging. Jade is a girl. This is the way I treat her like one." David and Lynn understood medical transition to be a way to help Jade align her physical body with her psyche, to complete her process of gender transition. Making a medical transition would assist Jade in assimilating in a world that expects these things to be congruent.

I interviewed Patti on the night before Avery, then fourteen, was scheduled to receive his first injection of Lupron, a synthetic GNRH (or gonadotropin-releasing hormone) antagonist, one of a class of drugs used to suppress the body's production of sex hormones and pause pubertal development. Patti told me the recent few weeks had been the most difficult for her. She frequently compared Avery to other transgender children she knew. She described other children who said, often with confidence, that they absolutely *are* girls, that there was some sort of mistake when they were born with the bodies they have. Avery used different language. Patti felt Avery was less confident in general, and that came across in his more reserved, less forceful responses about gender. But it also left Patti feeling uncertain about whether to proceed with hormone blockers for him, or instead, to let him go through puberty just to "see what happens." Patti and Avery's doctor had a series of conversations about whether to put him on blockers and wait it out or do nothing and see how he felt as puberty changed his body. Avery's doctor reminded Patti that people can transition later in life, but Patti worried that life would be much more difficult. She said, "But then you look like a transsexual, you know? You have this body and everyone can just tell."

Patti and many other parents described a feeling of working against the clock, in conditions of great uncertainty, while trying to decide whether to forestall or try to help children manage their natal puberty. On one hand, they feared the unknown long-term consequences of hormone therapies; on the other, they had copious evidence suggesting that previous generations of transgender adults suffered mightily when their bodies and identities didn't match in the eyes of others. They weighed competing versions of normativity, the chance for a cisgender adulthood versus the promise of a passing transgender adulthood.

There was no way to opt out of this decision-making process. The giving of gender extends to the body, and puberty is decisive. As one activist parent I interviewed said, "not making a choice is still making a choice." Once parents decided to facilitate gender nonconformity in their children, be it through providing them with new clothing or toys, disclosing their new identity to family or caregivers, or seeking gender-confirming medical care, they opened their families up to social disapproval. This is particularly acute in parts of the United States, like Texas, where lawmakers are attempting to restrict access to gender-related medical care.

THE CHANGING CLIMATE FOR TRANS YOUTH

I met Jerri, a grandparent caring for her son Scott's four children, when Phoebe was six years old. Scott and Dina, Phoebe's mother, were both active in the U.S. military, and Jerri had custody of the children while they ironed out the details of their divorce. The previous year, Phoebe had started kindergarten, and Jerri had been determined to help her attend school as a girl. After repeated hostile encounters with school officials and teachers who demonstrated resistance to incorporating a transgender child into the school, it became clear that the fewer people who knew about Phoebe's boy history, the safer the school environment would be. Jerri understood that Phoebe's school records were likely the first thing her new teachers would encounter and felt that the message they conveyed about who Phoebe was would set the stage for the treatment that followed.

Convincing the school to change those records was an uphill battle. "It was like everything I asked for, this woman said no." Jerri sighs. "I asked if they could change her name just on the roll call list. No. I asked, can we keep her medical and private information separate from her academic record? No." Jerri knew that medical information was protected by federal law, yet she didn't know how she was going to convince the school and the district to honor the law. She knew that one mention of Phoebe's gender history was all it would take to thwart her efforts at secrecy. "Once the cat's out of the bag, you can't really put it back in." Administrative records certified who Phoebe was in the environment of the school. They marked expectations for how she would be viewed by others and the kind of treatment she would receive. They could protect Phoebe from discrimination by certifying her femaleness and masking information about her past, or they could render her acutely vulnerable by leaving the decision about how to gender her to individual teachers and administrators to make on an ad hoc basis. The school finally relented after Jerri hired an attorney and threatened a lawsuit. She told me that she walked away from the battle with the school having learned two things:

one was the power of legal representation, and the other was the importance of a coherent legal identity.

For that reason, at the time we met, she and Scott were battling Dina for the right to legally change Phoebe's name. Dina neither supported nor recognized Phoebe's female identity, and because of the discord between Scott and Dina, each of the many small parenting decisions that related to her gender involved extensive review by the team of experts required by the state to adjudicate disagreements over parenting. Each adult party (Dina, Scott, and Jerri) had their own legal counsel. The local family court appointed a guardian ad litem and an attorney to represent Phoebe as well. Jerri's attorney worked to construct arguments to convince each of these people that every step they took to support Phoebe in making a social gender transition was correct. It took Jerri over two years to legally change Phoebe's name and gender. She emailed me when it was all finished to express her delight, and to share photos taken at a family party celebrating Phoebe and her new legal identity.

Local institutions, schools, and medical professionals viewed legal gender as if it were simply a fact. Government identification with gender markers would set the terms by which Phoebe was viewed in the environments she inhabited and the expectations for treatment by teachers and administrators and would minimize the amount of information others would need to have about her transition. Phoebe's gender continued to be a site of some struggle within the family. But the family court system, in ordering the change to Phoebe's public records, made it possible for her to fully integrate into her community as a girl. Jerri and Scott made active use of the state to assist them in negotiating issues related to their child's gender with parents who rejected their child's trans identity. The modern era is characterized by ever-more-complete state monitoring of its citizens,[11] and part of the process involves the creative utilization, by individuals, of these regulatory powers. Some parents I met had found creative ways to use those systems to intervene in supportive ways to legislate the facilitation of a child's gender transition.

They were, however, in the minority. For the most part, parents went on the defensive once state agencies entered their lives.[12] Some parents faced administrative intrusions into their family lives by social services agencies, often because some adult in their community—a teacher, a doctor, even a neighbor— disapproved of their facilitative parenting and reported them to the police. These allegations often arose during moments when families tried to intervene in some institutional process, like changing school records, educating medical practitioners, and advocating for inclusion in religious contexts. Investigations, even when quickly resolved, were terrifying and disruptive to family life, leaving parents in a state of hypervigilance.

A Peculiar Vulnerability

As intersectional theorists have elaborated for decades, gender traffics in race. Claims to gender legitimacy are always already claims to racial legitimacy, and the lives of transpeople of color often look different than those of white transpeople. My families were no exception. Sean, a white single gay dad from a large West Coast city, adopted two black children from a foster-to-adoption program in his city. Michael was eleven at the time his state-appointed therapist suggested that Sean make an appointment at a university hospital to discuss puberty blockers. The day before their appointment with a pediatric endocrinologist, Sean, who was out of town, received a call that Children's Services had pulled Michael out of school to interview him about the appointment.

Sean knew that Michael had been removed from three previous foster homes after such interviews revealed actual evidence of abuse, so he hastily boarded a plane and spent the next twelve months fighting these spurious allegations. Sean's story was not unique. Families with children of color were far more likely to report that the state intervened in their efforts to facilitate their kids' transitioning. These interventions were the most violent in cases where families lacked financial resources to hire experienced attorneys or when one parent was gay or lesbian. As Sean succinctly put it, "I figured I'd have to protect him from bullies at school, not from doctors and social workers. It's a peculiar kind of vulnerability."

Most gender changes require the consent of a host of institutional actors. This kind of state regulation exists in both positive and negative forms. As C. Riley Snorton and Jin Haritaworn have written, most universalist depictions of coming out/transitioning, visibility and recognition practices fail to recognize the ways these depictions are yoked to forms of neoliberal legislation, gentrification, and policing practices that bear down most heavily on people of color. Race affects who is permitted to assert a trans identity and who is able to do so safely.

The state confers recognition, in the form of legal name changes and gender changes, antidiscrimination laws and protections, disability rights paradigms, which can be useful in schools. In this way, we can see gender as a resource distributed by the state.[13] On the other hand, the state also both regulates and punishes deviance. This happens through the formal regulation of Departments of Children's Services and reveals both the differential vulnerabilities of certain families to intrusion and the role of the state in moderating parenting practices and family disputes. Some families I met faced administrative inquiries initiated by the state into their parenting practices because someone, sometimes a mandated reporter like a doctor or teacher, sometimes a nosy neighbor, disapproved of their choice to allow their child to transgress gender norms and alerted children's services. Families with black children, those with a gay or lesbian parent, and adoptive or foster families with preexisting relationships characterized by state surveillance were the typical targets of such intrusions. On the other side, some families used the apparatus of the state to enforce the recognition of a child's reassigned gender. Those parents were typically white and educated The difference between the character of state intervention in these two cases illustrates both the centrality of institutional recognition in gendered life and the disparities in how that recognition is distributed.

When I did the research for *Trans Kids*, most families I encountered imagined that things were getting better and better for young gender-nonconforming people in the United States. I did hear stories of conflict, within families, with institutions like schools, and even with the state, but my participants mostly thought these would ultimately be the kind of tales we told in the past tense, remnants of a time when we fundamentally misunderstood transpeople and their lives. At a moment where states across the country are banning access to trans-related health care, prohibiting trans youth from participating in gender-segregated activities like sports, and even threatening criminal sanctions against doctors, psychologists, teachers, and parents for simply affirming trans identities, many parents I know, like Katie, are either living in daily fear or turning their lives upside down to move their children to safer ground.

NOTES

1. Meadow (2018).
2. Krishnakumar (2021).
3. Munce (2021).
4. West and Zimmerman (1987).
5. Kane (2006); Martin (2005); Rahilly (2015).
6. Ward (2010).
7. Whitley (2013).
8. Sedgwick (1991).
9. Drescher and Pula (2014).
10. Richardson (2007); Seidman (2002).
11. Foucault (1975).
12. Reich (2005).
13. Meadow (2010).

27

Beyond Sons and Daughters

Nonbinary Experiences with Family[1]

Emily Via, Daniela Guerrero Rodriguez, Ni'Shele Jackson, Barbara J. Risman, and William Scarborough

I remember my mom calling me a little girl. Even if that wasn't a part of my experience. I remember my parents just being like, you're a cute little girl, you know, like, kind of having that placed on me pretty early.

—Aster, 43, white

My parents would let me paint my toenails sometimes, because I would also paint my mom's nails. We would just sit around and I would do her nails. And but also my grandpa would let us paint his toenails (laughs). And so there's a lot of stuff like that, that was just kind of like, this is goofy and adorable and cute and like, we're just gonna let it happen. But I can't really think of any times when clothing that was highly gendered was supported in me wearing it. It was like if you put it on it was funny, but it wasn't . . . no one's rooting for me.

—Aiden, 27, white

From the moment we are born, and even before, gender plays a central role in our lives. Those around us gender us, place expectations on us based on that gender, and expect us to grow from young boys and girls into men and women. Even if this gendering is more covert, like Aster's (43, white) mother calling them a little girl, these expectations still influence us and our self-conceptions.

Though we are all influenced by gendered expectations as children, these expectations can uniquely affect those who reject gender categories of man or woman and who come to identify as nonbinary.

In the last decade, increasing numbers of people, especially young people, have rejected being categorized as women or men. They identify as nonbinary, or between gender categories, and sometimes use nongendered pronouns such as *they* instead of *he* or *she*. According to the Williams Institute, in 2021 around 1.2 million adults in the United States identified as nonbinary; most are under the age of twenty-nine. Pew Research Center similarly found that in 2022, around 5 percent of adults under thirty were trans and/or nonbinary. Given how long we have presumed that everyone in modern society was either a woman or a man, this is a major change for individuals and families. We know little about nonbinary people's relationships with their families of origin and extended kin. While *family* has many definitions, we use *family of origin* here to refer to those people we grow up around, whom we interact with as children and often remain emotionally intimate with long into adulthood. How have families changed now that gender no longer necessarily involves exclusively being a man or a woman, a husband or a wife, a son or a daughter?

To answer that question, we wonder, in particular, how do gendered expectations shape these relationships? Gendered expectations are not one-dimensional, and families enforce gender differently. Sometimes, these expectations are complex and contradicting, as they were for Aiden (27, white). Aiden was allowed to paint their nails and their grandfather's nails, and this family bonding was celebrated. However, other kinds of nonconforming behavior, while not met with outright hostility, wasn't celebrated or encouraged. We talked to nonbinary people to learn more: for many of our participants, these contradictions were common in their stories about growing up in their families.

We interviewed forty nonbinary young adults living in one Midwest city. We asked about three basic issues to learn about their family relationships. First, how do they remember their childhood socialization? Do they remember being coerced into femininity or masculinity? Or were their parents open to letting them explore all aspects of themselves? Second, how open are they with those in their immediate and extended family about being nonbinary? Has disclosing their identity negatively affected family relationships? And finally, how do they navigate their family relationships currently? What are the characteristics of families that are open and welcoming to nonbinary members? Alternatively, what are the characteristics of families that refuse to recognize their nonbinary members' identities and perhaps even stigmatize them?

There is no one pattern that describes how all nonbinary people relate to their families. These relationships are complicated, as are the processes of socialization within families and of navigating "outness." In this chapter, we review prior research and offer details about how we did our research. We focus on what we learned about nonbinary people and their families, their childhoods, their navigation of outness (or not) with their families, and the quality of their relationships with parents, siblings, and other family members. This leads us—and we hope you—to some thoughts about how having a nonbinary identity may reshape family life in the future.

LITERATURE REVIEW

Studies of Gender-Nonconforming Children and the Families

Despite the recent increase in the visibility of nonbinary people, there is little research on family relationships. That doesn't mean that there is no relevant research on closely aligned topics. Many nonbinary people also identify as transgender, and there have been two informative books about trans children in the last few years. Travers's *The Trans Generation* (2018) included interviews with trans kids and their parents. They report that trans kids' crises can often be traced to restrictive sex and gender norms enforced upon them by others even when their parents are supportive. In *Trans Kids: Being Gendered in the Twenty-First Century* (2018), Tey Meadow interviews parents, kids, and medical providers, and describes similar crises for transgender children (see Chapter 26). Both institutional and interpersonal environments threatened trans kids, and their families as parents had to make strategic negotiations about how their kids should or could present themselves as gendered based on potential retaliation. Not all, or even most, nonbinary people in our sample identified as such during childhood, but these studies shed light on the difficulties for those who do. In addition, most nonbinary people identify within the LGBTQ community, and so research on LGBTQ families is also informative. A growing literature on LGBT families is available, but much of it has focused on LGB children of non-LGBT parents or on two-parent cisgender lesbian and gay men couples (Few-Demo et al. 2016).

LGBTQ Youth Experiences

As LGBTQ acceptance rose, researchers established there is no correlation between same-sex parents and negative childhood outcomes (Knight et al. 2017; Manning, Fettro, and Lamidi 2014). LGBTQ youth continue to be at risk of more negative life outcomes compared with their heterosexual peers, especially when it comes to their psychological and emotional health. Researchers, therefore, have begun to study families as both a source of risk and a shield against negative outcomes. One study surveyed 53 parents and their GLB (gay, lesbian and bisexual) youth and found that parental approval of their children's identities was correlated with self-esteem and feelings of community acceptance (D'amico et al. 2015). Youth who had supportive parents were more likely to come out in other social situations and less likely to be suicidal. Youth whose parents were less approving tended to express more internalized homophobia. Causality can be tricky: the authors did *not* claim to be able to determine whether accepting parents influenced their children's experiences, or whether children who were more assertive prompted more accepting parents. Qualitative literature regarding LGBTQ+ youth's mental and health outcomes confirms that family of origin is repeatedly found to be an important factor in the life outcomes of LGBTQ+ youth (Wilson and Cariola 2020). As above, the causality between supportive families and positive mental health and social outcomes for children is not always clear. And keep in mind: these studies, and others, have tended to neglect young people outside of the gender binary—which is why we did our study.

Closets and Strategic Outness

Research on how nonbinary people navigate coming out to others is also limited (see Barbee and Schrock 2019 and Darwin 2017 for notable exceptions). Therefore, we turned again to related research about LGBTQ youth. Coming out is not a linear or singular phenomenon encapsulated by a singular moment (Guittar and Rayburn 2016; Brumbaugh-Johnson and Hull 2019). It can be broadly defined as the process by which LGBTQ people inform others of their status as LGBTQ. While popular TV and movies sometimes show coming out as a state that is achieved at once and forever after celebrated, decades of research have refuted coming out as such a singular linear experience (Coleman 1982; Gagné, Tewksbury, and McGaughey 1997). LGBTQ individuals tend to have a series of coming-out experiences, where they may strategically assess the safety of coming out, do so multiple times, to some people but not others, and in some settings but not others.

An important framework that helps with understanding the complexity of nonbinary experiences is Eve Sedgwick's *Epistemology of the Closet* (1990). Being out of the closet is generally understood as revealing one's sexual and gender identity. One can be in the closet in certain aspects of their life while out in others. Sedgwick critiques the symbolism of the closet as a consistent oppressive presence in the life of gay people. Sedgwick argues that the simple dualistic notion of being *in or out* of the closet fails to capture the complexities of queer life. Similarly, sociologist Jason Orne (2011) encourages a shift from thinking of coming out as identity development to identity *management*—or *strategic outness*. In Orne's research, gay participants talk about navigating their level of outness strategically, assessing different risks and benefits and the quality of their social relationships before disclosing their sexualities. Strategic outness is defined by managing and negotiating coming out differently in each social context.

Literature on LGBTQ experiences with family and the coming out research helped us create our questions about family life for nonbinary individuals. We pay special attention to how nonbinary individuals' families of origin shape their experiences with identity and overall well-being. Following the narrative lead of our respondents, we also examine how nonbinary individuals manage identity in a world that is often, but not always, normatively cisgendered, binary, and heterosexual.

METHODS

Our interviews were part of a larger three-city project. The forty interviews we share here were gathered by the authors and student researchers in a major metropolitan city in the Midwest. We imposed as few limitations as possible for inclusion. Anyone over the age of eighteen was eligible if they identified as nonbinary or any other identity that was between or outside of the gender binary. Flyers calling for participants were posted in LGBTQ public spaces and to social media groups designated solely for those who are nonbinary, and the call for participants was announced at meet-up groups for nonbinary folks. The people we interviewed were encouraged to share information about the research project with their social networks and refer others to the research team. We asked everyone for written consent. We took field notes about our experiences, and we provided compensation for participating in the interview. These in-depth, semi-structured interviews collected life histories and lasted one to two hours.

Whom did we talk to? Our recruiting methods gave us a diverse group of interview participants. Table 27.1 provides an overview of the forty nonbinary people we interviewed between 2019 and 2021 of varying ages, races, and levels of education. Most participants were twenty-five to thirty-four, with the youngest age twenty and the oldest age forty-three. The majority (thirty-four) of our sample were raised as girls, which means that we have less to say about the experiences of people who were raised as boys. This is a common pattern in studies like ours: other research about nonbinary people also reports samples primarily, but not exclusively, of people raised as girls (Hammack et al. 2022).

Once interviews were completed, the research team transcribed each interview, coded them, and tested for reliability across coders. Regular team meetings

Table 27.1 | Participant Demographics

Pseudonym	Age	Gender Socialized	Pronouns	Race	Social Class*
Aardvark Jackson	24	Girl	they/them and any	Black	Middle
Aiden Edwards	27	Boy	they/them	White	Upper-Middle
Alita Klein	33	Girl	she/her	White	Upper-Middle
Amethyst Smith	24	Girl	they/them	Black	Middle
Anzle	28	Girl	they/them	White	Middle
Aqua Farie	27	Girl	they/them/ theirs and fae/fem/ faers	Mixed	Middle
Ashley California	32	Girl	they/them and she/her	Mestiza	Working
Aster	43	Girl	they/them	White	Working
Betty Brickhouse	27	Girl	she/her and they/them	White	Upper-Middle
Black Table	34	Girl	they/them	White	Middle
Blue Music	21	Girl	they/them	White	Working
Camil Williams	24	Girl	she/they	White	Upper-Middle
Carol Fernandez	22	Girl	they/them	Multiracial	Middle
Crow Samsung	29	Girl	they/them	White	Middle
Ella	30	Girl	they/them	Asian	Working
Elle Silver	34	Girl	she/her and they/them	White	Working
GD	32	Girl	they/them	White	Upper-Middle
Georgia Argula	23	Girl	they/them and he/him	Black	Upper-Middle
J. Smith	24	Girl	they/them	White	Working
Jack Cassidy	22	Boy	they/them	White	Middle
Jay B.	26	Girl	they/them	Afro-Latin	Middle
Konny Reynolds	36	Boy	they/them	White	Upper-Middle
Lapis Lazuli	31	Girl	they/them	White	Working
Lilli Whitley	42	Girl	she/they	White	Working

continued

Luna Sol	27	Boy	they/them	Latinx	Working
Maru Mosca	20	Girl	name and they/them	Andean	Working
Matcha Green	34	Girl	they/them and she/her	Black	Working
Michael Alexander	35	Boy	they/them	White	Upper-Middle
Mx. Jones	27	Girl	xe/hir	White	Middle
Naveah	23	Girl	they/them	Black	Working
Ralphie James	39	Girl	they/them	White	Middle
Riv Boston	31	Girl	they/them	White	Upper-Middle
River	36	Boy	they/them	Black	Middle
Rose Red	23	Girl	they/them	Black	Middle
Shane	29	Girl	they/them	Black	Upper-Middle
Sherry Belmont	31	Girl	she/her	White	Middle
Sweeny Daniels	25	Girl	they/them and he/him	White	Working
Velmira	22	Girl	they/them	Black	Working
Violet Tam	31	Girl	they/them	Chinese	Upper-Middle
YR	26	Girl	they/them	Mestizo	Working

*Parent class inferred from parents' jobs.

were held where coding was discussed, and mutual agreement was reached on any questions that arose. All the names we use in this paper are pseudonyms chosen by the respondents.

GENDER SOCIALIZATION AND GENDERED EXPECTATIONS

Gender socialization is a never-ending process of learning how to behave according to societal expectations of one's gender. Beginning from birth and constantly reinforced through the course of life, gender socialization tells us not only how we should ourselves behave but also what sorts of behaviors and beliefs to expect from others. Gender socialization covers many aspects of life, including aesthetics (or style), behavior, work, and sexualities. While gendered socialization is a major influence on our lives, it is not deterministic. Individuals often reject socialized ways of being. In many instances, we accept some aspects of our socialization while rejecting others. Even so, socialization shapes our lives. This was revealed in our interviews with nonbinary participants, who reported that their parents—as do nearly all parents—covertly and overtly set gender expectations for them in a variety of ways.

Overt and Covert Gender Socialization

All participants reported generally being socialized as the gender they were assigned at birth. Participants being raised as girls reported restrictions on their clothing, their activities, the sex of acceptable partners, and their household responsibilities. These instances of gender socialization could be covert, such as it was for Aster (43, white), quoted at the opening of this chapter, who mentioned their mother gendering them as a little girl as early as they could remember.

Participants reported being aware of gendered expectations, like Black Table (34, white), who remembered their short hair being called a "bold" choice, which they felt was indicative of the expectation for people raised as girls to have long hair. Another respondent, Konny (36, white), recalled their parents laughing at their brother for wanting to be a "queen" when he grew up. Consequently, Konny internalized the lesson that boys should not aspire to fulfill feminine roles, even powerful ones such as a queen.

Other participants described having overt experiences of the gender expectations set for them, such as Maru (20, Andean):

> Like, there's this one time that my brother was hungry and made himself food. And [my grandmother] got mad at me because he made himself food. And she thought that I was the one who was supposed to cook for him.

For Maru, gendered expectations were not covert or expressed indirectly, but plainly stated. Being socialized as feminine or masculine happens in both *overt* and *covert* ways, as you will read in the next stories we share.

Being Socialized as Feminine

Many participants raised as girls (twenty-one out of thirty-four) told us that they were either pressured to dress in traditionally feminine ways or reprimanded for failing to do so, especially early in their childhoods. For example, Jay (26, Afro-Latin) told us, "I only wore like pants and hoodies. Even like, 100-degree weather because I just hated being like looked at, you know what I mean? And my mom hated it." However, some were able to adopt traits or styles traditionally conceived as masculine at least sometimes, and the term *tomboy* was mentioned by nine of the nonbinary people we interviewed that were socialized as girls. They identified with the description of being a tomboy, and others often identified them as such. Aardvark (24, Black), for example, said, "Yeah, I always identified as a tomboy first. I know tomboy isn't a gender. . . . But that's one title that I always vibed with." *Tomboy* is a generally accepted term to describe girls who do not embody normative femininity. The fact that more than a quarter of the respondents raised as girls identified with this term shows that gender socialization is understood through binaries, even when the traditional binary is subverted. Many of our participants challenged gender expectations in their childhoods but in ways that were viewed in conventional terms by those around them.

Another example of a participant who was raised as a girl but felt able to engage in traditionally masculine activities was Blue (21, white), who recounts,

> I wasn't one of those kids who, like, play with only one-gender toys, which . . . gave me a very big hint of mine when I found out [what nonbinary was]. I literally was one of those kids who, like, put on concerts for their adult and then crashed cars into everything.

Similarly, J. Smith (24, white) reported being encouraged to be handy and to build things with their dad, saying, "I was raised putting in this new sprinkler system in the backyard with my dad. That's what he was doing when I was three. That's what I did when I was three."

Still, many of our participants raised as girls remembered being expected to dress in normatively feminine ways. Notably, much of family gender socialization was focused on aesthetic and sexual expectations. The following two quotes show how our respondents remembered parents socializing them to behave and to present themselves in feminine ways. Ralphie (39, white) told us,

> Yeah, I mean, I think a lot of my appearance, they, my mom was very strict about. And I wasn't allowed to, you know, dress a certain way or look a certain way. I couldn't get my ears pierced for a very long time. So I never really had full control over a lot of my decisions, but certainly my appearance.

Sweeny (25, white) had a similar experience to Ralphie (39, white), emphasizing their parents' control over their fashion and aesthetics:

> I typically have a set fashion sense. But [my dad] would get really, really strict, or not strict, but really hard on my style. I'm not saying, you know, this was like, you know, Paris during Fashion Week or anything like that. I'm like, hoodie, jeans, and shoes. Like, that's my thing. Like *Wayne's World*–type fashion. Um, so it's just like I buy you all these clothes to express yourself, express your beauty. And you wear this all the time. I am like, this is what I am comfortable in.

Being Socialized as Masculine

A common pattern among the six participants socialized as boys was a constant pressure to perform normative masculinity. Socialization was remembered as even more oppressive by the respondents raised as boys. Aiden (27, white) explained at the chapter's opening how they were permitted to explore femininity only when that femininity was part of a joke, but not if the expression was in earnest. Aiden also reported being bullied for being "effeminate." They explained how they were only allowed to paint their grandpa's toenails in the context of it being abnormal and "goofy." It was framed as young childhood play—a not-very-subtle message that feminine behavior among boys was not allowed and was even ridiculous.

The pressure to *enforce* normative masculinity was experienced by participants socialized as boys—even when they did not have particularly oppressive parents. While Jack Cassidy (22, white) reported that their parents were "less concerned" with enforcing their ideas of masculinity on Jack, they still felt compelled to police others' masculinity when they were younger:

> Well, I'm sitting here with a manicure I got last week and I'm a male-bodied individual. But like, also, I don't know, I've been guilty of enforcing masculinity as well. Like, yeah, because, you know, there was one time when my little cousin came over with his toenails painted red. And I was like, well, what are you doing? And they were just like, he just wanted to?
>
> Interviewer: How long ago was that?
>
> Jack: Oh, I was maybe twelve. And I thought it was weird. Because I had masculinity forced down my throat for twelve years.

Jack remembers reactively questioning their cousin's choice to wear nail polish. Even though Jack's parents hadn't enforced gender expectations, Jack (22, white) had learned that boys are not supposed to wear nail polish and had chastised their younger cousin. This illustrates how gender expectations and stereotypes come from multiple sources, including schools, the media, or extended family.

Gender Revolution Continues?

In a promising sign for the gender revolution, nearly half of our sample (nineteen out of forty participants) reported not feeling rigid gender expectations from their parents. YR (26, Mestizo) reflected on how their parents were different from many other Mexican families:

> I feel like I'm grateful to say that my parents, in terms of, like, our cultural background, because I think a lot of Mexican families have a lot of these strict, like, rules

around what girls in the families can do. And I didn't grow up with any of that. I have friends who would be like, "Oh, yeah, they won't let me wear this or they won't let me go outside. And I have to be home at a certain time" And these are adults.

YR was grateful that, unlike their friends raised in a similar culture, YR's parents didn't enforce many rules around certain gender expectations.

Those who were socialized with less rigid expectations often mentioned how their parents' expectations were less about the quality of their gender conformity and more about character traits, such as working hard or being responsible. At least nineteen of our forty participants reported feeling as though their families emphasized developing a strong character and values, with less explicit gender rules. Some reported even being encouraged to defy established gender norms. For example, when asked if their parents were feminists interested in nongendered child-rearing, J. Smith (24, white) replied, "I don't think it was specifically intentional so much as . . . raise a kid to be a strong independent person."

Other respondents reported that their parents treated them as boys or girls but didn't enforce gendered expectations rigidly. For example, when asked when they realized they were being socialized as a boy, Jack Cassidy (22, white) responded,

> I wouldn't say I necessarily got it from home. Because like, while I was raised as a boy, like, my parents were less concerned with like, be a man and more concerned with like, be a decent human being. . . . My parents didn't really, like enforce gender on me. They just sort of were like, all right, well, you know, they treated me as a boy, but like, they didn't insist that I perform, you know, classical masculinity all the time.

River (36, Black) communicated that their parents were more focused on River becoming self-sufficient, saying, "Other than making money, that was it. Yeah, like that was their only main goal, I think was to make sure I can support myself financially." Jack and River remembered their parents felt it was more important to pass down traits such as responsibility and independence rather than be strict enforcers of gendered expectations. And yet, even when participants reported not being subjected to rigid gender expectations, normative gendered expectations arose. Sweeny (25, white) explained,

> I learned how to take care of myself. I learned how to cook like through a microwave. . . . With my mom, I learned how to take care of others. With my dad, I learned how to take care of myself. So it's, like, completely two different ends of the spectrum. . . . If anything, from the two of them combined, I learned how to take care of both. If that makes sense.

While Sweeny reported growing up in an environment without strict gender expectations, their parents modeled distinct gendered differences in the skills needed to be a responsible and caring human being.

How Race and Class Affect Gender Socialization

Class mattered. Respondents whose parents were working class (fifteen people) and middle class (fourteen people) reported less rigid gender socialization experiences than more upper-middle-class participants. Half of the working- and middle-class participants' parents were not stringent enforcers of gendered expectations and norms. However, those with multiple siblings in financially vulnerable households sometimes reported their parents relied on them to take care of their siblings. We heard from respondents from working-class families that parents prioritized safety, care for their siblings, and financial stability over the more intricate or aesthetically focused details of gendered socialization. That is, even if they took on "feminine" responsibilities like housework and child care, our participants often thought this was more about supporting their household than gendered socialization. For example, Matcha (34, Black) explained their life situation and didn't even mention gender expectations in the following memories:

> I felt like I was a co-parent in a lot of ways. Up until the time when I was 16, and I moved out to go live with my father. He bought a house, and he had a house for a while. And my mother just pushed me to my limit. So, I went to live with my father. And then we just lived as roommates. Because at that point, you know, I've been a co-parent for so long or whatever and doing all that, it wasn't hard for him to just be like, "Oh, hey, you need to have the dishes washed before, before the end of the night." Or "Hey, need to make sure you like do such and such." It wasn't like him looking at my homework or anything like that. Like for the next, however long I was there, it was just like, "Hey, I'm be late today" or "Hey, I'm gonna work in a double shift. So I'll see you in the morning" or whatever. Like we were just roommates basically.

While parents may not be remembered as strictly enforcing gendered norms, they did apply gendered standards when assigning tasks. Children being raised as girls were often designated to undertake child care. Ralphie (39, white), who was raised as a girl, stated, "I was given a lot more responsibility. . . . Yeah, I was seen as kind of the older child, though I was the middle one." Ralphie was made the lead caretaker of their siblings, even though they had an older brother. None of the people raised as boys in our sample reported being asked to act as caregivers for their siblings.

Our respondents often told us stories about how their gender socialization was intertwined with their racial socialization. River (36, Black), who was raised as a boy and whose parents were generally relaxed about gendered expectations, reported that their parents did not allow them to play hockey, not because they associated the sport with any one gender, but because "they say Black people don't play hockey, which is false." Velmira (22, Black) reflected on the expectations around gender for Black women and the complicated relationship among race, skin color, and gender, saying, "I know that I feel outside of my gender. But is that because I feel outside of my gender? Or is that because Black women are not allowed to be perceived as feminine, especially dark-skinned ones?" Another participant, Naveah (23, Black), had trouble answering some questions and interjected, "These questions are so weird because they're, like, asking me questions about gender in a way that is separate from my race." And when asked to elaborate, they mentioned how the degree of femininity they felt they were achieving in society was based on expectations of whiteness:

> My clothes are masc-ish, or not like, feminine. Like maybe my hair changes to, like, have balance . . . but changing my hair in a lot of ways is about, like, depending on where I'm going, or what I'm doing is about meeting standards of femininity that are set by white women.

Naveah echoed a sentiment expressed by Velmira: that standards of femininity were related to whiteness, and that their Blackness put them at odds with these standards of femininity. Both participants described their experience of gender as entangled with their racialization.

White participants often had less to say about their own racialization as children or within their families, though a few did remark on gender and whiteness. Riv (31, white), for example, described how their mother's focus on appearances through sending Christmas cards was specific to her being a white woman:

> My mom has every year a Christmas card called a brag letter where she'll put pictures of us and then brag about all the things that we did over the course of the year to prove how much better we are than our cousins and other people that she knows. . . . Apparently, a lot of white ladies do this.

Camil (24, white) similarly talked about their sister as being different from them, describing her as "a much more conventional femme kind of dresser, like just imagine like a straight white woman." Though Camil is also white, they seemed to view their sister's femininity as specifically a white femininity and acknowledged that proper femininity is often linked to whiteness.

More often, white participants recognized their white privilege in terms of interactions with police or other authority figures growing up. Some made general statements about how gender is tied to institutional racism. For example, Aster (43, white) reflected on gender as a whole when they said, "I just think gender is a construct that was created by patriarchy, and like white supremacy, to subjugate people, and I don't think it's necessary. I think that we could live without it." Though participants of color usually were more cognizant of race in their upbringing, many of our participants overall were aware of the intersections between race and gender.

Unequal Gender Enforcement between Parents

Participants also described how their fathers and mothers often held different gender expectations. Sometimes a participant's father would be a strict enforcer of gender in opposition to the mother. This was the case for Mx. Jones (27, white)

> My dad didn't have any like specific lessons in mind as much as he wanted us to be like well-behaved little girls. . . . Not like fully functional adults, but like scared little girls who will do what people tell them to do. And my mom wanted us to, like, speak up for ourselves and be strong and independent.

Maru (20, Andean) also reported feeling less traditional gender expectations from their mother, stating, "I always lived with [my mom], and I just like always kind of felt safe and like discovering myself." They said that their dad was "a different question."

There were no instances in our interviews where the mother was a strict enforcer of traditional gender expectations while a father outrightly opposed them, though sometimes mothers were less strict than fathers or neither parent enforced strict expectations. While both mothers and fathers expressed a range of beliefs about gender norms, fathers tended to be less involved in child care and therefore gender socialization overall. This, too, taught children about gender: that women are meant to be nurturers.

Even in cases where both parents were committed to feminist principles of raising children without gender constraints, participants would sometimes emphasize one parent's involvement over the other. Michael (35, white) had an unusual case of both parents being involved and being generally progressive. While Michael's parents both "made a really rigorous point of kind of treating everyone equally," Michael emphasized that this egalitarian attitude was especially prevalent from their "dad's side." It was uncommon for both parents to have the same expectations for gender socialization, which may reflect a broader pattern of the division of labor and an imbalance in parenting responsibilities in families. For Aster (43, white), both parents were supportive of Aster's gender-nonconforming behavior during their childhood. He explained, "My parents are really awesome. I'm very, very lucky to be a queer trans person with parents who loved me and have always supported me." Still, much of the support that Aster described involved their mother. For example, Aster recounted the time when their mother supported them in buying boxers in the men's department even though they were being raised as a girl. When asked about their dad, they replied, "He just wasn't involved in that." While both parents may have been a part of creating either a progressive or conservative gender environment, the degree of direct involvement in child-rearing varied, with mothers often the more involved parent. This was true for most American families at the time these adults were raised—and that continues to be the case today.

We interviewed two people whose parents did not adhere to traditional gender expectations. Aiden (27, white) reminisces that their parents "really didn't stick to the exact, like, compartmentalized gender roles of a man and woman who are married and have a kid." Aiden reported that their mother handled finances and was "head of the household," while their father cooked all their meals, modeling an alternative to dominant gendered expectations. Aiden's own gender socialization experience therefore was complicated: "So like, that was another interesting kind of like flip reversal of what you'd expect in the standard, you know, whatever the standard cross section of an American family is that's, we kind of fit it but then also had our little aberrations." Konny (36, white) also told us, "My mom teaches carpentry. . . . I do not have a strong sense of like dressing behaviors like indicating one gender or another."

Gender socialization in families tended to be complex. Participants all experienced gendered expectations. But those raised as girls were more likely to be allowed to express themselves in traditionally masculine ways. While nearly half our participants reported having parents who did not strictly police their gender, the other half reported childhoods filled with rigid gender expectations. Furthermore, even participants whose parents held progressive attitudes toward gender socialization still often experienced instances where they were expected to dress or behave in a way that aligned with their assigned gender at birth. Finally, whether parents policed gender strictly, many still embodied traditional gendered family roles. No matter their ideology, parents' normatively gendered practices were often models for their children.

Navigating Strategic Outness

Nonbinary folks have diverse experiences with sharing their identity across social contexts. Many come out strategically, over and over again, as they move between groups. Our participants reported weighing the benefits of coming out to family members against concerns for their safety and comfort. Many decided to disclose being nonbinary only to specific family members, in specific times and places. Consistent with how LGBTQ people come out, our respondents came out in an ongoing process. For example, Riv (31, white) talked about how they came out as bisexual a few times and then later came out again as nonbinary:

> The first time I came out, I was in high school, and I came out as bi. And that is kind of still, I identify as like bi pansexual queer, like, you know, umbrella term. I like many different people with many different sexualities and gender. But I came out that way in high school and the first time I did it my mom thought I was like kidding, like joking. . . . So then I had to come out to her a second time and be like, No, I'm not joking. And like, here's what's going on. So like, that was its whole thing. And then I visited from college, I think I was in my junior year of college. When I told them, specifically my mom, that I was nonbinary, and to use they/them pronouns for me, and that didn't go well. She's, like, what do you mean? Like you're an alien? Like, you're an it? Like, you don't have a sex or gender? What does that mean?

Amethyst (24, Black) acknowledged that outness is not just a personal decision, but one with "politics" involved:

> I didn't think I would come out to my mom. But she seemed understanding. I have changed my approach. I didn't think I was going to come out at college, or—what is this—post-grad or grad school, but I did, because I saw other people were out. So yeah, just trying to be more out. I was gonna say more brave. But I don't think being out is the same as being brave. Because I think that there's so much politics around outness. And I think it's less about braveness and more about if I want you to know me intimately or not.

For Riv (31, white), Amethyst (24, Black), and most participants, their decision to come out was based on both safety and comfort level with others. When asked if they were out to their sibling and mother, Blue (21, white) responded, "I'm not out and about. Basically, it didn't go well for them [a friend]. So I was like, Nope, not doing this."

These experiences of navigating outness are a good example of Orne's concept of "strategic outness," discussed earlier in the context of sexual identity. As with LGBTQIA+ people's discussion of sexual identities, our respondents were constantly negotiating to whom—and when—to disclose their gender identities. Nonbinary people *strategically* choose to "come out" to family, often slowly, and to different family members in different ways. Culture, language, and religion also play a role in if, how, and when nonbinary people come out to their families.

Family Reactions to Coming Out

Participants reported a variety of reactions when coming out to family members, both close and distant relatives. Eleven participants had at least one positive reaction from a family member when coming out and thirteen had at least one negative reaction. The most common reaction—for more than half—was ambivalence. These reactions were not all negative or all positive. Rather, parents struggled to use new names and pronouns for their children. Mainly, these parents were poised to eventually accept their child's new identity. Other parents shrugged off their child's coming out without much emotion either positively or negatively.

Negative reactions to their disclosure put stress on some participants, as they did for Rose (23, Black):

> My parents just didn't, neither one of our parents [Rose's parents and the parents of Rose's first girlfriend] just handled it well at all. They both were very verbally abusive. My parents were physically abusive when they found out. Yeah, they just did not handle it well, and it definitely, I think, made both of us hide who we are . . . for a very long time, which is obviously not good.

Some participants were hesitant to come out to family members because they anticipated negative reactions. Rose (23, Black) is not out to all family members in part because of their parents' and brother's negative reactions:

> I know my family are gonna have their issues. I actually came out to my brother. He didn't talk to me for about a month, and then when he reached out, it was no acknowledgment.

When parents reacted harshly, that clearly affected the relationship with our respondents. It was common for participants who received negative reactions from family members to have strained relationships with family for a long time.

Some participants reported positive reactions. In these cases, participants reported feeling safe and seen, which led to closer family relationships. When asked what the positive aspects of living at home with their mom are, Maru (20, Andean) stated,

> That she's welcoming, and . . . that she's, like, very open-minded to my identity and is very accepting. When I was younger, I never, I never felt scared of being queer. Like because of my mom. . . . I always lived with her, and I just always kind of felt safe in, like, discovering myself

The acceptance of new pronouns and sometimes new names was a critical aspect of the coming-out experience. Whether parents and other family members accepted their new identity influenced whether participants remained on good terms with their families. For example, Sweeny (25, white) wasn't too worried about their family using their new pronouns:

> I'm gonna be me no matter what you call me. . . . My family hasn't really gotten (laughs) they/them/their down. I don't think they're going to be okay with him/ he. Or his, whatever. So it's just, it's kind of like that radical acceptance. . . . I get that [I'll] always be a "she" or your granddaughter, your daughter, or your sister, or whatnot. But just know that I may not always look it.

Most participants received ambiguous or unclear reactions. On these occasions, family members were not clear about their support, or parents were confused and ignorant about what nonbinary meant without espousing negativity. Elle (34, white) described their father's reaction: "My dad's a little bit . . . I just don't think he understands. Like I don't think he grasps the concept." Other times some family members were supportive while others were not. Sometimes relatives' reactions changed over time. Lilli (42, white) noted that while their dad was supportive of their being in a queer relationship, their stepmother was less so:

> My parents were very, very supportive. My dad was really sweet. He was basically, just like, "We're glad you're happy. She's really nice." My stepmom . . . she's a little bit of a loose cannon. My stepmom was like, I just hope you're not gonna be one of those butch lesbians, and I was like, well, I'm gonna continue to be what you see right now. So if this is too butch for you . . . fuck off (laughs). Like, I'm not going to change. I am already what I am. But that was a long time ago.

Language, Culture, and Religion

Participants reported that a factor that influenced their coming-out decision and process was language. The existence of terminology that facilitates the description of one's identity became important when choosing to whom to come out and

how. This factor was particularly relevant to the experiences of Latinx participants, who claimed a lack of nonbinary terminology in Spanish-speaking environments. As an example, when asked about their coming-out process, Ashley
(32, Mestiza) stated,

> I think it is harder because my mom is from Mexico. She only speaks Spanish,
> and we don't really have a nonbinary word. I don't think that she would be able to
> understand. I mean if, in the future, there is a word that can describe it correctly,
> I would share this with her. But I don't think that this will happen anytime soon.

Luna (27, Latinx) expressed similar feelings about coming out to their immediate
family, citing language as a barrier:

> I haven't told my immediate family, like blood family, about it. And I don't know
> how they'd react in that way. I haven't told them. Maybe if . . . if I find the language
> in Spanish to do so. But I just know if I explain it to them in English, they won't
> understand. So maybe if I can, like, be confident in who I am as a person to be
> able to find the language needed to be able to clearly explain it to them in Spanish.
> Maybe, but I don't foresee that for, like, at least another five years.

Religion also played a role in the negative reactions some participants faced from
their families when coming out as nonbinary. Luna was outed as gay after their
parents discovered them watching gay pornography as a teenager. They were
subjected to conversion therapy, and Luna made clear connections between their
parents' religiosity and their negative reaction to Luna's queerness:

> I came out and like she [my mom] went straight to the pastor, and . . . my pastor told
> me she needs to talk to me. And that she can do therapy when she wasn't licensed
> to be a therapist. So I had to meet with her every week. And I was basically, it was
> just a lot of repetitive Bible verse writing for homework and then talking and then
> she would like, give me a sermon. . . . She always referred to where in the Bible it
> claims that homosexuality was a sin or whatever.

Georgia (23, Black) also had religious parents who reacted negatively to their
coming out as nonbinary. They described the conversations they must now navigate with their father where he pulls on religious doctrine to negate their nonbinary identity:

> Before I left for my trip, my dad, I told him that I am nonbinary. . . . He is, like,
> always quoting Genesis something about, like, in the beginning, God created men

and women. So it's just it's a binary shit. And so I'm, like, well, there's a difference between sex and gender, and also, like, sex isn't binary as well.

Overall, nonbinary people strategically negotiate outness many times and in many different contexts throughout their lives. Rather than one single instance of coming out, participants often found themselves self-disclosing different identities to their families as those identities evolved over time. Parents of nonbinary people in our sample had a variety of reactions to their children coming out as nonbinary. Most often, parents were either ambivalent or expressed mixed feelings. Culture, language, and religion influenced how family members reacted and also shaped participants' willingness to come out as nonbinary to their family members.

THE QUALITY OF FAMILY RELATIONSHIPS

Our participants reported more negative relationships with parents than with siblings. Overall, twenty-six participants (two-thirds) described their relationship with at least one of their parents as negative, and fourteen (one-third) described their relationship with at least one of their parents as positive. About half the participants had positive relationships with at least one of their siblings; the other half had negative relationships with at least one sibling. While there were a variety of stressors on these relationships, respondents often cited their gender identity as an issue. Some participants noted that their families attempted to support them but had trouble, while others described more blatant animosity. Religion was sometimes, although not usually, cited as a source of stress and animosity in their relationships. Still, some parents and siblings were very supportive of their nonbinary child or sibling, and participants with queer siblings noted especially positive and supportive sibling relationships.

Parental Relationships

Participants in our sample often described their relationships with their parents as both positive and negative. While many of our participants described strained relationships with their parents, not all the problems were connected to gender or queerness. Sometimes participants acknowledged that their parents accepted their nonbinary or queer identities but were unkind, manipulative, or abusive in other ways. Nonbinary participants' relationships with their parents are complex, just as all parent-child relationships are.

For many of our participants, identifying as nonbinary often added a source of stress in their relationships with their parents. Such stress ranged from a lack of understanding to blatant stigma and rejection. Elle (34, white) explained that their dad still called them his daughter, and this bothers them because they "don't think he quite understands." Camil (24, white) feels similarly about their parents:

> They're not like, you know, they're not like super xenophobic or like super conservative or anything like that. But they have had some moments of . . . ignorance and queerphobia in their own ways. Like they don't understand nonbinary pronouns, even though I use them.

In both these instances, nonbinary respondents told us that their parents weren't being malicious; they were just ignorant. In these cases, they still maintained relationships with their parents.

Participants often had to pick their battles when it came to their parents, including deciding what level of contact to continue and what concessions each side could make. Some resigned themselves to tentative relationships with their parents without broaching issues of queerness, because they knew it would be a losing battle. For example, Sweeny (25, white) said of their mom,

> No, she hasn't really accepted. And it's not something I really talked about with her. And it's kind of why I just accepted, like, people are going to call me whatever they want to call me. Like, I can't force them. And I don't feel like going into this huge class of teaching them and, like, this is why I want to be called this.

Others were more defensive in the face of their parents' lack of acceptance. For instance, Riv (31, white) decided not to disclose anything about their gender and transition to their parents, anticipating their negative reactions:

> They don't know I've had top surgery. They don't know I've had a hysterectomy. Like they don't know I legally changed my name in 2017. Like, they don't know any of that. Because honestly, they don't deserve it. Like, you will use it as a weapon against me. So you don't deserve it.

Over a third of our participants had either ended all communication with one or both of their parents or maintained the relationship with little contact. Some people had little contact with their parents for other reasons, such as abuse or manipulation. For example, Velmira (22, Black) said they had an abusive mother, an abusive grandmother, and a father complicit with their abuse, so they had to cut off ties with their family. The abuse wasn't overtly related to queerness. In fact, Velmira reported that their parents had no negative reactions to their coming out.

Five participants experienced negative relationships with their parents because of traditional religious beliefs. For example, Ella (30, Asian) explained that their parents "were very anti-sex because of the [Christian] upbringing that they had." Riv (31, white) noted that their mother was constantly joining cults throughout their childhood, and River (36, Black) cited their mother's "God-fearing" personality as a reason why she would not be "emotionally mature" enough to handle their coming out. Georgia (23, Black) and Luna (27, Latinx) had the most to say about their parents' religiosity. Georgia said,

> My parents have basically no boundaries between the congregation and us. These are intertwined with each other. And so, like, if I were to leave my congregation, my parents would stop talking to me. Or, like, they would definitely probably start communicating with me less and would be, like, well, if you're not in this congregation, like, what exactly are you doing? . . . And I don't even mention transphobia, like, just how they dispose of people who don't follow God as they want them to.

Luna's case was perhaps most extreme. After their parents found out they had been watching gay pornography as a teenager, they enlisted the help of their congregation to put Luna into conversion therapy. Luna said of the experience,

> They made me do conversion therapy with a pastor. And again, no privacy, like the entire church congregation knew my personal business. And they were praying for me, putting me at the very front of the congregation and doing all that. . . . My social workers affirmed that it was not the best environment for me anymore, because it was beginning to really take a toll on me. So I was looking at paperwork to start my emancipation process.

While not typical, Luna's parents' reactions to Luna's teenage identity as gay illustrate the most extreme lengths to which religiosity affected parental relationships. While Luna still kept up relationships with their parents, this was true only long after having left their parents' home.

While half of our respondents told a positive story overall, five participants described little gender- and sexuality-related strain at all in their relationships with their parents. Their parents were supportive of their gender and the decisions they made related to gender. Crow (29, white) described how their mother was supportive of their haircut:

> My mother actually wrote this long Facebook post about [cutting my hair], how it was symbolic of me taking control of my own life and the fact that it was on my bucket list for years and I finally decided to do it and how [it] was emblematic of

the fact that I wanted to die without regrets. She cried. She thought it was beautiful. She was like, Go, honey, I love you. Like she was great.

While not the norm for participants, some parents were outwardly accepting of their children's queerness.

Sibling Relationships

Overall, thirty-four participants had siblings, while six were only children. Over half of those with siblings (nineteen) had a positive relationship with at least one of their siblings, and about the same number had a negative relationship with at least one of their siblings. Like parental relationships, sibling relationships turned negative for a variety of reasons beyond gender acceptance. For example, Ashley (32, Mestiza) cites an age difference between them and their sibling as a source of strain in their relationship. Sherry (31, white) says their sister is estranged, but then clarifies that she is "estranged kind of from everybody." However, gender and queerness were sources of strain for others. GD (32, white) had cut off all contact with their biological family. They explained that their parents and siblings refused to respect their gender:

> Basically, I've been trying to get away since I was much younger, hoping, you know, whatever, you know, I got away and for a while trying to have a relationship still with my parents, try to kind of tell them about who I actually am instead of who I was pretending to be, you know, growing up. And you know, it didn't go well. . . . They don't respect my boundaries, and they don't—I mean, there was a lot of drama growing up also. . . . Most of my siblings are, you know, like my parents.

Riv (31, white) didn't like one of their sisters and said the feeling was mutual, because "she's got a husband and a job and is successful in this hetero patriarchy." Riv similarly disliked their brother, who is a heterosexual police officer. Riv's dislike of their siblings is not necessarily due to their sexuality; rather, it's because Riv sees them as supportive of oppressive structures like the patriarchy and heteronormativity. River (36, Black) explained, "I'm not coming out to [my family] because I want to enjoy my transition and coming out and doing all this fun stuff. So they're very close minded. A bit judgmental."

In general, participants had more positive relationships with their siblings than they did with their parents. Sometimes, this was despite the negative relationships participants had with their parents. For example, Luna (27, Latinx), whose parents forced them into conversion therapy, had a good relationship with their younger sister, explaining that she "really likes makeup and I do drag so

I like give her tips without my mom knowing and, like, pretending that I'm a makeup artist professionally, so . . . she, like, bonds with me over that." Though Riv (31, white) hardly communicated with their parents and described most of their family as bigoted, including some of their siblings, they still maintained a strong relationship with their youngest sibling, who is also queer.

Three participants had queer siblings with whom they had quite positive relationships. Lilli's (42, white) youngest sibling is queer, and because of a wide age gap, they serve as a source of support for them. Crow explained that they're "out as everything to my adoptive brother, but you know, he's gay as shit. So he's not gonna judge me." Riv (31, white) said of their nonbinary youngest sibling,

> We're both queer. We get along. We respect each other's pronouns. They want to get the hell out of there, which is fair. They still live with my parents in Nebraska. And they're, like, rattling the cage door. They're like, "Let me out."

Participants with queer siblings overall spoke fondly of their queer siblings and either saw themselves as a source of support for their sibling or saw their queer sibling as a source of support, especially if their parents were not accepting of their gender.

Participants had complex relationships with their families of origin, often describing some aspects as positive and some aspects as negative. Though gender was a source of strain for many, participants cited other reasons for strained relationships as well, like manipulation and abuse. In general, participants had more positive relationships with their siblings than with their parents, and had more supportive relationships with siblings, especially queer ones. Families' conservative religious beliefs were a source of stress for a few participants, and sometimes those beliefs even led to abusive behaviors such as being forced into conversion therapy.

CONCLUSION

Nonbinary people have complex relationships with their families, as do we all. However, nonbinary gender identity can often be a source of added stress in relationships. While some participants reported their parents held rigid traditional gender beliefs, many participants reported their family did not have rigid gender expectations for them growing up. Still, even parents who tried not to impose gender stereotypes on their children often modeled gendered behavior in their own lives. But not all; other participants told us that their parents broke typical gender norms. Our respondents' gender socialization experiences overall seem similar to others in the millennial generation, to which most respondents belonged (see Risman's *Where the Millennials Will Take Us* [2018] for more on gender socialization among millennials).

Eventually, however, our respondents began to identify as nonbinary. The coming-out process for our participants was just that—an ongoing process. Though participants could point to some distinct moments when they had come out or were outed, many found themselves coming out to family multiple times as their understanding of their gender and sexuality developed over time. Participants based the strategic outness (Orne 2011) on a variety of complex social factors. Our findings about nonbinary people's coming-out experiences mirror previous findings about other LGBTQ groups, though our participants faced unique difficulties with coming out: the language they have for describing their identities is new, and it is changing.

Our nonbinary participants expressed both positive and negative aspects of their relationships with parents and siblings. Participants negotiated the boundaries of these relationships carefully, being strategic about their contact and levels of outness with family. Parental relationships were more strained for all. Sibling relationships were more positive, especially when participants had queer siblings whom they supported or who supported them.

Our findings suggest a shifting consciousness about gender among parents. Though we did not interview parents about the expectations they had for their kids, we noticed that participants' recollections of their socialization experiences included many parents who did not strictly enforce gendered expectations. Combined with findings about the parents of trans kids (Meadow 2018; Travers 2018), this may indicate a shift in how at least some parents deal with gender and child-rearing.

As our nonbinary participants demonstrated, their relationships with families varied. Family relationships can be a source of support as well as a challenge for nonbinary people. Future researchers will, we hope, interview parents of nonbinary people to understand their perspectives on raising nonbinary kids. We also hope future researchers will explore how nonbinary parents choose child-rearing techniques as they begin to raise their own children in our very gendered world.

NOTE

1.   This research was supported by a grant from the National Science Foundation to two of the co-authors, Professor Barbara J. Risman and Professor William Scarborough.

In Other Words

WHEN PARENTS SHOW UP TO SUPPORT THEIR LGBTQ ADULT CHILDREN

Amy L. Stone, March 29, 2022 / CCF@TSP

At the first Mardi Gras ball I attended in Baton Rouge, Louisiana, my host, Ernest, appeared in elaborate drag at the end of the event, debuting as the queen of the ball. His parents and siblings from rural Louisiana crowded at two tables to celebrate his entrance. They wore pins signifying that they were the parents of the queen, and they wore crowns from their own experiences as royalty at Mardi Gras events. They stood and celebrated the entrance of Ernest onto the raised stage in a convention hall filled with over one thousand guests.

When I started my research on lesbian, gay, bisexual, transgender, and queer (LGBTQ) involvement in Mardi Gras in the Gulf South, I had no idea that family would be a central part of my research. Mardi Gras or Carnival season is celebrated throughout the Gulf South from mid-January to the start of Lent. Private organizations called krewes or social aid and pleasure clubs organize the festival by hosting parades and private balls. There is a long history of LGBTQ krewes throughout the Gulf South that dates back to the early 1960s. In my book *Queer Carnival*, I analyze how these festival events are central to how LGBTQ people make a place for themselves in the Southern city. I argue that involvement in Carnival is fundamentally about cultural citizenship, cultivating a sense of belonging in one's own city.

But just as important is the way that these events are an opportunity for LGBTQ adult children to connect with their parents and other family members. Over two-thirds of the LGBTQ adults I spoke to for my research had family members who attended their festival event. Discussions about family involvement in krewe events were the most emotional parts of my interviews, as interviewees often cried when they talked about their parents attending. Largely, these family members were not "PFLAG parents"—parents, families, and friends of lesbians and gays—or people who identify as strong allies, yet they showed up to publicly support their LGBTQ children.

Parents were involved in many aspects of festival events. Several lesbian festival queens and kings received money from family to help with costs, particularly for their royalty expenses. The mother of one white lesbian paid for her royalty gown and train with funds that had originally been put aside for her wedding. I was conducting this project as same-sex marriage was being legalized statewide, and many interviewees described family support as equivalent to the money and attention they might have lavished on a wedding.

These connections can even be reconciliatory, repairing damage done to parent-child relationships after volatile reactions to coming out. The most dramatic story came from James, a younger white gay krewe member in Baton Rouge. James had an ambivalent relationship with his mother. When he came out at age eighteen, she kicked him out of the house. A tumultuous decade later, James was costuming for the first time and invited his mother to attend the ball. James bought her a ball gown, had her come early so that the krewe could do her hair and makeup, and made sure her favorite cocktail was on hand. "She had a day, it was nice," James told me. He did what I have termed "comfort work" to make attendance at the ball comfortable for her. James reported that after the ball, she was immediately enthusiastic and told him she wanted to help him decorate his table and make the food for the event next year. James's mother attended his mostly LGBTQ house party during a neighborhood festival parade the next weekend. His mother hung out in his kitchen during the party, making gumbo, and insisted later that James's friends refer to her as "Mama Zee."

Mardi Gras is an unexpected space that allows parents to show up for their LGBTQ children. This project pushed me to think more broadly about the ways that parents may support their LGBTQ adult children and youth. I think more about the myriad ways that parents show up (or don't) for their children. ▄

28

Adoptive Parents Raising Neoethnics and Demonstrating Whose Rights Matter

Pamela Anne Quiroz

Increasing attention to the formation of families through transnational adoption raises the question as to whether transnational adoption is in the public interest: there are many unresolved issues about human rights and social justice On the one hand, children gain material and social advantage through adoption. On the other hand, many, if not most, of these children lose their name. contact with family and community of origin, native language, and culture. Both sending and receiving countries have raised issues about the commodification of children and child trafficking, erosion of national interests, and damaging of children's identity.[1] Perhaps the most powerful critique of transnational adoption has emerged from adolescent and adult adoptees, whose narratives reveal the profound effects of being raised by ethnic "others."[2] Their stories compel us to examine the processes that produce the problems they describe in their lives and how culture and race were dealt with by their adoptive parents.

In this chapter, you will read three sections. The first answers the question *How do adoptive parents think and discuss international adoption?* The second answers the question *How has transnational adoption changed in the past three decades?* And the third addresses the question *How have U.S. adoptive parents addressed foster care and adoption of Latino children in the context of the family separations that have happened at the U.S.-Mexico border?* For the first question, I use data from my study (2006–2008) of parent interactions in three online adoption forums and transnational adoption workshops to show how parents interpret race, ethnicity, and culture in regard to their children. For the second question, I review trends in international adoption. And for the final question, I use

2012–2014 data from an online domestic Latino adoption forum and interviews with foster and adoptive parents to assess whose rights matter. In this final case, you will see how adoption raises a moral dilemma. This moral dilemma refers to the "sending" immigrant families in this time period who did *not* seek to place their children into the adoption process. Rather, parents were either detained or deported and their children were placed into foster care and adoption without the permission or knowledge of their biological parents.

Some Concepts: Symbolic Ethnicity and Neoethnics

Practices described by parents help us understand how the symbolic ethnicity of adoptive parents affects the identity formation of their adopted children. *Symbolic ethnicity* is typically associated with white Americans who have a great deal of choice in terms of their ethnic identities and who bear little social cost for their identification with different white ethnic groups (such as Irish or Polish).[3] Forum interactions also provide a firsthand account of adoptive parents, who are typically white ethnics, as selective participants in the cultural socialization and racial assignment of their adopted children. Through these practices, transnational adoptive families produce a unique group of migrants that I call *neoethnics*: people whose identities have literally been re-created through the act of adoption. These identities reflect the intersection of race, class, gender, sexuality, citizenship, adoptive status, and sometimes even a disability. Like symbolic ethnics, neoethnic adoptees are socialized to choose their individual affiliations and to embrace racial identity as voluntary, flexible, and symbolic. Yet research on adoptees tells us they live on the margins of multiple worlds and the complex political histories of immigration.[4] In this chapter I explore how parents and adoption professionals deal with these complicated issues. I end with some suggestions for future practices for parents and professionals.

Transnational Adoptive Families: A New Frontier

Between 1989 and 2009, adoptive parents in the United States, who are predominantly white, adopted more than 270,000 children from other countries. During this time, 50–75 percent of transnational adoptions came from four sending countries: China, Russia, Guatemala, and Korea.[5] In Table 28.1 you can see how the numbers of children from those countries shifted each year throughout this period. This resulted in a substantial number of children who have been raised by parents whose race is different from theirs.

Table 28.1 | U.S. Transnational Adoptions from Top Four Sending Countries

FY	China	Russia	Guatemala	Korea	Total Adoptions
1993	330	745	512	1,775	7,377 (45%)
1994	787	1,530	436	1,795	8,333 (55%)
1995	2,130	1,896	449	1,666	9,679 (63%)
1996	3,333	2,454	427	1,516	11,340 (68%)
1997	3,597	3,816	788	1,654	13,621 (72%)
1998	4,206	4,491	911	1,829	15,583 (73%)
1999	4,101	4,348	1,002	2,008	15,719 (72%)
2000	5,053	4,269	1,518	1,794	18,857 (67%)
2001	4,681	4,279	1,609	1,870	19,647 (63%)
2002	5,053	4,939	2,219	1,779	21,378 (65%)
2003	6,859	5,209	2,328	1,790	21,654 (75%)
2004	7,044	5,865	3,264	1,176	22,990 (75%)
2005	7,903	4,631	3,783	1,628	22,734 (79%)
2006	6,492	3,702	4,135	1,373	20,680 (76%)
2007	5,453	2,303	4,727	938	19,609 (68%)
2008	3,911	1,857	4,122	1,065	17,475 (63%)
2009	3,001	1,586	756	1,080	12,753 (50%)

Sources: Bureau of Consular Affairs, U.S. Department of State, Intracountry Adoption, Statistics, adoption.state.gov/about_us/statistics.php (accessed September 23, 2010); and the Donaldson Adoption Institute, Annual Reports, adoptioninstitute.org/supportus/annual-reports/ (data from 1993–2005).

Transnational adoptions have now declined by more than 90 percent from 22,290 in 2004, to 8,668 in 2012, and 1,785 adoptions in 2021. Why this decline? Improved economic conditions of sending countries, reports of child trafficking, and highly publicized incidents of child abuse shifted sentiment in sending countries to opposing transnational adoption.[6] It is also possible that biases toward marital status and sexuality have played a role, as single women accounted for a third of adoptive parents by the late 1990s. For example, additional new restrictions by China and other countries have eliminated adoption by single persons, and Russia has eliminated all adoptions by U.S. citizens. Since 2020, the COVID-19 pandemic slowed international adoption even more. Indeed, in the past twenty-five years, over 40 percent of all sending countries either completely shut down or temporarily restricted transnational adoptions.[7] Whether one views transnational adoption as a global gift or a neocolonialist mistake, the consequences for children deserve serious attention.

The large number of transnational adoptions to the United States and the fact that most transnational adoptees occupy a different status from their adoptive parents in the U.S. racial hierarchy have stimulated researchers to pay special attention to the impact of adoption on racial/ethnic identity formation.[8] Some studies have found positive indicators of adoptive parents' interest in promoting a bicultural orientation for their children, while others have highlighted discrepancies between parents' and adoptees' perceptions of parents' attempts at cultural socialization. Still, our knowledge of how parents address race and cultural socialization and how these processes affect adoptees' experiences remains limited.

QUESTION 1: HOW DO ADOPTIVE PARENTS TALK ABOUT INTERNATIONAL ADOPTION?

Because many people look to the internet as a means of creating identity and a sense of community, I explored adoptive parent practices involving race and culture by looking at interactions in adoption forums. Some of the advantages of using forum interactions to explore identity formation are that they are "public by default, but private through intent," as participants speak to people they believe are similarly situated. Table 28.2 gives a profile of adoption (in the period around when the study was conducted) in the United States that helps ground our reading of these adoption forums. In these virtual spaces, parents discuss a variety of topics that range from the mundane to the highly sensitive. These forum posts are unscripted, and the topics of discussion (threads) are generated by participants' concerns. Because they are speaking to one another, parents may use greater candor in these discussions than they would with researchers conducting

Table 28.2 | Adoptive Families in the United States*

- 2.5% of children in the United States are adopted (1.7 million children)
- 18% of these households contained members of different races (308,000)
- 71% adopted children under 18 lived with a white (non-Hispanic) head of household
- 1.8% of households have adopted children
- $56,000 = median income of households with adopted children
- 43 years = average age of parents of adopted children

*U.S. Census Bureau (2003); Pew Internet and American Life Project (2006).
Source: Census 2000 PHC-T-21, Adopted Children and Stepchildren: 2000, www.census.gov (retrieved on October 3, 2003).

interviews or surveys. Consequently, participants serve both as framers of identity and as audience for identities presented by other participants.

As with all data collected by social scientists (see Cohen, Chapter 2; Cowan, Chapter 3; and Burton, Chapter 4), there are limitations to how much forum data can help us understand adoptive parenting. During the time frame of this study (2006–2008), the U.S. adoptive parent population was relatively small (3–4 percent), and adoptive parents who participated in forums were likely to be an even smaller and self-selected group. Additionally, online posts for any particular topic may number in the hundreds, but the number of participants can be quite small. For example, threads revolving around ethnoracial consciousness in the Guatemalan forum generated 805 posts, but there were only eighty-five individuals who participated in these discussions. This kind of analysis cannot capture the nonverbal cues available in face-to-face interactions.

Also, because thread topics are discrete, it is not possible to determine whether the practices conveyed by parents represent a coherent and consistent set of practices or whether they are unique to a particular situation or moment. Therefore, the most common orientations of forum posts are analyzed rather than individual parents. Nevertheless, patterns found in these forums mirror patterns found in other qualitative studies of adoptive parents, and the insights into cross-racial parenting are valuable, as participants provide a way to gauge how they negotiate race and culture in transnational and transracial families.

Where did I find these threads? I used archived threads from adoption forums posted on Adoption.com, the largest online adoption directory, offering information, referrals, and community. Adoption.com's home page provided guidelines for interaction in the forums, and the forums generated literally thousands of interactions across a vast array of topics. The majority of participants self-defined as either parents or prospective parents. The large number of threads and lengthy discussions necessitated a circumscribed, two-year period of study (2006 to 2008). Forums for three of the four largest "sending" countries between 1989 and 2009 were selected: China, Russia, and Guatemala. These countries have also been the subject of a number of studies on adoption.[9]

An independent coder assisted me, and we engaged in multiple iterations of coding that began with thread topics generated by participants and resulted in identifying four parenting processes related to racial assignment and cultural socialization. Interactions were sometimes brief but typically extensive: while a few participants posted only once, threads often included a small number of participants who posted multiple times, giving the interaction a conversational tone. Different threads tended to generate greater involvement by different subsets of participants. It was not possible to quantify participants by race, ethnicity, or gender, as they did not always state either or all of those identities. However, most of those who did identify themselves in these forums indicated that they were white, which reflects the majority of U.S. adoptive parents. Because women more than men tend to use the internet to seek and form relationships, I inferred that most of the participants in these adoption forums were white women. Because different parents posted in each thread, individuals could not be assessed. What could be assessed was the number of different people posting on each topic. Frequent overlap in discussion threads and individual posts occurred. When this happened, the post was categorized under the dominant theme. For example, a thread about family acceptance included posts about color blindness or color consciousness. However, because the dominant focus of the thread was family acceptance, the post was placed in this category.

In addition to analyzing internet data, I also observed five transnational adoption workshops offered by private adoption agencies. Three workshops were in Illinois and two were in Texas. Though they were located in different states, workshop formats were similar, and each workshop lasted approximately two hours. Workshops consisted of presentations by facilitators, followed by either a panel of adult adoptees or some mix of adoptive parents and their adolescent and adult children who presented their perspectives on transnational adoption. Presentations were typically followed by a question-and-answer session with prospective and adoptive parents. Notes were taken during these sessions, and a variety of brochures, pamphlets, articles, and guides (for example, adoption language guides) were also gathered and examined. These observations supplement the analysis of forum posts and offer a look at the role of adoption agencies in shaping parent involvement. They also reveal discrepancies between parents and adoptees.

Using both kinds of data, I identified four general and overlapping activities regarding identity: choosing, avoiding or cultural distancing, keeping, and purchasing. *Choosing* refers to which children adoptive parents were willing to adopt and how they arrived at their decisions. Choosing also refers to the variety of decisions parents made that directly and indirectly affected identity. These decisions include both minor and substantive decisions, such as where to live, which schools to attend, and what languages to learn, among other practices, such as circumcision. *Avoiding* refers to cultural distancing and the silence surrounding children's birth origins, culture, and race. Most of the posts in each forum indicated that parents either did not address their child's origins or addressed them in a perfunctory manner. *Keeping* refers to parents who subscribed to and engaged in activities to help their children retain a sense of native group identity. *Purchasing* refers to the use of cultural symbols, activities, media, and artifacts as a means of providing the basis of racial/cultural identity for adopted children.[10] I noted the frequency of posts within each category by participants who explicitly identified as parents and the number of people posting on each topic. Posts used here are presented verbatim and typify the most common set of responses within each category. Only spelling or punctuation has been modified to clarify comments. Posts suggest well-intentioned efforts to understand and accommodate children while at the same time balancing parents' preferences and the demands of the complex social contexts within which they lived.

PARENTS' DOMINANT PRACTICES: CULTURAL SOCIALIZATION AND RACIAL ASSIGNMENT

The practices described by forum participants are presented here as separate, but in fact, each represents one aspect of the cultural socialization process, and they overlap with one another. Tensions between these practices became apparent as many parents struggled to balance their values and the interests of their children.

Choosing

The practice of choosing relates to decisions made by adoptive parents regarding their adopted child.[11] Parents described how they chose their adoption program or country, and even their child's gender, race, and health status. These choices were embedded in parents' constructions of their ideal child and their own identities, as well as their views and their family's views on race and culture. For example, many parents in the Russian forum found that the Russian cultural practice regarding circumcision conflicted with their own practice, so they weighed the emotional consequences for their adopted sons against their personal preferences and the perceived appropriateness of engaging in this practice. Most of those who posted on this topic elected to circumcise their adopted sons; however, discussions were not without some debate as parents moved between choosing, distancing, or avoiding the norms of their sons' culture of origin.

> Boys in Russia are almost never circumcised. Same with Eastern Europe. But for you, since it won't likely have been done, make your decision just as if you were having your own newborn. Circumcision is quite trivial at any age. It really is! It doesn't matter if it's 2 weeks, 2 months, 20 months or 4 years or older. I know because I've been there, not only with my adopted son (at 4 y/o), but also with an adult friend who did it at 21 and a Jewish friend's ceremony for their newborn son. After several months, when he was settled, I easily obtained a referral from my pediatrician to a urologist, and the urologist told me they do about one circ

(circumcision) a week and I shouldn't be uptight (I wasn't) because it's so common. (forums.adoption.com/russia-adoption, 11/25/2008)

I think often it is tempting for A-parents (adoptive parents) to try and erase a child's past and heritage in their efforts to make him more of *their* child. Please be assured that no matter whether your child's genitalia match your husband's or not, he will be completely your child. I sincerely hope that unless it is medically necessary you will not subject your son to an additional trauma, as he will already be going through a tremendous period of adjustment and acclimation. (http://forums .adoption.com/russia-adoption, 11/25/2008)

Several studies have shown how the process of choosing takes place in a racial system that defines which children are more acceptable and most likely to be integrated into extended families, so it is not surprising that this was reflected in adoption forums.[12] As Kazuyo Kubo[13] said, adoptive families not only provide "a space where racial integration can be created, they also tell us that it is a space where racial preference can be practiced."

I knew for me the Hispanic culture would have worked because I love it. I knew Russia would work because most of my family is from Russia. And I knew Africa would work because I live in an area with a large population of African Americans. I knew the Asian cultures had not fascinated me in the ways that the other cultures did. I had 9 years of infertility and adoption tribulation so it gave me an opportunity to educate my family on those things that would allow me to create my family. Not being willing to adopt certain nationalities may be a sign of bigotry but it may also be that parents have thought through the process and its consequences, and decided that certain things just would not work for them. (http://forums.adoption .com/Guatemala-adoptions, 11/2007)

Cultural Distancing

Across all forums, the dominant or modal practice described by parents was that of distancing themselves from their adopted child's birth origins by either failing to substantively address their child's race or culture or addressing it in a perfunctory manner. Such practices often occur when people are confronted with information that generates personal dissonance, a disjunction between current ideas, relations, and knowledge or beliefs. Transracial and transnational adoptions frequently result in personal conflicts and anxiety on the part of adoptive parents as intimate associations are disrupted by these adoptions. Conflicts may occur with extended family members who disapprove of an adoption, or even with close friends, neighbors, church members, or others who may not accept the adopted child or who may marginalize the adoptive family. It may also occur because of anxiety about how to navigate racial boundaries. Cultural distancing is an index of the feelings about the self and others, and in the case of adoption, how the child's "otherness" gets defined. Parents often alleviated this dissonance by promoting the child's engagement in choosing their own relationship to the culture of origin once they were grown.

> If we as parents decided to make contact, then we leave our children with the potential burden of the effects and outcomes of that contact. Suppose we choose to offer some type of financial support; then our children may feel pressured to continue that support down the road. I absolutely agree that the decision should be made by the adoptee when he or she is ready. . . . But as adoptive parents, we should always let our children know that we are there and will support and assist them if they choose to make contact. (http://forums.adoption.com/guatemala -adoptions, 3/2008)

Other distancing activities involve emphasizing the child's sameness with the adoptive family instead of discussing their difference, keeping silent about the child's birth family, and avoiding or downplaying the significance of racial incidents such as name-calling or bullying at school. Whether by design or default, these rhetorical strategies allowed parents to relinquish responsibility for keeping culture, assured distance from birth families and birth origins, and left the burden of racial identity to adoptees. It was apparent that the identities of parents were as much a focus of these processes as were the identities of their children.

Keeping

Many parents claimed a desire to achieve some degree of cultural literacy and to support their child's identification with their native culture, as described in Heather Jacobsen's book *Culture Keeping*.[14] Activities that involved *keeping* include retaining the child's birth name, learning about their child's country and culture of origin, learning their child's native language, visiting the sending country, and engaging in cultural activities such as ethnic celebrations.

> We take language lessons with our daughter because we want to be able to be part of her culture, at least as much as we can. It does take driving a ways to get there, and of course, it would be easier to just say, well, she's in America now, but it's one of the many things that brings us closer and makes us a family. We consider ourselves a Chinese American family, not an American family with a Chinese child. (http://forums.adoption.com/China adoption, 11/20/2007)

Rarely did parents describe a sense of "shared fate" with their children or profound alterations in lifestyles on behalf of their adopted children, for example,
changing churches, learning a language, or moving to a new neighborhood or
city. Learning what it means to be Chinese, Guatemalan, or Russian did not seem
to involve having friendships with members of their child's birth group. Instead,
parents helped their child construct a racial and cultural identity through a set
of practices that involved other adoptive parents and by purchasing cultural artifacts and "ethnic" experiences. Participants in both forums and workshops spoke
about relying on adoptive parent support groups such as Red Thread or Raising
China Children. Parents typically looked to each other, adoption agencies, and
adoption experts to help them with culture keeping. Even more pronounced was
parents' use of cultural artifacts to mark inclusivity.

Purchasing

Purchasing was a natural outgrowth of two features of adoption: parents' limited
knowledge of their child's culture of origin and the fact that adoptive parents are
the primary consumers in the adoption industry. Consequently, adoptive parents purchased products sold by the adoption industry, such as books, artwork,
toys, music, clothes, food, bedroom decorations, and experiences such as ethnic
folk dancing, culture camp, and "Roots" or Heritage trips instead of engaging
in more authentic ongoing cultural practices, such as making attempts to meet
members of their child's country of origin.

In general, forum interactions presented cultural socialization as an opaque
set of practices as parents engaged in balancing conflicting identities, reserving
some decisions for themselves and deferring others to their adopted children.
Whether acknowledged or even recognized, these processes reflected adoptive
parents' position as symbolic ethnics. As parents, they could selectively engage
culture and ethnicity for themselves and also select their adopted child's race/
ethnicity and the cultural representations, practices, and contacts that were available to their child.

PARENT-CHILD INTERACTIONS AT WORKSHOPS

Parent-child interactions in adoption workshops augment our understanding of
these processes. These workshops made clear that adoptive parents' perceptions
of successful socialization differed significantly from their adopted child's perceptions. Two examples of these discrepancies extend our observations of forum
interactions. In the first, the facilitator of a transnational adoption workshop, who

was also an adoptive parent of a child from India, provided a moving rendition of her family's successful negotiation of culture. The social worker/mother offered examples of what she deemed to be culture keeping, such as learning about the history of India, learning to cook Indian food, and enrolling her daughter in Indian folk-dance classes, which she claimed her daughter loved. After this discussion, her daughter (in her late twenties) participated on a panel with three other adult adoptees and completely contradicted her mother's narrative. The daughter assessed her experiences as lacking real cultural understanding. She also contradicted her mother's positive version of the cultural activities chosen for her and described them as difficult and isolating. Far from feeling accepted, the daughter claimed that the other Indian children in her folk-dance class regarded her as white, and therefore, she was ostracized. Struck by these contrasting narratives, I observed the social worker/mother while her daughter spoke but saw no perceptible response regarding the discrepancies between their narratives.

A similar situation occurred with an adoptive mother and adolescent son (fourteen years old) in a workshop where three families presented in separate thirty-minute sessions. Again, the mother presented first and described the family's various efforts at culture keeping. These included decorating her son's room with artwork, piñatas, and artifacts brought home from Guatemala. It even included a photograph of the son's birth mother and siblings, whom the adoptive mother had met. Because at least some effort had been made to learn about her son's circumstances, this adoptive mother believed that her family had created and sustained a link to her son's family of origin and that through other efforts his culture was being honored. Unlike the daughter in the prior example, this son did not directly contradict his mother. However, he did express feelings of marginality with respect to both his adoptive siblings and biological siblings. Instead of confirming his mother's description of successful cultural socialization, this adoptee talked about his struggle with the knowledge that he was the only one of his biological siblings who had been placed for adoption.

Raising Neoethnics

Interactions in these adoption forums and workshops help us understand that the lack of strong cultural/racial identities among adult adoptees is partially the result of the sources of identity construction, the identities of adoptive parents, and the tools parents use to socialize their children. I refer to these adoptees as a rather unique group of involuntary migrants, or *neoethnics*. Neoethnics are people whose identities have been literally re-created through the act of adoption and who typically do not experience direct links to their culture and ethnicity of origin. They are socialized as symbolic ethnics who choose their individual affiliations, yet neoethnics also continue to be defined by their group affiliations. Studies show that adult transnational adoptees typically experience everyday life as members of U.S. minority groups even though they may not identify with these groups or have lives that mirror their native group or even the transplanted cultural group. Identification with these groups may be more a function of adoptees' racialized experiences in their adopted country.

Tobias Hubinette's study of Swedish adult adoptees of color found that they did not claim the same status or economic position of their adoptive Swedish parents, who were typically of high socioeconomic status.[15] Instead, adoptees of color typically occupied low socioeconomic status, did not marry, and remained childless. Though research on adult adoptees of color in the United States lacks the detail of the Swedish census to make similar comparisons, we also find that adoptees perceive themselves as members of a marginalized group. Adoptees are both involuntary migrants and members of minority groups who may be schooled in the performance of whiteness but whose experiences continue to be influenced by race. Neoethnics are not likely to visit their countries of origin, speak their native language, or establish or sustain intimate relationships with members of their first family or country or even form close social ties to members who have migrated from their communities of origin. We know from numerous autobiographical accounts that those who do try to reclaim their past must often engage in this process alone or with the help of friends rather than family or other institutional supports.[16]

QUESTION 2: HOW HAS TRANSNATIONAL ADOPTION CHANGED IN THE PAST THREE DECADES?

In the past thirty years, we have witnessed a 90-plus percent decline in U.S. transnational adoptions (see Table 28.3). Restrictions from primary sending countries, changing economic conditions, new social movements against transnational adoption, and the worldwide pandemic have shifted the attention of adoptive parents in the United States to new locations. Between 2007 and 2017, adoptions from Africa nearly tripled, as parents adopted children from Ethiopia, South Africa, Liberia, Nigeria, and Madagascar. Between 2003 and 2010, more than 35,000 children were adopted from African countries, with the majority (22,282) from Ethiopia.[17] However, African adoptions declined as Ethiopia joined the Hague and eventually banned international adoptions in 2018.

During this time, other trends in transnational adoption emerged as a consequence of immigration policies that sharpened my recognition of the moral dilemma referenced in the introduction. The Obama administration's

Table 28.3 | Changes in Transnational Adoptions from Primary
Sending Countries

Country	Peak Adoptions	Adoptions in the U.S. (2012)
China	7,903 in 2005	2,697
Russia	5,865 in 2004	748
Guatemala	4,727 in 2007	7
Korea	2,008 in 1999	627
Ethiopia	2,275 in 2009	1,568

Adoption statistics for 2007 = number of adoptions from October 2006 through September 2007 (the timeline for yearly visa count).

Source: Bureau of Consular Affairs, U.S. Department of State. Statistics. travel.state.gov/content /adoptionsabroad/en/about-us/statistics.html (accessed November 2013).

detainment and deportation of over 400,000 Latinos resulted in another group of children who have been affected by foster care and adoption. According to Race Forward: The Center for Racial Justice Innovation, in 2011, more than 5,000 Latino children were in foster care or in the process of being adopted because their parents had been detained or deported. At that time, Race Forward projected that another 15,000 children would be in this situation within the next five years.[18] African adoptees and Latino children caught in these processes would face the dilemma of cultural socialization as they became the newest neoethnics. Unfortunately, the predictions of Race Forward came true.

In 2016 we saw a shift in U.S. immigration policy with large numbers of citizen and immigrant children separated from their (detained or deported) parents and placed in the child welfare system. In this political climate, where children were forcibly separated from their parents, the risks for Latino children (and their families) were substantial. Deportation and detention in large numbers provided a *new means* of satisfying the desire for children when there were diminishing numbers of children available in the transnational market.

Despite laws that prohibit families from adopting children of migrants, investigative reporters (Dreby 2013) and a small study conducted with adoptive and foster parents (Quiroz 2019) revealed the foster placement and adoption of migrant children. These activities not only indicate who the newest "neoethnics" are but also offer a new mirror on human rights and the tensions between family-building through adoption and the processes through which adoptive families are formed.

No longer are we talking about child trafficking as something exclusive to international adoption and "third world" countries. Now our adoption headlines involve stories of detention, children in cages, deportation, and children suffering from post-traumatic stress syndrome as enforcement of U.S. immigration policy results in family separation and child placement. This reality forces us to revisit the complex political and sociological nature of adoptive parenting that is too often ignored—the building of family and identity that occurs through the loss of family (and identity).

As an adoptive parent who has engaged in both domestic and international adoption, I voice observations from my lived experience in the hope that it leads to greater understanding and feeling for those about whom we write. In other words, I am implicated in the dynamics of these processes. The separation and placement of children from immigrant families is the latest chapter in the history of U.S. adoption that underscores the involuntary nature of immigration for children (via adoption) and the various social and political factors that enter into these processes.

QUESTION 3: HOW HAVE ADOPTIVE PARENTS THOUGHT AND TALKED ABOUT ADOPTION IN THE CONTEXT OF THE FAMILY SEPARATIONS THAT HAVE HAPPENED AT THE U.S.-MEXICO BORDER? EXPLORING THE CREATION OF NEW NEOETHNICS

As an adoptive parent, I was approached in 2013 by one of four Chicago adoption agencies that were trying to place Latino children with foster and adoptive parents. I later asked to interview participants to understand their perspectives on parenting citizen-children and children of undocumented parents who ended up in the Illinois child welfare system. Only a small number of participants responded (fourteen). I was drawn to the stories of Latino children who were entering foster care and adoption, and I was inspired by the book *Shattered Families* and the changing transnational adoption landscape. I was also moved by my personal experience of being Latino, being an adoptive parent, and being solicited to foster a Latino child. As such, I returned to the internet to explore a domestic Latino adoption forum (2012–2014) and conducted interviews with a small convenience sample of adoptive and foster parents to see how participants engaged in this process. I focused specifically on parent participation in fostering and adopting citizen-children and children of Latino immigrants.

Adoptive parent forums highlighted the different perspectives and practices expressed by adoptive parents and prospective parents. Together these data revealed the ways we describe and value children based on their race/ethnicity and nationality. The value of online data is that they reveal unscripted viewpoints and practices of adoptive parenting. These forums give us access to organic discussions of shifting policies of immigration, detention, and deportation.

Language is a particularly important element of forums because terminology can evoke positive or negative attitudes toward groups. Terms can soften harsher images of persons or generate images and responses to those images. For example, the following posts described biological parents as "criminal" or "illegal." A small sample of thread titles include "Illegal Immigrant Bio Parents," "Adopting Illegal Children," "Illegal Aliens? Foster Care and Adoption," "Adopting an Illegal Immigrant," and "Deportation of BIOS while Children Are in Foster Care." Much of the discussions focused on information seeking, specifically how adoptive and foster parents could secure their rights. Information and the act of adopting or fostering was justified by criminalizing or minimizing the biological parents. Because discursive analyses assume that language can have social consequences, and language regarding immigration is a contentious issue, it is notable that the term *illegal* was the most commonly used term instead of *undocumented* or *unauthorized*. Accompanying the reference to "illegal" parents is a sense of indignation on the part of participants and reluctance to address or admit to the broader social and economic realities of the children and their families.

> I'm in Denver and we had a newborn drug-addicted girl whose mother wouldn't work her plan and her dad is an illegal alien. We were told by the first caseworker that he wouldn't get her because he's illegal. . . . NOT TRUE. The case was transferred to the Spanish-speaking division and everything changed. I will avoid the Spanish division as long as I can (long, long story about another child). Luckily, the only reason cases go there is if the parents do not speak English. DHS does not care about alien status for parents. They do not report to immigration and [our daughter] now lives with her dad. HE speaks no English, we speak no Spanish, but we are lucky enough to get her every weekend. [Colorado]
>
> One of my friends is currently going through something similar. The Biological dad was deported. A home study was completed in Mexico for the grandma. The kid had lived with my friend on and off for years (failed RU). My friend said the home study in Mexico was a joke. The kid doesn't even know his grandmother. CPS told her the kid was illegal anyway and costing the state money. Nice. She was pretty broken up about it. [peaceforall]

Similar to transnational adoption discussions in other forums, several discussions in the Latino forum distanced foster and adoptive parents from the children's biological families, thus helping to validate rights to a child and mitigate guilt about the circumstances under which we become adoptive parents.

> In Missouri, incarceration is not a valid reason to terminate rights. . . . It is my understanding that after the TPR [Termination of Parental Rights] hearing, the Biological parents may still contest it for up to 30 days. Our county has heard contested

TPR's past the 30-day period; however, most counties also will look for a relative placement once the child is free for adoption. If no suitable relative placement can be found, foster parents usually have the first option to adopt the children, if the "team" is in agreement. . . . Hang in there. It can be a long process. Our case worker has a friend who filed last year to adopt their foster child and on the last day of the appeal time frame, the Biological Dad decided to appeal it, from jail. It has taken 11 months to go through. But keep your chin up. I know for us, it will be worth it once our little girl is finally ours! God knows your child's destiny and he knows where your child needs to be in order for His will to be accomplished in his/her life [Cali].

The United Nations Convention on the Rights of the Child guarantees children the right to preserve their identity and cultural heritage, yet adoption forums remind us we cannot assume that complex issues of race and cultural assignment have been either addressed or transcended merely by the act of adoption. These issues are not divorced from power: who controls the narrative and who gets to determine whose rights matter—the biological parents, particularly when they are unauthorized immigrants, or the U.S. adoptive parents?

Where Do We Go from Here?

In the first study, forum interactions and observations of workshops provided a nuanced understanding of adoptive parent practices regarding cultural socialization. They illustrated the processes through which parents' views are expressed, debated, and potentially modified, and provided the link to understanding adolescent and adult adoptees' challenges with group identification and feelings of racial exceptionalism. Forum interactions illustrated how parents convey the guidelines for adoptees' racial subjectivity. Choosing, cultural distancing, keeping, and purchasing are the processes by which adoptees learn the scripts for their new social position within the adoptive family and society. Despite survey results that indicate the willingness of adoptive parents to discuss race and culture with their children, qualitative studies have found considerable variation in the manner, degree, and quality of these discussions.

Online, some parents described incidents they initially regarded as uneventful as making them aware of the new niche they were carving as multiracial families. While cultural distancing was the most common response by parents, this was not always their perception: many genuinely felt themselves to be doing what was best for their child and claimed efforts at acquiring cultural literacy.

For a small number of parents, self-perceptions changed dramatically and shifted into a new identity that incorporated their child's identity of origin.

In transnational adoptive families in the United States, cultural socialization is predominantly in the hands of white adoptive parents who rarely describe living in or interacting within the "other's" domain. Online, a significant number of parents indicated that acceptance comes at a price because children are separated from their culture, and we begin to see how families formed through transnational adoption may simultaneously reflect race-mixing while allowing the current racial hierarchy to remain firmly in place. As you see from data about the declining rates of transnational adoption, all of this occurs in a global context in which people are shifting their views and concerns.

My final study, of the adoption of children in border situations, makes clear that there remains interest in transnational adoption. The line between transnational and *domestic* (adoption within the United States) has blurred, as the loss of connection to their family for children of unauthorized immigrants is not located in some distant past or vague set of memories. As adoptees have increasingly demanded to be included in the conversation about transnational adoption, we are becoming aware of the complexities of this family form.

Here's where these studies take me: To contribute to the debate about the impact of adoption on identity formation, one has to believe that as a set of symbolic, social, and material resources, *culture matters and the rights of biological parents are paramount.* We must remember to keep a critical eye on who has the right to adopt or foster and which groups end up being fostered and adopted, and under what circumstances, along with the profound impact of physical, legal, and social relocation on adoptees. If one accepts this, then perhaps adoption forums, workshop interactions, and even judicial procedures can provide a way of understanding that something is uniquely lost to transnational adoptees and adoptees of unauthorized immigrants.

Reconsidering Whose Rights Matter

Because parents typically look to one another, adoption agencies, and adoption experts for guidance on how to navigate culture keeping, we must update these entities to help honor social policies that aim to secure the rights of children. The ways that agency and expert providers help shape the practices of adoptive parents are typically ignored. Unlike biological parents, adoptive parents require the approval of an agency social worker and the state, which must be willing to designate them as worthy, competent, and in the case of transnational adoption, *culturally literate.*

However, this designation relies primarily on a home study, an intercountry workshop, and parent education. Therefore, adoption professionals need to help adoptive parents move beyond a banal understanding of transnational adoption to an understanding of the political and social realities of the families and countries from which children are adopted. Aside from providing home studies and workshops on intercountry adoption, adoption agencies also promote reading adoption books as part of the ongoing education of adoptive parents. And while it is probably impossible to find a modern adoption book that completely ignores race or culture, it is rare to find a book that addresses these issues in any substantive manner, or that incorporates all the voices of adoption participants, including parents, birth parents, children, and siblings of adopted children. More importantly, these books frequently invoke race and culture as a "dilemma" rather than as a value-add. We need better books for this. Adding different perspectives and different voices, including those of birth parents and members of the child's community, can help adoptive parents understand the complexity of crossing race and culture.

Adoptive parents also need workshops that address issues of power and privilege in the formation of family. Those who adopt and those who are adopted occupy radically different cultural, economic, social, and racial spaces. These workshops should include multiple voices and multiple perspectives.

More than 4 million Latino children face the possibility of having a parent deported, and already hundreds of thousands of children have had this experience (American Immigration Council 2017; ARC 2011; Foley 2014; DePillis 2015). We can now add to this number those separated from their families under the Trump administration and placed into foster care and adoption. As prospective parents seek available children, and as their willingness to adopt Latino children has increased significantly, it is important that they understand the social and political circumstances in which the children they adopt or foster are embedded.

It is easy to wonder what impact detention, deportation, and separation of families might have on prospective parents looking to adopt. Whereas the majority of transnational and private adoptions cost more than $40,000, foster care adoptions are typically free or they have a minimal cost or are subsidized. This may serve the interests of prospective adoptive parents, but it does little to reduce the trauma of children whose first families are torn apart. We must gain a more substantive understanding of the emotional and health-related costs of adoption for these children.

Finally, we need to consider modeling transnational adoption after U.S. domestic open adoption, where children maintain some degree of contact with their biological families, and remind adoptive parents that culture keeping is a child's right and an enriching experience for both parents and children. In short, we are in need of an adoption policy framework that provides for more substantive practices regarding power and privilege, and their intersections with multiple dimensions of inequality, including race, culture, sexuality, disability, and gender. As anthropologist Claudia Fonseca suggests, the meaning of adoption and family are largely defined by Western standards. True social justice may require creating more spaces for a plurality of views and practices.

NOTES

1. Cardello (2009); Hearst (2010); Leifson (2008); Smolin (2005).
2. Brian (2012); Lee et al. (2010). McGinnis et al. (2009); Samuels (2009); Tuan and Shiao (2011).
3. Waters (1990).
4. Hubinette (2012); McGinnis et al. (2009); Palmer (2011).
5. Quiroz (2012).
6. Briggs (2006); Fonseca (2002); Leifson (2008); Meier and Zhang (2008); Smerdon (2008).
7. Smolin (2004).
8. Lee et al. (2010); Tuan and Shiao (2011); McGinnis et al. (2009).
9. Dorow (2006); Gailey (2009); Jacobsen (2008); Rotabi et al. (2012).
10. Quiroz (2012).
11. Sweeney (2013).
12. Brian (2012); Dorow (2006); Ortiz and Briggs (2003); Sweeney (2013).
13. Kubo (2010).
14. Jacobsen (2008).
15. Hubinette (2012).
16. Trenka, Oparah, and Shin (2006).
17. Selman (2012).
18. Race Forward: The Center for Racial Justice Innovation (2011).

29

Parents as Pawns

Intersex, Medical Experts, and Questionable Consent

Georgiann Davis

id you have a boy or a girl? New parents are routinely asked this question. The assumption is that boys have penises and girls have vaginas, making the question seem simple when, in fact, gender is far more complex than what is between our legs. To start with, gender and sex are not synonymous. Gender is a culturally specific phenomenon expressed in different ways, for example in our clothing choices. Baby boys are routinely dressed in blue jumpers, whereas baby girls are more commonly spotted in pink dresses. These displays of gender are meant to signal a baby's sex, which is commonly understood through strict biological definitions. Males are assumed to have penises, testes, and XY sex chromosomes, while females are said to have vaginas, ovaries, a uterus, and XX sex chromosomes.

However, this line of thinking simultaneously oversimplifies gender and sex. Correlating them with each other is flawed, especially when one considers those born with intersex traits that surface as "ambiguous" external genitalia or sexual organs, and/or as sex chromosomes that do not match normative expectations. For example, those born with complete androgen insensitivity syndrome, an intersex trait, have vaginas, but they also have XY sex chromosomes and testes (usually internal and undescended). Historically, individuals with intersex traits were referred to as "hermaphrodites," but today, that term is considered derogatory by some in the intersex community. Terms less contentious include *intersex* and *intersexuality*. More recently, some have embraced new medical terminology—disorders of sex development, DSDs for short—to name their condition. I explore these terminological tensions in my book *Contesting Intersex:*

The Dubious Diagnosis (2015). Regardless of the terminology one uses, intersex traits make it explicitly clear that the "boy or girl" question is deeply problematic.

In this chapter, I draw on sixty-five in-depth interviews I conducted from 2008 to 2011 across the United States with parents of intersex children, adults with intersex traits, and medical experts. Most of my participants were recruited from the Androgen Insensitivity Syndrome Support Group–USA,[1] Organisation Intersex International, Accord Alliance, and the Intersex Society of North America. I rely on these interviews to describe the complexities of parental experiences within the medical management of intersexuality. I begin with a brief history of intersex medical care and the birth of intersex activism. I discuss how medical professionals present intersex traits to parents of newly diagnosed children as medical emergencies that can be fixed only with irreversible surgical treatments. I then describe how parents of children with intersex traits understand their child's diagnosis. I argue they often consent to medical recommendations with minimal hesitation because the condition is presented as a medical emergency. However, when parents eventually learn more about intersex traits, they often regret consenting to medical interventions that they come to realize were elective procedures rather than medically necessary interventions.

A BRIEF HISTORY OF INTERSEX MEDICAL CARE

The medical community views individuals born with intersex traits as needing medical care, even though many of these traits rarely pose a health threat.[2] Since medical professionals have had the technological tools to discover and rid the body of intersex traits, they have surgically and hormonally erased their existence. There simply is no room for the intersex body in a world that assumes male and female bodies are mutually exclusive and must be neatly categorized. For example, we now know that testosterone isn't present only in the male body, just as we know that estrogen isn't found only in the female body. If we took a sample of men, we would find lots of variation in their genitals. We would also find genital variation if we examined women's bodies. Penises and vaginas are not one size fits all. Despite this obvious overlap in male and female bodies and natural variation across penises and vaginas, bodies around the world continue to be categorized as male or female.

Since medical professionals also categorize bodies as either male or female, their first response when encountering an intersex trait usually involves "treating" it by surgically erasing it. Medical professionals are not evil people who run down hospital corridors with scalpels in hand searching for "abnormal" genitals. But this does not mean that their actions should not be carefully examined, nor does it mean that their actions are appropriate. Rather, it means that their decision to medically treat intersex traits by erasing them is much more complicated than it appears. Because ideologies about sex maintain we must be either male or female with absolutely no overlap, medical providers justify their treatment of intersex traits as helping individuals born with these conditions fit into society.

In the early 1990s, everything seemed to change. Feminist critiques of the medical treatment of intersex bodies fueled the birth of the intersex rights movement. An individual with an intersex trait by the name of Cheryl Chase, who was angry about how the medical profession treated her when she was young (specifically, surgically modifying her body and lying to her about her condition as she got older), met similarly bodied others.[3] They shared criticisms of the everlasting effects of medically unnecessary interventions, including loss of sexual pleasure and emotional harm caused by the absence of full disclosure. The U.S.-based intersex rights movement was fueled by these connections, which evolved into activist organizations and peer support groups. Intersex activists organized protests at medical association meetings, and when possible, relied on the media to raise awareness about how they were treated by the medical community. Feminist scholars, such as Suzanne Kessler and Anne Fausto-Sterling, were standing with intersex activists as they offered similar critiques from a scholarly platform in ways that legitimized the intersex rights movement.[4] With such collective activism, medical professionals could no longer operate under the radar as they performed irreversible procedures on the basis that they were helping individuals unfortunate enough to be born with such "abnormalities."

With a decade of protests by adult intersex activists and scholarly critiques from feminist scholars, medical experts were under public scrutiny. The American Academy of Pediatrics issued a formal statement on the medical management of intersex conditions,[5] which at first glance seemed to be evidence of progress. The document had a number of recommendations, including that intersex infants "should be referred to as 'your baby' or 'your child'—not 'it,' 'he,' or 'she.'"[6] The guidelines advised doctors to inform parents that their baby's "abnormal appearance can be corrected and the child raised as a boy or a girl as appropriate."[7] Surgery was still an option. The guidelines also stated that a number of factors should be considered when determining which "gender assignment" should be recommended for a given intersex child. Most notably, these factors included "fertility potential" and "capacity for normal sexual function."[8] The medical definition of normal sexual function assumed that there is only one way to experience sexual pleasure—penile-vaginal penetration. This is inaccurate. Oral sex gives many people pleasure, as do other kinds of sexual activity that do not rely on penile-vaginal penetration. The medical community approaches gender assignment and the interventions that follow with the belief that one's genitals (internal and external) must match gender expression. The standard of medical care that dominated intersex treatment before the birth of intersex activism continued despite increased public attention and scrutiny from feminist scholars and those born with intersex traits.

In 2006, there once again seemed to be a ray of hope. The American Academy of Pediatrics again revised its policy on intersex medical care due to "progress in diagnosis, surgical techniques, understanding psychosocial issues, and recognizing and accepting the place of patient advocacy."[9] The organization offered new recommendations in this policy revision, including introducing the option of avoiding unnecessary surgical interventions and the implementation of new nomenclature—disorders of sex development (DSD)—which I have shown in other scholarly work has replaced "intersex" language in virtually all corners of the medical profession.[10] However, despite this formal revision of the 2000 protocol, evidence suggests that medically unnecessary surgeries continue.[11]

Between October 2008 and April 2011, I set out on a journey to understand how intersex was treated and experienced in contemporary U.S. society. As I am a feminist who was born with an intersex trait, this journey was especially close to my heart. Before I started this project, I had met only one other person with an intersex trait who was as secretive about her condition as I was. Today, after traveling all across the country meeting so many individuals with intersex traits, their parents, and medical experts, I feel liberated and not at all ashamed about my intersex trait. In fact, it has become a central component of my identity.

During this methodological journey, I interviewed sixty-five individuals affiliated with four key organizations in the intersex community: the Intersex Society of North America (ISNA), Accord Alliance, the Androgen Insensitivity Syndrome Support Group–USA (AISSG-USA), and Organisation Intersex International (OII). I targeted these four organizations because, based on my initial assessment of their websites, each organization appeared to be involved in the intersex rights movement in a different way. For instance, ISNA and OII are activist organizations, while AISSG-USA is a support group, and Accord Alliance is an organization that seeks to distribute educational resources to medical professionals. I also asked participants to refer me to others who might share different views from their own—a methodological recruitment process known as snowball sampling. In addition to the in-depth interviews, I spent over three hundred hours in the public meeting spaces of intersex organizational meetings recording informal observations.

In the sections that follow, I rely on this qualitative approach to understand why parents usually consent to these medically unnecessary interventions—especially irreversible surgery. I found that when doctors describe the condition to parents as a medical emergency, parents are likely to defer to medical expertise and willingly consent to medically unnecessary interventions. There is one exception, however. If parents connect with the intersex community before they consent to medically unnecessary interventions, they are likely to delay or even

refuse such recommendations after hearing of the pain and suffering such procedures cause in one's life.

A MEDICAL EMERGENCY

When a baby is born, parents immediately want reassurance that their child is
healthy. Since medical professionals are health experts, new parents often turn
to them for such reassurance, beginning with the all-too-familiar decision (especially in the Western world) to medicalize the entire pregnancy process from
prenatal laboratory tests to ultrasonography to labor and delivery. In this section, I take you on a walk into medical consultation rooms, where we hear how
medical providers describe intersex traits to parents who, of course, want nothing
more than for their child to be healthy. What you will hear when reading these
accounts is that when a medical professional discovers a child has an intersex
trait, the provider usually presents the trait as a medical emergency that needs to
be corrected.

Imagine your friend has just given birth to a baby. After a routine labor and
delivery, it is discovered that the new baby has atypical genitalia. There are many
possibilities for how the intersex trait could be discussed with the parents. For
example, a doctor could describe the intersex trait as a natural and normal variation of the body. During this discussion, the doctor could reassure the parents
that the presence of an intersex trait, in most cases, does not mean there is an
immediate health concern. However, this is not what typically happens in medical consultation rooms. Instead, the focus tends to be on whether the baby is
male or female, as if biological sex is simple and the most important question.
Medical professionals could approach intersex in a way that problematizes the
sex binary. Instead, they tend to use the sex binary to problematize intersex.

When I asked Dr. D. to describe what happens when she encounters a baby
with an intersex trait, she explained:

> We try to find out as much biochemical and genetic data as we can, *as fast as we
> can* [emphasis added]. We look at the phenotypic appearance of the exterior of the
> child. We try to figure out . . . if we know their biochemical basis or what we think
> it is, what is likely to happen to them at puberty.

Dr. I. elaborated:

> The family is aware that we are getting additional data. We have to wait for labs to
> come back, karyotypes to come back. We let the family know that the emergency,

which would have been a salt-wasting CAH [congenital adrenal hyperplasia], is or is not the concern. Once you say there's no medical emergency here, then we say, let's get some more data.

Although Dr. I. explained that the possible "medical emergency" in this situation is salt-wasting CAH, which could potentially be life-threatening, it is important to note that ruling out this possibility neither ends nor postpones the need for immediate investigation. Rather, as Dr. I. explained, the search for "more data" continues, which reinforces the assumption that intersex is a medical emergency rather than a natural biological variation.

This search for hard scientific data about one's body is supposed to help decide if the child born with the intersex trait should be assigned a male or female gender identity. However, gender identity isn't so neatly tied to biology. Gender, itself, is culturally and contextually specific. Young women who grew up in the 1950s, for example, were expected to wear dresses and skirts. Today, teenage girls can be perfectly girly wearing the ever-so-popular "boyfriend" jeans. Neither genes nor jeans are perfectly correlated with gender identity.

Since medical professionals construct the emergency, they also create a situation that only they have the authority and power to address. For example, when a dentist tells us at a routine cleaning that we have a cavity that needs to be filled that we didn't even know we had, she reestablishes herself as the expert who is exclusively capable of fixing the cavity. Of course, we already view the dentist as an expert, but the fact that she uncovered a problem we didn't even know we had reinforces her authority and reestablishes the power she has to fix the problem that she has discovered. In the case of intersexuality, the emergency response involves a number of modern medical techniques designed to force the baby into the sex binary and disallow the existence of intersex bodies, even though, as Dr. F. shared, there is not "a good scientific way to make a choice. I don't think it matters what the chromosomes are. I don't think you can tell [gender identity] from the hormones." The question this raises is, why do medical professionals continue to search for medical markers of gender when they themselves acknowledge such markers can't easily be predicted?

Although there is no clear medical marker in the body that can predict one's gender identity—how could we even expect that, given gender is culturally specific and changes over time and context?—the authority that resides within the medical profession still justifies medical investigation. For example, Dr. A. was convinced that their "obligation as healthcare providers is to provide people with very complete information about what we know about the biology of DSDs, about the implications of DSDs for later development of sexual preference and sexual identity." Yet the allegedly "very complete information" that is delivered includes no social explanations of sex, gender, or sexuality, nor does it involve connecting individuals and their families with peer support groups. Instead, a "case conference," as Dr. F. called it, is held, where the medical professionals rely exclusively on medical markers to justify and necessitate their interventions on the intersex body.

Dr. I. described the goal of these case conferences as follows:

> [We] meet as a team and think about what are the options, which option we feel is medically in their best interest, and then we present the options to the family. And then we help the family reach a decision as soon as possible.

The problem with such an approach is that by the time the medical team meets with parents, they have already made decisions about which interventions are "medically in [the child's] best interest." For example, Dr. I.'s comments indicate that a decision has already been made for the intersex child *before* medical professionals meet with the parents. Parents are not included in the team meetings. They are included in discussions only *after* the team has reached their decisions. Although the medical experts are clearly the decision makers here, they assume no responsibility for the decisions they recommend. Instead, they shift all the responsibility onto parents.

DOCTOR KNOWS BEST

Think back to the last time you were being treated by a medical professional. Maybe you were getting a physical, had a cold, or were simply under the weather and sought medical care to feel better. I recently sought out medical care hoping to get some relief from uncontrollable allergy symptoms: sneezing, itchy eyes, scratchy throat, and headaches. The symptoms were so debilitating, I could hardly get any work done. I made an appointment with my primary care physician, who during my visit wrote me a prescription that promised relief. After my visit, I drove directly to the pharmacy, where I anxiously waited for my prescription to be filled. Soon thereafter, I was medicated and waiting for the relief I had been promised.

I'd argue my experience with something as mundane as seeking care for my allergy symptoms is relevant to intersex medical care. Why? To begin with, it is an obvious example of how we defer to medical expertise. When was the last time you questioned the prescription a doctor was writing for you? When was the last time you did your own independent research before following your doctor's recommendations? Hardly ever, I'd imagine. And, if you have questioned a medical provider's recommendations, you likely faced some pushback. In part, there is a shared understanding that medical professionals are the experts. They did go through all that school, after all. They are body experts. We, on the other hand, tend to defer to their expertise, and perhaps we should in some cases.

In the case of intersex medical care, when irreversible and medically unnecessary interventions are being performed on children's bodies, it is important to present the most complete information to parents—which ought to include the fact that it is acceptable to do nothing. A child with an intersex trait that is not life threatening is perfectly healthy as born. There is no need to immediately perform any type of intervention. Yet, the birth is presented as a medical emergency, and parents defer to medical expertise. In this section, I highlight how doctors shift all the responsibility for medical interventions onto parents, who in turn explain they were following medical recommendations with little hesitation under the assumption that *doctor knows best*. Medical professionals do not usually accept primary responsibility for performing unnecessary interventions on healthy intersex bodies. Rather, they present treatment options to the parents of intersex children in ways that appear to be exclusively informational.

For example, in explaining that medical intervention was performed out of respect for parents' wishes, Dr. A. said,

> Some families, for cultural, religious, or psychological reasons, may feel very strongly about the importance of trying to have their child look more typically male or female. Under those circumstances, I would counsel them to defer surgery. I wouldn't oppose surgery.

While Dr. A. seems to be taking some responsibility by counseling parents to delay their decision about surgical intervention, he still makes it appear to be exclusively their decision. However, Dr. A. is involved in the decision-making process and, as a medical expert, in a very important way. He could have, for example, informed the parents that the surgical interventions they desire may down the road be emotionally or physically harmful. Instead, he only counseled parents to defer, rather than avoid, surgery. While deferring surgery is a better alternative than going forward with immediate surgical interventions, it still frames surgery as an appropriate medical response.

When I asked the medical professionals how they justified irreversible and medically unnecessary interventions, they tended to explain that they were fulfilling parents' beliefs that sex, gender, and sexuality ought to be perfectly correlated. For example, Dr. G. shared,

> The hard part [for this family] is that every time this mom changes the diaper of her baby girl, she sees these testes. . . . It's this daily reminder. Some families could accept that, but for this family, it's just really getting debilitating.

Dr. D. further explained that "parents [of intersex children raised as boys] complain to me that they wanna wear their sister's dresses and play with the dolls; they don't wanna go out and play with other boys." Dr. A., on the other hand, shifted the responsibility to parents more directly by citing their beliefs about sex, gender, and sexuality:

> I generally think it's up to parents to pick [a sex and ultimately a gender] based upon what information we have available at the time. The most important counseling that we can give to people is help them understand that the gender of rearing may or may not turn out to be much related to sexual preference and behavior later on. And parents need to appreciate the ambiguity involved.

When consulting with parents, medical professionals like Drs. G., D., and A. do not challenge the idea that sex, gender, and sexuality must be neatly correlated even though they acknowledge the "ambiguity involved." This is likely because they, too, hold narrow understandings of such phenomena and a deep desire to see two, and only two, sexes.

Let us not forget that medical professionals present the intersex trait to the parents of newly diagnosed children by inundating them with medical information. For example, Dr. B. explained:

> I feel like we pretty immediately—when we do the initial education with families— talk about what we know about the sources of these problems, and we talk a little bit about what we know about what determines sexual orientation and what determines, and what would determine, sexual function.

If medical professionals believe the sex, gender, and sexuality of an infant can be captured by diagnostic testing, and they are the experts who discover and then disclose the intersex traits to parents, we cannot reasonably expect parents to challenge their recommendations for how to "treat" the intersex trait. Medical professionals did acknowledge the difficulty parents face when making their decisions. Dr. B. described the process: "We kind of go through, here are the two choices, and get parents pretty actively involved. I think sometimes we overwhelm them a little bit with information, but I don't know how else you do it. I'm not sure." Dr. I. further explained:

> So for family, it's hard. They are forced to make certain decisions—not all decisions—some decisions with the best available data we have at this time. And that's hard. That's what parents do all the time. We just do the best we can [in our recommendations] with the data we have.

Although it was common for medical professionals to acknowledge that decision making could be a difficult process for the parents, they still placed the responsibility for the decision entirely on the parents—thereby escaping any responsibility. When Dr. B. was asked what could be done to make the decision-making process easier for parents, she suggested that "better" data could help parents make their decisions: "I mean, I'm really saying that we could give better information to parents 'cause they make the decision."

There were a few medical professionals who acknowledged that at least some parents were resistant to medical intervention. Describing one particular case, Dr. F. explained, "The mother is really torn about which sex to raise this child." Dr. F. further articulated the problem:

> Surgeons want to do a surgery to repair the hypospadias and make the child look more typically male now, and the mother is concerned that if she does that, that the child may somehow later in life reject that, or may want to change to a female sex of rearing, and [would] have gone through all this surgery unnecessarily. So the mother is disinclined to do any surgery, and the surgeon is trying to hint her into the direction of doing surgery.

Dr. E. similarly shared with me that "parents are really pressured . . . from doctors" to raise their intersex children to "conform to a gender role."

What happens when parents resist medical recommendations? Although it's not common given that most parents defer to medical expertise, what I learned is that the parents who do challenge medical recommendations are likely to face harsh criticism from medical providers. For example, Dr. C. recounted a recent consultation with a family that was very critical of his recommendations:

> The father said, "[Doctor], can I ask you a question?" I said, "Absolutely, this is your forum. I'm at your disposal. You're hiring me." He said, "Why should we do anything?" And I acted physically surprised, I'm sure I did. And I said, "Well, I'm concerned that if you raise this child in a male gender role without a straight penis, he's not going to see himself as most other males and he's not going to certainly be able to function as most other males." And the father said, "Well, in our family we like to celebrate our differences and not try to all be the same and feel the social pressure to do everything like everyone else does." . . . I said, I do have to say one thing, and I think it's of key importance, that you both see a psychiatrist.

This harsh criticism is evidence of the pushback parents experience if they are brave enough to question medical recommendations. While the 2000 and 2006 medical statements introduced earlier warned against performing medically unnecessary interventions on intersex bodies, these surgeries continue. In the section that follows, we hear directly from the parents and learn that when they connect with the intersex community, they question the necessity of medical interventions, delaying and in some cases denying consent for such procedures.

ADVICE FROM THE COMMUNITY

I think it is fair to assume most parents are guided by their own life experiences and the best of intentions when they make parenting decisions. For most parents of children with intersex traits, they face an important parental decision—to consent or refuse to consent to irreversible medical interventions—without, in most cases, any of their own life experiences to guide their decision. For many parents, intersex is something they've never heard of before their child's diagnosis. This is further complicated when we are reminded that medical professionals frame intersex as a medical emergency that demands immediate action. Some parents do question the necessity of acting immediately, and in turn, usually find themselves connected with the intersex community and diverse viewpoints from other parents, adults with intersex traits, and professional allies from both within and outside of medicine. They are not inundated with more medical diagnostics. Instead, they hear personal accounts in ways that shape how they understand intersex medical care. More specifically, parents connected to intersex communities learn about the consequences of irreversible medical interventions, and as discussed below, are less likely to allow medical providers to perform suggested procedures. The parents who connect with the intersex community after they've allowed medical professionals to perform irreversible medical interventions are also affected by the personal accounts, but since they've already consented to such procedures, they are left feeling responsible for earlier decisions they've made.

As described earlier, in the 1990s the intersex rights movement was formed. In many ways, the movement has been so successful in its formation because it formed as the internet was gaining momentum and becoming more affordable for the average person to access. If one has access to the internet, a simple Google search of "intersex," for example, would lead you to a number of intersex activist and support group organizations throughout the United States and even the world. Today, intersex activist organizations and support groups exist all over the internet, allowing many parents of newly diagnosed children—and even adults with intersex traits—to get connected to the community and learn about the condition by communicating with those also personally affected.[12]

Parents who connect with the intersex community learn quite quickly that most adults with intersex traits are openly critical of unnecessary medical interventions. This criticism offers insight into the consequences of medically unnecessary interventions, which most medical providers seem to ignore or not care to share. For example, Pidgeon, a young adult with an intersex trait, offered this advice that many in the community share:

> Never let them touch you in terms of surgery. That's number one. If they ask about surgery or ask your opinion, don't do that. Don't do surgery, no matter what they say. . . . You'll love your body somehow, some way, and you don't need surgery to love your body and love yourself. . . . If you fuck with your body, you can never change that. But if you don't fuck with your body, you can change your acceptance of your body.

Parents in the community tended to offer similar advice geared to other parents. Hope explained:

> Just breathe. Take a deep breath and don't feel like you have to rush into anything. . . . Let [your child be]. Get all the information you can and then wait. Don't feel like you have to rush and make your decisions.

One of the reasons for the criticism from community members about medically unnecessary surgical interventions is that it creates an incredible amount of trauma in one's life. Ana, an adult with an intersex trait, shared:

> When I was 12 . . . I was told [by my parents and doctors] that my ovaries had not formed correctly and that there was a risk of cancer and that they needed to be removed. And I had lots of examinations, including of my genitals, but I was never made aware [prior to surgery] that anything was going to be taken away [from down] there. So it was a big shock to me [when I woke up after surgery]. And I really had some work to do when I was eventually ready to do it . . . from the trauma that I had from waking up from my surgery to realize that what was between my legs was gone.

As you might imagine, parents are deeply moved when they hear these personal accounts from adults with intersex traits and their parents. In turn, this influences how parents who are faced with the decision to consent or refuse to consent to suggested medical interventions respond. For those who are contemplating their consent, they usually end up refusing or, at the very least, delaying consent to medically unnecessary interventions. Laura, a parent of a child with an intersex trait, explained:

> [My husband] wanted [anything male] gone. Anything male, he wanted it out of our daughter 'cause he considered it male, and our daughter a separate entity. . . .

But the more I was reading, and I guess on the [intersex support group] webpage and then on the parent group talking about it. . . . "Your daughter's natural hormone maker [should be left alone]. . . . It's better than being on a pill all your life. Sometimes kids with the pill have a difficult or more difficult puberty." There wasn't any doubt about it that I wanted to keep [her as is after that]. I think it was . . . it took me a little while to convince [my husband] we needed to keep it.

Shelby and her husband, Drew, parents of a young baby with an intersex trait, shared a similar experience. Drew explained:

When we met [an adult with an intersex trait], he said . . . "Hey, keep them in as long as you can." I think I'm going to listen to a guy like that a little bit more. . . . It sounds like there's probably more benefits to having them than less benefits.

However, Shelby and Drew experienced pushback from some medical experts. One doctor told them that their daughter "would be very psychologically damaged if [they] don't remove her testes immediately."

Michelle, a parent of a teenager with an intersex trait, had a comparable experience with medical professionals:

They told us that they needed to remove the gonads at one month. So she had surgery because they said "this is what you do" and we had no clue. Now I wish that we would've waited just because of all the information that we have now.

Jeff, a father of a young adult with an intersex trait, stated, with obvious emotion, that medical professionals advised:

Basically immediate surgery, for certain things . . . and you know we found out that that wasn't really necessary. . . . They didn't get into whether [she] would need surgery or not need surgery. . . . The big fear right away is . . . this is the fear that the pediatric endocrinologist put into us, is "Oh, she's got to have it taken out right now or she's going to have cancer. Right now." And then when you start finding out [from] people who've dealt with these situations for a long time, over many, many years . . . they're like "That's not true." The risk is no different than anybody else.

Laura, a parent introduced earlier, shared,

My big turnaround was when I met you guys [in the support group]. It showed me that it all works out in the end. It does all work out. You guys all lead great lives and you're not so worried all the time.

Drew had a similar experience:

> I think the [intersex support group] conference reassured me the most. To see . . .
> I mean, those girls, it seems like they're all accomplished people that are doctors,
> people that are whatever they want to be. Nothing's going to hold them back.

With respect to parents who found the intersex community after already consenting to such procedures, there appears to be some guilt, albeit with an understanding that their decision was anything but informed. For example, Susan, a parent, shared that "parents aren't making an informed decision" when doctors treat it "like, oh, you got to do it right now." Jen, a parent, explained:

> The only reason we did [the surgery] then was that was what we were told eleven
> years ago. Oh, you have them taken out because . . . you either make a decision, or
> you wait for [your] teen to decide. . . . [The] word "cancer" came up enough and
> that did it. So we took them out.

As I've shown in this section, parents could benefit in the decision-making process if they were connected to the intersex community. However, for this to happen, medical experts need to be willing to refer parents to intersex support groups.

PARENTS AS PAWNS

Parents seem to be pawns in the case of intersex medical care because medical professionals tend to place all the responsibility for unnecessary surgical interventions on their shoulders. Medical professionals rarely accept responsibility in the decision-making process. Instead, as I've shown, they tend to inundate parents with *medical information* and myths about cancer risks associated with intersex traits. While it may be the case that some intersex traits have the potential to increase one's risk of developing gonadal (or other related) cancer,[13] these claims have inconsistent support. It is also true that the mere risk of developing cancer should not be reason enough to surgically modify healthy bodies. We don't, for example, go around removing breast tissue from newborn babies to eliminate their possibility of developing breast cancer.

What parents could benefit from is not more *medical information* but rather *personal experiences* from those in the community—especially adults with intersex traits. When parents learn that irreversible medical interventions are not always necessary and can even cause emotional and, in some cases, physical pain for those who have been surgically modified, they choose to delay or even refuse such procedures. Those who are exposed to such personal experiences after already consenting to irreversible interventions, on the other hand, are left with some guilt even though they were acting with the best of intentions and merely following medical recommendations.

Given parents are affected by the personal experiences of those in the intersex community, shouldn't doctors want to connect parents with similarly situated others as they contemplate irreversible interventions? Wouldn't this approach, coupled with the medical information doctors provide, offer parents the most complete pool of information and assist them in their decision-making process? If medical professionals do not begin to refer parents to support groups when there is evidence such connections influence the parental decision-making process about medical interventions, they are, on these grounds alone, acting *irresponsibly* and might even be *legally liable* for their actions. Medical professionals must present parents with a diverse pool of information even if some of that information resides outside of medicine—otherwise, parents will continue to be played like pawns in a chess game of medical authority and jurisdiction over the intersex body.

Notes

1. Androgen Insensitivity Syndrome Support Group-USA was recently renamed AIS-DSD Support Group.
2. See Cools et al. (2006); Pleskacova et al. (2010).
3. Chase (1998).
4. Some of the first feminist scholarship on the medical management of intersex traits is as follows: Fausto-Sterling (1993); Kessler (1990). For more contemporary feminist scholarship, see Karkazis (2008); Preves (2003).
5. Committee on Genetics: Section on Endocrinology and Section on Urology (2000).
6. Committee on Genetics: Section on Endocrinology and Section on Urology (2000), p. 138.
7. Committee on Genetics: Section on Endocrinology and Section on Urology (2000), p. 138.
8. Committee on Genetics: Section on Endocrinology and Section on Urology (2000), p. 141.
9. Lee et al. (2006).
10. Davis (2011).
11. Davis (2011).
12. Preves (2004).
13. See Cools et al. (2006); Pleskacova et al. (2010).

In Other Words

THE MESSAGES AFRICAN AMERICAN MOTHERS AND FATHERS GIVE ADOLESCENTS ABOUT RACE ARE SHAPED BY THEIR OWN EXPERIENCES WITH RACIAL DISCRIMINATION AND THEIR OBSERVATIONS AND FEARS OF RACIAL DISCRIMINATION

Kathleen Holloway and Fatima Varner, June 28, 2022 / CCF@TSP

African American parents commonly socialize their adolescent children about race, ethnicity, and interracial relations. These racial socialization messages include communications about potential racial barriers—known as preparation for bias—and messages about African American culture, history, and heritage—known as cultural socialization.

Cultural socialization has been linked to adolescents' academic achievement, fewer problem behaviors, and better psychological functioning. Though the evidence is somewhat weaker than for cultural socialization, preparation for bias has been linked to reduced problem behaviors, increased self-esteem, and increased well-being in the presence of racial discrimination.

African American individuals can experience racial discrimination directly or vicariously. In addition, they can fear future discrimination, also known as anticipated discrimination. These race-related stressors may, in turn, influence African American parents' racial socialization messages. For example, after parents are exposed to others' racial discrimination experiences (for example, the death of Trayvon Martin), they may prepare their children to cope with racial stressors. Moreover, parents' worries about experiencing future racial discrimination may lead them to communicate about race with their children.

How parents view their race and think others view them—their racial identity—as well as whether they are a mother or father, can influence the relationship between race-related stressors and the racial socialization messages that they give their children. For example, previous research has found that parents who believe others view their race negatively (they report low public regard for African Americans) are more likely to communicate with their children about racial discrimination. Similarly, parents who hold positive views of their own race (they report high private regard for African Americans) share more positive messages about being Black with their children.

This research brief reports on a recent study that examined how parents' race-related stressors, racial identity, and gender shape the racial socialization messages they give their adolescents. The researchers analyzed online survey data from a national sample of 567 African American parents of adolescents.

Key Findings

Levels of discrimination: African American parents reported moderate levels of personal racial discrimination and vicarious racial discrimination experiences. They reported moderately high levels of anticipating future racial discrimination.

Personal and vicarious racial discrimination experiences were related to the messages parents gave their adolescent children about African American culture, history, and heritage. However, anticipated racial discrimination was not associated with these cultural socialization messages.

Among mothers who held positive views about African American people, higher reported experiences of vicarious racial discrimination were associated with more cultural socialization messages for their adolescents.

The following groups had higher preparation for bias messages; that is, they did more to prepare their adolescent children for bias:

- parents who believe that others view their race negatively who also experienced high vicarious racial discrimination
- mothers who reported higher anticipated racial discrimination
- fathers who hold positive views about African American people who also had high levels of personal racial discrimination experiences

Policy Implications

Race-related stressors, particularly those associated with vicarious and anticipated racial discrimination, are common among African American parents and likely influence how they socialize their children about race. Reducing discrimination and helping African American parents cope with these race-related stressors would benefit parents and their children. Ways to achieve these goals include increasing resources available to schools, mental health providers, and institutions that serve African American families.

African American parents often relay messages about race to their adolescents that promote pride in their ethnic-racial group and that warn of possible racial barriers. The color-blind approaches (for example, "I only see one race, the human race") that are sometimes emphasized in schools are in conflict with these racial socialization messages that African American parents share with their children. Therefore, schools should strongly consider curricula that include racial socialization messages to both spark students' pride in their racial-ethnic group and prepare them for bias.

Finally, African American parents' racial messages to their children vary based on personal characteristics such as gender and racial attitudes as well as their exposure to different race-related stressors. More funding for culturally relevant training and interventions is needed to support African American families, with attention to how exposure to and processing of racialized experiences may influence Black mothers and fathers differently. ▰

In Other Words

MOTHERING WHILE BLACK

Dawn Marie Dow, October 22, 2019 / CCF@TSP

It is common for observers to talk about a "stalled revolution" in family life. Most American mothers raising small children now work outside the home, but the "ideal worker" remains a man who has no obligations at home because he has a wife to take care of his children; and many Americans believe that the "ideal parent" is a mother who takes primary responsibility for the home. Much has been written about the guilt and conflict that mothers feel when they work for pay outside the home. But for some mothers in America, working outside the home was not a revolution but a long-standing norm. Whereas significant numbers of middle-class white mothers joined the workforce only during World War II and again in the early 1960s, African American mothers, including middle-class ones, have always worked for pay or as enslaved people. Thus, statements such as "mothers think," "mothers feel," or "mothers are seen" might be appropriate for racially, ethnically, or economically homogeneous nations, but not for the United States. Here, the impact of race and class on mothers' experiences and perspectives makes such claims suspect.

For my book *Mothering While Black: Boundaries and Burdens of Middle-Class Parenthood*, I interviewed sixty African American middle-class mothers about their work, family, and parenting experiences. They talk very differently than white mothers about what it means to be a good mother. Although caregiving was an essential part of these mothers' identities, they and their communities often assumed they would work outside the home. Although balancing the demands of paid employment and child-rearing did not become easier, this did mean that these mothers often viewed working outside the home and economically providing for their families as part of the duties of motherhood, rather than as a detraction from them. Indeed, contrary to research and popular discourse that depicts working mothers as feeling compelled to justify their employment, these mothers generally did not do so. In fact, African American middle-class stay-at-home mothers often felt as though they had to justify their decision *not* to work.

Patricia Hill Collins and Bart Landry have described how African American women were historically not able or encouraged to reduce or eliminate their paid employment. In response, African American women produced their own distinct and positive visions of womanhood and motherhood that incorporated the needs of their communities and supported their work outside the home. Landry describes how, long before Betty Friedan and the women's rights movement of the 1960s and 1970s, African American female activists from the nineteenth and twentieth

centuries, such as Ida B. Wells, Mary Church Terrell, and Anna Cooper, were proponents of an ideal of womanhood that combined family, career, and community and,
in part, explained why African American women's rates of employment were higher
than those of white women.

Indeed, the majority of African American middle- and upper-middle-class mothers I talked to, including both employed mothers and stay-at-home mothers, did
not feel isolated in their mothering. Instead they experienced motherhood within a
community they were already connected to or worked to create. Many of the mothers I interviewed expected support from extended family and community members
when raising their children. They felt secure having kin and community members
care for their children, and that assistance facilitated their paid employment.
Although these networks of care were not available to all mothers, those who had
them generally used them. Research on middle-class families often focuses on self-
sufficient traditional heterosexual nuclear families consisting of a mom, dad, and
children, with extended kin called on only in emergencies. In my interviews, informants described extended family and community networks as sources of assistance
that were valued for their own benefit, not merely used as backup. Such networks
play an essential role in helping these women balance the competing demands of
paid employment and child-rearing.

The middle- and upper-middle-class African American mothers I studied made
decisions about work and family against a familial and community backdrop that
presumed working for pay was one aspect of mothering. They often grew up in
households in which two or more incomes were necessary to counter racial discrimination in the labor force. They were connected to communities in which being a
strong independent woman is seen as a virtue. Their families and communities generally view positively their decision to engage in paid labor and provide emotional
and instrumental support by helping with child care. Indeed, instead of expressing guilt or ambivalence about their work, African American mothers employed in
middle-class professional careers described themselves as role models of female
independence and self-reliance for both their sons and daughters. The positive
expectation that mothering responsibilities include breadwinning supports their
comfort with paid employment. Ironically, such expectations can also lead stay-at-
home mothers to feel the need to explain their choice.

Of course, structural shifts such as changes in workplace functioning and new
family-friendly laws and policies are necessary to reduce the challenges all parents
face in the workplace. But my research with African American middle-class mothers shows that it is also important to encourage cultural expectations and community supports that validate women's need and desire to combine paid work and
caretaking. ■

30

Parenting Adult Children in the Twenty-First Century

Joshua Coleman

W*hen I was growing up in the 1960s and '70s, my friends and I couldn't stand our parents' music, clothing, and more than a few of their friends. We would have no sooner put on a Bing Crosby record than they would have worn a tie-dyed T-shirt, smoked a bong, or waxed poetic about the intensity of a Jimi Hendrix solo. They were the ADULTS—foreign, unfathomable, living in a world we scarcely deigned to penetrate except to get the keys to their cars.[1]*

In addition, our parents had little interest in our music and weren't terribly concerned with what we thought about their taste in clothing. They expected us to respect them and didn't spend a lot of time worrying whether their parenting mistakes would ruin our love for them. They also didn't spend endless hours reading parenting books or watching experts on television, and they weren't terribly concerned about respecting our rights or infringing on our autonomy.

A few generations have passed, and I'm now a parent to adult children and a clinical psychologist who has addressed and studied generation gaps. As the saying goes, "My, how times have changed."

It is not just since the 1960s: for more than a century, we have witnessed a profound change in our perception of children and how they should be parented. Prior to the twentieth century, parents viewed children as resilient and robust, and they also believed that the rigors of life would make children stronger and more capable. Fast-forward through many generations and, for a variety of reasons, including smaller family size, the prevalence of divorce, the advent of parenting experts, a decrease in opportunities after college, and a perception of an increasingly dangerous world, today's parents believe that children are fragile and vulnerable, requiring a close and carefully managed childhood in order to succeed. Since the 1960s, there has been a gradual blurring of the boundaries between parents and children as families moved to a more democratic structure where the child's opinions and feelings became far more valued. Parents' expectations of what they want from their children have also changed.

In the twenty-first century, generational boundaries are more likely to exist in poor, working-class, and other more marginalized families. As Patricia Sanchez-Connally describes in Chapter 32, immigrant families use duty and closeness as a resource for mobility—even if that style of familism isn't always valued in dominant social institutions. Historian Steven Mintz explained (in an email): "Many immigrant families, especially those in the first generation, still value interdependence and filial duty. However, in recent decades the majority of American families who have been here for several generations or more have experienced weakening [extended] kin ties and high rates of mobility and dispersion." There's still great variety, but for the middle class, generational markers that were common as recently as four or five decades ago, like I described in my childhood, have largely disappeared.

The twentieth century brought us unprecedented improvements in the quality of children's lives, yet in the twenty-first century, today's middle-class parents are worried. They obsess over the slightest error in parenting and worry that they may have forever blighted their child's life with a comment made in anger or exhaustion. The constant broadcast of parenting advice causes new parents to feel as though they are practically committing child abuse if they don't obsessively read every available book on pregnancy, early childhood development, and acing the SATs. Parents worry that if they don't closely monitor the academic implications of every grade from preschool through high school, their child will get crowded out of the increasingly tight bottleneck of colleges and the shrinking opportunities for secure, good jobs.[2] They are terrified of doing something to turn their child against them or of forever losing their love. Parents everywhere worry about drug and alcohol addiction, internet porn, attention deficit disorder (ADD), sexual predators, and a whole slew of psychiatric disorders.[3] As Gerson (Chapter 36) and Jacobs and Dunatchik (Chapter 38) explain, dads and moms are more involved, but the bulk of the burden and worry still falls on moms. Prior generations of parents felt that their job was finished once children left home, yet many parents today continue to worry long afterward. As a psychologist in private practice, I see parents struggling to understand their adult children, and many are fighting to find ways to keep them in their lives. The confusion about how to remain close to adult children has spawned an explosion of new self-help books in just the past few years with titles such as *Walking on Eggshells, You're Wearing That?, Don't Bite Your Tongue, Setting Boundaries with Your Adult Children,* and my own books, *When Parents Hurt* and *Rules of Estrangement.*

FROM RESILIENCE TO FRAGILITY

In the nineteenth and early twentieth centuries, the task of children was to prepare themselves for adult work by following the instructions appropriate to their class, race, and gender. Historian Mintz points out (in Chapter 7 of this volume) that at the end of the nineteenth century, Americans began to see children as independent beings with their own needs and rhythms of development. In addition, Americans shifted from believing that it was the obligation of children to meet the family's needs to believing that the family should meet the children's needs.[4]

From the 1920s to the 1970s, Americans steadily changed their child-rearing emphasis from valuing conformity, church attendance, loyalty, and obedience to focusing on children's autonomy, tolerance, and ability to think for themselves.[5] This change was accompanied by a transformation in the family climate of the middle class from authoritarian to more democratic and permissive. Children went from being quietly kept in the background to being loudly and proudly paraded into the foreground. In many households, children became the axis upon which the household turned.[6]

Distrust of parents emerged early in the twentieth century. Sigmund Freud, who founded psychoanalysis at the dawn of the twentieth century, and the experts who followed him popularized the idea that parents could be a corrupting influence on the fragile psychological development of the child. According to Freud, children could be easily led into neurosis (that is, a mild level of mental disturbance that isn't related to a biological source), if not psychosis, by parents who failed to adequately address the challenges posed by each stage of development.[7] This perspective put pressure on parents and made them worry that a small mistake would consign their child to a life spent in a therapist's office, or worse.

Nevertheless, for the first half of the twentieth century, parents continued to believe not only that children could handle the stresses created by struggle, adversity, and competition but that these would strengthen and prepare them for the challenges they would later face.[8] Phrases such as "building backbone," "strengthening character," and "improving moral fiber" were all used to characterize the outcome of a childhood and adolescence exposed to these elements.

Hothouse Parenting

Over the past forty to fifty years, our view has slowly changed, and we now perceive children as fragile and requiring a kind of "hothouse parenting" in order to thrive.[9] Sociologist Annette Lareau describes this type of middle-class parenting as "concerted cultivation," characterized by the parents' active organization of children's leisure activities and the frequent engagement of verbally intensive interactions geared to increase a sense of entitlement and mutuality with adults. One of the goals of concerted cultivation is helping children understand the parents' decisions and assisting children in understanding their own inner words.[10] While this form of parenting originated in the middle class, recent studies show that it has become common across social classes.[11]

But it doesn't work the same for all. As sociologist Jessica Calarco shows, this norm of entitlement doesn't work in poor and working-class families as well as it does for the middle class.[12] Poor and working-class parents don't have the same resources to provide their children with the kinds of opportunities available to the children of parents with greater resources. In addition, families with fewer resources and those who face greater discrimination may require children to help the parent or parents more.

Mintz writes that with the notable exceptions of the Quakers and Native Americans, strategies that motivated children by using guilt, shame, or pain dominated American parenting up through the Victorian era. During the twentieth century, these strategies gradually gave way to approaches that emphasized negotiating with children to help them understand their behavior and motivation.[13] In the twentieth century, the negotiating style became de rigueur. As a result of this shift, parents began to feel tremendous pressure to produce a child who was self-aware but who was not unduly fettered by the corrosive effects of guilt, self-consciousness, and the burdens of "codependency," or the inclination to worry so much about the well-being of the other that you consistently put their needs above yours.

Parents as Problems in the Late Twentieth Century

This new focus on raising self-aware children created a slew of relational and parenting experts to help people overcome the guilt, anxiety, and fear that came as they began to wrestle with this new kind of identity. One of the central obstacles to this individualistic perspective became the problematic parent, as we first heard about from Freud. Parents began to be viewed as potential baggage to be contained, if not eliminated, in the quest for self-esteem, psychological health, and personal fulfillment. A visit to any bookstore shows the success of this enterprise.

In fact, the field of psychology has probably done more to create parental, especially maternal, anxiety and guilt than any other institution. For example, in the 1960s, the influential child psychologist Bruno Bettelheim wrote that childhood autism was caused by mothers who couldn't relate to their children.[14] Psychologist Jay Haley and colleagues, along with anthropologist Gregory Bateson, argued that schizophrenia resulted from mothers who communicated in contradictory, "double-binding" fashions with their children.[15] Both theories, popular at their time, have been disproved or shown to be highly flawed.

Remember the guilt that was used by parents to control children? The tables turned. Parents' capacity to provide their children with entertainment became an effective and guilt-inducing tool to market products to parents. In addition, it became another way that children could later fault their parents. The statement "I'm bored" grew to be a statement that reflected on the parents' adequacy and worth. Children could now judge parents by how well they provided opportunities and, therefore, how deserving they were of the child's love and respect. Children could later, rightly or wrongly, blame parents for the ways that they turned out or failed.[16] They could attribute parents' failure to provide "formative opportunities" as being far more central than they may have been.

For example, in Steven Spielberg's movie *Hook*, a 1991 remake of *Peter Pan*, Captain Hook attempts to curry favor with Michael by arranging a baseball game. When Michael is up to bat, Hook motivates him by saying, "This is for all of the baseball games that your father never attended!" The child snarls in righteous anger and hits a home run.

This is a major reversal. Where prior generations of children were expected to earn the *parents'* love and respect, today's parents are worried that they won't have their *children's* love and respect because they're not good *enough*: not sensitive enough, not fun enough, not "there" enough.[17] They're worried, often correctly, that their real or imagined mistakes in parenting may one day come back to haunt them. And compared with the past, parents have far fewer support systems of kin and neighbors to help them strike the right balance in raising their child.[18]

THE ISOLATED FAMILY

In the past few decades, the financial and emotional resources that were once exchanged with extended kin, neighbors, religious institutions, and friends have become increasingly concentrated in the nuclear family. Only half as many people said that they had four to five confidants in 2004 compared with those who had that number of confidants in 1985, and the number of people stating that there is *no one* with whom they discuss important matters has tripled in that same time frame.[19] In the time of COVID, families became even more isolated. In 2021, 12 percent of people reported having no close friendships beyond their family.[20]

Whereas the family and the identity of its members once existed in a rich ecosystem fed and nourished by a community of supports, American families have more and more begun to stand alone. Much of the time and energy that once went into socializing with neighbors and kin has been transferred into parenting.

According to sociologists Suzanne Bianchi, John Robinson, and Melissa Milke, today's mothers spend twice as much time with their children—from a higher base rate—and fathers three times as much time as they did in the supposedly halcyon days of the mid-1960s.

Parents, especially mothers, increase their time with their children by giving up time for themselves, sacrificing sleep, friendships, and time with their spouses.[21] At the same time, there has been a 40 percent reduction in the amount of time that children play outside, leaving parents with much more time under the same roof with their children.[22] These changes, combined with smaller family sizes, have increased the demands on parents to play the emotional, educational, and socializing roles that siblings, neighbors, and friends once filled.

These changes have benefited some families. A greater amount of time spent between parent and child offers the potential for more intimacy, understanding, and shared meaning. Many of today's parents are able to have long-term friendships with their children after they leave home that are enriched by the close and involved years that they spent together before the children moved out.[23]

Yet this intensive parenting may test the limits of what couples can reasonably ask of each other and may place an undue burden on the parent-child relationship. When parents spend less time with their friends and communities, many of them may turn to their offspring for fulfillment, intimacy, and long-term security. More time and more involvement create the possibility for more conflict, resentment, and disappointment on the part of both parent and child. Ironically, a close, intimate relationship with a parent may make it harder to separate from that parent and, as a result, may tempt the adult child to push away more aggressively in order to launch their own adult life.

While parents are expected to provide an even greater investment in child care, entertainment, protection, college, and after-college care than prior generations of parents, there are few guidelines for what they might expect in return. Parents may feel betrayed if they do not get the love and gratitude they look forward to and believe that they deserve. But children can also review their childhoods from the calculus of how supportive or affectionate their parents were and may declare the relationship null and void if they evaluate it as something less than they needed or deserved.

SOULMATE PARENT

The combination of the democratization of the family form, fewer opportunities after children leave home, a culture that blames parents for child outcomes, a more dangerous world, and an increase in parental guilt and anxiety have together created an environment where parents believe that they have to be everything for their children. From this perspective, the modern middle-class parent has much in common with another cultural icon, *the soulmate*. The soulmate ideology goes like this: one's future spouse is supposed to be sexy (though not insatiable), independent (but not too independent), intimate (but not cloying), funny (but not obnoxious), well educated (but not arrogant), and sensitive (but not wimpy).

In parallel, the soulmate ideal requires parents to be sensitive (but not intrusive), tolerant (though not neglectful), forgiving (though not weak), current on child development (though not a pedant), a good playmate (but not trying to live their life through the child), and a good mentor (without using the word *mentor*). Parents are also supposed to be enthusiastic fans of whatever artistic, sporting, or academic endeavor is pursued by the child.

The romantic soulmate and the soulmate parent suffer from fundamental problems: (1) most individuals don't have the bounty of traits, attitudes, and attributes to bring to any one relationship; (2) what we want and need from a person at one point in time is often quite different from what we may need from them at another; and (3) our own character flaws, genetics, and moods may cause us to wittingly or unwittingly shut down or greatly inhibit the other's capacity to provide the interaction that we may so desperately crave. In addition, parents and children can have very different outlooks and opinions due to cultural, racial, or sexual identification differences. For example, you can read about the experiences of nonbinary youth coming out to their families in Chapter 27.

WHEN THE CHILD REJECTS THE PARENT

In the past decade, I have seen an explosion in my clinical practice of parents who have come to me because they were cut off by their grown children. While some of these parents made terrible mistakes, many of them were loving and reasonable. What explains this increase in cases of parental rejection?[24]

Divorce is one common factor. Parents are more concerned than in the past about their children's individual happiness, and they are also looking out for their own happiness. As a result, they increasingly feel free to leave marriages that are insufficiently supportive, meaningful, or affectionate.

In some circumstances, a divorce creates the ability to be a more involved, less distracted parent.[25] Numerous studies show that children benefit from a divorce if their parents had a high-conflict marriage.[26] In this situation, a divorce may enable the children to have better relationships with their parents. Constance Ahrons found that some adult children felt that their relationships with their fathers either improved or remained stable over time after a divorce.[27]

But divorce also offers a variety of ways for parents and children to become distant or estranged. Numerous studies show that after a divorce, the relationship between father and daughter is more at risk than the mother-daughter relationship.[28] These feelings may become especially inflamed after a parent remarries, or with increased interparental conflict, father remarriage, or low father involvement in the early post-divorce years. And in their old age, divorced fathers usually get much less care and attention from their daughters than do mothers.[29] Divorce increases fathers' vulnerability to anxiety and depression.[30] Mothers or fathers who feel angry or hurt by the divorce, and who use their children as a way to punish the other parent, often alienate adult children. Mentally ill parents may successfully cause the adult child to believe that closeness with the other parent is a selfish or disloyal act.[31]

But divorce is not the only source of tension between parents and their adult children. Many of the causes are built into today's high expectations of parent-child relations and the greater isolation of nuclear families. Both high expectations and greater isolation create more opportunities for disappointment and fewer places to turn to compensate for problems in the parent-adult relationship. These tensions have been exacerbated in the past thirty years by a decline in the prospects for youthful economic independence. Adult children have become more economically dependent on their parents, and parents are less able to understand the lives and decisions of their young adult children.

"WHEN I WAS YOUR AGE ..."

Prior to the 1970s, a young man could reasonably expect to leave high school and, even without a college degree, marry and support a family. College grads were likely to get permanent work shortly after graduation and could expect to send their kids to an even better university than they attended. Women did not have the same opportunities, but they expected to marry, and for most, marriage seemed the best economic investment in their future.

As historian Stephanie Coontz notes (see Chapter 6), many of the young men starting families after World War II were eligible for veterans' benefits that allowed an unprecedented number of them to enter the middle class. The federal government was also active in helping families by underwriting low down payments and long-term mortgages to boost homeownership. This, in combination with well-paid union jobs, allowed many working-class families to gain entry into the middle class (see Fremstad, Chapter 10, for more on this). Still, barriers to education and homeownership remained in place for African Americans. Nonetheless, women and minorities also began to believe that they might claim their fair share of opportunities as a result of the women's movement and the civil rights struggle of the 1950s and 1960s.[32]

This is radically different from the opportunities that greet today's high school and college graduates. Deindustrialization and economic restructuring during the past forty years have altered the educational and vocational requirements needed to support a family. Whereas a high school degree was once the basic requirement for successful employment, now a college degree is considered the baseline.[33] Even a college degree may not be enough to manage the vagaries of today's changing economic market. For example, as Jones and Schmitt wrote in 2014, a college degree is no guarantee—and Black graduates don't obtain good jobs or good pay at the rate that white graduates do.[34]

These recent economic changes may strain the relationship between parents and their adult children because many parents fail to understand or sympathize with the very different social and economic world that greets their newly minted adults. They may believe that their adult children's economic problems stem more from a lack of character than a new social reality. A *New Yorker* cartoon illustrated this dynamic. It showed two parents standing over their twentysomething-year-old, who was watching television in their living room. The caption, addressed to the reclining son, read, "When I was your age, I was an adult." The cartoon reflects a sentiment that many parents feel and often express to their adult children.

Many of today's parents don't understand the extent to which the job market has changed. While prior generations of children assumed they would one day earn more than their parents did, this experience is becoming less and less common. The headline for an article in the satirical paper *The Onion* says it all: "Most Americans Falling for 'Get Rich Slowly over a Lifetime of Hard Work' Schemes."[35] Prior generations of parents relied on their children's higher earnings to help provide for those parents in old age. But due to skyrocketing costs for health care and housing, low pay for entry-level jobs, and the erosion of job benefits, many of today's young adults find themselves barely able to support themselves, let alone help support their parents. These changes in the economy have also removed an important way that adult children shared a sense of obligation and connection to their parents over the life course.

Of course, many young people do go on to earn very good wages, but the lengthening transition to adulthood means that their ability to do so often depends on their parents' willingness and ability to subsidize them. A study by the Institute for Social Research at the University of Michigan found that 34 percent of young adults between the ages of eighteen and thirty-four receive financial assistance on a regular basis from their parents. According to government statistics gathered in 2017, middle-income parents can expect to spend $290,000 (in 2022 dollars) on each child through the age of seventeen, not including college. But parents can anticipate spending more over the next seventeen years—which makes the transition to adulthood quite different for twenty-somethings whose parents can continue this support. Even parents who cannot afford these expenditures are helping out more than in the past. Today's parents spend nine weeks of their time each year helping adult children aged eighteen to thirty-four with babysitting, transportation, and laundry.[36]

Just as tensions may rise when parents are not able to understand why their kids aren't self-supporting, young adults may resent their parents, either because they can't help or because they feel that there are strings attached to the help from their parents. They may also be tempted to blame parents for their difficult circumstances because they were raised in a culture that views parents as the most important causal agent in child development.

INDIVIDUALISM AND DEPRESSION

Less than one-fifth of Americans see class, race, or gender as important in getting ahead in life. The majority believe that what matters most is individual initiative.[37] But what happens when individual initiative is insufficient to support a family? Psychologist Martin Seligman has shown that individualistic attributions of causality that focus on enduring, personal traits can be useful in creating feelings of optimism and happiness when events go well. But they can generate feelings of depression and pessimism when events turn out poorly because they engender self-blame.[38]

One of the strategies to defend against feelings of self-blame is to blame someone else—what psychologists refer to as *externalization*. Externalization can be a healthy defense mechanism, and as a result, most therapists work hard to help their clients find reasonable explanations that direct blame away from the self. Unfortunately, in today's culture, this often occurs by blaming parents. Parent-blaming can miss the point that our history lessons provide: that larger systems have a lot to do with how opportunities are experienced.

While parents are clearly important in how children turn out, they are less so than our current culture leads us to believe. As historian Stephanie Coontz writes, we live in a culture "that expects us single-handedly, or at most two-parently to counter all the comic ups and downs, social pressures, personal choices, and competing demands of a highly unequal, consumption-oriented culture dominated by deteriorating working conditions, interest-group politics, and self-serving advertisements for everything from toothpaste to moral values."[39] An overemphasis on parental responsibility ignores compelling evidence that children are also affected by their peer groups, neighborhoods, class status, genetics, and siblings.[40] Yet most of the stories that end up in the media feature parents who are (or were) selfish, abusive, neglectful, alcoholic, drug addicted, intrusive, or weak.

While psychotherapy provides a way to externalize blame onto parents, there are few culturally prescribed ways for parents to externalize their feelings of guilt and inadequacy when they feel, rightly or wrongly, that they have caused their child to suffer or to fail. This is probably why so many parents suffer from depression when their children don't thrive as adults or when their children cut off contact with them.[41] While a certain level of selfless devotion comes with the job of being a parent, we need a more accurate lens for people to evaluate their adulthoods other than whether mom or dad did a good-enough job. Perspectives that blame child outcomes on parents are especially problematic when applied to the poor, since the social dynamics of poverty make it harder for parents to protect their children and provide them with the assortment of educational, enrichment, and therapeutic opportunities that are available to the children of parents with greater resources.[42]

INCREASING THE UNDERSTANDING

It is unlikely that the social origins of conflict between parents and their adult children will become part of the public dialogue anytime soon. For this reason, I advise parents who have been cut off or consistently criticized by their adult children to work toward not being defensive, to try to understand their children's complaints, to take responsibility for their parenting mistakes (large and small), and to continue to reach out to their adult children.

Many parents feel challenged by these suggestions. For example, I recently worked with a sixty-three-year-old mother who was frustrated by her thirty-five-year-old daughter's complaints that she wasn't encouraging enough of her when she was growing up. "When I was a child, you got what you got and you were glad for it," she told me. "I wouldn't have even *thought* about my mother not encouraging me enough." Many older parents feel confused and resentful, like this mother, when their parenting is held to the ideal of today's much more intensive parenting standard.

They struggle not to say any one of the following to their complaining adult child:

"Your childhood was a dream compared to mine."

"After everything that I sacrificed for you, this is what I get in response?"

"I didn't have all of the information about parenting that you have these days. It's unfair to have expected me to have known things that weren't part of the culture at the time."

"You had your own contributions to make to our relationship. You weren't an easy child."

I discourage parents from saying any of these statements, because they sound defensive. As with marriage, communication is the most effective when people work to understand, reflect on what was said, and empathize. I also let parents know that even if it feels as though an adult child has all the power, the parent is still a powerful figure in the adult child's mind, even if the parent feels impotent.

There are many reasons why an adult child might cut off or criticize a parent. As with marriage, it is now a game negotiated between equals, and as such, it requires more patience, more respect, and less reliance on the invocations of parental authority. From adult children, it requires an understanding that much more is being asked of today's parents than was asked in prior generations. In the same way that there are numerous forces that affect a child's development, there are many forces affecting an individual's capacity to parent. The more parents and their adult children can empathize with the separate realities of the other, the more closeness and shared understanding can occur going forward.

THE FUTURE OF TENSIONS

What about the future? This chapter shows you that every family story is complicated by history, resources, social class, and inequality. That does not seem to be getting better. At the time of this writing, the United States has the highest rates of social inequality of all the G7 nations.[34] While social inequality is especially hurtful to poor and working-class families, economists note that it has a negative effect on the well-being of middle- and upper-income families as well.[44] There is little in the current political climate to inspire optimism that this will change any time soon. As a psychologist, I see every day how larger context plays a role in personal relationships.

On the other hand, parents and adult children are more in contact today than they've been in many generations. This is due to the financial or domestic needs of the adult child, but it also reflects a more affectionate relationship between parents and adult children caused by more careful, conscientious, and informed parenting over the past few decades.

Notes

1. Coleman (2003).
2. Coleman (2007).
3. Stearns (2003).
4. Zelizer (1994).
5. Coltrane (1996).
6. Stearns (2003).
7. Freud (1926).
8. Stearns (2003).
9. Marano (November/December 2004).
10. Lareau (2003).
11. Ishizuka (2018).
12. Calarco (2018).
13. Mintz (2004).
14. Bettelheim (1967).
15. Bateson (1980).
16. Stearns (2003).
17. Ehrensaft (1997).
18. Ishikuza (2018).
19. Coontz (2006); Putnam (2000).
20. Cox (2021).
21. Bianchi, Robinson, and Milke (2006); Sullivan and Coltrane (2008).
22. Mintz (2006).
23. Pew Research Center (2006).
24. Coleman (2021).
25. Hetherington and Kelly (2002).
26. Amato and Booth (1997); Hetherington and Kelly (2002).
27. Ahrons (2004); Ahrons and Tanner (2003).
28. Nielsen (2004); Hetherington and Kelly (2002).
29. Lin (2008).
30. Amato and Sobolewski (2004); Baum (2006).
31. Hetherington and Kelly (2002); Nielsen (2004).
32. Coontz (2008).
33. Flanagan (2006); Danziger and Gottschalk (2005).
34. Jones and Schmitt (2014).

35. "Most Americans Falling for 'Get Rich Slowly over a Lifetime of Hard Work' Scheme," *The Onion* 41, no. 49 (December 7, 2005): 2.

36. Bahney (2006) and updated with LaPonsie (2022).

37. Wilson and Darity (2022).

38. Seligman (1996).

39. Coontz (1997).

40. Dunn and Plomin (1990); Harris (1999); Reiss, Neiderhiser, Hetherington, and Plomin (2000).

41. Knoester (2003).

42. Coontz (1997).

43. Schaeffer (2020).

44. For example, see Wilkinson and Pickett (2010) and Doepke and Zilibotti (2019).

In Other Words

KEEPING TIES WITH PROBLEMATIC PARENTS

Emma Bosley-Smith and Rin Reczek, November 29, 2022 / CCF@TSP

Relationships with parents are immensely central to children's life experiences. Parents are understood as the de facto caregivers to children and young adults, and the quality of the parent-child relationship shapes children's entire life trajectories. Norms around parenting emphasize that parents should feed, clothe, and love their children. However, parents can also be sources of strain, rejection, fear, and trauma. What is remarkable is that even the most problematic parent-adult child relationships are expected to be—and often are—maintained. Our book *Families We Keep: LGBTQ People and Their Enduring Bonds with Parents* explores why and how the parent-adult child bond remains intact—even when it maybe shouldn't.

Families We Keep centers the voices of seventy-six LGBTQ adults and forty-four of their parents, who volunteered to be interviewed (separately) about their parent-child relationships. On average, LGBTQ people have more strained relationships with parents than cisgender heterosexual adult children due to parents' homophobia, biphobia, transphobia, and the other gender- and sexuality-related stigmas. In fact, many LGBTQ adults' ties with their parents are so bad that LGBTQ people create "chosen" families to supplement the support and love missing in family-of-origin ties. Still, even when LGBTQ adults form chosen families, many also maintain their ties with parents. This is what *Families We Keep* calls a culture of "*compulsory kinship*": the assumption and social expectation that family-of-origin relationships—especially ties with parents—are natural, inevitable, and the most central. *Families We Keep* provides new insight into why and how this is the case.

LGBTQ adults provide three rationales for why they keep ties with parents in line with compulsory kinship. First, LGBTQ adults and their parents draw on what are contemporary ideals of family as spaces of unconditional love and closeness—even when faced with unloving or unclose behavior. Second, LGBTQ people draw on notions of growth—of "it's getting better"—to explain why they maintain these ties, even when the current state of the relationship is still bad. And third, LGBTQ adults think of parents as unique (you only get one mom), and therefore this tie must be kept, even if it hurts. In showing these collective reasonings, *Families We Keep* highlights how the social forces of compulsory kinship frame parent-adult child relationships as natural, inevitable, and enduring *regardless* of the quality. Notably, the ways in which compulsory kinship operates is deeply racialized, with historic and ongoing structural racism subjecting individuals to different levels of stigma and discrimination and increasing importance of family ties.

The second part of the book explores the type of work—specifically "conflict work"—that LGBTQ adults do to keep these relationships intact. For LGBTQ adults, this work revolved around managing, minimizing, or coping with parental homophobia or transphobia, including avoiding or minimizing discussion of their LGBTQ identity or educating their parents about their LGBTQ identity. The work to keep these bonds close fell heavily on the shoulders of LGBTQ adults, creating even more stress in an already strained family situation.

Overall, *Families We Keep* is a book about the importance of compulsory kinship in sustaining what is considered family, structuring choices about who we *should* be in family ties with even if family bonds are harmful or strained. This book is critical in showing the social forces that bond parents and their adult children and should be considered in concert with a large and important scholarship on children who are forcibly removed from their parents, particularly in communities of color. In fact, in contrast to the parents of LGBTQ adult children found in this book, many parents of color have fought and are currently fighting for their rights to keep their own children, including Indigenous peoples who had their children removed from their homes and placed in often deadly residential schools, Black parents who lost children due to an unjust child welfare system and disproportionate incarceration, and immigrant parents who were legally separated from their children. While many children are forcibly removed from parents, other children and adults are in vulnerable positions by an unsafe but compulsory parent-child tie. These two trends—one of the state removing children from people of color and one of compulsory kinship keeping parents and adult children together despite abuse—can be viewed together as a broader system that works to control the family lives of adults. As such, *Families We Keep* ends with a call for wider social supports for all adults, especially those most vulnerable to economic insecurity, ultimately with the goal of giving all people the opportunity to choose the relationships and life that are most fulfilling to them. ◼

PART SEVEN

Leveling the Playing Field

31

Student Loans, Families, and the Unequal
Transition to Adulthood

Arielle Kuperberg and Joan Maya Mazelis

Family economic position has long played an influential role in college attendance in the United States. As described in *A History of American Higher
Education* (Thelin 2019), early college students were young men from wealthy
families; although tuition was not expensive, few families could afford to lose the
help their children provided for the family farm or business. Efforts to expand
college access to the growing middle and upper-middle classes began in the latter part of the nineteenth century. The Morrill Act of 1862 provided land to all
states for the establishment of public colleges. Although still out of reach for
most of the working class, tuition at even prestigious colleges was relatively cheap
from the 1880s to the 1920s (Thelin 2019). The GI Bill of 1944 further expanded
access to higher education by providing veterans with up to four years of tuition
and a living allowance, with higher allowances for married veterans. More than
2 million World War II veterans took advantage of this program, causing enrollments at many universities to double between 1943 and 1946. However, because
most veterans were men, and enrollment in many colleges in the 1940s and 1950s
was restricted to White men, women and veterans of color continued to have
more limited access to higher education (Thelin 2019).

Expanding college access to women and people of color in the mid-twentieth
century transformed the demographic makeup of college students between 1960
and 1980 (Thelin 2019). The high school graduation rate for Black students rose
from under 39 percent in 1960 to 71 percent in the mid-1970s, cutting the Black-
White gap in the high school graduation rate in half and also reducing racial
gaps in college enrollment (Karen 1991). The rapid growth of public universities,

which were more affordable than private schools, diminished the importance of family wealth in college attendance and helped increase access to higher education. By 1980, 78 percent of college students attended public universities, and almost half of recent high school graduates enrolled in college, including 42 percent of recent Black high school graduates and 50 percent of recent White high school graduates (Snyder 1999). The year 1980 was also one of the first years that women became more likely to enroll in college than men (Snyder 1999).

Yet soon after more colleges opened their doors to women and people of color, state governments began a decades-long trend of defunding public higher education through direct cuts to funding and limited budget increases that did not match increased costs and demand (Elliott and Lewis 2015; McGhee 2021). As a result, tuition increased at a rate that far outpaced inflation (Barr and Turner 2013). In addition, starting in 1978, the focus of federal financial aid programs also shifted from grants, which do not have to be repaid, to loans (Thelin 2019).

Before this change, in the late 1970s, approximately 70 percent of the cost of higher education was covered by state and federal governments, and students from low-income backgrounds could rely on grants to cover most of the cost of college (Archibald and Feldman 2012; Elliott and Lewis 2015). But by 2012 less than half of college costs were covered by the government, leaving the remaining burden to students and their families, who increasingly relied on loans (Elliott and Lewis 2015). State budget cuts during the Great Recession worsened these trends so that between 2008 and 2019 the average amount of loan debt at graduation rose by 25 percent (Hanson 2022). (Note: readers who want to look at more recent student debt information can find the latest national and state-level data on the Institute for College Access & Success website here: https://ticas.org/our-work/student-debt/.)

By 2019, 63 percent of students graduating from four-year colleges had some loan debt, and the average public university student with loans took on more than $30,000 in debt to finish their degree (Hanson 2022). The amounts borrowed are only part of what students must later pay, as interest and fees can increase repayment costs considerably. President Biden's student debt policy change, announced in 2022, may reduce or eliminate interest burdens for many borrowers of public (but not private) loans, though the future of the policy remains unclear given ongoing legal battles. College attendance rates are also high, with 66 percent of adults over twenty-five having attended some college (U.S. Census Bureau 2018). Loans therefore affect a substantial number of adults. Our analysis of national U.S. data from 2019 to 2020 (described further below) found that 40 percent of all adults ages thirty-five to forty had taken out at least some student loans to attend college at some point in their lives. Among the two-thirds of people in that age group who had attended at least *some* college, 60 percent had taken out loans. And among those who had *graduated* with a four-year degree (which was around one-third of all adults in that age group), 69 percent had taken out loans. Fewer than 10 percent of adults in their late thirties had managed to both finish a four-year college degree and avoid taking out loans.

As the share of college costs paid by individuals and their families has increased, the role of families—and family wealth—in influencing the college prospects of young adults has regained the high level of importance it had in the early days of university education in the United States. Some students' families have the wealth to pay for college, allowing students to avoid loans or reduce their debt burden. Those without enough help from family must pay these costs themselves, often with student loans—or else forgo a college education, likely reducing their future income considerably. After college, student debt can increase young adults' dependence on parents, decrease their financial stability, and impede romantic relationships, marriage, and childbearing (Kuperberg and Mazelis 2021a; Mazelis and Kuperberg 2022). Delays in achieving these common symbolic markers of the *transition to adulthood* can undermine young adults' well-being by curtailing their ability to build the adult lives or families they want and to achieve the financial stability they hoped for when they first decided to attend college. Loans therefore perpetuate intergenerational class inequalities, even though they also reduce inequalities by allowing young adults without family or personal wealth to attend college (Furstenberg et al. 2004; Mazelis and Kuperberg 2022).

The student debt system also helps perpetuate racial inequalities across generations. Due in no small part to historical and ongoing racial discrimination in employment and housing, Black and Latino families have less wealth than White families in the United States (Conley 1999; Oliver and Shapiro 2006; Wolff 2017). Though the college enrollment and graduation rates of Black and Latino young adults have grown over time, they have not yet met the rates of White students (Irwin et al. 2022), in part because lack of wealth hinders many young adults from pursuing a college degree.

Once they enroll in college, Black students are much less likely to get family help with paying for tuition, are more likely to rely on student loans, and have greater debt burdens (Houle and Addo 2019; Koeze and Russell 2022; Kuperberg 2023). Black students on average pay more for college because of their lack of inherited wealth and their resulting tendency to rely on loans that charge interest (McGhee 2021). After college, Black young adults with loans also tend to earn less and have a harder time repaying their loans compared with White students; as a result, they end up carrying their debt for much longer (Addo et al. 2016; Houle and Addo 2019). Though graduating college is widely believed to reduce inequalities, student debt serves to perpetuate or widen racial disparities.

In this chapter we discuss how student loans, higher education, and families interact to reproduce inequality across generations. We will begin by exploring how family assets, structure, and help are related to whether and how much debt students take on to attend college. Next, we discuss how loans are related to the transition to adulthood during and after college, and how the help that young adults get from and give to their families influences this transition. We then turn to in-depth explorations of how student debt affects marriage, childbearing, and romantic relationships. We end by discussing the implications of our findings for the intergenerational transmission of inequality and the ability of young adults to advance their class positions relative to their parents' class.

In addition to reviewing scientific studies conducted by other researchers, we will discuss our own research on student loan debt and families. Our research has three components (see Kuperberg 2023; Kuperberg and Mazelis 2021a, 2021b, 2022; Mazelis and Kuperberg 2022):

First, we examined the 1997 cohort of the National Longitudinal Survey of Youth (NLSY97), a nationally representative dataset of U.S. young adults born between 1980 and 1984. We refer to this survey as "national data" in this chapter. NLSY first surveyed 8,984 teenagers in 1997 and has been surveying the same group of people every one or two years since then. In the most recent survey available, collected in 2019–2020, the oldest respondents were forty years old.

Second, in spring 2016 we interviewed twenty-four seniors with loans at two regional public universities, one located in the northeast and one in the southeast. We interviewed them shortly before they graduated and have followed up with them annually since then. In this chapter we discuss findings from four waves of interviews, collected each year from 2016 through 2019.

Third, in spring 2017 we surveyed all undergraduates enrolled at the two universities where we had conducted interviews, receiving 3,282 complete responses. In summer 2018, we sent a follow-up survey to the students who completed the first survey and had been about to graduate in spring 2017. A total of 196 graduates responded. This second survey allowed us to see how the students' lives had changed fifteen months after graduation. We refer to these results as "our surveys" in this chapter.

How Do Families Influence Student Loan Debt?

Loan debt is related to families in multiple ways. Family background determines who goes to college in the first place; young adults whose parents have more education are more likely to attend college themselves (Gilbert 2018). In national data, we found that young adults who had a parent with a bachelor's degree (but no graduate degree) were the most likely to take out loans, in part because they had some of the highest college attendance rates (compared, for example, with young adults whose parents did not complete college). The only group with higher college attendance rates were students whose parents had a graduate degree, but their parents' high earnings enabled a larger proportion of this group to avoid loans.

In our surveys and in national data, among young adults who *attended* college, the people most likely to have student loans were those with a parent who had a high school degree or some college but who did *not* finish a four-year degree. Those whose parents had a college or graduate degree were less likely than those with a parent with only a high school degree or some college to take out loans, as were the small number of college attendees whose parents did not complete high school. Though students whose parents have very little education may have greater access to financial aid programs, they are also more reluctant to attend college if doing so requires them to take on debt (Goldrick-Rab 2016).

For most people who attend college, their parents' class position (shaped by their wealth, income, education, and occupation) strongly affects whether they will have family help with paying for college, which can help some students avoid loans entirely (Brown et al. 2011; Millett 2003). Many of our interview participants (who all had loans) noted that they did not have relatives who were able to give them money. As one interview participant, Flo,[1] told us, "Nobody's got it. My whole family's broke. . . . Everybody's poor. I'm probably the richest, and I'm in debt."

Because of their class backgrounds, instead of getting help *from* their families, many young adults with loans give help *to* their families (Mazelis and Kuperberg 2022). In our surveys, we found that around half of college students and graduates with loans said they were helping their families by giving them money, compared with about one-third of students without loans and just over a quarter of graduates without loans. When comparing students whose parents had the same level of education, those with parents who had taken out loans for college were more likely to have taken out loans themselves. Parents' own loan debt may limit their ability to save for their children's education. Our surveys found that 42 percent of undergraduates with loans and 24 percent of graduates with loans said they would save money for their (future) children's college tuition if their loans were forgiven.

Parental wealth and income also determine eligibility for need-based college funding programs like Pell Grants. Pell Grants, first established in 1972, provide funds for tuition and living expenses based on an "expected family contribution," determined by parents' assets until the year students turn twenty-four (U.S. Department of Education 2020). Pell can help some students avoid loans, especially those from very low-income backgrounds, but these grants only rarely cover the entire difference between "expected family contributions" (now renamed the "Student Aid Index") and college expenses. Many parents earn too much money for their children to be eligible for Pell but not enough to pay for all (or any) college costs (Goldrick-Rab 2016; Thelin 2019).

Students' family structures—whether they are cohabiting, are married, or have children of their own—also affect both Pell Grant eligibility and their families' level of assistance with college expenses. Child care costs and number of children in the household are factored into the Student Aid Index (U.S. Department of Education 2020). When students marry or have children, parents' assets are no longer considered even if the students are younger than twenty-four because it is assumed that married or parenting students will not receive tuition assistance from their own parents (U.S. Department of Education 2020). This can expand students' eligibility for Pell, unless they marry a spouse with income that exceeds their parents' expected contributions (students' income is considered whether or not they are married). The assumption that parents will not help married or parenting students as much reflects reality: our surveys found that students who were married, had children, or moved in with a partner were less likely to get help from their parents with paying for college, even when compared with students of the same age and background. But likely because parenting students were more likely to be awarded Pell funding, and married students were more likely to get help paying for college from a romantic partner, our surveys did not indicate that marriage and parenthood affected student loan debt.

On the other hand, our surveys revealed that students who were cohabiting with (but not married to) a romantic partner were the most likely to take out loans—more so than married students *or* students not living with a romantic partner. Without a legal marriage, these students did not have expanded eligibility for Pell Grants, but they didn't get as much help from their parents as students who weren't living with a romantic partner, nor did they receive as much help from their romantic partners as the married students. Couples on weaker financial footing also tend to move in with each other faster because of financial difficulties or housing needs and are more likely to live together before marriage and live together for longer before marrying, if they do eventually marry (Kuperberg 2018, 2019; Sassler and Miller 2017).

Parents' marital status was also associated with whether students took out loans. In our surveys, students with divorced or never-married parents were more likely to take out loans than those with married parents. This likely reflects the strong association of marital status with income and wealth. Financial strain reduces the likelihood of marriage and increases the risk of divorce; divorce, in turn, can further deplete financial assets (Cooper and Pugh 2020).

Student Loans, Family Help, and the Transition to Adulthood

Socially defined symbolic markers of adulthood include completing education, achieving financial independence, and moving out of parents' homes; many also consider marriage and parenthood to be markers that one is an adult (Furstenberg et al. 2004; Settersten and Ray 2010; Shanahan 2000), though sense of adulthood is subjective and nuanced (Katsiaficas 2017; Manzoni 2016; Mazelis and Kuperberg 2022). Young adults value these traditional markers of adulthood, but growing economic uncertainty and the education required to attain financial stability have led to delays in achieving them (Furstenberg et al. 2004; Harknett and Kuperberg 2011). Student loans can delay the transition to adulthood in several ways. By encouraging college attendance and completion, student loans delay the completion of education, which is a key marker of the transition to adulthood. Student debt also delays the transition to adulthood by increasing financial instability among those who take out loans, compared with similarly educated people without debt (Furstenberg et al. 2004; Houle and Warner 2017).

College students and graduates often rely on family for help—especially with money or for a place to live as they navigate higher education and the transition out of college—but this help can diminish their sense of having reached adulthood (Aquilino 2006; Fingerman et al. 2017; Furstenberg et al. 2004; Mazelis and Kuperberg 2022; Settersten and Ray 2010). Attaining a college degree can also be a marker of adulthood and can increase potential earnings, but when that degree is accompanied by substantial debt, the financial independence that is a central signifier of adulthood may remain out of reach.

Financial help from parents can allow students to avoid loans and graduate college debt-free (Rauscher 2016). When parents do not provide financial support, student debt increases (Zissimopoulos et al. 2020). Therefore, financial dependence on parents during college can help facilitate financial independence after college (Mazelis and Kuperberg 2022). We found in our surveys that students without loans were more likely to get an allowance during college but were less likely to get funds from family after graduation compared with students with loans.

In many cases, achieving some markers of adulthood—such as college completion and financial stability—requires forgoing others, such as living independently (Furstenberg et al. 2004; Mazelis and Kuperberg 2022; Shanahan 2000). Though our interview participants generally thought that paying bills *and* living independently defined the transition to adulthood, many were unable to live independently while paying their other bills. Some had used loans to pay for housing in college, increasing their independence for a time, but after graduation were living with their parents, giving their parents money or paying some household bills while also saving to live independently again later on. Social norms regarding living apart from parents and becoming financially independent led some participants to feel they had not quite arrived at adulthood. At the same time, they felt confident that living with their parents might make their transition to adulthood more stable and lasting, enabling them to reach adulthood with greater independence.

Living with family is a frequent strategy among those who take on student debt but do not achieve a degree (Houle and Warner 2017), but it is also common among those with degrees. Our surveys found that 24 percent of college students with loans anticipated living with parents for longer than they wanted as a result of their debt. This expectation was realized by a similar proportion of graduates with loan debt; 23 percent reported that their debt caused them to live with parents longer than they wanted.

Many of our interview participants lived with their families. Rather than pay rent, they usually contributed by helping around the house or paying one recurring household bill. Living with family members was common and welcome, especially because some participants reported not wanting to ask their families for direct financial support. Participants who believed that their families did not have extra money to share were especially appreciative that they had a place to live rent-free or for a small amount of money. Those we interviewed shared with us that their parents described these living arrangements as an opportunity to help their children repay debt and save for the future, rather than as a disappointment or burden.

Loans delay financial independence after college, and those seeking to avoid loans in college may delay residential independence by living at home during or after college to save money. Support from family may enable a more secure and durable—albeit later—transition to adulthood. Over the course of our study, some participants were able to use the money they saved by living with family to later buy a home or pay off their loan debt entirely. But the help from their families led to ambivalence about their status as adults. Some who were receiving support from family, especially if it was in the form of a place to live, felt they might be violating societal norms of adulthood, but they also recognized that they would not reach the goal of financial independence and *eventually* fulfill the social norm of living independently as adults *without* this support.

Helping out around the house or with the bills in minor ways helped some of those living with their families manage their sense of their own adulthood by symbolically taking on a more adult role. However, some participants felt that their families expected so much help in return that at times it felt burdensome. And of course, providing money to family members can limit graduates' ability to save money, which can further delay the transition to adulthood. Family support can therefore both facilitate and delay the transition to adulthood, and family support during college can reduce the need for this support afterward.

As large a role as family support can play, social ties with family members are complicated. Some people avoid asking for help, and when financial need is dire and individuals' dependence on family members for assistance is high, arguments or embarrassment over money or shared housing can create difficulties in relationships (Mazelis 2017). We found that students who reported they did not like asking their parents for money were more likely to have taken out loans.

Loans and Family Formation

Past research found that student loan debt is associated with delayed marriage and childbearing, especially among women (Bozick and Estacion 2014; Gicheva 2016; Min and Taylor 2018; Nau et al. 2015). We found only trivial differences in marriage rates by student loan debt among college graduates in the national data we examined, although it is important to note that our sample is older than some other samples used in other research.

We did, however, find evidence in national data that loans were related to timing and rates of parenthood among women (but not men) who attended college, though the patterns were complex. In their twenties, women who were enrolled in college with loans were more likely to have children than women in college who didn't have loans. But after graduation this trend reversed, and by age thirty-five about 63 percent of women who had gotten a college degree without taking out loans had at least one child, compared with 56 percent of college graduates with loans. By age forty, these numbers were 67.5 percent for women graduates without loans versus 60 percent for those with loans. And among women who graduated college and *did* have children, those with loans were less likely to be married when they first gave birth. Children whose parents are married at the children's birth experience a range of social and economic benefits (Brown 2004; Carlson and Corcoran 2001); the lower marriage rate at the children's birth and lower birth rate among women graduates with loans therefore extends inequalities to a third generation.

Why might student loan debt lead to delays in family formation (partnering, marriage, or having children)? We developed four related hypotheses to explore this question. The *career focus hypothesis* posits that those with loan debt are more career focused than similarly educated young adults without loans, because they know they will have debt to repay, or because their career focus motivated them to take out more student debt to begin with. This strong focus on building a career in early adulthood leads to delays in family formation. However, our survey showed this explanation is unlikely: students with loans were more likely to report they wanted to have children than students without loans and weren't more likely to choose a major based on whether they thought it would help them earn more money.

Second, the *social norms hypothesis* posits that those with student loan debt delay marriage and parenthood because of cultural beliefs about how people with loan debt *should* behave. In our survey, we asked college students whether they thought people *should* put off marriage and having children if they have loan debt to repay. About a quarter (23 percent) thought marriage should be delayed, and nearly half—47 percent—thought people should put off having children if they had debt to repay. When we probed further and asked if people shouldn't have children at all if they wouldn't be able to repay their loans until their fifties, fewer agreed. Still, 17 percent—nearly one in five—thought that those with remaining loan debt in their fifties should forgo having children entirely.

When it came to marriage, many interviewees said people should have begun paying off some loan debt before getting married, but they didn't think delaying marriage until loans were *completely* paid off was necessary or desirable. PJ said, "No. You both are in it together, so you can both help each other out." And Jason explained, "In a way, I think being married would probably help in that circumstance. . . . Just having dual income would be helpful for that. . . . I think a typical arrangement would be that my debt would become her debt and her debt would become my debt."

Although they were in the minority, a substantial number of students believed loans *should* lead to a delay in marriage and having children. And beliefs about how people in general *should* behave can affect how individuals themselves *do* behave. We asked students with loans if they thought they would put off relationships, marriage, or having children because of their loans, and around 8 percent thought they would put off having serious romantic relationships, 19 percent thought they would postpone marriage, and 32 percent thought they would delay having children. Those who believed that people with loan debt *should* put off marriage or childbearing were over twice as likely to say they themselves *would* put off marriage or having children because of their loan debt compared with those who did not agree with this statement. When we checked in with graduates fifteen months after graduation, 15 percent reported they were delaying serious romantic relationships, 23 percent said they were delaying marriage, and 28 percent were putting off having children as a result of their debt. The graduates who said in college that those with loan debt *should* delay marriage or parenthood were also more likely to later report they *were* themselves delaying relationships, marriage, and children.

A third hypothesis—the *disposable income hypothesis*—posits that loans reduce young adults' disposable income and sense of financial stability, which are known, in turn, to lead to delays in family formation (Furstenberg et al. 2004; Harknett and Kuperberg 2011; Sassler and Miller 2017). Instead of saving for a house, a wedding, daycare bills, or other expenses that may come with having a child, those who leave college with loans are spending some of their income on those loans until they are paid off—which can take decades. Even if they had the same income as those who left college without loans, they would be on shakier financial ground because of their loan payments. And as our analysis of national data found, graduates with loans earn *lower* incomes than college graduates without loans—although they earn much higher incomes than people who don't attend or finish college. Past research found that college graduates with loans were more likely to take jobs that paid more in the short run but less in the long run (Minicozzi 2005). And in our survey of graduates, almost 22 percent of those with loans said they were delaying graduate school or had decided not to attend at all because of their debt. Some of our interviewees also took very low-paying jobs to take advantage of ten-year public service loan forgiveness programs. These decisions, shaped by debt, may affect income and careers long after that debt is repaid.

NAVIGATING LOANS IN ROMANTIC RELATIONSHIPS

Financial instability and debt can also reduce marriage prospects because other people find debt to be unattractive and because people with less money are less able to purchase services or goods that may increase their appeal to a romantic partner (such as a fancy date or a nice haircut). A fourth hypothesis is the *negative partner reaction hypothesis*, which asserts that debt elicits negative reactions among partners, which may lead to breakups or family formation delays. In our survey, we asked college students how they would react to a hypothetical serious romantic partner who told them they had a large amount of student loan debt. If they were considering getting engaged to a serious romantic partner and then found out their partner had $75,000 in student loan debt, only slightly more than a third (36 percent) stated it would not affect their marriage plans; 18 percent would put off marriage, 2.6 percent would not marry the partner at all, and the most common answer—43 percent—was that a partner's loans may affect marriage plans, depending on the circumstances.

Qualitative interviews revealed what those circumstances might be. Commonly mentioned: how responsible their partners seem, if they had a plan for repaying the debt, what the student loans were for (how many years, what kind of degree), what type of job they had and how much money they were earning, how serious the relationship was, and if they felt they had been purposely misled.

As Rose said, "I feel like already that far into it, then you are already in it for the long run, I guess. I mean, it would definitely make me very mad if they didn't say it in the beginning." But she added, "I still think I would marry them if we were already that serious." Simone told us, "I would reevaluate what they were doing with their life. If they weren't even near finishing school or if they didn't have a practical career lined up or goals, I would break up with them. I would be like, 'So, this isn't going to work out if you don't have a set plan on how you're going to be able to pay this off.'"

When we asked survey participants how they would react to a partner they had been dating for six months who told them they had $100,000 in debt, only about a third, 36 percent, said it would not affect how they felt about that person. Almost two-thirds (63 percent) said they would have a talk with them about how they planned to pay it off. Nearly a quarter (23 percent) reported they would hold off on moving in together, 34 percent would hold off on marrying them until they had paid off some of their debt, and 8 percent said they would hold off on legal marriage until they had paid off *all* their debt. Another 6 percent said they would consider breaking up with them, but only 0.7 percent would definitely break up. Another common reaction was avoiding taking expensive trips or doing expensive activities with them (38.5 percent)—activities that may increase the chance of a relationship persisting. More than a quarter (26 percent) reported they would feel bad for their partner and 17 percent would feel closer because they both had debt. But 14 percent said they would pay for more things in the relationship, and 13.5 percent said they would be worried their partner was irresponsible with money, potentially increasing financial tensions in the relationship.

Students nearly universally thought loans should be discussed with romantic partners. Less than 2 percent of those surveyed said it did not have to be disclosed, along the lines of what Alice told us: "I don't think they should bring it up anytime soon. I don't think it is their business." Though most reported that loans should be discussed with romantic partners, they differed on the appropriate timing of that discussion. Most agreed it wouldn't be the right time to tell someone about $100,000 in loans right at the beginning of a relationship. Only around 3 percent of survey respondents thought loans should be disclosed before even beginning to date someone. Flo said it should be disclosed on the first date. She elaborated, "I feel like if you really want someone to love you for who you are, you put everything out on the table. . . . If you can't bring that up to somebody, there's something wrong. You need to have that conversation. Be transparent. Otherwise, you're living a lie." Ashley said, "I feel like if they're both recent college graduates and if they have built this relationship with each other, number one, they should probably know that that should kind of be something you say up front if you're getting serious, like you want to move in with each other."

In survey data, there was not a strong consensus on when to disclose loan debt in a relationship. Among the college students we surveyed, 99 percent thought loans should be brought up before marriage, but only 29 percent thought loans should be brought up "right away when the relationship begins to be serious." Another 47 percent thought debt should first be discussed when discussing or making concrete plans to move in together, 17 percent thought it should be brought up when discussing marriage, and 2.5 percent thought they should wait until a formal engagement. Different expectations about how to manage debt in a relationship can potentially cause problems in relationships, reducing the chances those relationships will last.

STUDENT LOAN DEBT AND THE INTERGENERATIONAL TRANSMISSION OF INEQUALITY

Rising student debt has reshaped adulthood for college graduates. Though President Biden announced the cancellation of some student loan debt and a reduction of interest on loan payments in 2022, he left in place the system of funding higher education through loans. As of the writing of this chapter, his plan is also in legal limbo. With higher education budget cuts related to COVID-19 (Jackson and Saenz 2021), college costs—and student debt—may continue to grow. Compared with those without loans, college graduates with loans have less wealth, are less likely to have savings and investments or to own a home, and are more likely to declare bankruptcy (Baker et al. 2017; Gicheva and Thompson 2015; National Association of Realtors 2017). They also depend on parents for longer, report they are delaying marriage and childbearing, and ultimately end up less likely to have children, with their children more likely to be born in nonmarital relationships (Kuperberg and Mazelis 2021a, 2021b, 2022; Mazelis and Kuperberg 2022). Loan debt affects romantic relationship prospects and can complicate relationships and numerous other aspects of adult life.

Those who take on student loan debt have parents who are less financially secure, and loans have far-reaching effects on the lives of people who take them out, often exacerbating their difficulties. Loans allow them to enjoy the rewards of a higher education—but not as fully as those who can attend college debt-free. Loans therefore contribute to the *intergenerational transmission of inequality* (Kuperberg and Mazelis 2022) and restrict *class mobility*—the ability of individuals to improve their class position relative to that of their parents (Gilbert 2018). There are also strong and enduring racial disparities in wealth due to past and present racial discrimination and persistent, cumulative inequalities (Fischer et al. 1996; McGhee 2021; Oliver and Shapiro 2006; Taylor 2019;

Zucchino 2020). Given the strong ties between wealth and race in the United States, the current student loan system not only fails to increase class mobility; it also increases racial disparities, helping to perpetuate racial inequalities (Addo et al. 2016; Seamster and Charron-Chénier 2017).

Although loans enable college attendance for those who might not otherwise be able to go, college does not always lead to mobility, and class differences in family background persist even after completion of a college degree (Witteveen and Attewell 2017). Loans can even leave those whose loan payments exceed the income boost that their college education provides worse off than they were before college. Loans generate a "class divide" among college attendees and graduates, resulting in multiple forms of inequalities among the highly educated (Kuperberg and Mazelis 2022). Delays in the transition to adulthood and family formation are important manifestations of this inequality; so are some of the complexities in romantic relationships. Young adults with loans must consider when, whether, and how to disclose their debt to their romantic partners. As our surveys showed, they also face the risk that such a disclosure may cause their partners to end the relationship. Student loan debt can have ripple effects, influencing romantic partnerships and decisions about childbearing, where to live, what to do for a living, and how to approach the future. It affects the number of children born and the circumstances they are born into; it may be no coincidence that fertility rates have recently dipped to record lows as student loan debt has reached record highs (Hamilton et al. 2019).

Student loan debt complicates sociological ideas about higher education, social class, mobility, and the intergenerational transmission of inequality. The outsized role of family resources in shaping higher education prospects, which has grown even larger in the face of declining government funding for public higher education, helps perpetuate intergenerational inequalities. Assistance from family, expectations from family, resources available through family connections, and financial literacy allow class background to shape one's chances of attending college and having loans, loan amounts, and experiences repaying loans. College attendance is traditionally seen as a path to upward class mobility, and loans allow students to attend college who otherwise could not. Yet, educational debt hinders them from achieving the financial security and stability of those who can attend college *without* student loans, restricting their mobility.

A college degree is not a guarantee of wealth. Those who manage to earn a college degree still often struggle to repay student debt, hindered in their launch into adulthood by loan payments. Those who leave college with debt but no degree struggle even more. As they confront the stigma of compounding debt and delayed financial independence, they must navigate multiple situations, obstacles, and institutions that those without student debt never encounter, such as dealing with loan offices and researching programs to help pay off debt. Others, whose parents had the will, interest, and (most importantly) ability to save enough to pay for their children's college education or who can otherwise avoid loans, launch into adulthood with a college degree but *without* student debt. The advantages that enable them to avoid loans also help pave their way to successful careers and financial stability and security—which in turn helps them form the families they want to have when they choose to have them. Families thus both shape and are shaped by student loan debt.

NOTE

1. All participant names are pseudonyms chosen by participants.

32

Sí Puedes

Latinx Families and Higher Education

Patricia Sánchez-Connally

L atinx have made important advances in higher educational attainment during the last decade, yet they still lag behind other groups in earning four-year degrees (Gramlich 2017). By 2019, more than one in five Latinx ages twenty-five to twenty-nine had at least a bachelor's degree; in 2010, the rate was just one in ten.[1] On the one hand, higher education is a pathway to opportunity, even if the benefits are not as great as they once were. On the other hand, educational institutions often don't recognize how to support Latinx students in the very opportunities they are set up to offer. My research is motivated by an interest in enhancing higher education opportunities by focusing on *resources* in the lives of Latinx students rather than deficits. A wealth of research grounded in critical race theory[2] motivates this framework, as does my own experience. I am a first-generation immigrant college graduate—and now I am also a professor, researcher, and scholar activist.

SOME CONCERNING NUMBERS

The dilemma is this: according to the U.S. Department of Education's National Center for Education Statistics (2021), Hispanic[3] students had the highest dropout rate (7.7 percent) of all racial/ethnic groups. Compare that with 4.1 percent for white students and 5.7 percent for Black students. Often, the educational gap and failure of Latinx students within the academic system are blamed on the lack of capital, resources, and interest of families. *Capital* conventionally refers to money (economic capital), connections (social capital), and knowledge and shared values (cultural capital).[4] As a scholar studying Latinx immigrant students' success and higher educational attainment, I see discussions of "capital" in terms of the culture of Latinx families presented mainly from a *deficit perspective*. Newer work presented here aims to correct this.

Four critical elements define the deficit perspective in education: a blame-the-victim orientation, a blindness to larger complex systems of oppression, a pervasive and often implicit nature that leaves the perspective unexamined, and reinforcement of hegemonic systems (the "status quo") (Davis and Museus 2019). Deficit thinking has real effects on the way families experience and connect to schools and education. For example, the voices of Latinx parents are silenced within schools through the implementation of bureaucratic requirements such as informal expectations of parental involvement and overall disregard of their knowledge and culture through language-based racism (Villenas and Deyhle 1999). Think of parents who do not speak English: they are excluded. Think of biased and objectifying language used in assignments discussing immigration: families may be alienated, and parents may be unable to protest. The list goes on.

Scholars and activists can advance anti-deficit perspectives and empower students by critiquing deficit logic in institutions and by centering the voices and experiences of historically marginalized and oppressed people. Applying knowledge from marginalized communities, such as first-generation immigrant Latinx students, provides a way to better understand different aspects of educational processes. This allows us to unveil structural and social inequalities and the practices and narratives that sustain them. And it leads us to better strategies of inclusion and support for Latinx students and their families.

In recent work on social inequalities, scholars find strength in using critical race theory (CRT) to overturn existing, failing approaches. New work relies on its methods for deep, empirical, systematic observations developed within marginalized communities. I review work that uses these techniques and builds on CRT-related methods in my own research.

In particular, my research challenges the misconceptions around Latinx families' involvement in their children's academic lives, college planning, and career aspirations. Over the past decade, I conducted interviews with over one hundred students that focused on where and how they find motivation to persist in predominantly white educational institutions. The participants either were in high school or were first-generation college students and either had migrated to the United States or were children of immigrants.

As I analyzed my data, I relied on the community cultural wealth (CCW) paradigm that also builds on CRT. This model is a counter to the conventional versions of "capital" and explores how Latino culture is an asset for succeeding in higher education. The CCW model recognizes knowledge, skills, and networks used by communities of color in educational settings (Yosso 2005). Finally, the resource thinking approach begins with the recognition that Latinx immigrant families are no different from any other families in valuing postsecondary education. This investigation highlights *how* families serve as motivators for academic achievement.

Familism in Latinx Families

Some key lines of research—on *familism* and on *gendered familism*—inform my analysis. Latinx families are characterized by familism—a cultural value that is often a target in the deficit perspective. *Familism* means pride, loyalty, and closeness in the family, which in turn results in family obligations coming before any individual needs (Valenzuela and Dornbusch 1994). Familism contrasts with the values of individuality and independence present in American culture and instead requires an individual family member to make personal sacrifices for the sake of their family. Numerous studies show how family obligations are positive for young people. One study found that young adults who did not do well in high school were more likely to stay in college when their sense of family obligation emphasized their role in supporting and assisting their family (Fuligni and Pedersen 2002). Another study found that Latina college students who spent more time with their families while attending college had higher achievement and lower school-related stress (Sy 2006). These studies show that familism may be positive when students are able to use it for emotional and mental strength.

Gender, however, complicates the story. Other scholars argue that familism can also have negative outcomes if it discourages young people, especially women, from following their dreams and places the family's needs first. This emphasis on personal sacrifice is further reinforced among Latinas by *marianismo*, which "emphasizes the self-sacrificing role of females and highlights the role as family caretaker" (Sy 2006, p. 369). Latina students often suffer greater stress during their college career than Latino men (Sy 2006). Consequently, many Latinas experience conflicts between following the traditional female role and the nontraditional role of pursuing higher education. Even though research has shown that Latinx parents value higher education, daughters may experience extra pressure to continue to fulfill their family obligations as they make the transition to college (Sy 2006). This added time demand and stress can make the transition to higher education institutions challenging.

Effects on Academic Trajectories

The extent to which students experience different forms of familism may influence students' academic trajectory and career aspirations. Specifically, families' ideas of gender and strict gender roles shape not only the messages that students receive about the role of education but also the college pathways that students may pursue. Ovink (2014) discusses the importance of looking at the "(re)production of intersecting gender and racial/ethnic beliefs, attitudes and behaviors"—a process she calls *gendered familism* (p. 4). Her work with Latinx high school students shows how gendered familism influenced the way students interpreted the value and meaning of higher education in their lives. Latinas were more likely to view a college degree as a path to financial independence and therefore were more likely to enroll in and attend four-year institutions in order to obtain a bachelor's degree. Latinas also reported feeling more pressure from parents to succeed educationally and financially. Latinas reported fulfilling caregiving and breadwinner roles while attending college full-time, while Latinos reported wanting to fulfill academic goals in order to provide for their future families. López (2003) found that men, regardless of age, were rarely expected to assume family caretaking obligations; thus, their frame of reference was different from that of women. Young men did not personally identify with their mother's struggles and therefore had a difficult time evaluating choices about education, career, and family life (López 2003, p. 132). For scholars, advocates, and mentors, as well as for students directly, these findings can be helpful in recognizing how families impact students' educational experiences. When working with Latinx students, we must gauge their family's involvement and make use of the importance of family knowledge and participation in students' academic and career decision making.

RECOGNIZING AND VALUING FAMILIAL KNOWLEDGE

How do we turn a story of deficit into a rich plan of action grounded in family resources? A study of Chicano/a college students examines how students develop strategies for navigating college—and offers a road map to learning about familial capital (Delgado Bernal 2002; Yosso 2005). The Chicano/a students used the knowledge from family and community to successfully confront discrimination and the other obstacles they encountered in higher education. An adaptation of CRT, Latino critical theory takes an alternative approach to family features, such as bilingualism and family obligations, which are routinely perceived as deficits in predominantly white culture. Instead, researchers uncover how Latinx family features serve as resources. By considering household knowledge such as bilingualism, biculturalism, and commitment to communities as part of a valuable knowledge base, the study showed how household knowledge "interrupts the transmission of official knowledge and even helps students navigate their way around educational obstacles" (Delgado Bernal 2002, p. 113). Indeed, biculturalism or the ability to identify and function in two cultures is associated with psychological benefits such as perspective taking from another point of view (Schwartz et al. 2013). Delgado Bernal (2002) found that students who embraced biculturalism and recognized that they served as role models for younger siblings, cousins, and other family members were better equipped to persist in college. In addition, commitment to helping their communities and families served as a form of inspiration to fight through struggles.

Experiences and skills passed on by family are important when considering student achievement. *Familial capital* refers to family experiences and skills that are nurtured among kin and carry a sense of community history and memory (Yosso 2005; Delgado Bernal 1998). Familial capital is a form of cultural wealth that provides a commitment to community and relates the meaning of family to encompass a broader understanding of kinship. Extended family such as uncles, aunts, grandparents, and friends help nurture this knowledge and help students access resources within the community. Still more forms of familial capital that help students are moral, emotional, educational, and occupational consciousness and strategies for coping and caring (Yosso 2005, p. 79). This consciousness is fostered and transferred within and between different families and through school and community settings.

The acquisition of familial capital gives way to *aspirational capital*, which is another form of cultural wealth. Yosso (2005) describes it as the ability to "maintain hopes and dreams for the future, even in the face of real and perceived barriers" (p. 77). Aspirational capital manifests in different ways, but a good example comes from the work of scholars who show that although the Latinx community may have low educational outcomes, they still maintain high aspirations for the future (López 2003; Gandara 1995; Yosso 2005).

The cumulative evidence reviewed here, uncovered by using CRT and Latino critical theory, points to the benefits for Latinx students and their families of shifting from deficit thinking to resource thinking. What does it look like when we center first-generation students, their families, and their forms of knowledge? My interviews focus on how students' parents and extended family pass on different stories related to life in their native country, survival in the United States, challenges within the workforce, and most importantly, sacrifices for their student. My findings show that students' aspirations and goals were influenced by immigrant stories that parents shared mostly in the context of reminding students why they should dedicate themselves to academic success. Stories were students' familial capital, allowing them to develop a sense of possibility (Bettie 2002; Gandara 1995). Validating immigrant students' motivation from their siblings, community members, parents, and other family members is an example of how we can use this framework to give voice to this segment of students.

SHAPING ASPIRATIONS: ONE STORY AT A TIME

Two themes from my interviews exemplify how Latinx families provide familial knowledge and how students interpret and use that knowledge to create educational aspirations. Specifically, familial capital in the form of educational expectations was expressed by (a) sharing immigrant stories and providing a dual frame of reference (*nuestro sacrificio*)[5] and (b) insisting that young women earn a degree in order to achieve financial independence and reminding students that they are responsible for providing financial support to the family (*pa' que me mantengas*).[6]

Nuestro Sacrificio

A common way that immigrant parents verbalized educational expectations was by recounting how they immigrated to the United States and reminding students about the sacrifice they made in leaving their native country. Jade, a Dominican eighteen-year-old high school senior, describes her mom's scolding:

> She was like "You know how much we try? We give you guys everything you guys want and you guys can't even do this; you can't even bring a solid A report card home. There is no need for that. We work overtime just to give you guys whatever you need. You know how many kids in DR can't afford a notebook and a pencil, and you guys have them here roaming around everywhere! Like, there is no need for that."

Jade's mom expresses her dissatisfaction with her kids not being able to bring home an A and reminds them that most children in the Dominican Republic do not have the resources that Jade and her brother have. Jade herself argues with her younger sibling over his grades. She mentions that she encourages her brother, saying, "You need to take all that into consideration; you know how much they are working." Jade feels responsible for her own academic success, which she sees as a form of repayment for her mom's sacrifice.

The expected exchange between parents and children/students is voiced often, and it involves the narrative that parents made a sacrifice to come to this country, left family behind, and work long hours doing jobs they do not want to do. Students see part of their obligation as children to seize academic opportunities, like participating in after-school and summer programming, as a way to reward their parents for their sacrifice. Most importantly, there's an understanding that children and parents are engaged in a reciprocal financial relationship (Gonzales 2011). In many interviews, this story was repeated in myriad ways: accountability was an engine of achievement.

Pa' Que Me Mantengas

In her study of second-generation West Indian, Haitian, and Dominican youth, Nancy López concluded that young women consistently evaluated both educational and employment goals against their mothers' experiences with hardships (López 2003). All students in my sample, both men and women, were well aware of the limited opportunities their parents had because they had immigrated to the United States. Nicole, a Dominican college student, explained, "College is important to me [because] I watched what happens when you don't go to college. I've watched my mom suffer . . . because she doesn't have money." Nicole's words resonated with a number of my participants. Respondents discussed not wanting to be in the restricting financial positions their parents or family members experienced. In describing their reasons for wanting to go to college, both men and women acknowledged their parents' hard work, but women were more vocal about wanting to succeed and not having to work as hard as their moms or sisters, while men talked about rewarding parents by attending college.

Samantha, a Puerto Rican graduating high school senior, described why college is important to her:

> I think college is important because basically I look at my parents, especially my mom, because she always comes home tired. . . . [She'd] have to clean like one hundred rooms in one day. . . . I started looking at that and I really don't want to be like that at all. I don't want to have that job where I clean after people.

Nicole and Samantha recognize their parents' financial struggles and low status within their occupations, and they both desire a different economic future. Other research also finds that students' family realities and community contexts help to form and shape expectations about financial aspirations (Carter 2005, p. 97). My participants were anxious to take whatever opportunities were granted to them so that they would not have to work as hard as their parents. Parents were very vocal about their expectations. Jade noted, "My mom was always telling me you need to go to college; you need to be someone later on in life '*pa' que me mantenga*' this and that." Anabel, a first-generation college student born to Dominican immigrants, explained, "I think about my parents. They say, 'If you bring a C here, we are going to have problems!' That's what motivated me academically."

Parents and extended family reminded students that they were expected to achieve academically, strive for financial success, and serve as role models while doing it. This was notable among the women I interviewed, who shared the messages they received from other women in their families (mainly mothers and older sisters). First, they should not depend on men for financial stability. Second, romantic relationships should be delayed, if not avoided at all costs, while in college. When asked about how her mother inspires her, Kiki, a junior in high school, said, "[Mami] tells me to forget about boys. They're not important. Don't listen to the guys. If you date a guy, remember that school comes first, and the relationship comes second." This form of familial capital geared toward women is an example of gendered familism (Ovink 2014). As discussed earlier, Latinas in Ovink's study reported feeling pressure to succeed educationally and financially at higher rates than Latinos. This pressure can serve as motivation to persist, as it did for Kiki, when experiencing stress related to academic and financial responsibilities while in college.

White native-born adults between the ages of eighteen and twenty-four tend to receive more financial help from parents (Rumbaut and Komaie 2010). Immigrant young adults often do not live with parents, and they experience some of the highest levels of poverty in the United States. Studies show that the pattern of financial support among immigrant young adults is quite reciprocal and more often reversed (Rumbaut and Komaie 2010). For example, Fuligni's (2002) study of over one thousand immigrant and nonimmigrant families found that immigrant children with high levels of academic motivation had a greater sense of indebtedness and financial obligation to their families. Moreover, young adults who were classified as Latinx were significantly more likely to provide financial support to their parents and siblings than nonimmigrant people. Students in my sample voiced their determination to attain higher education, their struggle to graduate college, and their desire to secure a job that would allow them to live comfortably and help other family members.

While first-generation immigrant students may receive scholarships from their institutions, many do not receive any financial support from their family. The students I worked with all had at least a part-time job while attending school full-time. Ashley shared that "leaving college was not an option" and that she had to work over thirty hours a week to make ends meet:

> I was very busy. I took every job I can find and kept switching jobs to get better pay. When I came home from work, my roommates would be setting up parties or partying. I couldn't do that. I had to study and do homework. I thought it was unfair and I had to suck it up. At the end that wasn't the first memory I had in college but that was a memory that I was angry and had to [financially] support myself.

Ashley realized that her college experience wasn't the same as that of her peers. She had different priorities than her roommates had. Having to work in order to stay in college allowed her to appreciate her family's struggle. Students who had experienced financial uncertainty understood the responsibility they had to their family. Leaving home and going to college for an education that could lead to more job opportunities were significant risks they were willing to take if it meant that they'd be able to financially support their parents in the future. This is in opposition to the deficit-model notion that familism can hinder socioeconomic success and that it limits opportunities for growth. Instead, my findings show how familism can serve as a source of positive support for both academic achievement and college attendance (Valenzuela and Dornbusch 1994).

CONCLUSION

From a resource perspective, I have asked, *What keeps Latinx students persisting in their education?* I interviewed over one hundred high school and college students who had immigrated to the United States or whose parents had immigrated shortly before the students were born. They told me they relied on *family expectations* to motivate themselves. These interviews added to the knowledge of CRT and Latino critical theory scholars who resisted seeing familism in Latinx culture as a deficit and thereby recognized the resources that support educational persistence.

When parents or other family members shared their immigrant experience, they created a sense of duty in students to fulfill future expectations. By comparing life in their native country to life in the United States, parents created a dual frame of reference for students. This is important for two reasons. First, the current literature continuously portrays family obligations as *obstacles* for students, especially women. My work shows that, to the contrary, this familism is crucial in shaping and achieving educational goals. I used an alternative framework for understanding how and why students, especially women, who experience high levels of family obligations are academically succeeding and attending four-year institutions. While support from friends, mentors, academic support programs, and teachers is considered important, the majority of respondents identified family as the main motivator for academic success.

Make a Difference with Latinx Family Stories

There are cultural and ethnic practices shared by Latinx immigrant families and communities that do not get attention. My findings provide evidence of the ways that youth embrace their own immigrant experience and use it to frame a positive outlook on their life chances. Focusing on the strengths that immigrant families provide through their storytelling, for example, can be useful in discussing future academic goals with students. This can be helpful to academic and career counselors, teachers, and community workers, because it provides an opportunity to value and validate first-generation students' experiences. For first-generation students, their professors, or their classmates reading this chapter, I believe you can use this knowledge—and add to it—as you press for more inclusive systems that help you succeed.

NOTES

1. Postsecondary National Policy Institute (2021).

2. Critical race theory is a framework that challenges dominant ideas such as colorblindness and meritocracy and shows how these ideas operate to disadvantage people of color and further advantage Whites (Delgado and Stefancic 1994).

3. *Hispanic* is tied to the Spanish language. *Latino* is tied to geographic region and includes non-Spanish-speaking people. *Latinx* is a gender-neutral word.

4. See, for example, Annette Lareau (2011), *Unequal Childhoods: Class, Race, and Family Life*, Second Edition *with an Update a Decade Later* (Berkeley, CA: University of California Press).

5. "Our sacrifice."

6. "So you can support me."

In Other Words

CENTERING STUDENT VOICES PROVIDES CAUTIOUS OPTIMISM ABOUT THE FUTURE OF RACIAL SEGREGATION

Chantal A. Hailey, September 20, 2022 / CCF@TSP

Every spring 80,000 NYC eighth-graders receive their matched high school offer. The offer ends a monthslong process during which families search for potential schools and submit an application to the NYC Department of Education ranking their top twelve preferred schools. And every spring, the high school match season sparks an impassioned conversation about how NYC school choice policies abate, reflect, and exacerbate racial inequities and segregation. Although students are key policy recipients and actors in school choice and segregation, student perspectives are often absent from this policy debate.

I wanted to understand students' opinions of high schools. Unlike with elementary and middle school selections, students are deeply involved in their high school selections. I conducted an experiment with more than 1,000 NYC families of eighth-graders to understand their preferences regarding high schools. I separately asked parents and students about their willingness to attend hypothetical majority-White, majority-Latinx, and majority-Black schools with randomized graduation rates and safety indicators. These schools were essentially the same on all indicators except their racial compositions.

I found that students express different race-based preferences for schools than their parents do. White and Latinx students' school preferences were less anti-Black than were White and Latinx parents'. White and Latinx parents' aversion to attending the majority-Black school compared to White and Latinx schools was two to three times stronger than White and Latinx students' preference to avoid the majority-Black school. The differences in White and Latinx parents' and students' race-based school preferences could be driven by younger generations being less likely to desire racially segregated schools and to endorse anti-Black sentiments and stereotypes. Using race as a signal of a school's academic quality, parents may also feel anxious about making educational decisions that might somehow jeopardize students' socioeconomic future.

Black students preferred to avoid the majority-White school relative to the other school options, while Black parents did not express race-based preferences for schools. Black students' caution about attending majority-White schools could be rooted in concerns about facing racial biases, discrimination, and violence in White social spaces.

Students' perspectives of schools yield cautious optimism about the future of segregation. We could see racial segregation decline as this generation of White and Latinx students mature into adulthood. They could continue to be less anti-Black than their parents and less determined to avoid schools, universities, neighborhoods, and jobs with more Black people. However, as White and Latinx youth become parents, they could also adopt the same socioeconomic-based anxieties and anti-Black preferences as their parents. They could avoid Black spaces and, accordingly, school and residential racial segregation could persist.

As Black youth continue to grapple with publicized racial violence and discrimination, they may choose to avoid predominately White universities and neighborhoods and to attend historically Black colleges and universities (HBCUs) and reside in Black neighborhoods. These students could also eventually believe, like Black parents, that there is no right choice that shields them from structural and individual racism.

Across the country, in cities like New York, Chicago, and San Francisco, politicians, education administrators, and parents intensely debate school choice policies and segregation. However, it is imperative that we center student voices in these conversations about the future of educational equity. ▬

33

Between a Rock and a Hard Place

Undocumented Immigrants and Mixed-Status Families Negotiating Migration Returns to Visit Ill and Dying Family Members

Cassaundra Rodriguez

What if you couldn't say farewell to a dying parent? On the other hand, what if you are able to see your dying parent but in doing so, risk being separated from your partner and children? For undocumented immigrants in the United States who have parents abroad, these questions are lived realities. Much attention has been paid to how undocumented immigrants in the United States are vulnerable to forced removal or deportation from the country. However, another issue undocumented immigrants face is restrictions regarding travel. Although they may be able to voluntarily exit the United States, reentry would likely be unauthorized[1] and therefore dangerous, costly, and in some cases, fatal.[2] Estimates suggest that approximately seven thousand migrants perished crossing the U.S.-Mexico border between 1998 and 2020.[3] As immigrants attempt to escape detection by border agents, they follow more dangerous routes that can take them into desert and hostile terrains, which can lead to dehydration, heat-related illness, and accidents.[4] These serious risks present a dilemma for undocumented Mexican immigrants who have made roots in the United States but have not been able to physically visit their loved ones who remained in their country of origin. As the *Washington Post* recently described, "The elderly parents of the estimated 5 million undocumented Mexicans in the United States are dying alone in Mexico while their children remain stuck on the other side of the border."[5]

This chapter outlines how family members in mixed-status families—or families that include both U.S. citizens and undocumented immigrants—negotiate the family process of whether to visit ill or dying family members abroad. To understand this complex issue, the chapter will review some immigration policies and demonstrate how long-term undocumented immigrants have been blocked from legalizing their status despite having U.S. citizen children. This chapter then shows the complex ways that immigrants and their loved ones negotiate competing obligations and the emotions of guilt, anger, love, and grief. Undocumented immigrants are not just workers and parents but also loving sons and daughters who wish to honor their own parents and say farewell.[6]

IMMIGRATION STATUS TERMS

The term *undocumented* refers to immigrants who do not have legal authorization to reside in a country. In the United States, there are at least two ways an immigrant can be undocumented. One way is for an immigrant to enter the country without authorization. This means that they did not access a visa or other sort of permission from a government to enter the country. Another way for an immigrant to be undocumented is to enter the country with a visa but remain longer than allowed. Some undocumented young people have access to DACA, or Deferred Action for Childhood Arrivals. This program includes a number of benefits, such as legal access to work, government identification, and protection from deportation. However, this status is temporary and needs to be renewed about every two years, assuming the program is active.[7] Legal permanent residents have legal authorization to reside and work in the country, and some may be able to apply for U.S. citizenship eventually. U.S. citizens have the greatest legal access to live and work in the United States and many can vote and participate in other civic responsibilities. A mixed-status family includes members with a mix of these and other immigration statuses.

CREATING AN UNDOCUMENTED AND MIXED-STATUS FAMILY POPULATION

To understand how mixed-status families are formed, it is imperative to learn how a number of policies end up creating undocumented immigrants in the United States. Undocumented immigrants are part of a process related to community histories, immigration policies, labor demands, and transnational exchange. Long before any heated talks about undocumented Mexican migration, large parts of the United States were originally part of Mexico, including California, Texas Nevada, Utah, and parts of Arizona, New Mexico, and Colorado. Most of these states became U.S. territory with the signing of the Treaty of Guadalupe-Hidalgo in 1848. In the decades that followed, Mexicans and Mexican Americans continued to have an intimate relationship with the United States. Those who lived on or near the border crossed easily between each side to work, go to school, shop, and visit relatives. It wasn't until 1924 that the Border Patrol was established, placing greater restrictions on crossing. But Mexican immigrants continued to migrate to the United States in search of work opportunities and to be with family.[8]

Then the Bracero Program (1942–1964) established a U.S.-Mexico partnership where seasonal laborers from Mexico could temporarily and legally work on U.S. soil. This program created a system of family networks that would further normalize Mexican labor migration to the United States. For Mexicans, seasonal labor became a gendered and familial expectation for men who had families to economically support. When the program was terminated in the 1960s, demand for immigration remained high, but legal visas became much harder to access for Mexicans, thereby encouraging the flow of undocumented migration.[9] At the same time, for aspiring migrants, there remained a desire to migrate because of economic need, violence in their home country, or family reunification.

This background helps explain why undocumented immigration occurs, but it's important to note that many undocumented immigrants today are settled, long-term residents of the United States, not the seasonal come-and-go immigrant workers who characterized migration in earlier years. The sources of this change were several key policies that made the U.S.-Mexico border more rigid and unauthorized crossing more difficult. This started with the Immigration Reform and Control Act (IRCA) of 1986. One of the outcomes of IRCA was a tightening of the border via increased immigration enforcement. As a result, it became harder for immigrants to cross the border without authorization. Into the 1990s, the Illegal Immigration Reform and Immigration Responsibility Act (IIRIRA)[10] subsequently served to make unauthorized crossing more difficult. In addition, the border became militarized, meaning that technologies of surveillance and other military-grade practices were used to monitor the border. As a result, immigrants who normally would have participated in temporary or seasonal migration realized that once they successfully made it to the United States, they would rather avoid undertaking such an arduous, costly, and dangerous journey again. Even those who initially migrated with a visa but overstayed it also understood that an exit and a subsequent return to the United States could involve an unauthorized crossing. Once immigrants worked and lived in the United States, many ultimately decided to stay indefinitely even though they may have originally planned to work in the United States for a short time and then return home to reunite with their loved ones. This is part of the reason why mixed-status families exist today. When immigrants settle, they establish roots and families in their new country. Because children born on U.S. soil are citizens, mixed-status families can be formed when parents do not share their children's citizenship or immigration status.

It is estimated that there are about 16 million people in mixed-status households.[11] About 63 percent of undocumented immigrants have been in the United States for ten years or more, and many of them are also parents of American (or American-raised) children.[12] Data from 2019 estimate that about 25 percent of the undocumented population is forty-five years of age or older.[13] As short-term migrations to the United States transform into permanent stays, undocumented immigrants age and can become part of two transnational families—the families they have created (families of procreation/nuclear families) in the United States and their families of origin who have remained in their homeland.[14]

LEARNING FROM MIXED-STATUS FAMILIES

I did not initially set out to understand how mixed-status families tackle the possibility of returning to visit an ill or dying family member. Instead, back in 2015, I conducted a qualitative research project to understand how members of mixed-status families—undocumented immigrants and U.S. citizens specifically—experience belonging in the United States. I moved from Western Massachusetts, where I was in graduate school, to Los Angeles, California, to carry out this research. As I was doing this study, I immersed myself in immigrant spaces and immigrant homes and carried out in-depth interviews with members of mixed-status families across L.A. County. In total, I conducted sixty-seven interviews with members of mixed-status families, including forty-two U.S. citizens, seven DACA recipients, and eighteen undocumented immigrants. Participants had ties to Mexican-origin families, although six participants also identified as Salvadoran, Guatemalan, or Armenian.

Many of my interview questions were about belonging, migration and family histories, immigration status differences, and perspectives on immigration policies. For this chapter, many of the data were derived from responses that pertained to interviewees' perspectives on immigration reform, hopes or thoughts on legalization, and their unprompted narratives about travel and transnational grieving. Further demonstrating how these negotiations are a salient family process, many of the narratives are from family members who witnessed how painful it was for an undocumented loved one to experience transnational grieving. All names used here are pseudonyms to protect the identity of the participants.

LEGALIZATION HOPES AND REALITIES

The undocumented immigrants I interviewed desired the ability to freely move throughout the country and exit the United States and return legally and safely. Many in the study reported thinking of their migration to the United States as a temporary stay that would allow them to earn wages and save funds before returning to their country to reunite with family. Instead, many immigrants eventually decided to settle in the United States after forming nuclear families there. Gustavo, an undocumented father, explained how this happened in his life:

> G: I think everyone wants to visit this country because everyone sings this country's praises. This is a beautiful country. I think the majority of us come here to get to know this country and then you end up staying here. In my case, I have my son now, my home, and so it's difficult to return even if you miss your family, your parents, your brothers. Here I am by myself because I don't have my family [of origin] here. I don't even have a single brother here.
>
> C: They are in your country?
>
> G: All of them are in my country. I am the only one here. It is difficult because one would like to see family. Even if it's just one day, I would like to see my family, but it can't be done. Hopefully in the future it can be possible. It is important for the laws to change so we can go and return like a lot of people do. What can I tell you? Thanks be to God we are here surviving. We have good days and bad days, like everyone else. We are striving to move forward.

Gustavo remained hopeful that he could legalize his status and visit his parents and siblings one day. In the meantime, he focuses on being an active father, a loving husband, and a hardworking provider for his family. Unfortunately, Gustavo's son is much too young to help him change his immigration status. However, there are other families that include adult-age citizen children.

Adult children who are U.S. citizens knew that they could potentially help their undocumented parents access legal permanent residency via immigration sponsorship.[15] If successful, adult children knew their parents would travel and reestablish bonds with their families of origin. This was especially key because adult citizen children understood that their grandparents abroad were aging and that there might be limited time to reunite with them. Kevin, for example, had been thinking about this. He had not reached the eligible age of twenty-one to sponsor his immigrant parents, but he knew that taking on that responsibility would be very meaningful to them. Kevin explained,

> [My parents] have been here longer than nineteen years. [My father] wants to go back [to Mexico] because he hasn't seen his family over there. That's one thing he has mentioned every now and then. . . . He says that he just hopes I am able to help them out so that they can see their families safely.

When Kevin explains helping his family, he is referring to plans to consult with a lawyer about how or whether to sponsor his parents for their legal permanent residency.

Although it is yet to be determined whether Kevin will eventually be able to help his parents in this matter, other interviewees who were at least twenty-one had not done so. Citizen young adults in my study reported challenges to immigration sponsorship. This stands in contrast to a strand of virulent anti-immigrant narratives that paint undocumented parents as bearing "anchor baby" children on U.S. soil so that they can access legal status for themselves. The *anchor baby* term is an offensive slur that persists despite evidence that suggests this practice is primarily a myth.[16] The reality is that even though family members prefer not to remain undocumented, it can be difficult to help undocumented parents access their legal permanent residency.[17] Adult-age children encountered roadblocks to sponsoring their undocumented parents because they came to learn their parents would probably have to leave the United States and wait out a ten-year ban before being able to return to the United States with authorization.[18] Aside from this challenge, immigration sponsorship entails meeting certain eligibility requirements, financial costs and obligations, and family cooperation. Consequently, it is not uncommon for undocumented parents to remain undocumented, even when their children reach the eligible age to serve as immigration sponsors. When families experience roadblocks to legalization, concerns relating to visiting an ill or dying family member remain, at least in terms of immigration restrictions.

THE DECISION TO RETURN

The decision of whether to visit a dying family member as an undocumented immigrant is a negotiation precisely because there are so many individual and familial factors to consider. The decision to leave is emotionally fraught because of concerns related to the risks of returning to the United States. These negotiations powerfully affect nuclear families because spouses/partners and children often witness a loved one on the emotional rollercoaster of grieving and making hard choices.

Juliana, an undocumented mother of citizen children, has been in the United States for over fifteen years, along with her husband, Vicente. She and her husband had to endure this problem when Vicente got word that his father was very ill. Vicente, also an undocumented immigrant, spent some time deciding what to do. Juliana shared what this experience was like from her perspective:

> [My husband] went through something horrible because he had not been to Mexico in such a long time. . . . [My father-in-law] became very ill. My husband could not go see him. He was basically between a rock and a hard place because he couldn't go. He couldn't leave his job here and, of course, he had no way to return. So, we talked about it. His mom told him to prepare emotionally because his father was very sick. That time for us was so hard because [my husband] did not sleep. He was like a zombie. He would come home from work and then shut himself in the bathroom. He would eat every now and then, but it wasn't the same. He wouldn't sleep and then when I would wake up, he would be locked in the bathroom. Sometimes I would wake up in the middle of the night and see him in bed but completely awake. So, he would tell me: "I don't know what to do." I couldn't really give him an opinion, because if I told him not to go, and his father dies, I will feel guilty. On the other hand, if I tell him to go, he's going to have to pay to come back, and what if something happens to him?

The expression "between a rock and a hard place" perfectly captures how undocumented immigrants in this situation are wedged between emotional commitments to their families of origin and their nuclear families precisely because of immigration status restrictions. That is to say, immigrants want to visit their ill and dying family members back home, but they risk not being able to return and see the families they have formed in the United States. It was an emotionally charged period for Vicente, who struggled with what to do. Certainly, giving advice would also be complicated for Juliana given her concerns about her family and compassion for her husband. To make matters more difficult, Juliana was not actively in the workforce, so her husband's return to Mexico, and the risks involved, could have dire emotional and financial consequences for her and their children.

Juliana ultimately advised Vicente to make the decision that felt right for him, and eventually, Vicente returned to Mexico to bid his father farewell. It was the return back to the United States that proved complicated. Without a legal way to return to the United States, Vicente crossed the border without authorization using a *coyote*, or human smuggler. However, the coyote abandoned him with a group of people in the desert. Although Juliana did not share—or perhaps did not know—what ensued, she experienced the emotional turmoil of not knowing the whereabouts of her husband, assuming the worst. "I spent a whole week without knowing anything about him, I'm saying nothing, nothing about him." Thankfully, Vicente did return to her safely. Juliana recounts, "He came back and said: 'I have returned and thank God I am safe. If God wants to take my father, he at least gave me the chance to see him one last time.'" A short time later, Vicente's father did pass, and it seemed that the visit was able to ameliorate the family's grief, especially because Vicente was able to see firsthand how much his ill father was suffering because of his rapidly deteriorating health. Overall, it was a difficult circumstance, and in this case, a return was made.

A return, clearly, is not a decision that is taken lightly. It entails a certain amount of risk and separation from U.S.-based family. For some immigrants, a return may also involve more significant long-term risk. For example, Penelope, a young adult with DACA, noted how her father's return to visit her dying grandfather is complicating her father's attempt to legalize his status. "We just went to a lawyer this week and the lawyer basically said my dad can't fix his status because he went back [to Mexico] in 2003, so that automatically bars him from fixing his status." Penelope continued, "He went in 2002. His dad was really sick, and he wanted to see him. He went back, saw his dad, and sure enough his dad died a couple of months later. He came back and he was caught, so we are in the process of trying to see if he has a deportation order or not." Penelope's father tried to return to the United States and did not make it the first time. Because he was apprehended or "caught" at the border on his first attempt, Penelope's family is concerned that this action might make legalization impossible or much harder.

THE DECISION TO REMAIN

Many undocumented immigrants who experience the news of a dying or ill parent abroad make the difficult decision not to return to bid farewell to their loved ones. This decision is not borne out of a disregard for their departing family member but instead is made based on immigration status restrictions. Liliana tearfully explained how her stepfather has endured prolonged separation from his family of origin.

> L: His entire family, his brothers, his sisters, his dad are in Mexico City. His mom actually died a couple of years ago and it was really, really hard on him. Just—[starts tearing up] I am sorry I am getting emotional. . . . Just seeing what he went through because he couldn't say bye to his mom was hard.

C: Because he wasn't able to go?

L: He wasn't able to go. He told us that he wanted to so badly go to at least bury his mom, but he couldn't do it. That was really hard.

C: How did your mom and you and your siblings help support him at the time?

L: We just let him go through whatever he needed to go through, you know? I mean, I think he was able to talk to me about it because I lost my father, but I couldn't relate in the sense that you can't bury your parent. . . . I think he's still dealing with it on a day-to-day basis. I think he is angry at the way things are set up. I think he is angrier than ever because the rules are set up in a way that he can't even go see his mom. It's not like he has a criminal record, but they are considered criminals because . . . [starts crying]. It's hard.

For Liliana's stepfather, the emotional effects of not being able to visit his mother, or bury her, remain. In this case, Liliana's stepfather feels anger about how immigration policies have not allowed him a pathway to legalize his status or at least an opportunity to visit family members outside the United States safely. It should be noted that Liliana's stepfather did try to legalize years prior but was unsuccessful. In the absence of large-scale immigration reform, he has not had the opportunity to change his immigration status in more recent years.

For a lot of undocumented parents, especially fathers, the decision not to return also entails concerns about the costs associated with their absence and the exorbitant fees tied to undocumented crossing. These financial concerns are critical to fathers, who understand the gendered role they play as breadwinners to their families, specifically the financial risk involved if they were unable to return to their families in the United States. Carmen, a mother of three, explained this situation and how her husband could not attend his mother's funeral:

My husband could not go to the funeral. When he got the news, we had just bought a house . . . and he just felt too much responsibility and didn't want to leave us, so he said: "I just can't go, because if I go, it's just too dangerous to come back. I know I can get the money. I can borrow the money and I can pay someone to get across, but it's just too dangerous." We decided against it, and we had already heard of sad stories of people coming through, and yes, there are successful stories, but there is always a risk, so in the end, he said he didn't want to do it. The little one was maybe two or three, so we decided against it.

As Carmen puts it, the decision not to return was partly based on her husband's feeling of responsibility—to her and their young children and also his financial commitment regarding the home they had just purchased. There is also the physical risk involved in a loss. The "sad stories" Carmen refers to can be immigrants who have died in their attempt to cross.[19]

Carmen explains that if her husband were a single man he would have probably returned to Mexico. Without a family to financially support or feel committed to returning to, the decision to travel to Mexico would be less complicated. With a sigh of sadness, Carmen ponders out loud what it would feel like if any of her children left home and migrated at a young age and what it would feel like for her to pass without them. Recognizing the emotional trauma her husband endured, she does her best to try to use these family experiences as an opportunity to encourage her children to have compassion. Sometimes, Carmen tells her children about what their father withstood so that they can develop empathy for the immigrant experience and understand their family roots. "Whenever I tell [my children] that story—because they grew up without grandmas—so whenever I tell them that story it is definitely something sad. I said: 'Imagine leaving your house at nineteen and not being able to see your mom again.'" Carmen's husband remains undocumented, but the family is hopeful that one day his status will be legalized through a widespread amnesty program or possibly via family sponsorship.

GUILT AND STATUS PRIVILEGE

Although my study's undocumented parents managed difficult choices shaped by legal status constraints, family love, and competing obligations, other members of mixed-status families had greater opportunity to travel internationally. Some DACA recipients were able to access some (albeit limited) travel opportunities through advance parole. Although advance parole has not always been available, some DACA recipients can apply to this program so that they may travel internationally and then return to the United States lawfully. Generally, advance parole is granted when DACA recipients travel internationally for educational, humanitarian, or employment purposes.

For DACA recipients, the possibility of advance parole allowed for a newfound privilege to travel, but this was not something extended to their parents. As a result, some youth felt guilty about having this access when they felt their parents deserved it much more. Amber, a DACA recipient, explained this to me:

> I've been seeing a lot of people go to their birth places with advance parole. I have been thinking, my grandma is sick and I haven't seen her for a long time, so

maybe I want to go and I'll get to visit where my brother is resting and all these things, but then it's like: Why do I get to go? Why do I get to go when my parents have a stronger attachment to Mexico? So, it's constant guilt of having something you can't share with the people you most love and most care about. This is especially the case because it is something that we don't talk about, and my mom said something, and I actually asked her: "Would you go if you could?" She used really emotional words to say of course she would. She said she wants to go see the cemetery where my brother is and go back. So, it's very conflicting to know you have the possibility of going, even if it's for a couple of days and then other people who have a stronger desire to go, can't. So I feel very privileged, and I wish I could take this [DACA] away from me and kind of give it to them. That is how I feel about DACA. I am glad it's helping me out, but I also wish I had the chance to give it to them instead.

Amber's feelings of guilt are not unlike what other undocumented youth have shared with researchers about their experience with DACA and advance parole.[20] Many undocumented youth wish that the possibilities provided with DACA—such as advance parole—could be shared with parents who have even stronger transnational family attachments.

Guilt was also experienced by adult citizen youth who had even greater opportunity to travel internationally than their DACA recipient peers. The adult citizen children of undocumented parents, for example, could travel freely so long as they had the economic resources and time to do so. This was not a privilege they took lightly, knowing full well that their undocumented loved ones did not have this same access. When Alexander became an adult, he made it a point to travel back to Mexico to visit family there. He also shared this experience by inviting his sister so that she could participate in the trip too. His ability to partake in such a visit inspired mixed feelings. "I felt like I was being selfish, just because I knew [my parents] couldn't go, you know?" He continued, "For so long I thought I was being selfish because my parents can't go, but in the end, I was like, me going kind of gives them hope that one day they can go back." In some ways, Alexander felt like the family representative on these trips to visit family: "I go and people tell me: 'Ooh, I haven't seen your mom in so long. It's good to see you. Good to see you guys are healthy.' At the end of the day, we all have our problems, but they get to see me and my little sister are good." In this way, Alexander and other youth who have greater access to legal travel can become what scholars have called "family ambassadors"[21] because they can represent their parents on these important trips and can exchange greetings, photos, and family news and facilitate video chats between family members across borders.

CLOSING THOUGHTS

While news and debates concerning undocumented immigrants are ubiquitous, very little of this coverage focuses on immigrants as both loving parents *and* devoted sons and daughters. Some undocumented immigrants care for the families they create in the United States but deeply cherish and miss the families that remain in their home country. Much scholarship and media focus on how immigrants fear or experience detention and deportation, which can also entail family separation, physical containment, and emotional trauma. The experiences described here focus on another related aspect of being undocumented—the feeling of being stuck within U.S. borders and the lack of legal, safe, and affordable options to move freely to honor transnational family bonds.

Although my data did not capture this, some families do get to experience successful legalization and subsequently experience joyful returns to their home countries. On social media sites such as TikTok, some adult children chronicle their immigrant parents' return to their home country after they have experienced decades of living as undocumented immigrants. In these brief clips, sometimes viewers learn that adult children were able to help their parents become legal permanent residents. In these short clips, the climax is when immigrant parents finally embrace their own mothers and fathers in what is typically an emotional, heartfelt, and sometimes surprise reunion. When family reunions are not possible, undocumented immigrants report using communication or virtual meeting technologies to witness or participate in family grieving rituals.[22]

Sometimes reunions between undocumented immigrants and their parents can occur in the United States. For example, since 2017, some Mexican elders have been granted visas to visit their undocumented children in the United States for a three-week stay.[23] This program is new and limited and has not been officially endorsed by the U.S. State Department, but it has allowed some reunions to occur. Therefore, while it is true that many undocumented immigrants find themselves "between a rock and a hard place" when it comes to family separation, some immigrants do ultimately find themselves in the loving embraces of loved ones. Unfortunately, immigration laws put undocumented immigrants in those difficult spaces that challenge emotional well-being and make transnational family bonds harder to honor. Still, families do their best to express love and commitment in the face of such grief and adversity.

Notes

1. In this context, I am not referring to when an immigrant goes through the steps of consular processing and has authorization to return to the United States or when someone with DACA has advance parole and therefore has permission to lawfully reenter the United States.

2. Holmes (2013); Missing Migrants Project (2023).

3. Missing Migrants Project (2023).

4. Riggle-van Schagen and Vaquera (2022).

5. Sieff (2019).

6. In this context, I am referring to a farewell as a final in-person meeting between loved ones, but it could also include travel to participate in any collective grieving rituals, such as attending a viewing, funeral, or burial.

7. Hipsman, Gómez-Aguiñaga, and Capps (2016).

8. Ngai (2003).

9. Calavita (1992); Ngai (2003); Massey (2009).

10. Legal Information Institute (n.d.).

11. Mathema (2017).

12. Taylor et al. (2011).

13. Migration Policy Institute (2023).

14. Not all families experience this form of transnational separation. For example, some families migrate together or eventually reunite as immigrants in the United States.

15. USCIS (2020).

16. Chavez (2013, 2017); Rodriguez (2016).

17. Rodriguez (2019); Schmalzbauer and Andrés (2019); García Valdivia (2022).

18. USCIS (2019).

19. See Getrich (2019) and Guzman Garcia (2020).

20. Ruth and Estrada (2019).

21. Ruth and Estrada (2019).

22. Bravo (2017).

23. Sieff (2019).

In Other Words

HOW IMMIGRATION STATUS SHAPES FAMILY NEGOTIATIONS

Vanessa Delgado, August 12, 2022 / CCF@TSP

Growing up with undocumented parents can place children at a disadvantage. Indeed, studies find that children with undocumented parents are more likely to experience poverty, depression and anxiety, housing instability, and educational barriers. As these youth come of age, they often take on additional responsibilities for the family, including providing financial support, sponsoring undocumented parents for lawful permanent residency (LPR), and sharing immigration policy updates. However, it remains unclear how the *immigration status* of the young adults shapes the types of support they provide to their undocumented parents. *In other words, how does parental support differ between citizen young adults and undocumented young adults?*

My recent study examines how U.S.-born citizen and DACAmented college students manage parental illegality in their families. This qualitative study draws on forty-one semistructured interviews with Latinx college students who vary in immigration status. All participants had at least one undocumented parent and lived in Southern California at the time of the interview.

The findings suggest that young adults' legal status shaped the strategies they used to mediate parental illegality. Young adults engaged in various tactics to support their undocumented parents, including informing undocumented parents about their legal rights, sharing tips about how to navigate interactions with police or Immigration and Customs Enforcement (ICE), easing fears about family separation, and devising strategies to minimize threats of deportation or detention. The in-depth interviews revealed that citizen young adults' and DACAmented young adults' support was facilitated or constrained by their own immigration status.

Citizen young adults attempted to use their protected legal status to support their undocumented parents in two ways. First, citizens investigated the immigration petition process and sought out possible options for adjusting their parents' legal status. Participants detailed how they looked up information about sponsorship on the web, discussed the family's case with lawyers, and strategized about how to cover the costs of sponsorship. Only three participants were able to successfully petition their parents for lawful permanent residency, with the vast majority unable to do so due to state-sanctioned restrictions. Second, citizens helped their undocumented parents by stepping in to shield them from threats of deportation.

The most commonly used tactic was driving undocumented parents through and around checkpoints. The strategies used by citizens underscore the advantages and drawbacks of citizenship in mixed-status Latinx immigrant families.

DACAmented young adults shared legal capital and immigration policy updates with their undocumented parents. Respondents' unique social characteristics as acculturated bilingual college students with DACA shaped the set of tactics they used to help their undocumented parents. Access to DACA allowed these young people to help in similar ways to that of citizen young adults. For instance, both DACAmented and citizen young adults were able to provide financial support by working part-time jobs and opening credit cards that their parents could use. However, DACA's temporary and unstable nature during the Trump administration left DACAmented respondents in a state of precarity wherein their safety and futures were threatened. In response to this uncertainty, DACAmented young adults made use of legal resources on college campuses. These youth were able to access targeted on-campus resources and programming for undocumented students, including a centralized resource center, classes, conferences, scholarships, legal services, housing, DACA renewal clinics, professional development, academic consultation, support groups, and immigrant rights organizations. These resources enabled DACAmented young adults to acquire legal capital. They then shared these resources with their undocumented parents with the intention of mediating the harmful effects of illegality in their families.

In the context of a restrictive sociopolitical climate, this study sheds light on how the adult children of undocumented immigrants develop strategies to combat threats of family separation, detention, and deportation. Young adults draw on resources available to them to support their undocumented parents, albeit some are better positioned to provide legal knowledge than others. The strategies implemented by the adult children of undocumented immigrants highlight the need for policies that address the legal vulnerability of undocumented and mixed-status families. Until then, children of undocumented immigrants will continue to endure the burden of navigating a broken immigration system. ∎

34

Queer(ing) Intimate Partner Violence through
Transgender Inclusion

Xavier Guadalupe-Diaz

Understanding how gender informs violence in intimate relationships has been central to family theory, research, policy, and service provision. Today, intimate partner violence (IPV) is understood as a pattern of emotional/psychological, physical, and sexual abuses that occur within the context of a current or former romantic relationship that can feature many factors, including financial abuse, coercion, and stalking (Chen et al. 2020). These "understandings" aren't just academic exercises—they tell us how it is that people continue to be victims of violence and give us important ideas for how to create more effective, compassionate, and inclusive communities of prevention and repair.

The work of understanding IPV has come in waves and is marked by successes and failures. During the 1970s, second-wave feminists, intent on equality, cultivated a movement highlighting how patriarchal power fueled problems such as violence against women. Patriarchal power is characterized by male rule in institutions and in personal life. Second-wave feminists, and especially a subset referred to as radical feminists, framed gender as the primary source of oppression for *all* women and asserted that traditional patriarchal family structures facilitated inequity in relationships that put women at higher risk for violence by male partners.

Black feminists and other feminists of color problematized the idea of *all* and the exclusive focus on gender. The idea of *all* had the effect of minimizing other aspects of life that are associated with violence. They highlighted how gender intersected with race and other systems of oppression to create unique experiences across marginalized women and beyond—an intersectional approach.

This led to calls to see IPV as a family abuse problem that could be experienced by people of *any gender* and *any sexual orientation*. The hetero and cisnormative assumptions of early radical feminist thought relied on a gender binary—or the idea that there are only two genders (man and woman) that align with two sexes assigned at birth: male and female. The binary doesn't accurately portray the range of genders, and the consequences are profound. The gender binary made invisible the abuse that existed in same-gender intimate relationships, including gay, lesbian, bisexual, and queer relationships, and in relationships in which at least one of the partners identified within the broader transgender umbrella including transgender women/men, nonbinary, and genderqueer people.

Since then, decades of work and activism have documented lesbian, gay, bisexual, transgender, and queer (LGBTQ) IPV and have elevated our understanding of intimate partner violence and the contexts in which it occurs. However, within the early radical feminist work on IPV, gender remains largely unexamined beyond the binary of cisgender man and woman. This cisnormative bias is evident in the small body of transgender-inclusive research and service provision. If gender is central to understanding IPV, why has the field struggled to incorporate more diverse understandings of gender that are inclusive of transgender experiences?

Transgender people are more visible now than at any point in U.S. history. For example, researchers at Pew recently found that a record 42 percent of Americans personally know someone who is transgender (Minkin and Brown 2021). Transgender activists have advocated for centuries for social, cultural, and political progress around a diverse range of intersectional gender issues. In a recent, alarming turn, transgender people are being scapegoated by far-right extremists who have banned books on transgender topics, criminalized parents of transgender children, banned transgender people from sports, and more. Those actions are motivated by the myth of a gender binary.

An inclusive social understanding of gender goes beyond improving how we think about IPV. Challenging the cultural myth of the gender binary directly implicates the patriarchal power structure that, in part, facilitates many forms of violence and inequality. As you will read, history shows that the best work toward gender justice and IPV justice requires that we challenge the myth of a gender binary. A gender binary holds that there are two and only two distinct genders and that social institutions and intimate relationships are structured heteronormatively around this. Studying and addressing IPV in the lives of transgender people, in fact, helps us see that the gender binary is embedded within patriarchal power structures—and this in turn facilitates many forms of violence and inequality.

How do we do this? This chapter introduces you to a powerful tool, *queer(ing) gender.* Although a generation ago the word *queer* was offensive, now it is a focal term for updating limited concepts of gender. As is often the case with newer, emerging perspectives, what it means to *queer* dominant perspectives is the subject of much debate. For some, queering has simply involved the addition of nonheterosexual, noncisgender perspectives and experiences. This is sometimes referred to as an "add queer and stir" approach to methods, theory, and practice (Compton et al. 2018). For others, queering has also involved disrupting all forms of normative thinking and rigid, totalizing perspectives that present a one-size-fits-all explanation to social and cultural phenomena. And combinations of these two approaches have sought to integrate more LGBTQ (or nonheterosexual, noncisgender) perspectives and experiences while disrupting normative thinking, binary frameworks, and assumptions that one group in society has all the power while others have none.

The *queer(ing) gender* approach to IPV illuminates distinct realities faced by transgender survivors. By queering how gender is conceptualized, you will see that power is structured by patriarchy, it is situational, and it is informed by systems of oppression that intersect to create distinct realities for relationships that are not made of straight (heterosexual) or cisgender partners. Ultimately, when we shift how we think about gender, power, and relationships, we learn more about the types of abuse transgender people experience in intimate relationships and subsequently offer stronger recommendations for intervening in and preventing IPV.

BACKGROUND: EVOLUTION OF FEMINIST THOUGHT ON IPV

Social problems are products of the systems and culture around us, and IPV is no exception. For much of human history, violence within families has taken on many meanings. Within a Western, U.S.-centric framework, violence in families has been documented since early colonization through the present day. Family violence has historically been a normalized aspect of private life. Violence in intimate relationships was long considered a private problem. This very privacy emboldened men to use violence within the family. Despite several notable moments throughout U.S. history, such as the temperance movement's focus on alcohol and family abuse and the introduction of abuse as grounds for limited divorce options, a broad-scale movement against IPV did not take hold until the 1970s.

Radical feminists rallied through storytelling and shared experiences around rape, sexual assault, sexual harassment, and IPV. Many of these activists developed a critical, power-based critique that focused on how patriarchy structured gender inequality and fostered cultural environments hostile to women. Radical feminists of the time maintained a hetero and cisnormative perspective that framed issues like IPV as a heterosexual, cisgender women's problem. Even more, fearing the mischaracterization of all radical feminists as lesbians, mainstream feminist discourse was palpably hostile toward queer perspectives (Shulman 1980).

These critiques focused on gender as an equally oppressive construct for all women, yet Black and other feminists of color pushed back on the notion that gendered power was the same for all women. Black, Indigenous, and other people of color (BIPOC) highlighted how gendered racism created divergent realities of oppression for women of color. For example, the racialized patriarchy had created a hierarchy in which white heteronormative femininity was revered while Black femininity was pathologized. Since the early colonial era and for centuries after, Black women were deemed "unrapeable" by U.S. courts and went largely unprotected by laws criminalizing sexual assault (Roberts 2021).

There were critiques from other groups too. By the early 1980s, challenges to radical feminist perspectives of IPV included family violence scholars who argued that violence between married heterosexual spouses was gender symmetrical. Family violence scholars argued that large national samples of violence in households revealed that cisgender women were equally violent as cisgender men (Gelles and Straus 1987). They rejected ideas about gendered power differences and did not consider how violence functions differently in different contexts. Two dominant camps had formed: radical feminist scholars and family violence scholars. These opposing frameworks dominated the scholarly debate around the role of gender in IPV for years to come. They were unified in their neglect of transgender people. Much energy was dedicated to determining how influential gender and patriarchy were in issues of IPV, and the debate remained entirely cis and heteronormative. In some cases, gay and lesbian IPV scholars joined family violence scholars in critiquing the centrality of gender, emphasizing individual psychology and noting that because same-gender IPV existed, this meant that gender played little or no role in explaining such violence (see Island and Letellier 1991). Other gay and lesbian IPV scholars took a more social psychological approach, arguing that patriarchal structure informs all types of violence, including same-gender IPV (Merrill 1996).

By the 1990s, scholars such as Michael Johnson (2010) were finding that radical feminists and family violence scholars were measuring different types of IPV and assuming that experiences were universal. More specifically, family violence scholars were capturing more situational violence that failed to adequately show context, severity, and injury, which were all gendered outcomes. Radical feminist scholars were capturing more severe violence, or intimate terrorism, which researchers would find in samples from shelter services and elsewhere. They shifted attention to the context of power and control yet missed something important. While gender was the focus of IPV studies, few scholars and advocates considered the full range of gender diversity that today's queer(ing) gender IPV work includes. And despite critiques from BIPOC, queer, and transgender communities, the public discourse had centered IPV as an exclusively cisgender, heterosexual women's problem.

Politics of the day further enveloped IPV as part of the broader movement to end violence against women. Within the emerging "tough on crime" political climate of the 1970s and '80s, mainstream feminists merged their interests in addressing violence against women with the growing arm of the criminal-legal system in the United States. The feminist agenda converged with a growing political drive to increase law enforcement, toughen penalties, and incarcerate more people, and this led to new criminal procedures to address IPV (Kim 2020).

As one of those feminist criminal-legal accomplishments, the Violence Against Women Act of 1994 (VAWA) became the first federal legislation to fund the expansion of policing and punishment of IPV. It created a federal Office on Violence Against Women, expanding shelter grants and other service provisions. Scholars refer to the convergence of the feminist agenda and mass incarceration as *carceral feminism*: the feminist movement had leveraged the power of a racist, classist, and biased criminal-legal system to more proactively intervene in crimes such as IPV, sexual assault, and rape (Whalley and Hackett 2017). Although the feminist movement to end IPV had made significant accomplishments in the criminal-legal and human services realm, their methods fell short. Many of the interventions relied on a limited understanding of how IPV affects diverse groups. Gender had been cemented as a focal point. Gender remained binary, cis and heteronormative, even while scholarly work on gay and lesbian IPV grew.

The gay liberation movement in the United States, sparked by the Stonewall Riots of 1969, highlights queer and trans liberation. Despite being led by and centering BIPOC transgender activists, the political mainstreaming of lesbian and gay rights quickly marginalized BIPOC transgender activists and adopted more "palatable" cisnormative, middle-class, and white agendas (Stryker 2017). Similarly, the growing attention to gay and lesbian IPV retained a largely cisgender framework that continued to marginalize transgender survivors. While queer perspectives expanded greatly in the 1990s, the field of IPV was limited to the inclusion of same-gender violence. The field had not yet taken on questioning the gender binary.

QUEER(ING) GENDER, POWER, AND INTIMATE PARTNER VIOLENCE

This earlier feminist work did much to highlight the gendered nature of violence against women. In summary, the history of thought and activism on IPV centered patriarchal culture as *the* dominant explanation for violence. Yet the rigid framework of patriarchy as culprit and gender as a binary marginalized the violence experienced between partners of the same gender and made transgender survivors of IPV invisible.

For example, as reviewed above, mainstream feminist thought assumed that gender was the primary social factor of oppression for *all* women. Intersectional and queer perspectives challenged that rigidity by introducing how gender was experienced differently across race, sexual orientation, class, and other identities. This means that mainstream feminism assumed that patriarchal power structures were the primary explanation for IPV, sexual assault, and rape. Intersectional and queer approaches recognized that these problems were framed as cisgender, heterosexual women's issues.

As you can see from this history, queer(ing) how gender and power are understood helps us address a wider range of experiences and realities. Queering gender in IPV perspectives requires us to look at the very words that institutions as well as the people in them use to establish who does and does not have power (Guadalupe-Diaz 2019). Queering done in social research does not hesitate to question the status quo—and when effective, it "highlight[s] the instability of taken-for-granted meanings and resulting power relations" (Browne and Nash 2010, p. 4).

Queer(ing) perspectives prompts us to examine transgender experiences with IPV. First, queering challenges the words used in laws, caregiving systems, counseling, and research that persistently construct IPV as a cisgender, heterosexual woman's problem. Second, by examining language and discourse, queer perspectives show us how abuse is fostered by systems of oppression: the way we talk about things is like the air we breathe—it is everywhere and it is invisible. It gives a view to how oppression operates "out there" in larger systems as well as "in here" in close relationships. Analyzing language that flows through our daily lives allows us to see and hear how oppression in larger systems facilitates the *situational* leveraging of power in intimate relationships. Yet queering doesn't mean ending the investigation by looking at new ways to blame larger systems for personal troubles. It allows us to see things hidden in plain sight too. Queering allows us to examine how individuals sometimes weaponize power situationally, regardless of assumed hierarchies in society.[1]

For transgender people, the criminal-legal system and social services create power that can be used to dominate individuals through institutions. The very words used by institutions inform how violence is experienced because language constructs the meaning, for example, of who can and cannot be seen or treated like a victim. For transgender people, not being seen as a victim generates distinct vulnerabilities. Consider how rape victims are presented to courts of law: victims are expected to verbalize their experiences using legal jargon that follows the contours of heterosexual scripts; failure to represent experiences through the language of the court may result in the case not advancing even when such language marginalizes the survivor (Arrigo and Bernard 1997). Similarly, the language that upholds various other social systems, including education, marriage, and labor markets, reflects a cisnormative discourse that shapes opportunities for violence, how such violence is interpreted and experienced, and the subsequent barriers to structural responses for transgender survivors. For example, domestic violence laws of the past used gendered language to define victims as women and perpetrators as men, excluding others from protection. As another example, shelter services may define services as only for cisgender women, neglecting others in need.

Transgender IPV—What Do We Know?

Queering is hard to understand when you are new to it, precisely because of the taken-for-granted power of our gender binary systems. Queer(ing) IPV moves beyond the consideration of non-normative genders and sexual orientations and interrogates how power in intimate relationships actively reflects ways of knowing through both language and structure. Queering perspectives makes it possible to see more of our human experience.

Much work in recent decades sought to reduce cisgender biases in IPV research and to center transgender survivors. Several measurement challenges continue to make an "apples to apples" comparison between cisgender and transgender IPV difficult. Primary among those challenges is that the most generalizable national surveys typically do not include gender measures that capture transgender populations. This means that comparisons are largely left to convenience samples or cross-study comparisons that may not be easily comparable. Given the safe assumption that the transgender population in the United States is relatively small, targeted sampling offers larger samples but not necessarily more generalizability.

One of the most generalizable prevalence estimates for transgender IPV (T-IPV) comes from the U.S. Transgender Survey (USTS) 2015, which found that 54 percent of the 27,715 transgender respondents had experienced at least one form of IPV (James et al. 2016). A review of several lifetime IPV victimization prevalence estimates among transgender people showed that 44–57 percent reported psychological IPV, 20–35 percent physical IPV, 8–47 percent sexual IPV, and 27–73 percent anti-transgender IPV (Messinger and Guadalupe-Diaz 2021). The wide ranges by IPV type reflect the fact that different surveys use different methods and sampling techniques. General population surveys that opt for randomized sampling techniques often do not capture large enough transgender samples to offer useful comparisons. National studies conducted on cisgender samples typically find lower rates of IPV when compared with transgender samples. For example, in the CDC's National Intimate Partner and Sexual Violence Survey, 35.6 percent of cisgender women and 28.5 percent of cisgender men reported having experienced IPV in their lifetime (Black et al. 2011).

The higher rate of IPV experienced by transgender people reveals their distinct vulnerability to violence. Several contextual factors—including intersecting power structures that can shape situational dynamics in intimate relationships (including in unexpected ways)—elevate the risk. By reliably examining abusive power dynamics across a wider range of relationships and identities, a queer(ing) approach gives us a fuller account of the distinct risk factors faced by transgender people.

Using the USTS, our work (Guadalupe-Diaz and West 2021) examined IPV within the context of various intersecting forms of violence that increased vulnerability to abuse. Queering approaches showed how larger oppressive contexts shape the high rates of interpersonal violence experienced by transgender people. We found that forms of structural violence, including poverty, housing and employment insecurity, and health care disparities, were more common for transgender people, and these inequitable and unjust forms of structural violence were linked to IPV. These societal conditions often limit agency and result in relying on precarious survival work, periods of homelessness, and more (Kritz 2021). Severe economic marginalization may be associated with a greater risk for abuse and partially explain the high rates of violence experienced by transgender people.

Added to structural violence is a related concept of institutional violence. Institutional violence can stem from social institutions such as the educational system, the carceral state, and public accommodations. Increasingly, the backlash against the minimal gains made by transgender rights activists in recent years has further weaponized social institutions. Far-right politics have rapidly harnessed anti-transgender sentiments within the context of the normalization of white nationalist fascism in the United States. As part of this backlash, conservative politicians have passed a number of anti-trans executive orders and laws aimed at leveraging the power of institutions to maintain cisgender domi-nance. These policies include sports bans and restrictions against transgender athletes, bans on books covering gender and sexuality, and the criminaliza-tion of gender-affirming care (Lenning and Guadalupe-Diaz, forthcoming). Within the context of growing authoritarianism in U.S. institutions and around the world, Haider (2018) noted that "those who fiercely advocate for eradicat-ing transgender people are fighting to retain a world under the regime of male hegemony. In such an environment, autocrats and their accompanying oligar-chies are sustained."

Together, structural and institutional forms of violence are shaped by the intersections of race and ethnicity. BIPOC transgender people report distinctly high rates of discrimination, isolation, economic marginalization, and other fac-tors associated with heighted risk for abuse (West and Guadalupe-Diaz 2021). These compounding forms of violence highlight how transgender people experi-ence unique vulnerability to IPV. The broader context of power and marginaliza-tion informs the daily lives and intimate relationships of transgender people and limits choices and opportunities.

DYNAMICS OF ABUSE

Why do we look at these larger contexts? The dynamics of abuse are often informed and specified by a victim's situation (Walker 2015). Potential abusers of transgender partners may leverage the power and violence of structure and insti-tutions with the added threat of more interpersonal violence. For transgender people, this makes it possible for abusers to tailor their abusive tactics to further undermine their partner. Although broad categories of abuse, including physical, sexual, emotional, psychological, and verbal abuses, are well documented across all types of relationships, transgender people may be subject to additional abuses that emerge as a result of intense societal and cultural marginalization.

Emotional and psychological abuses are documented across relationships of all sexual orientations and genders. But with transgender people, queer(ing) researchers find novel patterns of abuse, especially the anti-trans aspect of iden-tity abuse. Woulfe and Goodman (2021, p. 3) defined identity abuse as "the set of tactics of IPV that leverage heterosexism and cissexism against LGBTQ sur-vivors." Identity abuse against transgender partners includes multiple forms of emotional, verbal, and psychological violence that is often experienced in tan-dem with physical or sexual violence. Transgender IPV is further exacerbated by abusers' transphobic abuse (Roch, Ritchie, and Morton 2010). The variety of tactics includes the undermining of transgender identity, blocking medical

appointments or gender-affirming care, and threatening to out transgender partners to employers, family, or friends.

When transgender survivors tell their stories, we hear about patterns of *transphobic* and *genderist* attacks (Guadalupe-Diaz 2019). Their descriptive accounts
illustrated that abusers of transgender people often use transphobic and genderist
tactics. Transphobic attacks include derogatory and prejudiced attitudes toward
transgender people. Genderist attacks involve the regulation and policing of
a transgender partner's gender and how their gender is expressed.

Identity abuse is also used to undermine transgender partners and entrap
them in violent relationships. Although sociologists find that all humans engage
in the active construction of various identities, known as identity work, transgender people are subjected to greater scrutiny for living their authentic truths.
Identity construction is social in the sense that our internal sense of self is a
product of social definitions and our identities adapt or reflect the social feedback
that we receive from others. For example, transgender survivors of IPV often
see their abusive experiences as discrediting identity work (Guadalupe-Diaz and
Koontz Anthony 2017). By listening for concerns regarding identity, queer(ing)
researchers recognize how abusers of transgender people employ altercasting. In
this case, *altercasting*—something that happens when one person projects onto
another a particular role—is a process whereby the abusers place the victim in an
unwanted category or role and target the tools (or sign-vehicles) their transgender
partners use to express gender, such as chest binders, makeup, clothing, medications such as hormone therapy, and other material objects used to signify gender
or other aspects of their identities.

As part of discrediting identity work, abusers of transgender people manipu-
late already marginalized and vulnerable identities in an attempt to further erode
a victim's confidence and self-worth. By (often) centering a victim's transition or
gender, abusers can exploit insecurities, or guilt and shame. For example, abusers
may make victims feel undesirable or unworthy of love because of their transgender identity. Similarly, when abusers target sign-vehicles, they destroy objects that
function as extensions of self (Allen-Collinson 2011).

Queer(ing) perspectives in IPV research has disrupted traditional understandings of power and control in intimate relationships. The old way of thinking,
from radical feminist approaches, saw power and structures in such a way that
supported the idea that men are perpetrators and women are victims. While
recognizing that patriarchal structures shape all our lives, queer(ing) IPV work
does not stop there. This work has shown how individual identities do not always
result in neat hierarchal categories in which one person can be assumed to have
all the power and another has none of the power. Queer(ing) IPV work allows us
to see that women can be abusive, that men can be victims, and that a wide range

of intersectional identities creates different opportunities for abuse to arise in relationships regardless of the abuser or victim's particular placement in society.

Author X. Quinn (2020) described his own experiences of being abused as a trans man by someone who had even less societal privilege than he did. In his account, his abuser had significantly less privilege than he did regarding economics, citizenship status, and health. In a review of tactics, Quinn described how abusers can sometimes be poorer than victims or economically dependent on victims, how some abusers could even be more racially marginalized than their victims, or how victims may have a variety of other privileges that an abuser may not have, such as citizenship or legal residency status. Furthermore, some abusers who made transphobic or genderist attacks and discredited transgender identity work were *themselves* transgender or otherwise queer or gender nonconforming (Guadalupe-Diaz 2019). These dynamics highlight that abusers of all identities can weaponize structural vulnerabilities against their partners. Even a transgender abuser can use transphobic attacks against a transgender partner to gain control or undermine their partner's sense of self.

Queer(ing) IPV also disrupts some of the binary thinking around the victim/offender dichotomy. The human services and criminal-legal responses to IPV often attempt to create neat categories out of complex abusive situations. For example, many survivors of IPV report that they fight back in self-defense or even preemptively strike when they feel their abuser is about to lash out (Potter 2008). Although self-defense or even a preemptive strike does *not* mean that there is no "real" victim in the relationship, it does illustrate that the binary categories of victim and offender are often problematic in the criminal-legal realm. This is one way in which many IPV survivors find themselves being wrongfully labeled as the abuser by law enforcement or judges. Criminal-legal narratives around victimization require that survivors present neatly packaged experiences in which they are encouraged to tell their story in a way that makes them "deserving" of help. As a result, many survivors of all genders may not feel that they are "true" victims. Transgender survivors of IPV have reported that the gendered connotation of "victim" (the assumption that only women or otherwise feminine people can be victims) made it difficult for them to identify as a victim and be seen as deserving of resources (Guadalupe-Diaz and Jasinski 2017).

Queer(ing) Help Responses

The criminal-legal and human services approach to IPV intervention has led to a proliferation of resources that involve shelters, victim advocacy, law enforcement, and carceral responses. Although these formal response avenues successfully serve some survivors, many survivors report re-victimization and re-traumatization by formal help avenues such as domestic violence shelters and the police (Guadalupe-Diaz and Jasinski 2017). In addition, research using the USTS has shown that among transgender IPV survivors, only 2 percent reported having used a domestic violence shelter or rape crisis center (Messinger, Guadalupe-Diaz, and Kurdyla 2022). Other research has shown that transgender IPV survivors are reluctant to report abuse to the police for fear of transphobic, racist, or anti-immigrant responses by the system (Guadalupe-Diaz and Jasinski 2017; Langenderfer-Magruder et al. 2016). Although much work has been done to make the criminal-legal and human services response to IPV more inclusive, calls for queer(ing) help responses will benefit from more abolitionist perspectives.[2] Such approaches turn away from incarceration as we know it and seek to empower communities, center survivor needs, and foster forms of accountability that are removed from the carceral state (Kim 2018).

One aspect of queer(ing) IPV help responses focuses on the mutual aid that communities can provide to survivors. Mutual aid involves a network of grassroots community resources that are offered to those in need while working in tandem with social movements addressing social harms and inequalities (Spade 2020). Given that research has found that informal networks such as friends, family, neighbors, and colleagues are a primary source of help for transgender IPV survivors, more can be done to empower communities to serve as support systems for victims who may not want to involve the human services or criminal-legal system. Mutual aid models are increasingly used to leverage the collective power of communities invested in addressing violence, among other issues, by centering survivor needs. For example, mutual aid networks expanded greatly during the COVID-19 pandemic as communities became more reliant on social support systems. These models include provisions for housing, child care, food, health care, clothing, and other material needs required for safety planning.

Similarly, abolitionist models addressing IPV rely on community participation to meet survivor needs and establish accountability for the person doing the harm. Models such as *Creative Interventions Toolkit* (Creative Interventions 2012) enable communities to develop people-led help structures without relying on criminal-legal and human services institutions. The tool kit identifies the role(s) of the (1) survivor, (2) community allies, (3) person doing harm, and (4) facilitator in a mutual process of achieving safety and accountability, identifying needs, goals, and other players.

While formal systems individualize the problem of violence and often isolate survivors from their communities, abolitionist interventions actually leverage the very sources that IPV survivors often report as most helpful—neighbors, friends, and family. *Creative Interventions Toolkit* notes that "help comes from those closest to you" (p. 16). This toolkit emphasizes that we all have a role to play in reducing IPV against transgender people and people of all identities. Community education on the history of violence in the family, the dynamics of abuse, and the complications of interlocking systems of violence could serve to empower more people to serve as resources.

Overall, the societal response to violence in intimate relationships has undergone many developments in recent decades. Systemic responses to IPV remain heavily hetero and cisnormative and dependent on problematic institutions; yet, increasingly, more creative approaches are changing how the public perceives gender, transgender people, abuse and power, and conventional systems of punishment. Queer(ing) IPV has not only opened up research, theory, and practice to include a broader range of relationship experiences but also broadened the call for interventions to include the realities of all people.

Notes

1. For example, Foucault (1980) argued that power was not just embedded in social structure but instead that dominant narratives, language, and ways of knowing were the root of power.

2. Abolitionists seek to reduce the reliance on the criminal-legal system for interventions in IPV and focus on community accountability, survivor-centered needs, and other noncarceral alternatives to healing. For further discussion, see Whalley, Chapter 40.

In Other Words

UNDERSTANDING BLACK QUEER MALE SURVIVORS' EXPERIENCES OF SEXUAL ASSAULT

Doug Meyer, June 16, 2022 / CCF@TSP

Sexual assault has received increased attention since #MeToo spread on social media in 2017 in response to sexual abuse allegations against Harvey Weinstein. Some scholars have noted, however, that much of this advocacy and media attention has focused on women with race and class privilege despite the fact that it was a Black woman, Tarana Burke, who initially used the phrase, back in 2006. #MeToo's focus on primarily white women survivors has led some scholars to argue that Burke's contributions have been sidelined, and that gender inequality has been privileged in sexual assault advocacy over other forms of oppression, such as institutional racism. This emphasis on white women's experiences of assault does not reflect the actual distribution of this violence. For example, as I note in my book *Violent Differences: The Importance of Race in Sexual Assault against Queer Men*, nationally representative data in the United States has shown that Black men experience sexual victimization at higher rates than white women. Research has also shown that queer men in general experience high rates of sexual assault and that queer people of color experience sexual assault at higher rates than their white counterparts.

In *Violent Differences*, I examine queer men's experiences of sexual assault, based on interviews I conducted with sixty queer male survivors. A majority of the respondents, thirty-seven, self-identified as Black or African American. Many of their experiences differed from traditional representations of sexual assault. For instance, Ornell (a pseudonym) a thirty-seven-year-old Black gay man, talked about how he met and fell in love with a man, Andres, while living in a homeless shelter at age twenty-one; they moved in together after dating for a few months. Ornell described a process of escalating verbal disputes that eventually resulted in Andres being physically abusive. A few weeks after the physical abuse began, Andres raped Ornell, forcibly holding him down by the throat and covering his mouth.

Several weeks after the sexual assault, a neighbor called the police when Ornell and Andres were arguing. When the officers came to their apartment, Ornell explained that they had been arguing in part about the rape, which he said that the officers "turn into a joke," with one of them asking, "You're sitting here wearing earrings, and you expect us to take you seriously?" Ornell described his gender expression as "feminine," and Black gender-expansive or gender-nonconforming men in this study often described profiling experiences in which they perceived the police as targeting their gender expression as well as their racial identity. The complexities of such experiences would be flattened or obscured through an approach that focused only on race, gender, or sexuality; instead, these experiences require deeper consideration of their overlap.

White queer male survivors' experiences undoubtedly revealed a lack of some institutional support as well; for example, the vast majority of white participants had negative experiences when reporting a sexual assault to the police. However, I show that queer men of color described feeling "lonely" after their assaultive experiences to a much greater extent than their white counterparts, as the former felt more isolated from a variety of domains, such as LGBTQ communities and institutional resources provided by groups such as the police. Focusing on the forms of marginalization that Black queer men experience reveals the extent to which many survivors are not supported in a U.S. context.

For this reason, work attempting to reduce sexual assault would benefit from continuing to expand feminist understandings of sexual violence to include a wider range of survivors beyond white and middle-class heterosexual women. Otherwise, we will continue to marginalize survivors who are harmed by systems of oppression other than gender inequality. Understanding sexual assault in relation to multiple dimensions of inequality helps explain high rates of assault experienced by multiple marginalized individuals such as Black women and LGBTQ people of color. This recognition of sexual assault as rooted in multiple systems of oppression also facilitates a better understanding of how it operates, allowing feminist and intersectional work to account for acts in which gender inequality may be less apparent and to examine how assailants' actions may emerge from several social hierarchies at the same time. Advocacy and scholarship that tackles multiple power relations can benefit a wider range of survivors and reveal the limitations of privileging one form of inequality over others. ◼

35

Mass Incarceration and Family Life[1]

Bryan L. Sykes, Becky Pettit, and Daniela Kaiser

You have likely read about or studied high incarceration rates in the United States—and in this book, you have read extensively about changes in family life. We ask, how does the high number of people who are imprisoned—and who have been imprisoned—in the United States affect our families? American families have experienced tremendous demographic and economic change since the mid-twentieth century. Scholars of the American family have drawn attention to how increases in women's labor market involvement, the decline in manufacturing, wage stagnation, suburbanization, and other important large-scale economic, social, and political changes influence family life.[2] Five decades of growth, from 1970 until 2020, in the prison and jail population represents a critical institutional intervention in the lives of American families but one that has attracted relatively little scholarly attention. Although the rate of incarceration has declined in the United States since its peak in 2009, the impact of mass incarceration on people's lives and their families, as well as inequalities in the distribution of harm, persist. The United States continues to be the world leader in incarceration.

Crime is at historic lows, yet the number of people in prison and jail remains near record highs. Close to 1.7 million Americans are behind bars—representing 1 percent of the adult population in the United States.[3] Sociologist David Garland has coined the term *mass incarceration* to characterize the uniquely modern American social phenomenon of extraordinarily high incarceration rates.[4]

Incarceration is highly concentrated among men, African Americans and Hispanics, as well as those with low levels of education. Moreover, inequality in incarceration among adults is mirrored in inequality in parental incarceration among children. Black and Hispanic children are three to six times more likely than white children to have had a parent in state or federal prison for at least a year.

This dramatic impact brings us to this chapter, where we investigate race and class inequality in incarceration and its effects on families and children. We begin by reviewing trends in crime and punishment and illustrate inequality in exposure to the criminal justice system and incarceration. We then consider the consequences of incarceration for family life and child well-being. Parental incarceration is linked to family instability, economic insecurity, and an increased risk of behavioral problems, especially among boys. Children of incarcerated parents are overrepresented in foster care, and high rates of incarceration in disadvantaged communities negatively impact educational attainment even among children who themselves do not have an incarcerated parent. Finally, we consider how inequality in exposure to incarceration creates and exacerbates race and class inequalities in family life.

TRENDS IN CRIME AND PUNISHMENT

Trends in crime in the United States bear only modest resemblance to trends in incarceration. By any measure, crime is down significantly from its peak. However, different measures of crime and victimization have risen and fallen at different rates and to different levels over the past few decades. Figure 35.1 displays crime rates since 1960. Violent crime rates grew from the early 1970s through 1981 during the early years of the penal buildup. As Figure 35.1 shows, violent crime rates ebbed and then grew into the early 1990s. Violent crime rates exhibited steep declines after 1993. The most reliable measure of violent crime—the murder rate—peaked in the United States in 1980, fluctuated through the 1980s, and had been declining since 1991 until the COVID-19 pandemic, when homicide rates increased even though the total violent crime rate remained low.

Figure 35.1 also shows trends in property crime rates. Like violent crime rates, property crime experienced surges in the 1960s through the 1980s. Property crime is more common than violence; the rate of these incidents is nearly seven times as high, as indicated by the main scale. Like violent crime rates, property crime rates began to decline in the early 1990s. Despite some discrepancies in the time series across measures, the trend in crime rates over the past several decades is unmistakable. There were crime surges by most measures in the early 1980s and 1990s, but all measures of crime are down from their historic heights. Even during the economic downturn that started in the last quarter of 2007, crime rates continued to be on par with levels observed in the late 1960s and

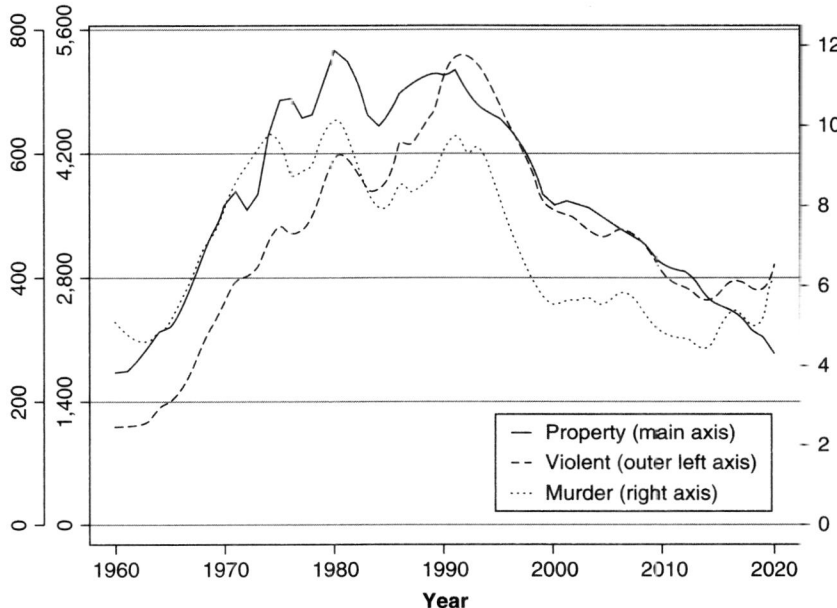

Figure 35.1 | Crime Rates per 100,000 Inhabitants, United States, 1960–2020

Source: Author calculations using data from the Survey of Inmates, Current Population Survey, and Bureau of Justice Statistics.

early 1970s. As noted, the same is true for the unrest and upheaval during the COVID-19 pandemic.

At the same time, contemporary incarceration rates are at historic highs Figure 35.2 documents the incarceration rate in the United States since the early 1970s. When statistics on the size of the prison population were first recorded in 1925, seventy-nine out of every one hundred thousand Americans were held in federal or state prisons, generating an imprisonment rate of 0.079. The imprisonment rate, or the percentage of Americans housed in federal or state prisons, hovered close to 0.1 (or 100 in 100,000) until the mid-1970s. The long-term stability in the imprisonment rate prompted some well-known criminologists to claim the existence of a "natural" or stable incarceration rate.[5]

Theories of stable incarceration rates were upended during the prison expansion that began in the mid-1970s. Between 1975 and 2009, the U.S. imprisonment rate grew an average of 4.7 percent annually. This is a stunning increase considering the imprisonment rate adjusts for population growth over the period. The incarceration rate, which includes inmates housed in local jails, grew almost

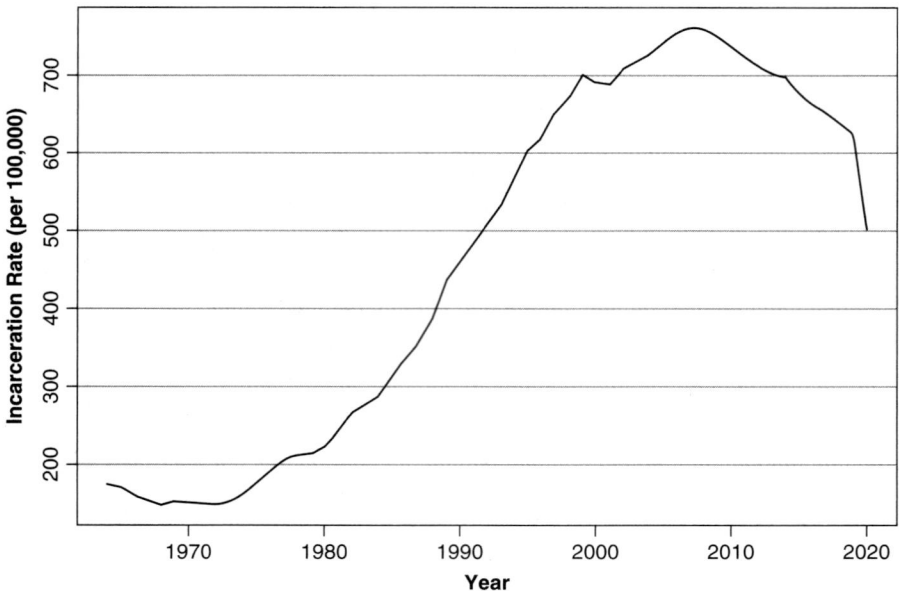

Figure 35.2 | Incarceration Rate per 100,000 Inhabitants, United States, 1964–2020

Source: Author calculations using data from the Survey of Inmates, Current Population Survey and Bureau of Justice Statistics.

as briskly. Figure 35.2 shows the steep increase in the incarceration rate in the United States that continued, unabated, even after the crime rate began declining in the early 1990s. Contrasting trends in Figures 35.1 and 35.2 illustrate the decoupling of crime and incarceration in the United States by the mid-1990s.

As of 2020, just under 1.7 million Americans were behind bars, representing approximately 1 percent of the adult population in the United States. Roughly 39 million more men and women are under the supervision of the criminal justice system through parole, probation, or other forms of community-based corrections.[6] That means approximately 2.1 percent of the U.S. population—or one in forty-seven adults—is under some form of correctional supervision or criminal justice surveillance.

Mass incarceration is not only a contemporary development; it is also distinctly American. Until the mid-1970s, the incarceration rate in the United States was similar to the incarceration rate in France and Germany, among other industrialized nations.[7] Now, after five decades of penal expansion, the United States

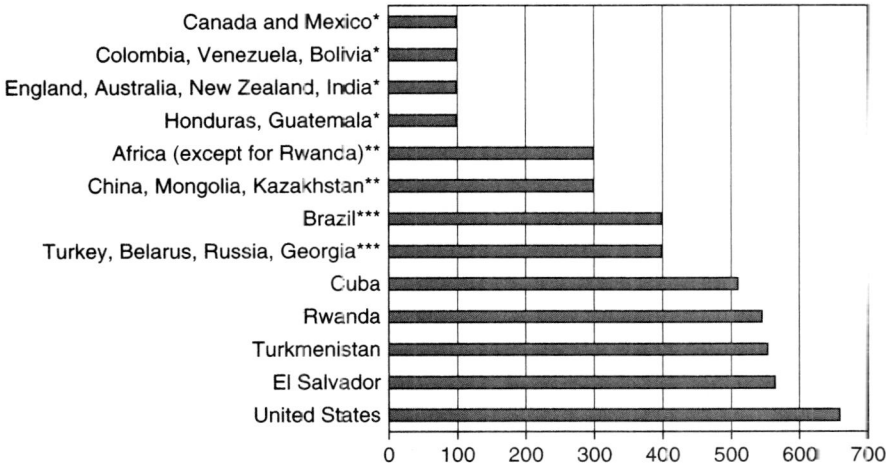

Figure 35.3 | Incarceration Rate per 100,000 Inhabitants, Select Countries

Source: J. Gramlich "America's Incarceration Rate Falls to Lowest Level since 1995," Pew Research Center, August 16, 2021. www.pewresearch.org/short-reads/2021/08/16/americas-incarceration -rate-lowest-since-1995.

*Rates between 0 and 99.

**Rates between 200 and 299.

***Rates between 300 and 399.

is the world leader in incarceration.[8] Figure 35.3 shows the incarceration rate for select countries and regions in 2020. In the late 2000s, the United States incarcerated a higher proportion of its population than any other advanced industrialized country. In fact, the incarceration rate in the United States is over ten times the incarceration rate in Sweden, Norway, Slovenia, Finland, and Denmark. This pattern continued into the 2020s,[9] even though the incarceration rate declined significantly in United States during 2020, as jails and prisons released more people during the COVID-19 pandemic.

The decoupling of crime rates and incarceration rates suggests that the growth in the penal population cannot simply be explained by large-scale changes in crime or criminality. Instead, shifts in policing, prosecution, and criminal justice policy at the local, state, and federal levels are important for understanding the expansion of the prison system. Over the past few decades, law enforcement agencies have stepped up policing, prosecutors have more actively pursued convictions, and a host of changes in sentencing policies now mandate jail or prison time.[10] Recent claims of decreased federal involvement in the lives of Americans[11] are at odds with the expansion of the criminal justice system; mass incarceration, as a policy intervention, has *increasingly* affected millions of adults and their families. In the following sections, we document inequality in exposure to the criminal justice system and its implications for American family life.

Patterns in Exposure to the Criminal Justice System

Although explanations for contemporary prison and jail growth remain a source of debate, growth of the criminal justice system itself is indisputable. Even in the face of steep crime declines through the 1990s, the penal system continued its historic expansion into the twenty-first century. While women and Hispanics represent some of the fastest-growing segments of the incarcerated population, spending time in prison or jail continues to be most heavily concentrated among men, African Americans, and those with low levels of education.[12] Incarceration rates among black men are about seven times higher than those for white men. In 2008 the civilian incarceration rate among black men ages eighteen to sixty-four was 8 percent, compared with 1.2 percent among non-Hispanic white men. Among young men ages twenty to thirty-four, the incarceration rate of African American men was 11.4 percent, compared with 1.7 percent for non-Hispanic white men. Among those with the lowest levels of education, 37.2 percent of black men and 12 percent of white men were incarcerated.

The lifetime risks of imprisonment have also grown during the period of prison expansion. Moreover, the risks of imprisonment are increasingly concentrated among African American men without a high school diploma.[13] Five percent of white men and 27 percent of black men born between 1989 and 1993 spent at least a year in prison before reaching age thirty-five. The risks of spending time in prison for this birth cohort were significantly higher among high school dropouts: 28 percent of white and 68 percent of black dropouts had spent at least a year in prison by 2009.

Exposure to imprisonment now rivals or exceeds exposure to other social institutions long thought vital to the transition to adulthood, such as the completion of schooling, employment, or marriage. Young, black, male high school dropouts are more likely to spend at least a year in prison than they are to get married, and spending time in prison has become more common than completing a four-year college degree or serving in the military.[14] In short, among some groups of black men, spending time in prison has become a normative life event.

Just as the number of adults who are incarcerated has grown, so has the number of children with an incarcerated parent. Figure 35.4 shows the number of minor children with a parent incarcerated, by race. In 1980, roughly half a

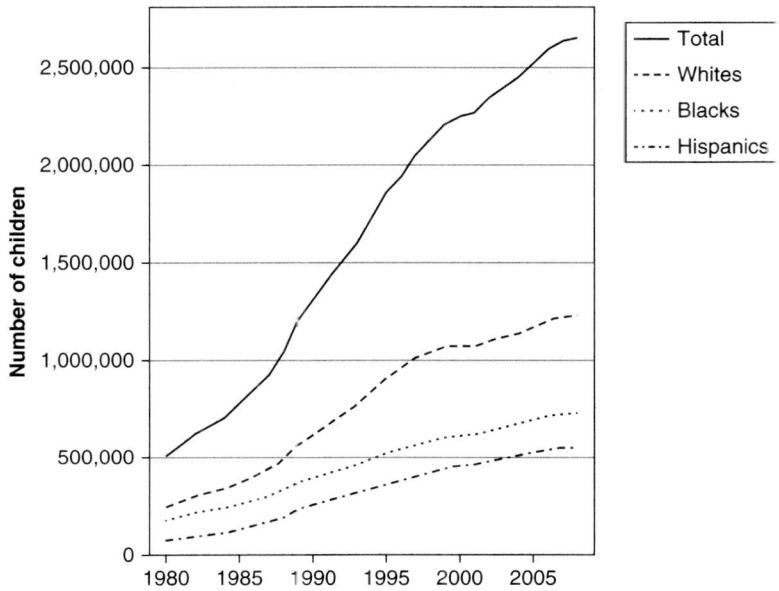

Figure 35.4 | Number of Minor Children with an Incarcerated Parent, by Race, 1980–2008

Source: Author calculations using data from the Survey of Inmates, Current Population Survey, and Bureau of Justice Statistics.

million children had a parent behind bars. By 2008, nearly 2.6 million children had at least one parent in prison or jail. While the number of children with an incarcerated parent has increased for all racial groups, black children experienced the fastest and largest growth in parental incarceration. In 1980, there were 245,000 black children with a parent in custody; by 2008, that figure had more than quintupled to over 1.23 million children, only slightly less than the combined total of white and Hispanic children.

Figure 35.4 illustrates how racial inequality in incarceration among adults is mirrored in racial inequality in children's chances of having an incarcerated parent. The figure shows the percentage of minor children with an incarcerated parent, by race. Between 1980 and 2008, the percentage of children in the United States with a parent behind bars increased from 0.8 percent to 3.6 percent. Yet there is enormous racial inequality in parental incarceration for children. By 2008, nearly one in eight black children (roughly 12 percent) had a parent behind bars, compared with one in fifty white and one in twenty-five Hispanic children.[15]

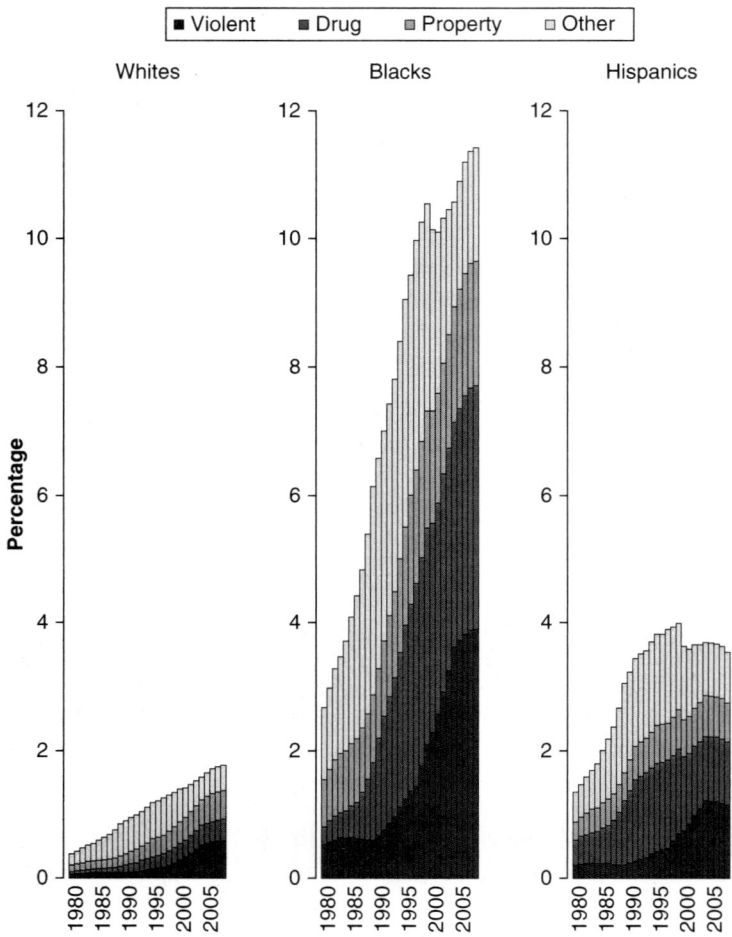

Figure 35.5 | Percentage of Minor Children with a Parent Incarcerated by Offense Type and Race, United States, 1980–2008

Source: Author calculations using data from the Survey of Inmates, Current Population Survey, and Bureau of Justice Statistics.

Increases in the jail and prison population are largely attributable to non-violent offenses. Figure 35.5 shows the percentage of minor children with an incarcerated parent, by offense type. While the percentage for any race group is the same as reported in Figure 35.4, we can investigate how much of parental incarceration is due to violent, drug, property, and other offense types. Several points are worth noting. First, violent offenses comprise no more than one-third of the total offenses for which parents are incarcerated. Second, the share of parents incarcerated for drug offenses has increased considerably since 1980, particularly for non-white parents. Drug offenses now explain one-third of parental incarceration for black children.

The risk of having a parent imprisoned at some point during childhood has also grown over time. Table 35.1 compares the risk of parental imprisonment by age seventeen for children born before the expansion of the penal system and for children born during its height. In 1980, less than 0.5 percent of white children and less than 3 percent of black children experienced parental imprisonment by age seventeen. By 2009, those numbers had increased dramatically. In the column for "overall," the table shows that approximately 4 percent of white children and about 25 percent of black children had a parent in prison at some point in

Table 35.1 | Cumulative Risk of Parental (Paternal and Maternal) Imprisonment by Age Seventeen, by Parents' Educational Attainment, Percent of Children (Adjusted for Adult and Child Mortality)

	All	Less than High School	HS/GED	College
1980				
NH-White	0.44	1.27	0.49	0.14
NH-Black	2.89	5.52	2.23	1.17
Hispanic	1.72	2.31	1.26	0.99
1990				
NH-White	1.27	3.40	1.46	0.52
NH-Black	8.16	15.09	6.53	4.38
Hispanic	4.79	5.64	3.83	4.38
2000				
NH-White	3.02	7.49	3.37	1.26
NH-Black	19.97	37.64	16.73	9.39
Hispanic	10.34	13.32	8.76	5.37
2009				
NH-White	3.95	14.56	3.68	1.35
NH-Black	24.19	62.05	16.12	9.85
Hispanic	10.68	17.35	6.80	4.78

Note: NH stands for "non-Hispanic." The 1980 cohort is born 1960–1964; the 1990 cohort is born 1970–1974; the 2000 cohort is born 1980–1984; the 2009 cohort is born 1989–1993. *Hispanic* is the term used by the U.S. Census and Current Population Survey at this time. Finally, the numbers in the table are percentage points.

their childhood. The numbers are staggering for children with parents with less education. Among recent cohorts of children of high school dropouts, 14.5 percent of white and 62 percent of black children had a parent who went to prison before the child reached age seventeen.

Other research has documented similar levels of, and racial inequality in, exposure to parental incarceration. Data from the National Longitudinal Survey of Adolescent Health (Add Health) indicate that as many as 12 percent of recent cohorts of children have had a biological father in prison or jail at some point in their childhood.[16] And these findings are consistent with Wildeman's analysis of the risk of parental imprisonment, which found that one-quarter of recent cohorts of black children can expect to have a parent imprisoned during their childhood.[17]

Mass incarceration is a uniquely modern American phenomenon that has disproportionately affected the lives of black men with low levels of education. However, the reach of the criminal justice system extends well beyond offenders and now infiltrates the lives of children and other family members. Thus, mass incarceration has become an increasingly important institution to consider in the study of American family life.

THE COLLATERAL CONSEQUENCES OF INCARCERATION FOR CHILDREN AND FAMILIES

A large and growing body of research investigates the consequences of criminal justice contact for individuals who have been incarcerated, their families, and their communities. Mass incarceration affects an inmate's community as well as an inmate's wages, employment, health, and political participation, as well as national election outcomes.[18] The impact of parental incarceration on children and families may be the least well understood, yet most consequential, implication of mass incarceration.[19]

Regardless of the crime committed, parental incarceration is likely to contribute to instability in family life. Over half of all prisoners have children under the age of eighteen, and about 45 percent of those parents were living with their children at the time they were sent to prison. In addition to the forced separation of incarceration, the post-release effects on economic opportunities leave formerly incarcerated parents less equipped to provide financially for their children. Incarceration is known to depress marriage and cohabitation among unwed parents.[20]

Many qualitative studies have effectively demonstrated how incarceration affects the family lives and children of those involved in the criminal justice system. By spending extended periods of time with inmates, former inmates, and their families, and conducting in-depth interviews, researchers have gathered an impressive body of evidence documenting the effects of incarceration on families and children, carefully considering the pathways through which incarceration influences family life. Research draws attention to how removing individuals from their families, and the associated economic hardship and social stigma, influences parenting and partnering.

Hagan and Dinovitzer argue that the loss of a father to incarceration changes the family's status to that of a single-parent family, ushering in effects similar to those brought on by the death of a parent or divorce, such as financial instability as well as emotional and psychological effects on the children and partner.[21] These issues are examined in Donald Braman's book *Doing Time on the Outside*.[22] In the book, Braman provides an account of how mass incarceration affects family and community in Washington, D.C. He demonstrates that incarceration levies financial costs that extend well beyond the individual incarcerated and that the psychological and social stigma associated with having a family member in prison or jail undermines the social fabric of urban communities.[23]

In *Doing Time Together*, Megan Comfort details the experiences of women attempting to maintain relationships with men at San Quentin State Prison.[24] Although the women she studied were free to leave San Quentin after their visits, the prison—and the men they loved who lived there—shaped their experiences and opportunities, burdening them financially and psychologically. Using the Fragile Families and Child Well-Being Study, Amanda Geller and colleagues confirm, with quantitative data, the extent to which incarceration incapacitates fathers from the labor force, making them unable to contribute financially to their partners and children.[25]

Although the financial effects of paternal incarceration may be greatest during periods of incapacitation, financial hardship affects previously incarcerated inmates and their families long after release.[26] In her book *My Baby's Father*, Maureen Waller demonstrates how men's poor economic opportunities—shaped by previous contact with the criminal justice system—structure their involvement in their children's lives.[27] Fathers' involvement in their children's lives may be curtailed, she argues, by their limited employment prospects and inability to contribute to the financial well-being of their children. Geller and colleagues also demonstrate that fathers' ability to contribute to the financial well-being of the family is curtailed even after release from prison or jail.[28]

Evidence suggests that fathers who have been incarcerated are much less likely to be cohabiting or married a year after the birth of their children.[29] Incarceration can also trigger higher risk of divorce or separation. Drawing on data from the National Longitudinal Survey of Youth (1979), Lopoo and Western find that the likelihood that a marriage will fail in the year a man is incarcerated is over three times higher than that for a man who is not incarcerated (13 percent compared with 4 percent).[30] Incarceration is thought to affect cohabitation and marriage directly through its incapacitative effect and indirectly through its implications on economic opportunities and social stigma.[31]

The effects of incarceration on children's well-being are only beginning to be understood. Children of incarcerated fathers are more likely to receive public assistance and to experience material hardship and disruptive residential mobility, and they are also at greater risk for developmental outcomes such as aggressive behavior.[32] Children of incarcerated parents are commonly pushed into kinship care or formal foster care.[33] Arditti and colleagues find that families of inmates were at risk for financial and mental health instability even before incarceration, emphasizing how incarceration elevates the risks of hardship among the already vulnerable.[34]

Comfort finds that seeing a father arrested, visiting him in prison, and dealing with parental absence traumatizes children.[35] Children of incarcerated fathers, Comfort argues, witness parental disempowerment and must contend with the emotional and psychological effects of their parent's abrupt removal as well as the quasi-imprisonment associated with the many rules and procedures involved in visiting a parent in correctional facilities. Nurse illustrates that incarcerated fathers' involvement in their children's lives is shaped by the children's mother and that hostility between young parents can have negative implications for children.[36] Wildeman demonstrates that recent and prior paternal incarceration is associated with significantly higher levels of physically aggressive behaviors for boys at age five.[37] In a review of existing research, Wakefield and Wildeman find that children who have had a parent incarcerated experience increases in mental health and behavioral problems as well as increases in levels of physical aggression.[38]

Despite important insights gleaned from existing research, the social scientific and policy communities have been slow to respond to shifts in family life associated with mass incarceration and collect nationally representative data designed to investigate the implications of incarceration for families and children. Few national surveys collect information about reasons for father absence, and no national statistics exist on the number of children living in single-parent families because of parental incarceration. Although data from Add Health and the Future of Families and Child Well-Being Study[39] have advanced our understanding of the effects of incarceration on families with young children, there is still much we do not know and cannot understand from existing large-scale data sources.

Children of incarcerated parents, particularly boys, are at greater risk of developmental delays and behavioral problems.[40] Paternal incarceration is associated with increased physical aggression for boys, thereby contributing to the intergenerational disadvantage fathers and sons are likely to experience. The effects of paternal incarceration are not confined to increased aggression; children with incarcerated fathers also exhibit increased attention problems. The experience of parental incarceration is very different and more pronounced than other forms of father absence.

Children of incarcerated parents are also at significant risk of homelessness and food insecurity. A research brief on fragile families in America by *The Future of Children* showed that father incarceration is associated with increased odds of child homelessness even after accounting for a multitude of important social background characteristics like family income, social welfare support, characteristics of the mother, and other measures of housing insecurity.[41] Race differences in child homelessness are an artifact of increasing racial inequality in imprisonment. The risk of homelessness for black children is particularly high. Compared with children who never experienced paternal incarceration, the odds of black youth experiencing housing instability are 144 percent higher if they have a father incarcerated. Cox and Wallace show that the likelihood for food insecurity increases by 4 to 15 percentage points in households with adults and children where at least one parent has been incarcerated.[42]

CONCLUSION

A growing body of research implicates the criminal justice system in structuring and reproducing social inequality in the lives of American children. Almost half of all youths in the correctional system have a parent in the adult system,[43] and the likelihood of incarceration is five to six times greater among children with a parent in prison than it is for children of never-incarcerated parents.[44] Father absence due to incarceration is associated with increased aggressive behaviors and attention problems for children.[45]

The intergenerational effect of having a parent behind bars disrupts and alters the life course trajectories of children. Parental imprisonment decreases the educational attainment of children in emerging adulthood.[46] Youth from these families are cumulatively disadvantaged. The social exclusion they face includes homelessness, lack of health care coverage, and political nonparticipation, all of which severely disconnect these children from important means of transitioning to adulthood.[47] Mass incarceration, particularly for nonviolent offenses, reproduces social inequality, thereby ensuring a vicious cycle wherein criminal justice contact recurs across generations.[48]

Current and former inmates constitute a Weberian status group: in particular, their social and economic differentiation, due to a lack of power and prestige to alter their current and future lives, solidifies them as a social class whose life chances have been fundamentally altered due to criminal justice contact.[49] Because of inmates' reduced opportunities for employment and housing, the children of inmates and former inmates are indirectly implicated as "legal bystanders" subjected to the effects of the legal system.[50] This invisible inequality produces a number of negative familial and community outcomes, particularly because over half of all fathers expect to live with their children and families when they exit the criminal justice system.[51]

While the long reach of the criminal justice system affects inmates and their families, newer research suggests that parole supervision may generate significant residential mobility. Harding and colleagues find that among Michigan parolees, less than one-third of former inmates return to an address within half a mile of their pre-prison residence, indicating that intermediate sanctions—jail, treatment programs, and residential facilities for parole rule violators—produce upward mobility in the lives of these disadvantaged men and women.[52] Despite this positive and promising side effect of criminal justice contact, the overwhelming experience of incarceration is largely negative for families and communities.

The marked status of having criminal justice contact extends into the lives of children and lowers the quantity and quality of social capital they will receive. Scholars of social inequality have documented a host of negative educational and social outcomes for children associated with different parenting styles. Lareau shows that "concerted cultivation"—practices and opportunities that promote, and stimulate, the cognitive and social development of children—is largely exercised by middle-class families, ensuring the solidification of their social advantage.[53] Lower-class families, in contrast, follow a path of "natural growth" that allows children to structure their own time and resources and does not imbue them with the same levels of social capital enjoyed by middle- and upper-class families. Because incarcerated men and women are marked and stigmatized for having a criminal record long after their sentence is completed,[54] the social inequality associated with parental incarceration will affect children during their formative years. Social policies are needed to address and mitigate the disruptive effects of parental imprisonment on the lives of disadvantaged children.

NOTES

1. Please direct correspondence to Bryan Sykes (blsykes@cornell.edu).

2. Wilson (1987).

3. Kluckow and Zeng (2022).

4. Garland (2001).

5. Blumstein and Cohen (1973).

6. Glaze (2010); Guerino, Harrison, and Sabol (2011).

7. Whitman (2003).

8. Walmsley (2011).

9. Kluckow and Zeng (2022).

10. Mauer (2006); Tonry (1995); Western (2006).

11. Western (2006).

12. Western (2006).

13. See also Pettit and Western (2004).

14. Pettit and Western (2004).

15. Pettit, Sykes, and Western (2009).

16. Foster and Hagan (2007).

17. Wildeman (2009).

18. Alexander (2010); Clear (2007); Johnson and Raphael (2009); Massoglia (2008); Pettit (2012); Rosenfeld et al. (2011); Sykes and Piquero (2009); Uggen and Manza (2002); Western (2006).

19. Hagan and Dinovitzer (1999).

20. Edin, Nelson, and Paranal (2004); Lopoo and Western (2005); Western and Pettit (2005); Western, Lopoo, and McLanahan (2004); Wilson (1987).

21. Hagan and Dinovitzer (1999).

22. Braman (2004).

23. Braman (2004).

24. Comfort (2008).

25. Geller et al. (2009).

26. Comfort (2008).

27. Waller (2002).

28. Geller et al. (2011).

29. Western et al. (2004).

30. Lopoo and Western (2005).

31. See, for example, Edin and Kefalas (2005).

32. Geller et al. (2012).

33. Freudenberg (2001).

34. Arditti (2012); Arditti, Smock, and Parkman (2005).

35. Comfort (2008).

36. Nurse (2004).

37. Wildeman (2010).

38. Wakefield and Wildeman (2011).

39. Previously known as the Fragile Families and Child Well-Being Study.

40. Geller et al. (2011); Geller et al. (2012); Wildeman (2010).

41. Wildeman (2014).

42. Cox and Wallace (2013).

43. Mumola (2000).

44. Springer, Lynch, and Rubin (2000).

45. Geller et al. (2012); Wildeman (2010).

46. Cho (2010); Foster and Hagan (2009); Hagan and Foster (2012).

47. Foster and Hagan (2007).

48. Wildeman and Western (2010).

49. Wakefield and Uggen (2010).

50. Comfort (2008).

51. Foster and Hagan (2009).

52. Harding, Morenoff, and Herbert (2013).

53. Lareau (2003).

54. Pager (2003); Alexander (2010).

PART EIGHT

Unfinished Gender Revolution

36

Why Can't Anyone "Have It All"?

The Colliding Worlds of Work and Caregiving

Kathleen Gerson

orking at a job and caring for others are arguably the most central activities that give structure, purpose, and meaning to life in the modern world. Yet in twenty-first-century America, these fundamental human pursuits are on a perilous collision course. If the predominant mid-twentieth-century image of a typical worker depicted a breadwinning father (overwhelmingly white) who held a secure nine-to-five job, today's predominant image depicts a harried parent (of any race and gender) putting in long workdays while wondering if the job will last. When it comes to caregiving, the predominant mid-twentieth-century image portrayed a nonemployed or part-time employed mother (again, overwhelmingly white) who depended on a husband's earnings and dedicated herself to the care and feeding of the family. Today that portrait more likely depicts an overwhelmed woman rushing to care for the household while also bringing home a paycheck to keep it afloat. These portrayals may overgeneralize when describing the way things were, especially for those who did not conform to such idealized images, but they reveal a core truth about the ways things are: paid employment and unpaid caregiving must now compete for everyone's time and attention. Workers and parents increasingly find that earning a living and caring for others are incompatible and even antagonistic pursuits.

The conflicts that result from this collision are now so common that they can seem inevitable to younger generations of American workers and parents. Yet work and caregiving need not be antagonistic. Instead, the deepening tension between these core life realms is a predictable consequence of institutional structures that presume and sustain domestic and occupational inequality. In the realm of paid employment, the "new economy," which typically involves the rise of new digital technologies and the growth of knowledge- and service-based work rather than the production of tangible goods, has undermined the secure jobs and steady paychecks that once allowed broad swaths of middle- and working-class men to support their families. In the realm of private life, household structures have diversified and a growing proportion of families now depend on a woman's earnings.[1] Glynn reports that 41 percent of today's mothers are either the sole or primary breadwinner for their families, and Glass, Raley, and Pepin report that 70 percent of mothers will become a family breadwinner at some point in their children's first eighteen years.[2] Yet most mothers, including breadwinning ones, continue to perform the lion's share of unpaid caregiving. In the absence of new institutional supports, this changed economic and family landscape has created new work-care conflicts that are taking a serious toll on American workers and families.

For all the attention these conflicts now receive, the debate surrounding their causes and solutions remains mired in outdated assumptions about gender and class. The most popular refrain is that women still cannot "have it all," although some argue that contemporary women are now able to do so if they wish.[3] This framing of the problem is far too narrow. Most obviously, it implies that work-care conflicts only apply to middle-class women. Less obviously, it implies that the problem is one of *having* it all rather than *doing* it all. Such a framework depicts women's struggle to attain a measure of personal autonomy as a selfish pursuit rather than a necessary means to achieving a secure and satisfying life for themselves and those who depend on them.

In a parallel way, it also implies that men already can and do have it all. Yet, just as women of all stripes continue to face exclusion from full participation in public life, most men continue to face exclusion from full participation in private life. What's more, men and women alike face growing economic precarity. By limiting our vision in these ways, the frame of "having it all" creates a discourse that denigrates women's rightful desire to seek what privileged men continue to take for granted while also ignoring the men who might also desire new avenues for integrating work and care. Equally important, it avoids the more fundamental questions: Why have our social institutions failed to respond effectively and humanely to the irreversible economic and social changes that have created such serious conflicts, and what can we do to address this failure to achieve work-family justice for all?

An important roadblock to addressing these issues effectively is a lack of agreement on what is happening. Some conceive the core problem to be a "gender stall," as women's labor force participation plateaus, a glass ceiling persists at work, and women continue to perform the bulk of caregiving at home.[4] Others focus on the decline of men's breadwinning, as their earnings erode, their labor force participation drops, and they fall behind women in educational attainment and career aspirations.[5] To put this debate in more political terms, progressives lament the persistent traditionalism that leaves women mired in second-class citizenship, while family-values conservatives see the elevation of women's personal autonomy as dangerous—not only because it undermines the notion that traditional marriage is superior to other family forms but also because it threatens the once accepted belief that men should have primary access to steady, well-paying jobs. These opposing views reflect different moral visions about where the problem lies and, in turn, create an impasse about how to define the challenges we face. To move beyond this stalemate, we need a more inclusive picture of the emerging economic and family landscape and the strategies people are fashioning in response.

Rather than asking whether women can have it all, it is time to pose a different set of questions: Why have institutional forces put work and care on a collision course? How are Americans of all kinds responding to the intractable conflicts this collision has created? And what structural and cultural realignments do we need to make to address the ensuing threats to American workers and families? The answers to these questions are neither obvious nor universal. And because work-care conflicts take different forms for different social groups, their responses are also varied. Some—overwhelmingly women—may pull back from paid work to care for others or take on the twin tasks of simultaneously supporting and caring for their families. Others may limit their caregiving responsibilities by remaining childless or minimizing their involvement with their children.[6] Still others—a smaller but noteworthy group—may strive to share work and care in more egalitarian, less gendered ways.

To gain a more comprehensive picture of how adults are negotiating new work and caregiving conflicts, I went to the heart of the new economy, where these conflicts are playing out in their most concentrated form. Accordingly, I conducted 120 face-to-face, in-depth interviews with a randomly selected group of residents in Silicon Valley (stretching from San Jose to the East Bay) and the New York metropolitan area.[7] I focused on (self-identified) women and men between the ages of thirty-three and forty-seven, ages at which American adults are most likely to be building—or not building—commitments to jobs and families. This approach yielded a group with diverse racial, economic, and educational backgrounds who were living in a variety of family arrangements, including singles, cohabitors, and married couples. This approach made it possible to decipher the shape of the emerging landscape, where new forms of working and caregiving are emerging alongside the persistence of more traditional jobs and family structures.

My interviews revealed four general patterns. At one end of the spectrum, close to a fifth (18 percent) of my participants adopted a *hyper-traditional* strategy.

This group engaged in a traditional division of paid work and caregiving and did so in an exaggerated way. In these households, fathers worked very long hours while mothers devoted a similarly high level of attention to their children. At the other end of the spectrum, slightly more than a third (36 percent) decided to *limit caregiving* either by remaining childless or by withdrawing from parenting involvement in the wake of a breakup. Taken together, slightly more than half (54 percent) of the interviewees exemplify the two trends—resurgent traditionalism and rising individualism—that contemporary debates tend to highlight.

The remaining participants, however, followed very different paths. A quarter (25 percent) were in a relationship in which *she does it all*. These homes depended on a woman's earnings—either as a co- or sole breadwinner—while also relying on her to provide the bulk of the caregiving. The remaining group (21 percent) also depended on a woman breadwinner, but they had created partnerships that transgressed traditional gender boundaries. These *gender pioneers* were either doing their best to share earning and caregiving equally or had reversed responsibility for the two realms.

It might be tempting to conclude that personal preferences led people to follow their particular paths, but only about a third of the interviewees arrived at the destinations they had hoped to reach when they first set out on the road through adulthood. Instead, a set of distinct obstacles and opportunities allowed some to achieve their early goals while others were forced to shift their life paths in unexpected ways. The following vignettes exemplify the contrasting ways that the rise of new economic and relationship uncertainties have reshaped the options for workers and parents.

BECOMING HYPER-TRADITIONAL

Among those who ultimately created hyper-traditional arrangements, only a third had planned to pursue any kind of traditional gender division, and even those who did were not envisioning the extreme version they found themselves practicing. Kyra's story reveals how roadblocks for women at work and pressures for men to work excessively push even disinclined couples to adopt an exaggerated version of the homemaker-breadwinner pattern.

Reared primarily by her mother after her father died when Kyra was a preschooler, Kyra always assumed she would support herself. After working her way through a small local college in the Rust Belt, she found full-time work in a small public relations firm where her energy, managerial skills, and outgoing personality propelled her to a series of increasingly influential and better-paying positions. A decade later, her future career prospects were bright. Indeed, after fleeing an unhappy marriage to an unreliable partner, she felt comfortable raising their son on her own.

After several years as a single mom, Kyra met Tony, an industrial engineer who hoped to become a car designer. During a year of dating, their relationship grew stronger, and they decided to live together. When they married several years later, Kyra continued to work full-time and to help support Tony as he moved from job to job in the unpredictable world of design consultancies. They also decided to have a child. Yet just as Kyra became pregnant, Tony received an offer for a "dream job" at a startup in California. Although this was no time for Kyra to make a career change, she could not ask Tony to give up this once-in-a-lifetime opportunity. So, with a baby on the way, they moved across the country.

After arriving on the West Coast, Kyra immediately began job hunting. Yet with her pregnancy apparent to all, her job interviews went nowhere. Despite her obvious talents and experience and her concerted efforts, attempts to restart her career in a new locale came to a halt. Instead, she found herself out of work and at home with a baby and a school-age son.

Kyra notes, with a mix of frustration and cynicism, that no one is concerned about Tony's status as a father. To the contrary, his employer expects him to spend long days at work and to be on call when he is home. He feels pressured to work from early morning into the night and to answer emails and phone calls at any time. As Tony labors to keep his job, Kyra devotes all her time to caring for their children and feels like she has become a single mother again.

Kyra's story demonstrates how a series of unforeseeable events can lead people to a work-care arrangement they did not seek and do not prefer. A combination of her husband's work pressures and fear of job loss and the roadblocks she has encountered as a woman and a mother have left Kyra little choice but to forgo a flourishing career and become an intensive parent.[8] In contrast, Tony has had to cope with the mirror image of Kyra's situation. Finding himself on the other side of the work-care divide, he feels pressure to work long hours, fears losing a job he has always wanted, and regrets the time he is missing with his young daughter. Both Kyra and Tony are contending with a division of work and care that neither intended nor desire.

Not all traditional couples prefer another arrangement, but most of those I interviewed do.[9] Their stories remind us that we should never assume people's behavior reflects their preferences. To the contrary, these couples make it clear that the institutions that create an exaggerated division of work and care are out of sync with the needs and desires of most contemporary workers and parents. Concerns about job security prompted hyper-traditional husbands to put in extremely long workweeks—ranging from sixty to as many as a hundred hours— just to assure employers of their worthiness. In a parallel way, the penalties men face if they take time for caregiving force mothers to overcompensate for their partners' absence. The result is that hyper-traditional mothers and fathers find themselves overworked in their separate spheres because the risks of doing otherwise seem too high.

DECIDING TO LIMIT CARE COMMITMENTS

In contrast to hyper-traditional couples, a larger proportion of my interviewees decided to limit their caregiving responsibilities. Although most of these "care limiters" were single, close to 40 percent were in a committed relationship. Most of those with limited care commitments had decided to forgo parenthood altogether, but biological parents who were not involved in their offspring made up 10 percent of this group. Notably, among those who ultimately eschewed such caregiving commitments, only 30 percent had anticipated this outcome as a young adult. Although this group contained a roughly equal percentage of women and men, they differed in their reasons for deciding to avoid caregiving. The stories of Camille and Jason illustrate these differences.

Growing up in a mid-sized Southern city, Camille enjoyed a comfortable upbringing as the only child of middle-class African American parents. Her father's entrepreneurial skills provided a reliable family income, while her mother focused on Camille's care. Yet the financial stability and parental commitment she took for granted suddenly crumbled as Camille neared her last year of high school. Her father's small business failed, and he soon left the household to live with another woman. Her mother had not worked for a paycheck in decades and, lacking credentials or an employment record, needed to take a string of "terrible jobs" to keep the household afloat. Camille had long wished to pursue a design career, and observing her mother's fate only strengthened her resolve to seek financial independence and purpose through work.

After working her way through college, Camille secured a promising job at an architectural firm and looked forward to an upward climb. She also met an young, ambitious lawyer who shared her hopes for combining marriage and parenthood with a meaningful career. When they decided to become engaged after dating for several years, the future looked bright. Yet the life she had anticipated hit a series of unexpected bumps. She encountered a glass ceiling at work that barred the upward movement she had planned, and she began to have second thoughts about her relationship. The prospect of entering a marriage with a partner who worked nights and weekends began to raise warning signs. What would it be like to raise a biracial child in a city riven by racial divisions, and how could she do so with a partner who worked all the time?

As these concerns mounted, Camille received an attractive job offer from a New York firm—a potential solution to her concerns, but only if her fiancé agreed to relocate. Yet he believed his success depended on local ties, which precluded any possibility of moving with her. Faced with a choice between pursuing her own ambitions and staying with the person she loved, she decided to accept the job and reluctantly broke her engagement. She knew she would never be happy relinquishing her aspirations for his.

After settling in New York, Camille held a series of jobs and landed a part-time side job teaching at a prestigious design school. To gain more autonomy and time for teaching, she eventually decided to start her own business. Along the way, she has also had some serious relationships, but none that equaled the intensity of the one she left behind. There were moments when she considered returning to her fiancé but knew she could not surrender the life she had worked so hard to build. At thirty-nine, she is unlikely to have the child she once hoped to bear—an outcome that prompts mild regret. Yet her close-knit circle of friends feels like a family, and her pets—a dog named Wayne and a cat named Cleo—feel like her children. Looking forward, she is optimistic that her freelance business will thrive and hopeful that her job teaching design will lead to a full-time appointment.

Like Camille, Jason has also minimized his caregiving obligations. At forty-two, he is also single and childless. Yet the path he has taken and his feelings about where he has arrived stand in stark contrast to Camille's story.

Growing up in a suburban neighborhood of tract housing in Southern California, Jason felt shy and reticent in most social situations. Good at math, he won a scholarship to a local college, where he learned the language of computer coding. Several years later, when a teacher recommended him for a job at a nearby small startup, he left school without a degree to make his way in the growing high-tech world. A Silicon Valley employer made him an offer when he was in his late twenties, and he jumped at the opportunity to move there.

Over the last decade, Jason has moved through a series of jobs, as the companies he has joined have downsized, gone out of business, or simply changed direction and no longer needed his skills. He has had a series of relationships that he describes as "not serious." He lived briefly with his last girlfriend until she was able to find a job and pay her own rent, but it felt more like an arrangement of convenience. With an erratic job history, he has preferred to remain free of any long-term commitment that would require his financial support and emotional attachment.

Now single again after his last girlfriend moved out, Jason lives alone with his cat. Out of work after being laid off from his job as a programmer over a year ago, he goes to a local coffee house every day and works on his laptop amid a scattering of similarly occupied regulars. Here he engages in the solitary pursuit of developing a new app that might jumpstart his fading tech career. Considering his work history, Jason has concluded that his marginal employment and modest social skills leave him ill-positioned to find a stable job. Consequently, he expects the coffee house to remain his workplace and his second home. He plans to live off his savings until he can "get back in the game" or make it big on his own. He does not feel "entitled" to a family as long as his finances remain so precarious.

Although the women who chose to limit caregiving typically did so to pursue other opportunities, the men in this group were more likely to be responding to limited and unpredictable economic opportunities. Although these women came to value autonomy so much that the costs of caregiving seemed too high, the men were either unable or unwilling to take on the financial and emotional responsibilities that marriage and parenthood would bring. As a result, the women largely felt liberated by their choice, while the men were more likely to feel isolated.

If hyper-traditional couples are recreating traditional gender patterns in an extreme form, care limiters are opting to preserve their independence by avoiding them altogether. Yet together these two patterns account for only 54 percent of participants. The remaining interviewees endeavored to combine paid work and caregiving, albeit in contrasting ways.

Defaulting to Her

A quarter of my participants were in dual-earner partnerships that relied on a woman's earnings while also depending on her for the bulk of the caregiving. Rather than "having it all," women in these relationships "did it all." By adding a "second shift" of unpaid domestic work onto women's first shift as a paid worker, these arrangements reflect the simultaneous decline of the sole male breadwinner alongside the persistence of the female caregiver norm.[10] It should come as no surprise that none of the women in the group wished for such an imbalanced outcome, but it is also worth noting that neither did many of the men. Yet, as the following two vignettes exemplify, the rise of women breadwinners coupled with the demands of increasingly insecure jobs have left women overworked at home and men risking their livelihoods if they are inclined to share responsibilities.

Although Michelle always expected to have a child, she never imagined doing it on her own. Reared in the Midwest by lower-middle-class parents who had a traditional marriage, she was an average student who knew the importance of attending college and becoming self-sufficient. After graduation and a few uninspiring sales jobs, she decided to move to the West Coast, where she could live with an aunt until she found work and could pay her own bills. Another series of dead-end jobs made it possible for Michelle to find her own place, but they left her feeling bored and adrift. In search of more challenging work, she took some night courses in business and found an entry-level position at a small nonprofit firm providing services for the poor and disabled.

Finally at a job she found meaningful, Michelle proved to be a gifted administrator and moved steadily up the organization's ladder. After several years, she landed the top spot when the director retired. Being responsible for the survival and smooth operation of the organization left little time for life outside the office, but the payoff of helping people made the hard work worthwhile.

In contrast to her work life, Michelle's personal life did not proceed as smoothly. As she entered her mid-thirties, a series of ill-fated relationships left her wondering if she would ever find a life partner. Then, on a business trip, she met Gary and began a whirlwind courtship. Though separated by many miles, they took turns visiting each other and began to consider ways to be together. After years of seeking a job she loved and a relationship with a promising future, she felt she had finally achieved both. Then, unexpectedly, she found herself pregnant.

Though her pregnancy was unplanned, Michelle was ready to start a family and greeted the news with ambivalence. When she informed Gary, however, he immediately made it clear that he did not wish to have a child and would take no responsibility if she decided to have the baby. After much soul-searching, Michelle decided that she would not let her single status prevent her from having a child. Although the circumstances were far from ideal, she concluded this might be her "last chance." If Gary had greeted the news of her pregnancy with enthusiasm, Michelle might have found herself in Kyra's shoes—moving to a new city with a young child, limited employment options, and a partner too busy to share caretaking. Instead, she became a single mother.

Today, Michelle is rearing her daughter, Courtney, with the help of a dedicated paid caretaker and a network of close friends but with no financial support or involvement from Gary. She remains single, although she recently began dating a divorcee who shares custody of his son. She has no regrets about her decision to have a child, but becoming a single mother has required unanticipated changes at work. Although she continues to work full-time, she reluctantly relinquished her directorship to take a less inspiring job in human resources at a well-established firm (where, not coincidentally, women at her company are concentrated). Her new position offers neither the influence nor challenges she once enjoyed, but it provides better pay, more job security, fewer demands, and a more predictable schedule, all of which make it easier to meet the twin responsibilities of supporting and caring for Courtney.

While Michelle is meeting the responsibilities of both work and parenthood without the help of a partner, Tim faces a different set of constraints. He is married to a work-committed partner and expected to share the care of their young son, but unanticipated work pressures upended these plans.

Although he grew up in a traditional household to parents of modest means, Tim has long wished to share earning and caregiving. Accordingly, since he met and married Margaret in his mid-twenties, he has fostered her work aspirations and she has fostered his. For Tim, this has meant supporting Margaret through many years of medical school and subsequent training. For Margaret, this has meant supporting him as he found his feet in public relations. When Margaret's training brought them to the West Coast, Tim landed a series of jobs with local companies whose fortunes rose and fell in the boom-and-bust tech sector. For most of their married life, the financial security and earnings of Margaret's career have enabled Tim to seek and take jobs with less certain prospects.

As they entered their thirties and decided it was time to start a family, they realized that their long workweeks, which had once seemed an acceptable fact of life, were now a big drawback. With their first child on the way, they both sought ways to cut back the time they spent at their jobs but soon discovered that only Margaret had that option. As part of a large practice, her partners agreed to share the patient workload to provide the flexibility she needed. Tim's employers did not welcome any arrangement that would reduce his time on the job. To do so would signal that he put his care responsibilities before his commitment to building the company. Indeed, his manager informed him that it would be easy to replace him with "someone overseas who will work for a third of what we're paying you."

Now the father of two, including a toddler, Tim worries about the fate of both his marriage and career. Margaret is content to keep her workweek to four long days in order to have an extra day devoted to caring for their sons, but she has grown frustrated and worried about his lack of involvement. He understands the reasons for her resentment and wants to take on his share of the load, but he feels greater pressure to prove his worth at work by putting in the time they expect. Amid the pressures of an uncertain job market, he cannot afford to pull back without risking his paycheck.

It is hardly news that carrying the load of both the first and second shifts left women feeling overwhelmed, disheartened, and resentful. Although some men openly acknowledged being "spoiled" (in the words of one interviewee), most noted that their avoidance of caregiving took a toll on their relationships. Of course, "care limiters" such as Tony avoided the blowback that unequal caregiving creates by severing all ties to their partners and offspring. Most of these men, however, were in dual-earner partnerships where they could not escape the domestic strains this imbalance created. Instead, they had to weigh these costs against the risks to their financial prospects if they shifted their priorities. Because a "flexibility stigma" continues to penalize workers—especially professionals—who pull back even slightly to engage in domestic care, these are understandable fears.[11]

Becoming a Gender Pioneer

Unlike those who relied on a woman to do it all, the remaining fifth (21 percent) of my participants were endeavoring to create and sustain a more egalitarian arrangement. All these "pioneers" were couples who were committed to sharing work and care, but equality is difficult to define and can take different forms. Most were attempting to divide earning and caregiving equally, but a quarter had come to rely on a gender-reversed arrangement. Danny exemplifies one shape that equality can take.

Danny grew up in a bedroom community near San Francisco with his parents and two siblings. His father, an accountant, worked hard to pay the family's bills and provide a modest standard of living, and his mother enjoyed tending their home and socializing with friends. As Danny neared high school graduation, his father suffered a stroke that left him not only unable to work but also in need of constant care. Danny had always known he would have to put himself through college, but his father's illness meant delaying those plans for several years. Eventually, he was able to enroll at a local college and obtain a business degree.

After graduating with a degree in finance, Danny took a job at a large brokerage firm, where his disciplined work habits and outgoing personality served him well. He liked the environment, especially because he met his wife, Francesca, who worked on a different floor. He found his "soul mate" and realized he was ready to "settle down." He described himself as "old-fashioned," and they did not live together until they married several years later. By then, Danny had set up his own financial consultancy, and Francesca had begun her climb up the managerial ranks at another firm. Each had found work they enjoyed, and they relied on both incomes.

As soon as they knew a baby was on the way, Danny and Francesca agreed to share in the care of their daughter, Alyssa. Neither wished to short-circuit the other's budding career, but local child care options were scarce and very expensive. They were both wary of paying someone else to "raise their child," so they decided instead to trade off so that one of them would always be with her. Danny decided to work at home in the mornings, and Francesca arranged to leave her office early and take over in the afternoons.

They have done their best to share Alyssa's care equally while continuing to hold two demanding jobs. Danny is proud of their arrangement and harbors no regrets, but he wonders how long they can maintain this juggling act. He would like to have another child but doubts they can manage the additional time, money, and energy without endangering their relationship and careers.

Carmen also shares work and care with her spouse, Julio. In her case, however, they did not have their own biological children but assumed responsibility for her niece and nephew when her siblings were unable to care for them.

Carmen grew up in Colorado in a large, close-knit family, overseen by her father, a military man who retired, and her mother, who emigrated from the Philippines. Without funds for college, she joined the military after high school and spent the next decade living in different parts of the country and the world. By the time she decided to return to civilian life, she had moved to Northern California and had decided to stay.

Drawing on skills developed during her military service, Carmen quickly found a job as an office manager at a small tech startup. Her organizational skills and ability to motivate others more than compensated for her lack of technical acumen, and she proved to be an adept administrator and a valued member of the team. When the company floundered, she drew on the contacts she had made and moved to another startup. This pattern repeated itself, providing Carmen with a widening network of contacts that finally led her to a startup so successful that a major firm with a global presence eventually acquired it. Carmen and her coworkers moved as a group, and she became the administrative head of their division.

In the midst of this series of jobs, Carmen met and married Jose—the "love of [her] life." As a construction worker and small contractor, Jose has never been able to match Carmen's earnings, but he has worked steadily doing what he enjoys, and he values the flexibility and autonomy his job provides. Their marriage has proved strong and stable. Having two incomes has provided a sense of security as they have both moved from job to job, and Jose's construction skills have made it possible to maintain a home large enough to become the center of their extended families.

When Carmen's sister fell on hard times as her marriage unraveled, leaving her feeling unable to care for her children, Carmen and Jose welcomed Carmen's niece and nephew into their home and became their full-time caretakers. They have relished the opportunity and made every effort to share the load amid their frenetic schedules. With more flexibility during weekdays, Jose gets the kids to school and prepares dinner, while Carmen steps in on the weekends.

Balancing her job and her "surrogate children," Carmen marvels at how far she has come. She takes pleasure and pride in both commitments as well as in the strength of her relationship with Jose. She knows her current employer could decide at any time to "take a different direction" and leave her looking once more for another position. Yet her past experiences have taught her to view this possibility as just another opportunity.

Carmen and Danny are gender pioneers. By sharing work and care, they have come closer to achieving their aspirations than their hyper-traditional, unencumbered, and unequal dual-earner peers. They nevertheless face many obstacles. With few institutional supports to draw on and no clear path to follow, they must devise their own strategies for both the short and longer terms. Danny is willing to forgo sleep and personal time to juggle work and care, and Carmen has opted to care for her sibling's children rather than having her own. Given the pressures at home and in the labor force and the dearth of structural underpinnings for sharing work and care, practicing equality is not the same as "having it all." It entails risks and sacrifices that leave work-care egalitarians wondering how long and at what cost they can sustain their efforts.

Different Responses to Shared Dilemmas

Despite the differences, all these strategies represent attempts to grapple with conflicts that few can escape. Rising economic insecurity has upped the ante for breadwinners, who face pressures to put in long hours or risk employment, and for caregivers, who worry that only intensive parenting can prepare their children to successfully navigate an uncertain future.[12] Despite their varied efforts, none of the strategies adopted by my interviewees could fully resolve conflicts rooted in structural arrangements and cultural pressures. Given the realities of the new economy, which relies on women workers but has eroded job security for men and women alike, *every* work-care strategy is bound to pose some wrenching trade-offs. It is thus not surprising that each strategy produced some degree of dissatisfaction. Yet some work-care arrangements produce more dissatisfaction than do others, and gender shapes perceptions about which arrangements are deemed more or less satisfying.

Figure 36.1 presents the percentage of women and men in each category who say they prefer their current arrangement to the alternatives. If we think of the difference between a person's current situation and the one they prefer as a "satisfaction gap," it is clear that the size of this gap differs for each work-care pattern. Additionally, the size of the satisfaction gap among women and among men converges in some categories and diverges in others. The proportion who prefer a hyper-traditional arrangement is quite low for both women (27 percent) and men (36 percent), while the proportion of gender pioneers who prefer their arrangement is quite high for both groups (80 percent for women and 73 percent

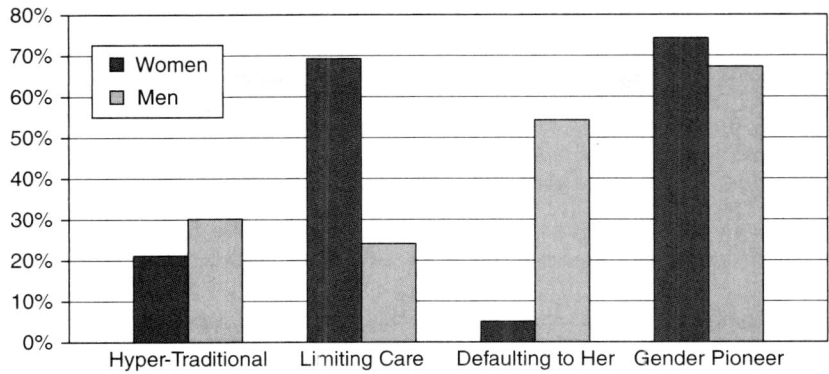

Figure 36.1 | The Satisfaction Gap: Percent Who Prefer Current Arrangement, by Gender

for men). Like the hyper-traditionals, the pioneers faced difficult trade-offs, but they were much more likely to view their difficulties as worth the effort.

In contrast to both the hyper-traditionals and gender pioneers, where women and men largely agree, a gender divide emerges in the other two arrangements. Among those who had limited their caregiving responsibilities by either remaining childless or distancing themselves from offspring, three-quarters of the women preferred their situation, compared with only 30 percent of the men. Among those who relied on a woman to do it all, the gender divide reverses. Not surprisingly, only a tenth of the women preferred this arrangement, compared with three-fifths of the men. It is easy to understand why men in dual-earner relationships would be more satisfied when their partners do most of the caregiving. Perhaps the more surprising finding is that 40 percent of the men would prefer a different arrangement in which they assumed more responsibilities. Like the pioneers who concluded the sacrifices were worth the payoff, unencumbered women valued their independence even though it entailed limiting their caregiving ties.

Taken together, these findings suggest that—apart from the work-care pioneers—a great deal of dissatisfaction pervades the work-care conflict landscape. They reveal the dangers of clinging to social yardsticks that measure a man's worth by his breadwinning prowess and a woman's worth by her willingness to be a selfless caregiver. The solution to today's work-care conflicts is not to shore up and intensify an outdated system but to address the inequalities and insecurities created by the emerging one. An essential step in this process is to jettison the tired lens of "having it all" and reframe the work-care debate. Any lens that depicts earning and caregiving as incompatible goals—and the (mostly) women who seek to combine them as selfish or unrealistic—implicitly blames struggling workers and parents for conditions beyond their control. It also diverts attention away from the fundamental sources of the work-care crisis, which are rooted in the inexorable changes wrought by the economic and gender revolutions. In this context, the only humane, just, and effective response is to restructure our work and caregiving institutions so that everyone can forge a more equal, balanced, and secure integration of work and caregiving. Judging from the experiences of my interviewees, everyone will bear the collective costs if we fail to do so.

NOTES

1. Women in Black households have always provided crucial earnings, but over the last half-century, this pattern has spread to virtually all racial and ethnic groups.

2. Glass, Raley, and Pepin (2021); Glynn (2019).

3. See, for example, the conflicting arguments about whether or not contemporary women have achieved equality. Anne-Marie Slaughter's much cited article in *The Atlantic*, "Why Women Still Can't Have It All" (2012), details the manifold ways that equality continues to elude American women. In contrast, Mississippi's attorney general Lynn Fitch's press release supporting that state's effort to limit abortion rights declares that "a lot has changed in five decades. In 1973, there was little support for women who wanted a full family life and a successful career. . . . In these last fifty years, women have carved their own way to achieving a better balance for success in their professional and personal lives."

4. England et al. (2020).

5. Edsall (2021); Yang (2022).

6. Brown (2021).

7. The participants were selected from zip codes with a relatively high concentration of people working in new economy jobs in the tech, service, and gig sectors, while excluding the zip codes of highly affluent neighborhoods where financial resources allow people to avoid the conflicts that other workers and caregivers face.

8. For thorough discussions of the rise of intensive parenting, see Hays (1996) and Lareau (2003).

9. Recent studies report that fathers are likely to express feeling as much conflict as mothers. Parker and Stepler (2017) find that the pressure on men to support their families has not abated even though their earnings are eroding.

10. Hochschild (1989) was the first to refer to women's unpaid work at home as a "second shift" added onto the first shift as a paid worker.

11. Williams, Blair-Loy, and Berdahl (2013).

12. Although the current stereotype may depict middle-class mothers as "helicopter parents" who hover too closely, Ishizuka (2019) reports that the norm of intensive parenting actually spans the class structure and includes working-class parents as well as their middle-class peers.

In Other Words

MINE AND YOURS, OR OURS: ARE ALL EGALITARIAN RELATIONSHIPS EQUAL?

Daniel L. Carlson, April 25, 2022 / CCF

Which marriages and relationships are happiest? And is it the same for men and women? These questions have come to the forefront of conversations about intimate partnerships in recent decades as the roles of men and women in families have shifted dramatically.

In 1960, 70 percent of married-parent households consisted of a male income-earner and a female homemaker. At the time, family experts believed that this was not only the most efficient way to organize society but the best predictor of marital stability and happiness. Nobel Prize-winning economist Gary Becker argued that labor specialization among heterosexual partners maximized the product of men's and women's labor, making for greater efficiency and leading to more satisfying and stable partnerships.

For several decades, research seemed to support Becker's suppositions. Couples with a "traditional" division of household labor reported higher marital and sexual satisfaction than couples who shared housework, and earnings equality in intimate partnerships actually raised the risk of relationship dissolution.

Today, "breadwinner-homemaker" families constitute less than one-third of married-parent families, while 60 percent of families are headed by dual earners. Gender responsibilities for paid work have become more evenly divided, and so have responsibilities for unpaid domestic work, though to a much lesser extent. On average, married mothers do half as much routine housework as they did in 1965 (16 hours versus 32 hours per week), while married fathers do twice as much (5 hours versus 2 hours). Among dual-earning couples, mothers do 13.5 hours of housework, compared with 9.5 hours for fathers.

Contrary to the expectations of scholars such as Becker, the decline in marital specialization has not hurt marriages. As of the 1990s, the increased risk of divorce for couples where wives earn as much or more than their husbands has disappeared. Additionally, couples who share child care responsibilities report greater relationship and sexual satisfaction than couples where mothers are solely responsible for child care. Since the 1990s, sexual intimacy among those who share housework equally has increased, whereas it has decreased among couples where female partners do the majority of housework.

Despite the seemingly positive impact of egalitarian relationships, movement in this direction has stalled in the past couple of decades. Although the gendered division of labor in families is much more equal than it was in the 1960s, there has been little change in women's labor force participation or men's housework in the last three decades. The COVID-19 pandemic threatened to reverse the progress of the gender revolution by thrusting domestic labor back into homes. Though fathers increased their domestic labor during the early days of the pandemic, so, too, did mothers, and the loss of in-person school and daycare was associated with significant decreases in mothers' labor force participation.

Some people suggest that we have reached an upper limit to the benefits of equal sharing, beyond which men in particular are not willing to go without relationship quality suffering. Others argue that relationships would be happier if work policies and social norms encouraged more couples to share the housework as evenly as they now share income-earning.

Resolving this question is not as easy as it might seem. The research is fairly consistent in demonstrating that women are happier in relationships where routine housework responsibilities, including cooking, cleaning, laundry, dishes, and shopping, are shared. But the findings are more mixed when it comes to men. Although some research finds that men report the greatest relationship satisfaction in couples where routine housework is shared equally, others find that men are happiest in arrangements where they have *no* responsibilities for routine housework. Still other studies find no difference in men's happiness between arrangements where they do no housework and those where they share it equally.

These contradictory findings on the relationship between egalitarian housework and relationship satisfaction may stem from the fact that the way housework is currently measured doesn't capture variations in how partners craft their housework arrangements. Conventional measures of housework simply calculate each partner's total time spent on all tasks. Yet "housework" is actually an amalgamation of several distinct tasks. Because of this, partners can accomplish an equal division of tasks in many different ways. Some egalitarian couples may divide tasks between partners, with each partner doing all of some tasks and none of the tasks done by the other. Others may share equally in the completion of all tasks. For instance, each partner may do the laundry, the cooking, and the cleaning half the time. A fundamental question, therefore, is *how do couples, egalitarian couples especially, actually construct their housework arrangements? And does this matter for relationship satisfaction?*

In a study in the journal *Sex Roles*, I use data from two nationally representative surveys of married and cohabiting U.S. adults to examine the degree to which partners share in the completion of routine housework tasks and how men's and women's relationship quality, including feelings of fairness, satisfaction with housework arrangements, and overall relationship satisfaction, varies by the number of routine housework tasks they both take equal responsibility for versus the number that they divvy up, with each focusing on a different set of tasks.

My findings suggest that when it comes to analyzing the impact of the division of labor on people's satisfaction, we need to do more than count the total time that each partner puts into housework or the overall proportion of overall household each partner does. There is significant variation in the extent to which couples, especially those in egalitarian arrangements, share or divide up tasks. As one might expect, there is little sharing in traditional housework arrangements, meaning those where men do less than 40 percent of housework. In such households, even when men do take on some of the routine tasks, 75 to 85 percent of partners equally share no tasks or only one. There is much more variation in task-sharing in egalitarian households, referring to those households where women and men do roughly equal amounts of the housework, varying between 40 and 60 percent. Only 20 to 30 percent of egalitarian partners equally share no tasks or only one task with each other, while upwards of 40 percent equally share all or nearly all tasks.

As it turns out, the number of equally shared tasks matters a great deal for both men's and women's relationship quality. Indeed, among recent cohorts, there is evidence to suggest that it matters as much if not more than each partner's overall proportion of housework. For both men and women, the number of equally shared tasks is associated with a greater likelihood of (a) feeling their relationship is fair to both partners, (b) feeling satisfied with their own housework arrangement, and (c) feeling satisfied with the relationship overall.

This pattern explains some of the contradictory research findings from earlier studies. Using the same data, I find that increases in men's proportion of overall housework are positively associated with women's reports of relationship quality but negatively associated with men's reports. From this, one could conclude that men feel less satisfied in equal domestic arrangements compared with traditional arrangements. But looking at the association of men's satisfaction with the number of equally shared tasks, one could conclude that equality is associated with greater relationship satisfaction for men.

Indeed, when considering both the number of tasks that partners share and the proportion of overall housework each partner does, it appears that satisfaction in egalitarian relationships compared with traditional relationships depends on the number of tasks that the couple shares. Men in traditional arrangements who do no housework are significantly more satisfied with their relationships than men in egalitarian arrangements who equally share only two or fewer tasks. But egalitarian men who equally share at least three tasks with their partner are as fully satisfied with their relationships and housework arrangements as men who do no housework at all.

Women's responses also confirm that not all egalitarian arrangements are created equal. Compared with women in traditional arrangements, women in egalitarian arrangements who equally share at least one task are significantly more satisfied with their relationships. However, women who *divide* housework equally with their male partners but do not equally *share* any tasks are no more satisfied than women who do *all* of the housework.

My findings suggest that the most mutually beneficial housework arrangement for the dyadic relationship is one where all tasks are shared equally. Men may be equally satisfied doing no housework or sharing all or most tasks equally, but since women's highest satisfaction is when all or most tasks are shared, the route to a happy relationship appears to lie in sharing.

Why might sharing the tasks equally create more satisfaction than dividing the tasks so that each partner specializes in a different set of tasks? One likely answer is that tasks vary in how onerous or enjoyable people find them to be—think doing the laundry or cleaning the bathroom versus cooking—and the unpleasant ones are less likely to be shared than other more enjoyable ones. As such, egalitarian partners who divide up tasks run the risk of delegating particularly onerous tasks to just one person, lowering feelings of fairness and relationship satisfaction. Even when couples try to divide the onerous tasks equally, it is hard for someone to assess whether their partner's contribution is the same as their own when doing different things at different times. Sharing all tasks equally eliminates these sources of resentment or misunderstanding, ensuring that each partner feels their arrangement is equitable and satisfying. ◾

37

When Men Stay Home

Household Labor in Female-Led Indian Migrant Families

Pallavi Banerjee

G lobal mobility of labor is marked by temporary workers on work visas residing in various parts of the world, including the United States. Each year
the United States issues various types of visas—for students, workers, families,
and tourists. High-skilled migration of workers to the United States is made possible through the issuance of various types of nonimmigrant work visas. In 2021,
a total of 471,932[1] people arrived in the United States to work on visas; about
13 percent (61,569)[2] were issued H-1B visas, or skilled workers' visas. It is important to note that this is considerably lower than previous years, perhaps due to the
COVID-19 pandemic. In 2020, 27 percent of all work visas went to temporary
skilled workers. In this chapter, I report findings from my study of migrant nurses
from India on temporary skilled workers' visas. Indian nurses came to the United
States due to a projected shortage of nurses and later brought their families with
them on dependent visas.

In response to the rising demand for skilled workers such as doctors, nurses,
computer engineers, analysts, and programmers, the Immigration Act of 1990
introduced the distinctive category of nonimmigrant skilled workers' visas or
the H-1B visas. Although Indian male high-tech workers have been the largest
recipients of the skilled workers' visas, they are not the only Indians who come
to the United States on such visas. Less attention has been paid to the migration of Indian nurses, who have been migrating to the United States since the
1970s. Beginning in the 1990s, Indian women nurses have been migrating to the
United States on skilled workers' visas and have been bringing their husbands

and children on the "dependent visa" or the H-4 visa. The dependent visa puts many restrictions on the spouses of skilled workers. Men or women who enter the United States on a dependent visa are not allowed to work for pay until their husband or wife has gained permanent residency in the United States, a process that can take anywhere between five and fifteen years.

Mostly women are the recipients of these dependent visas, thereby creating families that look like the 1950s nuclear family in which dad goes off to work and mom stays home to care for the children. When foreign women move to America to work, however, their husbands hold these visas. These visas have created families where men stay home as dependents and women, like the nurses in my study, are the main wage earners. Policy makers very rarely think about how different kinds of visas affect lives and gender relationships in migrant families. The gender dynamics become particularly complex when the skilled working migrant is a woman who is joined by her husband as a dependent. In my research, I ask: How do gender dynamics in the family change when women are the ones leading migration as the primary providers in the home? What do the family dynamics look like when men are legally defined as dependents?

In this chapter, I present findings from in-depth interviews with Indian migrant women nurses and their husbands. To foreshadow my main findings, I find that in these families, despite the visa-enforced gender status reversal, the traditional gendered division of labor changes only in terms of child care. The traditional family division of labor remains intact, including housework, cooking, and decision-making power of the men. The nurses ignore their own economic power and accept male dominance within the household because they feel intense guilt for being absentee mothers and nontraditional wives. They voluntarily work double shifts—at work and then at home—and emphasize the masculine role of their husbands in the family to overcompensate for what they perceive as their own inadequacy for not being a "dutiful wife."[3]

The men use different strategies to reassert male privilege as heads of households and maintain their masculinity. The dependent husbands refuse to take on any purely "wifely" or "househusband" role. They don't clean or cook or support their wives' careers; however, they do take on the role of the primary caregiver for their children. They adopt this role out of necessity more so than desire. I show how, framed this way, men are able to justify their "nontraditional" role in the family by describing themselves as "sacrificial fathers." A paradox exists because caregiving and nurturance are at the very core of what defines stereotypical femininity. I suggest that even though the husbands refuse to become domestic partners, they still are somewhat disrupting gendered norms by becoming caring nurturers.

INDIAN NURSES MIGRATE TO THE UNITED STATES: PUSH AND PULL FACTORS

U.S. health care organizations have systematically hired foreign professional nurses in response to the cyclical shortage of nurses in U.S. hospitals and nursing homes.[4] With the elderly population in the United States projected to grow exponentially in the coming years, the demand for nurses will likely increase as well.[5] Countries with a large English-speaking population—such as the Philippines, Canada, Ireland, India, and the West Indies—have been the main suppliers of qualified nurses for the U.S. market since the Immigration Act of 1965.[6] Internationally educated nurses "increased from around 50,000 in the mid-1970s to an estimated 165,000 (5.4 percent of all nurses) in 2008, mostly from the Philippines, Canada, the United Kingdom, and India."[7] While Indian nurses have been migrating to the United States since the 1970s, in the early 2000s, U.S. recruiters increased their efforts to hire Indian nurses as other sources started drying up.[8] The last available data on Indian nurses in the United States suggests that in 2005–2006, of all international nurses, Indian nurses represented the second-largest group, with 3,800 nurses qualifying for the licensure exam.[9] Only the Philippines sends more nurses to the United States.[10]

In response to rising demand from wealthier nations and the global market for well-trained, English-speaking Indian nurses, the Indian health care industry and Indian nursing schools have developed themselves for business process outsourcing (BPO), producing nurses trained for the foreign markets.[11] In 2004 there were more than one thousand accredited nursing schools in India, which collectively graduated 1,422,452 nurses, and this number has been growing consistently. Many of these graduates receive further training by the BPOs to be foreign nurses. Out of all the nurses trained each year, about 75 percent immigrate to different parts of the world. Most of these nurses immigrate to the Gulf countries, the United States, Australia, New Zealand, Singapore, Ireland, and the United Kingdom, in that order.[12] The training and recruitment of nurses for the international health care industry occur across all the big cities in India. However, most of the nurses are from one southern state in India called Kerala, and most of them are Christians.[13]

The BPOs are heavily invested in the training and recruitment of nurses for the foreign markets, but their recruitment practices are not always fair and sometimes result in extremely difficult situations for the nurses.[14] The Indian nurses who talked to me corroborated past research with their description of how Indian nurses are hired by contracts and often sent to hospitals in rural areas for three years with relatively low pay. In these first assignments, they are not allowed to bring their families. Some of my participants described the isolation, fear, and pain they felt for the period of their contracts (ranging from three to six years) when they were separated from their families, including sometimes their children. If they tried to break their contracts, they often had to pay up to $60,000 in fines to the recruiters.

I asked these nurses why, despite these difficulties, they decided to migrate instead of working in India. I received three overlapping responses.[15] First, nursing is a low-paid profession in India with low occupational prestige and slim chances of upward mobility. Most of my participants cited the "much higher pay" as a foreign nurse as one of the primary reasons to emigrate. Second, in India, nurses are looked down upon as women who engage in the dirty work of touching unclean bodies. This codification of nursing as dirty work is culturally related to two dominant religions in India, Hinduism and Islam, which both consider working with bodies as impure. Third, and most important, the nurses in my research told me about the severe lack of opportunities in their home state of Kerala. Kerala has been governed by the Communist Party of India for more than fifty years. During the first twenty, there was little foreign investment or industrialization in the state. The economy in Kerala in the first few years after Indian independence was predominantly agricultural. However, in the last ten years Kerala's economy has grown exponentially because of remittances from emigrants. Most of the nurses and their husbands come from poor, rural farming families. Christian women in Kerala for years have taken up nursing to lift their immediate and extended families out of poverty. Most women from Kerala still emigrate as nurses either to the Gulf countries or North America. This has been women's attempt at upward social mobility for fifty years.[16] With the demand from wealthier nations for Indian nurses, migration has become the most viable economic option for nurses and their families. As one of my nurse participants put it,

> I only became a nurse so that I could get a job abroad and give my family, my children a chance to live better. It was very hard to leave, but now my parents, my brothers and sisters, my husband's family all are doing better, and my children will have a better future than me or my husband.

Visas: More than a Travel Document

All the nurses in my research arrived in the United States on either H-1B skilled workers' nonimmigrant visas or immigrant skilled workers' visa, EB-3. This chapter focused on their husbands, who joined them on dependent visas, specifically the H-4 visa or the immigrant dependent E-34 visa, which does not have the same restrictions as the H-4 visa.[17]

You might wonder, as I did, about whether and how gender issues came up for nurses and their husbands who held H-1B and H-4 visas, respectively. The formal definition of the skilled worker's temporary nonimmigrant visa as put forth by the U.S. Immigration and Citizenship Services is, "H-1B applies to people who wish to perform services in a specialty occupation, services of exceptional merit." The H-4 or dependent visa is available to the "spouse and unmarried children under 21 years of age of H-1B workers. . . . Family members in the H-4 nonimmigrant classification may not engage in employment in the United States."[18] These definitions or the clauses of the visa laws do not specifically mention husbands or wives, so they are legally gender neutral. My research, however, shows that the ways in which immigration experts (such as lawmakers, lawyers, and activists) and the general public understand these laws are gendered. In my discussion about the H-1B visas with immigration experts, they often implied that the recipients of these skilled workers' visas are mostly men. As one immigration activist in talking about high-skilled workers, put it, "We offer these men the opportunity to come develop their skills." The general assumption therefore is that the high-skilled migrant workers are men, and hence their spouses on dependent visas are women. While it is statistically true that most recipients of the H-1B visas are men,[19] as my research and other research[20] have shown, female nurses also arrive in the United States as high-skilled migrants.

In talking about dependent visas, the default assumption among immigration experts, including legal opinions, and the public is that the dependent visa holders are women. When the proposal[21] for making changes to H-1B skilled workers' visa laws was floated in Congress in 1996, one of the proposed changes was to ease the process of procuring H-4 dependent visas, particularly for high-tech workers to allow "the wife" to migrate, as it is "important for the well-being and productiveness of the transnational high-skilled employee." Given that men have also been arriving on dependent visas, my research asks how this gender reversal affects the well-being of families. I am also interested in how institutional policies impact the everyday lives of transnational families.

DATA AND METHODS

This chapter is part of a research project that involved two and a half years of extensive qualitative methods. I did in-depth interviews, ethnography, and archival research between the summer of 2009 and winter of 2013. My fieldwork for this paper primarily involved conducting observations in the communities of Indian nurses in and around Chicago for a year. Most of my nurse participants migrated to the United States from the southern state of Kerala. They are called Malayalees and are usually Christians.

I began my fieldwork in three different Malayalee churches in the suburbs of Chicago. Access to this community was not easy. I learned that being Indian was not enough to gain access into this community. I am from north India and am non-Christian, and this made me an outsider in their community. However, with the assistance of an undergraduate at the University of Illinois at Chicago (UIC) who was originally from Kerala, I was eventually welcomed into their community.

The undergraduate student became my research assistant. (She gained field research experience as part of UIC's undergraduate research training, and as her mentor, I gained a junior partner in my research. It was a win-win situation.) She accompanied me to church every Sunday for about six weeks. I approached the church pastor, who announced my research from the pulpit and asked his flock to cooperate. Both the presence of my Malayalee research assistant and the pastor's support changed how the nurses and their families reacted to me.

After three months of attending church every Sunday and participating in community events, I finally was accepted into this community. Nurses and their husbands were more inclined to talk to me now, though given my gender and my status as a sociologist, the nurses were more forthcoming than their husbands. During the year I spent in the communities of nurses, I conducted hours of observations while participating in community events. The participant observations were conducted mostly in public events such as social gatherings at the churches or at nurses' homes.

During the participant observations, I focused on two questions. First, how did family gender dynamics work? I observed who had control over what aspect of the social events, the division of household labor among spouses at the events, discussions that men and women had about their work and family lives, and how men and women interacted with each other. I also listened for talk about immigration status or visa status. I took detailed field notes of my observations and my emotional reactions.

I also conducted in-depth interviews with nurses who were primary family breadwinners and with their dependent husbands. I asked them individually about their lives before migration, their experiences with the migration process, their work experiences, their household division of labor, and their views and understanding of visa policies. After interviewing each of the spouses separately, I interviewed them together. I interviewed twenty-five nurses and their husbands, fifty individuals total. I also interviewed ten immigration experts, including lawyers, activists, and policy makers, to understand their views on visa policies and immigration of high-skilled workers.

In this chapter, I discuss three key themes that emerged from the analysis of my data, all of which were related to struggles about gender expectations: (1) nurses wrestling with how to accept themselves as main providers and not primarily as wives and as their children's primary caretakers, (2) men struggling with their masculinity, and (3) the division of household labor within families. In each of these areas, the families struggled with role reversals. The one arena where men accepted their new responsibilities was as primary caretakers of their children.

Nurses Wrestling with Gender

It was a hot summer Saturday afternoon in a Chicago suburb. I was in the house of Shija, a floor nurse in a suburban hospital. I sat on a bar stool across the kitchen counter, sipping on chilled coconut water, interviewing Shija while she cooked for her family for the week. Saturday was Shija's only day off, and she asked me to come at that particular time because her children had a play date in a local park where her husband had taken them. Shija had four burners on a stove and an oven, and all were on. The air-conditioning was off. In the sweltering heat, the aroma of the Keralite food filled the house. As she cooked, she offered me a taste of what she was cooking, and I happily accepted. During the interview, she told me that even though it was hard on her to spend her only day off cooking, she felt good doing it. She explained,

> This is the only, most real way I can show my kids and my husband that I care for them. Also, I want my kids to grow up eating Malayalee food. It is big part of who we are. I grew up eating my mother's home-cooked meals and so should they.

This was a regular occurrence in their household. Only when Shija didn't have a day off from work to cook for the week would her husband take care of meals. Shija went on to explain that her husband didn't do much of the cleaning in their large four-bedroom suburban house. I could see it had a spacious living room and large kitchen. She explained, "He sometimes does, but because he does everything for the children, I try to do the other things myself."

This was the story in nearly every family. Even though the nurses worked full-time while the husbands either did not work or had minimal part-time jobs, the nurses were still responsible for housework and cooking. While the men refused to count the hours they spent doing household labor, the nurses told me the men were doing about thirty to forty hours of housework every week. Like Shija, all my nurse participants said that they did most of the cleaning and cooking for their family on their days off. Some of the nurses (eight out of the twenty-five in my sample) had either parents or in-laws living with them who often helped out, but even then, the nurses emphasized that cooking was primarily their responsibility. When I asked if this was something the family expected of them, most said they felt good cooking for their families. Rosa, one of the nurses, told me, "This is the least I can do for my children and my family—give them food cooked by mom. I work so much that I am never home. This is the only way I can give them mother's touch." Another nurse, Alma, told me that it would be hard to teach her husband to cook because "he's never cooked or done anything in the house. It would be more work teaching him to cook so I prefer cooking myself." Many of the nurses even opted for night shifts so that they didn't appear to be absentee mothers during the day.

Given the hours that nurses were required to put in at work, they felt they were not fulfilling their mothering duties. In talking about their children and motherhood, many of the nurses broke down in tears, saying that they were "bad mothers" or that they were "losing out on the children's childhood." In a heart-wrenching remark, Jenny said,

> I picked this life so that I have a better life than my mother, but now I am losing my children. I like it that they are close to their father, but my heart bleeds every time they run to their father when they need something and don't come to me even when I am there. It is like I am the person who makes money but is never there for them. That is not what a mother is [trails off in sobs].

The nurses also expressed a deep sense of guilt and shame when their husbands had to accompany them to the United States on dependent visas. In their guilt, the nurses often tried to overcompensate. Alma shared that she has been doing night shifts for three years "so that the kids don't think their mom brings money and dad sits at home." Gina, another nurse whose husband was on a dependent visa, said,

> I was only able to come here because my husband decided to support me. It was more his decision to move here. It is because of his sacrifice that I am here, and I am . . . able to work. I have two kids, five and eight. If it were not for my husband, I would not be able to do anything. We are all in it together—we just want our family to live better. I am very lucky to have Joseph as my husband.

Like Gina, other nurses whose husbands were dependents—either from their visa status or because they were stay-at-home husbands and dads—tried to assert that the husbands were still the heads of the household despite their economic dependence. In all the families with men on dependent visas, the women handed the reins of the family finances to their husbands. Many of the nurses told me that they did not even know their salaries and that their husbands "managed all money issues." Gina explained, "I only bring in the money. The rest is up to him." When I asked Lily what her income was, she said,

I am not quite sure; you have to ask my husband. He is the one who handles all the money things. My salary goes into our account and then he manages it—does what he thinks best. We are still a traditional Indian family. He is still the master of the house. Any major decisions about the kids or money, he makes those decisions. It is important for us as a family to give him that respect. Just because he cannot work because of the visa, we don't want him to feel he is not the head of the family.

The nurses' emphasis on the men being the "head of the family" shows a desire to maintain a semblance of the patriarchal familial structure that the visa laws threatened to alter. The insistence on cooking for their family shows internalized gendered cultural beliefs. In raising an immigrant family, the nurses felt it was important to impart the ethnic/regional food culture to their children even though they were growing up in the United States. The nurses construed "cooking for their children" as an essential part of motherhood. Opting for night shifts at work, engaging in second shifts[22] at home, and handing over finances to their husbands were all attempts to maintain the image of a normal traditional Indian family.

Almost all the nurses downplayed and often refused to even acknowledge their contribution toward their children and family—that is, providing material existence—home, food, education, and medical care. This behavior reveals a deeply internalized gendered understanding of what a family should look like.

Dependent Men Battle with Masculinity

The dependent husbands told me how they found it hard to cope with their loss of status as head of the household. Many of the men refused to come to the United States on dependent visas and preferred to live in India. Rather than compromise their masculine status by being labeled a dependent spouse, they visited their wives in the United States once a year. When they did come, they tried to negate their dependency by emphasizing that it was because of their "support," "insistence," and "permission" that their wives were able to accept the jobs and come to the United States. George, a husband on a dependent visa, said,

When my wife got this opportunity, she was not sure if she should take it because you know for a while I won't be able to work. But I knew it was important for our children and family. I gave her permission to take the job and then we moved here. It is easier because I can keep a watch on the children and while this is a bad policy, it is the way. What can we do?

Another husband on a dependent visa said,

> As a man I needed to make sure my family is OK, and my wife was getting this opportunity to help our family, and for that I would have to sacrifice a little and I was ready for that. I don't think about these things. Government does what it has to—it is no point getting depressed about this. I am doing my duty of keeping my family secure. That is what a man should do.

This attempt by the dependent men to establish maleness in the family context could be interpreted both as a deep-seated gendered belief about a man's role in the family and as a mechanism for coping with the perceived emasculation they experienced as dependent men.

When they claimed to contribute to housework as the dependent spouse, they expressed resentment for having to do so. Shijo, a husband who was on an H-4 visa but now had a work permit, stated,

> My wife works forty to sixty hours depending on how much she is on call. She only has time to cook. I have to do the rest. No choice nah [no]? When you marry a nurse, you know you will be servant of the house [laughs]. But see, I can never say this to my friends and family in Kerala because they laugh at me, say, "You became a woman or what?" But what will you do? If I earned like her, we would get a maid, but my English is not strong, and my diploma is not good here. So I stay home. I don't want to work in gas station like others. I want to start a business later. But for now, I am being houseboy.

The resentment expressed by Shijo about his changed role as the keeper of the house upon migration was a common sentiment among most of the husbands, even when they were eligible for employment. However, it was more pronounced among the few husbands who were on H-4 dependent visas. Johnny, an unemployed, separated husband of a nurse, who had been on H-4 for five years (but was now a permanent resident) and was drunk at the time of the interview, shared,

> I agreed to marry Maria without dowry because I thought she was my ticket to being rich and escaping from Kerala poverty. But when people have power, even a lamb acts like a tiger. That is what happened to Maria. It was the biggest mistake of my life; you better write that down [trailing off].

Johnny's drunkenness might discount his views, but I found similar, if less aggressive, rhetoric in my other interviews with men on H-4 visas. When I asked George what his day looked like, he responded angrily:

Why do you even ask, to shame me? . . . I am like the wife, OK? I wake up in the morning, make tea, feed breakfast to my son, get him ready for school and then drop him [off]. My wife does night shift, so by the time I come back, she is home and I warm breakfast for her—you are thinking, it should be the other way round. Not in this house. And then she sleeps. I warm lunch, eat, clean the house, and do laundry and then it is time to go pick up my son and take him for soccer and then drop my wife at the hospital and do the evening chores and go to bed. That is my life, not what a man's life should be. But I see it as a sacrifice for my family, my son. You know if you are woman in Kerala and a nurse you can do much more for the family. If you are man, you have nothing. It was my decision that we come here, but I should not have come, like some of the people in my village did. They stayed back till they got green cards. But I did not want my son not to have a good life, so I came, so it is all for him. I am learning to be dependent, but it is not easy because you can't talk about it to anyone. Not many of the men are on this visa. Even if you don't work, but if you are not on this visa, you have prestige. And it is not Mary's fault. She tries a lot . . . but what can she do? I did not ever drink or smoke—I have to now. It's bad but what to do. Please don't tell her anything. Please. I talked a lot with you.

George's unhappy confession, that he has taken to drinking and smoking to deal with his dependent status or, as he calls it, his role of "wife," shows the extent to which the men had internalized gendered norms about masculinity. The dependent men deeply lamented their loss of male privilege within the household even when their working wives strived against their own well-being and interests to maintain the patriarchal status quo. Some men took on under-the-table employment, jeopardizing the legal status of the entire family. However, they saw this as a subversive act to reclaim their dominant status within the family and the household.[23]

HOUSEHOLD LABOR: GENDERED INTERACTIONS WITHIN THE FAMILIES

It was about 9:30 p.m. on a breezy fall Saturday night in a northwestern suburb of Chicago. I was leaning on the kitchen counter at Amy's house, chatting with Amy's friend and colleague Rosa. Amy is a petite woman of thirty-eight and a nurse in an inner-city hospital. That particular night, all the women were clad in colorful silk saris. The men wore shirts and trousers. Amy owned a large five-bedroom house, which the family bought new about six years ago. It had a spacious kitchen with granite countertops, aluminum-finished gadgets, a large living and dining area, and a fully finished basement that served as a children's playroom. The house was spotless and had heavy, ornate furniture. Adjoining the kitchen was a living area with a fifty-inch plasma television and couches. Amy's house was typical of most of the nurses' houses I visited for my interviews and observations, including the layout, the furniture, and the family pictures that hung in the living room.

On this weekend night, about fifteen families were having a get-together. All the families had nurses as the lead migrant and the main breadwinner. Three of the husbands in this group were on dependent visas. The rest of the husbands had work permits or were legal permanent residents or citizens, but very few had full-time jobs. Six were stay-at-home fathers. I was invited by Amy to this party to conduct observations as well as interviews.

Like all other community events in the Malayalee community, this event was distinctly gender segregated. The men gathered in one area of the house—in this party, it was in the living space adjoining the kitchen—where some drank beer and chatted while watching Malayalee programming on TV. The women gathered in the kitchen or the living room. The children were often sent to the basement to play. The women usually took charge of warming and serving the food. Multiple dishes (seven to ten) were served, most of them cooked by the host family and a few brought by the guests. The women (nurses) cooked most of the food, but the husbands often declared that they had cooked the meat dishes. Cooking meat was understood to be a mark of masculinity. As I helped Amy[24] lay out the food, she whispered to me with a chuckle that her husband usually helps around the kitchen, but when he is with other men in the community "it is not the 'done' thing to help in the kitchen." If the men helped in the kitchen at social gatherings, it was seen as a sign of not being man enough.

This scenario presents the various forms of gendered interactions that occur among couples in families of nurses and in the Malayalee community. Gender-segregated social gatherings were common in the community. Dependent men and their wives were very protective of the men's male privilege in the presence of community members. The performance of masculinities among the nurses' husbands that fit gendered expectations of male heads of households was common in public and social events, including at the church.[25]

Breaking Gendered Expectations: Dads as Nurturers

Within the family, nurses did a major share of the household chores. The men, however, were responsible for child care. All the couples I interviewed had at least one child, and given that the nurse mothers had highly demanding jobs and long hours, the fathers had to step in to do child care. The families could not afford paid child care, and parental care was considered more culturally appropriate. As one of the men put it, "Someone has to feed the child and put him to bed. If the mother is not there, I have to do it. The child can't go hungry." The men often took care of feeding the children, putting them to bed, dropping them off and picking them up from school and other extracurricular activities like music and dance lessons, arranging and taking them to playdates, reading to them, drawing with them, taking them to parks, or doing other recreational activities. Mothers stayed informed about what was happening in their children's lives but joined in the activities only on their days off. Nurses who taught Sunday school at the church had more time with their own children at community and church events.

While men shunned housecleaning and cooking, they assumed the responsibility of child care without much complaint. Some of the men even took pride in the fact that their children were closer to them than to their mothers. John shared,

> My children really love me. If they need anything or if they have to share anything, the first person they run to is me, not their mother. It makes me feel important. It is a wonderful feeling to be loved by your children.

The nurses also felt that the children were closer to their fathers and shared regret and pain for being what they believed were absentee mothers. Some of the nurses were vocal in saying that it was important that the men contributed equally in the household chores. Missy, a floor nurse in a suburban hospital who is married to a mail sorter in the local post office, thought it was very important that her husband shared equally in the household labor. She explained,

> We are not living back in days and not living in the village in Kerala. It is impossible to run a family when both people are working, and in our families, we as nurses work more, to say that the women will still take care of the house. I now know how much hardship my mother had to go through because of this attitude, and I am happy that has changed. Arun [husband] does a lot in the house—takes [care] of the children and that is very good if you ask me. I don't think Arun is unhappy. [Arun nods in consent.]

In a similar story, Jenny shared that she decided to marry Thomas, who was less educated than she and came from a humble background, because she did not want to end up like her mother. She tearfully said,

I only wanted to become a nurse and leave my village so that I could help my mother and save her from my father. You know she was the one, worked like a donkey both for the family and at the farm and yet my father would yell at her, push her around, sometimes even beat her. I did not want that for me, which is why I married Thomas even if he was lower status than me. I wanted a man who would be understanding and would take care of my home and children and not be like my father. Thomas is a great husband, and I am happy that he does not think it is bad to take care of children and family.

Indeed, Thomas was one of the few men who did not complain about doing household chores.

In terms of social interactions and emotional work, the men in the families of nurses assumed more public responsibilities, such as organizing events at the church or organizing community picnics and games. While the men said that the church played an important role in their lives, they also unanimously complained that neither the church nor community provided the same sort of social support they had in India. Yet, keeping in touch with family and friends in India was still the primary responsibility of the wives. In fact, the men avoided talking to family and friends in India—perhaps it was one way for them to protect their already vulnerable masculinity from being further challenged.

The social and political expectation that a worker with a dependent spouse would be able to delegate household duties to the spouse was trumped by their gendered cultural beliefs and expectations for traditional Indian families. The only time they willingly overcame these gendered cultural expectations was in nurturing their children. The dependent men jumped in to take charge of the children, and many of them enjoyed it and took pride in their relationships with their kids.

DISCUSSION AND CONCLUSION

In this chapter, I presented an analysis of the consequences of visa policies for female-led Indian migrant families. I have shown that female-led migration disrupted the traditional gender order: women were the breadwinners; men became caregivers. The story wasn't that simple, however. Instead, what emerged in these families was a set of complicated gender dynamics. Challenges to traditional expectations threatened men's sense of their own masculinity. Female primary breadwinners were still expected to cook and clean while giving as much care to their children as they could fit into their schedule.

The husbands of the nurses resented being dependents. Most of these men from rural Kerala believed in strict rules about men's and women's positions in the family, and in their homeland, men were always the heads of their households. The nurses, too, described the family structure in Kerala as strictly patriarchal with the father as an iron-fisted patriarch. The men still believed that male honor rested in being a provider and the head of the household. Visa-imposed dependency therefore meant loss of male privilege and honor for the men. They were often resentful and depressed about this loss of status.

The dependent husbands of the nurses refused to take on any purely "wifely" or househusband role. But they did not resist adopting the role of a caregiver for their children; they believed their children needed care in the absence of their mother. These families—both the husbands and the wives—were very child oriented.

The most common reason the families had moved to the United States was to provide a better and brighter future for their children. The men see the logic in taking the reins of child care, claiming they are strong, able, and sacrificial fathers. The paradox of the situation is that most sociologists and psychologists view child care, including caregiving and caretaking, to be the very definition of femininity. It seems, then, that the men are challenging gender norms by becoming caring nurturers, even if they would shy away from admitting it. Their behavior shows us how society has socially constructed the meaning of gender itself.

Still, most of the dependent men assert their male privilege as heads of households. They and their wives actively perform traditional gender by insisting that their families remain patriarchal. Husbands continue to be the symbolic heads of the household, even though without their wives, their families could not survive economically or remain in their homes.

The nurses emphasized that becoming a nurse was their way to escape a life of poverty and patriarchal oppression in rural Kerala. They saw a career in nursing in a developed country as a way to improve the lives of their children and families, both here and in India. They, however, still held on to traditional gender beliefs. They believed that household work was women's work. The nurses felt guilty for being the reason for their husbands' migration as dependents. They also felt intensely unhappy at being employed mothers with long and erratic hours. Their long working hours made them feel as though they were absentee mothers. But as the main family breadwinners, they felt compelled to fulfill all their employer's demands. They did not feel they had the option to refuse these demands. The gender identity of mother remains strong among nurses; they envied the time fathers had with their children. The belief that men and women should have distinct family roles leaves nurses uncomfortable with reversed roles and keeps them from insisting household labor be more equitably divided.

Even though they were written in gender-neutral language, the institutional constraints of the visa structures are based on gendered presumptions that men bring wives with them. Visa laws, no matter how gender neutral they may seem, have gendered consequences for families. The nurses and their husbands hold on to traditional gendered beliefs about male providership and motherhood. As a result, the nurses work for a living and do most of the work in their households.

Seemingly gender-neutral visa policies have oppressive gendered consequences for individuals and for the way people *expect* to interact with each other and the way institutions interact with visa holders. I have shown the unintended consequences of visa laws on immigrants: rather than creating stable families, these visas create families full of anxiety and despair. Advocacy by women dependent visa holders, and the results of research such as this, led President Obama to pass an executive order that resulted in a shorter term of dependence for spouses with dependent visas. However, given it was an executive order (that is, changeable), this ruling was under constant threat of being rescinded during the Trump era.[26] If we are truly concerned with the interests of migrant families, these visa laws must be completely overhauled. We should no longer stand for forced economic and social dependency that creates deeply gendered families and oppressive conditions for both women and men, but especially women, in immigrant families.

Notes

1. U.S. Department of State (2021a), Table XV(A), Nonimmigrant Visas Issued by Classification, travel.state.gov/content/dam/visas/Statistics/AnnualReports /FY2021AnnualReport/FY21_TableXVA.pdf.

2. U.S. Department of State (2021b), Table XV(B), Nonimmigrant Visas Issued by Classification, travel.state.gov/content/dam/visas/Statistics/AnnualReports /FY2021AnnualReport/FY21_%20TableXVB.pdf.

3. Most nurses resented doing housework but avoided asking their husbands to do it.

4. See Aiken (2007); Aiken, Buchan, Sochalski, Nichols, and Powell (2004); Brush and Berger (2002); Polsky, Ross, Brush, and Sochalski (2007).

5. Brush, Sochalski, and Berger (2004).

6. Aiken (2007); George (2005); Khadria (2007).

7. Masselink and Jones (2014), 1.

8. Banerjee (2022); Rai (2003).

9. Sharma (2011); Banerjee (2022).

10. Walton-Roberts (2015).

11. Khadria (2007).

12. Khadria (2007).

13. Banerjee (2022); George (2005); Khadria (2007).

14. Pittman, Folsom, and Bass (2010).
15. See George (2005); Kurien (2002); Walton-Roberts (2012).
16. George (2005); Kurien (2002); Walton-Roberts (2012); Walton-Roberts (2020); Bhalla and Meher (2019).
17. Banerjee (2022).
18. The definitions are taken from the U.S. Citizenship and Immigration Services (USCIS) website at www.uscis.gov.
19. Biao (2005).
20. See Banerjee (2022); Dicicco-Bloom (2004); George (2005); Khadria (2007).
21. The proposal was to add fixed quotas of H-1Bs for each sending country, limiting the number of years on the visa to three years and then a continuation for three years and making the process of procuring H-4 dependent visas easier.
22. Hochschild (1989).
23. Banerjee (2019).
24. I did not address most of the nurses by their first names. I added *chechi* (the Malayalam term for "big sister") after their first names for the women and *chetian* (the Malayalam term for "big brother") for the men. The community viewed me as a younger woman, though I was not markedly younger than most of the women and men I interviewed. But I learned quickly that it was disrespectful to address my participants by their first names.
25. Banerjee (2022); George (2005).
26. Banerjee (2022); Banerjee and Sengupta (2020).

In Other Words

MORE DADS ARE HOME TAKING CARE OF CHILDREN THAN EVER BEFORE—ARE VIEWS ABOUT GENDER AND WORK CHANGING?

Arielle Kuperberg and Pamela Stone, September 27, 2022 / CCF@TSP

In 2021, the number of stay-at-home dads in the United States reached record highs. Does this mean that cultural views about gender, masculinity, work, and family—particularly the idea that men should be breadwinners—are changing? Not necessarily.

Our research in *Gender & Society* assesses cultural views of stay-at-home fathers over three decades by examining their portrayal in leading newspapers and magazines between 1987 and 2016. We found that news portrayals of stay-at-home dads have indeed become more positive over time. But the growing support for full-time caregiver fathers is conditional. Dads who lost their jobs because of involuntary unemployment are viewed sympathetically, especially since the Great Recession. But dads who can work but choose to stay home with children instead are still described negatively. As much as we'd like to think that the gender-bending phenomenon of (slightly) increasing numbers of dads at home is a harbinger of more fundamental gender liberalization, our results suggest that this is not unambiguously the case.

News articles about stay-at-home dads often focused on the stigma and hardships that these dads faced in their everyday lives. In the ninety-four articles we analyzed, stay-at-home dads discussed being laughed at, dismissed, or even accused of being a pedophile while at the playground with their child. They were often described as being shunned by mothers and ridiculed by their friends. Fathers discussed feeling like "less of a man" because they could not financially provide for their families, and over half reported feeling isolated and experiencing stress because of their role. Many recounted being called "Mr. Mom," the title of a 1980s movie about an inept stay-at-home dad. This phrase reinforced the idea that active parenting was something that women do, not men. Further reinforcing this idea, some dads were instead excessively praised for doing the most basic chores with their child (like bringing them to the grocery store).

But the focus on stigma lessened over time, as more dads began to stay home with children. After the Great Recession resulted in high rates of unemployment, dads who lost their jobs and took on caretaking roles at home were no longer described as experiencing stigma and were discussed sympathetically and supportively.

Accounts of stigma experiences didn't disappear, however; instead, they were mostly reserved for another type of stay-at-home dad—a father who had *chosen* to stay home with his children and hadn't been forced into the role by lay-offs.

In our article, we also compared stay-at-home dads' personal experiences to demographic trends. In Figure 37.1, we extend this analysis to 2021 to include another major economic shock—the COVID-19 pandemic. What is clear is that the rate at which fathers were at home rose in the wake of economic downturns, but it eventually reversed course and reverted to near pre-downturn levels upon economic recovery. Over the period we studied, staying home became more common among dads—especially after the Great Recession of 2007–2009. But the number of dads who reported they were home specifically to take care of children was still very low—less than 2 percent in 2021. And prior to the pandemic, rates of staying

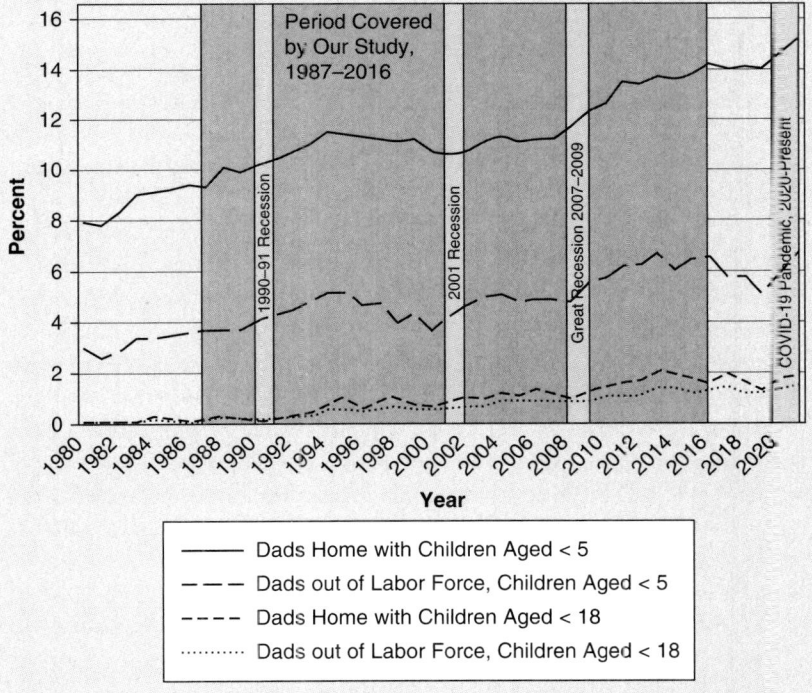

Figure 37.1 | Percent of U.S. Fathers Out of the Labor Force and Percent of Fathers Out of the Labor Force Specifically to Care for Children, 1980–2021

Source: Authors' analysis of Current Population Survey—March Supplement Data.

home had begun to go down among dads of younger children, declining almost to pre–Great Recession levels by 2019. These patterns also suggest that the post-recession increase in dads staying home was not a result of long-lasting changes in attitudes and ideologies about gender and work but rather was a temporary response to economic precarity.

Taken together, our findings indicate that cultural views of stay-at-home dads may be changing, but mostly for dads who stay home because they don't have any other choice. The stigma surrounding stay-at-home dads has been reduced, but only because more dads are out of the workforce due to broader economic circumstances that make it impossible for them to be breadwinners. Dads who choose to stay home and not contribute financially to the family are still stigmatized, presumably seen as failures as breadwinners or as deadbeats for ducking this responsibility entirely. But dads who began to stay home because of the pandemic (or other future economic events) are likely to be viewed sympathetically, suggesting some relaxing of strong male-breadwinner social norms.

And cultural views may continue to change. A 2021 report from the Council on Contemporary Families found that over 70 percent of mothers will spend at least part of their children's childhood as the main financial provider, with the average mother spending six years in this role. The pandemic also reversed the beginning of a decline in staying-home rates among fathers of young children, and dads are now out of the labor force and home with kids at record-high rates. The sustained rate of dads staying home with kids may reduce the stigma of this role even further as more children grow up with dads at home as caregivers for at least some portion of their childhoods.

On the other hand, support for dads staying home may be reduced if economic conditions improve more broadly, reducing the number of men in that role involuntarily. And during the pandemic, while more dads withdrew from the labor force and increased the time they spent on housework and child care, in 70 percent of families it was mothers who were primarily responsible for homeschooling when schools went virtual. Mothers were also far more likely than fathers to withdraw from the workforce or reduce their hours in paid work. These pandemic trends reinforce the idea that the recent uptick in dads staying home is not an auger of radical gender change, but rather a reflection that traditional ideas about gender and parenting and divisions of labor are still going strong. Until these ideas change, and the stigma surrounding men who voluntarily stay home with children is reduced, few men will be willing to take on this role, preventing advancement toward full gender equality in work and family roles. ∎

38

Gender Inequality in the United States during the COVID-19 Pandemic

Allison Nicole Dunatchik and Jerry A. Jacobs

The COVID-19 pandemic disrupted lives as well as economic and social arrangements throughout the world. It altered where people work, where they shop, how they eat, whom they can see, and how they think about their futures. Yet despite its universal sweep, the pandemic affected people in radically different ways depending on their particular circumstances. Some lost their lives or family members, while some lost their jobs or businesses. Some workers were able to shift to remote work, and they lost important connections and supports. Others, in workplaces ranging from hospitals to grocery stores, were deemed "essential"; these workers and their families were put at risk on a daily basis.

While the pandemic continues to evolve,[1] and the aftermath of it shapes our lives, the early days of the pandemic were ripe for understanding inequalities, including gender inequality. In the United States, as well as many countries around the world, gender proved to be an enduring cleavage in how people experienced the pandemic. While men had a greater age-specific risk of mortality from COVID-19, a pattern partially offset by the concentration of women among older adults, women suffered more job losses than men did, particularly women without a college degree. Not only were women concentrated in hard-hit service-sector jobs, but they also suffered the loss of child care and schooling—essential supports for the primary caregivers of children (Zamarro, Perez-Arce, and Prados 2021). As a result, mothers of young children were more likely than fathers to reduce their paid work hours, become unemployed, and exit the labor force during the pandemic (Collins et al. 2020; Landivar et al. 2020). In many families, the move of schooling and child care into the home also increased the burden of unpaid work borne by mothers, exacerbating existing gender inequalities in the domestic division of labor. Still, some aspects of pandemic-induced changes in work and care, such as expanded opportunities to work from home, also offered fathers new opportunities for involvement in domestic work and parenting.

In this chapter, we ask how families with children experienced and responded to abrupt changes in paid and unpaid work in the early months of the pandemic, with particular attention to how these practices varied among families in different circumstances and their implications for gender equality at home. We draw on nationally representative survey data from 478 partnered parents and 151 single parents collected in April 2020 to examine how the loss of child care and in-person schooling affected the amount of time parents spent on housework, child care, and children's remote learning. We also examine how parents felt about the sudden responsibility for their children's schooling.[2]

The evidence largely indicates that although responses to the pandemic reinforced and even widened gender disparities in the domestic division of labor, there is also some reason for cautious optimism. The pandemic may prompt new discussions of these issues by exposing the depth of gender inequality in caregiving and the inadequacy of support provided by our work and caregiving institutions. Some of the changes prompted by the pandemic—such as options for remote work—may enable employed parents to develop new ways of combining and sharing paid work and caregiving. Yet reducing inequality and building a stronger infrastructure of care depends on understanding how the pandemic played out in diverse family contexts.

ANTICIPATED EFFECTS OF THE PANDEMIC ON GENDER INEQUALITY AT HOME

The COVID-19 pandemic substantially increased time demands at home among parents. Child care center closures relocated the responsibility for care of young children to the home, and the transition of many schools to a virtual format necessitated greater supervision by parents of their children's learning. At the same time, greater health and hygiene concerns, alongside the closure of many dining options outside the home, increased the burden of housework in many families. How these additional responsibilities would be divided within families and their impact on gender inequality at home was the source of some debate.

There were a variety of reasons to believe that the pandemic would have negative consequences for gender equality in housework and child care. First, these activities are strongly gendered within different-sex couples. Performing domestic work and care (or not) is an important way that individuals enact their gender to meet societal norms and expectations about appropriate gender roles within the family (Berk 1985; West and Zimmerman 1987). Despite increases in fathers' contributions to unpaid work over recent decades, prior to the pandemic mothers still carried out the majority of housework and child care in the United States even among dual-earner couples (e.g., Collins 2019; Raley et al. 2012; Yavorsky et al. 2015).

Second, the pandemic disproportionately affected women's employment (Yavorsky, Qian, and Sargent 2021). The economic recession sparked by the pandemic substantially reduced employment in nonessential service industries (such as food services, retail, and hospitality) that disproportionately employ women (IWPR 2020). As a result, women suffered greater job losses in the wake of the pandemic, and their employment was slower to rebound as the economy reopened (IWPR 2021). In addition, prior research has shown that during periods of unemployment, women's domestic labor increases more than does men's (Gough and Killewald 2011; Rao 2020). These patterns provide further indication that mothers would be more likely than fathers to absorb the additional unpaid work created by the pandemic. In addition to greater risk of unemployment, increased demands at home pushed many mothers to reduce their employment hours or leave the labor force altogether during the pandemic (Zamarro et al. 2021; Collins et al. 2020), underscoring the interconnected nature of gender inequalities in paid and unpaid work.

Still, some of the large-scale disruptions associated with the pandemic, such as greater opportunities to work from home, offered possible opportunities to increase gender equality in the division of care and domestic work. Many work-family scholars have placed the option to work remotely at least some of the time high on their list of recommended reforms, arguing that such an option would not only reduce commuting time but would also allow for more flexibility in integrating domestic and employment responsibilities (Correll et al. 2014; Kaduk et al. 2019; Mas and Pallais 2017). Additionally, as remote work decreases the need for "face time" at the office, classic rationales justifying an unequal division of domestic labor may also recede. For example, one explanation for the persistence of gendered divisions of household labor is that men tend to spend more time than women away from the home in paid employment Consequently, much of the housework and care done at home is simply invisible to men. Working from home, therefore, may make previously unnoticed domestic work more visible to men and encourage greater contribution to these activities. Men's greater physical presence at home may also allow them greater opportunity to respond to housework and care needs as they arise throughout the day when they would have otherwise been unavailable. Importantly, however, even if remote work facilitates greater gender equality for remote workers, access to this arrangement remains a largely white-collar privilege that limits the scope of such potential gains.

Still, as other research has pointed out, in a context of prevailing social norms and pressures regarding mothers as primary caregivers, remote work may work to the detriment of women's employment by increasing women's already disproportionate share of unpaid workloads within households (Noonan and Glass 2012). Indeed, one study found that mothers spent significantly more time doing housework and caring for children during their working hours during the pandemic than they did before (Lyttelton, Zang, and Musick 2022). And telecommuting mothers spent twice as much worktime with their children present than telecommuting fathers did.

Finally, the consequences of the loss of child care and in-person schooling will likely be particularly severe among single parents, who must reconcile paid work responsibilities and additional unpaid work without a partner to share the burden and with limited access to the networks of support that single parents depend on (Tach and Edin 2017). Some research has found that single mothers reported greater stress in managing employment and domestic responsibilities during the pandemic compared with parents in multi-adult households and were more likely to report feeling their productivity had suffered as a result (Hertz et al. 2020). However, others have found that single mothers reported greater satisfaction with their balance of paid and unpaid work during the pandemic compared with before (Craig and Churchill 2021). With 81 percent of single-parent households headed by women (Livingston 2018), considering the impact of the pandemic on these families is critical to gaining greater understanding of the implications of the pandemic for gender inequality more broadly.

DATA AND METHODS

The data in this study come from an online poll conducted by Morning Consult on behalf of the *New York Times* from April 9 to 10, 2020, during the early weeks of school closures and lockdown measures in the United States (Morning Consult and the *New York Times* 2020; Miller 2020). The sample of 2,200 adults, including 629 parents of resident, dependent children, was weighted to reflect the adult population in terms of age, education, gender, race, and region. We focus on the 478 partnered parents with dependent children in the household and then turn to the experiences of 151 single parents (consisting of 109 single mothers and forty-two single fathers).

Housework and child care involve a number of complex tasks. Our data focus on several important dimensions, including the amount of time spent on child care and housework, who assumes responsibility for these tasks, and how people feel about the domestic work they perform. We address a range of issues:

- whether respondents spent more time on housework (cooking and cleaning) and child care during the pandemic

- who was primarily responsible for housework and child care in respondents' households

- whether respondents increased their responsibility for housework or child care during the pandemic

- who spent more time helping children with distance learning

- how pressured parents felt to oversee their children's distance learning

Our analysis asks how respondents' varying family arrangements and employment statuses shaped changes in gendered time allocation and household divisions of housework and child care during the early stage of the pandemic. First, we examine key trends in gender inequality in housework and child care, focusing on the extent to which the gender gap varies by parents' employment status and whether respondents and their partners were working remotely. We then briefly examine the experiences of single parents, again distinguishing between those working remotely and those not able to do so.

PANDEMIC PARENTING AMONG PARTNERED PARENTS

How did the pandemic alter housework and domestic responsibilities? Many parents in two-parent households reported spending more time on housework and child care during the pandemic than they did before. Partnered mothers were more likely to increase their housework time (55 percent) compared with fathers (45 percent), but mothers and fathers were equally likely to report spending more time on child care (36 percent and 33 percent, respectively).

In addition to actual time spent, it is important to consider the sense of responsibility that parents feel about these tasks. Mothers and fathers were nearly equally likely to state that their responsibility for housework and child care within their household increased during the pandemic: 15 percent of mothers and 14 percent of fathers reported greater responsibility for housework, and 16 percent of mothers and 15 percent of fathers reported increased responsibility for child care.

Although the pandemic appeared to increase responsibility for and time spent on housework and child care similarly for mothers and fathers in two-parent households, the division of responsibility for these tasks remained starkly gendered during the pandemic. Nearly 80 percent of partnered mothers said they were *primarily* responsible for housework in their household during the pandemic compared with just 28 percent of partnered fathers. Similarly, 66 percent of mothers were *primarily* responsible for child care compared with 24 percent of fathers.

Helping children with their homework took on added dimensions during the early phases of the pandemic as many schools closed. In some cases, this meant that parents essentially took on the responsibility for homeschooling their children. In other cases, parents were tasked with helping children with homework that may not have been clearly understood as a result of remote lessons. Mothers took on the lion's share of these tasks. Three-quarters (73 percent) of partnered mothers (regardless of employment status) stated they spent more time on home education than did others in their household, compared with one-third (34 percent) of partnered fathers. Mothers were also more likely to say they felt "some" or "a lot" of pressure regarding their children's home learning (57 percent) compared with fathers (45 percent).

The impact of the pandemic was particularly acute among employed parents. Among two-parent households, a majority (62 percent) of employed mothers reported spending more time on housework than before the pandemic and 47 percent reported spending more time on child care, compared with 47 percent and 35 percent among employed fathers, respectively. One might expect that mothers who work for pay might take on fewer household responsibilities. But the evidence points to the opposite conclusion. In fact, the great majority—77 percent—of employed mothers reported being mainly responsible for housework, 61 percent reported being mainly responsible for child care, and 78 percent reported taking the lead on helping with their children's remote learning. The additional domestic demands created by the pandemic affected employed parents—and especially employed mothers. Most employed mothers (64 percent) and half of employed fathers (50 percent) felt "some" or "a lot" of pressure related to their children's home learning.

The particularly intense gendering of housework, child care, and home learning among employed partnered parents is surprising given that working mothers had less time available to absorb the additional unpaid work required during the pandemic relative to nonworking mothers. However, assessing how these patterns varied depending on whether employed mothers and fathers worked remotely provides some clarity.

Responses to the pandemic were most gender egalitarian in families where both parents worked remotely. Both mothers and fathers in dual remote-worker households reported increases in the time spent on housework and child care (see Figures 38.1a and 38.1b). However, the nearly equal increase among both women and men leaves the overall preexisting gender gap largely unchanged.

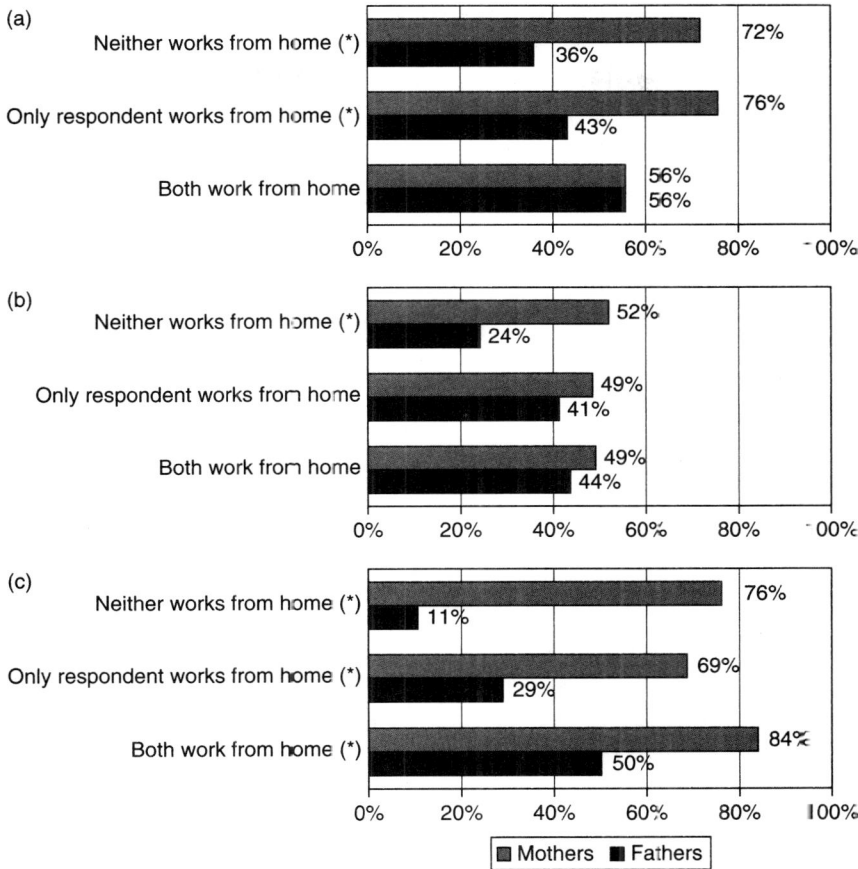

Figure 38.1 | Proportion of Respondents Who Report Spending More Time on (a) Housework, (b) Child Care, and (c) Children's Home Learning during the COVID-19 Pandemic Compared with before the Pandemic

Note: N = 336 partnered working parents; *gender differences are statistically significant at p = 0.05.

In addition, mothers in dual remote-working households were more likely than fathers to take charge of children's home learning, with 84 percent of mothers spending more time on schooling than other household members compared with 50 percent of fathers (Figure 38.1c).

This finding emphasizes that mothers still feel largely responsible for education and child care even when both parents are physically present in the home and, therefore, theoretically available for these tasks. Among couples who both worked from home, 72 percent of mothers said they were primarily responsible

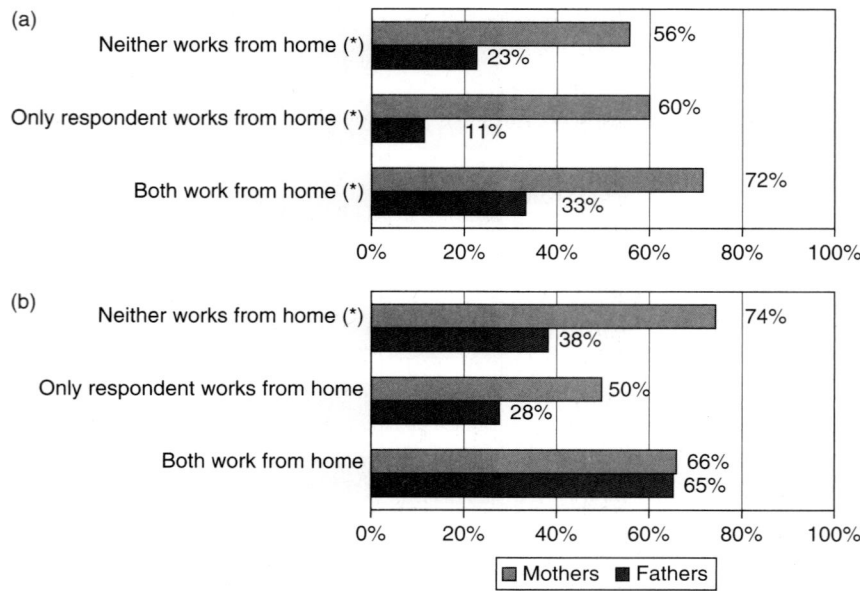

Figure 38.2 | Proportion of Respondents Who Report Feeling (a) Primarily Responsible for Child Care in Household, and (b) "Some" or "a Lot" of Pressure regarding Children's Home Learning during the COVID-19 Pandemic Compared with before the Pandemic

Note: N = 336 partnered working parents; *gender differences are statistically significant at p < 0.05.

for child care since the beginning of the pandemic compared with 33 percent of fathers (Figure 38.2a). In sum, even when both parents worked from home, a gendered division of labor persisted. Despite this gendered division of care work, mothers and fathers in dual remote-worker households felt nearly equal amounts of pressure around children's schooling: 66 percent of mothers and 65 percent of fathers reported "some" or "a lot" of pressure regarding their children's home learning (Figure 38.2b).

Gender disparities in housework, child care, and home education were even more pronounced when only one spouse worked remotely. When fathers alone worked from home, they reported far less involvement in domestic work than mothers did when working from home alone. Among mothers who worked from home (but whose spouse did not), 76 percent reported more time doing housework and 69 percent reported spending more time on their children's home learning compared with 43 percent and 29 percent of similarly situated fathers, respectively. Gendered norms appear to protect teleworking fathers, but not mothers, from extra domestic labor as well as from the stress of their children's remote learning—*even when fathers were the sole parent working from home*

What happened when both parents were working in-person? Here again, the pandemic reinforced gender disparities. When domestic workloads increased and neither parent worked from home, employed mothers were the ones who mostly picked up the slack—particularly for housework and home learning. Among couples where neither partner worked remotely, 72 percent of mothers reported doing more housework during the pandemic and 79 percent reported being primarily responsible for housework, compared with 36 percent of fathers who increased their housework and 25 percent of fathers who said they were mainly responsible for housework. In households where no parent worked remotely, most mothers (76 percent) reported taking on the majority of home-learning activities for their children, compared with 11 percent of fathers. Consequently, mothers not working remotely were twice as likely as fathers not working remotely to say they felt "some" or "a lot" of pressure regarding children's home learning (74 percent compared with 38 percent, respectively).

Single Parenting during the Pandemic

The pandemic posed a distinct set of challenges for single parents, including declining access to the networks of support single parents depend on (Tach and Edin 2017). Just under half (49 percent) of single mothers reported doing more housework compared with the pre-pandemic period and just under one-quarter (24 percent) reported spending more time on child care. Two-fifths (41 percent) reported feeling "some" or a "lot of" pressure regarding their children's education, which is considerably less than partnered mothers (57 percent). While the increase in domestic work is notable among single mothers, these effects of the pandemic were more muted than those reported by partnered peers, perhaps because single mothers were already shouldering such a high level of responsibility before the pandemic.

Single parents nevertheless had to address the challenge of working and parenting without the help of a partner, forcing some to cut back on their working time. One in four (26 percent) single mothers reported working fewer hours per week for pay. And although the percent of partnered moms who reported reducing working time was even higher (39 percent), single parents are much less likely to have another source of income to cushion the financial blow. It is thus no surprise that more than one-third of single mothers (36 percent) said they would take paid leave if it were available, which is the same rate as partnered mothers.

How do single mothers compare with single fathers? The results, based on small sample sizes, are mixed, so we can't draw firm conclusions. Single mothers working remotely were more likely to report working more during the pandemic (27 percent) compared with single, remote-working fathers (9 percent). Among single, employed parents, mothers working from home were more likely (62 percent) than either fathers working remotely (46 percent) or mothers working in-person (52 percent) to report spending more time on housework than they had before the pandemic. Yet remote-working single mothers were less likely to report spending more time on child care (22 percent) than remote-working single fathers (36 percent) and single mothers working in-person (33 percent).

When it came to homeschooling, remote-working single mothers were more likely to report taking on the majority of home-learning responsibilities (83 percent) compared with single fathers working from home (59 percent). Among those working in-person, however, single mothers and fathers were similarly likely to report having primary responsibility for home learning (47 percent vs. 51 percent, respectively). Regarding their psychological well-being, remote-working single mothers and fathers reported similar levels of stress, with 55 percent of mothers feeling "some" or "a lot" of pressure about their children's schooling compared with 50 percent of fathers. In general, single parents working at home reported feeling more pressure about their children's home learning compared with single parents working outside the home (35 percent and 40 percent, respectively). Whether the focus is on gender differences or differences between remote and commuting workers, these mixed findings point to the varied ways the pandemic intensified the difficulties facing single parents, who are especially vulnerable to changes in their work situation and any loss in their care support system.

OVERALL: THE GENDER GAP AT HOME WIDENED BUT MORE FOR SOME FAMILIES THAN OTHERS

Overall, our findings indicate that the pandemic reinforced gender disparities in housework and child care. Among families with dependent children, both mothers and fathers reported doing more housework and child care in the early months of the pandemic. However, in two-parent families, employed mothers were more likely than employed fathers to report taking on additional domestic tasks, widening the gender gap at home.

Our results also demonstrate considerable variation according to families' circumstances. Responses to the pandemic were most gender egalitarian in families where both parents were able to work from home. In these families, both mothers and fathers reported increasing their contributions to housework and child care.

However, these changes preserved pre-pandemic gender inequalities in the division of domestic work. In contrast, gender inequalities increased among couples where neither parent worked from home and where mothers alone worked from home. In these households, mothers became the stopgap who absorbed most of the additional caring and schooling of children. Furthermore, responsibility for these tasks also remained gendered.

Unsurprisingly, single mothers and fathers also reported spending more time on housework, child care, and children's remote learning during the pandemic. Perhaps more surprising, however, was that single mothers were less likely than partnered mothers to report having increased their time on these activities despite partnered mothers having a spouse available—in theory—to share the domestic burden. This may be because single mothers were already shouldering a high level of domestic responsibility before the pandemic, leaving little time in the day to increase time spent on these activities.

Although the longer-term consequences of the pandemic remain to be seen, our findings indicate that gender was a powerful force in determining how—and by whom—housework and care were carried out in the early months of the pandemic. Although some have argued that the rise of remote work would prompt more domestic equality in child care and housework, especially among dual-earner couples, we find that the domestic division of labor did not become markedly more equal during this disruptive period. When the jobs of both parents moved into the home, the gender gap neither increased nor decreased.

These results may also indicate that access to remote work may have the potential for longer-term positive effects. Perhaps fathers' presence in the household will foster an increased willingness to contribute to housework and parenting. Still, our findings emphasize that remote work is hardly a panacea for gender equality: fathers working from home alone were generally better able than similarly situated mothers to protect themselves from the demands of unpaid care work. Going forward, these results suggest that the implications of remote work for gendered divisions of domestic labor beyond the pandemic will likely depend on the varied forms it takes in individual families.

NOTES

1. At the time of writing, the COVID-19 pandemic had entered a new phase in the United States and most COVID-19 mitigation measures (such as mandatory remote work, mask mandates, and school closures) had been lifted. Because this chapter focuses on the early days of the pandemic, we refer to the pandemic (and its effects) in the past tense although we acknowledge it is still ongoing.

2. This chapter draws on research originally reported in Dunatchik et al. (2021).

In Other Words

THE CHOICE TO CONCEIVE, LGBTQ FAMILIES, AND COVID-19

Penny Harvey, August 24, 2021 / CCF@TSP

The appointments were all scheduled, the preliminary tests were done, the co-parenting agreements were signed, and the flights were booked. My wife and I were counting the days until our sperm donor, Steffan, would arrive in the United States. This was February 2020. Steffan was due to arrive in April to provide his sperm donation. We planned to start our journey to grow our family several months later, in August 2020.

Then came March 2020, and with it came COVID-19. Now fertility clinics were closed, international travel was limited, and our carefully thought out, well-timed plans had come to a screeching halt. Like many couples planning to conceive in 2020, the new reality drastically changed what was already a nerve-wracking endeavor.

Family building for LGTBQ folks has never been easy. For most cis/het couples who don't face infertility issues (85 to 90 percent), the process is ideally a time for connection, romance, and the inevitable lovemaking. But for LGBTQ folks, the process involves legal forms, doctors' visits, psychological tests, and major financial decisions. Yes, technology has eased this process given the relative accessibility of assisted reproductive technology (ART), the availability of sperm banks, and the advent of online support groups. You hear less and less about the queers making children in an awkward, often substance-filled, turkey baster situation. However, there are still major structural barriers and a series of daunting hurdles we need to traverse.

The average cost of a single fertility treatment without insurance ranges from $12,000 to $75,000. This presents a significant barrier for many LGBTQ families, who are, on average, more likely to have lower incomes and less wealth than cis/het families. This means that LGBTQ families face heightened financial barriers from the get-go. Even if LGBTQ families choose not to follow the reproductive route, adoptions can cost upward of $15,000 to $40,000 depending on the state.

LGBTQ families also face additional structural barriers, from donor/surrogate selection, to added testing, to increased FDA-regulated wait times for directed or known donor sperm (six months compared to no wait for sexually intimate partners). And on top of these barriers, LGBTQ families must navigate a draconian legal maze as they seek to secure their family choices with individual legal protections to affirm parental rights, ensure various kinds of access and birth certificate recognitions, and correct parental genders. For families who desire to have three or more recognized parents, there may be no legal protections to ensure that all parties are recognized appropriately. All these barriers are coupled with additional challenges like finding a donor or surrogate and finalizing co-parent agreements. LGBTQ folks are also at higher risk of fertility issues than cis/het couples, as LGBTQ people are more likely to start trying to conceive later in life and are more likely to have engaged in substance use, both of which significantly affect fertility.

In March 2020, most fertility clinics closed their doors due to the risk of COVID, the lack of medical equipment and supplies, and the unknown risk of virus transmission through sperm. This was a devastating blow to many prospective parents planning to conceive during this time. Every missed cycle was a missed chance to try for a child. I saw firsthand the impact the pandemic was having in my many "how to conceive" support groups. I felt all my plans slipping away. I had waited so long to try to start a family. There was so much in my life I could not control, from an uncertain job market, to publications, to finishing my PhD. Before COVID the choice to at least try to start a family felt in my grasp. So as an academic, I stepped back, critiqued the systems, and turned my frustration and fears into research. My co-author and I began compiling news stories and academic research to make sense of everything we were witnessing.

We found that in the United States and many other countries, fertility clinics closed due to uncertainty about procedure safety and lack of medical equipment. While we support a brief initial closure, many closed for an extended period, citing fertility treatment as a "nonessential medical service." Other clinics opened but did not take in new patients, forcing many prospective families, both cis/het and LGBTQ, to put their plans on an indefinite hold. In addition to fertility-center closures, prospective LGBTQ families uniquely had nonmedicalized methods interrupted or halted.

Social distancing, lockdown, and travel laws meant that many people could not make the necessary connections to provide or receive biological materials. This affected lesbian couples who were unable to drive a state away to collect a sperm deposit, gay couples whose surrogate was in another country and barred from entering the United States, and multiparent families whose households were not allowed to meet—or felt it was too dangerous to meet—to try to conceive.

There were, of course, other effects as well. Recent research has shown that having fertility plans put on hold is psychologically equivalent to a miscarriage, and this situation is exacerbated when there is no definitive date to resume.

Experts forecast that it's not unlikely that we will encounter other pandemics over the coming years or, at the very least, a series of local and global disasters!

Therefore, we have several recommendations that will benefit both LGBTQ families (and cis/het folks) facing infertility:

1. Access to fertility treatments should not be deemed nonessential, which would include addressing the problem of medical gatekeeping to ensure that treatment is accessible to all who desire it.

2. Federal guidelines for donor waiting periods should be significantly reduced or removed and replaced with informed consent risk awareness procedures.

3. Medical and insurance companies should redefine infertility to include all families who cannot conceive without medical assistance.

4. Federal aid should be provided to stem growing inequality caused by the pandemic.

My story has a happy ending, for which I'm deeply grateful, given the barriers that affect so many LGBTQ+ folks. During the height of the pandemic, my wife and I were privileged to fly to my home country of England. With the help of Steffan and his wife, Laura, we created our tiny human. Avril was born almost one year later in April 2021. ▄█

39

The Power of Queer

How "Guy Moms" Challenge Heteronormative Assumptions about Mothering and Family

Raine Dozier

When my daughter was younger, a friend of mine joked that she was going to nominate my YouTube channel for *Best YouTube Channel* in the Trans-Guys Community Awards. These awards are designed to honor excellence and achievement by transgender men on the internet.[1] She said she thought my channel showed the real life of a trans[2] person. Rather than detailing my transition journey (common on YouTube), my channel consists of my daughter's piano performances and some vacation videos.

Human beings are complex, and I am no exception. I have multiple identities—as a white sociologist who studies gender and inequality, a mother, a single parent, a queer butch, and a transgender person. My trans identity is relatively uncomplicated; internally, I feel like a man and don't identify with being a woman. Although I've had top surgery, I've never used hormones and am generally perceived as a masculine woman. Because not much research investigates social locations such as "guy mom," my position can offer insight into areas typically examined within a heterosexual framework, specifically gender and its relationship to mothering and the family. In this chapter, I combine some of my own vantage point with existing research on same-sex parenting and my own research on gender and gender diversity. Doing so highlights the opportunities that guy mom, like other gender-transgressive categories, brings to those who seek to understand and transform gendered family structures.

Much of the sociological research about gender focuses on what it means to be a man or woman in a particular society and how gender affects our interactions, position in the social structure, access to power, and life outcomes. This type of research often assumes that our sex (whether we are male or female), our gender identity (man/woman), our gender expression (masculine/feminine), and our sexual orientation (gay/lesbian or heterosexual) align in one expected configuration. In addition, it assumes that each of these categories is binary—you are either one or the other. A growing body of work considers gender within the context of marginalized identities such as transgender and other gender-diverse people and lesbian, gay, or queer[3] individuals.[4] Often the purpose of this work is to "trouble the waters," calling into question our assumptions about binary categories as natural, essential, and neatly aligned with one another. Whether focusing on typical or marginalized identities, examining gender in the context of social institutions like the family can help us see more clearly how gender is not biologically determined but socially constructed.

DOING GENDER

The concept of *doing gender* views gender as something created in interaction with others, and a performance for which we are all held accountable.[5] We learn to do gender in childhood but also learn, relearn, and revise how we do gender over time and depending on the social situation. For example, how a person expresses masculinity at five years old might be very different from their enactment at fifteen. In addition, how we do gender at work might differ depending on whether our job is in an office, on a construction site, or at a strip club. Our cultural and ethnic identities and other factors figure into these performances too. For example, what it means to do masculinity as an affluent Black teen will differ from masculinity as a rural, impoverished white teen. Also, these adolescent masculinities might differ based on gender—whether the teen enacting them is a boy or a girl.

In addition to our own performance of gender, others interpret our behaviors through the lens of gender. For example, if I am grocery shopping with a toddler and perceived as a woman, my behavior is relatively unremarkable. If I am perceived as a man, then my behavior is worth remarking on—and, in fact, people do. Gay fathers report that when out with their children, people often praise them for "giving mom the day off."[6] When men care for children, they are perceived as generous and remarkable, while women are expected to provide the same level of care as a matter of course. Tasks associated with maintaining the family are often gendered, making the family an important site for creating and sustaining both gender and gender inequality.

Parents do gender in a variety of ways, ranging from how they choose to dress their children to how they divide the work involved in running a household.

Although couples are becoming more egalitarian in the division of household labor, when they become parents, men and women in heterosexual relationships increasingly specialize, with women doing a disproportionate share of child care and housework.[8] Some people argue that this division of labor is natural, based on a mother's need to be at home with an infant due to the physical demands of breastfeeding and childbirth, yet the majority of mothers with infants work outside the home.[9] And mothers in heterosexual relationships who have infants still do the majority of the child care and housework—even when working full-time.[10]

Trying to decipher what is driven by physical necessity and what is doing gender can be difficult. Studies that look at the division of labor among lesbian and heterosexual parents find that lesbians have a more egalitarian distribution of household labor, even when one of them has physically given birth, implying that gendered ideas about family participation might contribute to inequality among heterosexual parents.[11]

In an effort to control for biological aspects of new parenting, one study investigated changes in the division of household labor among heterosexual and same-sex couples who recently adopted infants. Although no member of these couples was nursing or physically recovering from birth, the study still found inequality in child care and household tasks, especially among heterosexual couples. For all couples, the more the primary parent worked, the more equitable the distribution of child care, yet heterosexual couples had greater inequality in the division of household labor, including cleaning, cooking, doing laundry, washing dishes, and running errands. Among both same-sex and heterosexual couples, the parent who made more money (not worked more hours) was less likely to engage in housework relative to the primary parent, and this was especially true for heterosexual parents. Having economic power, then, means the primary earner is less obligated to do menial labor at home.[12] This study illustrates that the unequal division of labor in heterosexual families is not based on biology but on a combination of gendered behavioral expectations and privilege accorded to the person with the greatest economic power.

HETERONORMATIVE VIEWS OF FAMILY LIFE

Families are a significant site for the manufacture of heteronormative values and practices. Heteronormativity can be conceptualized as assumptions and practices grounded in the belief that heterosexuality is the norm and that an individual's sex, gender, sexual orientation, and gendered social positions align in expected ways. Heteronormativity asserts the primacy of certain lifestyles, such as the nuclear family (i.e., being heterosexually married with children) and delineates expectations about appropriately gendered behavior (e.g., women are responsible for the domestic sphere). A minority of families meet this dominant cultural value. For example, a significant number of people, especially people of color, live in extended families, some families have only one parent, and Black women have always been more likely than white women to work.[13] Due to economic shifts, a minority of families have a stay-at-home mom, and the number of households with children is declining.[14]

Heteronormativity is the cultural ideal that defines behavioral expectations and also organizes social, political, and economic structures. If the heteronormative family model includes a married, heterosexual couple with a stay-at-home mother, then even as structural realities change, women are still held accountable for this idealized norm. Despite remarkable growth in women's participation in the workforce, they still bear the brunt of what is termed the "second shift," doing the majority of household labor in addition to their paid work.[15]

Heteronormativity doesn't just influence the structure of heterosexual families; it can also affect same-sex and queer[16] families in a variety of ways, such as by excluding them from fully participating in everyday life and denying them legal rights. The legalization of same-sex marriage has improved the legal landscape for same-sex and queer families, yet it relies on a specific family form that approximates the heterosexual nuclear family. And even when a child has been born into a same-sex relationship, legal sources advise that the nonbiological parent adopt their own child to ensure legal rights.[17] However, legal rights don't always assure equity. In 2007, a lesbian mother spent her dying hours alone after collapsing from an aneurysm in Florida while on vacation. Even with legal documents, including adoption papers and a health care proxy, her children and partner of eighteen years were not allowed to be with her during her final hours. As the hospital social worker told her partner, "This is an anti-gay city and an anti-gay state, and you are not going to get to see her or know her condition."[18] Heteronormativity, then, organizes social life by creating norms and expectations about family structure and gendered behavior, and sanctioning individuals and families who do not comply.

QUEERING FAMILY AND MOTHERHOOD

Any aspect of social life that is gendered can be "queered" when people participate in gendered social positions in unexpected ways. Queering is "whatever is at odds with the normal, the legitimate, the dominant."[19] It involves a transgressive position or something that might destabilize accepted ideas about the way things work. Queering motherhood, then, describes any act of mothering that deconstructs norms around mothering. If we accept this definition, then single motherhood, mothering in extended families or transracial families, mother as primary earner, and many other types of mothering are queer. The danger of defining *queer* as generally at odds with the dominant form, though, is that it removes queer from the realm of sexual orientation and gender identity. Mothering as a gay, lesbian, bisexual/pansexual, queer, transgender, or nonbinary person is a particular position, at odds in a specific way with the heteronormative institution of motherhood and family. Queering motherhood can both illuminate and deconstruct what is assumed normal and natural in family life.

Families with same-sex parents challenge unexamined assumptions about mothering and families. They destabilize what is considered essential to create a family: biological features, one father, one mother, and the gendered division of labor. Some families with same-sex parents may have no interest in radicalizing the family structure; instead, they might aspire to marriage, the white picket fence, PTA meetings, and all the trappings of conventional family existence. Regardless of intention, though, having two mothers—or, in the case of gay men, having no mother at all—queers the family. Whether LGBTQ+ families seek to challenge heteronormative assumptions about the family as a deliberate political act or seek a relatively heteronormative lifestyle, they challenge accepted notions of family and motherhood simply by engaging in everyday family life. Mignon Moore writes of her experience carving out a place for her lesbian family in a Black Pentecostal church that is the center of her extended family's social life. She shows up in a space that opposes same-sex relationships with her gender-nonconforming partner and their children. She rejects the notion that participating in heteronormative or homophobic institutions is an attempt to conform, but instead views participation as "radical, even revolutionary behavior."[20]

When a parent edits a form that asks for the names of "Mother" and "Father," it is a small but deliberate act that makes visible unexamined notions about motherhood and family structure. The now numerous lesbian and gay parents who have had their children rejected from faith-based schools or prohibited from participating in Boy Scout activities have queered the family, drawing public attention both to heteronormative assumptions about family and to the marginalization of families outside the heteronormative form. These everyday acts of resistance can lead to political and social change.

For example, after an eight-year-old boy was rejected from a Catholic elementary school because of his lesbian mothers, the archdiocese of Boston clarified its policy. In response to public outcry, the new admissions policy states that Boston's parochial schools must not "discriminate against or exclude any categories of students."[21] In another case, a five-year-old recently adopted by a married lesbian couple was rejected from a Baptist school in Louisiana. Other faith-based schools took the opportunity to explicitly state their support for same-sex families and offer the kindergartener a seat at their school.[22] By engaging in everyday family life, same-sex couples with children challenge the heteronormative framework of major social institutions. Even the relatively conservative act of enrolling a child in a faith-based school or participating in a Pentecostal church can disrupt assumptions about parenting and generate a broader societal conversation about same-sex and queer families and inequality.

QUEERING FAMILY STRUCTURE

In addition to assumptions about the structure of families and the division of labor, heteronormativity also privileges biology—viewing "real" parents as those who have a biological connection to their children. Due to biology, queer family formation challenges the nuclear-normative family model. Because transgender people cannot procreate within the sex with which they identify and same-sex couples need a third party to procreate, reproduction in queer families often requires more than two people. Trans folks who procreate, with a trans woman providing sperm or a trans man gestating the pregnancy, trouble the relationship between gender and reproduction or mothering.

While heterosexual couples can decide whether and when to disclose that an egg or sperm donor was involved in their child's conception, same-sex couples do not have this choice—the lack of biological connection between family members is visible. As a result, families with same-sex parents must continually have discussions with individuals and systems about biology, legitimacy, and the definition of motherhood and family. Same-sex families are often called upon to explain their family configuration to strangers at the playground, in the doctor's office, to acquaintances who want details, and to family members who contest the legitimacy of nonbiological family connections.[23]

The relationship of a same-sex couple to an egg or sperm donor or a surrogate or birth mother can take many forms. When children have a significant relationship to a donor dad or a shared parenting arrangement with a biological parent who is not romantically involved with the same-sex couple, it demonstrates possibilities for family structure beyond the heteronormative model. It can also illuminate assumptions about biology, pregnancy, and motherhood. For example, if one person in a same-sex couple donates an egg and the other person carries and births the baby, who's the "real" mother? The biological mother is often referred to as the "real" mother in situations such as adoption, yet in the case of egg donation, the biological mother's claim is less certain.[24] In fact, fertility clinics often require the parent providing the egg to relinquish all parental rights before embryo transfer—even when they will be a parent to the resulting child.[25]

Some studies address the issue of legitimacy among female same-sex parents and illustrate the overreliance on biological ties to define families. Among lesbian couples, the nonbiological mother's role can be contested by relatives and devalued within institutions such as schools and health care settings.[26] Sometimes relatives seek to "heterosexualize" the family by treating the sperm donor as a more significant family member than the nonbiological mother. Often in public and social situations, people attempt to ascertain who the "real" mother is through intrusive questioning.[27] Although these situations can be uncomfortable, frustrating, and demeaning for same-sex parents, they can destabilize a basic tenet of heteronormative family structures—the biological basis of kinship and the gendered family structure.

Lesbian and gay individuals have a long history of creating "chosen families" (see Chapter 40 by Whalley). As people who historically faced family and community rejection, lesbian and gay individuals developed strong family relationships with people unrelated by biological or legal ties.[28] A de-emphasis on biology and a privileging of social connection may make same-sex couples an especially good fit for foster and adoptive parenting. Same-sex couples are more likely to adopt, and to adopt transracially, relative to heterosexual couples.[29] Perhaps the inability to base a family on biological connection encourages other obvious disruptions of biology like transracial adoption. Research also suggests that an increasing number of queer people practice polyamory; that is, they have more than one romantic or sexual relationship.[30] This can expand the family to incorporate other significant adults such as more than one partner and metamours (partners of partners) as well as the children of parents' partners and metamours.

Because same-sex and queer families are more likely to have atypical configurations—often with important adults beyond the two-parent norm and family members who are not related biologically—they queer notions of family when engaging in everyday activities. When queer family configurations interact with institutions like schools, health care organizations, and the legal system, they draw attention to unexamined beliefs about families and mothering, including their biological basis and the essential nature of the gendered division of labor. For example, when schools call parents who help in the classroom "room moms," gay father volunteers illuminate gendered assumptions about who helps children.[31] When a female parent is called "Dad" by her child, schools must re-examine their tradition of "moms' night" and "dads' night" if they want to be inclusive. And forms and policies become problematic when children have a third parent figure who is significantly involved in schooling. Whether they want to assimilate or not, a queered family configuration does not fit into hetero-normative boxes on forms or within social institutions and exposes unexamined assumptions about gender and families.

THE POLITICS OF SAMENESS

Because same-sex parents are more vulnerable to legal challenges to their parent-hood, there has been a heavy investment in showing that they do not differ from heterosexual parents. Families that include one mother, one father, and their biological children are assumed to be the "gold standard"[32] to which same-sex families must measure up. Multiple studies, particularly of lesbian mothers, find few differences between children of same-sex parents and children of different-sex parents in their mental health, school outcomes, sexual behavior, substance abuse, peer victimization, or family relationships.[33]

Unfortunately, the investment in asserting sameness has made it difficult to investigate potentially meaningful differences in LGBTQ+ parents and their children. Overall, evidence suggests that families headed by same-sex parents[34] have unique strengths. Several studies find they have greater parental investment in child-rearing and fewer parenting disagreements with their co-parent.[35] Chil-dren adopted by lesbian and gay parents perceive themselves to be more accept-ing and compassionate toward others.[36] Lesbian mothers are more likely to foster connected, open relationships with their children and to seek to instill pro-social, egalitarian behaviors in their children. In addition, their children display fewer gender-typical behaviors.[37] Finally, adolescents of planned lesbian families have greater social and academic competence, fewer social problems and external-izing behaviors, and a greater sense of connection to people at school relative to their counterparts with heterosexual parents.[38]

Because previous research has been used to discriminate against same-sex parents, it creates pressure to focus on similarities and minimize differences in lifestyle, family structure, and outcomes in new studies. As a result, it is difficult to know what interesting differences researchers might find if they did not have to consider the safety of same-sex and queer families. For example, there is little research regarding gender expression—that is, masculinity and femininity—in same-sex relationships and its influence on mothering and families. In addition, few studies explore transgender parents and potential differences in their parent-ing styles or children's outcomes, especially in socioemotional functioning and justice-related values.

The need to measure up to heteronormative standards can create pressure for same-sex parents to be accountable for their children's gender performance, sexual orientation, and general functioning. Historically, lesbian and gay parents have been viewed as a threat to their children's heterosexual orientation, and a significant focus of research has addressed the sexual orientation of their children. This scrutiny can make LGBTQ+ parents feel extra pressure to raise children who are "perfectly normal," especially in gender expression.[39] One gay father reported,

> We make sure our girls' hair is done nice. We put them in dresses or nice dress shoes. Especially with the girls. I make sure that they see that a father can do the "mom thing" and dress their kids up. . . . I paint their fingernails.[40]

The "mom thing," then, includes socializing children into the gender binary, and same-sex parents are especially held accountable for their children's gender expression. When parents or children hold multiple marginalized statuses, the pressure to conform can be even greater due to the surveillance faced by many marginalized groups.[41] For example, a queer Latina mom faced significant backlash on social media when she posted a photo of her two-month-old son wearing a ribbon with a glitter-covered flower in his hair. Even with pushback, Nydia Pabón-Colón remains committed to "mothering queerly" and sees her feminist, queer Latina knowledge as holding "revolutionary, 'world-making' powers."[42]

The tenuous social position of same-sex and queer-headed families can create the pressure to conform—in family structure and gendered behavior. It also encourages researchers to focus on similarities between same-sex and different-sex parents and families. Generally, research addresses whether same-sex and queer families "measure up" to heterosexual families, even though evidence suggests that children of lesbian and gay parents may have more positive outcomes in some areas. There is little pressure for heterosexual parents to measure up to same-sex parents in these areas.

HOMONORMATIVITY: THE NEW NORMAL?

As same-sex couples and families become more visible and gain access to rights and privileges such as marriage, they may experience greater acceptance. Gaining social acceptance, however, increases the pressure to assimilate to heteronormative practices and structures. *Homonormativity* refers to societal acceptance of gays and lesbians based on their ability to express heteronormative values and behaviors.[43] Gays and lesbians are legitimized and included as long as they are "gender conventional, as long as we link sex to love and marriage-like relationship, as long as we defend family values, personify economic individualism, and display national pride."[44]

The strategy of emphasizing sameness, that "love is love," has been successful in securing legislative victories; however, homonormativity also creates a hierarchy of sexual orientation and gender expression. The "new normal" is affluent, monogamous, and conventional in every way except for sexual orientation. The closer a couple and family resemble a heteronormative family, the greater they are valued. For example, gay men who are not feminine, mothers who are not masculine, parents who are not poor, and families with two (and only two) significant, married adults will reap social and legal rewards. As privileges and social acceptance become available to same-sex families, socioeconomic status, immigration status, race/ethnicity, and gender identity and expression influence who gains privileges and who does not, similar to other sites of social inequality.

TRANSGRESSIVE MOTHERING

Some families and mothers hold a more radical conception of gender, sexual orientation, and family, either as a conscious political act or because they are far from "the new normal." Their masculinity, femininity, gender identity, or relationship configuration does not align with hetero- or homonormative standards. Their inability to assimilate queers their interactions with the social institutions of mothering and the family. Surprisingly, there is little research engaging these individuals and families.

One important aspect of queering is its focus on expressions of gender, sexual behavior, or identities at the margins—in this case, parents who do not neatly align with the categories of binary sex, gender, and sexual orientation or the heteronormative goal of monogamous marriage. When considering mothering and families, queer positions are rarely represented in research, yet they have much to offer our understanding. Looking at motherhood and families through a queer lens is useful not just in thinking about same-sex parents but in examining accepted notions of how we do the work of mothering in families. My social position as a "guy mom"—a masculine (or butch), trans-identified mother—queers the concepts of mothering, nurturing, families, and the "natural" division of labor. Because of this, I would like to share some thoughts derived from my experiences.

As a guy mom, I believe my participation in everyday mothering queers notions of gender, motherhood, and the family. When I wake up in the morning, put on men's clothing, then rush around preparing breakfast and making a school lunch, it's queer. Lucal suggests that gender-nonconforming individuals who position themselves in gender-typical situations challenge the gender binary by their very existence.[45] In her case, she is referring to public bathrooms and whether, as a gender-nonconforming person, the act of using the women's bathroom challenges the gender order. In my case, I am referring to the institution of motherhood and whether simply participating in it as a masculine female disrupts the sex/gender binary.

When I walk into the mother-dominated PTA meeting with a tray of brownies, it illuminates assumptions about both masculinity and femininity. I do not identify as a woman: I appear masculine, yet I am existing in space created and occupied by women. When I explain that I am not in the wrong bathroom to other mothers at the middle school, it dislocates their assumptions about the natural and normal alignment of sex, gender, and mothering. I visibly don't look feminine, yet I am doing women's work. My inability to conform to the gender binary creates constant "gender trouble" for individuals interacting with me, especially in sites dominated by mothers and focused on children.

Gay men are in a similar situation. Their mere presence in everyday parenting life challenges heteronormative beliefs regarding gender, sexual orientation, and the "natural" gender order of the family. Consider the meaning of the expression "fathering a child."[46] Gay fathers are doing far more than fathering children (and in fact they may not have fathered their children at all); instead, their everyday parenting activities look very much like mothering. In one study, more than half of gay male parents "considered themselves mothers and were comfortable accepting the title"[47] not because they felt like women, but because their social position most closely resembled that of a mother.

When a gender-atypical person does mothering, everyday actions in public space require re-examination of commonly held notions about gender, biology, and mothering. In one blog, the author recounted her observations of her genderqueer partner in the public pool with their son.[48] The juxtaposition of a genderqueer person, shirtless with a surgically modified chest, being called "Mommy" and playing rough-and-tumble games with children disrupts unexamined beliefs about sex, gender, and who can participate in the binary that includes "mother" and "father." In another post, the genderqueer partner explained:

> "Mommy" is the word I used as a kid to describe the person who could take all the pain away or support me when I needed it. . . . So when our son . . . was born, I chose "Mommy" as a name because I loved the idea of being that force for someone in this crazy world of ours. . . . I love to hear the word "mommy" and to be called "mom" sometimes. But that has no real bearing as to how I feel in my body.[49]

Interacting with mothers who are not clearly women (or in the case of gay men, not women at all) calls for a radical reconsideration of gender and the family, including the division of labor and the "natural" ability of women to mother as well as broader assumptions about sex, gender, and the organization of social life.

Trans, nonbinary, and masculine mothers disrupt the idea that femininity and motherhood naturally align and that women, particularly feminine women, are uniquely qualified to engage in mothering. My particular case also challenges the reliance on femininity or womanliness as a signal for reproductive ability. I've been asked repeatedly who my children's birth mother is or when I adopted because of the persistent association of gender expression (masculinity and femininity) with sex and reproductive capability. In another example, a trans man I interviewed for a study gave birth to a baby. The social impossibility of this meant that no one saw past his facial hair to interpret his body as pregnant. He explained, "When you have facial hair you can pass regardless of what your body looks like. I mean, I was nine months pregnant walking around and people were like, 'Ooh, that guy's fat.'"[50]

These examples illustrate that masculine appearance coupled with mothering disrupts the association of reproduction, mothering, and femininity. On a broader level, it illuminates the fallacy of gender. Although gender is socially constructed, people often rely on biology to explain why men and women behave in particular ways. Masculine female, gay male, lesbian dad, and trans parents challenge biological explanations for the ability to mother and, more broadly, the essential nature of gender.

GUY MOMS, GENDER, AND SINGLE MOTHERHOOD

In my previous research with trans men, I asserted that gender was a balance of perceived sex (whether you are perceived as male or female) and masculine and feminine behaviors.[51] I have come to realize that my conceptualization of gender as composed of behavior and appearance was not completely accurate. It misses a crucial aspect of gender—our various social positions. Social position refers to the statuses one has in relation to individuals and institutions such as employers, family, school, or the legal system. My social position as a mother has affected my personal life far more than my gender identity or expression. Gendered social positions—social positions generally ascribed to one sex—inescapably influence our lives. When a social position is highly correlated with being male or female, social policy, laws, and culture develop in response and can result in structural inequality.

"Mother" and "single mother" are specific social locations; the words evoke particular expected behaviors in families as well as in interactions with social institutions such as schools, the labor market, and the legal system. The physical and economic constraints of single parenthood and the legal status of a primary parent with fewer assets is a uniquely gendered situation. Single parenthood is generally women's work and comes with the attendant hazards of poverty, legal troubles, and strained resources as the crises and costs of parenting fall disproportionately on one set of shoulders. The gendered social position "single mother" affects individuals not because they are feminine or identify as women but because there are gender differences in access to power and resources.[52]

I identify as transgender in the most stereotypical of ways: I feel like a man and don't relate to being a woman at all. Yet even with this relatively black-and-white conception of gender identity, I do not think of myself as a father, but rather as a mother within the context of particular political, social, and legal systems. For example, as a single parent with a young child, I was embroiled in a legal dispute over child support. These disputes are commonplace; whether the noncustodial parent is a man or a woman, masculine or feminine, influences the predicament less than the socio-structural position of the custodial parent, commonly described as "single mother." Regardless of gender identity, then, as a primary parent and a single parent, I find myself strongly allied with the plight of mothers, a distinctly *female* social position associated with less power in many major social institutions, including the family, the economy, and the legal system. I proudly claim the identity of "single mother" and all that entails in resources, time use, legal history, oppression, resistance, and life chances while retaining my masculine and male gender identity. Surely, this is queering motherhood.

QUEERING CHILDHOOD—UNEXAMINED POSSIBILITIES

Research suggests that children raised by lesbian mothers differ in small but meaningful ways regarding gender; for example, the children make fewer gendered toy choices and boys raised by lesbian mothers are more empathetic. But it is difficult to know what effects radical departures from heteronormative attitudes and structures might have. Based on my own observations, I would like to suggest a few areas for consideration that could be better understood with additional research.

The Necessity of Gender Role Models

A common concern raised by relatives, strangers, and sometimes same-sex parents themselves is whether a child can have healthy development without a male role model and, in the case of gay male parents, a female role model. Some claim this fixation on a male role model for children in lesbian-headed families "seems to suggest that any model of maleness is preferable to none."[53] It is widely believed that male and female role models are necessary to socialize children into gender. The fear appears to be that without a male role model, boys won't grow into "real men." Evidence suggests this may be true to a certain extent; boys raised by lesbians are more empathetic, are more open to difference, and value egalitarian relationships.[54] Are these differences we would like to inhibit or foster in boys and men? If we identify them as strengths, perhaps researchers could investigate how these characteristics are developed and try to replicate them in boys from heterosexual families.

The definition of a desirable male role model can vary based on culture, subculture, and personal values. For example, in one study, Swedish lesbian couples articulated a very different view of male role models when describing their process for choosing a sperm donor (donors are often involved in parenting in Sweden). The couples viewed gay men as healthier role models because they challenge stereotypical notions regarding manhood and masculinity. As a result, lesbian parents believed gay donor dads would be less likely to engage in sexist behavior, providing a positive male role model for children.[55]

The oft-voiced concern that children need both male and female role models within the family also implies that children do not foster meaningful relationships outside the family, ignoring children's significant involvement in schools and communities. When my daughter was a tween, an acquaintance learned she didn't have a father and said reassuringly, "Well, I'm sure you have male role models though." Confused, she quietly replied, "Not really." Later, as she was thinking over the incident, she quipped, "I should have told him, 'Sure I have male role models—Strangely (a not typically masculine circus performer), Gabe (a young trans guy), and my mom!'"

If I am responsible for doing "guy things" with the children—going to stock car races, showing them how to put brakes on the car, and playing football—am I an adequate male role model? What about a man who shows my daughter how to knit and apply makeup—is he a male role model because he is biologically male? Although the unspoken assumption is that a male or female role model will teach a child how to grow up appropriately gendered, it is unclear what they must do to assure this.

The Lie of Gender Differentiation

Parents often seek role models for their children in the belief that behavior observed by children can influence future behavior and development. Certainly, childhood experiences can influence adult outcomes. For example, while the unequal division of household labor in heterosexual couples endures, there is evidence that viewing a different model in childhood can have lasting effects. Research finds that men whose parents had a more equitable distribution of household tasks or had working mothers spent more time on housework as adults relative to other men.[56] This implies that early experiences with more equitable expressions of gender may have long-lasting effects on behavior and will reduce gender inequality. In addition, perhaps childhood exposure to masculinity and femininity that is decoupled from sex and gender identity could result in adults with more diverse sets of behaviors and altered worldviews. I recall an incident when my child was a preschooler that illustrates how children might grapple with the complexities of gender at a young age. They (they are nonbinary) were amused that I was wearing their sister's flowery flip-flops. "Look, George," they exclaimed to a neighbor, "my mom looks like a drag queen!" In this case they recognized there were gender differences, yet they were complex and unassociated with sex—a feminine person could include both their sister and a drag queen, but not their mother. As they have grown up with exposure to trans and gender-diverse people, they've learned both that gender is not binary and that appearance is not congruent with identity, sex, or social position. This consistent exposure to queering sex and gender has left them with a less gendered framework relative to females raised in heteronormative family structures and offers more possibilities regarding their identit(ies) and lifestyle.

When one is speculating about the effects of queering motherhood, the little evidence available suggests that explicitly discussing gender and inequality (which is more likely in same-sex families) may result in children who are more aware of gendered scripts and feel less accountable to gender. Men and women who grew up with lesbian and gay parents report more diverse, less gender-typical interests, which they attribute to their upbringing.[57] In my personal experience, this leads to an ongoing awareness that gendered behaviors and social roles are optional, not inevitable. My daughter, who grew up in the 1990s, reflected,

> When I went through puberty, I remember being really conscious that shaving your legs was a choice and that other girls didn't feel this way. I chose not to shave my legs. There are many things like that that have come up over the years—where I realized I had a choice to do or not to do something. It wasn't as automatic.

Although there is risk in drawing conclusions from personal experience, the lack of research calls for some initial thoughts about the possible effects of radical departures from hetero- or homonormative parenting. Clearly, this is an area that calls for further investigation, both in how families who exist outside sexual orientation and gender norms differ in their child-rearing and what enduring differences might result in their children.

Conclusion

While theoretical discussions help advance our understanding of both gender and family, it is important to note that queer motherhood, lesbian motherhood, and heterosexual motherhood look fairly similar in everyday life. The majority of mothering involves basic tasks such as supervising homework, transporting children, cooking, and cleaning; our social identities often do not come into play. As I'm fond of saying, "It doesn't matter whether I feel like a man changing diapers or a woman changing diapers—I'm still changing diapers!" Although gender identity may not affect the daily process of many mothering tasks, it does influence who does them, how they are interpreted, and the value placed on them by society. For this reason, upending expected gendered behaviors and family structures allows individuals and institutions to reexamine heteronormative systems that perpetuate gender inequality.

Notes

1.   "Trans Guys of the Year," TransGuys.com, retrieved May 10, 2013, web.archive.org /web/20130328234929/http://transguys.com/features/transguys-of-the-year.

2.   *Trans* is an umbrella term that can include individuals with a variety of identities. I am using the term to describe individuals who do not solely identify with the gender (man/ woman) associated with the sex (male/female) assigned to them at birth. They may or may not take hormones, have surgeries, or be socially recognized as the gender with which they identify. In this article, I use *trans* to include transgender, nonbinary, and other gender-diverse individuals.

3.   *Queer* is a term for people who do not identify as heterosexual and/or see themselves as living outside the confines of traditional notions of sexual orientation and/or gender. The term has been popularized because the growing diversity in gender identity and expression makes it more challenging to discuss sexual orientation in traditional terms (*gay, straight, bi*) because they rely on a gender binary.

4.   Anderson (2020); Dozier (2005); Lampe, Carter, and Sumerau (2019).

5.   West and Zimmerman (1987).

6.   Carroll (2018). 3421.

7.   To avoid confusion for the reader, I am choosing to primarily use the term *heterosexual couples* rather than *different-sex couples*. However, it is important to note that not all individuals in different-sex couples are heterosexual; one or both of the members could identify as bisexual, queer, or pansexual. This also applies to my usage of the terms *lesbian* and *gay* in this chapter.

8.   Baxter, Hewitt, and Haynes (2008); Ciciolla and Luthar (2019); Kluwer, Heesink, and van de Vliert (2002).

9. National Women's Law Center (2017).

10. Ascigil, Wardecker, Chopik, and Edelstein (2021); Bartley, Blanton, and Gilliard (2005); Bianchi and Milkie (2010); Ciciolla and Luthar (2019).

11. Bartley, Blanton, and Gilliard (2005); Bianchi and Milkie (2010).

12. Goldberg, Smith, and Perry-Jenkins (2012).

13. Banks (2019); Kramer (2019); Zonta (2016).

14. Sullivan (2020); VanOrman and Jacobsen (2020).

15. Carlson, Petts, and Pepin (2022); Hochschild and Machung (2003).

16. I'm using *same-sex* and *queer* here because not all parents neatly align with the gender/sex binary. *Queer* also includes families with parents who are transgender or gender-nonconforming.

17. National Center for Lesbian Rights (2019).

18. James (2009), para. 7.

19. Halperin (1995), 62.

20. Moore (2019), 77.

21. Wangsness (2011), para 1.

22. Hudson (2022).

23. Haines et al. (2018); Kelsall-Knight and Sudron (2020); McInerney, Creaner, and Nixon (2021).

24. Epstein (2018); Grant (2009); McInerney, Creaner, and Nixon (2021).

25. Epstein (2018).

26. Kelsall-Knight and Sudron (2020); McInerney, Creaner, and Nixon (2021).

27. Haines et al. (2018); O'Neill, Hamer, and Dixon (2012); Radis and Nadan (2021).

28. Dempsey (2010); Weston (1997).

29. Goldberg et al. (2018); Lev (2010).

30. Pain (2020); Pallotta-Chiarolli, Sheff, and Mountford (2020).

31. Goldberg, Allen, and Carroll (2020).

32. Stacey and Biblarz (2001), 162.

33. Bos, van Balen, and van den Boom (2007); Mazrekaj, De Witte, and Cabus (2020); Reczek, et al. (2017); Wainright and Patterson (2006).

34. Most research on LGBTQ families has focused on lesbian-headed households because, historically, they have been more common than families headed by gay men.

35. Biblarz and Stacey (2010); Chan et al. (1998); Gartrell and Bos (2010); Johnson (2012); Mazrekaj, De Witte, and Cabus (2020); Vanfraussen, Ponjaert-Kristofferson, and Brewaeys (2002).

36. Cody et al. (2017).

37. Averett (2016); Goldberg and Garcia (2016); Johnson and O'Connor (2002).

38. Gartrell and Bos (2010); Prickett, Martin-Storey, and Crosnoe (2015).

39. Averett (2016); Bergstrom-Lynch (2020); Cody et al. (2017); Gartrell and Bos (2010); Johnson (2012).
40. Giesler (2012), 130.
41. Baughman et al. (2021).
42. Nydia Pabón-Colón (2017), 73.
43. Duggan (2002).
44. Seidman (2002), 189.
45. Lucal (1999).
46. Fathering a child means impregnating a woman.
47. Brinamen (2000), 67.
48. Schilt (2012).
49. Schilt (2009), para. 4.
50. Dozier (2005), 305.
51. Dozier (2005).
52. Elizabeth, Gavey, and Tolmie (2012); Waller (2020).
53. Saffron (1996), 186.
54. Cody et al. (2017); Goldberg (2007); Johnson (2012); Lev (2010).
55. Ryan-Flood (2005).
56. Cordero-Coma and Esping-Andersen (2018); Gupta (2006); McGinn, Castro, and Lingo (2018).
57. Goldberg (2007); Goldberg, Kashy, and Smith (2012); Tasker and Golombok (1997).

In Other Words

NOT JUST KID STUFF: BECOMING GENDERED

Heidi M. Gansen and Karin A. Mart n, August 7, 2018 / CCF

Children are gendered by parents before the children are borr. What does that mean? As soon as parents know if "it's a boy!" or "it's a girl!" they start to imag ne different children and childhoods. From birth, children are treated differently by gender and learn to "do" their gender from families, peers, school, and media. Par- ents and families buy different clothes and toys for boys and girls and decorate their rooms differently. Observers ascribe different traits (for example, toughness and bravery) to a baby who is assumed to be a boy (even if it's not) than to a baby perceived to be a girl.

We Don't Even Know We Are Doing This

Things we do not think of as constructing gender differences do, as we write in "Becoming Gendered" in the *Handbook of the Sociology of Gender*. For example, preschools are heightened incubators of gender difference. Preschool teachers have differential responses to boys' and girls' behaviors, such as permitting informal behaviors for boys (lying down during circle time and being loud) and requiring more formal school behaviors for girls (using indoor voices and sitting up straight).

Except When We Do

In some preschools, the curriculum is explicitly gendered. Beginning in preschool, some teachers see instructing children about their gender's behavioral expecta- tions or responsibilities as an explicit component of their curriculum and teaching practices. Gansen interviewed and observed teachers in three preschools (nine preschool classrooms total). She found that teachers in the three preschools disci- plined boys and girls differently and created gendered stories to account for and justify their gendered beliefs, expectations, and disciplinary practices.

For example, in all three preschools that Gansen observed, when girls were not following a teacher's instructions to clean up, girls were disciplined by having to clean up an area by themselves. In one classroom, if there was nothing left for girls to clean up, teachers would have a child or teacher dump a container of toys on the floor. These dumped-out toys were then the girls' "responsibility" to clear up on their own. However, in none of the nine classrooms that Gansen observed did teachers discipline boys by having them clean up without assistance from their peers or a teacher. Instead, teachers in these nine classrooms frequently asked other children (almost always girls) to help boys clean up.

In another classroom, the teachers had boys do push-ups when they were physically fighting or being aggressive with their classmates. The teacher would ask the boys involved to take a break, come to the middle of the classroom, and do five push-ups. This teacher held gendered expectations for children's behavior. She viewed boys as having physical energy they needed to release, and she implemented a gendered disciplinary practice (push-ups) to accommodate what she perceived as a behavioral "need" for preschool-aged boys. By contrast, in all nine classrooms, teachers immediately sent girls to timeout or moved them to a different play activity when they engaged in physical behaviors.

Freeing Children from Boy versus Girl Discipline Creates Stronger Individuals

Beginning in preschool, disciplinary interactions between teachers and students guide the construction of gender difference in young children. Gendered expectations and differential treatment of children at the young ages of three to five years old create and maintain gender inequality by constructing gender differences as natural, normal, and unchangeable. Perhaps if we change our gendered expectations and disciplinary responses to boys' and girls' behaviors in various contexts, such as at home and in school, we will open the door for children's identities to be shaped in more individualized, and less gendered, ways. ▄

40

Queering Family Sexual Violence

Elizabeth Whalley

I n 2019, Hollywood director Bryan Singer agreed to pay $150,000 to resolve a lawsuit filed in 2017 that asserted he raped Cesar Sanchez-Guzman, a then-seventeen-year-old boy, in 2003. Singer, who identifies as bisexual, leveraged his industry connections during their interaction. Sanchez-Guzman explained his decision not to report the assault to the authorities as due to a fear of being outed as gay: although he had come out to his close friends, he had not yet disclosed his sexuality to his family. Sanchez-Guzman told a close friend about the assault but not his family or the police. His strict Pentecostal family had previously sent him to a gay conversion camp, and he believed that by reporting Singer to formal authorities, his family would have learned that he was gay. Sanchez-Guzman explained, "That was not an option. . . . I knew if I did, the consequences would be worse for me" (Garcia-Roberts 2017). What can we learn about families from this example of sexual violence? What can we learn about sexual violence from this example of family?

The perpetration of family sexual violence is conventionally defined within two categories of abuse, demarcated by the age of the victim: intrafamilial child sexual abuse (CSA) and marital rape. This understanding of family violence relies on an understanding of family based in genetic and institutional markers that uphold the power of the state (through the institution of marriage or legal adoption) and biological essentialism.[1] Analyzing Sanchez-Guzman's experience from a conventional family perspective would be limited to a discussion of homophobia within his biological family and his nondisclosure of the assault to them. This restricted understanding of family causes queer sexual violence, such as that experienced by Sanchez-Guzman, to be labeled as occurring outside his family rather than an issue of sexual violence within the family of the LGBTQ community. If family sexual violence is distinguished from other types of sexual violence by the betrayal of trust and safety, how do the limitations placed on the understanding of family restrict our understanding of the harm of sexual violence?

Further, much of sexual violence research would likely categorize Sanchez-Guzman as having disclosed to his friends but not his *family*. Yet for LGBTQ people, close queer friends are often their chosen kinship-based family. The erasure of the familial nature of these dynamics flattens our understanding of the harm of familial sexual violence and reflects the need for discussions of sexual violence within families to be expanded to include kinship and queer community-based families.

The dynamics at play within instances of sexual violence can be expanded by queering our approach to family sexual violence.[2] This chapter proposes the understanding of family sexual violence be queer(ed) in two ways: (1) by expanding the definition of family to include the queer community and chosen families that LGBTQ people historically and currently inhabit and (2) by constructing an understanding of power within sexual violence that is structural rather than tied to binary sex and gender categories. What happens to sexual violence when the victim and perpetrator share a chosen or community-identified family? How does a queered understanding of family inform our larger understanding of how sexual violence occurs within families and is responded to? What can be learned about the different types of betrayal, harm, and healing within family sexual violence when the definitions of both family and sexual violence are queered?

This chapter has four parts. First, to introduce you to the approach of *queering*, the chapter queers the understanding of family. In particular, we examine the history and meaning of family within LGBTQ communities. Second, we queer sexual violence by disrupting traditional understandings of gender, power, and family sexual violence. Third, we turn to research on the occurrence of and responses to sexual violence within an expanded understanding of families and structural power. Fourth, the chapter concludes by offering solutions, laying out a transformative roadmap to address the harm of sexual violence in our communities.

To queer a subject is to question *hegemonic* (dominant and inescapable) forms of knowing and understanding our social world. In this chapter, queering is accomplished in two ways: (1) by highlighting the impact of including LGBTQ and nonnormative sexualities and genders in family sexual violence, where such identities are often erased, and (2) by challenging the assumptions and constructions of power used in normative language, institutions, behavior, and culture at large (Ball 2014). In the case of much existing family and sexual violence scholarship, queering foregrounds the frequent reliance on heteronormative conceptualizations of family based in biological and matrimonial connections and widens the field. (For more on queering, see Chapter 34 by Guadalupe-Diaz.)

Much scholarship has traced the evolution of the definition of family over time and across cultures. While definitions of family vary wildly based on historical and geographic locations, nearly every society uses its localized definition of family to justify the distribution and restriction of rights, privileges, and requirements to groups of individuals (Coontz 2015). These classifications normalize the hegemonic definitions of family that serve the powerful while solidifying understandings of family that often sustain the power of the state and entrench racial, class, citizenship, and sexual hierarchies. Throughout this volume, authors use different approaches to challenge some common conceptualizations of family, with an aim at seeing families as they really are. This chapter uses another approach to contest the traditional understandings of family, using the interconnection of queerness and community.

TRADITIONAL DEFINITIONS OF U.S. FAMILIES

In the United States, the mainstream and legal definitions of family require establishment through biological and matrimonial codifications—blood and marriage. This is most obvious within the heteronormative ideal of the nuclear family, a heterosexual marriage resulting in biologically related children (Dozier 2015). As a reflection of this cultural understanding, much mainstream family literature operates within this limited heteronormative approach to families. As a result, cultural, policy, and academic debates around matters of the family are centralized around topics such as divorce, parenthood, marriage, and birth rates (Cowan and Cowan 2015). The connections between legal understandings of marriage and heterosexist understandings of family are often explicit, as seen in the focus on same-sex parental ability in discussions of the legality of same-sex marriage in *Obergefell v. Hodges* (Fish and Russell 2018), the U.S. Supreme Court decision that made same-sex marriage available in all U.S. states. Allegiance to government documents in family establishment, such as birth certificates and marriage licenses, also latently reinforces the state as the natural and inevitable arbiter of individuals' relationships. These heteronormative parameters reaffirm heterosexuality and patriarchal power; they also naturalize cultural values of objectivity and biological essentialism.

Progressive, deconstructed definitions of family move away from normative conceptions only to then focus on using that new definition to expand state recognition of different forms of families (see Struening 2015). Implicit in such goals is the assumption that the state serves a protective purpose and that legalization of families can provide equal protection to all. But does it? There remains a need to queer the understanding of the family and the functions of state power while expanding the definition of care and community that human beings provide for one another.

QUEERING FAMILY—WELCOME TO THE (CHOSEN) FAMILY

In this chapter, queering family takes two forms: (1) folding the concept of chosen family or "family-of-choice" networks into definitions of family and (2) considering how the queer community functions as a community-level family. This analysis offers a more nuanced understanding of all families, as queering traditional approaches to families "allows prevailing notions of 'the family' to be deconstructed and illuminates diversity amongst queer and all families" (Fish and Russell 2018, p. 3). In this way, the process of queering expands the understanding of not just LGBTQ families and communities but *all* family structures and arrangements.

"Is she family?" is a common phrase within queer vernacular and is used by LGBTQ-identifying individuals to discuss if someone belongs to the larger LGBTQ community. This expression is also reflective of the belief that the queer community is a type of family at large that expansively includes even fellow queers who do not know each other personally. Many LGBTQ people identify their families as including kinship groups that are more closely defined by strength of friendship than by biological or legal certification. Despite this, the fields of sexual violence and family research both often conduct research at the individual and group level rather than the community level. Cowan and Cowan (2015) problematized normative understandings of family, writing, "What is left out of too many contemporary family policy discussions is a concern with family process—the quality of patterns of interactions among family members" (359). A queered understanding of family allows for the interpersonal connections, such as the strength of emotional support, within a family to be centered.

Nonbiological and extralegal conceptions of families are not novel: from the Middle Ages through the eighteenth century, *family* was commonly understood as referring to larger kinship groups sharing a residence in a household. It was only in the mid-nineteenth century that the word *family* took on the more familiar understanding seen today, meaning a married couple with their children (Coontz 2015).

LGBTQ communities have used familial language to distinguish kinship ties for over a century. In his historical analysis of gay men's culture in New York, Chauncey (1994) observed the use of terms such as *auntie* and *sister* in reference to close friends as early as the 1920s. Beginning in Harlem in the 1950s, Black and Latinx queer Ballroom culture was seen as forming much of the basis for queer family structure. This is most famously chronicled in the 1990 documentary film *Paris Is Burning*. A major tenet of the Ballroom or house culture is the founding of family-like structures, called houses, where house mothers and fathers provide support for their children through social supports, friendship networks, and expansive expression of genders and sexualities (Arnold and Bailey 2009). These houses formed in response to rejection and marginalization from their families of origin, communities, and society at large. Rather than accepting the normative definitions of family, in these spaces "the concepts of home and family are redrawn to meet the needs of its members . . . constructing both homes and families for themselves" (Arnold and Bailey 2009, p. 3). In this way, queer definitions of family do not only expand to include LGBTQ community but also re-create formulations of family that operate entirely outside of state conceptualizations.

While founded in Black and Latinx Harlem, these kinship families have evolved to encompass many members of the LGBTQ community. The phrase "chosen family" first emerged within Kath Weston's *Families We Choose* (1991) to describe the ways that fictive kin were legible as actual family ties. In a study of friendship structures, De Vries and Megathlin (2009) found that gay men and lesbians were more likely than heterosexual individuals to include cognitive (loyalty, trust) and affective (care, compatibility) processes in their discussions of kinship. The creation of kinship-formed families often, but not always, emerged in response to LGBTQ members' rejection from their families of origin. However, family rejection is not a prerequisite for the formation of a chosen family; often individuals who form chosen families retain connections to their families of origin. These kinship structures have been said to help individuals manage racism, heterosexism, and transphobia from the outside world (Allen and Mendez 2018).

Indeed, this approach is queer family theory. Queer family theory has tackled the use of traditional family definitions in scholarship. Using this approach, scholars define family "through social interaction rather than solely by legal or consanguineous relationships" (Allen and Mendez 2018, p. 71) and "by intentionality, identity, and community connection rather than biological relation" (Hammack, Frost, and Hughes 2019, p. 60). Now that we've updated our definitions of family, we can apply this queered definition of family to family sexual violence.

The Cultural Discovery of Family Sexual Violence

The process of "queering" sexual violence requires more than just including queer communities, families, and individuals in scholarship. Our understanding of sexual violence must also be deconstructed to "queer our understandings of violence itself" (Ball 2014, p. 4). Queering sexual violence allows for the examination of the central role of power structures in all forms of sexual violence. How did understandings of sexual violence and power develop? How can they evolve to be more inclusive?

Feminist power analysis in sexual violence scholarship emerged in the 1970s from the white feminist movement commonly known as second-wave feminism. Within this social movement, power was understood as centrally rooted within patriarchy, which was seen as the root cause of violence against all ciswomen (Guadalupe-Diaz and Whalley 2022). This framing of power was applied to family sexual violence in Susan Brownmiller's *Against Our Will* (1975), widely considered the first scholarship that positioned sexual violence as a widespread social problem. Brownmiller asserted that the cause of family violence was embedded in the patriarchal power structure, describing child sexual abuse as "rooted in the same patriarchal philosophy of sexual private property that shaped and determined historic male attitudes towards rape. For if woman was man's original corporal property, then children were, and are, a wholly owned subsidiary" (1975, p. 281). In this way, sexual violence was narrowly understood as a gendered form of patriarchal control in which ciswomen (and their children) were the only recognized victims of cismen perpetrators. Gender and sexuality, in this formulation, were invisibly and inextricably tied, excluding many gender-nonconforming people from receiving attention and care.

Exclusively focusing on gender structures left out other categorizations such as race, class, and sexuality and how they created vastly different experiences of violence and power. Women of color had been experiencing public racialized and gendered exploitation for centuries before the second-wave movement brought widespread awareness to (white women's) sexual assault (Tillman et al. 2010; Davis 1981; Moraga and Anzaldúa 1981). A sexual violence framework focused solely on the gender hierarchy ignored the long history of racialized sexual violence that occurred because of chattel slavery, which Black feminist scholars cited as foundational to the causes of sexual violence. Angela Davis (1981) discussed how during slavery, slave women were treated as "breeders" whose value could be calculated based on their reproductive ability, "an uncamouflaged expression of the slaveholder's economic master and the overseer's control over Black women as workers" (7). This sexual degradation of enslaved Black women, Davis argued, led to widespread sexual abuse in the United States. To limit a power analysis of sexual violence to gender was to dismiss the existence of racial hierarchies that are at the core of all forms of sexual assault. Further, Black feminists asserted that a theoretical framework exclusively focused on gender divisions required false divisions between Black women and Black men, erasing collective oppressions, such as white supremacy, that are faced across gender.[3]

It was under this second-wave understanding of gender and power that marital rape emerged as a social problem—a type of sexual violence that remains core to the understanding of family sexual violence. Diana Russell's 1982 *Rape in Marriage* dispelled the idea that marital rape was rare. In fact, Russell found that one in seven married women had experienced "wife rape." This type of scholarship served as the foundation for second-wave feminist efforts to overturn marital rape exemption laws, which were founded in patriarchal ownership of women through marriage. Simultaneously, this activist focus became part of a long legacy of carceral feminist efforts that rely on criminalization through the criminal-legal system to address the social problem of sexual violence.[4] Rose Corrigan (2013) described the turn of the mainstream feminist movement toward the carceral state as an interest convergence between conservatives and feminists, bringing state logics into the movement while being aware that these systems cause and perpetuate sexual violence.

To understand family sexual violence, we learn more from a framework that identifies patriarchal power alongside intersectional understandings of power in interpersonal and institutional dynamics (Guadalupe-Diaz and Whalley 2022).

QUEERING FAMILY SEXUAL VIOLENCE

Queer perspectives on sexual violence push against the assumptions of heterosexuality and cisnormativity while drawing attention to the structures of oppression. Power is not all in one place; power can be held by individuals as well as by social structures. It can reside within institutions and be expressed through the social distribution of resources.

Power is fundamentally racialized, classed, and gendered in ways that enable more privileged people to use their power to abuse people who are more marginalized than themselves (Guadalupe-Diaz and Whalley 2022). This conceptualization of power can explain why cisgender girls and women, who are more often socially subordinated, are disproportionately sexually assaulted by cismen. In a queered understanding of power, feminine subordination can be extended beyond ciswomen, providing attention to more people through this nuanced and comprehensive critique of masculinity and power.

Recall Singer's assault of Sanchez-Guzman, discussed at the opening of this chapter. Now you can understand it as a multifaceted enactment of power Singer's power as a white man assaulting a Latino teenage boy; the power within the twenty-one-year age difference between Singer and Sanchez-Guzman; Singer's power in an exclusive industry that he was offering access to if Sanchez-Guzman stayed silent; and the power of the religious and cultural homophobia within

Sanchez-Guzman's family. Also, given their shared in-group membership in the larger LGBTQ family, one can recognize the harm Singer caused by violating Sanchez-Guzman's sense of safety and community.

A QUEERED ASSESSMENT OF SEXUAL VIOLENCE AND THE FAMILY

A queered definition of family helps us see the betrayal of trust within *all* family sexual violence. In this section, this framework will be applied to the two types of violence that comprise standard definitions of family sexual violence — marital rape and child sexual abuse (CSA). By queering the conception of family to include kinship and community ties, we look at the layers of betrayal involved when an individual is sexually assaulted by someone they trusted, felt safe with, and love(d). This understanding also lends insight into how families and communities respond to disclosures of each type of family sexual victimization.

Queering Marital Rape

Regarding adult sexual assault, the vast majority of sexual violence is perpetrated by someone known to the victim, most frequently a current or former partner (Filipas and Ullman 2001; Fisher and Cullen 2000). Despite this frequency, this broad category of sexual violence is only considered *family* sexual violence if the victim has had their relationship legislated by the state through the institution of marriage. In so doing, the betrayal and violation of trust inherent in sexual violence between intimate partners is decentered. Queering the definition of family to not rely on state institutions of marriage allows us to address more deeply the levels of harm this type of sexual violence can cause to an individual, family, and community. Regardless of marital status, to be assaulted by someone whom you love and trust is a family experience of sexual violence. Queering our understanding of sexual violence and the family does not only serve LGBTQ inclusion but also gives us a deeper way of understanding all types of non-stranger sexual violence as betrayals of trust, safety, and vulnerability.

The vast majority of sexual assault survivors eventually disclose their assault to another person, and these disclosures are most commonly made to family and friends (Ahrens et al. 2007). The response to these revelations is significant; positive or negative reactions have been found to have a mediating effect on the development of symptoms of post-traumatic stress disorder (Ullman 2010).

Family members of origin have been found to be more likely than other close contacts to respond to a sexual assault disclosure by engaging in victim blaming, controlling behavior (such as forcing the victim to report the assault to the police), egocentric reactions, the promotion of rape myths, and attempts to distract the victim from the topic (Lorenz et al. 2018). The rape myths most often employed by families include questions about what the victim was wearing and why they were alone, and assertions that rape is not possible by a boyfriend or husband. For LGBTQ victims of sexual assault, the potential for a negative, shaming, stigmatizing reaction to their assault is compounded by implications of the assault on the family member's understanding of the victim's sexuality (Guadalupe-Diaz 2014). In one study of social reactions to sexual assault disclosures, victims described wishing their family-of-origin members had been more encouraging of them to talk and better able to provide emotional support and validation (Filipas and Ullman 2001). A queered framework of family sexual violence allows us to see the power structures within a family that enable a family member to de-center the victim. We also see the power embedded in the use of cultural understandings of rape that rely on sexism, homophobia, and patriarchal ownership over sexual autonomy.

The reactions of *friends* to disclosures of sexual assault have been found to be the most positively influential on a victim's recovery. Victims report feeling far more comfort and support from their friends than their family, describing friends as better able to listen and provide high levels of emotional support tangible aid, and information. Victims also describe how friends sharing their own experiences with sexual violence was very helpful (Lorenz et al. 2018; Filipas and Ullman 2001). From a queered perspective, the strength of these kinship disclosures can be highlighted as familial, as they emphasize the healing power of the cognitive and emotive bonds often found in queer chosen-family structures

Queering Intrafamilial Child Sexual Abuse

Traditional definitions of child sexual abuse define intrafamilial as those related to the child either biologically or through marriage. Using this metric, approximately one-third of CSA is perpetrated by family members, most often fathers and stepfathers (Rice and Harris 2002). Research suggests the presence of a stepfather in a household is a significant risk factor for child sexual abuse (McCloskey and Bailey 2000; Finkelhor and Baron 1986). By centering the definition of intrafamilial sexual assault on genetically or matrimonially related cismen, the power of the state to define families using narrow cis- and heteronormative language is maintained. This framework centers the *taboo* of incest as the harm, rather than the violations of trust and safety at the root of family sexual violence. Yet the very focus on stepfathers within the literature suggests that it is not biological incest at issue within CSA, but instead the violation of normative expectations of children's sexual safety in their homes. Within a queered definition of family sexual violence, power dynamics that are uncoupled from the state can be centered. Therefore, sexual abuse by a parent's fiancé, long-term partner, or boyfriend would all be considered forms of family sexual violence.

Responses to disclosures of family CSA are characterized by silence and secrecy at interpersonal, family, community, and cultural levels. Children whose families believe them fare better than children whose families deny their reports (Malloy et al. 2016). The cultural value of the sanctity of family means that CSA victims, in disclosing their abuse, are themselves violating the normative expectation to protect one's family. Aishah Shahidah Simmons (2019) illuminated the irony of this expectation, explaining that "in the name of familial love and loyalty, child sexual abuse survivors are overtly and covertly encouraged to remain silent" (16). It is this silence around family CSA, Simmons argues, that creates cultures of sexual violence throughout all social institutions, including religious and academic organizations.

QUEER LIBERATORY SOLUTIONS TO SEXUAL VIOLENCE IN FAMILIES

What do we do? I have looked for alternatives in the transformative justice movement because sexual violence scholars have documented how carceral sexual assault solutions—prosecution and prison—perpetuate sexual violence (Bumiller 2008; Corrigan 2013; Simmons 2019; Whalley 2020). Increased criminalization of sexual abuse through greater penalties and broader criminal statutes, for example, has not increased conviction rates or curbed rates of adult or child sexual assault (Lonsway and Archambault 2012; Belknap 2010). On the contrary, laws passed in the name of protecting victims have had the effect of frequently revictimizing and punishing survivors of sexual violence (Kaba 2021).

How could state violence associated with punishment within the carceral state be used to reduce sexual violence? It cannot, because the structural causes of sexual violence—such as white supremacy, heteropatriarchy, and transmisogyny—are embedded in the legal-penal codes of the state. State responses operate through the same strategy as is used in the perpetration of sexual violence: nonconsensual imposition, coercion, and selective use of brute force. As such, state solutions to violence that rely on domination and control cannot provide the safety, trust, liberation, or self-determination that victims require (Whalley and

Hackett 2017). Nor can the state center victims' voices, create space for trust-building, or provide resources through community connection that families need in order to heal from sexual abuse. Through the exclusive promotion of the criminal-legal system to address sexual violence, sexual violence continues unabated. There is a clear need for strategies for responding to sexual violence within families that are helpful, restorative, and healing for all victims, families, and communities.

The transformative justice movement has formulated responses to the harm of family sexual violence that exist outside of the state. Transformative justice and community accountability are a set of radical interventions proposed by activist-scholars of color in direct response to solutions to interpersonal violence that require the use of state violence. Transformative justice is rooted in the awareness that structural oppressions are the core drivers of all violence and harm. Drawing on expansive definitions of family, transformative justice uses community education, organizing, and accountability to address harm while dismantling structures of violence. In her anthology of transformative solutions to child sexual abuse, Aishah Shahidah Simmons calls for "ideas, visions, and strategies for how we can address, disrupt, and ultimately end child sexual abuse without solely relying upon systems that have continuously harmed diasporic Black people and other marginalized communities" (Simmons 2019, p. 1). In her work, Simmons disrupts the traditional binary language used in understanding the effects of CSA, explaining that "for me, and for many survivors of child sexual abuse, the family is simultaneously a source of deep pain and love. I am committed to creating models of holding family members accountable without suppressing that love. And I am not alone" (17). To queer our understanding of responses to family sexual violence, conceptions of families must be expanded to account for both love and pain, good and bad, trust and betrayal, and accountability with transformation.

Many of the abolitionist community-based social movements seeking to end sexual violence understand violence as a collective behavior rather than an individualized issue (Heiner and Tyson 2017). One such organization focused on solutions to family violence is the Bay Area Transformative Justice Collective (BATJC), which is based in Northern California. The BATJC was founded in 2013 with the specific mission of responding to child sexual abuse using transformative justice practices "where everyday people can intervene in incidences of child sexual abuse in ways that not only meet immediate needs but also prevent future violence and harm" (BATJC, n.d.). The BATJC has created a set of tools to guide families and communities to intervene in situations of child sexual abuse. Using education, community labs, skill building, and direct interventions, the BATJC supports both those who have been harmed and those who have enacted the harm of CSA, resisting the carceral binaries of victim and offender to build accountability for CSA based in the prevention of future harm. One of BATCJ's most popular tools, Pod Maps, helps individuals think through whom they can turn to if violence were to occur and helps identify areas where networks need to be strengthened to be able to respond well to an incident of violence. The BATJC is one of many community accountability groups that help families and communities respond to and prevent violence *without enacting violence*, extending the definition of family to kinship and community while resisting the enactment of state violence.

This *queering* lens moves us away from reliance on state institutions for our understanding of family sexual violence. This lens leads to a liberatory definition of family and violence, one that is inclusive and does not replicate the state systems of heterosexism, cisgenderism, racism, and biological essentialism. You have read about the connection among these power hierarchies and sexual violence: because we want to fix family sexual violence, we must also look out for these links. Discussions of the carceral state ask you to keep in mind that these queered definitions are not in and of themselves liberatory. If queered understandings of family sexual violence are then made part of criminal justice systems that are part of these power hierarchies, the causes of family sexual violence will endure.

NOTES

1. When you read the term *state* in this chapter, it means a government and its laws, policies, and institutions as well as the culture that surrounds it. For example, marriage is part of the state because it is regulated by the government through access and documents; it is influenced by government through policies such as the tax code. It is also supported by culture by the idealizing and even the commercialization of such forms. We can see the state in other things such as punishment, education, or health.

2. This chapter uses the word *queer* as an overarching term for nonheterosexual, noncisgender identities, including lesbian, gay, bisexual, transgender, and queer (LGBTQ) people, and as an operational concept that disrupts common assumptions within normative language (Guadalupe-Diaz and Whalley 2022).

3. For more on the legacy of slavery and sexual violence, see Angela Davis, *Rape, Racism and the Myth of the Black Rapist* in *Women, Race and Class* (New York: Random House, 1981).

4. Carceral feminism refers to feminist organizing focused using the criminal-legal system to gain protection for some women, under the guise of representing all women. In appealing to the state for legal rights, mainstream feminist organizers believe patriarchal violence toward "all" women can be reduced through legislation, greater police reporting, and a general expansion of penal power. The state in this case is a "carceral state." For more on this topic, see Whalley and Hackett (2017).

Contributors

Elizabeth A. Armstrong is Sherry B. Ortner Collegiate Professor of Sociology at the University of Michigan. Armstrong's research focuses on the reproduction of gender, class, and race inequalities. She examines these processes in the domain of sexuality and within the organizational context of the university. With Laura T. Hamilton, she is author of *Paying for the Party: How College Maintains Inequality*. She is currently working with colleagues on identifying and describing "situationships" as a new relationship type.

Alison Ash is a trauma-informed intimacy coach and educator and the founder of TurnON .love. She works with individuals and couples to support their capacity to create and sustain intimacy. In addition to lecturing at Stanford University, she offers a wide range of workshops, courses, and retreats to individuals and businesses outside of academia. With Lily Zheng, she is the author of *Gender Ambiguity in the Workplace: Transgender and Gender-Diverse Discrimination*.

Pallavi Banerjee is Associate Professor in the Department of Sociology at the University of Calgary. Her research is situated at the intersections of immigration, gender, families, unpaid and paid labor, intersectionality, and transnationalism. She is the author of *The Opportunity Trap: High-Skilled Workers, Indian Families and the Failures of Dependent-Visa Policy* (New York University Press, 2022). Her award-winning research has been published in many peer-reviewed journals, including the *American Behavioral Scientist*; *Contexts*; *Sociological Forum*; *Gender, Work and Organization*; and *Women, Gender, and Families of Color*, among others. She directs the Critical Gender, Intersectionality and Migration Research Group at the University of Calgary, and her research is supported by the Social Sciences and Humanities Research Council of Canada (SSHRC) and Immigration, Refugees and Citizenship Canada (IRCC).

Amy Blackstone is Professor of Sociology at the University of Maine. She studies gender, the childfree choice, civic engagement, and workplace harassment. Dr. Blackstone is the author of *Childfree by Choice* (Dutton, 2019). She is passionate about bringing a sociological perspective to public dialogue and has contributed to a variety of media platforms, including the *New York Times*, the *Washington Post*, NPR, the BBC, *Al Jazeera*, CNBC, and others.

Catherine Bolzendahl is Professor of Sociology and Director of the School of Public Policy at Oregon State University. As a political sociologist, the bulk of Bolzendahl's work examines public support for egalitarian family policies and gendered inequalities in political engagement, typically from a cross-national perspective. She is a co-author of the award-winning book *Counted Out* and recently co-edited and contributed two papers to a special issue of the *European Journal of Politics & Gender* on nonbinary measures of gender and politics. She is currently co-authoring a book on gender differences in political engagement in Western Europe.

Amy Brainer is Associate Professor and Director of Women's & Gender Studies and LGBTQ+ Studies at the University of Michigan–Dearborn. She is the author of *Queer Kinship and Family Change in Taiwan* (Rutgers University Press, 2019), for which she received the Ruth Benedict Prize from the Association for Queer Anthropology. Her current research follows queer and trans individuals and couples as they navigate marriage-based immigration to the United States. At UM–Dearborn, she is faculty adviser to Pride and teaches courses on the LGBTQ+ religious experience; family diversity and power; colonialism, race, and sexuality; and other topics.

Jenifer L. Bratter is Professor of Sociology at Rice University and the founding director of BRIDGE (Building Research on Inequality and Diversity to Grow Equity). Her research interests include race/ethnicity, racial inequality, demography, and family. She is the co-editor of *Unmaking Race and Ethnicity* (Oxford University Press), and she has co/authored over thirty peer-reviewed articles exploring dynamics of race and racial mixture, as well as conceptualization. Her work appears in *Demography, Ethnicities, Journal of Comparative Family Studies*, the *Du Bois Review, Ethnic and Racial Studies, Journal of Marriage and Family*, and other outlets.

Linda M. Burton is Dean of Berkeley Social Welfare and holds the Eugene and Rose Kleiner Chair for the Study of Processes, Practices and Policies in Aging. Dean Burton is a preeminent scholar on child welfare and poverty whose program of research is conceptually grounded in life course, developmental, and ecological perspectives and focuses on three themes concerning the lives of America's poorest urban, small-town, and rural families: (1) intergenerational family structures, processes, and role transitions; (2) the meaning of context and place in the daily lives of families; and, (3) childhood adultification and the accelerated life course. Her methodological approach to exploring these issues is comparative, longitudinal, and multi-method.

Philip N. Cohen is Professor of Sociology at the University of Maryland. He has published extensively on family structure, gender inequality in families and the labor force, and health disparities. He has written for such publications as the *New York Times*, the *Washington Post*, and the *Atlantic* and has appeared on radio and TV, including NPR and MSNBC. He writes the blog FamilyInequality.com.

Joshua Coleman is a psychologist in private practice in the San Francisco Bay Area and a Senior Fellow with the Council on Contemporary Families. He has written for the *New York Times*, the *Atlantic*, NBC Think, the *Behavioral Scientist*, CNN, MarketWatch, the *San Francisco Chronicle, Greater Good Magazine*, AEON, *Huffington Post, Psychology Today*, and more. He is the author of numerous peer-reviewed articles and chapters and has written four books, most recently *The Rules of Estrangement: Why Adult Children Cut Ties and How to Heal the Conflict* (Penguin Random House). A frequent guest on the *Today Show* and NPR, he has also been featured on *Sesame Street, 20/20, Good Morning America*, PBS, and numerous news programs for FOX, ABC, CNN, and NBC.

Marilyn Coleman is Distinguished Curators' Professor Emerita of Human Development and Family Science at the University of Missouri. Dr. Coleman is a Fellow in the National

Council on Family Relations. She has conducted research on stepfamilies for over forty-five years. Her recent work has focused on the development and maintenance of effective step-relationships. Dr. Coleman has co-authored over 300 articles and book chapters as well as ten books. Dr. Coleman is a past editor of the *Journal of Marriage and Family.*

Stephanie Coontz is Director of Research and Public Education at the Council on Contemporary Families. Professor Emerita at Evergreen State College in Olympia, Washington, and former Woodrow Wilson Fellow, she has authored seven books on marriage and family life, including *The Way We Never Were: American Families and the Nostalgia Trap* and *Marriage, A History,* which was cited in the Supreme Court decision on marriage equality. She also edited *American Families: A Multicultural Reader.* A new book of essays, *For Better AND Worse: The Problematic Past and Uncertain Future of Marriage,* will be out in 2024. Her many articles for the *New York Times,* CNN, and other outlets can be found at stephaniecoontz.com.

Carolyn Pape Cowan is Adjunct Professor of Psychology Emerita at the University of California, Berkeley. She has co-directed three longitudinal intervention studies of how family relationships affect children's adaptation. She, with Philip Cowan and later with Marsha Kline Pruett and Kyle Pruett, developed and evaluated couple groups led by mental health professionals and followed the families over time to track the effects. Seven trials in the United States, Canada, the United Kingdom, and Malta revealed positive benefits for the parents' and children's development. She is co-author of *When Partners Become Parents: The Big Life Change for Couples* and numerous scientific journal articles. She is also co-editor of *Fatherhood Today: Men's Changing Role in the Family* and *The Family Context of Parenting in Children's Adaptation to Elementary School.* She consults internationally on the development and evaluation of interventions for partners who are parents.

Philip A. Cowan is Professor of Psychology, Emeritus, at the University of California, Berkeley. Since 1979, he and Carolyn Pape Cowan have been co-directors of three longitudinal studies of couples group interventions, led by mental health professionals, which were found to have had long-term positive effects on the couples and their children. In collaboration with Marsha Kline Pruett and Kyle Pruett, they created and evaluated the Supporting Father Involvement project—a group intervention for low-income couples. Professor Cowan is the author of *Piaget: With Feeling,* co-author with Carolyn Pape Cowan of *When Partners Become Parents: The Big Life Change for Couples,* co-editor of four additional books and monographs, and the author or co-author of numerous research articles in scientific journals.

Christina J. Cross is Assistant Professor of Sociology at Harvard University. Her research falls at the intersection of families, race/ethnicity, and social inequality. She examines how family structure, change, and dynamics influence individuals' life chances, particularly among minoritized and economically disadvantaged populations. Her work has appeared in outlets such as *Social Problems, Demography,* and the *Journal of Marriage and Family.* Her research has been supported by organizations such as the National Institutes of Health, the National Science Foundation, the Ford Foundation, the Andrew W. Mellon Foundation, and the JPB

Foundation. Her research has received numerous awards, including from the American Sociological Association, the Population Association of America, the National Council on Family Relations, and the Society for the Study of Social Problems. Cross holds a PhD in Public Policy and Sociology from the University of Michigan.

Georgiann Davis is Associate Professor of Sociology at the University of New Mexico. Her research and teaching are at the intersection of sociology of diagnosis and feminist theories. She is the author of *Contesting Intersex: The Dubious Diagnosis*. She is also a former board president of interACT: Advocates for Intersex Youth and a past president of InterConnect Support Group.

Raine Dozier is a sociologist and Professor of Human Services at Western Washington University. His research interests include transgender health, gender, sexual orientation, and inequality. She has published widely, including in *Gender & Society*, *Social Forces*, *Psychology of Women Quarterly*, and *Journal of Homosexuality*. Dozier is a queer/trans mother of two with a long history of activism, parenting, intellectual inquiry, and laundry.

Allison Nicole Dunatchik is a dual PhD candidate in sociology and demography at the University of Pennsylvania. Her research interests center on gender, work, and family, with a particular focus on how social policies affect gender inequalities inside and outside the household. Dunatchik's current work uses large-scale, cross-national data to explore how gender inequalities in earnings and employment are produced and reproduced within different-sex couples in the context of changing gender norms and changing patterns in family demography across high-income countries.

Paula England is Dean of Social Science at New York University Abu Dhabi. Her research interests include gender inequality, families, and sexualities. She is the author of over a hundred articles and two books, including *Households, Employment, and Gender: A Social, Economic, and Demographic View*. England is a former president of the American Sociological Association and a member of the National Academy of Sciences.

Donna L. Franklin has held academic appointments at the University of Chicago, Smith College, Howard University, and the University of Southern California. She was a member of the founding board of the Council on Contemporary Families and was one of its national chairs. Her first book, *Ensuring Inequality* (Oxford University Press, 1997), won two major awards: the American Sociological Association's William J. Goode Distinguished Book Award for "outstanding scholarship on the family" and *Choice* magazine's award for "outstanding academic book." She was the first African American author to win the ASA award. Her second book, *What's Love Got to Do with It? Understanding and Healing the Rift between Black Men and Women* (Simon & Schuster, 2000), was one of the first books to include a historical analysis of gender relations in the African American community.

Shawn Fremstad is trained as an attorney and is Director of Law and Political Economy and Senior Advisor at the Center for Economic and Policy Research in Washington, D.C. His expertise covers inequality and poverty; social security and assistance programs; immigration; family policy; and class, gender, race, and disability. Fremstad has worked in direct service at the local level, policy advocacy at the state level, and policy research and analysis at the federal level.

Marni Fritz is a PhD candidate in sociology at the University of Illinois at Chicago She studies inequality, organizations, whiteness, social movements, and racism. Her current work focuses on the racialization of social justice organizations and takes an intersectional approach to understanding how organizations facilitate inequality both within themselves and on a societal level.

Lawrence Ganong is Professor Emeritus of Human Development and Family Science and Nursing at the University of Missouri–Columbia. He has co-authored more than three hundred journal articles and book chapters and ten books. He has also received multiple grants from federal institutes and private foundations. His primary research program has focused on how postdivorce family members, especially in stepfamilies, develop and maintain satisfying and effective relationships. He is a fellow in the National Council on Family Relations and the Gerontological Society of America. Ganong has served on the board of directors of the National Council on Family Relations, the Council on Contemporary Families, and the Stepfamily Association of America.

Lorena Garcia is Associate Professor of Sociology and Latin American and Latino Studies at the University of Illinois at Chicago. Her research interests include gender, sexuality, race, intersectionality, U.S. Latinas, and youth. She is the author of *Respect Yourself, Protect Yourself: Latina Girls and Sexual Identity* (New York University Press, 2012) and a co-editor of the NYU Press book series Critical Perspectives on Youth. Her work has also been published in *Gender & Society*, *Social Problems*, and *Latino Studies*, among other journals. She is currently working on her second book project, which focuses on the parenting perspectives and practices of newly middle-class Latina/x/os.

Claudia Geist is Associate Professor of Sociology and Gender Studies at the University of Utah. Her research lies at the intersection of gender, families, and inequalities. Her current work examines the gendered division of labor, family formation, the social construction of gender, and sexuality. She is a co-author of the award-winning book *Counted Out* and has published articles in *Contraception*, *Demography*, *Journal of Marriage and Family*, *PLOS One*, and *Social Forces*.

Kathleen Gerson is Collegiate Professor of Arts & Science and Professor of Sociology at New York University. Her work focuses on the sources, shapes, and consequences of the intertwined revolutions in gender, work, and private life in the United States and across the globalizing world. She is the author or co-author of six books, including the award-winning book *The Unfinished Revolution* and most recently *The Science and Art of Interviewing* (with Sarah Damaske). She is currently at work on a book tentatively titled *Why No One Can Have It All*.

Abbie E. Goldberg is Professor of Psychology at Clark University in Worcester, Massachusetts. Her research examines diverse families, including LGBTQ-parent families and adoptive-parent families. Her most recent book is *LGBTQ Family Building: A Guide for Prospective Parents* (APA, 2022). She has served as a visiting fellow at the Williams Institute at the UCLA School of Law and the Rudd Adoption Program at the University of Massachusetts Amherst.

Amy Greenleaf graduated from the University of Maine in 2012, where she earned BAs in both psychology and sociology. She was also a student at Walden University's master's program in Marriage, Couples, and Family Therapy and has worked in behavioral health in New England.

Xavier Guadalupe-Diaz (he/him/his) is Associate Professor of Sociology and Criminology at Framingham State University. His research examines intimate partner and sexual violence within LGBTQ+ communities with a focus on transgender victimization. He's the author of *Transgressed: Intimate Partner Violence in Transgender Lives* (2019) and is co-editor of *Transgender Intimate Partner Violence: A Comprehensive Introduction* (2020), both from New York University Press. His work has been featured in the journals *Interpersonal Violence*, *Critical Criminology*, and the *Journal of Homosexuality* and has been mentioned in the *Washington Post*, *Insider*, CNN's *Forensic Files*, and other media outlets.

Melanie Heath is Associate Dean of Graduate Studies and Associate Professor of Sociology at McMaster University. Her research interests include sexuality, gender, family, and politics. She is the author of *Forbidden Intimacies: Polygamies at the Limits of Western Tolerance* and *One Marriage Under God: The Campaign to Promote Marriage in America*. She has published articles on family, gender, and sexuality in *Gender & Society*, *Sociological Quarterly*, and *Sociological Perspectives*, among other places.

Ni'Shele Jackson is a doctoral graduate student in the sociology program at the University of Illinois at Chicago. Their research interests include fat studies, intersectional theory, queer theory, sociology of health and medicine, and sociology of the body. Their current work attempts to contextualize constructions of fatness within a larger biopolitical project that seeks to maintain race, gender, sexuality, and class hierarchies.

Jerry A. Jacobs is Professor of Sociology at the University of Pennsylvania and is the co-founder and first president of the Work and Family Researchers Network. Jacobs has served as editor of the *American Sociological Review*, president of the Eastern Sociological Society, and co-president of Sociologists for Women in Society and has won several awards for his scholarship and professional contributions. Jacobs has written extensively about women's careers and work-family issues. His six books include *The Time Divide: Work, Family and Gender Inequality* (2004) with Kathleen Gerson, *The Changing Face of Medicine: Women Doctors and the Evolution of Health Care in America* (2008) with Ann Boulis, and *Revolving Doors: Sex Segregation and Women's Careers* (1989). His current projects include a study of technology and elder care, which features interviews with family caregivers during the pandemic, and a multifaceted exploration of the future of work.

Todd Jensen is a Research Assistant Professor in the School of Social Work, the Associate Director for Research in the Collaborative for Implementation Practice, and a Family Research and Engagement Specialist in the Jordan Institute for Families at the University of North Carolina at Chapel Hill. His scholarship focuses on promoting family well-being in diverse contexts, strengthening family-serving systems, and centering equity in family research, practice, and policy. He is co-founder and co-chair of the Diverse Family Structures Focus Group of the National Council on Family Relations, which has amassed over 130 scholars across the country and globe aiming to align research, practice, and policy with the complex realities of family relationships.

Daniela Kaiser is a doctoral student in the Department of Criminology, Law and Society at the University of California, Irvine. Her research explores how contact with criminal justice and child welfare systems shapes the well-being of families and children, as well as a wide array of collateral effects brought about by the involvement with these systems.

Arielle Kuperberg is Professor of Sociology at the University of North Carolina at Greensboro and Chair of the Council on Contemporary Families. Her research explores social change and inequalities in romantic and sexual relationships, families, and young adulthood, especially topics related to premarital cohabitation and marriage; college hookups and dates; gender, work, education, and parenthood; and the transition to adulthood with student loan debt. She has published in the *Journal of Marriage and Family, Gender & Society, Social Forces, Archives of Sexual Behavior*, and *Journal of Sex Research*, among other places.

Joan Maya Mazelis is Associate Professor of Sociology and Director of the Gender Studies Program at Rutgers University–Camden. Her research explores poverty, social ties, reciprocity, inequality, student debt, and the varied understandings and experiences of the American Dream. She is the author of *Surviving Poverty: Creating Sustainable Ties among the Poor*. She received the 2022 Public Sociology Award from the Eastern Sociological Society and the 2022 Michael Harrington Award from the Poverty, Class & Inequality Division of the Society for the Study of Social Problems.

Tey Meadow is Associate Professor of Sociology at Columbia University. Her work examines the relational nature of gender and sexual identities and categories. She is the author of the award-winning book *Trans Kids: Being Gendered in the Twenty-First Century* and the co-editor of *Other, Please Specify: Queer Methods in Sociology*.

Steven Mintz is a leading authority on familial change and the history of the life course as well as Professor of History at the University of Texas at Austin. He is also the author and editor of fifteen books, including *Domestic Revolutions: A History of American Family Life, Huck's Raft: A History of American Childhood*, and *The Prime of Life: A History of Modern Adulthood*.

Mignon R. Moore is the Ann Whitney Olin Professor of Sociology at Barnard College. Her work and academic interests lie at the intersections of race and gender, family formation and processes, LGBTQ populations, aging, and qualitative research methods. She is the author of *Invisible Families: Gay Identities, Relationships, and Motherhood among Black Women* and has received grants from the National Institutes of Health and the Woodrow Wilson Foundation to support her work. In 2022–23 she was in residence at the Russell Sage Foundation to complete *In the Shadow of Sexuality: Social Histories of African American Lesbians and Gay Men, 1950–1979*, a book on the development of community for Black sexual minority women in the mid-twentieth century. She is the 2021 President of Sociologists for Women in Society.

Adina Nack is Professor of Sociology at California Lutheran University. As a medical sociologist, she has focused her research on reproductive and sexual health. She has published articles on topics such as abortion stigma and patient-practitioner interaction styles. She is the author of *Damaged Goods? Women Living with Incurable Sexually Transmitted Diseases* (Temple University Press). Most recently, she collaborated on a public health study of maternal morbidities for NYC's Department of Health and Mental Hygiene.

Becky Pettit is the Barbara Pierce Bush Regents Professor of Liberal Arts at the University of Texas at Austin. She is the author of *Invisible Men: Mass Incarceration and the Myth of Black Progress* (Russell Sage Foundation, 2012), which investigates how decades of growth in America's prisons and jails obscures basic accounts of racial inequality. She edited *Social Problems*, the official journal of the Society of the Study of Social Problems, from 2011 to 2014 and was on the advisory board of the General Social Survey from 2017 to 2021. She holds a PhD in sociology from Princeton University and a BA in sociology from the University of California at Berkeley.

Brian Powell is the James H. Rudy Professor of Sociology at Indiana University. His research focuses on family, sexuality, gender, and higher education. He is coauthor—with Catherine Bolzendahl, Claudia Geist, and Lala Carr Steelman—of *Counted Out: Same-Sex Relations and Americans' Definitions of Family*. He also is coauthor—with Natasha Quadlin—of *Who Should Pay? Higher Education, Responsibility, and the Public*. His research has been featured in the *Los Angeles Times*, the *New York Times*, the *Washington Post*, *USA Today*, ABC World News Tonight, C-SPAN, and National Public Radio, among other outlets.

Pamela Anne Quiroz is Executive Director of the national research consortium the Inter-University Program for Latino Research (IUPLR). She is also Director of the University of Houston's Center for Mexican American and Latino/a Studies and CLASS Distinguished Professor of Sociology. Her book *Dating, Mating and Relating: Personal Advertising and Romance in Modern Society* (McFarland Press, 2022) is the result of seventeen years of research on modern dating activities. She is also the creator of Latino cARTographies, the country's first portable, bilingual, and interactive digital board that maps the Latino visual artists of Houston.

Jennifer Randles is Professor and Chair of Sociology at California State University, Fresno. Her research interests include families, childhood, gender, race, poverty, and welfare policy.

She is the author of *Proposing Prosperity: Marriage Education and Family Inequality in America* and *Essential Dads: The Inequalities and Politics of Fathering*. Her current book project focuses on diaper inequalities and the national diaper bank movement.

Barbara J. Risman is College of Liberal Arts & Sciences Distinguished Professor at the University of Illinois at Chicago. Her expertise includes gender inequality, work and family policies, and gender identity. She is currently Editor in Chief of *Gender & Society*; she sits on the U.S. National Chapter Advisory Board for the Scholars Strategy Network; and she has led many organizations, including being President of the Board of Directors and Executive Officer of the Council on Contemporary Families, President of Sociologists for Women in Society, President of Southern Sociological Society, and Vice President of the American Sociological Association. Her most recent book is *Where the Millennials Will Take Us: A New Generation Wrestles with the Gender Structure* (Oxford, 2018). Two major active projects include the study COVID & Caregiving (with Jerry Jacobs, Kathleen Gerson, and Jennifer Glass) and an international study of people who reject gender categories (with Emanuela Abbatecola, Arantxa Grau, Lucy Nichols, and William Scarborough).

Cassaundra Rodriguez is Assistant Professor of Sociology at the University of Nevada, Las Vegas. She specializes in the areas of Latinx sociology, immigration and citizenship, family race, and gender. She is the author of *Contested Americans: Mixed-Status Families in Anti-Immigrant Times*, which investigates how members of mixed-status families—that is, families that include U.S. citizens and undocumented immigrants—experience belonging and manage illegality in their lives. She was a 2020–21 fellow in the Institute for Citizens & Scholars Career Enhancement Fellowship Program.

Daniela Guerrero Rodriguez received her bachelor's degree from the University of Illinois at Chicago in December 2022. They graduated with a BA in Public Policy with specializations in Environmental Policy and Foreign & Global Policy, a BA in Political Science with a concentration in Laws & Courts, a BA in Sociology, and minors in International Studies, Gender & Women Studies, and Sustainable Cities. Daniela currently works as a digital organizer for the grassroots organization Just Transition Northwest Indiana and aspires to continue working in advocacy to promote and secure environmental protections, immigration, and LGBTQIA+ rights.

Virginia E. Rutter has been Professor of Sociology at Framingham State University for sixteen years and continues teaching and conducting research as Emerita. She is a senior scholar and was a long-term member of the Board of the Council on Contemporary Families. Her books, articles, columns, and engagement of public sociology through CCF and Sociologists for Women in Society aim to do what she does as an award-winning teacher at FSU: to make clear and accessible the best available social science research on families, sexuality, and inequality. Along with leading the editorial team on *Families as They Really Are*, Third Edition, she was co-author or co-editor of *Families as They Really Are*, Second Edition, *The Gender of Sexuality*, and *The Love Test* and founding editor of CCF's The Society Pages home (CCF@TSP). She was Vice President and Director of her local union chapter of the Mass State College Association (MTA/NEA) for six years. Rutter was the 2012 FSU Distinguished Faculty for Teaching Award recipient, and in 2016 she was the FSU Distinguished Faculty for Scholarship and Writing Award recipient. She lives in Washington, D.C.

Patricia Sánchez-Connally is Associate Professor of Sociology at Framingham State University. Her interests are race and ethnicity, Latinx studies, higher education, and immigration. Her current project is a collaboration that looks at issues of legality and access among immigrant college students. Her research has been published in *Race, Class, & Gender* and the *Journal of Education and Social Policy*.

Caroline Sanner is Assistant Professor of Family Science at Virginia Tech. She studies family complexity, including how structurally complex families—for example, post-divorce families and stepfamilies—adapt to change and transition. Her research seeks to (a) name invisible processes in complex families and (b) understand how these processes are shaped by taken-for-granted aspects of culture and society, including cultural norms, ideologies, policies, and institutions.

William J. Scarborough is Assistant Professor of Sociology at the University of North Texas. His research examines variation in gender norms and their intersection with race. He is the author of *Gendered Places: The Landscape of Local Gender Norms across the United States* and co-editor, with Barbara Risman and Carissa Froyum, of the *Handbook of the Sociology of Gender*. His research on shifting gender attitudes, the challenges facing working mothers, and individuals' support for workplace diversity policies has been published in journals such as the *American Sociological Review*, *Gender & Society*, and *Social Science Research*.

Pepper Schwartz is Professor Emerita at the University of Washington. Her areas of concentration are intimate relationships, sexuality, and gender. Her newest book is *Relationship Rx* (Rowman and Littlefield, 2023), which she co-authored with Jessica Griffin. She has served as President of the Pacific Sociological Association and President of the Society for the Scientific Study of Sexualities. She has received awards from the American Sociological Association for Public Understanding of Sociology and the Simon-Gagnon award for excellence in research on sexualities.

Laura Simon is Assistant Professor of Sociology at Mercer University. Her research interests include race, health, family, and social connection. She teaches courses on the sociology of health, sociology of race and ethnicity, and sociological theory. Her current work uses an intersectional approach to examine disruptions in social connections and community building during the COVID-19 pandemic, the strategies individuals used to navigate disruptions, and the overall impact on well-being.

Brittany Stahnke is Assistant Professor of Social Work at Limestone University. She specializes in mental health with research interests in suicide, marriage, OCD, and life satisfaction.

She is author of *The Doubting Disease: How One Person Took Charge of the Mental Disorder that Plagued Her Decisions for a Decade, Finally Embraced the Unknown, and Found the Power of Choice*. She was the 2022 recipient of the Faculty Excellence Award at her past university. She feels it is her life purpose to guide students along their individual paths.

Lala Carr Steelman is Distinguished Professor Emerita at the University of South Carolina. Her research focuses on the integral role that families assume in children's well-being. With Brian Powell, Catherine Bolzendahl, and Claudia Geist, she was the recipient of multiple awards, including the American Sociological Association Family Section's William J. Goode Book Award, for *Counted Out: Same-Sex Relations and Americans' Definitions of Family*.

Bryan L. Sykes is Associate Professor in the Department of Sociology and the Jeb E. Brooks School of Public Policy at Cornell University. He studies racial inequality, mass incarceration, demography, law and society, population health, and research methodology.

Sejin Um is a doctoral student in sociology at New York University. Her research interests include gender, work, family, and organizations. She is currently studying how young women and men in large organizations construct varied work trajectories using qualitative methods.

Nicholas Velotta is a PhD student in the Sociology Department at the University of Washington. Their research focuses on the intersections of intimate relationships, sexuality, and gender. They are currently examining how people navigate sex and connection, eroticism, and intimacy in long-term relationships as well as in individuals' dating lives. Outside of academia, Velotta works as the Head of Relationship Research at a couple's wellness online platform.

Emily Via is a graduate student in sociology at the University of Illinois at Chicago. Their research focuses on trans and nonbinary experiences of gender, as well as norms around trans and nonbinary gender. Their continuing work focuses on the medicalization of trans identities and organizations associated with providing trans-specific medical care.

Elizabeth Whalley is Assistant Professor in the Department of Sociology and Criminology at Framingham State University. Her research interests include the enactment of and institutional responses to gendered and sexual violence. After years of volunteering as a rape crisis advocate, her activism and scholarship are now rooted in community-based responses to the harm of violence that do not replicate the violence of the prison system. Whalley and Guadalupe-Diaz recently co-authored a chapter on queering #MeToo, where they call upon the social movement to return to its original aim of expanding the frames of thinking around sexual violence by centering the marginalized.

Deadric T. Williams is Associate Professor of Sociology at the University of Tennessee, Knoxville. His research lies at the intersection of racism, families, and inequality. His current work not only critiques conventional approaches on racial inequality in family life but also offers a path forward by applying critical race theory to race and family research. His work has been published in *Journal of Marriage and Family*, *Journal of Family Issues*, *Family Relations*, *Social Problems*, and *Population Research and Policy Review*, among other publications. He was also recently selected as a William T. Grant Scholar.

Kristi Williams is Professor and Chair of the Department of Sociology at the Ohio State University. Her scholarship examines how the changing intersections of union formation and fertility shape health and well-being across the life course and across generations. Her most recent research explores the effects of adverse childhood experiences on life course developmental processes, including marriage and parenthood, with consequences for midlife health. She is a Senior Scholar at the Council on Contemporary Families and former editor in chief of *Journal of Marriage and Family*. Her work has been published in academic outlets such as *American Sociological Review*, *Journal of Health and Social Behavior*, and *Demography* and featured in media outlets such as the *New York Times*, the *Atlantic*, and *Time*.

References

CHAPTER 2: How Do We Tell What's True?
by Philip N. Cohen

Bak-Coleman, Joseph B., Mark Alfano, Wolfram Barfuss, Carl T. Bergstrom, Miguel A. Centeno, Iain D. Couzin, Jonathan F. Donges, et al. 2021. "Stewardship of Global Collective Behavior." *Proceedings of the National Academy of Sciences* 118, no. 27. doi.org/10.1073/pnas.2025764118

Baldwin, Melinda. 2018. "Scientific Autonomy, Public Accountability, and the Rise of 'Peer Review' in the Cold War United States." *Isis* 109, no. 3: 538–558.

Bergstrom, Carl T., and Jevin D. West. 2020. *Calling Bullshit: The Art of Skepticism in a Data-Driven World*. Illustrated ed. New York: Random House.

Cohen, Philip N. 2015. "Children in Same-Sex Parent Families, Dead Horse Edition." *Family Inequality* (blog). February 13, 2015. familyinequality.wordpress.com/2015/02/13/children-in-same-sex-parent-families/.

———. 2019. "Scholarly Communication in Sociology." March. doi.org/10.21428/43882.9e.

———. (@demfactaday). 2022. "In the last 10 years, the US child poverty rate has fallen dramatically." Twitter, November 14, 2022.

Creamer, John, Emily A. Shrider, Kalee Burns, and Frances Chen. 2022. "Poverty in the United States: 2021." P60-277. Current Population Reports. Washington, DC: U.S. Census Bureau. www.census.gov/library/publications/2022/demo/p60-277.html.

DePillis, Lydia, and Jason DeParle. 2022. "Pandemic Aid Cut U.S. Poverty to New Low in 2021, Census Bureau Reports." *New York Times*, September 13, 2022, sec. Business. www.nytimes.com/2022/09/13/business/economy/income-poverty-census-bureau.html.

Fraser, Nicholas, Liam Brierley, Gautam Dey, Jessica K. Polka, Máté Pálfy, Federico Nanni, and Jonathon Alexis Coates. 2021. "Preprinting the COVID-19 Pandemic." *BioRxiv*, February, 2020.05.22.111294. doi.org/10.1101/2020.05.22.111294.

Germani, Federico, and Nikola Biller-Andorno. 2021. "The Anti-Vaccination Infodemic on Social Media: A Behavioral Analysis." *PLOS ONE* 16, no. 3: e0247642. doi.org/10.1371/journal.pone.0247642.

Giddens, Anthony. 1990. *The Consequences of Modernity*. Stanford, CA: Stanford University Press.

Isaacson, Walter. 2007. *Einstein: His Life and Universe*. New York: Simon & Schuster.

Mead, Lawrence M. 2020. "Poverty and Culture." *Society*. doi.org/10.1007/s12115-020-00496-1.

Merriman, Ben. 2021. "Peer Review as an Evolving Response to Organizational Constraint: Evidence from Sociology Journals, 1952–2018." *American Sociologist* 52, no. 2: 341–366.

Moxham, Noah, and Aileen Fyfe. 2018. "The Royal Society and the Prehistory of Peer Review, 1665–1965." *Historical Journal* 61, no. 4: 863–889.

Murray, Ellie. n.d. "Coronavirus Experts." Twitter. Accessed July 17, 2021. twitter.com/i /lists/1220869298631200769.

Nishikawa-Pacher, Andreas. 2022. "Who Are the 100 Largest Scientific Publishers by Journal Count? A Webscraping Approach." *Journal of Documentation* 78, no. 7: 450–463.

Publons. 2018. "Global State of Peer Review." Clarivate Analytics. doi.org/10.14322/publons .GSPR2018.

RELX. 2021. "RELX Annual Report and Financial Statements 2021." www.relx.com/~/media /Files/R/RELX-Group/documents/reports/annual-reports/relx-2021-annual-report.pdf.

Sagan, Carl. 1997. *The Demon-Haunted World: Science as a Candle in the Dark*. Reprint, New York: Ballantine Books.

Wilcox, W. Bradford. 2020. "Family Stability and the American Dream (Statement before the Joint Economic Committee)." American Enterprise Institute. www.aei.org/wp-content /uploads/2020/02/Wilcox-JEC-FamilyStability-2-25.pdf.

Williams, Deadric T., and Regina S. Baker. 2021. "Family Structure, Risks, and Racial Stratification in Poverty." *Social Problems* 68, no. 4: 964–985.

CHAPTER 3: When Is a Relationship between Facts a Causal One?
by Philip A. Cowan

Cherlin, Andrew J., P. Lindsay Chase-Lansdale, and Christine McRae. 1998. "Effects of Parental Divorce on Mental Health throughout the Life Course." *American Sociological Review* 63: 239–249.

Cowan, Philip A., and Carolyn Pape Cowan. 2002. "Interventions as Tests of Family Systems Theories: Marital and Family Relationships in Children's Development, and Psycho-pathology." *Development and Psychopathology, Special Issue on Interventions as Tests of Theories* 14: 731–760.

Cummings, E. Mark, and Patrick Davies. 1994. *Children and Marital Conflict: The Impact of Family Dispute and Resolution*. New York: Guilford.

Emery, Robert E. 1999. *Marriage, Divorce, and Children's Adjustment*. 2nd ed. Thousand Oaks, CA: Sage.

Gottman, John M., and Clifford I. Notarius. 2002. "Marital Research in the 20th Century and a Research Agenda for the 21st Century." *Family Process* 41: 159–197.

Waite, Linda J., and Maggie Gallagher. 2000. *The Case for Marriage: Why Married People Are Happier, Healthier, and Better off Financially*. New York: Doubleday.

CHAPTER 5: Racism, Family Structure, and Black Families
by Deadric T. Williams, Caroline Sanner, Todd Jensen, and Laura Simon

Acock, Alan, and David Demo. 1994. *Family Diversity and Well-Being*. Thousand Oaks, CA: Sage Publications.

Addo, F. R., and D. T. Lichter. 2013. "Marriage, Marital History, and Black–White Wealth Differentials among Older Women." *Journal of Marriage and Family* 75, no. 2: 342–362.

Alvarado, S. E. 2020. "The Complexities of Race and Place: Childhood Neighborhood Disadvantage and Adult Incarceration for Whites, Blacks, and Latinos." *Socius* 6, 2378023120927154.

Baker, R. S. 2022. "The Historical Racial Regime and Racial Inequality in Poverty in the American South." *American Journal of Sociology* 127, no. 6: 1721–1781.

Baker, R. S., D. Brady, Z. Parolin, and D. T. Williams. 2021. "The Enduring Significance of Ethno-Racial Inequalities in Poverty in the US, 1993–2017." *Population Research and Policy Review*, 1–35.

Baker, R. S., and H. A. O'Connell. 2022. "Structural Racism, Family Structure, and Black–White Inequality: The Differential Impact of the Legacy of Slavery on Poverty among Single Mother and Married Parent Households." *Journal of Marriage and Family*. doi-org.utk.idm.oclc.org/10.1111/jomf.12837.

Billingsley, A. 1994. *Climbing Jacob's Ladder: The Enduring Legacies of African-American Families*. New York: Touchstone.

Bloome, D., and S. Ang. 2020. "Marriage and Union Formation in the United States: Recent Trends across Racial Groups and Economic Backgrounds." *Demography* 57, no. 5: 1753–1786.

Bonilla-Silva, E. 1997. "Rethinking Racism: Toward a Structural Interpretation." *American Sociological Review* 62, no. 3: 465–480.

———. 2017. *Racism without Racists: Color-blind Racism and the Persistence of Racial Inequality in America*. Lanham, MD: Rowman & Littlefield.

Brady, D. 2019. "Theories of the Causes of Poverty." *Annual Review of Sociology* 45: 155–175.

Bratter, J., and T. Zuberi. 2001. "The Demography of Difference: Shifting Trends of Racial Diversity and Interracial Marriage 1960–1990." *Race and Society* 4, no. 2: 133–148.

Braveman, P. A., E. Arkin, D. Proctor, T. Kauh, and N. Holm. 2022. "Systemic and Structural Racism: Definitions, Examples, Health Damages, and Approaches to Dismantling." *Health Affairs* 41, no. 2: 171–178.

Brown, S. L. 2010. "Marriage and Child Well-Being: Research and Policy Perspectives." *Journal of Marriage and Family* 72, no. 5: 1059–1077.

Brown, S. L., W. D. Manning, and K. K. Payne. 2017. "Relationship Quality among Cohabiting versus Married Couples." *Journal of Family Issues* 38, no. 12: 1730–1753.

Bryant, C. M., K. A. S. Wickrama, J. Bolland, B. M. Bryant, C. E. Cutrona, and C. E. Stanik. 2010. "Race Matters, Even in Marriage: Identifying Factors Linked to Marital Outcomes for African Americans." *Journal of Family Theory & Review* 2, no. 3: 157–174.

Burton, L. M., E. Bonilla-Silva, V. Ray, R. Buckelew, and E. Hordge Freeman. 2010. "Critical Race Theories, Colorism, and the Decade's Research on Families of Color." *Journal of Marriage and Family* 723: 440–459.

Crenshaw, K., N. Gotanda, G. Peller, and K. Thomas. 1995. *Critical Race Theory: The Key Writings That Formed the Movement*. New York: New Press.

Cross, Christina J. 2020. "Racial/Ethnic Differences in the Association between Family Structure and Children's Education." *Journal of Marriage and Family* 81, no. 2: 691–712.

Cross, C. J., P. Fomby, and B. Letiecq. 2022. "Interlinking Structural Racism and Heteropatriarchy: Rethinking Family Structure's Effects on Child Outcomes in a Racialized Unequal Society." *Journal of Family Theory and Review* 14, no. 3: 482–501.

Darity, W. 2011. "Revisiting the Debate on Race and Culture: The New (Incorrect) Harvard /Washington Consensus." *Du Bois Review: Social Science Research on Race* 8, no. 2: 467–476.

Delgado, R., and J. Stefancic. 2017. *Critical Race Theory: An Introduction*. New York: New York University Press.

Edin, K., and M. Kefalas. 2005. *Promises I Can Keep: Why Poor Women Put Motherhood before Marriage*. Berkeley: University of California Press.

Few-Demo, A. L. 2007. "Integrating Black Consciousness and Critical Race Feminism into Family Studies Research." *Journal of Family Issues* 28, no. 4: 452–473.

——. 2014. "Intersectionality as the 'New' Critical Approach in Feminist Family Studies: Evolving Racial/Ethnic Feminisms and Critical Race Theories." *Journal of Family Theory & Review* 6, no. 2: 169–183.

Franke, K. M. 1999. "Becoming a Citizen: Reconstruction Era Regulation of African American Marriages." *Yale Journal of Law and the Humanities* 11: 251.

Frankel, N. 1999. *Freedom's Women: Black Women and Families in Civil War Era Mississippi.* Bloomington: Indiana University Press.

Gans, H. J. 2011. "The Moynihan Report and Its Aftermaths: A Critical Analysis." *Du Bois Review: Social Science Research on Race* 8, no. 2: 315–327.

Geronimus, A. T. 2003. "Damned If You Do: Culture, Identity, Privilege, and Teenage Childbearing in the United States." *Social Science & Medicine* 57, no. 5: 881–893.

Gibson-Davis, C. M., K. Edin, and S. McLanahan. 2005. "High Hopes but Even Higher Expectations: The Retreat from Marriage among Low-Income Couples." *Journal of Marriage and Family* 67, no. 5: 1301–1312.

Golash-Boza, T. 2016. "A Critical and Comprehensive Sociological Theory of Race and Racism." *Sociology of Race and Ethnicity* 2, no. 2: 129–141.

Hamilton, D., W. Darity Jr., A. E. Price, V. Sridharan, and R. Tippett. 2015. *Umbrellas Don't Make It Rain: Why Studying and Working Hard Isn't Enough for Black Americans.* New York: New School.

Hardeman, R. R., P. A. Homan, T. Chantarat, B. A. Davis, and T. H. Brown. 2022. "Improving the Measurement of Structural Racism to Achieve Antiracist Health Policy: Study Examines Measurement of Structural Racism to Achieve Antiracist Health Policy." *Health Affairs* 41, no. 2: 179–186.

Haskins, R. 2009. "Moynihan Was Right: Now What?" *The Annals of the American Academy of Political and Social Science* 621, no. 1: 281–314.

Hawkins, A. J., P. R. Amato, and A. Kinghorn. 2013. "Are Government-Supported Healthy Marriage Initiatives Affecting Family Demographics? A State-Level Analysis." *Family Relations* 62, no. 3: 501–513.

Hill, S. A. 2006. "Marriage among African American Women: A Gender Perspective." *Journal of Comparative Family Studies*, 421–440.

Howell, E. A. 2018. "Reducing Disparities in Severe Maternal Morbidity and Mortality." *Clinical Obstetrics and Gynecology* 61, no. 2: 387.

Hunt, M. O. 2007. "African American, Hispanic, and White Beliefs about Black/White Inequality, 1977–2004." *American Sociological Review* 72, no. 3: 390–415.

Hunt, M. O., P. R. Croll, and M. Krysan. 2022. "Public Beliefs about the Black/White Socioeconomic Status Gap: What's 'Upbringing' Got to Do with It?" *Social Science Quarterly*, no. 1: 82–89.

Hunter, T. 2017. *Bound in Wedlock: Slave and Free Black Marriage in the Nineteenth Century.* Cambridge, MA: Belknap Press of Harvard University Press.

Iceland, J. 2019. "Racial and Ethnic Inequality in Poverty and Affluence, 1959–2015." *Population Research and Policy Review* 38: 615–654.

Jensen, T. M., and C. Sanner. 2021. "A Scoping Review of Research on Well-Being across Diverse Family Structures: Rethinking Approaches for Understanding Contemporary Families." *Journal of Family Theory & Review* 13, no. 4: 463–495.

Johnson, M. D. 2014. "Government-Supported Healthy Marriage Initiatives Are Not Associated with Changes in Family Demographics: A Comment on Hawkins, Amato, and Kinghorn." *Family Relations* 63, no. 2: 300–304.

Jones, C. P. 2000. "Levels of Racism: A Theoretic Framework and a Gardener's Tale." *American Journal of Public Health* 90, no. 8: 1212–1215.

Kendi, I. X. 2017. "The Civil Rights Act Was a Victory against Racism. But Racists Also Won." *Washington Post*, July 2. www.washingtonpost.com/news/made-by-history/wp/2017/07/02/the-civil-rights-act-was-a-victory-against-racism-but-racists-also-won/.

Kramer, M. R., N. C. Black, S. A. Matthews, and S. A. James. 2017. "The Legacy of Slavery and Contemporary Declines in Heart Disease Mortality in the US South." *SSM-Population Health* 3: 609–617.

Krieger, N., G. Van Wye, M. Huynh, P. D. Waterman, G. Maduro, W. Li, R. C. Gwynn, O. Barbot, and M. T. Bassett. 2020. "Structural Racism, Historical Redlining, and Risk of Preterm Birth in New York City, 2013–2017." *American Journal of Public Health* 110, no. 7: 1046–1053.

Lemmons, B. P., and W. E. Johnson. 2019. "Game Changers: A Critical Race Theory Analysis of the Economic, Social, and Political Factors Impacting Black Fatherhood and Family Formation." *Social Work in Public Health* 34: 86–101.

Lenhardt, R. A. 2014. "Marriage as Black Citizenship." *Hastings Law Journal* 66: 1317.

———. 2015. "Race, Dignity, and the Right to Marry." *Fordham Law Review* 84, no. 1: 53–67.

———. 2016. "Black Citizenship through Marriage—Reflections on the Moynihan Report at Fifty." *Southern California Interdisciplinary Law Journal* 25: 347.

Letiecq, B. L. 2019. "Surfacing Family Privilege and Supremacy in Family Science: Toward Justice for All." *Journal of Family Theory & Review* 11, no. 3: 398–411.

Livingstone, G. 2018. "About One-third of U.S. Children Are Living with an Unmarried Parent." Pew Research Center, April 27. https://www.pewresearch.org/short-reads/2018/04/27/about-one-third-of-u-s-children-are-living-with-an-unmarried-parent/#:~:text=All%20told%2C%2024%20million%20U.S.,live%20with%20a%20solo%20father.

Lynch, E. E., L. H. Malcoe, S. E. Laurent, J. Richardson, B. C. Mitchell, and H. C. Meier. 2021. "The Legacy of Structural Racism: Associations between Historic Redlining, Current Mortgage Lending, and Health." *SSM-Population Health* 14: 100793.

Maralani, V. 2013. "The Demography of Social Mobility: Black-White Differences in the Process of Educational Reproduction." *American Journal of Sociology* 118, no. 6: 1509–1558.

McLanahan, S. 2004. "Diverging Destinies: How Children Are Faring under the Second Demographic Transition." *Demography* 41, no. 4: 607–627.

———. 2009. "Fragile Families and the Reproduction of Poverty." *Annals of the American Academy of Political and Social Science* 621, no. 1: 111–131.

McLanahan, S., and C. Percheski. 2008. "Family Structure and the Reproduction of Inequalities." *Annual Review of Sociology* 34: 257–276.

Mehta, N. K., H. Lee, and K. R. Ylitalo. 2013. "Child Health in the United States: Recent Trends in Racial/Ethnic Disparities." *Social Science & Medicine* 95: 6–15.

Moynihan, D. P. 1965. *The Negro Family: The Case for National Action*. Office of Policy, Planning, and Research, U.S. Department of Labor. www.dol.gov/oasam/programs/history/webid-meynihan.htm.

Neubeck, K. J., and N. A. Cazenave. 2002. *Welfare Racism: Playing the Race Card against America's Poor*. New York: Routledge.

O'Connell, H. A. 2012. "The Impact of Slavery on Racial Inequality in Poverty in the Contemporary US South." *Social Forces* 90, no. 3: 713–734.

Oliver, M. L., and T. M. Shapiro. 2006. *Black Wealth, White Wealth: A New Perspective on Racial Inequality*. New York: Taylor & Francis.

Pew Research Center. 2016. "On Views of Race and Inequality, Blacks and Whites Are Worlds Apart," June 27. www.pewresearch.org/social-trends /2016/06/27/on-views-of-race-and-inequality-blacks-and-whites-are-worlds-apart/.

Reece, R. L. 2020. "Whitewashing Slavery: Legacy of Slavery and White Social Outcomes." *Social Problems* 67, no. 2: 304–323.

Reskin, B. 2012. "The Race Discrimination System." *Annual Review of Sociology* 38: 17–35.

Roberts, D. E. 2017. *Killing the Black Body: Race, Reproduction, and the Meaning of Liberty*. 20th anniversary ed. New York: Vintage.

Saito, L. T. 2009. *The Politics of Exclusion: The Failure of Race-Neutral Policies in Urban America*. Stanford, CA: Stanford University Press.

Sanner, C., and T. M. Jensen. 2021. "Toward More Accurate Measures of Family Structure: Accounting for Sibling Complexity." *Journal of Family Theory & Review* 13, no. 1: 110–127.

Sharkey, P. 2008. "The Intergenerational Transmission of Context." *American Journal of Sociology* 113, no. 4: 931–969.

Trail, T. E., and B. R. Karney. 2012. "What's (Not) Wrong with Low-Income Marriages." *Journal of Marriage and Family* 74, no. 3: 413–427.

Umberson, D., and M. B. Thomeer. 2020. "Family Matters: Research on Family Ties and Health, 2010–2020." *Journal of Marriage and Family* 82, no. 1: 404–419.

Vasquez-Tokos, J., and P. Yamin. 2021. "The Racialization of Privacy: Racial Formation as a Family Affair." *Theory and Society* 50, no. 5: 717–740.

Walsdorf, A. A., L. S. Jordan, C. R. McGeorge, and M. O. Caughy. 2020. "White Supremacy and the Web of Family Science: Implications of the Missing Spider." *Journal of Family Theory & Review* 12, no. 1: 64–79.

Wildsmith, E., J. Manlove, and E. Cook. 2018. *Dramatic Increase in the Proportion of Births Outside of Marriage in the United States from 1990 to 2016*. Child Trends.

Williams, D. T. 2019. "A Call to Focus on Racial Domination and Oppression: A Response to 'Racial and Ethnic Inequality in Poverty and Affluence, 1959–2015.'" *Population Research and Policy Review* 38: 655–663.

———. 2020. "Rethinking Black Families in Poverty: Postcolonial Critiques and Critical Race Possibilities." In *Introduction to Africana Demography* (pp. 143–164). Brill.

Williams, D. T., and R. S. Baker. 2021. "Family Structure, Risks, and Racial Stratification in Poverty." *Social Problems* 68, no. 4: 964–985.

Wilson, W. J. 2009. "The Moynihan Report and Research on the Black Community." *Annals of the American Academy of Political and Social Science* 621, no. 1: 34–46.

Wood, R. G., S. McConnell, Q. Moore, A. Clarkwest, and J. Hsueh. 2012. "The Effects of Building Strong Families: A Healthy Marriage and Relationship Skills Education Program for Unmarried Parents." *Journal of Policy Analysis and Management* 31, no. 2: 228–252.

Zuberi, T. 2003. *Thicker than Blood: How Racial Statistics Lie*. Minneapolis: University of Minnesota Press.

Zuberi, T., and E. Bonilla-Silva. 2008. *White Logic, White Methods: Racism and Methodology*. Lanham, MD: Rowman & Littlefield.

CHAPTER 6: The Evolution of American Families
by Stephanie Coontz

Adams, David Wallace. 1988. *Education for Extinction: American Indians and the Boarding School Experience, 1875–1928*. Lawrence: University Press of Kansas.

Amott, Theresa L., and Julie M. Matthaei. 1991. *Race, Gender, and Work: A Multicultural Gender Economic History of Women in the United States*. Boston: South End Press.

Aswad, Barbara C., and Barbara Bilge. 1996. *Family and Gender among American Muslims: Issues Facing Middle-Eastern Immigrants and Their Descendants*. Philadelphia: Temple University Press.

Bailey, Beth L. 1989. *From Front Porch to Back Seat: Courtship in Twentieth-Century America*. Baltimore, MD: Johns Hopkins University Press.

Bianchi, Suzanne M., John P. Robinson, and Melissa A. Milkie. 2006. *Changing Rhythms of Family Life*. New York: Russell Sage Foundation.

Boydston, Jeanne. 1990. *Home and Work: Housework, Wages, and the Ideology of Labor in the Early Republic*. New York: Oxford University Press.

Burguiere, André, et al. 1996. *A History of the Family*. Cambridge, MA: Belknap Press.

Coontz, Stephanie. 1988. *The Social Origins of Private Life: A History of American Families, 1600–1900*. New York: W. W. Norton.

——. 1992. *The Way We Never Were: American Families and the Nostalgia Trap*. New York: Basic Books.

——. 2006. *Marriage, A History: How Love Conquered Marriage*. New York: Penguin Books.

Coontz, Stephanie, Maya Parson, and Gabrielle Raley, eds. 2008. *American Families: A Multicultural Reader*. New York: Routledge.

Cott, Nancy. 2000. *Public Vows: A History of Marriage and the Nation*. Cambridge, MA: Harvard University Press.

D'Emilio, John, and Estelle B. Freedman. 1997. *Intimate Matters: A History of Sexuality in America*. 2nd ed. Chicago: University of Chicago Press.

Gabaccia, Danna, and Vicki L. Ruiz. 2006. *American Dreaming, Global Realities: Rethinking U.S. Immigration History*. Chicago: University of Chicago Press.

Gallup, George, and Evan Hill. 1962. "The American Woman." *Saturday Evening Post*, December 22–29.

Gaspar, David Barry, and Darlene Clark Hine. 1996. *More than Chattel: Black Women and Slavery in the Americas*. Bloomington: University of Indiana Press.

Gottlieb, Beatrice. 1993. *The Family in the Western World from the Black Death to the Industrial Age*. New York: Oxford University Press.

Gullickson, Aaron. 2006. "Black/White Interracial Marriage Trends, 1850–2000." *Journal of Family History* 31, no. 3: 1–24

Hing, Bill Ong. 1993. *Making and Remaking Asian America through Immigration Policy, 1850–1990*. Stanford, CA: Stanford University Press.

Hirsch, Jennifer S. 2003. *A Courtship after Marriage: Sexuality and Love in Mexican Transnational Communities*. Berkeley: University of California Press.

Hua, Cai. 2001. *Society without Fathers or Husbands: The Na of China*. Cambridge, MA: MIT Press.

Ingoldsby, Bron B., and Suzanna D. Smith. 2006. *Families in Global and Multicultural Perspective*. 2nd ed. Thousand Oaks, CA: Sage.

Ishwaran, K. 1992. *Family and Marriage: Cross-Cultural Perspectives*. Toronto: Thompson Educational Publishing.

Katz, Michael J., Michael J. Doucet, and Mark J. Stern. 1982. *The Social Organization of Early Industrial Capitalism.* Cambridge, MA: Harvard University Press.

Kennedy, Cynthia. 2005. *Braided Relations, Entwined Lives: The Women of Charleston's Urban Slave Society.* Bloomington: Indiana University Press.

Lobo, Susan. 1998. *Native American Voices: A Reader.* New York: Longman.

Lott, Juanita Tamayo. 2006. *Common Destiny: Filipino American Generations.* Lanham, MD: Rowman & Littlefield.

Lyons, Clare A. 2006. *Sex among the Rabble: An Intimate History of Gender and Power in the Age of Revolution.* Chapel Hill: University of North Carolina Press.

Maffi, Mario. 1995. *Gateway to the Promised Lands: Ethnic Cultures on New York's Lower East Side.* New York: New York University Press.

May, Elaine Tyler. 1980. *Great Expectations: Marriage and Divorce in Post-Victorian America.* Chicago: University of Chicago Press.

———. 1988. *Homeward Bound: American Families in the Cold War Era.* New York: Basic Books.

McAdoo, Harriette Pipes. 2007. *Black Families.* 4th ed. Thousand Oaks, CA: Sage.

McCurry, Stephanie. 1995. *Masters of Small Worlds: Yeoman Households, Gender Relations, and the Political Culture of the Antebellum South Carolina Low Country.* Athens: University of Georgia Press.

McGhee, Heather. 2021. *The Sum of Us: What Racism Costs Everyone and How We Can Prosper Together.* New York: Penguin Random House.

Miles, Tiya. 2005. *Ties That Bind: The Story of an Afro-Cherokee Family in Slavery and Freedom.* Berkeley: University of California Press.

Mintz, Steven, and Susan Kellogg. 1988. *Domestic Revolutions: A Social History of American Family Life.* New York: Free Press.

Moran, Rachel. 2001. *Interracial Intimacy: The Regulation of Race and Romance.* Chicago: University of Chicago Press.

Mullings, Leith. 1997. *On Our Own Terms: Race, Class, and Gender in the Lives of African-American Women.* New York: Routledge.

Ngai, Mae M. 2004. *Impossible Subjects: Illegal Aliens and the Making of Modern America.* Princeton, NJ: Princeton University Press.

O'Day, Rosemary. 1994. *The Family and Family Relationships, 1500–1900.* London: Palgrave Macmillan.

Peters, Virginia Bergman. 1995. *Women of the Earth Lodges: Tribal Life on the Plains.* New Haven, CT: Archon Books.

Ritterhouse, Jennifer. 2006. *Growing Up Jim Crow: How Black and White Southern Children Learned Race.* Chapel Hill: University of North Carolina Press.

Rosen, Ruth. 2000. *The World Split Open: How the Women's Movement Changed America.* New York: Penguin Books.

Rubin, Lillian B. 1994. *Families on the Fault Line.* New York: HarperCollins.

Ruiz, Vicki, and Ellen Dubois. 2000. *Unequal Sisters: A Multicultural Reader in U.S. Women's History.* 3rd ed. New York: Routledge.

Ryan, Mary P. 1983. *Cradle of the Middle Class: The Family in Oneida County, New York, 1790–1865.* New York: Cambridge University Press.

Seccombe, Wally. 1992. *A Millennium of Family Change.* London: Verso.

Skolnick, Arlene S., and Jerome H. Skolnick. 2003. *Family in Transition.* 12th ed. Boston: Allyn & Bacon.

Stacey, Judith. 1990. *Brave New Families: Stories of Domestic Upheaval in Late Twentieth-Century America.* New York: Basic Books.

Stavig, Ward. 1995. "'Living in Offense of Our Lord': Indigenous Sexual Values and Marital Life in the Colonial Crucible." *Hispanic American Historical Review* 75, no. 4: 597–622.

Stevenson, Brenda E. 1996. *Life in Black and White: Family and Community in the Slave South.* New York: Oxford University Press.

Thorne, Barrie, and Marilyn Yalom. 1992. *Rethinking the Family: Some Feminist Questions.* Boston: Northeastern University Press.

Tung, Mae Paomay. 2000. *Chinese Americans and Their Immigrant Parents: Conflict, Identity, and Values.* Binghamton, NY: Haworth.

Vecchio, Diane C. 2006. *Merchants, Midwives, and Laboring Women: Italian Migrants in Urban America.* Champaign: University of Illinois Press.

Wallenstein, Peter. 2002. *Tell the Court I Love My Wife: Race, Marriage, and Law—An American History.* New York: Palgrave Macmillan.

Weiss, Jessica. 2000. *To Have and to Hold: Marriage, the Baby Boom, and Social Change.* Chicago: University of Chicago Press.

Wong, Bernard P. 2006. *The Chinese in Silicon Valley: Globalization, Social Networks, and Ethnic Identity.* Lanham, MD: Rowman & Littlefield.

Zinn, Maxime Baca, D. Stanley Eitzen, and Barbara Wells. 2008. *Diversity in Families.* 8th ed. Boston: Allyn & Bacon.

CHAPTER 7: American Childhood as a Social and Cultural Construct
by Steven Mintz

Ambramitsky, Ran, and Leah Boustan. 2022. "Why the Children of Immigrants Are the Ones Getting Ahead in America." *Time,* June 1. time.com/6182715/immigrants-children-us-mobility/.

American Psychological Association. n.d. "Undocumented Americans." www.apa.org/topics /immigration-refugees/undocumented-video.

Axtell, James. 1974. *The School upon a Hill: Education and Society in Colonial New England.* New Haven, CT: Yale University Press.

Belkin, Lisa. 2000. "The Making of an 8-Year-Old Woman." *New York Times,* December 24.

Burns, Kalee, Liana Fox, and Danielle Wilson. 2022. "Expansions to Child Tax Credit Contributed to 46% Declines in Child Poverty Since 2020." U.S. Census Bureau. www .census.gov/library/stories/2022/09/record-drop-in-child-poverty.html.

Center on Poverty and Social Policy at Columbia University. 2022. "3.7 Million More Children in Poverty Jan 2022 without Monthly Child Tax Credit." www.povertycenter .columbia.edu/news-internal/monthly-poverty-january-2022.

Charles, Rebecca, Sophie Collyer, and Christopher Wimer. 2022. "The Role of Government Transfers in the Black-White Child Poverty Gap." Center on Poverty and Social Policy at Columbia University. static1.squarespace.com/static/610831a16c95260dbd68934a1/62_ a300c46e382698827a2f1/1646932056576/Role-of-Government-Transfers-Black-White-Child-Poverty-Gap-CPSP-2022.pdf.

Child Trends. 2018. "Trends in Immigrant Children." December 28. www.childtrends.org /indicators/immigrant-children.

Chudacoff, Howard P. 1989. *How Old Are You? Age Consciousness in American Society.* Princeton, NJ: Princeton University Press.

Clement, Priscilla. 1997. *Growing Pains: Children in the Industrial Age, 1850–1890.* New York: Twayne.

Grant, Julia. 1998. *Raising Baby by the Book: The Education of American Mothers.* New Haven, CT: Yale University Press.

Herman-Giddens, Marcia E., E. J. Slora, R. C. Wasserman, C. J. Bourdony, M. V. Bhapkar, G. G. Koch, and C. M. Hasemeier. 1997. "Secondary Sexual Characteristics and Menses in Young Girls Seen in Office Practice: A Study from the Pediatric Research in Office Settings Network." *Pediatrics* 99, no. 4: 505–512.

Heywood, Colin. 2001. A *History of Childhood: Children and Childhood in the West from Medieval to Modern Times.* Cambridge, UK: Polity.

Hulbert, Ann. 2003. *Raising America: Experts, Parents, and a Century of Advice about Children.* New York: Knopf.

Illick, Joseph. 2002. *American Childhoods.* Philadelphia: University of Pennsylvania Press.

Ishizuka, Patrick. 2019. "Social Class, Gender, and Contemporary Parenting Standards in the United States: Evidence from a National Survey Experiment." *Social Forces* 98, no. 1: 31–58.

Jones, Kathleen W. 1999. *Taming the Troublesome Child.* Cambridge, MA: Harvard University Press.

Kett, Joseph F. 1977. *Rites of Passage: Adolescence in America.* New York: Basic Books.

Kline, Daniel T. 1998. "Holding Therapy." March 7. History-Child-Family Listserv (history-child-family@mailbase.ac.uk).

Kolata, Gina. 2001a. "Doubters Fault Theory Finding Earlier Puberty." *New York Times,* February 20.

———. 2001b. "2 Endocrinology Groups Raise Doubt on Earlier Onset of Girls' Puberty." *New York Times,* March 3.

Lareau, Annette. 2003. *Unequal Childhoods: Class, Race, and Family Life.* Berkeley: University of California Press.

Macleod, David I. 1998. *The Age of the Child: Children in America, 1890–1912.* New York: Twayne.

Mintz, Steven, and Susan Kellogg. 1988. *Domestic Revolutions: A Social History of American Family Life.* New York: Free Press.

Nasaw, David. 1985. *Children in the City: At Work and at Play.* Garden City, NY: Anchor Press/Doubleday.

Robertson, Stephen. 1994. *The Disappearance of Childhood.* New York: Vintage Books.

Russell, Stephen T., Lisa J. Crockett, and Ruth K. Chao. 2010. *Asian American Parenting and Parent-Adolescent Relationships.* New York: Springer.

Schultz, James A. 1995. *The Knowledge of Childhood in the German Middle Ages, 1100–1350.* Philadelphia: University of Pennsylvania Press.

Scraton, Phil, ed. 1997. *"Childhood" in "Crisis"?* London: University College of London Press.

Stansell, Christine. 1986. *City of Women: Sex and Class in New York, 1789–1860.* New York: Knopf.

Weissbourd, Richard. 1996. *The Vulnerable Child: What Really Hurts America's Children and What We Can Do about It.* Reading, MA: Addison-Wesley.

Wu, Fang, and Sen Qi. 2004. "Asian-American Parents: Are They Really Different?" Online submission, paper presented at the Annual Conference of the Chinese American Educational Research and Development Association (San Diego, CA, April 2004). files.eric.ed.gov/fulltext/ED489960.pdf.

CHAPTER 8: African Americans and the Birth of the Modern Marriage
by Donna L. Franklin

Berlin, Ira, and Leslie S. Rowland, eds. 1998. *Families and Freedom: A Documentary History of African-American Kinship in the Civil War Era.* New York: New Press.

Bernard, Jessie. 1966. *Marriage and Family among Negroes.* Englewood Cliffs, NJ: Prentice-Hall.

Bird, Carol. 1979. *The Two-Paycheck Family.* New York: Rawson, Wade.

Blumstein, Phillip, and Pepper Schwartz. 1983. *American Couples.* New York: Morrow.

Boris, Eileen. 1993. "The Power of Motherhood: Black and White Activist Women Redefine the Political." In *Mothers of a New World,* edited by Seth Koven and Sonya Michel, 213–245. New York: Routledge.

Bowen, William C., and Derek Bok. 1998. *The Shape of the River: Long Term Consequences of Considering Race in College and University Admissions.* Princeton, NJ: Princeton University Press.

Burbridge, Lynn C. 1995. "Policy Implications for a Decline in Marriage among African-Americans." In *The Decline in Marriage among African Americans,* edited by M. Belinda Tucker and Claudia Mitchell-Kernan, 229–260. New York: Russell Sage Foundation.

Butterfield, Fox. 2002. "Study Finds Big Increase in Black Men as Inmates Since 1980." *New York Times,* August 29.

Carby, Hazel V. 1987. *Reconstructing Womanhood: The Emergence of the Afro-American Woman Novelist.* New York: Oxford University Press.

Carlson, Shirley J. 1992. "Black Ideals of Womanhood in the Late Victorian Era." *Journal of Negro History* 77, no. 2: 61–73.

Clinton, Catherine, and Nina Silber, eds. 1992. *Divided Houses: Gender and the Civil War.* New York: Oxford University Press.

Conrad, Cecelia A. 2008. "Black Women: An Unfinished Agenda." *American Prospect* 15, no. 10: A12–A15.

Coontz, Stephanie. 2006. *Marriage, A History: How Love Conquered Marriage.* New York: Penguin Books.

Cooper, Anna Julia. 1990. *A Voice of the South.* Introduction by Mary Helen Washington. New York: Oxford University Press.

Cott, Nancy F. 2000. *Public Vows: A History of Marriage and the Nation.* Cambridge, MA: Harvard University Press.

Cuthbert, Marion. 1936. "Problems Facing Negro Young Women." *Opportunity,* February 2, 48.

Davis, Elizabeth Lindsay. 1933. *Lifting as They Climb: The National Association of Colored Women.* Washington, DC: National Association of Colored Women.

DuBois, W. E. B. 1924. *The Gift of Black Folk.* Boston: Stratford.

Epstein, Cynthia Fuchs. 1971. "Law Partners and Marital Partners: Strains and Solutions in the Dual-Career Family Enterprise." *Human Relations* 24, no. 6: 549–563.

Faust, Drew Gilpin. 1996. *Mothers of Invention.* Chapel Hill, NC: University of North Carolina Press.

Foner, Eric. 1988. *Reconstruction: America's Unfinished Revolution, 1863–77.* New York: Harper and Row.

Franklin, Donna L. 1997. *Ensuring Inequality: The Structural Transformation of the African-American Family.* New York: Oxford University Press.

———. 2000. *What's Love Got to Do with It? Understanding and Healing the Rift between Black Men and Women*. New York: Simon and Schuster.

Freeman, Elsie, Wynell Burroughs Schamel, and Jean West. 1992. "The Fight for Equal Rights: A Recruiting Poster for Black Soldiers in the Civil War." *Social Education* 56, no. 2: 118–120.

Giddings, Paula. 1985. *When and Where I Enter: The Impact of Black Women on Race and Sex in America*. New York: Bantam Books.

———. 2008. *Ida: A Sword among Lions: Ida B. Wells and the Campaign against Lynching*. New York: Amistad.

Gordon, Linda. 1991. "Black and White Visions of Welfare: Women's Welfare Activism, 1890–1943." *Journal of American History* 78: 559–590.

Hacker, Andrew. 1992. *Two Nations: Black and White, Separate, Hostile, Unequal*. New York: Ballantine Books.

Hall, Francine S. 1979. *The Two-Career Couple*. Reading, MA: Addison-Wesley.

Harley, Sharon. 1988. "Mary Church Terrell: Genteel Militant." In *Black Leaders of the Nineteenth Century*, edited by Leon F. Litwack and August Meier, 307–322. Urbana: University of Illinois Press.

Harris, Barbara J. 1978. *Beyond Her Sphere: Women and the Professions in American History*. Westport, CT: Greenwood.

Higginbotham, Evelyn Brooks. 1993. *Righteous Discontent: The Women's Movement in the Baptist Church, 1880–1920*. Cambridge, MA: Harvard University Press.

Holmstrom, Lynda Lytle. 1972. *The Two Career Family*. Cambridge, MA: Schenkman.

Jones, Jacqueline. 1985. *Labor of Love: Black Women, Work, and the Family from Slavery to Present*. New York: Basic Books.

Kennedy, Susan Estabrook. 1979. *If All We Did Was to Weep at Home: A History of White Working-Class Women in America*. Bloomington: Indiana University Press.

Kessler-Harris, Alice. 1982. *Out to Work: A History of Wage-Earning Women in the United States*. New York: Oxford University Press.

Landry, Bart. 2000. *Black Working Wives: Pioneers of the American Family Revolution*. Berkeley: University of California Press.

Lerner, Gerda. 1972. *Black Women in White America: A Documentary History*. New York: Vintage Books.

Litwack, Leon F. 1998. *Trouble in Mind: Black Southerners in the Age of Jim Crow*. New York: Knopf.

Loewenberg, Bert James, and Ruth Bogin, eds. 1976. *Black Women in the Nineteenth-Century American Life: Their Words, Their Thoughts, Their Feelings*. University Park: Pennsylvania State University Press.

Massey, Mary E. 1966. *Bonnet Brigades*. New York: Knopf.

Matthaei, Julie. 1982. *An Economic History of Women in America*. New York: Schocken Books.

McMurry, Linda O. 1998. *To Keep the Waters Troubled: The Life of Ida B. Wells*. New York: Oxford University Press.

Mills, C. Wright. 1959. *The Sociological Imagination*. New York: Oxford University Press.

Mintz, Steven, and Susan Kellogg. 1988. *Domestic Revolutions: A Social History of American Family Life*. New York: Free Press.

Moses, William Jeremiah. 1978. *The Golden Age of Black Nationalism*. New York: Oxford University Press.

Noble, Jeanne. 1956. "The Negro Woman's College Education." Ph.D. dissertation, Teachers College, Columbia University, New York.

Poloma, Margaret M., and T. Neal Garland. 1971. "The Married Professional Woman: A Study in the Tolerance of Domestication." *Journal of Marriage and the Family* 33, no. 3: 531–540.

Powdermaker, Hortense. 1939. *After Freedom: A Cultural Study in the Deep South.* New York: Viking.

Rapoport, Rhona, and Robert Rapoport. 1971. *Dual-Career Families.* Middlesex, UK: Penguin Books.

Rouse, Jacqueline A. 1989. *Lugenia Hope Burns: Black Southerner Reformer.* Athens: University of Georgia Press.

Ruffin, Josephine St. Pierre. 1895. "Address to the First National Conference of Colored Women." Charles Street A. M. E. Church. Boston, July 29.

Satcher, David, George E. Fryer Jr., Jessica McCann, Adewale Troutman, Steven H. Woolf, and George Rust. 2005. "What If We Were Equal? A Comparison of the Black-White Mortality Gap in 1960 and 2000." *Health Affairs* 24, no. 2: 459–464.

Scott, Ann Firor. 1970. *The Southern Lady from Pedestal to Politics: 1830–1930.* Chicago: University of Chicago Press.

Shaw, Stephanie J. 1996. *What a Woman Ought to Be and Do: Black Professional Women Workers during the Jim Crow Era.* Chicago: University of Chicago Press.

Smith-Rosenberg, Carol. 1985. *Disorderly Conduct: Visions of Gender in Victorian America.* New York: Knopf.

Vicinus, Martha. 1985. *Independent Women: Work and Community of Single Women, 1850–1920.* Chicago: University of Chicago Press.

Vinoskis, Maris A. 1989. "Have Social Historians Lost the Civil War? Some Preliminary Demographic Speculations." *Journal of American History* 76, no. 1 35–59.

Wells, Ida B. 1970. *Crusade for Justice: The Autobiography of Ida B. Wells,* edited by Alfreda M. Duster. Chicago: University of Chicago Press.

Wertheimer, Barbara M. 1977. *We Were There: The Story of Working Women in America.* New York: Pantheon Books.

Williams, Fannie Barrier. 1904. "The Women's Part in a Man's Business." *Voice* 1, no. 11 544.

Wilson, W. J., & Neckerman, K. M. 1987. "Poverty and Family Structure: The Widening Gap between Evidence and Public Policy Issues." In *The Truly Disadvantaged,* edited by W. J. Wilson, 232–259. Chicago: University of Chicago Press.

CHAPTER 9: Change That Counts: The Evolution of Americans' Definition of Family
by Claudia Geist, Catherine Bolzendahl, Lala Carr Steelman, and Brian Powell

Allport, Gordon W. 1954. *The Nature of Prejudice.* Reading, MA: Addison-Wesley.

Hart-Brinson, Peter. 2018. *The Gay Marriage Generation: How the LGBTQ Movement Transformed American Culture.* New York: New York University Press.

McCutcheon, Allen L. 1987. *Latent Class Analysis.* Newbury Park, CA: Sage.

Pettigrew, Thomas F., and Linda R. Tropp. 2006. "A Meta-Analytic Test of Intergroup Contact Theory." *Journal of Personality and Social Psychology* 90: 751–783.

Powell, Brian, Catherine Bolzendahl, Claudia Geist, and Lala Carr Steelman. 2010. *Counted Out: Same-Sex Relations and Americans' Definitions of Family*. New York: Russell Sage Foundation.

Smith, Dorothy E. 1993. "The Standard North American Family: SNAF as an Ideological Code." *Journal of Family Issues* 14: 50–65.

Weston, Kath. 1997. *Families We Choose: Lesbians, Gays, Kinship*. 2nd ed. New York: Columbia University Press.

CHAPTER 10: Labor Unions and Families, a Very Brief History
by Shawn Fremstad

AFL-CIO. n.d. "Mother Jones." aflcio.org/about/history/labor-history-people/mother-jones.

Associated Press. 1933. "Green Hits Choice of Miss Perkins." *Evening Star*, March 1, 3.

Bremner, Robert H. (Robert Hamlett). 1956. *From the Depths; the Discovery of Poverty in the United States*. New York: New York University Press.

Brown, Hayley. 2022. "A May Day Assessment of Union Membership in the United States— Center for Economic and Policy Research." *CEPR*, April 29. cepr.net/union-2022.

Clark, Peter Allen. 2022. "2022 Was Tech's Biggest Year Yet for Labor Unions and Workplace Organizing." *Axios*, December 12. www.axios.com/2022/12/12/tech-labor -movement-unions-2022.

Cooper, Melinda. 2017. *Family Values: Between Neoliberalism and the New Social Conserva-tism*. Princeton, NJ: Princeton University Press.

Farber, Henry S., Daniel Herbst, Ilyana Kuziemko, and Suresh Naidu. 2021. "Unions and Inequality over the Twentieth Century: New Evidence from Survey Data." *Quarterly Journal of Economics* 136, no. 3: 1325–1385.

Foner, Philip Sheldon. 1947. *History of the Labor Movement in the United States: From Colonial Times to the Founding of the American Federation of Labor*. New York: International Publishers.

———. 1979. *Women and the American Labor Movement*. New York: Free Press.

———. 1982. *Organized Labor and the Black Worker, 1619–1981*. New York: International Publishers.

Gonyea, Don. 2021. "House Democrats Pass Bill That Would Protect Worker Organizing Efforts." *NPR*, March 9. www.npr.org/2021/03/09/975259434/house-democrats -pass-bill-that-would-protect-worker-organizing-efforts.

Gramlich, John. 2021. "Majorities of Americans Say Unions Have a Positive Effect on U.S. and That Decline in Union Membership Is Bad." *Pew Research Center*, September 3. www.pewresearch.org/fact-tank/2021/09/03/majorities-of-americans-say-unions-have-a -positive-effect-on-u-s-and-that-decline-in-union-membership-is-bad/.

International Labour Organisation. 2022. "Statistics on Union Membership." *ILOSTAT*. ilostat.ilo.org/topics/union-membership/.

Karch, Andrew. 2013. "A Watershed Episode: The Comprehensive Child Development Act." In *Early Start: Preschool Politics in the United States*, 59–85. Ann Arbor, MI: University of Michigan Press.

Kessler-Harris, Alice. 1975. "Where Are the Organized Women Workers?" *Feminist Studies* 3, no. 1/2: 92–110.

Levine, Susan. 1983. "Labor's True Woman: Domesticity and Equal Rights in the Knights of Labor." *Journal of American History* 70, no. 2: 323–339.

McCarthy, Justin. 2022. "U.S. Approval of Labor Unions at Highest Point Since 1965." *Gallup*, August 30, 2022. news.gallup.com/poll/398303/approval-labor-unions-highest-point-1965.aspx.

Milkman, Ruth, ed. 1987. *Women, Work, and Protest: A Century of US Women's Labor History*. New York: Routledge.

National Labor Relations Board. 2022. "First Three Quarters' Union Election Petitions Up 56%, Exceeding All FY21 Petitions Filed." July 13. www.nlrb.gov/news-outreach/news-story/first-three-quarters-union-election-petitions-up-56-exceeding-all-fy21.

Neill, Charles Patrick. 1916. "Summary of the Report on Condition of Woman and Child Wage Earners in the United States." U.S. Department of Labor. Washington, DC: Government Printing Office.

Nixon, Richard. 1971. "Veto of the Economic Opportunity Amendments of 1971." *The American Presidency Project*. www.presidency.ucsb.edu/documents/veto-the-economic-opportunity-amendments-1971.

Organization for Economic Co-operation and Development. 2023. "Employment Rate: Aged 25–54: Females for France." Federal Reserve Bank of St. Louis. January 13, 2023. fred.stlouisfed.org/series/LREM25FEFRQ156S.

Ruggles, Steven. 2015. "Patriarchy, Power, and Pay: The Transformation of American Families, 1800–2015." *Demography* 52, no. 6: 1797–1823.

Trades Union Congress. 2014. "New TUC Guide Shows How Unions Improve Jobs and Build a Fairer Society." September 6, 2014. www.tuc.org.uk/news/new-tuc-guide-shows-how-unions-improve-jobs-and-build-a-fairer-society.

Troy, Leo. 1965. "Trade Union Membership, 1897–1962." *Review of Economics and Statistics* 47, no. 1: 93–113.

UE News. 2021. "UE Fought for Child Care as 'Infrastructure' as Far Back as WWII." May 9, 2021. www.ueunion.org/ue-news-feature/2021/ue-fought-for-child-care-as-infrastructure-world-war-two.

U.S. Bureau of Labor. 1910–1913. *Report on Condition of Woman and Child Wage-Earners in the United States: In 19 Vols*. Washington, DC: U.S. Government Printing Office.

U.S. Bureau of Labor Statistics. 2022. "Employment Characteristics of Families News Release—2021 Annual Results." April 20, 2022. www.bls.gov/news.release/famee.htm.

U.S. Census Bureau. 1909. "A Century of Population Growth from the First Census of the United States to the Twelfth, 1790–1900." Washington, DC: U.S. Government Printing Office.

U.S. Department of Agriculture. 2018. "Agricultural Statistics 2018." May 4, 2018. downloads.usda.library.cornell.edu/usda-esmis/files/j3860694x/2z10wz00c/9019s972q/Ag_Stats_2018.pdf.

Walker, Roger W. 1970. "The A.F.L. and Child-labor Legislation: An Exercise in Frustration." *Labor History* 11, no. 3: 323–40.

Woloch, Nancy. 2015. *A Class by Herself: Protective Laws for Women Workers, 1890s–1990s*. Princeton, NJ: Princeton University Press.

CHAPTER 11: Childfree Families
by Amy Blackstone, Brittany Stahnke, and Amy Greenleaf

Angeles, Luis. 2010. "Children and Life Satisfaction." *Journal of Happiness Studies* 11: 523–538.

Blackstone, Amy. 2013. "Setting the Record Straight on 6 Myths about Childless Adults." *Bangor Daily News*, September 17.

———. 2014. "Doing Family without Having Kids." *Sociology Compass* 8, no. 1: 52–62.

Bogenschneider, Karen. 2006. *Family Policy Matters: How Policy Making Affects Families and What Professionals Can Do*. Mahwah, NJ: Lawrence Erlbaum Associates.

Brown, A. 2021. *Growing Share of Childless Adults in U.S. Don't Expect to Ever Have Children*. Pew Research Center, November 19. www.pewresearch.org/fact-tank /2021/11/19/growing-share-of-childless-adults-in-u-s-dont-expect-to-ever-have-children/.

Burman, Bonnie, and Diane de Anda. 1986. "Parenthood and Non-parenthood: A Comparison of Intentional Families." *Lifestyles* 8: 69–84.

DeOllos, Ione Y., and Carolyn A. Kapinus. 2002. "Aging Childless Individuals and Couples: Suggestions for New Directions in Research." *Sociological Inquiry* 72: 72–80.

Dye, Jane Lawler. 2008. *Fertility of American Women: 2006*. Washington, DC: U.S. Census Bureau.

Gubrium, Jaber F., and James A. Holstein. 1990. *What Is Family?* Mountain View, CA: Mayfield.

Hansen, Thomas. 2012. "Parenthood and Happiness: A Review of Folk Theories versus Empirical Evidence." *Social Indicators Research* 108: 29–64.

Henslin, James M. 2010. *Sociology: A Down-to-Earth Approach, Core Concepts*. 4th ed. Boston: Pearson.

Horwitz, Steven. 2005. "The Functions of the Family in the Great Society." *Cambridge Journal of Economics* 29: 669–684.

Houseknecht, Sharon K. 1987. "Voluntary Childlessness." In *Handbook of Marriage and the Family*, edited by Marvin B. Sussman and Suzanne K. Steinmetz, 369–395. New York: Plenum.

Johnson, E., and S. Volsche. 2021. "COVID-19: Companion Animals Help People Cope during Government-imposed Social Isolation." *Society & Animals* 29, no. 2: 1–18.

Knox, David. 2011. *M&F*. Belmont, CA: Wadsworth, Cengage Learning.

Kramer, Laura. 2011. *The Sociology of Gender: A Brief Introduction*. New York: Oxford University Press.

Laslett, Barbara, and Johanna Brenner. 1989. "Gender and Social Reproduction: Historical Perspectives." *Annual Review of Sociology* 15: 381–404.

Monte, Lindsay M., and Renee R. Ellis. 2014. *Fertility of Women in the United States: 2012*. U.S. Census Bureau, July. www.census.gov/content/dam/Census/library/publica tions/2014/demo/p20-575.pdf.

Osborne, Ruth S. 2003. "Percentage of Childless Women 40 to 44 Years Old Increases since 1976, Census Bureau Reports." U.S. Census Bureau Press Release.

Oswald, Ramona Faith, Libby Balter Blume, and Stephen R. Marks. 2005. "Decentering Heteronormativity: A Model for Family Studies." In *Sourcebook of Family Theory and Research*, edited by Vern L. Bengtson, Alan C. Acock, Katherine R. Allen, Peggy Dilworth-Anderson, and David M. Klein, 143–165. Thousand Oaks, CA: Sage.

Oswald, Ramona Faith, and Elizabeth A. Suter. 2004. "Heterosexist Inclusion and Exclusion during Ritual: A 'Straight versus Gay' Comparison." *Journal of Family Issues* 25, no. 7: 881–899.

Somers, Marsha D. 1993. "A Comparison of Voluntarily Childfree Adults and Parents." *Journal of Marriage and the Family* 55: 643–650.

Stahnke, B., A. Blackstone, and H. Howard. 2020. "Lived Experiences and Life Satisfaction of Childfree Women in Late Life." *Family Journal* 28, no. 2: 159–167.

Stahnke, B., and M. Cooley. 2021. "A Systematic Review of the Association between Partnership and Life Satisfaction." *Family Journal* 29, no. 2: 182–189.

Stahnke, B., M. Cooley, and A. Blackstone. 2022. "A Systematic Review of Life Satisfaction Experiences among Childfree Adults." *Family Journal*: 1–9.

Tomczak, Lisa M. 2012. *Childfree or Voluntarily Childless? The Lived Experience of Women Choosing Non-motherhood.* Master's thesis, Northern Arizona University. Ann Arbor, MI: ProQuest.

Twenge, Jean M., W. Keith Campbell, and Craig A. Foster. 2003. "Parenthood and Marital Satisfaction: A Meta-Analytic Review." *Journal of Marriage and Family* 65: 574–583.

Valerio, T., B. Knop, R. M. Kreider, and W. He. 2021. *Childless Older Americans: 2018.* U.S. Census Bureau Current Population Reports.

Veevers, Jean E. 1980. *Childless by Choice.* Toronto: Butterworths.

Volsche, S. 2020. "Pet Parents and the Loss of Attachment." In *Pet Loss, Grief, and Therapeutic Interventions: Practitioners Navigating the Human-Animal Bond Book,* edited by L. Kogan and P. Erdman, 1: 55–69. Routledge.

Volsche, S., and P. Gray. 2016. "Dog Moms' Use Authoritative Parenting Styles." *Human-Animal Interaction Bulletin* 4, no. 2: 1–16.

West, Candace, and Donald Zimmerman. 1987. "Doing Gender." *Gender & Society* 1: 125–151.

Zagura, Michelle. 2012. *Parental Status, Spousal Behaviors and Marital Satisfaction.* Master's thesis, SUNY–Albany. Ann Arbor, MI: ProQuest.

CHAPTER 12: Stepfamilies as They Really Are
by Lawrence Ganong, Marilyn Coleman, and Caroline Sanner

Braithwaite, D. O., P. W. Toller, K. L. Daas, W. T. Durham, and A. C. Jones. 2008. "Centered but Not Caught in the Middle: Stepchildren's Perceptions of Dialectical Contradictions in the Communication of Co-parents." *Journal of Applied Communication Research* 36, no. 1: 33–55.

Chapman, A., C. Sanner, L. Ganong, M. Coleman, L. T. Russell, Y. Kang, and S. Mitchell. 2016. "Exploring the Complexity of Stepgrandparent-Stepgrandchild Relationships." *Contemporary Perspectives in Family Research* 10: 101–130.

Cherlin, A. 1978. "Remarriage as an Incomplete Institution." *American Journal of Sociology* 84, no. 3: 634–650.

Ganong, L., and M. Coleman. (2004) 2017. *Stepfamily Relationships: Development, Dynamics, and Interventions.* 2nd ed. New York:

———. 2018. "Studying Stepfamilies: Four Eras of Family Scholarship." *Family Process* 57, no. 1: 7–24.

Ganong, L., M. Coleman, and T. Jamison. 2011. "Patterns of Stepchild-Stepparent Relationship Development." *Journal of Marriage and Family* 73, no. 2: 396–413.

Ganong, L., M. Coleman, C. Sanner, and S. Berkley. 2022. "Effective Coparenting in Stepfamilies: Empirical Evidence of What Works." *Family Relations* 71, no. 3: 918–934.

Ganong, L., and C. Sanner. 2023. "A Review of Stepfamily Typologies." *Journal of Child and Family Studies.* doi.org/10.1007/s10826-023-02558-4.

Guzzo, K. B. 2016. *Stepfamilies in the U.S.* (FP-16-09). National Center for Family & Marriage Research. www.bgsu.edu/content/dam/BGSU/college-of-arts-and-sciences/NCFMR/documents/FP/guzzo-stepfamilies-women-fp-16-09.pdf.

Papernow, P. L. 1987. "Thickening the Middle Ground: Dilemmas and Vulnerabilities of Remarried Couples." *Psychotherapy: Theory, Research, Practice, Training* 24: 630–639.
———. 2018. "Clinical Guidelines for Working with Stepfamilies: What Family, Couple, Individual, and Child Therapists Need to Know." *Family Process* 57, no. 1: 25–51.
Reynolds, L. 2020. *Ten Years of Change in the U.S. Remarriage Rate, 2008 & 2018* (FP-20-20). National Center for Family & Marriage Research. doi.org/10.25035/ncfmr/fp-20-20.
Sanner, C., L. T. Russell, M. Coleman, and L. Ganong. 2018. "Half- and Stepsibling Relationships: A Systemic Integrative Review." *Journal of Family Theory & Review* 10, no. 4: 765–784.
Stykes, B., and K. B. Guzzo. 2015. *Remarriage & Stepfamilies* (FP-15-10). National Center for Family & Marriage Research. www.bgsu.edu/ncfmr/resources/data/family-profiles/stykes -guzzo-remarriage-stepfamilies-fp-15-10.html.

CHAPTER 13: When LGBTQ People Become Parents
by Abbie E. Goldberg

Adamson, K. 2013. "Predictors of Relationship Quality during the Transition to Parenthood." *Journal of Reproductive and Infant Psychology* 31: 160–171.
Alang, S. M., and M. Fomotar. 2015. "Postpartum Depression in an Online Community of Lesbian Mothers: Implications for Clinical Practice." *Journal of Gay & Lesbian Mental Health* 19, no. 1: 21–39.
Averett, K. 2016. "The Gender Buffet: LGBTQ Parents Resisting Heteronormativity." *Gender & Society* 30, no. 2: 189–212.
Belsky, J. 1990. "Children and Marriage." In *The Psychology of Marriage*, edited by F. Fincham and T. Bradbury: 172–200. New York: Guilford.
Belsky, J., and J. Kelly. 1995. *The Transition to Parenthood: How a First Child Changes a Marriage*. New York: Dell.
Belsky, J., and M. Rovine. 1984. "Social Network Contact, Family Support, and Transition to Parenthood." *Journal of Marriage and the Family* 46: 455–467.
Bergman, K., R. J. Rubio, R. J. Green, and E. Padron. 2010. "Gay Men Who Become Fathers via Surrogacy: The Transition to Parenthood." *Journal of GLBT Family Studies* 6, no. 2: 111–141.
Blackwell, L., J. Hardy, T. Ammari, T. Veinot, C. Lampe, and S. Schoenebeck. 2016. *LGBT Parents and Social Media: Advocacy, Privacy, and Disclosure during Shifting Social Movements*. Proceedings of the 2016 CHI conference on human factors in computing systems, 610–622.
Brainer, A., M. Moore, and P. Banerjee. 2020. "Race and Ethnicity in the Lives of LGBTQ Parents and Their Children: Perspectives from and beyond North America." In *LGBTQ-Parent Families: Innovations in Research and Implications for Practice*, 2nd ed., edited by A. E. Goldberg and K. R. Allen, 85–103. Cham, Switzerland: Springer.
Cao, H., W. R. Mills-Koonce, C. Wood, and A. M. Fine. 2016. "Identity Transformation during the Transition to Parenthood among Same-sex Couples: An Ecological, Stress-Strategy-Adaptation Perspective." *Journal of Family Theory & Review* 8: 30–59.
Carroll, M. 2018. "Gay Fathers on the Margins: Race, Class, Marital Status, and Pathway to Parenthood." *Family Relations* 67, no. 1: 104–117.
Chan, R., R. Brooks, B. Raboy, and C. Patterson. 1998. "Division of Labor among Lesbian and Heterosexual Parents: Associations with Children's Adjustment." *Journal of Family Psychology* 12: 402–419.

Cowan, C. P., and P. A. Cowan. 1999. *When Partners Become Parents: The Big Life Change for Couples*. Rev. ed. New York: Routledge.

DeMino, K. A., G. Appleby, and D. Fisk. 2007. "Lesbian Mothers with Planned Families A Comparative Study of Internalized Homophobia and Social Support." *American Journal of Orthopsychiatry* 77: 165–173.

Doss, B. D., G. K. Rhoades, S. M. Stanley, and H. J. Markman. 2009. "The Effect of the Transition to Parenthood on Relationship Quality: An 8-year Prospective Study." *Journal of Personality and Social Psychology* 96, no. 3: 601–619.

Downing, J. B., and A. E. Goldberg. 2011. "Lesbian Mothers' Constructions of the Division of Paid and Unpaid Labor." *Feminism & Psychology* 21: 100–120.

Ellis, S. A., D. M. Wojnar, and M. Pettinato. 2014. "Conception, Pregnancy, and Birth Experiences of Male and Gender Variant Gestational Parents: It's How We Could Have a Family." *Journal of Midwifery & Women's Health* 60, no. 1: 62–69. doi:10.1111/jmwh.12213.

Faisal-Cury, A., K. Tabb, and A. Matijasevich. 2021. "Partner Relationship Quality Predicts Later Postpartum Depression Independently of the Chronicity of Depressive Symptoms." *Brazilian Journal of Psychiatry* 43: 12–21.

Forenza, B., B. Dashew, and C. Bergeson. 2019. "LGB + Moms and Dads: 'My Primary Identity… Is Being a Parent.'" *Journal of GLBT Family Studies* 17: 18–29.

Frost, R., and A. E. Goldberg. 2020. "Adopting Again: A Qualitative Study of the Second Transition to Parenthood in Adoptive Families." *Adoption Quarterly* 23: 85–109.

Gartrell, N. K., A. Banks, J. Hamilton, N. Reed, H. Bishop, and C. Rodas. 1999. "The National Lesbian Family Study: 2. Interviews with Mothers of Toddlers." *American Journal of Orthopsychiatry* 69: 362–369.

Gartrell, N. K., J. Hamilton, A. Banks, D. Mosbacher, N. Reed, C. Sparks, and H. Bishop. 1996. "The National Lesbian Family Study: 1. Interviews with Prospective Mothers.' *American Journal of Orthopsychiatry* 66: 272–281.

Gartrell, N., C. Rodas, A. Deck, H. Peyser, and A. Banks. 2006. "The USA National Lesbian Family Study: Interviews with Mothers of 10-Year-Olds." *Feminism & Psychology* 16, no. 2: 175–192.

Goldberg, A. E. 2006. "The Transition to Parenthood for Lesbian Couples." *Journal of GLBT Family Studies* 2: 13–42.

——. 2009. "Lesbian and Heterosexual Preadoptive Couples' Openness to Transracial Adoption." *American Journal of Orthopsychiatry* 79: 103–117.

——. 2010a. *Lesbian and Gay Parents and Their Children: Research on the Family Life Cycle*. Washington, DC: American Psychological Association.

——. 2010b. "The Transition to Adoptive Parenthood." In *Handbook of Stressful Transitions across the Life Span*, edited by T. W. Miller, 165–184. New York: Springer.

——. 2012. *Gay Dads: Transitions to Adoptive Fatherhood*. New York: New York University Press.

——. 2013a. "'Doing' and 'Undoing' Gender: The Meaning and Division of Housework in Same-Sex Couples." *Journal of Family Theory and Review* 5: 85–104.

——. 2013b. "Predictors of Psychological Adjustment in Early Placed Adopted Children with Lesbian, Gay, and Heterosexual Parents." *Journal of Family Psychology* 27, no. 3: 431–442.

——. 2019. *Open Adoption and Diverse Families: Complex Relationships in the Digital Age*. New York: Oxford.

Goldberg, A. E., J. B. Downing, and H. B. Richardson. 2009. "The Transition from Infertility to Adoption: Perceptions of Lesbian and Heterosexual Preadoptive Couples." *Journal of Social and Personal Relationships* 26: 938–963.

Goldberg, A. E., J. B. Downing, and C. C. Sauck. 2008. "Perceptions of Children's Parental Preferences in Lesbian Two-Mother Households." *Journal of Marriage and Family* 70: 419–434.

Goldberg, A. E., R. Frost, M. Manley, and K. Black. 2018. "Meeting Other Moms: Lesbian Adoptive Mothers' Relationships with Other Parents at School and Beyond." *Journal of Lesbian Studies* 22: 67–84.

Goldberg, A. E., L. A. Kinkler, A. M. Moyer, and E. R. Weber. 2014. "Intimate Relationship Challenges in Early Parenthood among Lesbian, Gay, and Heterosexual Couples Adopting via the Child Welfare System." *Professional Psychology: Research & Practice* 45: 221–230.

Goldberg, A. E., L. A. Kinkler, H. B. Richardson, and J. B. Downing. 2011. "Lesbian, Gay, and Heterosexual Couples in Open Adoption Arrangements: A Qualitative Study." *Journal of Marriage and Family* 73: 502–518.

Goldberg, A. E., A. M. Moyer, L. A. Kinkler, and H. B. Richardson. 2012. "'When You're Sitting on the Fence, Hope's the Hardest Part': Experiences and Challenges of Lesbian, Gay, and Heterosexual Couples Adopting through the Child Welfare System." *Adoption Quarterly* 15: 1–28.

Goldberg, A. E., A. M. Moyer, E. R. Weber, and J. Shapiro. 2013. "What Changed When the Gay Adoption Ban Was Lifted? Perspectives of Lesbian and Gay Parents in Florida." *Sexuality Research and Social Policy* 10: 110–124.

Goldberg, A. E., and M. Perry-Jenkins. 2007. "The Division of Labor and Perceptions of Parental Roles: Lesbian Couples across the Transition to Parenthood." *Journal of Social and Personal Relationships* 24: 297–318.

Goldberg, A. E., and J. Z. Smith. 2008. "The Social Context of Lesbian Mothers' Anxiety during Early Parenthood." *Parenting: Science & Practice* 8: 213–239.

———. 2011. "Stigma, Social Context, and Mental Health: Lesbian and Gay Couples across the Transition to Adoptive Parenthood." *Journal of Counseling Psychology* 58: 139–150.

———. 2013. "Predictors of Psychological Adjustment in Early Placed Adopted Children with Lesbian, Gay, and Heterosexual Parents." *Journal of Family Psychology* 27, no. 3: 431–442.

———. 2014. "Preschool Selection Considerations and Experiences of School Mistreatment among Lesbian, Gay, and Heterosexual Adoptive Parents." *Early Childhood Research Quarterly* 29: 64–75.

Goldberg, A. E., J. Z. Smith, and D. A. Kashy. 2010. "Pre-adoptive Factors Predicting Lesbian, Gay, and Heterosexual Couples' Relationship Quality across the Transition to Adoptive Parenthood." *Journal of Family Psychology* 24: 221–232.

Goldberg, A. E., J. Z. Smith, N. McCormick, and N. Overstreet. 2019. "Health Behaviors and Outcomes of Parents in Same-Sex Couples: An Exploratory Study." *Psychology of Sexual Orientation & Gender Diversity* 6: 318–335.

Goldberg, A. E., J. Z. Smith, and M. Perry-Jenkins. 2012. "The Division of Labor in Lesbian, Gay, and Heterosexual New Adoptive Parents." *Journal of Marriage and Family* 74: 812–828.

Goldberg, A. E., E. R. Weber, A. M. Moyer, and J. Shapiro. 2014. "Seeking to Adopt in Florida: Lesbian and Gay Parents Navigate the Legal Process." *Journal of Gay and Lesbian Social Services* 26: 37–69.

Greif, G., J. Leitch, and M. Wooley. 2019. "A Preliminary Look at Relationships between Married Gay Men and Lesbians and Their Parents-in-Law: Five Case Studies." *Journal of Gay & Lesbian Social Services* 31: 290–313.

Katon, W., J. Russo, and A. Gavin. 2014. "Predictors of Postpartum Depression." *Journal of Women's Health* 23, no. 9: 23. doi.org/10.1089/jwh.2014.4824.

Kohn, J. L., W. S. Rholes, J. A. Simpson, A. M. Martin III, S. Tran, and C. L. Wilson. 2012. "Changes in Marital Satisfaction across the Transition to Parenthood: The Role of Adult Attachment Orientations." *Personality and Social Psychology Bulletin* 38, no. 11: 1506–1522.

Langdridge, D., P. Sheeran, and K. Connolly. 2000. "Understanding the Reasons for Parenthood." *Journal of Reproductive & Infant Psychology* 23: 121–133.

Lawrence, E., A. D. Rothman, R. J. Cobb, and T. N. Bradbury. 2010. "Marital Satisfaction across the Transition to Parenthood: Three Eras of Research." In *Strengthening Couple Relationships for Optimal Child Development: Lessons from Research and Intervention*, edited by M. S. Schulz, M. K. Pruett, P. K. Kerig, and R. D. Parke, 97–114. Washington, DC: American Psychological Association.

Lewin, E. 2009. *Gay Fatherhood: Narratives of Family and Citizenship in America*. Chicago: University of Chicago Press.

Logsdon, M. C., and A. B. McBride. 1994. "Social Support and Postpartum Depression." *Research in Nursing & Health* 17: 449–457.

Lynch, J. M. 2004a. "Becoming a Stepparent in Gay/Lesbian Stepfamilies: Integrating Identities." *Journal of Homosexuality* 48, no. 2: 45–60.

———. 2004b. "The Identity Transformation of Biological Parents in Lesbian/Gay Stepfamilies." *Journal of Homosexuality* 47, no. 2: 91–107.

Manley, M., A. E. Goldberg, and A. E. Ross. 2018. "Invisibility and Involvement: LGBTQ Community Connections among Plurisexual Women during Pregnancy and Postpartum." *Psychology of Sexual Orientation and Gender Diversity* 5: 169–181.

Manley, M. H., M. M. Legge, C. E. Flanders, A. E. Goldberg, and L. E. Ross. 2018. "Consensual Non-monogamy in Pregnancy and Parenthood: Experiences of Bisexual and Plurisexual Women." *Journal of Sex & Marital Therapy* 44: 721–736.

McKenzie, S., and K. Carter. 2013. "Does Transition into Parenthood Lead to Changes in Mental Health? Findings from Three Waves of a Population Based Panel Study." *Journal of Epidemiological Community Health* 67: 339–345.

Mitnick, D., R. Heyman, and A. Smith Slep. 2009. "Changes in Relationship Satisfaction across the Transition to Parenthood: A Meta-analysis." *Journal of Family Psychology* 23, no. 6: 848–852.

Moore, M. R. 2008. "Gendered Power Relations among Women: A Study of Household Decision Making in Black, Lesbian Stepfamilies." *American Sociological Review* 73: 335–356.

Nordqvist, P. 2015. "Out of Sight, out of Mind: Family Resemblances in Lesbian Donor Conception." *Journal of Family Issues* 36: 480–500.

Parfitt, Y., A. Pike, and S. Ayers. 2014. "Infant Developmental Outcomes: A Family Systems Perspective." *Infant and Child Development* 23, no. 4: 353–373.

Patterson, C. J., S. Hurt, and C. D. Mason. 1998. "Families of the Lesbian Baby Boom: Children's Contact with Grandparents and Other Adults." *American Journal of Orthopsychiatry* 68: 390–399.

Patterson, C. J., E. L. Sutfin, and M. Fulcher. 2004. "Division of Labor among Lesbian and Heterosexual Parenting Couples: Correlates of Specialized versus Shared Patterns." *Journal of Adult Development* 11: 179–189.

Pelka, S. 2009. "Sharing Motherhood: Maternal Jealousy among Lesbian Co-mothers." *Journal of Homosexuality* 56: 195–217.

Price Askeland, C. A., K. R. Bush, and S. J. Price. 2016. *Families and Change: Coping with Stressful Events and Transitions.* 5th ed. Thousand Oaks, CA: Sage.

Prickett, K. C., A. Martin-Storey, and R. Crosnoe. 2015. "A Research Note on Time with Children in Different- and Same-Sex Two-Parent Families." *Demography* 52, no. 3: 905–918.

Ross, L. E., C. Dobinson, and A. Eady. 2010. "Perceived Determinants of Mental Health for Bisexual People: A Qualitative Examination." *American Journal of Public Health* 100, no. 3: 496–502.

Ryan, M. 2009. "Beyond Thomas Beatie: Trans Men and the New Parenthood." In *Who's Your Daddy? And Other Writings on Queer Parenting,* edited by R. Epstein,139–150. Toronto, CA: Sumach.

South et al. 2019. "Relationship Quality from Pre to Post Placement in Adoptive Couples." *Journal of Family Psychology* 33, no. 1: 64–76.

Tasker, F., and E. Lavender-Stott. 2020. "LGBTQ Parenting Post-heterosexual Relationship Dissolution." In *LGBTQ-Parent Families: Innovations in Research and Implications for Practice,* edited by A. E. Goldberg and K. R. Allen, 3–23. Springer.

Timm, T., J. Mooradian, and R. Hock. 2011. "Exploring Core Issues in Adoption: Individual and Marital Experience of Adoptive Mothers." *Adoption Quarterly* 14: 268–283.

Titlestad, A., and R. Robinson. 2019. "Navigating Parenthood as Two Women: The Positive Aspects and Strengths of Female Same-Sex Parenthood." *Journal of GLBT Family Studies* 15: 186–209.

Tornello, S. L., B. N. Sonnenberg, and C. J. Patterson. 2015. "Division of Labor among Gay Fathers: Associations with Parent, Couple, and Child Adjustment." *Psychology of Sexual Orientation and Gender Diversity* 2, no. 4: 365–375.

Ward, M. 1998. "Impact of Adoption on the New Parents' Marriage." *Adoption Quarterly* 2: 57–78.

Wojnar, D. M., and A. Katzenmeyer. 2014. "Experiences of Preconception, Pregnancy, and New Motherhood for Lesbian Nonbiological Mothers." *Journal of Obstetric & Gynecological Neonatal Nursing* 43: 50–60.

CHAPTER 14: Reflections on Race, Family, and Identity: Is There Anything New about Multiracialism Today?
by Jenifer L. Bratter

Alba, R. 2020. *The Great Demographic Illusion: Majority, Minority, and the Expanding American Mainstream.* Princeton, NJ: Princeton University Press.

———. R. 2021. "The Surge of Young Americans from Minority-White Mixed Families and Its Significance for the Future." *Daedalus* 150, no. 2: 199–214.

Alba, R., B. Beck, and D. Basaran Sahin. 2018. "The US Mainstream Expands—Again." *Journal of Ethnic and Migration Studies* 44, no. 1: 99–117.

Baradaran, Mehrsa. 2017. *The Color of Money: Black Banks and the Racial Wealth Gap.* Cambridge, MA: Belknap Press of Harvard University Press.

Bernstein, Mary, and Kristine A. Olsen. 2009. "Identity Deployment and Social Change: Understanding Identity as a Social Movement and Organizational Strategy." *Sociology Compass* 3, no. 6: 871–883.

Bratter, J. L. 2007. "Will 'Multiracial' Survive to the Next Generation? The Racial Classification of Children of Multiracial Parents." *Social Forces* 86, no. 2: 821–849.

Bratter, J. L., and B. K. Gorman. 2011. "Is Discrimination an Equal Opportunity Risk?
Racial Experiences, Socioeconomic Status, and Health Status Among Black and White
Adults." *Journal of Health and Social Behavior* 52, no. 3: 365–382.

Bratter, J. L. and E. M. Whitehead. 2018. "Ties That Bind? Comparing Kin Support Availability for Mothers of Mixed-Race and Monoracial Infants." *Journal of Marriage and
Family* 80, no. 4: 951–962.

Bratter, J. L., R. Casarez, A. Farrell, S. K. Mehta, X. Zhang, and M. Carroll. 2022. "Counting
Families, Counting Race: Assessing Visible Family Structural Change among Multiracial Families, 1980–2018." *Journal of Contemporary Family Studies* 31: 609–622.

Buggs, S. G. 2019. "Color, Culture, or Cousin? Multiracial Americans and Framing Boundaries in Interracial Relationships." *Journal of Marriage and Family* 81, no. 5: 1221–1236.

Campbell, M. E. 2009. "Multiracial Groups and Educational Inequality: A Rainbow or a
Divide?" *Social Problems* 56, no. 3: 425–46.

Chang, S. 2015. *Raising Mixed Race: Multiracial Asian Children in a Post-Racial World.*
New York: Routledge.

Childs, Erica Chito. 2009. *Fade to Black and White: Interracial Images in Popular Culture.*
Lanham, MD: Rowman & Littlefield.

Choi, K., and R. E. Goldberg. 2020. "The Social Significance of Interracial Cohabitation:
Inferences Based on Fertility Behavior." *Demography* 57: 1727–1751.

Curington, Celeste Vaughan, Ken-Hou Lin, and Jennifer Hickes Lundquist. 2015. "Positioning Multiraciality in Cyberspace: Treatment of Multiracial Daters in an Online Dating
Website." *American Sociological Review* 80, no. 4: 764–788.

Curington, Celeste Vaughan, Jennifer Lundquist, and Ken-Hou Lin. 2021. *The Dating
Divide: Race in the Era of Online Romance.* Berkeley: University of California Press.

DaCosta, K. M. 2007. *Making Multiracials: State, Family, and Market in the Redrawing of the
Colorline.* Stanford, CA: Stanford University Press.

———. 2010. Review of *Framing Racial Inequality*, by William Julius Wilson. *Sociological
Forum* 25, no. 2: 377–381.

———. 2020. "Multiracial Categorization, Identity, and Policy in (Mixed) Racial Formations."
Annual Review of Sociology 46, no. 1: 335–353.

Davenport, L. D. 2016. "The Role of Gender, Class, and Religion in Biracial Americans'
Racial Labeling Decisions." *American Sociological Review* 81, no. 1: 57–84.

Doering, J. 2014. "A Battleground of Identity: Racial Formation and the African American
Discourse on Interracial Marriage." *Social Problems* 61, no. 4: 559–575.

Doyle, J. M., and G. Kao. 2007. "Are Racial Identities of Multiracials Stable? Changing
Self-identification among Single and Multiple Race Individuals." [In English.] *Social
Psychology Quarterly* 70, no. 4: 405–423.

Elliot, S. 2014. "An American Family Returns to the Table." *New York Times*, January 28. www
.nytimes.com/2014/01/29/business/media/an-american-family-returns-to-the-table.html.

Feagin, J. 2006. *Systemic Racism: A System of Oppression.* New York: Routledge.

Field, C. J., S. R. Kimuna, and M. A. Straus. 2013. "Attitudes toward Interracial Relationships
Among College Students: Race, Class, Gender, and Perceptions of Parental Values."
Journal of Black Studies 44: 741–776.

Foster-Frau, S., T. Melink, and A. Blanco. 2021. "'We're Talking about a Big Powerful
Phenomenon': Multiracial Americans Drive Change." *Washington Post*, October 8.
www.washingtonpost.com/nation/2021/10/08/mixed-race-americans-increase-census/.

Fu, V. K. 2008. "Interracial-Interethnic Unions and Fertility in the United States." *Journal of Marriage and Family* 70: 783–795.

Gardner, S. K., and M. W. Hughey. 2019. "Still the Tragic Mulatto? Manufacturing Multiracializing in Magazine Media, 1961–2011." In *The Mechanisms of Racialization Beyond the Black/White Binary*, edited by Bianca Gonzalez-Sobrino and Devon R. Goss, New York: Routledge.

Good, J. J., G. F. Chavez, and D. T. Sanchez. 2010. "Sources of Self-categorization as Minority for Mixed-race Individuals: Implications for Affirmative Action Entitlement." [In English.] *Cultural Diversity and Ethnic Minority Psychology* 16, no. 4: 453–460.

Gross, A. 2003. "Texas Mexicans and the Politics of Whiteness." *Law and History Review* 21: 195–205.

Gullickson, A. 2006. "Education and Black-White Interracial Marriage." *Demography* 43, no. 4: 673–689.

Herman, M., and M. Campbell. 2012. "I Wouldn't, but You Can: Attitudes toward Interracial Relationships." *Social Science Research* 41, no. 2: 343–358.

Hibbler, D. K., and K. J. Shinew. 2002. "Interracial Couples' Experience of Leisure: A Social Network Analysis." *Journal of Leisure Research* 34, no. 2: 135–156.

Hitlin, S., J. S. Brown, and G. H. Elder. 2006. "Racial Self-categorization in Adolescence: Multiracial Development and Social Pathways." [In English.] *Child Development* 77, no. 5: 1298–1308.

Hochschild, Jennifer L., Vesla M. Weaver, and Traci R. Burch. 2012. *Creating a New Racial Order? How Immigration, Multiracialism, Genomics, and the Young Can Remake Race in America*. Princeton, NJ: Princeton University Press.

Hodges, Graham. 1999. *Root and Branch: African Americans in New York and East Jersey, 1613–1863*. Chapel Hill: University of North Carolina Press.

Hollinger, David H. 1998. "National Culture and Communities of Descent." *Reviews in American History* 26, no. 1: 312–328.

Jackson, K. F., F. M. Mitchell, C. R. Snyder, and G. E. Miranda Samuels. 2020. "Salience of Ethnic Minority Grandparents in the Ethnic-Racial Socialization and Identity Development of Multiracial Grandchildren." *Identity* 20, no. 2: 73–91.

Jones, Jennifer A. 2011. "Who Are We? Producing Group Identity through Everyday Practices of Conflict and Discourse." *Sociological Perspectives* 54, no. 2: 138–161.

Kao, G., K. Joyner, and K. S. Balistreri. 2019. *The Company We Keep: Interracial Friendships and Romantic Relationships from Adolescence to Adulthood*. New York: Russell Sage Foundation.

Khanna, N. 2010. "'If You're Half Black, You're Just Black': Reflected Appraisals and the Persistence of the One-Drop Rule." *The Sociological Quarterly* 51, no. 1: 96–121.

Krysan, M., and K. Crowder. 2017. *Cycle of Segregation: Social Processes and Residential Stratification*. New York: Russell Sage Foundation.

Lee, Jennifer, and Frank D. Bean. 2004. "America's Changing Color Lines: Immigration, Race/Ethnicity, and Multiracial Identification." *Annual Review of Sociology* 30: 221–242.

———. 2010. *The Diversity Paradox: Immigration and the Color Line in Twenty-First Century America*. New York: Russell Sage Foundation.

Liebler, Carolyn A. 2016. "On the Boundaries of Race: Identification of Mixed-Heritage Children in the U.S., 1960 to 2010." *Sociology of Race and Ethnicity* 2, no. 4: 548–568.

Liebler C. A., S. R. Porter, L. E. Fernandez, J. M. Noon, and S. R. Ennis. 2017. "America's Churning Races: Race and Ethnicity Response Changes between Census 2000 and the 2010 Census." *Demography* 54, no. 1: 259–84.

Lin, Ken-Hou, and Jennifer Lundquist. 2013. "Mate Selection in Cyberspace: The Intersection of Race, Gender, and Education." *American Journal of Sociology* 119, no. 1: 183–215.

Livingston, G., and A. Brown. 2017. *Intermarriage in the U.S. 50 Years after Loving v. Virginia*. Washington, DC: Pew Research Center.

Loblack, Angelica. 2020. "'I Woke up to the World': Politicizing Blackness and Multiracial Identity through Activism." Master's thesis, University of South Florida.

Long, L., and R. Joseph-Salisbury. 2019. "Black Mixed-Race Men's Perceptions and Experiences of the Police." *Ethnic and Racial Studies* 42, no. 2: 198–215.

Malaney, Victoria K., and Kendra Danowski. 2015. "Mixed Foundations: Supporting and Empowering Multiracial Student Organizations." *JCSCORE* 1, no. 2: 54–85.

Masuoka, Natalie. 2008. "Political Attitudes and Ideologies of Multiracial Americans: The Implications of Mixed Race in the United States." *Political Research Quarterly* 61, no. 2: 253–267.

McCarthy, J. 2021. "U.S. Approval of Interracial Marriage at a New High – 94%." Gallup Poll. https://news.gallup.com/poll/354638/approval-interracial-marriage-new-high.aspx.

Mills, M. A. 2021. *The Colors of Love: Multiracial People in Interracial Relationships*. New York: New York University Press.

Morning, A., and A. Saperstein. 2018. "The Generational Locus of Multiraciality and Its Implications for Racial Self-Identification." *ANNALS of the American Academy of Political and Social Science* 677, no. 1: 57–68.

Nash, Gary B. 1995. "The Hidden History of Mestizo America." *Journal of American History* 82: 941–964.

Nayani, F. 2020. *Raising Multiracial Children: Tools for Nurturing Identity in a Racialized World*. Berkeley, CA: North Atlantic Books.

Nemoto, Kumiko. 2006. "Intimacy, Desire, and the Construction of Self in Relationships between Asian American Women and White American Men." *Journal of Asian American Studies* 9, no. 1: 27–54.

Nobles, M. 2000. *Shades of Citizenship: Race and Census in Modern Politics*. Stanford, CA: Stanford University Press.

Oliver, M., and T. Shapiro. 2006. *Black Wealth / White Wealth: A New Perspective on Racial Inequality*. New York: Routledge.

———. 2019. "Disrupting the Racial Wealth Gap." *Contexts* 18, no. 1: 16–21.

Onwuachi-Willig, A. 2013. *According to Our Hearts: Rhinelander v. Rhinelander and the Law of the Multiracial Family*. New Haven, CT: Yale University Press.

Osuji, C. 2019. *Boundaries of Love: Interracial Marriage and the Meaning of Race*. New York: New York University Press.

Parker, K., and A. Barroso. 2021. "In Vice President Kamala Harris, We See How America Has Changed." *Pew Research Center*, February 25. www.pewresearch.org/fact-tank/2021/02/25/in-vice-president-kamala-harris-we-can-see-how-america-has-changed/.

Parker, K., J. M. Horowitz, R. Morin, and M. H. Lopez. 2005. "Multiracial in America." *Pew Research Center*, June 11. www.pewresearch.org/social-trends/2015/06/11/multiracial-in-america/.

Pascoe, P. 2010. *What Comes Naturally: Miscegenation Law and the Making of Race in America*. New York: Oxford University Press.

Perez, A. D., and C. Hirschman. 2009. "The Changing Racial and Ethnic Composition of the US Population: Emerging American Identities." *Population and Development Review* 35: 1–51.

Pyke, Karen D., and Denise L. Johnson. 2003. "Asian American Women and Racialized Femininities 'Doing' Gender across Cultural Worlds." *Gender & Society* 17, no. 1: 33–53.

Qian, Z., and D. T. Lichter. 2007. "Social Boundaries and Marital Assimilation: Interpreting Trends in Racial and Ethnic Intermarriage." *American Sociological Review* 72, no. 1: 68–94.

Ray, Rashawn, and Alexandra Gibbons. 2021. "Why Are States Banning Critical Race Theory?" Brookings. Accessed March 10, 2023. www.brookings.edu/blog/fixgov/2021/07/02/why-are-states-banning-critical-race-theory/.

Rockquemore, K. A., and D. L. Brunsma. 2002. "Socially Embedded Identities: Theories, Typologies, and Processes of Racial Identity Among Black/White Biracials." *Sociological Quarterly* 43, no. 3: 335–356.

Rockquemore, K. A., and T. A. Laszloffy. 2005. *Raising Biracial Children*. Lanham, MD: Rowman Altamira.

Romano, R. C. 2003. *Race Mixing: Black-White Marriage in Postwar America*. Cambridge, MA: Harvard University Press.

Rosenfeld, M. J. 2008. "Racial, Educational and Religious Endogamy in the United States: A Comparative Historical Perspective." *Social Forces* 87: 1–31.

Roth, W. D. 2005. "The End of the One-Drop Rule? Labeling of Multiracial Children in Black Intermarriages." *Sociological Forum* 20, no. 1: 35–67.

———. 2018. "Unsettled Identities Amid Settled Classifications? Toward a Sociology of Racial Appraisals." *Ethnic and Racial Studies* 41, no. 6: 1093–1112.

Roth, W. D., and B. Ivemark. 2018. "Genetic Options: The Impact of Genetic Ancestry Testing on Consumers' Racial and Ethnic Identities." *American Journal of Sociology* 124, no. 1: 150–184.

Saperstein, A., and A. Gullickson. 2013. "A 'Mulatto Escape Hatch' in the United States? Examining Evidence of Racial and Social Mobility During the Jim Crow Era." *Demography* 50, no. 5: 1921–1942.

Schwartz, C. R. 2013. "Trends and Variation in Assortative Mating: Causes and Consequences." *Annual Review of Sociology* 39: 451–470.

Song, M. 2016. "Multiracial People and Their Partners in Britain: Extending the Link between Intermarriage and Integration?" *Ethnicities* 16, no. 4: 631–648.

———. 2020. "Rethinking Minority Status and 'Visibility.'" *Comparative Migration Studies* 8, no. 5: doi.org/10.1186/s40878-019-0162-2.

Spencer, Rainier. 2004. "Assessing Multiracial Identity Theory and Politics: The Challenge of Hypodescent." *Ethnicities* 4, no. 3: 357–79.

———. 2011. *Reproducing Race?: The Paradox of Generation Mix*. Boulder, CO: Lynne Rienner.

Steinbugler, A. C. 2012. *Beyond Loving: Intimate Racework in Lesbian, Gay, and Straight Interracial Relationships*. New York: Oxford University Press.

Stonequist, E. 1935. "The Problem of the Marginal Man." *American Journal of Sociology* 41, no. 1. doi.org/10.1086/217001.

Tabb, K. 2016. "Changes in Racial Categorization over Time and Health Status: An Examination of Multiracial Young Adults in the USA." *Ethnicity & Health* 21: 146–157.

Williams, D., J. Lawrence, and B. A. Davis. 2019. "Racism and Health: Evidence and Needed Research." *Annual Review of Public Health* 40: 105–125.

U.S. Census Bureau. 2020. Census Redistricting Data (Public Law 94-171) Summary File.
———. 2021. Census Redistricting Data (Public Law 94-171) Summary File.
Zhenchao, W., and D. T. Lichter. 2001. "Measuring Marital Assimilation: Intermarriage Among Natives and Immigrants." *Social Science Research* 30: 289–312.

CHAPTER 15: Queer Bat Signals: Families of Origin and Choice under Social Distancing and Lockdown
by Amy Brainer

AfroQueer Podcast. May 2020. "How Are You Doing?" https://afroqueerpodcast.com/2020/05/14/how-are-you-doing/ (last accessed October 2022).

Altay, Tunay. 2022. "The Pink Line across Digital Publics: Political Homophobia and the Queer Strategies of Everyday Life during COVID-19 in Turkey." *European Journal of Women's Studies* 29, no. 1S: 60S–74S.

Ara, Moshfec. 2022. "The Forbidden Word – the Life during COVID-19." In *COVID-19 Assemblages: Queer and Feminist Ethnographies from South Asia*, edited by N. Banerjea, P. Boyce, and R. Dasgupta. 45–51. New York: Routledge.

Bacon, Thomas. 2020. "The Secret Meaning of Batman's Bat Signal Revealed." *Comic News*, September. https://screenrant.com/batman-bat-signal-secret-meaning/ (last accessed October 2022).

Banerjea, Niharika, Paul Boyce, and Rohit Dasgupta, eds. 2022. *COVID-19 Assemblages: Queer and Feminist Ethnographies from South Asia*. New York: Routledge.

Banerjee, Debanjan, and T. S. Sathyanarayana Rao. 2021. "The Graying Minority: Lived Experiences and Psychosocial Challenges of Older Transgender Adults during the COVID-19 Pandemic in India." *Frontiers in Psychiatry* 11: 377–387.

Barrientosa, J., M. Guzmán-González, A. Urzúab, and F. Ulloac. 2021. "Psychosocial Impact of COVID-19 Pandemic on LGBT People in Chile." *Sexologies* 30: e35–341.

Berkhead, Samantha. 2020. "Quarantined with Family, Russia's LGBT Youth Face New Struggles." *Moscow Times*, June. www.themoscowtimes.com/2020/06/04/quarantined-with-family-russias-lgbt-youth-face-new-struggles-a70477 (last accessed September 2022).

Bettinger-Lopez, Caroline, and Alexandra Bro. 2020. "A Double Pandemic: Domestic Violence in the Age of COVID-19." Council on Foreign Relations Brief. www.cfr.org/in-brief/double-pandemic-domestic-violence-age-covid-19.

Cheded, Mohammed, and Alexandros Skandalis. 2021. "Touch and Contact during COVID-19: Insights from Queer Digital Spaces." *Gender, Work & Organization* 28 (S2): 340–347.

Garcia-Rabines, Diego, and Bruno Bencich. 2021. "Community-based Resistance Strategies among a Group of Trans Women in Lima, Peru during the COVID-19 Pandemic." *Journal of Homosexuality* 68, no. 4: 663–672.

Gato, Jorge, Daniela Leal, and Daniel Seabra. 2020. "When Home Is Not a Safe Haven: Effects of the COVID-19 Pandemic on LGBTQ+ Adolescents and Young Adults in Portugal." *Revista Psicologia* 3, no. 2: 89–100.

Gattamorta, Karina, John Salerno, and Roberto Roman Laporte. 2022. "Family Rejection during COVID-19: Effects on Sexual and Gender Minority Stress and Mental Health among LGBTQ+ University Students." *LGBTQ+ Family: An Interdisciplinary Journal* 18, no. 4: 305–318.

Gonzales, Gilbert, Emilio Loret de Mola, Kyle Gavulic, Tara McKay, and Christopher Purcell. 2020. "Mental Health Needs among Lesbian, Gay, Bisexual, and Transgender College Students during the COVID-19 Pandemic." *Journal of Adolescent Health* 67, no. 5: 645–648.

Gray, Mary. 2009. *Out in the Country: Youth, Media, and Queer Visibility in Rural America.* New York: New York University Press.

Hossain, Adnan. 2022. "Metaphor of Contagion: The Impact of COVID-19 on the Hijras in Bangladesh." In *COVID-19 Assemblages: Queer and Feminist Ethnographies from South Asia*, edited by N. Banerjea, P. Boyce, and R. Dasgupta, 100–106. New York: Routledge.

Hunte, Ben. 2020. "Coronavirus: 'I'm Stuck in Isolation with My Homophobic Parents.'" *BBC News*, March. www.bbc.com/news/uk-52039832 (last accessed September 2022).

Iyengar, Lakshmi, and Songqi Yu. 2020. "COVID-19 Is Further Disenfranchising China's Queer Youth." *Diplomat*, September. https://thediplomat.com/2020/09/covid-19-is-further-disenfranchising-chinas-queer-youth/ (last accessed September 2022).

Johnson, Madison. 2022. "The HIV Epidemic and the COVID-19 Pandemic: Conversations with LGBTQ+ Elders of Color on Two Public Health Crises." *Journal of Black Sexuality and Relationships* 8, no. 3: 23–46.

Labor, Jonalou, and Augustus Ceasar Latosa. 2022. "Locked Down Queer Love: Intimate Queer Online Relationships during the COVID-19 Pandemic." *Journal of Gender Studies* 31, no. 6: 770–781.

Maenzanise, Joyline (Jo). 2021. "How the Pandemic Has Complicated Life for LGBT Communities." *This Is Africa*, March. https://thisisafrica.me/african-identities/how-the-pandemic-has-complicated-life-for-lgbt-communities/ (last accessed September 2022).

Mallay, Rully, Benjamin Hegarty, Sandeep Nanwani, and Ignatius Praptoraharjo. 2021. "One Transgender Community's Experience of the COVID-19 Pandemic: A Report from Indonesia." *TSQ: Transgender Studies Quarterly* 8, no. 3: 386–393.

Mano, Pavan. 2021. "Rethinking the Heteronormative Foundations of Kinship: The Reification of the Heterosexual Nuclear Family Unit in Singapore's COVID-19 Circuit-Breaker Restrictions." *Culture, Theory and Critique* 62, no. 1–2: 142–153.

Mavhandu-Mudzusi, Azwihangwisi Helen, Tshimangadzo Selina Mudau, Thulile Shandu, and Nthomeni Dorah Ndou. 2021. "Transgender Student Experiences of Online Education during COVID-19 Pandemic Era in Rural Eastern Cape Area of South Africa: A Descriptive Phenomenological Study." *Research in Social Sciences and Technology* 6, no. 2: 110–128.

Oginni, Olakunle Ayokunmi, Kehinde Okanlawon, and Adedotun Ogunbajo. 2021. "A Commentary on COVID-19 and the LGBT Community in Nigeria: Risks and Resilience." *Psychology of Sexual Orientation and Gender Diversity* 8, no. 2: 261–263.

Paceley, Megan, Sloan Okrey-Anderson, Jessica Fish, Lauren McInroy, and Malcolm Lin. 2021. "Beyond a Shared Experience: Queer and Trans Youth Navigating COVID-19." *Qualitative Sociology* 20, no. 1–2: 97–104.

Patterson, Emmett. 2022. "Building Our Queer and Quarantined Sexual Worlds." In A. Shanker (ed.), *Crisis and Care: Queer Activist Responses to a Global Pandemic*. Oakland, CA: PM Press.

Perone, Angela, Keisha Watkins-Dukhie, and Judith Lewis. 2020. "LGBTQ+ Aging during COVID-19." *QED: A Journal in GLBTQ Worldmaking* 7, no. 3: 117–124.

Queer Rights Collective Nepal. 2022. "Untitled." In *COVID-19 Assemblages: Queer and Feminist Ethnographies from South Asia*, edited by N. Banerjea, P. Boyce, and R. Dasgupta, 182–188. New York: Routledge.

Santos, Betania, Indianarae Siqueira, Cristiane Oliveira, Laura Murray, Thaddeus Blanchette, Carolina Bonomi, Ana Paula da Silva, and Soraya Simões. 2021. "Sex Work, Essential Work: A Historical and (Necro)political Analysis of Sex Work in Times of COVID-19 in Brazil." *Social Sciences* 10, no. 2: doi.org/10.3390/socsci10010002.

Saria, Vaibhav. 2021. *Hijras, Lovers, Brothers: Surviving Sex and Poverty in Rural India.* New York: Fordham University Press.

Shanker, Adrian, ed. 2022. *Crisis and Care: Queer Activist Responses to a Global Pandemic.* Oakland, CA: PM Press.

Toomistu, Terje. 2022. "Thinking through the S(k)in: Indonesian Waria and Bodily Negotiations of Belonging across Religious Sensitivities." *Indonesia and the Malay World* 50, no. 146: 73–95.

UNIC Yangon. 2020. "LGBTIQ Community Faces New Challenges during COVID-19." Report for the United Nations Department of Global Communications, July. www.un.org/en/coronavirus/lgbtiq-community-faces-new-challenges-during-covid-19 (last accessed September 2022).

Weston, Kath. 1991. *Families We Choose: Lesbians, Gays, Kinship.* New York: Columbia University Press.

CHAPTER 16: Why Is Everyone (Still) Afraid of Sex?
by Nicholas Velotta and Pepper Schwartz

American Psychological Association. 2017. "Age of First Exposure to Pornography Shapes Men's Attitudes toward Women." Press release. www.apa.org/news/press/releases/2017/08/pornography-exposure.

Andrejek, N., T. Fetner, and M. Heath. 2022. "Climax as Work: Heteronormativity, Gender Labor, and the Gender Gap in Orgasms." *Gender & Society* 36, no. 2: 89–213.

Armstrong, E., P. England, and A. Fogarty. 2012. "Accounting for Women's Orgasm and Sexual Enjoyment in College Hookups and Relationships." In *American Sociological Review* 77, no. 3: 435–462.

Aviles, G. 2019. "'Fifty Shades of Grey' Was the Best-selling Book of the Decade." *NBC News*. December 20. www.nbcnews.com/pop-culture/books/fifty-shades-grey-was-best-selling-book-decade-n1105731.

Carras, C. 2021. "Emily Ratajkowski Accuses Robin Thicke of Sexual Assault." *Los Angeles Times*, October 4. www.latimes.com/entertainment-arts/books/story/2021-10-04/emily-ratajkowski-robin-thicke-sexual-assault-blurred-lines.

Centers for Disease Control and Prevention. 2015. "Trends in the Prevalence of Sexual Behaviors and HIV Testing National YRBS: 1991—2015." Youth Risk Behavior Survey.

England, P., and J. Bearak. 2014. "The Sexual Double Standard and Gender Differences in Attitudes toward Casual Sex among U.S. University Students." *Demographic Research* 30, no. 46: 1327–1338.

England, P., E. Shafer, and A. Fogarty. 2008. "Hooking Up and Forming Romantic Relationships on Today's College Campuses." In *The Gendered Society Reader*, edited by Michael Kimmel and Amy Aronson, 531–546. New York: Oxford University Press.

Finer, L. B. 2007. "Trends in Premarital Sex in the United States, 1954–2003." In *Public Health Reports* 122, no. 1: 73–78.

Fisher, T. D., Z. T. Moore, and M.-J. Pittenger. 2012. "Sex on the Brain? An Examination of Frequency of Sexual Cognitions as a Function of Gender, Erotophilia, and Social Desirability." *Journal of Sex Research* 49, no. 1: 69–77.

Foucault, Michel. 1980. *The History of Sexuality Volume 1: An Introduction.* First Vintage Books ed. New York: Random House.

Garcia, S. 2020. "Remembrance, Resilience, and Response: Addressing an Epidemic of Violence against Trans and Non-Binary People." *American Civil Liberties Union*, November 19. www.aclu.org/news/lgbtq-rights/remembrance-resilience-and -response-addressing-an-epidemic-of-violence-against-trans-non-binary-people/.

Geena Davis Institute on Gender in Media. 2021. *The Double-Edged Sword of Online Gaming: An Analysis of Masculinity in Video Games and the Gaming Community.* https://seejane.org/wp-content/uploads/gaming-study-2021-7.pdf.

Global Industry Analysts. 2022. *Sex Toys: Global Market Trajectory & Analytics* (No. 5140296). Research and Markets. www.researchandmarkets.com/reports/5140296/sex-toys-global-market-trajectory-and-analytics.

Hanson, R. E. 2016. *Mass Communication: Living in a Media World.* Thousand Oaks, CA: Sage.

Herbenick, D., T.-C. Fu, P. Wright, B. Paul, R. Gradus, J. Bauer, and R. Jones. 2020. Diverse Sexual Behaviors and Pornography Use: Findings from a Nationally Representative Probability Survey of Americans Aged 18 to 60 Years. *Journal of Sexual Medicine* 17, no. 4: 623–633.

Herbenick, D., M. Rosenberg, L. Golzarri-Arroyo, J. D. Fortenberry, and T. Fu. 2021. "Changes in Penile-Vaginal Intercourse Frequency and Sexual Repertoire from 2009 to 2018: Findings from the National Survey of Sexual Health and Behavior." *Archives of Sexual Behavior.* doi.org/10.1007/s10508-021-02125-2.

Hofmann, W., K. D. Vohs, and R. F. Baumeister. 2012. "What People Desire, Feel Conflicted About, and Try to Resist in Everyday Life." *Psychological Science* 23, no. 6: 582–588.

Human Rights Campaign Foundation. 2021. "An Epidemic of Violence 2021: Fatal Violence against Transgender and Gender Non-Confirming People in the United States in 2021." https://reports.hrc.org/an-epidemic-of-violence-fatal-violence-against-transgender-and -gender-non-confirming-people-in-the-united-states-in-2021.

Jane, E. A. 2016. *Misogyny Online: A Short (and Brutish) History.* Thousand Oaks, CA: Sage.

Kantor, L., and N. Levitz. 2017. "Parents' Views on Sex Education in Schools: How Much Do Democrats and Republicans Agree?" *PloS One* 12(7): e0180250–e0180250. PubMed. doi.org/10.1371/journal.pone.0180250.

Mallory, C., B. Sears, and L. A. Vasquez. 2021. "Banning the Use of Gay and Trans Panic Defenses." Williams Institute. https://williamsinstitute.law.ucla.edu/wp-content /uploads/Gay-Trans-Panic-Apr-2021.pdf.

Mantilla, K. 2015. *Gendertrolling: How Misogyny Went Viral.* Santa Barbara, CA: ABC-CLIO.

Match. 2021. "Singles in America." www.singlesinamerica.com/home.

Movement Advancement Project. n.d.. *Equality Maps: Panic Defense Bans.* The Democracy Maps. Retrieved July 28, 2022, from www.lgbtmap.org/equality-maps/panic_defense_bans.

Northrup, C., P. Schwartz, and J. Witte. 2012. *The Normal Bar: The Surprising Secrets of Happy Couples and What They Reveal about Creating a New Normal in Your Relationship.* New York: Harmony Books.

Orenstein, P. 2016. *Girls & Sex: Navigating the Complicated New Landscape*. New York: HarperCollins.

———. 2020. *Boys & Sex: Young Men on Hookups, Love, Porn, Consent, and Navigating the New Masculinity*. New York: HarperCollins.

Parker-Pope, T. 2020. "Masks, No Kissing and 'a Little Kinky': Dating and Sex in a Pandemic." *New York Times*, June 11. www.nytimes.com/2020/06/11/well/live/coronavi rus-sex-dating-masks.html.

Peitzmeier, S. M., M. Malik, S. K. Kattari, E. Marrow, R. Stephenson, M. Agénor, and S. L. Reisner. 2020. "Intimate Partner Violence in Transgender Populations: Systematic Review and Meta-analysis of Prevalence and Correlates." *American Journal of Public Health* 110, no. 9: e1–e14. doi.org/10.2105/AJPH.2020.305774.

Singh, O. 2020. "Miley Cyrus Spoke about Being Body-Shamed after 2013 MTV VMAs." *Insider*, March 19. www.insider.com/miley-cyrus-body-shamed-after-2013-mtv-vmas-reaction -2020-3.

Spell, S. A. 2017. "Not Just Black and White: How Race/Ethnicity and Gender Intersect in Hookup Culture." *Sociology of Race and Ethnicity* 3, no. 2: 172–187.

Stephens-Davidowitz, S. 2017. *Everybody Lies: Big Data, New Data, and What the Internet Can Tell Us About Who We Really Are*. New York: HarperCollins.

Taylor, J. 2020. "Biden Calls Anti-trans Violence an 'Epidemic That Needs National Leadership.'" *NBC News*, October 19. www.nbcnews.com/feature/nbc-out/biden-calls-anti -trans-violence-epidemic-needs-national-leadership-n1243932.

Thorpe, S., and A. Kuperberg. 2021. "Social Motivations for College Hookups." *Sexuality & Culture* 25, no. 2: 623–645.

Wade, L. 2017. *American Hookup: The New Culture of Sex on Campus*. New York: W. W. Norton.

Warner, M. 1999. *The Trouble with Normal: Sex, Politics, and the Ethics of Queer Life*. Cambridge, MA: Harvard University Press.

Wellings, K. 1995. "The Social Organization of Sexuality: Sexual Practices in the United States; Sex in America: A Definitive Survey." *British Medical Journal* 310, no. 6978: 540

Wolak, J., K. Mitchell, and D. Finkelhor. 2007. "Unwanted and Wanted Exposure to Online Pornography in a National Sample of Youth Internet Users." *Pediatrics* 119, no. 2: 247–257.

CHAPTER 17: Love (and Lust) in the Age of Viruses: Sexual Health and Relationships
by Adina Nack

Adler, Patricia A., and Peter Adler. 2006. *Constructions of Deviance: Social Power, Context, and Interaction*. 5th ed. Belmont, CA: Thomson Wadsworth.

Albrechtsen, Susanne, Svein Rasmussen, Steinar Thoresen, Lorentz M. Irgens, and Ole Erik Iversen. 2008. "Pregnancy Outcome in Women before and after Cervical Conisation: Population Based Cohort Study." *British Medical Journal* 337: a1343.

American Sexual Health Association. 2013a. "STDs/STIs Statistics." Research Triangle Park, NC: American Social Health Association. Retrieved June 8, 2013. www.ashasexual health.org/std-sti/std-statistics.html.

———. 2013b. "STDs/STIs Pregnancy." Research Triangle Park, NC: American Social Health Association. Retrieved June 8, 2013. www.ashasexualhealth.org/std-sti/Herpes/pregnancy .html.

———. 2022. "Herpes Treatment." Research Triangle Park, NC: American Social Health Association. Retrieved September 2, 2022 www.ashasexualhealth.org/herpes-treatment/.

———. n.d. "Herpes and Pregnancy." Research Triangle Park, NC: American Social Health Association. Retrieved July 19, 2022. www.ashasexualhealth.org/herpes-and-pregnancy/.

Awasthi, Sita, and Harvey M. Friedman. 2022. "An mRNA Vaccine to Prevent Genital Herpes." *Translational Research* 242: 56–65.

Bednarczyk, Robert A., Robert Davis, Kevin Ault, Walter Orenstein, and Saad B. Omer. 2012. "Sexual Activity–Related Outcomes after Human Papillomavirus Vaccination of 11- to 12-Year-Olds." *Pediatrics* 130, no. 5: 2–9.

Brouwer, Andrew F., Rachel L. Delinger, Marisa C. Eisenberg, Lora P. Campredon, Heather M. Walline, Thomas E. Carey, and Rafael Meza. 2019. "HPV Vaccination Has Not Increased Sexual Activity or Accelerated Sexual Debut in a College-Aged Cohort of Men and Women." *BMC Public Health* 19, no. 1: 821.

Centers for Disease Control and Prevention (CDC). 2013a. "CDC Fact Sheet: Incidence, Prevalence, and Cost of Sexually Transmitted Infections in the United States." Atlanta, GA: Centers for Disease Control and Prevention. Retrieved June 8, 2013. web.archive. org/web/20140213085827/https://www.cdc.gov/std/stats/STI-Estimates-Fact-Sheet-Feb-2013.pdf.

———. 2013b. "Genital Herpes Screening: Frequently Asked Questions." Atlanta, GA: Centers for Disease Control and Prevention. Retrieved June 8, 2013. www.cdc.gov/std/herpes /screening.htm.

———. 2013c. "Teen Vaccination Coverage: 2011 National Immunization Survey (NIS) – Teen." Atlanta, GA: Centers for Disease Control and Prevention. Retrieved June 8, 2013. www .cdc.gov/vaccines/who/teens/vaccination-coverage.html.

———. 2020. "Sex and Covid-19: Frequently Asked Questions." Atlanta, GA: Centers for Disease Control and Prevention. Retrieved July 27, 2022. https://npin.cdc.gov/publication /sex-and-covid-19-frequently-asked-questions.

———. 2021a. "Cancers Associated with Human Papillomavirus, United States—2014–2018." USCS Data Brief, no. 26. Retrieved March 17, 2023. www.cdc.gov/cancer/uscs/pdf /USCS-DataBrief-No26-December2021-h.pdf.

———. 2021b. "HPV Vaccine Safety and Effectiveness." Atlanta, GA: Centers for Disease Control and Prevention. Retrieved July 19, 2021. www.cdc.gov/vaccines/vpd/hpv /hcp/safety-effectiveness.html#:~:text=a%20syncopal%20event.-,HPV%20Vaccine%20 Effectiveness,women%20in%20their%20early%202020s.

———. 2021c. "National, Regional, State, and Selected Local Area Vaccination Coverage among Adolescents Aged 13–17 Years—United States, 2020" Atlanta, GA: Centers for Disease Control and Prevention. Retrieved July 19, 2021. www.cdc.gov/mmwr/vol umes/70/wr/mm7035a1.htm#:~:text=*%20Coverage%20with%20≥1%20dose,2019%20 to%2058.6%25%20in%202020.

———. 2021d. "Sexually Transmitted Infections Prevalence, Incidence, and Cost Estimates in the United States." Atlanta, GA: Centers for Disease Control and Prevention. January 25. www.cdc.gov/std/statistics/prevalence-2020-at-a-glance.htm.

———. 2022. "Safer Sex, Social Gatherings, and Monkeypox." Atlanta, GA: Centers for Disease Control and Prevention. Retrieved July 27, 2022. www.cdc.gov/poxvirus /monkeypox/prevention/sexual-health.html.

D'Souza, Gypsyamber, Yuri Agrawal, Jane Halpern, Sacared Bodison, and Maura L. Gillson. 2009. "Oral Sexual Behaviors Associated with Prevalent Oral Human Papillomavirus Infection." *Journal of Infectious Diseases* 199, no. 9: 1263–1269.

East, Leah, Debra Jackson, Kath Peters, and Louise O'Brien. 2010. "Disrupted Sense of Self: Young Women and Sexually Transmitted Infections." *Journal of Clinical Nursing* 19: 1995–2003.

Frank, Arthur W. 1991. *At the Will of the Body: Reflections on Illness*. Boston, MA: Houghton Mifflin.

Jakobsson, Maija, Mika Gissler, Jorma Paavonen, and Anna-Maija Tapper. 2009. "Loope Electrosurgical Excision Procedure and the Risk for Preterm Birth." *Obstetrics & Gynecology* 114, no. 3: 504–510.

Kalliala I., A. Anttila, T. Dyba, T. Hakulinen, M. Halttunen, and P. Nieminen. 2011. "Pregnancy Incidence and Outcome among Patients with Cervical Intraepithelial Neoplasia: A Retrospective Cohort Study." *British Journal of Obstetrics and Gynaecology* 119: 227–235.

Kreimer, Aimée R. 2009. "Oral Sexual Behaviors and the Prevalence of Oral Human Papillomavirus Infection." *Journal of Infectious Diseases* 199: 1253–1254.

Kyrgiou, M., G. Koliopoulos, P. Martin-Hirsch, M. Arbyn, W. Prendiville, and E. Paraskevaidas. 2006. "Obstetric Outcomes after Conservative Treatment for Intraepithelial or Early Invasive Cervical Lesions: Systematic Review and Meta-analysis." *Lancet* 367: 489–498.

Lichtenstein, Bronwen. 2003. "Stigma as a Barrier to Treatment of Sexually Transmitted Infection in the American Deep South: Issues of Race, Gender and Poverty." *Social Science & Medicine* 57, no. 12: 2435–2445.

Melville, J. L., S. Sniffen, R. Crosby, L. Salazar, W. Whittington, D. Dithmer-Schreck, R. DiClemente, and A. Wald. 2003. "Psychosocial Impact of Serological Diagnosis of Herpes Simplex Virus Type 2: A Qualitative Assessment." *Sexually Transmitted Infections* 79: 280–285.

Nack, Adina. 2000. "Damaged Goods: Women Managing the Stigma of STDs." *Deviant Behavior* 21: 95–121.

———. 2002. "Bad Girls and Fallen Women: Chronic STD Diagnoses as Gateways to Tribal Stigma." *Symbolic Interaction* 25, no. 4: 463–485.

———. 2008. *Damaged Goods? Women Living with Incurable Sexually Transmitted Diseases*. Philadelphia, PA: Temple University Press.

National Cancer Institute. 2013. "HPV and Cancer." Bethesda, MD: National Cancer Institute at the National Institutes of Health, U.S. Department of Health and Human Services. Retrieved June 8, 2013. www.cancer.gov/cancertopics/factsheet/Risk/HPV.

Rupp, R., S. Rosenthal, and L. Stanberry. 2005. "Pediatrics and Herpes Simplex Virus Vaccines." *Seminars in Pediatric Infectious Diseases* 16, no. 1: 31–37.

Rutter, Virginia, and Pepper Schwartz. 2011. *The Gender of Sexuality: Exploring Sexual Possibilities*. Plymouth, UK: Rowman & Littlefield.

Schneider, Joseph W., and Peter Conrad. 1981. "In the Closet with Illness: Epilepsy, Stigma Potential and Information Control." *Social Problems* 28, no. 1: 32–44.

Schwartz, Pepper. 2008. *Prime: Adventures and Advice on Sex, Love, and the Sensual Years*. New York: Collins.

Singhal, P., S. Naswa, and Y. S. Marfatia. 2009. "Pregnancy and Sexually Transmitted Viral Infections." *Indian Journal of Sexually Transmitted Diseases and AIDS* 30, no. 2: 71–78.

Temte, Jonathan L. 2007. "HPV Vaccine: A Cornerstone of Female Health." *American Family Physician* 75, no. 1: 28–30.

Vives, A., M. Cosentino, and J. Palou. 2020. "The Role of Human Papilloma Virus Test in Men: First Exhaustive Review of Literature." *National Library of Medicine* 44, no. 2: 86–93.

World Health Organization (WHO). 2022. "Hepatitis B." Geneva, Switzerland: World Health Organization. Retrieved July 19, 2022. www.who.int/news-room/fact-sheets/detail/hepati tis-b#:~:text=A%20safe%20and%20effective%20vaccine,chronic%20disease%20and%20 liver%20cancer.

CHAPTER 18: Orgasm in College Hookups and Relationships
by Elizabeth A. Armstrong, Paula England, and Alison Ash

Andrejek, Nicole, Tina Fetner, and Melanie Heath. 2022. "Climax as Work: Heteronormativity, Gender Labor, and the Gender Gap in Orgasms." *Gender & Society* 36(2):189–213.

Anonymous, M. D. 2006. *Unprotected: A Campus Psychiatrist Reveals How Political Correctness in Her Profession Endangers Every Student.* New York: Sentinel HC.

Bailey, Beth L. 1988. *From Front Porch to Back Seat: Courtship in Twentieth-Century America.* Baltimore: Johns Hopkins University Press.

Bogle, Kathleen A. 2007. "The Shift from Dating to Hooking Up in College: What Scholars Have Missed." *Sociology Compass* 1/2: 775–788.

———. 2008. *Hooking Up: Sex, Dating, and Relationships on Campus.* New York: New York University Press.

Boswell, A. Ayers, and Joan Z. Spade. 1996. "Fraternities and Collegiate Rape Culture: Why Are Some Fraternities More Dangerous Places for Women?" *Gender & Society* 10 (April): 133–147.

Braun, Virginia, Nicola Gavey, and Kathryn McPhillips. 2003. "The 'Fair Deal?' Unpacking Accounts of Reciprocity in Heterosex." *Sexualities* 6: 237–261.

Buss, David M. 1994. *The Evolution of Human Desire: Strategies of Human Mating.* New York: Basic Books.

Chodorow, Nancy. 1978. *The Reproduction of Mothering: Psychoanalysis and the Sociology of Gender.* Berkeley: University of California Press.

Crawford, Mary, and Danielle Popp. 2003. "Sexual Double Standards: A Review and Methodological Critique of Two Decades of Research." *Journal of Sex Research* 40: 13–27.

Darling, C. A., J. K. Davidson Sr., and D. A. Jennings. 1991. "The Female Sexual Response Revisited: Understanding the Multiorgasmic Experience in Women." *Archives of Sexual Behavior* 20: 527–540.

Denizet-Lewis, Benoit. 2004. "Friends, Friends with Benefits and the Benefits of the Local Mall." *New York Times*, May 30.

England, Paula, Emily Fitzgibbons Shafer, and Alison C. K. Fogarty. 2007. "Hooking Up and Forming Romantic Relationships on Today's College Campuses." In *The Gendered Society Reader*, 3rd ed., edited by Michael S. Kimmel and Amy Aronson. New York: Oxford University Press.

Fisher, Seymour. 1973. *The Female Orgasm.* New York: Basic Books.

Freitas, Donna. 2008. *Sex and the Soul: Juggling Sexuality, Spirituality, Romance and Religion on America's College Campuses.* New York: Oxford University Press.

Gagnon, John H., and William Simon. 1974. *Sexual Conduct: The Social Sources of Human Sexuality.* London: Aldine Transaction.

Gilmartin, Shannon K. 2005. "The Centrality and Costs of Heterosexual Romantic Love among First-Year College Women." *Journal of Higher Education* 76: 609–634.

Glenn, Norval, and Elizabeth Marquardt. 2001. *Hooking Up, Hanging Out, and Hoping for Mr. Right: College Women on Mating and Dating Today.* A report conducted by the Institute for American Values for the Independent Women's Forum, New York, NY

González-López, Gloria. 2005. *Erotic Journeys: Mexican Immigrants and Their Sex Lives.* Berkeley: University of California Press.

Hamilton, Laura, and Elizabeth A. Armstrong. 2009. "Gendered Sexuality in Emerging Adulthood: Double Binds and Flawed Options." *Gender & Society* 23, no. 5: 589–616.

Hite, Shere. 1976. *The Hite Report: A Nationwide Study of Female Sexuality.* New York: Seven Stories.

Holland, Dorothy C., and Margaret A. Eisenhart. 1990. *Educated in Romance: Women, Achievement and College Culture.* Chicago: University of Chicago Press.

Kasic, Allison. 2008. "Take Back the Date." Independent Women's Forum. Available at www .iwf.org/campus/show/20122.html.

Kass, Leon R. 1997. "The End of Courtship." *Public Interest* 126: 39–63.

Laumann, Edward O., John H. Gagnon, Robert T. Michael, and Stuart Michaels. 1994 *The Social Organization of Sexuality: Sexual Practices in the United States.* Chicago: University of Chicago Press.

Mah, Kenneth, and Yitzchak M. Binik. 2001. "The Nature of Human Orgasm: A Critical Review of Major Trends." *Clinical Psychology Review* 21: 823–856.

Martin, Karin. 1996. *Puberty, Sexuality, and the Self: Boys and Girls at Adolescence.* New York: Routledge.

Paul, Elizabeth L., Brian McManus, and Elizabeth Hayes. 2000. "'Hookups': Characteristics and Correlates of College Students' Spontaneous and Anonymous Sexual Experiences." *Journal of Sex Research* 37: 76–88.

Popenoe, David, and Barbara Defoe Whitehead. 2000. *The State of Our Unions, 2000: The Social Health of Marriage in America.* New Brunswick, NJ: National Marriage Project.

Richters, Juliet, Richard de Vissar, Chris Rissel, and Anthony Smith. 2006. "Sexual Practices at Last Heterosexual Encounter and Occurrence of Orgasm in a National Survey." *Journal of Sex Research* 43: 217–226.

Rupp, Leila J., Verta Taylor, Shiri Regev-Messalem, Alison C. K. Fogarty, and Paula England. 2013. "Queer Women in the Hookup Scene: Beyond the Closet?" *Gender & Society* 28, no. 2: 212–235.

Schalet, Amy. 2004. "Must We Fear Adolescent Sexuality?" *Medscape General Medicine* 6: 44.

———. 2009. "Subjectivity, Intimacy, and the Empowerment Paradigm of Adolescent Sexuality." *Feminist Studies* 35, no. 1: 133–160.

Schwartz, Pepper, and Virginia Rutter. 2000. *The Gender of Sexuality.* Lanham, MD: AltaMira.

Sessions Stepp, Laura. 2007. *Unhooked: How Young Women Pursue Sex, Delay Love, and Lose at Both.* New York: Riverhead Books.

Stombler, Mindy. 1994. "'Buddies' or 'Slutties': The Collective Sexual Reputation of Fraternity Little Sisters." *Gender & Society* 8: 297–323.

Tanenbaum, Leora. 1999. *Slut! Growing Up Female with a Bad Reputation.* New York: Seven Stories.

Tolman, Deborah L. 2002. *Dilemmas of Desire: Teenage Girls Talk about Sexuality*. Cambridge, MA: Harvard University Press.

Townsend, J. M. 1995. "Sex without Emotional Involvement: An Evolutionary Interpretation of Sex Differences." *Archives of Sexual Behavior* 24: 173–206.

Waite, Linda J., and Maggie Gallagher. 2000. *The Case for Marriage: Why Married People Are Happier, Healthier, and Better Off Financially*. New York: Doubleday.

Waite, Linda J., and Kara Joyner. 2001. "Emotional Satisfaction and Physical Pleasure in Sexual Unions: Time Horizon, Sexual Behavior, and Sexual Exclusivity." *Journal of Marriage and Family* 63: 247–264.

White, Emily. 2001. *Fast Girls: Teenage Tribes and the Myth of the Slut*. New York: Simon & Schuster.

Yancey Martin, Patricia, and Robert A. Hummer. 1989. "Fraternities and Rape on Campus." *Gender & Society* 3: 457–473.

CHAPTER 19: Independent Women: Equality in African American Lesbian Relationships
by Mignon R. Moore

Abdulahad, Tania, Gwendolyn Rogers, Barbara Smith, and Jameelah Waheed. 1983. "Black Lesbian/Feminist Organizing: A Conversation." In *Home Girls: A Black Feminist Anthology*, edited by B. Smith, 293–319. New York: Kitchen Table.

Blumstein, Philip, and Pepper Schwartz. 1983. *American Couples: Money, Work, Sex*. New York: Morrow.

Bulcroft, Richard A., and Kris A. Bulcroft. 1993. "Race Differences in Attitudinal and Motivational Factors in the Decision to Marry." *Journal of Marriage and Family* 55, no. 92: 338–355.

Carrington, Christopher. 1999. *No Place Like Home: Relationships and Family Life among Lesbians and Gay Men*. Chicago: University of Chicago Press.

Collins, Patricia Hill. 2004. *Black Sexual Politics: African Americans, Gender and the New Racism*. New York: Routledge.

Combahee River Collective. 1983. "A Black Feminist Statement." In *Words of Fire: An Anthology of African-American Feminist Thought*, edited by Beverly Guy-Sheftall, 232–240. New York: New Press.

Cornwell, Anita. 1983. *The Black Lesbian in White America*. Tallahassee, FL: Naiad.

Crenshaw, Kimberlé Williams. 1995. "Race, Reform, and Retrenchment: Transformation and Legitimation in Anti-Discrimination Law." In *Critical Race Theory: The Key Writings that Formed the Movement*, edited by Kimberlé Crenshaw, Neil Gotanda, Gary Peller, and Kendall Thomas, 103–122. New York: New Press.

Dang, Alain, and Somjen Frazer. 2004. "Black Same-Sex Households in the United States: A Report from the 2000 Census." New York: National Gay and Lesbian Task Force Policy Institute and the National Black Justice Coalition.

Dill, Bonnie Thornton. 1979. "The Dialectics of Black Womanhood." *Signs: Journal of Women in Culture and Society* 4: 543–555.

Esterberg, Kristin G. 1997. *Lesbian and Bisexual Identities: Constructing Communities, Constructing Selves*. Philadelphia: Temple University Press.

Ferree, Myra Marx. 1991. "The Gender Division of Labor in Two-Earner Marriages." *Journal of Family Issues* 12, no. 2: 158–180.

Gartrell, Nanette, Amy Banks, Nancy Reed, Jean Hamilton, Carla Rodas, and Amalia Deck. 2000. "The National Lesbian Family Study: 3. Interviews with Mothers of Five-Year-Olds." *American Journal of Orthopsychiatry* 70, no. 4: 542–548.

Gates, Gary. 2008. "Diversity among Same-Sex Couples and Their Children." In *American Families: A Multicultural Reader*, 2nd ed., Edited by Stephanie Coontz, with Maya Parson and Gabrielle Raley, 394–399. New York: Routledge.

Hequembourg, Amy. 2007. *Lesbian Motherhood: Stories of Becoming*. New York: Harrington Park.

Hochschild, Arlie Russell. 1989. *The Second Shift: Working Parents and the Revolution at Home*. New York: Viking.

Hunter, Andrea G., and Sherrill L. Sellers. 1998. "Feminist Attitudes among African-American Women and Men." *Gender and Society* 12, no. 1: 81–99.

Kamo, Yoshimore, and Ellen L. Cohen. 1998. "Division of Household Work between Partners: A Comparison of Black and White Couples." *Journal of Comparative Family Studies* 29, no. 1: 131–145.

Kenney, Catherine T. 2006. "The Power of the Purse: Allocative Systems and Inequality in Couple Households." *Gender and Society* 20, no. 3: 354–381.

Kessler-Harris, Alice. 2003. *Out to Work: A History of Wage-Earning Women in the United States*. New York: Oxford University Press.

King, Deborah. 1988. "Multiple Jeopardy, Multiple Consciousness: The Context of a Black Feminist Ideology." *Signs: Journal of Women in Culture and Society* 14, no. 1: 42–72.

Kurdek, Lawrence A. 1993. "The Allocation of Household Labor in Gay, Lesbian, Heterosexual, and Married Couples." *Journal of Social Issues* 49, no. 3: 127–139.

Landry, Bart. 2000. *Black Working Wives: Pioneers of the American Family Revolution*. Berkeley: University of California Press.

Mezey, Nancy J. 2008. *New Choices, New Families: How Lesbians Decide about Motherhood*. Baltimore, MD: Johns Hopkins University Press.

Moore, Mignon R. 2006. "Lipstick or Timberlands? Meanings of Gender Presentation in Black Lesbian Communities." *Signs: Journal of Women in Culture and Society* 31, no. 1: 113–139.

———. 2008. "Gendered Power Relations among Women: A Study of Household Decision-Making in Black, Lesbian Stepfamilies." *American Sociological Review* 73: 335–356.

Nelson, Fiona. 1996. *Lesbian Motherhood: An Exploration of Canadian Lesbian Families*. Toronto: University of Toronto Press.

Patterson, Charlotte. 1995. "Families of the Lesbian Baby Boom: Parents' Division of Labor and Children's Adjustment." *Developmental Psychology* 31, no. 1: 115–123.

Phelan, Shane. 1993. "(Be)Coming Out: Lesbian Identity and Politics." *Signs: Journal of Women in Culture and Society* 18, no. 4: 765–790.

Ransford, H. Edward, and Jon Miller. 1983. "Race, Sex, and Feminist Outlooks." *American Sociological Review* 48, no. 1: 46–59.

Schwartz, Pepper. 1994. *Peer Marriages: How Love between Equals Really Works*. New York: Free Press.

Sullivan, Maureen. 2004. *The Family of Woman: Lesbian Mothers, Their Children, and the Undoing of Gender*. Berkeley: University of California Press.

Tichenor, Veronica Jaris. 2005. *Earning More and Getting Less: Why Successful Wives Can't Buy Equality*. New Brunswick, NJ: Rutgers University Press.

Walby, Sylvia. 1990. *Theorizing Patriarchy*. Oxford, UK, and Cambridge, MA: Oxford University Press.

Wolf, Deborah Goleman. 1979. *The Lesbian Community*. Berkeley: University of California Press.

CHAPTER 20: Beyond Family Structure: Family Process Studies Help to Reframe Debates about What's Good for Children
by Philip A. Cowan and Carolyn Pape Cowan

Ahrons, C. R. 2004. *We're Still Family: What Grown Children Have to Say about Their Parents' Divorce*. New York: HarperCollins. 281.

Amato, P. R. 2000. "The Consequences of Divorce for Adults and Children." *Journal of Marriage and the Family* 62, no. 4: 1269–1287.

———. 2001. "Children of Divorce in the 1990s: An Update of the Amato and Keith (1991) Meta-analysis." *Journal of Family Psychology* 15, no. 3: 355–370.

Blankenhorn, D. 1995. *Fatherless America: Confronting Our Most Urgent Social Problem*. New York: Basic Books.

Booth, A., and P. R. Amato. 1994. "Parental Marital Quality, Parental Divorce, and Relations with Parents." *Journal of Marriage and the Family* 56, no. 1: 21–34.

Brazelton, T. B., and J. D. Sparrow. 2006. "Touchpoints Birth to 3: Your Child's Emotional and Behavioral Development." Cambridge, MA: Da Capo.

Brookings Working Group on Poverty and Opportunity. 2015. "Opportunity, Responsibility, and Security: A Consensus Plan for Reducing Poverty and Restoring the American Dream." Washington, DC: Brookings.

Cabrera, N. J., and C. S. Tamis-LeMonda, eds. 2013. *Handbook of Father Involvement: Multidisciplinary Perspectives*. 2nd ed. New York: Routledge.

Carlson, M., and S. McLanahan. 2002. "Fragile Families, Father Involvement, and Public Policy." In *Handbook of Father Involvement: Multidisciplinary Perspectives*, edited by C. S. Tamis-LeMonda and N. Cabrera, 461–488. Mahwah, NJ: Lawrence Erlbaum Associates.

———. 2006. "Strengthening Unmarried Families: Could Enhancing Couple Relationships Also Improve Parenting?" *Social Service Review* 80, no. 2: 297–321.

Casey, P., Philip A. Cowan, Carolyn P. Cowan, Lucy Draper, Naomi Mwamba, and David Hewison. 2017. "Parents as Partners: A U.K. Trial of a US Couples-Based Parenting Intervention for At-Risk Low-Income Families." *Family Process* 56, no. 3: 589–606.

Caspi, A., and G. H. J. Elder. 1988. "Emergent Family Patterns: The Intergenerational Construction of Problem Behaviour and Relationships." In *Relationships within Families: Mutual Influences*, edited by R. A. Hinde and J. Stevenson-Hinde, 218–240. Oxford: Clarendon.

Cherlin, A. J. 2009. *The Marriage-Go-Round: The State of Marriage and the Family in America Today*. New York: Alfred A. Knopf.

Conger, R. D., M. Cui, and F. O. Lorenz. 2011. "Intergenerational Continuities in Economic Pressure and Couple Conflict in Romantic Relationships." In *Romantic Relationships in Emerging Adulthood*, edited by Frank D. Fincham and Ming Cui, 101–122. New York: Cambridge University Press.

Cowan, C. P., and P. A. Cowan. 2000. *When Partners Become Parents: The Big Life Change for Couples*. Mahwah, NJ: Lawrence Erlbaum Associates.

———. 2020. "Breaking Down Silos in Family Policymaking and Service Delivery: Family Approaches that Enhance Children's Development." *Journal of Family Theory and Review* 11, no. 1: 92–111.

Cowan, C. P., P. A. Cowan, and G. Heming. 2005. "Two Variations of a Preventive Intervention for Couples: Effects on Parents and Children during the Transition to School." *The

Family Context of Parenting in Children's Adaptation to Elementary school. Mahwah, NJ: Lawrence Erlbaum Associates.

Cowan, C. P., Philip A. Cowan, Marsha Kline Pruett, and Kyle Pruett. 2007. "An Approach to Preventing Coparenting Conflict and Divorce in Low-Income Families: Strengthening Couple Relationships and Fostering Fathers' Involvement." *Family Process*. Special Issue Divorce and Its Aftermath 46, no. 1: 109–121.

Cowan, P. A., and C. P. Cowan. 2014. "Controversies in Couple Relationship Education (CRE): Overlooked Evidence and Implications for Research and Policy." *Psychology Public Policy and Law* 20, no. 4: 361–383.

Cowan, P. A., and G. Heming. 2005. "How Children and Parents Fare during the Transition to School." In *The Family Context of Parenting in Children's Adaptation to Elementary School*, edited by Philip A. Cowan, Carolyn Pape Cowan, Jennifer C. Ablow, Vanessa Kahen Johnson, and Jeffrey R. Measelle, 79–115. Monographs in Parenting Series Mahwah, NJ: Lawrence Erlbaum Associates.

Cowan, P. A., C. P. Cowan, M. K. Pruett, K. Pruett, and J. J. Wong. 2009. "Promoting Fathers' Engagement with Children: Preventive Interventions for Low-Income Families." *Journal of Marriage and Family* 71, no. 3: 663–679.

Cowan, P. A., C. P. Cowan, M. K. Pruett, K. Pruett, and P. Gillette. 2014. "Evaluating a Couples Group to Enhance Father Involvement in Low-Income Families Using a Benchmark Comparison." *Family Relations* 63, no. 3: 356–370.

Cowan, P. A., C. P. Cowan, M. K. Pruett, and K. Pruett. 2019. "Fathers' and Mothers' Attachment Styles, Couple Conflict, Parenting Quality, and Children's Behavior Problems: An Intervention Test of Mediation." *Attachment & Human Development* 21, no. 5: 532–550.

Dadds, M. R., S. Schwartz, and M. R. Sanders. 1987. "Marital Discord and Treatment Outcome in Behavioral Treatment of Child Conduct Disorders." *Journal of Consult Clinical Psychology* 55, no. 3: 396–403.

Davies, P. T., E. M. Cummings, and M. A. Winter. 2004. "Pathways between Profiles of Family Functioning, Child Security in the Interparental Subsystem, and Child Psychological Problems." *Development and Psychopathology* 16, no. 3: 525–550.

Dush, C. M. K. 2009. "An Examination of Child Well-Being in Stable Single-Parent and Married Families." New York: Columbia University Press.

Edin, K., and J. M. Reed. 2005. "Why Don't They Just Get Married? Barriers to Marriage among the Disadvantaged." *The Future of Children* 15, no. 2: 117–137.

Gannon, E. J., and M. Lawrence. 2018. "The Story of a Marriage." PsycCRITIQUES.

Ganong, L. H., M. Coleman, and C. Sanner. 2019. "Divorced and Remarried Parenting." In M. H. Bornstein (Ed.), *Handbook of Parenting: Being and Becoming a Parent*. pp. 311–344. New York: Routledge.

Golombok, S. 2015. *Modern Families: Parents and Children in New Family Forms*. Cambridge, MA: Cambridge University Press.

Harknett, K., L. Hardman, I. Garfinkel, and S. S. McLanahan. 2001. "The Fragile Families Study: Social Policies and Labor Markets in Seven Cities." *Children and Youth Services Review* 23, no. 6–7: 537–555.

Harold, G. T., D. Acquah, R. Sellers, and H. Chowdry. 2016. "What Works to Enhance Inter-Parental Relationships and Improve Outcomes for Children." London: Early Intervention Foundation.

Harold, G. T., L. D. Leve, K. K. Elam, A. Thapar, J. M. Neiderhiser, M. N. Natsuaki, D. S. Shaw, and D. Reiss. 2013. "The Nature of Nurture: Disentangling Passive Genotype–Environment Correlation from Family Relationship Influences on Children's Externalizing Problems." *Journal of Family Psychology* 27, no. 1: 12–21.

Haskins, R. 2018a. "A Better Way to Wage the War on Poverty." *Washington Post*, A17.

———. 2018b. "Evidence-Based Policy: The Movement, the Goals, the Issues, the Promise." *Annals of the American Academy of Political and Social Science* 678, no. 1: 8–37.

Hetherington, E. M., and J. Kelly. 2002. *For Better or for Worse: Divorce Reconsidered.* New York: W. W. Norton.

Lamb, M. E., and C. Lewis. 2013. *Father-Child Relationships,* New York: Routledge/Taylor & Francis Group.

Larzelere, R. E., A. S. Morris, and A. W. Harrist. 2013. "Authoritative Parenting: Synthesizing Nurturance and Discipline for Optimal Child Development." Washington, DC: American Psychological Association.

Lippman, L. 2014. "Five Myths about Moms and Families Worldwide." Child Trends, Washington, DC. https://www.childtrends.org/publications/5-myths-about-moms-and-families-worldwide.

Lundquist, E., J. Hsueh, A. E. Lowenstein, K. Faucetta, D. Gubits, C. Michalopoulos, and V. Knox. 2014. "A Family-Strengthening Program for Low-Income Families: Final Impacts from the Supporting Healthy Marriage Evaluation." In OPRE Report 2013-49A. Washington, DC: Office of Planning, Research and Evaluation, Administration for Children and Families, U.S. Department of Health and Human Services.

McLoyd, V. C., N. L. Aikens, and L. M. Burton. 2006. "Childhood Poverty, Policy, and Practice." In *Handbook of Child Psychology: Child Psychology in Practice.* Vol. 4, 6th ed.: 700–772.

Mincy, R., and H. Pouncy. 2002. "The Responsible Fatherhood Field: Evolution and Goals." In *Handbook of Father Involvement: Multidisciplinary Perspectives,* edited by C. S. Tamis-LeMonda and N. J. Cabrera. Mahwah, NJ: Lawrence Erlbaum Associates.

Parke, R. D. 2002. "Fathers and Families." In *Handbook of Parenting,* Vol. 3: *Being and Becoming a Parent,* 2nd ed., edited by M. H. Bornstein, 27–73. Mahwah, NJ: Lawrence Erlbaum Associates.

———. 2013. *Future Families: Diverse Forms, Rich Possibilities.* Malden, MA: John Wiley & Sons.

Parke, R. D., and J. T. Cookston. 2019. *Fathers and Families.* New York: Routledge/Taylor & Francis Group.

Perrone, L., S. D. Imrisek, A. Dash, M. Rodriguez, E. Monticciolo, and K. Bernard. 2021. "Changing Parental Depression and Sensitivity: Randomized Clinical Trial of ABC's Effectiveness in the Community." *Development and Psychopathology* 33, no. 3: 1026–1040.

Pickreign Stronach, E., S. L. Toth, F. Rogosch, A. Oshri, J. Todd Manly, and D. Cicchetti. 2011. "Child Maltreatment, Attachment Security, and Internal Representations of Mother and Mother-Child Relationships." *Child Maltreatment* 16, no. 2: 137–145.

Popenoe, D. 1993. "American Family Decline, 1960–1990." *Journal of Marriage and the Family* 55: 527–541.

Pruett, M., and R. Barker. 2009. "Children of Divorce: New Trends and Ongoing Dilemmas." In *The Wiley-Blackwell Handbook of Family Psychology,* edited by James H. Bray and Mark Stanton, 463–474. Malden, MA: Wiley-Blackwell.

Pruett, M. K., P. Gillette, and K. D. Pruett. 2016. "Supporting Father Involvement to Promote Co-parent, Parent and Child Outcomes in a Canadian Context." *Psychology & Psychological Research International Journal* 1, no. 1: 1–14.

Pruett, M. K., Philip A. Cowan, Carolyn Pape Cowan, Peter Gillette, Kyle D. Pruett. 2019. "Supporting Father Involvement: An Intervention with Community and Child Welfare–Referred Couples." *Family Relations* 68, no. 1: 51–67.

Schulz, M. S., et al. 2004. "Coming Home Upset: Gender, Marital Satisfaction, and the Daily Spillover of Workday Experience into Couple Interactions." *Journal of Family Psychology* 18, no. 1: 250–263.

Sheffield, Amanda M., et al. 2021. "We Know Even More Things: A Decade Review of Parenting Research." *Journal of Research on Adolescence* 31, no. 4: 870.

Stacey, J., and T. J. Biblarz. 2001. "(How) Does the Sexual Orientation of Parents Matter?" *American Sociological Review* 66, no. 2: 159–183.

Twenge, J. M., W. K. Campbell, and C. A. Foster. 2003. "Parenthood and Marital Satisfaction: A Meta-Analytic Review." *Journal of Marriage and Family* 65, no. 3: 574–583.

Waite, L. J., and M. Gallagher. 2000. *The Case for Marriage: Why Married People Are Happier, Healthier, and Better Off Financially*. New York: Doubleday. 260.

Wallerstein, J. S., J. Lewis, and S. Blakeslee. 2000. *The Unexpected Legacy of Divorce: A 25 Year Landmark Study*. New York: Hyperion.

Wikle, J. S., C. E. Leavitt, J. B. Yorgason, J. P. Dew, and H. M. Johnson. 2021. "The Protective Role of Couple Communication in Moderating Negative Associations between Financial Stress and Sexual Outcomes for Newlyweds." *Journal of Family and Economic Issues* 42, no. 2: 282–299.

Wilcox, W. B., and R. I. Lerman. 2014. *For Richer, for Poorer: How Family Structures Economic Success in America*. Washington, DC: Institute for Family Studies.

Wood, R. G., Q. Moore, A. Clarkwest, and A. Killewald. 2014. "The Long-Term Effects of Building Strong Families: A Program for Unmarried Parents." *Journal of Marriage and Family* 76, no. 2: 446–463.

CHAPTER 21: The Marriage Movement
by Melanie Heath and Jennifer Randles

Boo, Katherine. 2003. "The Marriage Cure," *New Yorker*, August 18.

Brooks, David. 2020. "The Nuclear Family Was a Mistake." *Atlantic*, March. www.theatlantic.com/magazine/archive/2020/03/the-nuclear-family-was-a-mistake/505536/.

Brotherson, Sean E., and William C. Duncan. 2004. "Rebinding the Ties That Bind: Government Efforts to Preserve and Promote Marriage." *Family Relations* 53: 459–468.

Brown, Susan. 2010. "Marriage and Child Well-Being: Research and Policy Perspectives." *Journal of Marriage and Family* 72, no. 2: 1059–1077.

Cherlin, Andrew J. 2009. *The Marriage-Go-Round: The State of Marriage and Family in America Today*. New York: Knopf.

Conger, Rand D., Katherine J. Conger, and Monica J. Martin. 2010. "Socioeconomic Status, Family Processes, and Individual Development." *Journal of Marriage and Family* 72: 685–704.

Coontz, Stephanie. 2005. *Marriage, a History: From Obedience to Intimacy, or How Love Conquered Marriage*. New York: Viking Press.

Edin, Kathryn, and Maria Kefalas. 2005. *Promises I Can Keep: Why Poor Women Put Motherhood before Marriage*. Berkeley: University of California Press.

Edin, Kathryn, and Timothy Nelson. 2013. *Doing the Best I Can: Fatherhood in the Inner City*. Berkeley: University of California Press.

Felder, Ben. 2022. "Oklahoma Is Pushing a Huge Surplus of Welfare Dollars to Community Programs." *Oklahoman*, April 3. https://eu.oklahoman.com/story/news/2022/04/03 /oklahoma-surplus-welfare-funds-being-sent-community-nonprofits-tanf-snap-wic /6847992001/.

Fry, Richard, and Kim Parker. 2021. "Rising Share of U.S. Adults Are Living without a Spouse or a Partner." Pew Research Center, October 5. www.pewresearch.org /social-trends/2021/10/05/rising-share-of-u-s-adults-are-living-without-a-spouse-or-partner/.

Halpern-Meekin, Sarah. 2019. *Social Poverty: Low-Income Parents and the Struggle for Family and Community Ties*. New York: New York University Press.

Hawkins, Alan. J., and Tamara A. Fackrell. 2010. "Does Relationship and Marriage Education for Lower-Income Couples Work? A Meta-Analytic Study of Emerging Research." *Journal of Couple & Relationship Therapy: Innovations in Clinical and Educational Interventions* 9: 181–191.

Heath, Melanie. 2012. *One Marriage under God: The Campaign to Promote Marriage in America*. New York: New York University Press.

Hymowitz, Kay S. 2007. *Marriage and Caste in America: Separate and Unequal Families in a Post-Marital Age*. New York: Rowman & Littlefield.

Hymowitz, Kay. 2021. "Our Conjugal Class Divide." *American Compass*, February 10. https://americancompass.org/essays/our-conjugal-class-divide/.

Kanter, Jeremy B., Deadric T. Williams, and Amy J. Rauer. 2021. "Strengthening Lower-Income Families: Lessons Learned from Policy Reponses to the COVID-19 Pandemic." *Family Process* 60: 1389–1402.

Livingston, Gretchen. 2018. "The Changing Profile of Unmarried Parents." Pew Research Center, April 25. www.pewresearch.org/social-trends/2018/04/25/the-changing-profile-of -unmarried-parents/.

McLanahan, Sara, Laura Tach, and Daniel Schneider. 2013. "The Causal Effects of Father Absence." *Annual Review of Sociology* 39: 399–427.

Office of Family Assistance. 2021. "About Healthy Marriage & Responsible Fatherhood." www.acf.hhs.gov/ofa/programs/healthy-marriage-responsible-fatherhood/about.

Pew Research Center. 2010a. Social & Demographic Trends Report, "The Decline of Marriage and Rise of New Families." November 18. Available from http://www.pewsocial trends.org/2010/11/18/the-decline-of-marriage-and-rise-of-new-families/.

———. 2010b. Social & Demographic Trends Report, "The Reversal of the College Marriage." October 7. Available from http://www.pewsocialtrends.org/2010/10/07/the-reversal -of-the-college-marriage-gap/.

Plummer, Ken. 2003. *Intimate Citizenship: Private Decisions and Public Dialogues*. Seattle: University of Washington Press.

Randles, Jennifer. 2014. "Partnering and Parenting in Poverty: A Qualitative Analysis of a Relationship Skills Program for Low-Income Unmarried Families." *Journal of Policy Analysis and Management* 33(2): 385–412.

———. 2017. *Proposing Prosperity? Marriage Education Policy and Inequality in America*. New York: Columbia University Press.

———. 2020. *Essential Dads: The Inequalities and Politics of Fathering*. Oakland: University of California Press.

Randles, Jennifer, and Orit Avishai. 2018. "Saving Marriage Culture 'One Marriage at a Time': Relationship Education and the Reinstitutionalization of Marriage in an Era of Individualism." *Qualitative Sociology* 41: 21–40.

Safawi, Ali, and Cindy Reyes. 2021. "States Must Continue Recent Momentum to Further Improve TANF Benefit Levels." Center on Budget and Policy Priorities. www.cbpp.org /research/family-income-support/states-must-continue-recent-momentum-to-further -improve-tanf-0.

Sager, Rebecca. 2010. *Faith, Politics, and Power: The Politics of Faith-Based Initiatives.* New York: Oxford University Press.

United States Congress. 1996. *The Personal Responsibility and Work Opportunity Reconcilia-tion Act.* (Public Law 104-193). Washington, DC: Government Printing Office.

Wang, Wendy, and W. Bradford Wilcox. 2017. "Marriage, Kids, and the 'Success Sequence' among Young Adults." Institute for Family Studies. www.aei.org/wp-content/uploads /2017/06/IFS-MillennialSuccessSequence-Final.pdf?x88519.

Waters, Rob. 2004. "The Citizen Therapist: Making a Difference — 5 Therapists Who Dared to Take on the Wider World." *Psychotherapy Networker*, Nov/Dec: Cover story.

Wilcox, Brad. 2010. *The State of Our Unions.* Available from http://www.stateofourunions.org.

Wilcox, W. Bradford, and Hal Boyd. 2020. "The Nuclear Family Is Still Indispensable." *Atlantic*, February. www.theatlantic.com/ideas/archive/2020/02/nuclear-family-still -indispensable/606841/.

Wood, Robert. G., Quinn Moore, Andrew Clarkwest, Alexandra Killewald, and Shannon Monahan. 2012. "The Long-Term Effects of Building Strong Families: A Relationship Skills Education Program for Unmarried Parents," Executive Summary. OPRE Report 2012-28B. Washington, DC: Mathematica Policy Research and the Office of Planning, Research, and Evaluation, Administration of Children and Families.

Wu, April Yanyuan, Quinn Moore, and Robert Wood. 2021. "Healthy Marriage and Relationship Education with Integrated Economic Stability Services: The Impacts of Empowering Families." OPRE Report 2021-224. Office of Planning, Research and Evaluation. U.S. Department of Health and Human Services. www.mathematica.org/publications /healthy-marriage-and-relationship-education-with-integrated-economic-stability- services-the-impacts.

CHAPTER 22: The Case for Divorce
by Virginia E. Rutter

Amato, Paul R., and Juliana M. Sobolewski. 2001. "The Effects of Divorce and Marital Discord on Adult Children's Psychological Well-Being." *American Sociological Review* 66: 900–921.

Ananat, E., and G. Michaels. 2008. "The Effect of Marital Breakup on the Income Distribu-tion of Women and Children." *Journal of Human Resources* 43(3): 611–629.

Becker, Howard S. 1973. *Outsiders: Studies in the Sociology of Deviance.* New York: Free Press.

Campbell, Jacquelyn C., ed. 1998. *Empowering Survivors of Abuse: Health Care for Battered Women and Their Children.* Thousand Oaks, CA: Sage Publications.

Carlson, L. 2021. "Age Variation in the Divorce Rate, 1990 & 2019." *Family Profiles*, FP-21 16. Bowling Green, OH: National Center for Family & Marriage Research. https://doi.org /10.25035/ncfmr/fp-21-16.

CBPP. 2022. "Robust COVID Relief Achieved Historic Gains against Poverty and Hardship, Bolstered Economy." February 24. www.cbpp.org/research/poverty-and-inequality /robust-covid-relief-achieved-historic-gains-against-poverty-and.

Centers for Disease Control and Prevention (CDC). 2023. "National Marriage and Divorce Rate Trends for 2000-2021." January 26. www.cdc.gov/nchs/nvss/marriage-divorce.htm.

Cherlin, Andrew J., Frank F. Furstenberg Jr., P. Lindsay Chase-Lansdale, Kathleen E. Kiernan., Philip K. Robins., Donna Ruane Morrison, and Julien O. Teitler. 1991. "Longitudinal Studies of Effects of Divorce on Children in Great Britain and the United States." *Science* 252: 1386–1389.

Cherlin, Andrew J., P. Lindsay Chase-Lansdale, and Christine McRae. 1998. "Effects of Parental Divorce on Mental Health through the Life Course." *American Sociological Review* 63: 239–249.

Choi, H., and N. F. Marks. 2008. "Marital conflict, depressive symptoms, and functional impairment." *Journal of Marriage and Family* 70(2): 377–390.

Coltrane, Scott, and Michele Adams. 2003. "The Social Construction of the Divorce 'Problem': Morality, Child Victims, and the Politics of Gender." *Family Relations* 52: 363–372.

Coontz, Stephanie, and Nancy Folbre. 2002. "Marriage, Poverty, and Public Policy." A Briefing Paper from the Council on Contemporary Families. Retrieved on June 24, 2008, from http://www.contemporaryfamilies.org/public/briefing.html.

Cowen, Tyler. 2007. "Matrimony Has Its Benefits, and Divorce Has a Lot to Do with That." *New York Times*, April 19. Retrieved on June 20, 2008, from http://www.nytimes.com /2007/04/19/business/19scene.html?_r=0.

Fomby, Paula, and Andrew Cherlin. 2007. "Family Instability and Child Well-Being." *American Sociological Review* 72(2): 181–204.

Gottman, J. M. 1994. *What Predicts Divorce?* Hillsdale, NJ: Lawrence Erlbaum Associates.

Greenberg, P. E., L. E. Stiglin, S. N. Finkelstein, and E. R. Berndt. 1993a. "Depression: A Neglected Major Illness." *Journal of Clinical Psychiatry* 54: 419–424.

———. 1993b. "The Economic Burden of Depression in 1990." *Journal of Clinical Psychiatry* 54: 405–418.

Hawkins, Daniel N., and Alan Booth. 2005. "Unhappily Ever After: Effects of Long-Term, Low-Quality Marriages on Well-Being." *Social Forces* 84(1): 451–471.

Hetherington, E. Mavis. 1999. "Should We Stay Together for the Sake of the Children?" In *Coping with Divorce, Single Parenting, and Remarriage: A Risk and Resiliency Perspective*, edited by E. Mavis Hetherington, 93–116. Mahwah, NJ: Lawrence Erlbaum Associates.

Hetherington, E. Mavis, and John Kelly. 2002. *For Better or For Worse: Divorce Reconsidered.* New York: W. W. Norton & Company.

Hetherington, E. Mavis, and P. Stanley-Hagan. 1997. "Divorce and the Adjustment of Children: A Risk and Resiliency Perspective." *Journal of Child Psychology & Psychiatry* 40: 129–140.

Heuveline, P. 2005. "The Tricky Business of Estimating Divorce Rates." A Briefing Paper from the Council on Contemporary Families. Last modified October 6, 2006. Retrieved on June 24, 2008, from http://www.contemporaryfamilies.org/public/briefing.html.

Kiecolt-Glaser, J. K., S. Kennedy, S. Malkoff, L. Fisher, C. E. Speicher, and R. Glaser. 1988. "Marital Discord and Immunity in Males." *Psychosomatic Medicine* 50: 213–299.

Li, Jui-Chung Allen. 2007. "The Kids Are OK: Divorce and Children's Behavior Problems." RAND Labor and Population Working Paper No. WR-489. Santa Monica, CA: RAND.

———. 2008. "New Findings on an Old Question: Does Divorce Cause Children's Behavior Problems?" A Briefing Paper from the Council on Contemporary Families. Retrieved on June 24, 2008, from https://contemporaryfamilies.org/wp-content/uploads/2013/11/2007 _Briefing_Allen-Li_The-impact-of-divorce-on-children-behavior.pdf.

Marino, Francesca A. 2022. "Divorce Rate in the U.S.: Geographic Variation, 2021." Family Profiles, FP-22-26. Bowling Green, OH: National Center for Family & Marriage Research. https://doi.org/10.25035/ncfmr/fp-22-26.

Meadows, S. O., S. McLanahan, and J. Brooks-Gunn. 2008. "Stability and Change in Family Structure and Maternal Health Trajectories." *American Sociological Review* 73(2): 314–334.

Mintz, Steven. 2004. *Huck's Raft: A History of American Childhood*. Cambridge, MA: Harvard University Press.

Osborne, C., and S. McLanahan. 2007. "Partnership Instability and Child Well-Being." *Journal of Marriage and Family* 69(4): 1065–1083.

Robles, T. F., and J. K. Kiecolt-Glaser. 2003. "The Physiology of Marriage: Pathways to Health." *Physiology and Behavior* 79(3): 409–416.

Ruggles, Steven. 1997. "The Rise of Divorce and Separation in the United States 1880–1990." *Demography* 34(4): 455–466.

Rutter, V. E. 2004. "The Case for Divorce: Under What Conditions Is Divorce Beneficial and for Whom?" Ph.D. diss. University of Washington.

Scafidi, B. 2008. *The Taxpayer Costs of Divorce: First-Ever Estimates for the Nation and All Fifty States*. New York: Institute for American Values.

Smock, Pamela J., Wendy D. Manning, and Sanjiv Gupta. 1999. "The Effect of Marriage and Divorce on Women's Economic Well-Being." *American Sociological Review* 64: 794–812.

Stevenson, B., and J. Wolfers. 2006. "Bargaining in the Shadow of Divorce Laws and Family Distress." *Quarterly Journal of Economics* 121(1): 267–288.

UN Women. n.d. "In Focus: Gender Equality in Covid-19 Response." Accessed May 3, 2023. www.unwomen.org/en/news/in-focus/in-focus-gender-equality-in-covid-19-response.

van Hemert, Dianne A., F. J. R. van de Vijver, and Ype H. Poortinga. 2002. "The Beck Depression Inventory as a Measure of Subjective Well-Being: A Cross-National Study." *Journal of Happiness Studies* 3(3): 257–286.

Veenhoven, Ruut. 2004. *World Database of Happiness: Continuous Register of Scientific Research on Subjective Appreciation of Life*. Rotterdam, Netherlands: Erasmus University. Available from http //www.isqols2009.istitutodeglinnocenti.it/Content_en /Veenhoven_WDH-Prospectus_2009.pdf.

Waite, Linda J., Don Browning, William J. Doherty, Maggie Gallagher, Ye Luo, and Scott M. Stanley. 2002. *Does Divorce Make People Happy? Findings from a Study of Unhappy Marriages* New York: Institute for American Values.

Wallerstein, J., and Sandra Blakeslee. 1988. *Second Chances: Men, Women, and Children a Decade after Divorce: Who Wins, Who Loses, and Why*. New York: Ticknor & Fields.

Weissman, M. M. 1987. "Advances in Psychiatric Epidemiology: Rates and Risks for Major Depression." *American Journal of Public Health* 77: 445–451.

Whisman, Mark A. 1999. "Marital Dissatisfaction and Psychiatric Disorders: Results from the National Comorbidity Survey." *Journal of Abnormal Psychology* 108: 701–706.

CHAPTER 23: Family Structure, Race, and Child Well-Being
by Christina J. Cross

Amato, P. R. 2005. "The Impact of Family Formation Change on the Cognitive, Social, and Emotional Well-Being of the Next Generation." *Future of Children* 15, no. 2: 75–96.

Amato, P. R., and B. Keith. 1991. "Parental Divorce and Adult Well-Being: A Meta-Analysis." *Journal of Marriage and the Family*, 53: 43–58.

Bobbitt, Z. 2021. "Correlation Does Not Imply Causation: 5 Real-World Examples." Statology, August 18. www.statology.org/correlation-does-not-imply-causation-examples/.

Brand, Jennie E., Ravaris Moore, Xi Song, and Yu Xie. 2019. "Why Does Parental Divorce Lower Children's Educational Attainment? A Causal Mediation Analysis." *Sociological Science* 6: 264–292.

Brown, Susan L. 2010. "Marriage and Child Well-Being: Research and Policy Perspectives." *Journal of Marriage and Family* 72: 1059–1077.

Carlson, Marcia J. 2006. "Family Structure, Father Involvement, and Adolescent Behavioral Outcomes." *Journal of Marriage and Family* 68, no. 1: 137–154.

Cherlin, Andrew, and Frank Furstenberg. 1994. "Stepfamilies in the United States—A Reconsideration." *Annual Review of Sociology* 20: 359–381.

Choi, Jeong-Kyun, Megan S. Kelley, and Dan Wang. 2018. "Neighborhood Characteristics, Maternal Parenting, and Health and Development of Children from Socioeconomically Disadvantaged Families." *American Journal of Community Psychology* 62: 476–491.

Coontz, Stephanie. 2006. *Marriage: A History.* New York: Penguin Books.

Cross, Christina J. 2020. "Racial/Ethnic Differences in the Association between Family Structure and Children's Education." *Journal of Marriage and Family* 81, no. 2: 691–712.

———. 2023. "Beyond the Binary: Intraracial Diversity in Family Organization and Black Adolescents' Educational Performance." *Social Problems* 70, no. 2: 511–532.

Cross, C. J., F. Fomby, and B. Letiecq. 2022. "Interlinking Structural Racism and Heteropatriarchy: Rethinking Family Structure's Effects on Child Outcomes in a Racialized, Unequal Society." *Journal of Family Theory and Review* 14, no. 3: 482–501.

Dunifon, R., and L. Kowaleski-Jones. 2007. "The Influence of Grandparents in Single-Mother Families." *Journal of Marriage and Family* 69: 465–481.

Farber, N., J. Miller-Cribbs, and M. Reitmeier. 2005. "Kin Networks in the South: A Comparison of Low-income, Rural African-American and White Women." *Rural Social Work and Community Practice* 10: 52–63.

Fomby, P., S. Mollborn, and C. Sennott. 2010. "Race/Ethnic Differences in Effects of Family Instability on Adolescents' Risk Behavior." *Journal of Marriage and Family* 72: 234–253.

Fox News. 2015. "Reporter Who Commented on 'Black Men Growing Up without Fathers' Suspended," January 8. www.foxnews.com/us/reporter-who-commented-on-black-men-growing-up-without-fathers-suspended.

Fremstad, Shawn, Sarah Jane Glynn, and Angelo Williams. 2019. "The Case against Marriage Fundamentalism: Embracing Family Justice for All." Washington, DC: Family Story. https://familystoryproject.org/case-against-marriage-fundamentalism/.

Ginther, Donna K., and Robert A. Pollak. 2004. "Family Structure and Children's Educational Outcomes: Blended Families, Stylized Facts, and Descriptive Regressions." *Demography* 41, no. 4: 671–696.

Hofferth, S. 2006. "Residential Father Family Type and Child Well-Being: Investment versus Selection." *Demography* 43, no. 1: 53–77.

"Jay-Z Blames Single Parent Households for Police Brutality." 2019. YouTube, September 2. Retrieved August 2, 2022. https://youtu.be/ByTkbZTYZaU.

Kalil, A., R. Ryan, and E. Chor. 2014. "Time Investments in Children across Family Structures." *ANNALS of the American Academy of Political and Social Science* 654, no. 1: 150–168.

Kearney, Melissa S., and Phillip B. Levine. 2017. "The Economics of Nonmarital Childbearing and the Marriage Premium for Children." *Annual Review of Economics* 9: 327–352.

Letiecq, Bethany L. 2019. "Surfacing Family Privilege and Supremacy in Family Science: Toward Justice for All." *Journal of Family Theory and Review* 11: 398–411.

Manning, W. D., and K. A. Lamb. 2003. "Adolescent Well-Being in Cohabiting, Married, and Single Parent Families." *Journal of Marriage and Family* 65, no. 4: 876–893.

McLanahan, Sara, and Christine Percheski. 2008. "Family Structure and the Reproduction of Inequalities." *Annual Review of Sociology* 34: 257–276.

McLanahan, Sara, and Gary Sandefur. 1994. *Growing Up with a Single-Parent: What Hurts, What Helps.* Cambridge, MA: Harvard University Press.

McLoyd, V. C., A. M. Cauce, D. Takeuchi, and L. Wilson. 2000. "Marital Processes and Parental Socialization in Families of Color: A Decade Review of Research." *Journal of Marriage and the Family* 62: 1070–1093.

National Center for Education Statistics. 2022. "Characteristics of Children's Families." Condition of Education. U.S. Department of Education, Institute of Education Sciences. Retrieved October 19, 2022. https://nces.ed.gov/programs/coe/indicator/cce.

Parolin, Zachary. 2019. "Welfare Money Is Paying for a Lot of Things Besides Welfare." *Atlantic*, June 13. www.theatlantic.com/ideas/archive/2019/06/through-welfare-states-are-widening-racial-divide/591559/.

———. 2021. "Temporary Assistance for Needy Families and the Black-White Child Poverty Gap in the United States." *Socio-Economic Review* 19, no. 3: 1005–1035.

Pittman, L. D. 2007. "Grandmothers' Involvement among Young Adolescents Growing Up in Poverty." *Journal of Research on Adolescence* 17: 89–115.

Sarkisian, N., and N. Gerstel. 2004. "Kin Support among Blacks and Whites: Race and Family Organization." *American Sociological Review* 69: 812–837.

Stack, C. B. 1974. *All Our Kin: Strategies for Survival in a Black Community.* New York: Harper & Row.

Stack, C. B., and L. M. Burton. 1993. "Kinscripts." *Journal of Comparative Family Studies* 24 157–170.

Taylor, R. J., A. D. Skipper, C. J. Cross, H. O. Taylor, and L. M. Chatters. 2022. "Racial Ethnic Variation in Family Support: African Americans, Black Caribbeans, and Non-Latino Whites." *Journal of Marriage and Family* 84, no. 4: 1002–1023.

U.S. Department of Health and Human Services Office of Family Assistance. 2019. "About TANF." July 19. www.acf.hhs.gov/ofa/programs/tanf/about.

Williams, Kristi. 2016. "Promoting Marriage among Single Mothers: An Ineffective Weapon in the War on Poverty?" In *Families as They Really Are*, 2nd ed., edited by B. J. Risman and V. Rutter. New York: W. W. Norton.

CHAPTER 24: The New (Post-COVID) Normal? Workplace Flexibility Matters
by Marni Fritz, Sejin Um, and Barbara Risman

Bloom, Nicholas. 2020. "How Working from Home Works Out." Stanford University Institute for Economic Policy Research. https://siepr.stanford.edu/publications/policy-brief/how-working-home-works-out.

Calarco, Jessica McCrory, Emily Meanwell, Elizabeth M. Anderson, and Amelia S. Knopf 2021. "By Default: How Mothers in Different-Sex Dual-Earner Couples Account for Inequalities in Pandemic Parenting." *Socius* 7. https://doi.org/10.1177/23780231211058783.

Collins, Caitlyn, Liana Christin Landivar, Leah Ruppanner, and William J. Scarborough. 2021. "COVID-19 and the Gender Gap in Work Hours." *Gender, Work & Organization* 28, no. S1: 101–112.

Daminger, Allison. 2019. "The Cognitive Dimension of Household Labor." *American Sociological Review* 84, no. 4: 609–633.

Dunatchik, Allison, Kathleen Gerson, Jennifer Glass, Jerry A. Jacobs, and Haley Stritzel. 2021. "Gender, Parenting, and the Rise of Remote Work during the Pandemic: Implications for Domestic Inequality in the United States." *Gender & Society* 35, no. 2: 194–205.

Hinchliffe, Emma. 2022. "The Women's Employment Crisis Is Far from Over—And January's Jobs Report Proves It." *Fortune*, February 7. https://fortune.com/2022/02/07/the-womens-employment-crisis-is-far-from-over-and-januarys-jobs-report-proves-it/.

Mooi-Reci, Irma, and Barbara J. Risman. 2021. "The Gendered Impacts of COVID-19: Lessons and Reflections." *Gender & Society* 35, no. 2: 161–167.

United Way Blog. 2020. "States with the Most Essential Workers." May 4. https://unitedwaynca.org/blog/us-states-with-the-most-essential-workers/.

U.S. Bureau of Labor Statistics. 2019. "Job Flexibilities and Work Schedules Summary: 2017–2018 Data from the American Time Use Survey." September 24. www.bls.gov/news.release/flex2.nr0.htm.

CHAPTER 25: "This Is Your Job Now": Latina Mothers and Daughters and Family Work
by Lorena Garcia

Ayala, Jennifer. 2006. "Confianza, Consejos, and Contradictions: Gender and Sexuality Lessons between Latina Adolescent Daughters and Mothers." In *Latina Girls: Voices of Adolescent Strength in the United States*, edited by Jill Denner and Bianca L. Guzmán, 29–43. New York and London: New York University Press.

Berridge, Clara W., and Jennifer L. Romich. 2010. "Raising Him to Pull His Own Weight." *Journal of Family Issues* 32: 157–180.

Cantú, Lionel. 2000. "Entre Hombres/Between Men: Latino Masculinities and Homosexualities." In *Gay Masculinities*, edited by Peter Nardi, 224–246. Thousand Oaks, CA: Sage Publications.

Carrillo, Héctor. 2002. *The Night Is Young: Sexuality in Mexico in the Time of AIDS*. Chicago: University of Chicago Press.

Carrington, Christopher. 1999. *No Place Like Home: Relationships and Family Life among Lesbians and Gay Men*. Chicago: University of Chicago Press.

Chafetz, Janet Saltzman. 1990. *Gender Equity: An Integrated Theory of Stability and Change*. Newbury Park, CA: Sage Publications.

Collins. Patricia H. 1987. "The Meaning of Motherhood in Black Culture and Black Mother-Daughter Relationships." *Sage: A Scholarly Journal on Black Women* 4: 3–10.

———1994. "Shifting the Center: Race, Class, and Feminist Theorizing about Motherhood." In *Mothering: Ideology, Experience, and Agency*, edited by Evelyn Nakano Glenn, Grace Chang, and Linda Rennie Forcey, 45–66. New York: Routledge.

Coltrane, S. 2000. "Research on Household Labor: Modeling and Measuring the Social Embeddedness of Routine Family Work." *Journal of Marriage and Family* 62: 1208–1233.

Deutsch, Francine. 2007. "Undoing Gender." *Gender & Society* 21(1): 106–127.

Dill, Bonnie Thornton. 1988. "Our Mother's Grief: Racial-Ethnic Women and the Maintenance of Families." *Journal of Family History* 13: 415–431.

Dreby, Joanne. 2010. *Divided by Borders: Mexican Migrants and Their Children*. Berkeley: University of California Press.

Erickson, Rebecca J. 1993. "Reconceptualizing Family Work: The Effect of Emotion Work on Perceptions of Marital Quality." *Journal of Marriage and Family* 55(4): 888–900.

———. 2005. "Why Emotion Work Matters: Sex, Gender, and the Division of Household Labor." *Journal of Marriage and Family* 67(2): 337–351.

Fine, Michelle, Lois Weis, and Rosemary Roberts. 2000. "Refusing the Betrayal: Latinas Redefining Gender, Sexuality, Culture, and Resistance." *Education/Pedagogy/Cultural Studies* 22: 87–119.

Garcia, Lorena. 2012. *Respect Yourself, Protect Yourself: Latina Girls and Sexual Identity*. New York: New York University Press.

George, Sheba. 2005. *When Women Come First: Gender and Class in Transnational Migration*. Berkeley: University of California Press.

Gerson, Kathleen. 2010. *The Unfinished Revolution: How a Generation Is Reshaping Family, Work and Gender in America*. Oxford: Oxford University Press.

Glenn, Evelyn Nakano. 1994. "Social Constructions of Mothering: A Thematic Overview." In *Mothering: Ideology, Experience, and Agency*, edited by Evelyn Nakano Glenn, Grace Chang, and Linda Rennie Forcey, 1–32. New York: Routledge.

González-López, Gloria, and Salvador Vidal-Ortiz. 2008. "Latinas and Latinos, Sexuality, and Society: A Critical Sociological Perspective." In *Latinas/os in the United States Changing the Face of America*, edited by Havidán Rodríguez, Rogelio Sáenz, and Cecilia Menjívar, 308–322. New York: Springer.

Hill, Shirley A. 1999. *African American Children: Socialization and Development in Families*. Thousand Oaks, CA: Sage Publications.

Hochschild, Arlie R. 1983. *The Managed Heart: Commercialization of Human Feeling*. Berkeley: University of California Press.

———. 1989. *The Second Shift: Working Parents and the Revolution at Home*. With Anne Machung. New York: Viking.

Hondagneu-Sotelo, Pierrette. 1994. *Gendered Transitions: Mexican Experiences of Immigration*. Berkeley: University of California Press.

———. 1997. "'I'm Here, But I'm There': The Meanings of Latina Transnational Motherhood." *Gender & Society* 11(5) 548–571.

Hurtado, Aida. 2003. *Voicing Chicana Feminisms: Young Women Speak Out on Sexuality and Identity*. New York: New York University Press.

Kane, Emily W. 2006. "'No Way My Boys Are Gonna Be Like That!' Parents' Responses of Children's Gender Nonconformity." *Gender & Society* 20(2): 149–176.

Lamont, Michèle. 2002. "Culture and Identity." In *Handbook of Sociological Theory*, edited by Jonathan H. Turner, 171–185. New York: Kluwer Academic/Plenum Publishers.

Lopez, Nancy. 2003. *Hopeful Girls, Troubled Boys: Race and Gender Disparity in Urban Education*. New York: Routledge.

Lorber, Judith. 2005. *Breaking the Bowls: Degendering and Feminist Change*. New York: W. W. Norton & Company.

Moore, Mignon. 2011. *Invisible Families: Gay Identities, Relationships and Motherhood among Black Women*. Berkeley: University of California Press.

Nelson, Fiona. 1996. *Lesbian Motherhood: An Exploration of Canadian Lesbian Families.* Toronto: University of Toronto Press.

Penha-Lopes, Vania. 2006. "'To Cook, Sew, to Be a Man': The Socialization for Competence and Black Men's Involvement in Housework." *Sex Roles* 54(3/4): 261–274.

Ridgeway, Cecilia. 2011. *Framed by Gender: How Gender Inequality Persists in the Modern World.* New York: Oxford University Press.

Risman, Barbara J. 1998. *Gender Vertigo: American Families in Transition.* New Haven, CT: Yale University Press.

Segura, Denise A. 1994. "Working at Motherhood: Chicana and Mexican Immigrant Mothers and Employment." In *Mothering: Ideology, Experience, and Agency*, edited by Evelyn Nakana Glenn, Grace Chang, and Linda Rennie Forcey, 211–233. New York: Routledge.

Segura, Denise A., and Jennifer Pierce. 1993. "Chicana/o Family Structure and Gender Personality: Chodorow, Familism, and Psychoanalytic Sociology Revisited." *Signs: Journal of Women in Culture and Society* 12(1): 62–91.

Shelton, B. A. 1992. *Women, Men and Time: Gender Differences in Paid Work, Housework, and Leisure.* Westport, CT: Greenwood.

Souza, Caridad. 2002. "Sexual Identities of Young Puerto Rican Mothers." *Dialogo* 6 (Winter /Spring): 33–39.

Sullivan, Maureen. 2004. *The Family of Woman: Lesbian Mothers, Their Children, and the Undoing of Gender.* Berkeley: University of California Press.

Sullivan, O. 2006. *Gender Relations, Changing Families: Tracing the Pace of Change Over Time.* Lanham, MD: Rowman & Littlefield.

Swidler, Ann. 1986. "Culture in Action: Symbols and Strategies." *American Sociological Review* 51 (April): 273–286.

———. 2001. *Talk of Love: How Culture Matters.* Chicago: University of Chicago Press.

Villeñas, Sofia, and Melissa Moreno. 2001. "To *valerse por si misma* between Race, Capitalism, and Patriarchy: Latina Mother-Daughter Pedagogies in North Carolina." *International Journal of Qualitative Studies in Education* 14: 671–687.

West, Candace, and Don H. Zimmerman. 1987. "Doing Gender." *Gender & Society* 1(2): 125–151.

Young, Alford A. Jr. 2004. *The Minds of Marginalized Black Men: Making Sense of Mobility, Opportunity, and Future Life Chances.* Princeton, NJ: Princeton University Press.

CHAPTER 26: Trans Kids and their Families: From the Kitchen Table to the Culture Wars
by Tey Meadow

Drescher, Jack, and Jack Pula. 2014. "Ethical Issues Raised by the Treatment of Gender Variant Prepubescent Children." *The Hastings Center Report* 44, Suppl. 4: 17–22.

Foucault, Michel. 1975. *Discipline and Punish: The Birth of the Prison.* New York: Random House.

Kane, Emily W. 2006. "'No Way My Boys Are Going to Be Like That!' Parents' Responses to Childhood Gender Nonconformity." *Gender & Society* 20, no. 2: 149–176.

Krishnakumar, Priya. 2021. "This Record-Breaking Year for Anti-transgender Legislation Would Affect Minors the Most." *CNN*, April 15. www.cnn.com/2021/04/15/politics /anti-transgender-legislation-2021/index.html.

Martin, Karen A. 2005. "William Wants a Doll. Can He Have One? Feminists, Child Care Advisors and Gender Neutral Child Rearing." *Gender & Society* 19, no. 4: 456–479

Meadow, Tey. 2010. "'A Rose is a Rose': On Producing Legal Gender Classifications." *Gender & Society* 24: 814–837.

———. 2018. *Trans Kids: Being Gendered in the Twenty-First Century.* Berkeley: University of California Press.

Munce, Megan. 2021. "Texas GOP Bills Targeting Transgender Children Have Exacted a Mental Health Toll, Even If They Don't Become Law." *Texas Tribune*, May 23. www .texastribune.org/2021/05/23/texas-transgender-legislation-sports-health-care/.

Rahilly, Elizabeth P. 2015. "The Gender Binary Meets the Gender Variant Child: Parents' Negotiations with Childhood Gender Variance." *Gender & Society* 29, no. 3: 338–361.

Reich, Jennifer A. 2005. *Fixing Families: Parents, Power and the Child Welfare System.* New York: Routledge.

Richardson, Diane. 2007. "Patterned Fluidities: (Re)Imagining the Relationship between Gender and Sexuality." *Sociology* 4, no. 3: 457–474.

Sedgwick, Eve. 1991. "How to Bring Your Kids Up Gay." *Social Text* 29, no. 1: 18–27.

Seidman, Steven. 2002. *Beyond the Closet: The Transformation of Gay and Lesbian Life.* New York: Routledge.

Ward, Jane. 2010. "Gender Labor: Transmen, Femmes and the Collective Work of Transgression." *Sexualities* 13, no. 2: 236–254.

West, Candace, and Don Zimmerman. 1987. "Doing Gender." *Gender & Society* 1: 125–151.

Whitley, Cameron T. 2013. "Trans-Kin Undoing and Redoing Gender: Negotiating Relational Identity among Friends and Family of Transgender Persons." *Sociological Perspectives* 56, no. 4: 597–621.

CHAPTER 27: Beyond Sons and Daughters: Nonbinary Experiences with Family
by Emily Via, Daniela Guerrero Rodriguez, Ni'Shele Jackson, Barbara J. Risman, and William Scarborough

Barbee, Harry, and Douglas Schrock. 2019. "Un/Gendering Social Selves: How Nonbinary People Navigate and Experience a Binarily Gendered World." *Sociological Forum* 34, no. 3: 572–593.

Brown, Anna. 2022. "About 5% of Young Adults in the U.S. Say Their Gender Is Different from Their Sex Assigned at Birth." Pew Research Center, June 7. www.pewresearch.org /fact-tank/2022/06/07/about-5-of-young-adults-in-the-u-s-say-their-gender-is-different -from-their-sex-assigned-at-birth/.

Brumbaugh-Johnson, Stacey M., and Kathleen E. Hull. 2019. "Coming Out as Transgender: Navigating the Social Implications of a Transgender Identity." *Journal of Homosexuality* 66, no. 8: 1148–1177.

Coleman, E. 1982. "Developmental Stages of the Coming Out Process." *Journal of Homosexuality* 7, no. 2–3: 31–43.

D'amico, E., D. Julien, N. Tremblay, and E. Chartrand. 2015. "Gay, Lesbian, and Bisexual Youths Coming Out to Their Parents: Parental Reactions and Youths' Outcomes." *Journal of GLBT Family Studies* 11, no. 5: 411–437.

Darwin, Helana. 2017. "Doing Gender beyond the Binary: A Virtual Ethnography." *Symbolic Interaction* 40, no. 3: 317–334.

Deterding, Nicole M., and Mary C. Waters. 2021. "Flexible Coding of In-Depth Interviews: A Twenty-First-Century Approach." *Sociological Methods & Research* 50, no. 2: 708–739.

Diamond, Lisa M. 2017. "Three Critical Questions for Future Research on Lesbian Relationships." *Journal of Lesbian Studies* 21, no. 1: 106–119.

Few-Demo, A. L., Á. M. Humble, M. A. Curran, and S. A. Lloyd. 2016. "Queer Theory, Intersectionality, and LGBT-Parent Families: Transformative Critical Pedagogy in Family Theory." *Journal of Family Theory and Review* 8, no. 1: 74–94.

Gagné, P., R. Tewksbury, and D. McGaughey. 1997. "Coming Out and Crossing Over: Identity Formation and Proclamation in a Transgender Community." *Gender and Society* 11, no. 4: 478–508.

Guittar, N. A., and R. L. Rayburn. 2016. "Coming Out: The Career Management of One's Sexuality." *Sexuality & Culture* 20, no. 2: 336–357.

Hammack, Phillip L., Sam D. Hughes, Julianne M. Atwood, Elliot M. Cohen, and Richard C. Clark. 2022. "Gender and Sexual Identity in Adolescence: A Mixed-Methods Study of Labeling in Diverse Community Settings." *Journal of Adolescent Research* 37, no. 2: 167–220.

Knight, Ken W., Sarah E. M. Stephenson, Sue West, Martin B. Delatycki, Cheryl A. Jones, Melissa H. Little, George C. Patton, Susan M. Sawyer, S. Rachel Skinner, Michelle M. Telfer, Melissa Wake, Kathryn N. North, and Frank Oberklaid. 2017. "The Kids Are OK: It Is Discrimination Not Same-Sex Parents That Harms Children." *Medical Journal of Australia* 207, no. 9: 374–375.

Manning, W. D., M. N. Fettro, and E. Lamidi. 2014. "Child Well-Being in Same-Sex Parent Families: Review of Research Prepared for American Sociological Association Amicus Brief." *Population Research and Policy Review* 33, no. 4: 485–502.

Meadow, Tey. 2018. *Trans Kids: Being Gendered in the Twenty-First Century*. Berkeley: University of California Press.

Newcomb, M. E., M. C. LaSala, A. Bouris, B. Mustanski, G. Prado, S. M. Schrager, and D. M. Huebner. 2019. "The Influence of Families on LGBTQ Youth Health: A Call to Action for Innovation in Research and Intervention Development." *LGBT Health* 6, no. 4: 139–145.

Orne, Jason. 2011. "'You Will Always Have to "Out" Yourself': Reconsidering Coming Out through Strategic Outness." *Sexualities* 14, no. 6: 681–703.

Reczek, C. 2020. "Sexual- and Gender-Minority Families: A 2010 to 2020 Decade in Review." *Journal of Marriage and the Family* 82, no. 1: 300–325.

Risman, Barbara J. 2018. *Where the Millennials Will Take Us: A New Generation Wrestles with the Gender Structure*. New York: Oxford University Press.

Sedgwick, Eve Kosofsky. 1990. *Epistemology of the Closet*. Berkeley: University of California Press.

Travers, Ann. 2018. *The Trans Generation: How Trans Kids (and Their Parents) Are Creating a Gender Revolution*. New York: New York University Press.

Umberson, D., M. B. Thomeer, R. A. Kroeger, A. C. Lodge, and M. Xu. 2015. "Challenges and Opportunities for Research on Same-Sex Relationships." *Journal of Marriage and the Family* 77, no. 1: 96–111.

Williams Institute. 2021. "1.2 Million LGBTQ Adults in the US Identify as Nonbinary." Williams Institute. https://williamsinstitute.law.ucla.edu/press/lgbtq-nonbinary-press -release/.

Wilson, C., and L. A. Cariola. 2020. "LGBTQI+ Youth and Mental Health: A Systematic Review of Qualitative Research." *Adolescent Research Review* 5: 187–211.

CHAPTER 28: Adoptive Parents Raising Neoethnics and Demonstrating Whose Rights Matter
by Pamela Anne Quiroz

Brian, Kristi. 2012. *Reframing Transracial Adoption: Adopted Koreans, White Parents, and the Politics of Kinship*. Philadelphia: Temple University Press.

Briggs, L. 2006. "Making 'American' Families: Transnational Adoption and U.S. Latin America Policy." In *Haunted by Empire: Geographies of Intimacy in North American History*, edited by Ann Laura Stoler, 606–644. Durham, NC: Duke University Press.

Cardello, Andrea. 2009. "The Movement of the Mother of the Courthouse Square: Legal Child Trafficking, Adoption and Poverty in Brazil." *Journal of Latin American and Caribbean Anthropology* 14(1): 140–161.

Dorow, Sarah. 2006. *Transnational Adoption: A Cultural Economy of Race, Gender and Kinship*. New York: New York University Press.

Fonseca, Claudia. 2002. "The Politics of Adoption: Child Rights in the Brazilian Setting." *Law & Policy* 24(3): 199–227.

———. 2006. "Traditional Influences in the Social Production of Adoptable Children: The Case of Brazil." *International Journal of Sociology and Social Policy* 26(3/4): 154–171.

Gailey, Christine. 2009. *Blue Ribbon Babies and Labors of Love: Race, Class, and Gender in U.S. Adoption Practice*. Austin: University of Texas Press.

Hearst, Alice. 2010. "Between Restavek and Relocation: Children and Communities in Transnational Adoption." *Journal of History of Childhood and Youth* 3(2): 273–292.

Hine, Christine. 2000. *Virtual Ethnography*. Thousand Oaks, CA: Sage Publications.

Hubinette, Tobias. 2012. "Post-racial Utopianism, White Color-blindness, and the Elephant in the Room: Racial Issues for Transnational Adoptees of Color." In *Intercountry Adoption: Policies, Practices, and Outcomes*, edited by Judith L. Gibbons and Karen Smith Rotabi, 221–229. Burlington, VT: Ashgate Publishing.

Jacobsen, Heather. 2008. *Culture Keeping*. Nashville, TN: Vanderbilt University Press.

Kim, Jodi. 2009. "An Orphan with Two Mothers: Transnational and Transracial Adoption, the Cold War, and Contemporary Asian American Cultural Politics." *American Quarterly* 61(4): 855–877.

Kim, Oh Myo, Reed Reichwald, and Richard Lee. 2013. "Cultural Socialization in Families with Adopted Korean Adolescents: A Mixed-Method, Multi-Informant Study." *Journal of Adolescent Research* 28(1): 69–95.

Kubo, Kazuyo. 2010. "Desirable Difference: The Shadow of Racial Stereotypes in Creating Transracial Families through Transnational Adoption." *Sociology Compass* 4(4): 263–282.

Lee, Richard M., A. Bora Yun, H. Choi Yoog, and K. Park Nelson. 2010. "Comparing the Ethnic Identity and Well-Being of Adopted Korean Americans with Immigrant/U.S.-born Korean Americans and Korean International Students." *Adoption Quarterly* 13(1): 2–17

Leifson, Esben. 2008. "Child Trafficking and Formalization: The Case of International Adoption from Ecuador." *Children & Society* 22: 212–222.

McGinnis, H., S. Livingston Smith, S. D. Ryan, and J. A. Howard. 2009. *Beyond Culture Camp: Promoting Healthy Identity Formation in Adoption.* New York: Evan B. Donaldson Adoption Institute.

Meier, Patricia, and Xiaole Zhang. 2008. "Sold into Adoption: The Hunan Baby Trafficking Scandal Exposes Vulnerabilities in Chinese Adoptions to the United States." *Cumberland Law Review* 39(1): 87–130.

Ortiz, Ana Teresa, and Laura Briggs. 2003. "The Culture of Poverty, Crack Babies, and Welfare Cheats: The Making of the 'Healthy White Baby Crisis.'" *Social Text* 21(3): 39–57.

Palmer, John. 2011. *The Dance of Identities: Korean Adoptees and Their Journey toward Empowerment.* Honolulu: University of Hawaii Press.

Pew Internet and American Life Project. 2006. *Internet Evolution: Internet Penetration and Impact.* Report 202-419-4500. April 26. Available from http://www.pewinternet.org.

———. 2008. *How Women and Men Use the Internet.* Report 202-419-4500. April 11. Available from http://www.pewinternet.org.

Quiroz, Pamela Anne. 2012. "Cultural Tourism in Transnational Adoption: Staged Authenticity and Its Implications for Adopted Children." *Journal of Family Issues* 33(4): 527–555.

Race Forward: The Center for Racial Justice Innovation. 2011. "Shattered Families: The Perilous Intersection of Immigration Enforcement and the Child Welfare System." Available from https://www.raceforward.org/research/reports/shattered-families.

Rotabi, Karen S., Joan Pennell, Jini L. Roby, and Kelley McCreery Bunkers. 2012. "Family Group Conferencing as a Culturally Adaptable Intervention: Reforming Intercountry Adoption in Guatemala." *International Social Work* 55(3): 402–416.

Samuels, Gina. 2009. "Being Raised by White People: Navigating Racial Difference among Adopted Multiracial Adults." *Journal of Marriage and Family* 71: 80–94.

Selman, Peter. 2012. "The Rise and Fall of Intercountry Adoption in the 21st Century: Global Trends from 2001 to 2010." *International Social Work* 52(5): 575–594.

Shiao, J. L., Mia Tuan, and Elizabeth Rienzi. 2004. "Shifting the Spotlight: Exploring Race and Culture in Korean-White Adoptive Families." *Race and Society* 7: 1–16.

Simon, Rita, and Rhonda M. Roorda. 2007. *In Their Parents' Voices: Reflections on Raising Transracial Adoptees.* New York: Columbia University Press.

Smerdon, Usha R. 2008. "Crossing Bodies, Crossing Borders: International Surrogacy between the United States and India." *Cumberland Law Review* 39(1): 1–85.

Smolin, David. 2004. "Intercountry Adoption as Child Trafficking." *Valparaiso University Law Review* 39(2): 281–325.

———. 2005. "Child Laundering: How the Intercountry Adoption System Legitimizes and Incentivizes the Practices of Buying, Trafficking, Kidnapping, and Stealing Children." Legal Repository. Retrieved on December 5, 2006, from http://law.bepress.com/expresso/eps/749.

Sweeney, Kathryn A. 2013. "Race-Conscious Adoption Choices, Multiraciality, and Color-blind Racial Ideology." *Family Relations* 62: 42–57.

Trenka, Jane J., Julia C. Oparah, and Sun Yung Shin. 2006. *Outsiders Within: Writing on Transracial Adoption.* Cambridge, MA: South End Press.

Tuan, Mia, and Jiannbin Lee Shiao. 2011. *Choosing Ethnicity, Negotiating Race: Korean Adoptees in America.* New York: Russell Sage Foundation.

U.S. Census Bureau. 2003. *Adopted Children and Stepchildren: 2000. Census 2000 Special Reports.* Washington, DC: U.S. Department of Commerce: Economics and Statistics Administration.

Volkman, Toby Alice. 2005. *Cultures of Transnational Adoption*. Durham, NC: Duke University Press.

Waters, Mary. 1990. *Ethnic Options: Choosing Identity in America*. Berkeley: University of California Press.

CHAPTER 29: Parents as Pawns: Intersex, Medical Experts, and Questionable Consent
by Georgiann Davis

Chase, Cheryl. 1998. "Hermaphrodites with Attitude: Mapping the Emergence of Intersex Political Activism." *GLQ: A Journal of Gay and Lesbian Studies* 4(2): 189–211.

Committee on Genetics: Section on Endocrinology and Section on Urology. 2000. "Evaluation of the Newborn with Developmental Anomalies of the External." *Pediatrics* 106: 138–142.

Cools, M., S. L. Drop, K. P. Wolffenbuttel, J. W. Oosterhuis, and L. H. Looijenga. 2006. "Germ Cell Tumors in the Intersex Gonad: Old Paths, New Directions, Moving Frontiers." *Endocrine Reviews* 27(5): 468–484.

Davis, Georgiann. 2011. "'DSD Is a Perfectly Fine Term': Reasserting Medical Authority through a Shift in Intersex Terminology." In *Sociology of Diagnosis*, edited by P. J. McGann and David Hutson, 155–182. Leeds, UK: Emerald.

Fausto-Sterling, Anne. 1993. "The Five Sexes: Why Male and Female Are Not Enough." *Sciences* 33(2): 20–25.

Karkazis, Katrina. 2008. *Fixing Sex: Intersex, Medical Authority, and Lived Experience*. Durham, NC: Duke University Press.

Kessler, Suzanne J. 1990. "The Medical Construction of Gender: Case Management of Intersexed Infants." *Signs* 16(1): 3–26.

Lee, Peter A., Christopher P. Houk, S. Faisal Ahmed, and Ieuan A. Hughes. 2006. "Consensus Statement on Management of Intersex Disorders." *Pediatrics* 118(2): 488–500.

Pleskacova, J. R. Hersmus, J.W. Oosterhuis, B. A. Setyawati, S. M. Faradz, M. Cools, K. P. Wolffenbuttel, J. Lebl, S. L. Drop, and L. H. Looijenga. 2010. "Tumor Risk in Disorders of Sex Development." *Sexual Development* 4: 259–269.

Preves, Sharon E. 2003. *Intersex and Identity: The Contested Self*. New Brunswick, NJ: Rutgers University Press.

———. 2004. "Out of the O.R. and into the Streets: Exploring the Impact of Intersex Media Activism." *Research in Political Sociology* 13: 179–223.

CHAPTER 30: Parenting Adult Children in the Twenty-First Century
by Joshua Coleman

Ahrons, C. 2004. *We're Still Family* New York: HarperCollins.

Ahrons, C., and J. L. Tanner. 2003. "Adult Children and Their Fathers Relationship Changes 20 Years after Parental Divorce." *Family Relations* 52: 340–351.

Amato, Paul R., and Alan Booth. 1997. *A Generation at Risk*. Cambridge, MA: Harvard University Press.

Amato, Paul, and Julie Sobolewski. 2004. "The Effects of Divorce on Fathers and Children: Nonresidential Fathers and Stepfathers." In *The Role of the Father in Child Development*, 4th ed., edited by Michael Lamb, 341–367. New York: John Wiley & Sons.

Bahney, Anna. 2006. "The Bank of Mom and Dad." *New York Times*, April 20. www.nytimes
.com/2006/04/20/fashion/thursdaystyles/the-bank-of-mom-and-dad.html.

Bateson, Gregory. 1980. *Steps to an Ecology of Mind*. New York: Ballantine.

Baum, N. 2006. "Postdivorce Paternal Disengagement." *Journal of Marriage and Family
Therapy* 32: 245–254.

Bettelheim, Bruno. 1967. *The Empty Fortress: Infantile Autism and the Birth of the Self*.
New York: Free Press.

Bianchi, Suzanne, John Robinson, and Melissa Milke. 2006. *Changing Rhythms of American
Family Life*. New York: Russell Sage Foundation.

Calarco, Jessica. 2018. *Negotiating Opportunities: How the Middle Class Secures Advantages
in School*. New York: Oxford University Press.

Coleman, Joshua. 2003. *The Lazy Husband: How to Get Men to Do More Parenting and
Housework*. New York: St. Martin's Press.

———. 2007. *When Parents Hurt: Compassionate Strategies When You and Your Grown Child
Don't Get Along*. New York: HarperCollins.

———. 2021. "A Shift in American Family Values Is Fueling Estrangement." *Atlantic*,
January 10. www.theatlantic.com/family/archive/2021/01/why-parents-and-kids-get
-estranged/617612/.

Coltrane, Scott. 1996. *Family Man: Fatherhood, Housework, and Gender Equity*. New York:
Oxford University Press.

Coontz, Stephanie. 1997. *The Way We Really Are: Coming to Terms with America's Changing
Families*. New York: Basic Books.

———. 2006. "How to Stay Married." *Times of London*, November 30.

———. 2008. *American Families: A Multicultural Reader*. 2nd ed. New York: Routledge.

Cox, Daniel A. 2021. "The State of American Friendship: Change, Challenges, and Loss."
The Survey Center on American Life. June 8. www.americansurveycenter.org
/research/the-state-of-american-friendship-change-challenges-and-loss/.

Danziger, S., and P. Gottschalk. 2005. "Diverging Fortunes: Trends in Poverty and Inequality." In *The American People: Census 2000 Series*, edited by R. Farley. New York: Russell
Sage Foundation and Population Reference Bureau.

Doepke, Matthias, and Fabrizio Zilibotti. 2019. *Love, Money, and Parenting: How Economics
Explains the Way We Raise Our Kids*. Princeton, NJ: Princeton University Press.

Dunn, J., and R. Plomin. 1990. *Separate Lives: Why Siblings Are So Different*. New York:
Basic Books.

Ehrensaft, Diane. 1997. *Spoiling Childhood: How Well-Meaning Parents Are Giving Children
Too Much—But Not What They Need*. New York: Guilford Press.

Flanagan, Constance. 2006. "The Changing Social Contract at the Transition to Adulthood:
Implications for Individuals and the Polity." In *Social and Political Change in Adolescent
Development*, edited by R. Silbereisen. Invited paper symposium for the biennial meet-
ings of the Society for Research on Adolescence, San Francisco, CA.

Freud, Sigmund. 1926. "Inhibitions, Symptoms, and Anxiety." In the *Standard Edition of the
Complete Psychological Works*, 20: 77–175. London: Hogarth Press.

Harris, Judith Rich. 1999. *The Nurture Assumption: Why Children Turn Out the Way They
Do*. New York: Touchstone.

Hetherington, E. Mavis, and John Kelly. 2002. *For Better or Worse: Divorce Reconsidered*.
New York: W. W. Norton & Company.

Ishizuka, Patrick. 2018. "Social Class, Gender, and Contemporary Parenting Standards in the United States: Evidence from a National Survey Experiment." *Social Forces* 98, no. 1: 31–58.

Jones, Janelle, and John Schmitt. 2014. "A College Degree Is No Guarantee." Center for Economic and Policy Research (CEPR). May 20. https://cepr.net/report/a-college-degree-is-no-guarantee/.

Knoester, Chris. 2003. "Transitions in Young Adulthood and the Relationships between Parent and Offspring Well-Being." *Social Forces* 81: 1431–1458.

Lacar, Marvi. 2006. "The Bank of Mom and Dad." *New York Times*, April 9.

LaPonsie, Maryalene. 2022. "How Much Does It Cost to Raise a Child?" *U.S. News and World Report*, September 7. https://money.usnews.com/money/personal-finance/articles/how-much-does-it-cost-to-raise-a-child.

Lareau, Annette. 2003. *Unequal Childhoods: Class, Race, and Family Life*. Berkeley: University of California Press.

Lin, I-Fen. 2008. "Consequences of Parental Divorce for Adult Children's Support of Their Frail Parents." *Journal of Marriage and Family* 70: 113–128.

Marano, H. E. 2004. "A Nation of Wimps." *Psychology Today*, November/December.

Mintz, Steven. 2004. *Huck's Raft: A History of American Childhood*. Cambridge, MA: Harvard University Press.

———. 2006. "How We All Became Jewish Mothers." *National Post*, February 17.

"Most Americans Falling for 'Get Rich Slowly Over a Lifetime of Hard Work' Schemes." 2005. *The Onion* 41(49), December 7.

Nielsen, L. 2004. *Embracing Your Father: How to Build the Relationship You've Always Wanted with Your Dad*. New York: McGraw-Hill.

Pew Research Center. 2006. *Adult Children and Parents Talking More Often*. February 23.

Putnam, Robert D. 2000. *Bowling Alone: The Collapse and Revival of American Community*. New York: Simon & Schuster.

Reiss, David, Jenae M. Neiderhiser, E. Mavis Hetherington, and Robert Plomin. 2000. *The Relationship Code: Deciphering Genetic and Social Influences on Adolescent Development*. Cambridge, MA: Harvard University Press.

Schaeffer, Katherine. 2020. "6 Facts about Economic Inequality in the U.S." Pew Research Center. February 7. www.pewresearch.org/fact-tank/2020/02/07/6-facts-about-economic-inequality-in-the-u-s/.

Schwartz, Barry. 2004. *The Paradox of Choice: Why More Is Less*. New York: Harper Perennial.

Seligman, M. E. P. 1996. *The Optimistic Child: Proven Program to Safeguard Children from Depression and Build Lifelong Resilience*. New York: Houghton Mifflin.

Stearns, Peter N. 2003. *Anxious Parents: A History of Modern Childrearing in America*. New York: New York University Press.

Sullivan, Oriel, and Scott Coltrane. 2008. "Men's Changing Contribution to Housework and Child-Care." Discussion paper prepared for the Council on Contemporary Families, Chicago, IL.

Wilkinson, Richard, and Kate Pickett. 2010. *The Spirit Level: Why Greater Equality Makes Societies Stronger*. New York: Bloomsbury.

Wilson, Valerie, and William A. Darity. 2022. "Understanding Black-White Disparities in Labor Market Outcomes Requires Models That Account for Persistent Discrimination and Unequal Bargaining Power." Economic Policy Institute.

Zelizer, Viviana, A. 1994. *Pricing the Priceless Child: The Changing Social Value of Children* Princeton, NJ: Princeton University Press.

CHAPTER 31: Student Loans, Families, and the Unequal Transition to Adulthood
by Arielle Kuperberg and Joan Maya Mazelis

Addo, F. R., J. N. Houle, and D. Simon. 2016. "Young, Black, and (Still) in the Red: Parental Wealth, Race, and Student Loan Debt." *Race and Social Problems* 8(1): 64–76.

Aquilino, W. 2006. "Family Relationships and Support Systems in Emerging Adulthood." In *Emerging Adults in America: Coming of Age in the 21st Century*, edited by J. J. Arnett and J. L. Tanner, 193–217. Washington, DC: APA Books.

Archibald, R. B., and D. H. Feldman. 2012. "The Anatomy of College Tuition." The American Council on Education. Retrieved February 20, 2017. www.acenet.edu/news-room /Documents/Anatomy-of-College-Tuition.pdf.

Baker, A. R., B. D. Andrews, and A. McDaniel. 2017. "The Impact of Student Loans on College Access, Completion, and Returns." *Sociology Compass* 11(6), e12480.

Barr, A., and S. E. Turner. 2013. "Expanding Enrollments and Contracting State Budgets: The Effect of the Great Recession on Higher Education." *The Annals of the American Academy of Political and Social Science* 650(1): 168–193.

Bozick, R., and A. Estacion. 2014. "Do Student Loans Delay Marriage? Debt Repayment and Family Formation in Young Adulthood." *Demographic Research* 30: 1865–1869.

Brown, S. L. 2004. "Family Structure and Child Well-Being: The Significance of Parental Cohabitation." *Journal of Marriage and Family* 66(2): 351–367.

Brown, S., A. Ortiz-Núñez, and K. Taylor. 2011. "Educational Loans and Attitudes towards Risk." SERP Working Paper 2011010. Department of Economics, University of Sheffield, Sheffield, United Kingdom.

Carlson M. J., and M. E. Corcoran. 2001. "Family Structure and Children's Behavioral and Cognitive Outcomes." *Journal of Marriage and Family* 63(3): 779–792.

Conley, D. 1999. *Being Black, Living in the Red: Race, Wealth, and Social Policy in America.* Berkeley: University of California Press.

Cooper, M., and A. J. Pugh. 2020. "Families across the Income Spectrum: A Decade in Review." *Journal of Marriage and Family* 82(1): 272–299.

Elliott, W., III, and M. K. Lewis. 2015. *The Real College Debt Crisis: How Student Borrowing Threatens Financial Well-Being and Erodes the American Dream.* Santa Barbara, CA: ABC-CLIO.

Fingerman, K. L., M. Huo, K. Kim, and K. S. Birditt. 2017. "Coresident and Noncoresident Emerging Adults' Daily Experiences with Parents." *Emerging Adulthood* 5(5): 337–350.

Fischer, C. S., M. Hout, M. S. Janowski, S. R. Lucas, A. Swidler, and K. Voss. 1996. *Inequality by Design: Cracking the Bell Curve Myth.* Princeton, NJ: Princeton University Press.

Furstenberg, F. F., S. Kennedy, V. C. McLoyd, R. G. Rumbaut, and R. A. Settersten Jr. 2004. "Growing Up Is Harder to Do." *Contexts* 3(3): 33–41.

Furuta, K. 2022. "Do Student Loans Compensate for Parental Resources? The Role of Student Loans in the Transition to Higher Education." *International Studies in Sociology of Education* 31: 1–24.

Gicheva, D. 2016. "Student Loans or Marriage? A Look at the Highly Educated." *Economics of Education Review* 53: 207–216.

Gicheva, D., and J. Thompson. 2015. "The Effects of Student Loans on Long-Term Household Financial Stability." In *Student Loans and the Dynamics of Debt*, edited by B. Hershbein and K. M. Hollenbeck, 287–316. Kalamazoo, MI: Upjohn Institute for Employment Research.

Gilbert, D. L. 2018. *The American Class Structure in an Age of Growing Inequality.* 10th ed. Thousand Oaks, CA: SAGE Publications.

Goldrick-Rab, S. 2016. Paying the Price: College Costs, Financial Aid, and the Betrayal of the American Dream. Chicago: University of Chicago Press.

Hamilton, B. E., J. A. Martin, M. J. K. Osterman, and L. M. Rossen. 2019. "Births: Provisional Data for 2018." *Vital Statistics Rapid Release*, no. 7. National Center for Health Statistics

Hanson, M. 2022. Student Loan Debt Statistics. EducationData.org. https://educationdata .org/student-loan-debt-statistics.

Harknett, K., and A. Kuperberg. 2011. "Education, Labor Markets and the Retreat from Marriage." *Social Forces* 90(1): 41–63.

Houle, J. N., and F. R. Addo. 2019. "Racial Disparities in Student Debt and the Reproduction of the Fragile Black Middle Class." *Sociology of Race and Ethnicity* 5(4): 562–577.

Houle, J. N., and C. Warner. 2017. "Into the Red and Back to the Nest? Student Debt, College Completion, and Returning to the Parental Home among Young Adults." *Sociology of Education* 90(1): 89–108.

Irwin, V., J. De La Rosa, K. Wang, S. Hein, J. Zhang, R. Burr, A. Roberts, A. Barmer, F. Bullock Mann, R. Dilig, and S. Parker. 2022. *Report on the Condition of Education 2022* (NCES 2022-144). U.S. Department of Education. Washington, DC: National Center for Education Statistics. Retrieved September 2, 2022. https://nces.ed.gov/pubsearch / pubsinfo.asp?pubid=2022144.

Jackson, V., and M. Saenz. 2021. "States Can Choose Better Path for Higher Education Funding in COVID-19 Recession." Center for Budget and Policy Priorities, February 17. www.cbpp.org/research/state-budget-and-tax/states-can-choose-better-path-for-higher -education-funding-in-covid.

Karen, D. 1991. "The Politics of Class, Race, and Gender: Access to Higher Education in the United States, 1960–1986." *American Journal of Education* 99(2): 208–237.

Katsiaficas, D. 2017. "'I know I'm an Adult When . . . I Can Care for Myself and Others': The Role of Social Responsibilities in Emerging Adulthood for Community College Students." *Emerging Adulthood* 5(6): 392–405.

Koeze, E., and K. Russell. 2022. "The Toll of Student Debt in the U.S." *New York Times*, August 26. www.nytimes.com/interactive/2022/08/26/your-money/student-loan -forgiveness-debt.html.

Kuperberg, A. 2018. "Premarital Cohabitation: From Countercultural Trend to a Strategy for the Financially Insecure: Changes in Premarital Cohabitation and Premarital Cohabitors, 1956–2015." *Council on Contemporary Families Brief Report*. https://sites.utexas .edu/contemporaryfamilies/2018/10/08/premaritalcohabitation/.

———. 2019. "Premarital Cohabitation and Direct Marriage in the United States: 1956–2015." *Marriage & Family Review* 55(5): 447–475.

———. 2023. "Selection into Different Methods of Payment for College." American Sociological Association Conference, Virtual Conference.

Kuperberg, A., and J. M. Mazelis. 2021a. "Student Loans, Education, and Family Formation." *SocArxiv.*

———. 2021b. "The Difference Debt Makes: College Students and Grads on How Student Debt Affects Their Life Choices—And What They Would Do Differently If It Were Forgiven." *Council on Contemporary Families Brief Report*. https://sites.utexas.edu /contemporaryfamilies/2021/03/24/college-student-debt-brief-report/.

———. 2022. "Social Norms and Expectations about Student Loans and Family Formation." *Sociological Inquiry* 92(1): 90–126.

Manzoni, A. 2016. "Conceptualizing and Measuring Youth Independence Multidimensionally in the United States." *Acta Sociologica* 59(4): 362–377.

Mazelis, J. M. 2017. *Surviving Poverty: Creating Sustainable Ties among the Poor.* New York: New York University Press.

Mazelis, J. M., and A. Kuperberg. 2022. "Student Loan Debt, Family Support, and Reciprocity in the Transition to Adulthood." *Emerging Adulthood.* Published online first.

McGhee, H. C. 2021. *The Sum of Us: What Racism Costs Everyone and How We Can Prosper Together.* New York: One World.

Millett, C. M. 2003. "How Undergraduate Loan Debt Affects Application and Enrollment in Graduate or First Professional School." *Journal of Higher Education* 74(4): 386–427.

Min, S., and M. G. Taylor. 2018. "Racial and Ethnic Variation in the Relationship between Student Loan Debt and the Transition to First Birth." *Demography* 55(1): 165–188.

Minicozzi, A. 2005. "The Short Term Effect of Educational Debt on Job Decisions." *Economics of Education Review* 24: 417–430.

National Association of Realtors, and American Student Assistance. 2017. *Student Loan Debt and Housing Report 2017: When Debt Holds You Back.* https://www.nar.realtor/sites /default/files/documents/2017-student-loan-debt-and-housing-09-26-2017.pdf.

Nau, M., R. E. Dwyer, and R. Hodson. 2015. "Can't Afford a Baby? Debt and Young Americans." *Research in Social Stratification and Mobility* 42: 114–122.

Oliver, M. L., and T. M. Shapiro. 2006. *Black Wealth/White Wealth: A New Perspective on Racial Inequality, Tenth-Anniversary Edition.* New York: Routledge.

Rauscher, E. 2016. "Passing It On: Parent-to-Adult Child Financial Transfers for School and Socioeconomic Attainment." *RSF: The Russell Sage Foundation Journal of the Social Sciences* 2(6): 172–196.

Sassler, S., and A. Miller. 2017. *Cohabitation Nation: Gender, Class, and the Remaking of Relationships.* Berkeley: University of California Press.

Seamster, L., and R. Charron-Chénier. 2017. "Predatory Inclusion and Education Debt: A New Approach to the Growing Racial Wealth Gap." *Social Currents* 4(3): 199–207.

Settersten, R. A., Jr., and B. Ray. 2010. "What's Going On with Young People Today? The Long and Twisting Path to Adulthood." *Future of Children* 20(1): 19–41.

Shanahan, M. J. 2000. "Pathways to Adulthood in Changing Societies: Variability and Mechanisms in Life Course Perspective." *Annual Review of Sociology* 26(1): 667–692.

Snyder, T. D. 1999. *1998 Digest of Education Statistics.* U.S. Department of Education. Washington, DC: National Center for Education Statistics.

Taylor, K. 2019. *Race for Profit: How Banks and the Real Estate Industry Undermined Black Homeownership.* Chapel Hill: University of North Carolina Press.

Thelin, J. R. 2019. *A History of American Higher Education.* 3rd ed. Baltimore: Johns Hopkins University Press.

U.S. Census Bureau. 2018. "Educational Attainment in the United States: 2018." Table 2: Educational Attainment of the Population 25 Years and Over, by Selected Characteristics: 2018. Current Population Survey, 2018 Annual Social and Economic Supplement. February 21, 2019. www.census.gov/data/tables/2018/demo/education-attainment/cps-detailed-tables.html.

U.S. Department of Education: Federal Student Aid. 2020. "The EFC Formula, 2021–2022." Retrieved December 2021. https://fsapartners.ed.gov/sites/default/files/attachments /2020-08/2122EFCFormulaGuide.pdf.

Witteveen, D., and P. Attewell. 2017. "Family Background and Earnings Inequality among College Graduates." *Social Forces* 95(4): 1539–1576.

Wolff, E. N. 2017. *A Century of Wealth in America.* Cambridge, MA: Belknap Press.

Zissimopoulos, J., J. Thunell, and S. Mudrazija. 2020. "Parental Income and Wealth Loss and Transfers to Their Young Adult Children." *Journal of Family and Economic Issues* 41: 316–331.

Zucchino, D. 2020. *Wilmington's Lie: The Murderous Coup of 1898 and the Rise of White Supremacy*. New York: Atlantic Monthly Press.

CHAPTER 32: *Si Puedes*: Latinx Families and Higher Education *by Patricia Sanchez-Connally*

Bettie, Julie. 2002. "Exceptions to the Rule: Upwardly Mobile White and Mexican American High School Girls." *Gender & Society* 16(3): 403–422.

Carter, Prudence. 2005. *Keepin It Real: School Success beyond Black and White*. New York: Oxford University Press.

Davis, Lori P., and Sam Museus. 2019. "What Is Deficit Thinking? An Analysis of Conceptualizations of Deficit Thinking and Implications for Scholarly Thinking." *Currents* 1(1). http://dx.doi.org/10.3998/currents.17387731.0001.110.

Delgado Bernal, Dolores. 1998. "Using a Chicana Feminist Epistemology in Educational Research." *Harvard Educational Review* 68(4): 555–582.

———. 2002. "Critical Race Theory, Latino Critical Theory, and Critical Raced-Gendered Epistemologies: Recognizing Students of Color as Holders and Creators of Knowledge." *Qualitative Inquiry* 8(1): 105–126.

Delgado, Richard, and Jean Stefancic. 1994. "Critical Race Theory: An Annotated Bibliography 1993, A Year of Transition Bibliography." *University of Colorado Law Review* 66: 159–193.

Fuligni, A. J., and Sara Pederson. 2002. "Family Obligation and the Transition to Young Adulthood." *Developmental Psychology* 38(5): 856–868.

Gandara, Patricia C. 1995. *Over the Ivy Walls: The Educational Mobility of Low-Income Chicanos*. Albany: State University of New York Press.

Gonzales, Roberto. 2011. "Learning to Be Illegal: Undocumented Youth and Shifting Legal Contexts in the Transition to Adulthood." *American Sociological Review* 76(4): 602–619.

Gramlich, John. 2017. "Hispanics Dropout Rate Hits New Low, College Enrollment at New High." Pew Research Center. http://pewrsr.ch/2x2wyy1.

López, Nancy. 2003. *Hopeful Girls, Troubled Boys: Race and Gender Disparity in Urban Education*. New York: Routledge.

Ovink, Sarah. 2014. "They Always Call Me and Investment Gendered Familism and Latino/a College Pathways." *Gender & Society* 28: 265–288.

Postsecondary National Policy Institute. 2021. "Factsheets Latino Students." https://pnp.org/latino-students/.

Rumbaut, Rubén G., and Golnaz Komaie. 2010. "Immigration and Adult Transitions." *Future of Children* 20(1): 43–66.

Schwartz, Seth, Alan Waterman, Adriana Umana-Taylor, Richard Lee, Su Yeong Kim, Alexander Vazsonyi, Que-Lam Huynh, Susan Krauss Whitbourne, Irene J. K. Park, Monika Hudson, Byron Zamboanga, Melina Bersamin, and Michelle Williams. 2013. "Acculturation and Well-Being among College Students from Immigrant Families." *Journal of Clinical Psychology* 69(4): 298–318.

Solórzano, Daniel G., and Tara J. Yosso. 2002. "Critical Race Methodology: Counter-Storytelling as an Analytical Framework for Education Research." *Qualitative Inquiry* 8(1): 23–44.

Sy, Susan R. 2006. "Family and Work Influences on the Transition to College Among Latina Adolescents." *Hispanic Journal of Behavioral Sciences* 28(3): 368–386.

U.S. Department of Education, National Center for Education Statistics. 2021. *The Condition of Education 2021* (NCES 2021-144). https://nces.ed.gov/programs/coe/indicator/coj.

Valenzuela, Angela, and Sanford Dornbusch. 1994. "Familism and Social Capital in the Academic Achievement of Mexican Origin and Anglo Adolescents." *Social Science Quarterly* 75: 18–36.

Villenas, Sofia, and Donna Deyhle. 1999. "Critical Race Theory and Ethnographies Challenging the Stereotypes: Latino Families, Schooling, Resilience and Resistance." *Curriculum Inquiry* (29)4: 413–445.

Yosso, Tara J. 2005. "Whose Culture Has Capital? A Critical Race Theory Discussion of Community Cultural Wealth." *Race, Ethnicity and Education* 8(1): 69–91.

CHAPTER 33: Between a Rock and a Hard Place: Undocumented Immigrants and Mixed-Status Families Negotiating Migration Returns to Visit Ill and Dying Family Members
by Cassaundra Rodriquez

Bravo, Vanessa. 2017. "Coping with Dying and Deaths at Home: How Undocumented Migrants in the United States Experience the Process of Transnational Grieving." *Mortality* 22(1): 33–44.

Calavita, Kitty. 1992. *Inside the State: The Bracero Program, Immigration, and the I.N.S.* New York: Routledge.

Chavez, Leo R. 2013. *The Latino Threat: Constructing Immigrants, Citizens, and the Nation.* 2nd ed. Stanford, CA: Stanford University Press.

———. 2017. *Anchor Babies and the Challenge of Birthright Citizenship.* Stanford, CA: Stanford University Press.

García Valdivia, Isabel. 2022. "Legal Power in Action: How Latinx Adult Children Mitigate the Effects of Parents' Legal Status through Brokering." *Social Problems* 69(2): 335–355.

Getrich, Christina M. 2019. *Border Brokers: Children of Mexican Immigrants Navigating U.S. Society, Laws, and Politics.* Tucson: University of Arizona Press.

Guzman Garcia, Melissa. 2020. "Mobile Sanctuary: Latina/o Evangelicals Redefining Sanctuary and Contesting Immobility in Fresno, CA." *Journal of Ethnic and Migration Studies* 47(19): 4515–4533.

Hipsman, Faye, Bárbara Gómez-Aguiñaga, and Randy Capps. 2016. "DACA at Four: Participation in the Deferred Action Program and Impacts on Recipients." Migration Policy Institute. Accessed June 2. www.migrationpolicy.org/research/daca-four-participation-deferred-action-program-and-impacts-recipients.

Holmes, Seth M. 2013. "'Is It Worth Risking Your Life?': Ethnography, Risk and Death on the U.S.-Mexico Border." *Social Science & Medicine* 99: 153–161.

Legal Information Institute. n.d. "Illegal Immigration Reform and Immigration Responsibility Act." Accessed June 2. www.law.cornell.edu/wex/illegal_immigration_reform_and_immigration_responsibility_act.

Massey, Douglas S. 2009. "Racial Formation in Theory and Practice: The Case of Mexicans in the United States." *Race and Social Problems* 1(1): 12–26.

Mathema, Silva. 2017. "Keeping Families Together: Why All Americans Should Care about What Happens to Unauthorized Immigrants." Center for American Progress. March 16. www.americanprogress.org/article/keeping-families-together/.

Migration Policy Institute. 2023. "Profile of the Unauthorized Population: United States." Accessed June 2. www.migrationpolicy.org/data/unauthorized-immigrant-population /state/US.

Missing Migrants Project. 2023. "Migration within the Americas." Accessed June 2. https://missingmigrants.iom.int/region/Americas.

Ngai, Mae. 2003. *Impossible Subjects: Illegal Aliens and the Making of Modern America.* Princeton, NJ: Princeton University Press.

Riggle-van Schagen, Courtney, and Elizabeth Vaquera. 2022. "More Migrants Are Dying along the US-Mexico Border, but It's Hard to Say How Big the Problem Actually Is." *Conversation*, February 22. https://theconversation.com/more-migrants-are-dying-along -the-us-mexico-border-but-its-hard-to-say-how-big-the-problem-actually-is-175886.

Rodriguez, Cassaundra. 2016. "Experiencing 'Illegality' as a Family? Immigration Enforcement, Social Policies, and Discourses Targeting Mexican Mixed-Status Families." *Sociology Compass* 10(8): 706–717.

———. 2019. "Latino/a Citizen Children of Undocumented Parents Negotiating Illegality." *Journal of Marriage and Family* 81(3): 713–728.

Ruth, Alissa, and Emir Estrada. 2019. "DACAmented Homecomings: A Brief Return to Mexico and the Reshaping of Bounded Solidarity among Mixed-Status Latinx Families." *Hispanic Journal of Behavioral Sciences* 41(2): 145–165.

Schmalzbauer, Leah, and Alelí Andrés. 2019. "Stratified Lives: Family, Illegality, and the Rise of a New Educational Elite." *Harvard Educational Review* 89(4): 635–660.

Sieff, Kevin. 2019. "My Daughter. My Grandchildren." *Washington Post*, May 24. www .washingtonpost.com/world/2019/05/24/my-daughter-my-grandchildren/.

Taylor, Paul, Mark Hugo-Lopez, Jeffrey S. Passel, and Seth Motel. 2011. "Unauthorized Immigrants: Length of Residency, Patterns of Parenthood." Pew Research Center, December 1. www.pewresearch.org/hispanic/2011/12/01/unauthorized-immigrant -length-of-residency-patterns-of-parenthood/.

U.S. Citizenship and Immigration Services (USCIS). 2019. "Unlawful Presence and Bars to Admissibility." Accessed June 2. www.uscis.gov/laws-and-policy/other-resources/unlawful -presence-and-inadmissibility.

———. 2020. "How to Apply for a Green Card." July 5. www.uscis.gov/green-card/how-to -apply-for-a-green-card.

CHAPTER 34: Queer(ing) Intimate Partner Violence through Transgender Inclusion
by Xavier Guadalupe-Diaz

Allen-Collinson, J. 2011. "Assault on Self: Intimate Partner Abuse and the Contestation of Identity." *Symbolic Interaction* 34(1): 108–127.

Arrigo, B. A., and T. J. Bernard. 1997. "Postmodern Criminology in Relation to Radical and Conflict Criminology." *Critical Criminology* 8(2): 39–60.

Ball, M. 2014. "Queer Criminology, Critique, and the 'Art of Not Being Governed.'" *Critical Criminology* 22(1): 21–34.

Black, M. C., K. C. Basile, M. J. Breiding, S. G. Smith, M. L. Walters, M. T. Merrick, J. Chen, and M. R. Stevens. 2011. "The National Intimate Partner and Sexual Violence Survey (NISVS): 2010 Summary Report." Atlanta, GA: National Center for Injury Prevention and Control, Centers for Disease Control and Prevention.

Browne, K., and C. J. Nash. 2010. *Queer Methods and Methodologies: Intersecting Queer Theories and Social Science Research*. New York: Taylor & Francis.

Chen, J., M. L. Walters, L. K. Gilbert, and N. Patel. 2020. "Sexual Violence, Stalking, and Intimate Partner Violence by Sexual Orientation, United States." *Psychological Violence* 10(1): 110–119.

Compton, D. L., T. Meadow, and K. Schilt, eds. 2018. *Other, Please Specify: Queer Methods in Sociology*. Berkeley: University of California Press.

Creative Interventions. 2012. *Creative Interventions Toolkit*. Retrieved July 1, 2022. www.creative-interventions.org/toolkit/.

Foucault, M. 1980. *Power/Knowledge: Selected Interviews and Other Writings, 1972–1977*. New York: Pantheon.

Gelles, R. J., and M. Straus. 1987. *The Violent Home*. Newbury Park, CA: Sage.

Guadalupe-Diaz, X. L. 2019. *Transgressed: Intimate Partner Violence in Transgender Lives*. New York: New York University Press.

Guadalupe-Diaz, X. L., and J. Jasinski. 2017. " 'I Wasn't a Priority, I Wasn't a Victim': Challenges in Help Seeking for Transgender Survivors of Intimate Partner Violence." *Violence against Women* 23(6): 772–792.

Guadalupe-Diaz, X. L., and A. Koontz Anthony. 2017. "Discrediting Identity Work: Understandings of Intimate Partner Violence by Transgender Survivors." *Deviant Behavior* 38(1): 1–16.

Guadalupe-Diaz, X. L., and C. M. West. 2021. "The Intersections of Race and Immigration." In *Transgender Intimate Partner Violence: A Comprehensive Introduction*, edited by Adam Messinger and Xavier L. Guadalupe-Diaz, 133–166.

Haider, M. 2018. "Authoritarians like Trump Target Trans People for a Reason." *Guardian*, October 22. www.theguardian.com/commentisfree/2018/oct/22/authoritarians-target-trans-people-democracy-patriarchy.

Island, D., and P. Letellier. 1991. *Men Who Beat the Men Who Love Them*. Binghamton, NY: Harrington Park Press.

James, S., J. Herman, S. Rankin, M. Keisling, L. Mottet, and M. A. Anafi. 2016. "The Report of the 2015 US Transgender Survey." National Center for Transgender Equality. Accessed June 3, 2023. https://transequality.org/sites/default/files/docs/usts/USTS-Full-Report-Dec17.pdf.

Johnson, M. P. 2010. *A Typology of Domestic Violence: Intimate Terrorism, Violent Resistance, and Situational Couple Violence*. Lebanon, NH: University Press of New England.

Kim, M. E. 2018. "From Carceral Feminism to Transformative Justice: Women-of-Color Feminism and Alternatives to Incarceration." *Journal of Ethnic & Cultural Diversity in Social Work* 27(3): 219–233.

———. 2020. "The Carceral Creep: Gender-Based Violence, Race, and the Expansion of the Punitive State, 1973–1983." *Social Problems* 67(2): 251–269.

Kritz, B. 2021. "Direct and Structural Violence against Transgender Populations: A Comparative Legal Study." *Florida Journal of International Law* 31(2): 2.

Langenderfer-Magruder, L., D. L. Whitfield, N. E. Walls, S. K. Kattari, and D. Ramos. 2016. "Experiences of Intimate Partner Violence and Subsequent Police Reporting among

Lesbian, Gay, Bisexual, Transgender, and Queer Adults in Colorado: Comparing Rates of Cisgender and Transgender Victimization." *Journal of Interpersonal Violence* 31(5): 855–871.

Lenning, E., and X. L. Guadalupe-Diaz. Forthcoming. "Monsters with Mommy Issues: How Hollywood Invented the 'Terroristic Tranny.'" In *The (Mis)Representation of Queer Lives in True Crime*, edited by Abbie E. Goldberg, Danielle C. Slakoff, and Carrie L. Buist. New York: Routledge.

Letellier, P., and D. Island. 2013. *Men Who Beat the Men Who Love Them: Battered Gay Men and Domestic Violence*. New York: Routledge.

Merrill, G. S. 1996. "Ruling the Exceptions: Same-Sex Battering and Domestic Violence Theory." *Journal of Gay & Lesbian Social Services* 4(1): 9–22.

Messinger, A. M., and X. L. Guadalupe-Diaz, eds. 2021. *Transgender Intimate Partner Violence: A Comprehensive Introduction*. New York: New York University Press.

Messinger, A. M., X. L. Guadalupe-Diaz, and V. Kurdyla. 2022. "Transgender Polyvictimization in the U.S. Transgender Survey." *Journal of Interpersonal Violence* 37: 19–20.

Minkin, R., and A. Brown. 2021. "Rising Shares of U.S. Adults Know Someone Who Is Transgender or Goes by Gender-Neutral Pronouns." Pew Research Center, July 27. www.pewresearch.org/fact-tank/2021/07/27/rising-shares-of-u-s-adults-know-someone -who-is-transgender-or-goes-by-gender-neutral-pronouns/.

Potter, H. 2008. *Battle Cries: Black Women and Intimate Partner Abuse*. New York: New York University Press.

Quinn, X. 2020. "Tactics and Justifications of Abuse Involving Transgender Individuals." In *Transgender Intimate Partner Violence: A Comprehensive Introduction*, edited by Adam Messinger and Xavier L. Guadalupe-Diaz, 35–61. New York: New York University Press.

Roberts, D. 2021. "Race." In edited by Nikole Hannah-Jones *The 1619 Project: A New Origin Story*. New York: One World.

Roch, A., G. Ritchie, and J. Morton. 2010. "Transgender People's Experiences of Domestic Abuse." LGBT Youth Scotland and the Equality Network. Accessed June 3, 2022. www .scottishtrans.org/wp-content/uploads/2013/03/trans_domestic_abuse.pdf.

Shulman, A. K. 1980. "Sex and Power: Sexual Bases of Radical Feminism." *Signs: Journal of Women in Culture and Society* 5(4): 590–604.

Smith, S. G., J. Chen, K. C. Basile, L. K. Gilbert, M. T. Merrick, N. Patel, M. Walling, and A. Jain. 2017. "The National Intimate Partner and Sexual Violence Survey (NISVS): 2010–2012 State Report." Atlanta, GA: National Center for Injury Prevention and Control, Centers for Disease Control and Prevention.

Spade, D. 2020. *Mutual Aid: Building Solidarity during This Crisis (and the Next)*. New York: Verso Books.

Stryker, S. 2017. *Transgender History: The Roots of Today's Revolution*. New York: Seal Press.

Walker, J. K. 2015. "Investigating Trans People's Vulnerabilities to Intimate Partner Violence /Abuse." *Partner Abuse* 6(1): 107–125.

Whalley, E., and C. Hackett. 2017. "Carceral Feminisms: The Abolitionist Project and Undoing Dominant Feminisms." *Contemporary Justice Review* 20(4): 456–473.

Woulfe, J. M., and L. A. Goodman. 2021. "Identity Abuse as a Tactic of Violence in LGBTQ Communities: Initial Validation of the Identity Abuse Measure." *Journal of Interpersonal Violence* 36(5–6): 2656–2676.

CHAPTER 35: Mass Incarceration and Family Life
by Bryan L. Sykes, Becky Pettit, and Daniela Kaiser

Alexander, Michelle. 2010. *The New Jim Crow: Mass Incarceration in the Age of Colorblindness.* New York: New Press.

Arditti, Joyce. 2012. *Parental Incarceration and the Family: Psychological and Social Effects of Imprisonment on Children, Parents, and Caregivers.* New York: New York University Press.

Arditti, Joyce, S. Smock, and T. Parkman. 2005. "It's Been Hard to be a Father: A Qualitative Exploration of Incarcerated Fatherhood." *Fathering* 3: 267–283.

Blumstein, Alfred, and Jacqueline Cohen. 1973. "A Theory of the Stability of Punishment." *Journal of Criminal Law and Criminology* 64: 198–206.

Braman, Donald. 2004. *Doing Time on the Outside: Incarceration and Family Life in Urban America.* Ann Arbor: University of Michigan Press.

Cho, Rosa Minhyo. 2010. "Maternal Incarceration and Children's Adolescent Outcomes: Timing and Dosage." *Social Service Review* 48(2): 257–282.

Clear, Todd. 2007. *Imprisoning Communities: How Mass Incarceration Makes Disadvantaged Neighborhoods Worse.* New York: Oxford University Press.

Comfort, Megan. 2008. *Doing Time Together: Love and Family in Shadow of the Prison.* Chicago: University of Chicago Press.

Cox, Robynn, and Sally Wallace. 2013. "The Impact of Incarceration on Food Insecurity among Households with Children." Fragile Families Working Paper 13-05-FF. Princeton, NJ: Princeton University Press.

Edin, Kathryn, and Maria Kefalas. 2005. *Promises I Can Keep: Why Poor Women Put Motherhood Before Marriage.* Berkeley: University of California Press.

Edin, Kathryn, Timothy Nelson, and Rechelle Paranal. 2003. "Fatherhood and Incarceration as Potential Turning Points in the Criminal Careers of Unskilled Men." In *Imprisoning America: The Social Effects of Mass Incarceration*, edited by Mary Patillo, David Weiman, and Bruce Western, 46–75. New York: Russell Sage Foundation.

Foster, Holly, and John Hagan. 2007. "Incarceration and Intergenerational Social Exclusion." *Social Problems* 54(4): 399–433.

———. 2009. "The Mass Incarceration of Parents in America: Issues of Race/Ethnicity, Collateral Damage to Children, and Prisoner Reentry." *Annals of the American Academy of Political and Social Science* 623: 179–194.

Freudenberg, Nicholas. 2001. "Jails, Prisons, and the Health of Urban Populations: A Review of the Impact of the Correctional System on Community Health." *Journal of Urban Health: Bulletin of the New York Academy of Medicine* 78(2): 214–235.

Garland, David. 2001. "The Meaning of Mass Imprisonment." In *Mass Imprisonment: Social Causes and Consequences*, edited by D. Garland, 1–3. London: Sage Publications.

Geller, Amanda, Carey E. Cooper, Irwin Garfinkel, Ofira Schwartz-Soicher, and Ronald B. Mincy. 2012. "Beyond Absenteeism: Father Incarceration and Child Development." *Demography* 49(1): 49–76.

Geller, Amanda, Irwin Garfinkel, Carey E. Cooper, and Ronald B. Mincy. 2009. "Parental Incarceration and Child Wellbeing: Implications for Urban Families." *Social Science Quarterly* 90(5): 1186–1202.

Geller, Amanda, Irwin Garfinkel, and Bruce Western. 2011. "Paternal Incarceration and Support for Children in Fragile Families." *Demography* 48(1): 25–47.

Glaze, Lauren. 2010. *Correctional Population in the United States, 2010*. Washington, DC: Bureau of Justice Statistics. Available from http://bjs.ojp.usdoj.gov/index.cfm?ty =pbdetail&iid=2237.

Guerino, P., Piege Harrison, and William Sabol. 2011. *Prisoners in 2010*. Revised. Washington, DC: Bureau of Justice Statistics. Available from http://bjs.ojp.usdoj.gov/index .cfm?ty=pbdetail&iid=2230.

Hagan, John, and Ronit Dinovitzer. 1999. "Collateral Consequences of Imprisonment for Children, Communities and Prisoners." *Crime and Justice: A Review of Research* 26: 121–162.

Hagan, John, and Holly Foster. 2012. "Intergenerational Educational Effects of Mass Imprisonment in America." *Sociology of Education* 85(3): 259–286.

Harding, David, Jeffery Morenoff, and Claire Herbert. 2013. "Home Is Hard to Find: Neighborhoods, Institutions, and the Residential Trajectories of Returning Prisoners." *Annals of the American Academy of Political and Social Science* 647: 214–236.

Johnson, Rucker, and Steven Raphael. 2009. "The Effects of Male Incarceration Dynamics on AIDS Infection Rates among African-American Women and Men." *Journal of Law & Economics* 52(2): 251–294.

Kluckow, Rich, and Zhen Zeng. 2022. "Correctional Populations in the United States, 2020—Statistical Tables." Washington DC: Bureau of Justice Statistics, https://bjs.ojp .gov/content/pub/pdf/cpus20st.pdf.

Lareau, Annette. 2003. *Unequal Childhoods: Class, Race, and Family Life*. Berkeley: University of California Press.

Lopoo, Leonard, and Bruce Western. 2005. "Incarceration and the Formation and Stability of Marital Unions." *Journal of Marriage and the Family* 67: 721–734.

Massoglia, Michael. 2008. "Incarceration, Health, and Racial Disparities in Health." *Law & Society Review* 42: 275–306.

Mauer, Mark. 2006. *Race to Incarcerate*. Washington, DC: Sentencing Project.

Mumola, C. 2000. *Bureau of Justice Statistics Bulletin: Incarcerated Parents and Their Children*. Washington, DC: U.S. Department of Justice.

Nurse, Anne. 2004. "Returning to Strangers: Newly Paroled Young Fathers and Their Children." In *Imprisoning America: The Social Effects of Mass Incarceration*, edited by Mary Pattillo, David Weiman, and Bruce Western, 76–96. New York: Russell Sage Foundation.

Pager, Devah. 2003. "The Mark of a Criminal Record." *American Journal of Sociology* 108: 937–975.

Pettit, Becky. 2012. *Invisible Men: Mass Incarceration and the Myth of Black Progress*. New York: Russell Sage Foundation.

Pettit, Becky, Bryan Sykes, and Bruce Western. 2009. *Technical Report on Revised Population Estimates and NLSY 79 Analysis Tables for the Pew Public Safety and Mobility Project*. Cambridge, MA: Harvard University Press.

Pettit, Becky, and Bruce Western. 2004. "Mass Imprisonment and the Life Course: Race and Class Inequality in U.S. Incarceration." *American Sociological Review* 69: 151–169.

Pew Charitable Trusts. 2008. *One in 100: Behind Bars in America 2008*. Available from http: //www.pewtrusts.org/en/research-and-analysis/reports/2008/02/28/one-in-100-behind -bars-in-america-2008.

Pew Research Center. 2021. "U.S. Incarcerates a Larger Share of Its Population than Any Other Country." August 16. http://www.pewresearch.org/fact-tank/2021/08/16 /americas-incarceration-rate-lowest-since-1995/ft_21-08-12_incarceration_2/.

Rosenfeld, Jake, Jennifer Laird, Bryan Sykes, and Becky Pettit. 2011. *Incarceration and Racial Inequality in Voter Turnout, 1980–2008.* Paper presented at the Population Association of American Annual Meetings, Washington, DC, and the Annual Meetings of the American Political Science Association, Seattle, OR.

Springer, David, Courtney Lynch, and Allen Rubin. 2000. "Effects of a Solution-Focused Mutual Aid Group for Hispanic Children of Incarcerated Parents." *Child and Adolescent Social Work Journal* 17(6): 431–442.

Sykes, Bryan, and Alex Piquero. 2009. "Structuring and Recreating Inequality: Health Testing Policies, Race, and the Criminal Justice System." *Annals of the American Academy of Political and Social Science* 623: 214–227.

Tonry, Michael. 1995. *Malign Neglect-Race, Crime, and Punishment in America.* London: Oxford University Press.

Uggen, Christopher, and Jeff Manza. 2002. "Democratic Contraction? Political Consequences of Felon Disenfranchisement in the United States." *American Sociological Review* 67: 777–803.

Wakefield, Sara, and Christopher Uggen. 2010. "Incarceration and Stratification." *Annual Review of Sociology* 36: 387–406.

Wakefield, Sara, and Christopher Wildeman. 2011. Mass Imprisonment and Racial Disparities in Childhood Behavioral Problems." *Criminology and Public Policy* 10(3): 793–817.

Waller, Maureen. 2002. *My Baby's Father: Unmarried Parents and Paternal Responsibility.* Ithaca, NY: Cornell University Press.

Walmsley, Roy. 2011. *World Prison Population List.* 9th ed. Retrieved on September 6, 2012, from http://www.prisonstudies.org/research-publications?shs_term_node_tid _depth=27.

Western, Bruce. 2006. *Punishment and Inequality in America.* New York: Russell Sage Foundation.

Western, Bruce, Leonard Lopoo, and Sara McLanahan. 2004. "Incarceration and the Bond between Parents in Fragile Families." *In Imprisoning America: The Social Effects of Mass Incarceration,* edited by Mary Pattillo, David Weiman, and Bruce Western. New York: Russell Sage Foundation.

Western, Bruce, and Becky Pettit. 2005. "Black-White Wage Inequality, Employment Rates, and Incarceration." *American Journal of Sociology* 111: 553–578.

Whitman, James. 2003. *Harsh Justice: Criminal Punishment and the Widening Divide between America and Europe.* London: Oxford University Press.

Wildeman, Christopher. 2009. "Parental Imprisonment and the Concentration of Childhood Disadvantage." *Demography* 46(2): 265–280.

———. 2010. "Paternal Incarceration and Children's Physically Aggressive Behaviors: Evidence from the Fragile Families and Child Wellbeing Study." *Social Forces* 89(1): 285–309.

———. 2014. "Parental Incarceration, Child Homelessness, and the Invisible Consequences of Mass Imprisonment." *Annals of the American Academy of Political and Social Science* 651(1): 74–96.

Wildeman, Christopher, and Bruce Western. 2010. "Incarceration in Fragile Families." *Future of Children* 20(2): 157–177.

Wilson, William Julius. 1987. *The Truly Disadvantaged.* Chicago: University of Chicago Press.

CHAPTER 36: Why Can't Anyone "Have It All"?
The Colliding Worlds of Work and Caregiving
by Kathleen Gerson

Acock, Alan C., and David H. Demo. 1994. *Family Diversity and Well-Being*. Thousand Oaks, CA: Sage Publications.

Amato, Paul R., and Alan Booth. 1997. *A Generation at Risk: Growing Up in an Era of Family Upheaval*. Cambridge, MA: Harvard University Press.

Amato, Paul R., and Bryndl Hohmann-Marriott. 2007. "A Comparison of High-and Low-Distress Marriages That End in Divorce." *Journal of Marriage and Family* 69(3): 621–638.

Barnett, Rosalind C., and Caryl Rivers. 1996. *She Works/He Works: How Two-Income Families Are Happier, Healthier, and Better-Off*. San Francisco: Harper.

Belkin, Lisa. 2003. "The Opt-Out Revolution." *New York Times Magazine*, October 26.

Bengtson, Vern L., Timothy J. Biblarz, and Robert E. L. Roberts. 2002. *How Families Still Matter: A Longitudinal Study of Youth in Two Generations*. New York: Cambridge University Press.

Bennetts, Leslie. 2007. *The Feminine Mistake: Are We Giving Up Too Much?* New York: Voice/Hyperion.

Bianchi, Suzanne M., John P. Robinson, and Melissa A. Milkie. 2006. *Changing Rhythms of American Family Life*. New York: Russell Sage Foundation.

Blankenhorn, David. 1995. *Fatherless America: Confronting Our Most Urgent Social Problem*. New York: Basic Books.

Booth, Alan, and Paul R. Amato. 2001. "Parental Predivorce Relations and Offspring Postdivorce Well-Being." *Journal of Marriage and Family* 63(1): 197–212.

Boushey, Heather. 2008. "'Opting Out?' The Effect of Children on Women's Employment in the United States." *Feminist Economics* 14(1): 1–36.

Brown, Anna. 2021. "Growing Share of Childless Adults in U.S. Don't Expect to Ever Have Children." Pew Research Center, November 19. www.pewresearch.org/short-reads/2021 /11/19/growing-share-of-childless-adults-in-u-s-dont-expect-to-ever-have-children/.

Coontz, Stephanie. 2005. *Marriage, a History: From Obedience to Intimacy, or How Love Conquered Marriage*. New York: Viking.

Edsall, Thomas B. 2021. "It's Become Increasingly Hard for Them to Feel Good about Themselves." *New York Times*, September 22. www.nytimes.com/2021/09/22/opinion /economy-education-women-men.html.

England, Paula, Andrew Levine, and Emma Mishel. 2020. "Progress toward Gender Equality in the United States Has Slowed or Stalled." *Proceedings of the National Academy of Sciences* 117(13): 6990–6997.

Fitch, Lynn. 2021. "Attorney General Lynn Fitch Files Brief in Dobbs v. JWHO." July 22. www.ago.state.ms.us/2021/07/22/attorney-general-lynn-fitch-files-brief-in-dobbs-v-jwho/.

Furstenberg, Frank F., and Andrew J. Cherlin. 1991. *Divided Families: What Happens to Children When Parents Part*. Cambridge, MA: Harvard University Press.

Galinsky, Ellen. 1999. *Ask the Children: What America's Children Really Think about Working Parents*. New York: Morrow.

Gerson, Kathleen. 2006. "Families as Trajectories: Children's Views of Family Life in Contemporary America." In *Families between Flexibility and Dependability: Perspectives for a Life Cycle Family Policy*, edited by Hans Bertram, Helga Kruger and Katarina Spiel. Farmington Hills, MI: Verlag Barbara Budrich.

———. 2010. *The Unfinished Revolution: How a New Generation Is Reshaping Family, Work, and Gender in America*. New York: Oxford University Press.

———. 2017. "Different Ways of Not Having It All: Work, Care, and Shifting Gender Arrangements in the New Economy." In *Beyond the Cubicle: Job Insecurity, Intimacy, and the Flexible Self*, edited by Allison J. Pugh, 155–178. New York: Oxford University Press.

Glass, Jennifer, R. Kelly Raley, and Joanna Pepin. 2021. "Mothers Are the Primary Earners in Growing Numbers of Families with Children, Including Married-Couple Families." Council on Contemporary Families, November 2. https://sites.utexas.edu /contemporaryfamilies/2021/11/02/breadwinning-mothers-brief-report/.

Glynn, Sarah Jane. 2019. "Breadwinning Mothers Continue to Be the U.S. Norm." Center for American Progress, May 10. www.americanprogress.org/article/breadwinning -mothers-continue-u-s-norm/.

Harvey, Lisa. 1999. "Short-Term and Long-Term Effects of Early Parental Employment on Children of the National Longitudinal Study of Youth." *Developmental Psychology* 35(2): 445–459.

Hays, Sharon. 1996. *The Cultural Contradictions of Motherhood*. New Haven, CT: Yale University Press.

Hetherington, E. M. 1999. *Coping with Divorce, Single Parenting, and Remarriage: A Risk and Resiliency Perspective*. Mahwah, NJ: Lawrence Erlbaum Associates.

Hirshman, Linda. 2006. *Get to Work*. New York: Viking.

Hochschild, Arlie R. With Ann Machung. 1989. *The Second Shift: Working Parents and the Revolution at Home*. New York: Viking.

Hoffman, Lois. 1987. "The Effects on Children of Maternal and Paternal Employment." In *Families and Work*, edited by N. Gerstel and H. E. Gross, 362–395. Philadelphia: Temple University Press.

Hoffman, Lois, Norma Wladis, and Lise M. Youngblade. 1999. *Mothers at Work: Effects on Children's Well-Being*. New York: Cambridge University Press.

Ishizuka, Patrick. 2019. "Social Class, Gender, and Contemporary Parenting Standards in the United States: Evidence from a National Survey Experiment." *Social Forces* 98(1): 31–58.

Lareau, Annette. 2003. *Unequal Childhoods: Race, Class, and Family Life*. Oakland: University of California Press.

Li, Allen J. 2007. "The Kids are OK: Divorce and Children's Behavior Problems." Working Paper WR 489. Santa Monica, CA: RAND.

Lorber, Judith. 1994. *Paradoxes of Gender*. New Haven, CT: Yale University Press.

McLanahan, Sara, and Gary D. Sandefur. 1994. *Growing Up with a Single Parent: What Hurts, What Helps*. Cambridge, MA: Harvard University Press.

Moen, Phyllis, and Patricia Roehling. 2005. *The Career Mystique: Cracks in the American Dream*. Lanham, MD: Rowman & Littlefield.

Moore, Kristin A., Rosemary Chalk, Juliet Scarpa, and Sharon Vandivere. 2002. *Family Strengths: Often Overlooked, But Real*. Washington, DC: Child Trends.

Parcel, Toby L., and Elizabeth G. Menaghan. 1994. *Parents' Jobs and Children's Lives*. New York: Aldine de Gruyter.

Parker, Kim, and Renee Stepler. 2017. "Americans See Men as the Financial Providers, Even as Women's Contributions Grow." Pew Research Center, September 20. www.pewre search.org/short-reads/2017/09/20/americans-see-men-as-the-financial-providers -even-as-womens-contributions-grow/.

Pew Research Center. 2007a. "As Marriage and Parenthood Drift Apart, Public Is Concerned about Social Impact." Retrieved on June 19, 2008, from http://pewresearch.org /pubs/526 /marriage-parenthood.

———. 2007b. "How Young People View Their Lives, Futures and Politics: A Portrait of the 'Generation Next.'" January 9. http://www.people-press.org/2007/01/09/a-portrait -of-generation-next/.

Popenoe, David. 1988. *Disturbing the Nest: Family Change and Decline in Modern Societies.* New York: Aldine de Gruyter.

———. 1996. *Life without Father: Compelling New Evidence that Fatherhood and Marriage Are Indispensable for the Good of Children and Society.* New York: Martin Kessler Books.

Popenoe, David, Jean B. Elshtain, and David Blankenhorn. 1996. *Promises to Keep: Decline and Renewal of Marriage in America.* Lanham, MD: Rowman & Littlefield.

Risman, Barbara J. 1998. *Gender Vertigo: American Families in Transition.* New Haven, CT: Yale University Press.

Roberts, Sam. 2007. "Fifty-one Percent of Women Are Now Living without Spouse." *New York Times,* January 16. https://www.nytimes.com/2007/01/16/us/16census.html.

Skolnick, Arlene, and Stacey Rosencrantz. 1994. "The New Crusade for the Old Family." *American Prospect,* 18(Summer): 59–65.

Slaughter, Anne-Marie. 2012. "Why Women Still Can't Have It All." *Atlantic,* July/August. www.theatlantic.com/magazine/archive/2012/07/why-women-still-cant -have-it-all/309020/.

Springer, Kristen W. 2007. "Research or Rhetoric? A Response to Wilcox and Nock." *Sociological Forum* 22(1): 111–116.

Stacey, Judith. 1996. *In the Name of the Family: Rethinking Family Values in the Postmodern Age.* Boston: Beacon Press.

Stone, Pamela. 2007. *Opting Out? Why Women Really Quit Careers and Head Home.* Berkeley, CA: University of California Press.

Waite, Linda J., and Maggie Gallagher. 2000. *The Case for Marriage: Why Married People Are Happier, Healthier, and Better Off Financially.* New York: Doubleday.

West, Candace, and Don H. Zimmerman. 1987. "Doing Gender." *Gender & Society* 1(2): 125–151.

Whitehead, Barbara D. 1997. *The Divorce Culture.* New York: Knopf.

Williams, Joan. 2000. *Unbending Gender: Why Family and Work Conflict and What to Do about It.* New York: Oxford University Press.

———. 2007. "The Opt-Out Revolution Revisited." *American Prospect,* March, A12–A15.

Williams, Joan C., Mary Blair-Loy, and Jennifer L. Berdahl. 2013. "Cultural Schemas, Social Class, and the Flexibility Stigma." *Journal of Social Issues* 69(2): 209–234.

Yang, Andrew. 2022. "The Data Are Clear: The Boys Are Not All Right" *Washington Post,* February 8. www.washingtonpost.com/opinions/2022/02/08/andrew-yang-boys-are -not-all-right/.

Zerubavel, Eviatar. 1991. *The Fine Line: Making Distinctions in Everyday Life.* Chicago: University of Chicago Press.

CHAPTER 37: When Men Stay Home: Household Labor in Female-Led Indian Migrant Families
by Pallavi Banerjee

Aiken, L. H. 2007. "U.S. Nurse Labor Market Dynamics Are Key to Global Nurse Sufficiency." *Health Services Research* 42(3p2), 1299–1320.

Aiken, L. H., J. Buchan, J. Sochalski, B. Nichols, and M. Powell. 2004. "Trends in International Nurse Migration." *Health Affairs* 23(3): 69–77.

Banerjee, P. 2019. "Subversive Self-Employment: Intersectionality and Self-Employment among Dependent Visas Holders in the United States." *American Behavioral Scientist* 63(2): 186–207.

——. 2022. *The Opportunity Trap: High-Skilled Workers, Indian Families, and the Failures of the Dependent Visa Program*. New York: New York University Press.

Banerjee, P., and P. Sengupta. 2020. "Trump's Suspension of H-1B Visas Is a Racist Attack on Immigrants—And a Bad Move for the Economy. *Conversation*, July 2. https://theconversation.com/trumps-suspension-of-h-1b-visas-is-a-racist-attack-on -immigrants-and-a-bad-move-for-the-economy-141329.

Bhalla, R., and S. Meher. 2019. "Education, Employment and Economic Growth with Special Reference to Females in Kerala." *Indian Journal of Labour Economics* 62(4): 639–658.

Biao, X. 2005. "Gender, Dowry and the Migration System of Indian Information Technology Professionals." *Indian Journal of Gender Studies* 12(2–3): 357–380.

Brush, B.L., and A. M. Berger. 2002. "Sending for Nurses: Foreign Nurse Migration, 1965–2002." *Nursing and Health Policy Review* 1(2): 103–115.

Brush, B. L., J. Sochalski, and A. M. Berger. 2004. "Imported care: Recruiting Foreign Nurses to U.S. Health Care Facilities." *Health Affairs* 23(3): 78–87.

Dicicco-Bloom, B. 2004. "The Racial and Gendered Experiences of Immigrant Nurses from Kerala, India." *Journal of Transcultural Nursing* 15(1): 26–33.

George, S. M. 2005. *When Women Come First Gender and Class in Transnational Migration*. Berkeley, CA: University of California Press.

Hochschild, A. R. 1989. *The Second Shift: Working Mothers and the Revolution at Home*. New York: Viking Penguin.

Khadria, B. 2007. "International Nurse Recruitment in India." *Health Services Research* 42(3p2): 1429–1436.

Kurien, P. A. 2002. *Kaleidoscopic Ethnicity: International Migration and the Reconstruction of Community Identities in India*. New Brunswick, NJ: Rutgers University Press.

Masselink, L. E., and C. B. Jones. 2014. "Immigration Policy and Internationally Educated Nurses in the United States: A Brief History." *Nursing Outlook* 62(1): 39–45.

Pittman, P. M., A. J. Folsom, and E. Bass. 2010. "U.S.-Based Recruitment of Foreign-Educated Nurses: Implications of an Emerging Industry." *American Journal of Nursing* 110(6): 38–48.

Polsky, D., S. J. Ross, B. L. Brush, and J. Sochalski. 2007. "Trends in Characteristics and Country of Origin among Foreign-Trained Nurses in the United States, 1990 and 2000." *American Journal of Public Health* 97(5): 895–899.

Rai, S. 2003. "Indian Nurses Sought to Staff U.S. Hospitals." *New York Times*, February 10. https://www.nytimes.com/2003/02/10/world/indian-nurses-sought-to-staff-us-hospitals .html.

Sharma, Rashmi. 2011. "Gender and International Migration: The Profile of Female Migrants from India." *Social Scientist* 39(3/4): 37–63.

U.S. Citizenship and Immigration Services. 2022. *Temporary (Nonimmigrant) Workers*. Retrieved from https://www.uscis.gov/working-in-the-united-states/temporary -nonimmigrant-workers.

U.S. Department of State. 2021a. Table XV(A), *Classes of Nonimmigrants Issued Visas (Including Border Crossing Cards), Fiscal Years 2017–2021*. Retrieved from https://travel .state.gov/content/dam/visas/Statistics/AnnualReports/FY2021AnnualReport/FY21 _TableXVA.pdf.

——. 2021b. Table XV(B), *Nonimmigrant Visas Issued by Classification (Including Border Crossing Cards), Fiscal Years 2017–2021.* Retrieved from https://travel.state.gov/content/dam/visas/Statistics/AnnualReports/FY2021AnnualReport/FY21_%20TableXVB.pdf.

Walton-Roberts, Margaret. 2012. "Contextualizing the Global Nursing Care Chain: International Migration and the Status of Nursing in Kerala, India." *Global Networks* 13(2): 175–194.

——. 2015. "International Migration of Health Professionals and the Marketization and Privatization of Health Education in India: From Push–Pull to Global Political Economy." *Social Science & Medicine* 124: 374–382.

——. 2020. "Student Nurses and Their Migration Plans: A Kerala Case Study." In *Governance and Labour Migration.* edited by S. Irudaya Rajan, 196–216. New Delhi: Routledge India.

CHAPTER 38: Gender Inequality in the United States during the COVID-19 Pandemic
by Allison Nicole Dunatchik and Jerry A. Jacobs

Berk, Sarah Fenstermaker. 1985. *The Gender Factory: The Apportionment of Work in American Households.* New York: Plenum.

Carlson, Daniel L., Richard J. Petts, and Joanna R. Pepin. 2022. "Changes in US Parents' Domestic Labor during the Early Days of the COVID-19 Pandemic." *Sociological Inquiry* 92(3): 1217–1244.

Collins, Caitlyn. 2019. *Making Motherhood Work: How Women Manage Careers and Caregiving.* Princeton, NJ: Princeton University Press.

Collins, Caitlyn, Liana Christin Landivar, Leah Ruppanner, and William J. Scarborough. 2020. "COVID-19 and the Gender Gap in Work Hours." *Gender, Work, & Organization* 28(S1): 101–112.

Correll, Shelley J., Erin L. Kelly, Lindsey Trimble O'Connor, and Joan C. Williams. 2014. "Redesigning, Redefining Work." *Work and Occupations* 41(1): 3–17.

Craig, Lyn, and Brendan Churchill. 2021. "Unpaid Work and Care During COVID-19 Subjective Experiences of Same-Sex Couples and Single Mothers in Australia." *Gender & Society* 35(2): 233–243.

Dunatchik, Allison, Kathleen Gerson, Jennifer Glass, Jerry A. Jacobs, and Haley Stritzel 2021. "Gender, Parenting and the Rise of Remote Work during the Pandemic: Implications for Domestic Inequality in the United States." *Gender & Society* 35(2): 1–12

Gough, Margaret, and Alexandra Killewald. 2011. "Unemployment in Families: The Case of Housework." *Journal of Marriage and Family* 73(5): 1085–1100.

Hertz, Rosanna, Jane Mattes, and Alexandria Shook. 2020. "When Paid Work Invades the Family: Single Mothers in the COVID-19 Pandemic." *Journal of Family Issues* 42(9): 2019–2045.

Institute for Women's Policy Research (IWPR). 2020. "Women Fall Further behind Men in the Recovery and Are 5.8 Million Jobs below Pre-COVID Employment Levels, Compared with 5.0 Million Fewer Jobs for Men." October. https://iwpr org/wp-content/uploads/2020/10/QF-Jobs-Day-October-dft-HM-Fact-Checked.pdf.

——. 2021. "Women and the COVID-19 Pandemic: Five Charts and a Table Tracking the 2020 She-Cession by Race and Gender." January 28. https://iwpr.crg/wp-content/uploads/2021/01/QF-Women-Jobs-and-the-COVID-19-Feb-to-Dec-2020.pdf.

Kaduk, Anne, Katie Genadek, Erin L. Kelly, and Phyllis Moen. 2019. "Involuntary vs. Voluntary Flexible Work: Insights for Scholars and Stakeholders." *Community, Work & Family* 22(4): 412–442.

Landivar, Liana Christin, Leah Ruppanner, William Scarborough, and Caitlyn Collins. 2020. "Early Signs Indicate that COVID-19 Is Exacerbating Gender Inequality in the Labor Force." *Socius* 6: 1–3.

Livingston, Gretchen. 2018. "The Changing Profile of Unmarried Parents." Pew Research Center, April 25. www.pewresearch.org/social-trends/2018/04/25/the-changing-profile-of-unmarried-parents/.

Lyttelton, Thomas, Emma Zang, and Kelly Musick. 2022. "Telecommuting and Gender Differences in Parents' Paid and Unpaid Work before and during the COVID-19 Pandemic." *Journal of Marriage and Family* 84: 230–249.

Mas, Alexandre, and Amanda Pallais. 2017. "Valuing Alternative Work Arrangements." *American Economic Review* 107(12): 3722–59.

Miller, Claire Cain. 2020. "Nearly Half of Men Say They Do Most of the Home Schooling. 3 Percent of Women Agree." *New York Times*, May 6. www.nytimes.com/2020/05/06/upshot/pandemic-chores-homeschooling-gender.html.

Morning Consult and the *New York Times*. 2020. National Tracking Poll #200424, April 9–10, 2020.

Noonan, Mary C., and Jennifer L. Glass. 2012. "The Hard Truth about Telecommuting." *Monthly Labor Review* 135: 38–45.

Raley, Sara, Suzanne M. Bianchi, and Wendy Wang. 2012. "When Do Fathers Care? Mothers' Economic Contribution and Fathers' Involvement in Child Care." *American Journal of Sociology* 117(5): 1422–1459.

Rao, Aliya H. 2020. *Crunch Time: How Married Couples Confront Unemployment*. Berkeley: University of California Press.

Tach, Laura, and Kathryn Edin. 2017. "The Social Safety Net after Welfare Reform: Recent Developments and Consequences for Household Dynamics." *Annual Review of Sociology* 43: 541–561.

West, Candace, and Don H. Zimmerman. 1987. "Doing Gender." *Gender & Society* 1: 125–151.

Yavorsky, Jill E., Claire M. Kamp Dush, and Sarah J. Schoppe-Sullivan. 2015. "The Production of Inequality: The Gender Division of Labor across the Transition to Parenthood." *Journal of Marriage and Family* 77: 662–679.

Yavorsky, Jill, E., Yue Qian, and Amanda Sargent. 2021. "The Gendered Pandemic: The Implications of COVID-19 for Work and Family." *Sociology Compass* 15(6): e12881.

Zamarro, Gema, Francisco Perez-Arce, and Maria Jose Prados. 2021. "Gender Differences in the Impact of COVID-19." *Review of Economics of the Household* 19: 11–40.

CHAPTER 39: The Power of Queer: How "Guy Moms" Challenge Heteronormative Assumptions about Mothering and Family
by Raine Dozier

Anderson, Steph M. 2020. "Gender Matters: The Perceived Role of Gender Expression in Discrimination against Cisgender and Transgender LGBQ Individuals." *Psychology of Women Quarterly* 44(3): 323–341.

Ascigil, Esra, Britney M. Wardecker, William J. Chopik, and Robin S. Edelstein. 2021. "Division of Baby Care in Heterosexual and Lesbian Parents: Expectations Versus Reality." *Journal of Marriage and Family* 83: 584–594.

Averett, Kate Henley. 2016. "The Gender Buffet: LGBTQ Parents Resisting Heteronormativity." *Gender & Society* 30(2): 189–212.

Banks, Nina. 2019. "Black Women's Labor Market History Reveals Deep-Seated Race and Gender Discrimination." *Economic Policy Institute Working Economics Blog*, February 19. www.epi.org/blog/black-womens-labor-market-history-reveals-deep-seated-race-and-gender-discrimination.

Bartley, Sharon J., Priscilla W. Blanton, and Jennifer L. Gilliard. 2005. "Husbands and Wives in Dual-Earner Marriages: Decision-Making, Gender Role Attitudes, Division of Household Labor, and Equity." *Marriage and Family Review* 37(4): 65–94.

Baughman, Charlotte, Tehra Coles, Jennifer Feinberg, and Hope Newton. 2021. "The Surveillance Tentacles of the Child Welfare System." *Columbia Journal of Race and Law* 11(3): 501–532.

Baxter, Janeen, Belinda Hewitt, and Michele Haynes. 2008. "Life Course Transitions and Housework: Marriage, Parenthood and Time on Housework." *Journal of Marriage and Family* 70(2): 259–272.

Bergstrom-Lynch, Cara. 2020. "Free to Be You and Me, Maybe: Lesbian, Gay, Bisexual and Transgender Parents Doing Gender with Their Children." *Journal of Gender Studies* 29(3): 282–294.

Bianchi, Susan M., and Melissa A. Milkie. 2010. "Work and Family Research in the First Decade of the 21st Century." *Journal of Marriage and Family* 72(3): 705–725.

Biblarz, Timothy J., and Judith Stacey. 2010. "How Does the Gender of Parents Matter?" *Journal of Marriage and Family* 72(1): 3–22.

Bos, Henny M. W., Frank van Balen, and Dyphmna van den Boom. 2007. "Child Adjustment and Parenting in Planned Lesbian-Parent Families." *American Journal of Orthopsychiatry* 77(1): 38–48.

Brinamen, Charles F. 2000. "On Becoming Fathers: Issues Facing Gay Men Choosing to Parent." *Dissertation Abstracts International* 61(5-B): 2794.

Bureau of Labor Statistics. 2020. "Labor Force Characteristics by Race and Ethnicity, 2019." *BLS Reports*. Washington, DC: U.S. Bureau of Labor Statistics. Retrieved on September 7, 2022. www.bls.gov/opub/reports/race-and-ethnicity/2019/home.htm.

Carlson, Daniel L., Richard J. Petts, and Joanna R. Pepin. 2022. "Changes in US Parents' Domestic Labor during the Early Days of the COVID-19 Pandemic." *Sociological Inquiry* 92(3): 1217–1244.

Carroll, Megan. 2018. "Managing without Moms: Gay Fathers, Incidental Activism, and the Politics of Parental Gender." *Journal of Family Issues* 39: 3410–3435.

Chan, Raymond W., Risa S. Brooks, Barbara Raboy, and Charlotte J. Patterson. 1998. "Division of Labor among Lesbian and Heterosexual Parents: Associations with Children's Adjustment." *Journal of Family Psychology* 12(3): 402–419.

Ciciolla, Lucia, and Suniya S. Luthar. 2019. "Invisible Household Labor and Ramifications for Adjustment: Mothers as Captains of Households." *Sex Roles* 81(7–8): 467–486.

Cody, Patricia A., Rachel H. Farr, Ruth G. McRoy, Susan Ayers-Lopez, and Kathleen J. Ledesma. 2017. "Youth Perspectives on Being Adopted from Foster Care by Lesbian and Gay Parents: Implications for Families and Adoption Professionals." *Adoption Quarterly* 20: 118–198.

Cordero-Coma, Julia, and Gøsta Esping-Andersen. 2018. "The Intergenerational Transmission of Gender Roles: Children's Contribution to Housework in Germany." *Journal of Marriage and Family* 80: 1005–1019.

Dempsey, Deborah. 2010. "Conceiving and Negotiating Reproductive Relationships: Lesbians and Gay Men Forming Families with Children." *Sociology* 44(6): 1145–1162.

Dozier, Raine. 2005. "Beards, Breasts, and Bodies: Doing Sex in a Gendered World." *Gender & Society* 19(3): 297–316.

Duggan, Lisa. 2002. "The New Homonormativity: The Sexual Politics of Neoliberalism." In *Materializing Democracy: Toward a Revitalized Cultural Politics*, edited by Russ Castronovo and Dana D. Nelson, 175–194. Durham, NC: Duke University Press.

Elizabeth, Vivienne, Nicola Gavey, and Julia Tolmie. 2012. "The Gendered Dynamics of Power in Disputes Over the Postseparation Care of Children." *Violence against Women* 18(4): 459–481.

Epstein, Rachel. 2018. "Space Invaders: Queer and Trans Bodies in Fertility Clinics." *Sexualities* 21: 1039–1058.

Gartrell, Nanette, and Henny Bos. 2010. "US National Longitudinal Lesbian Family Study: Psychological Adjustment of 17-Year-Old Adolescents." *Pediatrics* 126(1): 28–36.

Giesler, Mark. 2012. "Gay Fathers' Negotiation of Gender Role Strain: A Qualitative Inquiry." *Fathering* 10(2): 119–139.

Goldberg, Abbie E. 2007. "(How) Does It Make a Difference? Perspectives of Adults with Lesbian, Gay, and Bisexual Parents." *American Journal of Orthopsychiatry* 77(4): 550–562.

Goldberg, Abbie E., Katherine R. Allen, Kaitlin A. Black, Reihonna L. Frost, and Melissa H. Manley. 2018. "'There Is No Perfect School': The Complexity of School Decision-Making among Lesbian and Gay Adoptive Parents." *Journal of Marriage and Family* 80(3): 684–703.

Goldberg, Abbie E., Katherine R. Allen, and Megan Carroll. 2020. "'We Don't Exactly Fit In, but We Can't Opt Out': Gay Fathers' Experiences Navigating Parent Communities in Schools." *Journal of Marriage and Family* 82: 1655–1676.

Goldberg, Abbie E., and Randi L. Garcia. 2016. "Gender-Typed Behavior over Time in Children with Lesbian, Gay, and Heterosexual Parents." *Journal of Family Psychology* 30(7): 854–865.

Goldberg, Abbie E., Deborah A. Kashy, and JuliAnna Z. Smith. 2012. "Gender-Typed Play Behavior in Early Childhood: Adopted Children with Lesbian, Gay, and Heterosexual Parents." *Sex Roles* 67(9–10): 503–515.

Goldberg, Abbie E., JuliAnna Z. Smith, and Maureen Perry-Jenkins. 2012. "The Division of Labor in Lesbian, Gay, and Heterosexual New Adoptive Parents." *Journal of Marriage and Family* 74(4): 812–828.

Grant, Jaime. 2009. "Sex and the Formerly Single Mom." In *Who's Your Daddy*, edited by Rachel Epstein, 328–334. Toronto, ON: Sumach.

Gupta, Sanjiv. 2006. "The Consequences of Maternal Employment During Men's Childhood for Their Adult Housework Performance." *Gender & Society* 20(1): 60–86.

Haines, Kari M., C. Reyn Boyer, Casey Giovanazzi, and M. Paz Galupo. 2018. "'Not a Real Family': Microaggressions Directed toward LGBTQ Families." *Journal of Homosexuality* 65(9): 1138–1151.

Halperin, David M. 1995. *Saint Foucault: Towards a Gay Hagiography*. New York: Oxford University Press.

Hochschild, Arlie, and Annie Machung. 2003. *The Second Shift.* New York: Penguin Books.

Hudson, David. 2022. "School Kicks Out 5-Year-Old after She Is Adopted by Same-Sex Couple." *Queerty,* August 12. www.queerty.com/school-kicks-5-year-old-adopted -sex-couple-20220812.

James, Susan Donaldson. 2009. "Lesbians Sue When Partners Die Alone." *ABC News,* May 20. http://abcnews.go.com/Health/story?id=7633058&page=1#.UZlC06LBOi=.

Johnson, Susanne. 2012. "Lesbian Mothers and Their Children: The Third Wave." *Journal of Lesbian Studies* 16(1): 45–53.

Johnson, Susanne, and Elizabeth O'Connor. 2002. *The Gay Baby Boom: The Psychology of Gay Parenthood.* New York: New York University Press.

Kelsall-Knight, Lucille, and Ceri Sudron. 2020. "Non-Biological Lesbian Mothers' Experiences of Accessing Healthcare for Their Children." *Nursing Children and Young People* 32(2): 38–42.

Kluwer, Esther S., José A. M. Heesink, and Evert van de Vliert. 2002. "The Division of Labor Across the Transition to Parenthood: A Justice Perspective." *Journal of Marriage and Family* 64(4): 930–943.

Kramer, Stephanie. 2019. "U.S. Has World's Highest Rate of Children Living in Single-Parent Households." Pew Research Center, December 12. www.pewresearch.org/fact-tank /2019/12/12/u-s-children-more-likely-than-children-in-other-countries-to-live-with-just -one-parent/.

Lampe, Nik M., Shannon K. Carter, and J. E. Sumerau. 2019. "Continuity and Change in Gender Frames: The Case of Transgender Reproduction." *Gender & Society* 33: 865–887.

Lev, Arlene Istar. 2010. "How Queer! The Development of Gender Identity and Sexual Orientation in LGBTQ-Headed Families." *Family Process* 49(3): 260–290.

Lucal, Betsy. 1999. "What it Means to be Gendered Me: Life on the Boundaries of a Dichotomous Gender System." *Gender & Society* 13(6): 781–797.

Mazrekaj, Deni, Kristof De Witte, and Sofie J. Cabus. 2020. "School Outcomes of Children Raised by Same-Sex Parents: Evidence from Administrative Panel Data." *American Sociological Review* 85: 830–856.

McGinn, Kathleen L., Mayra Ruiz Castro, and Elizabeth L. Lingo. 2018. "Learning from Mum: Cross-National Evidence Linking Maternal Employment and Adult Children's Outcomes." *Work, Employment and Society* 33: 374–400.

McInerney, Anne, Mary Creaner, and Elizabeth Nixon. 2021. "The Motherhood Experiences of Non-Birth Mothers in Same-Sex Parent Families." *Psychology of Women Quarterly* 45(3): 279–293.

Moore, Mignon. 2019. "Reflections on Marriage Equality as a Vehicle for LGBTQ Political Transformation." In *Queer Families and Relationships after Marriage Equality,* edited by Michael W. Yarbough, Angela Jones, and Joseph Nicholas DeFilippis, 73–79. New York: Routledge.

National Center for Lesbian Rights. 2019. "Legal Recognition of LGBT Families." National Center for Lesbian Rights. Retrieved on September 8, 2022. www.nclrights.org/wp -content/uploads/2013/07/Legal_Recognition_of_LGBT_Families.pdf.

National Women's Law Center. 2017. "A Snapshot of Working Mothers." National Women's Law Center. Retrieved on September 8, 2022. https://nwlc.org/wp-content/uploads/2017 /04/A-Snapshot-of-Working-Mothers.pdf.

Nydia Pabón-Colón, Jessica. 2017. "Performing Queer Mamí on Social Media." *Performance Research* 22: 71–74.

O'Neill, Kristal R., Helen P. Hamer, and Robyn Dixon. 2012. "A Lesbian Family in a Straight World: The Impact of the Transition to Parenthood on Couple Relationships in Planned Lesbian Families." *Women's Studies Journal* 26(2): 39–53.

Pain, Emily. 2020. "Queer Polyfamily Performativity: Family Practices and Adaptive Strategies among LGBTQ + Polyamorists." *Journal of GLBT Family Studies* 16(3): 277–292.

Pallotta-Chiarolli, M., E. Sheff, and R. Mountford. 2020. "Polyamorous Parenting in Contemporary Research: Developments and Future Directions." In *LGBTQ-Parent Families*, 2nd ed., edited by Abbie Goldberg and Katherine R. Allen, 171–183. Cham, Switzerland: Springer.

Prickett, Kate C., Alice Martin-Storey, and Robert Crosnoe. 2015. "A Research Note on Time with Children in Different-and Same-Sex Two-Parent Families." *Demography* 52(3): 905–918.

Radis, Brie, and Yochay Nadan. 2021. "'Always Thinking about Safety': African American Lesbian Mothers' Perceptions of Risk and Well-Being." *Family Process* 60(3): 950–965.

Reczek, Corinne, Russell Spiker, Hui Liu, and Robert Crosnoe. 2017. "The Promise and Perils of Population Research on Same-Sex Families." *Demography* 54(6): 2385–2397.

Ryan-Flood, Róisín. 2005. "Contested Heteronormativities: Discourses of Fatherhood among Lesbian Parents in Sweden and Ireland." *Sexualities* 8(2): 189–204.

Saffron, L. 1996. *"What about the Children?" Sons and Daughters of Lesbian and Gay Parents Talk about Their Lives.* London: Cassell.

Schilt, Paige. 2009. "Genderqueer Mommy." *Bilerico Project* (blog), May 10. https://web.archive.org/web/20190709091125/https://bilerico.lgbtqnation.com/2009/05/genderqueer_mommy.php.

———. 2012. "Passing (Or Not) at the Pool." *Queer Rock Love: A Gay, Transgender, Rock-n-Roll Family Raising a Son in the Heart of the South* (blog), January 20. http://queerrocklove.com/2012/01/20/passing-or-not-at-the-pool/.

Seidman, Stephen. 2002. *Beyond the Closet: The Transformation of Gay and Lesbian Life.* New York: Routledge.

Stacey, Judith, and Timothy J. Biblarz. 2001. "(How) Does the Sexual Orientation of Parents Matter?" *American Sociological Review* 66(2): 159–183.

Sullivan, Julie. 2020. "Comparing Characteristics and Selected Expenditures of Dual- and Single-Income Households with Children." Bureau of Labor Statistics. Retrieved September 8, 2022. www.bls.gov/opub/mlr/2020/article/comparing-characteristics-and-selected-expenditures-of-dual-and-single-income-households-with-children.htm.

Tasker, Fiona L., and Susan Golombok. 1997. *Growing Up in a Lesbian Family: Effects on Child Development.* London: Guilford Press.

Vanfraussen, K., I. Ponjaert-Kristoffersen, and A. Brewaeys. 2002. "What Does it Mean for Youngsters to Grow Up in a Lesbian Family Created by Means of Donor Insemination?" *Journal of Reproductive and Infant Psychology* 20(4): 237–252.

VanOrman, Alicia, and Linda A. Jacobsen. 2020. "U.S. Household Composition Shifts as the Population Grows Older; More Young Adults Live with Parents." Population Reference Bureau, February 12. www.prb.org/resources/u-s-household-composition-shifts-as-the-population-grows-older-more-young-adults-live-with-parents/.

Wainright, Jennifer L., and Charlotte J. Patterson. 2006. "Delinquency, Victimization, and Substance Use Among Adolescents with Female Same-Sex Parents." *Journal of Family Psychology* 20(3): 526–530.

Waller, Maureen R. 2020. "Getting the Court in Your Business: Unmarried Parents, Institutional Intersectionality, and Establishing Parenting Time Orders in Family Court." *Social Problems* 67(3): 527–545.

Wangsness, Lisa. 2011. "Archdiocese Issues No-Discrimination Admissions Policy." *Boston Globe*, January 13. http://www.boston.com/news/education/k_12/articles/2011/01/13/archdiocese_issues_no_discrimination_admissions_policy/.

West, Candace, and Don Zimmerman. 1987. "Doing Gender." *Gender & Society* 1(2): 125–151.

Weston, Kath. 1997. *Families We Choose: Lesbians, Gays, Kinship*. New York: Columbia University Press.

Zonta, Michela. 2016. "Housing the Extended Family." Center for American Progress, October 19. www.americanprogress.org/article/housing-the-extended-family/.

CHAPTER 40: Queering Family Sexual Violence
by Elizabeth Whalley

Ahrens, Courtney E., Rebecca Campbell, N. Karen Ternier-Thames, Sharon M. Wasco, and Tracy Sefl. 2007. "Deciding Whom to Tell: Expectations and Outcomes of Rape Survivors' First Disclosures." *Psychology of Women Quarterly* 31(1): 38–49.

Allen, Samuel H., and Shawn N. Mendez. 2018. "Hegemonic Heteronormativity: Toward a New Era of Queer Family Theory." *Journal of Family Theory & Review* 10(1): 70–86.

Arnold, Emily A., and Marlon M. Bailey. 2009. "Constructing Home and Family: How the Ballroom Community Supports African American GLBTQ Youth in the Face of HIV/AIDS." *Journal of Gay & Lesbian Social Services* 21(2–3): 171–188.

Ball, M. 2014. "Queer Criminology, Critique, and the 'Art of Not Being Governed.'" *Critical Criminology* 22(1): 21–34.

Bay Area Transformative Justice Collective (BATJC). 2021, May 1. Bay Area Transformative Justice Collective. Retrieved June 25, 2022. https://batjc.wordpress.com/.

Belknap, Joanne. 2010. "Rape: Too Hard to Report and Too Easy to Discredit Victims." *Violence against Women* 16(12): 1335–1344.

Brownmiller, Susan. 1975. *Against Our Will: Men, Women and Rape*. New York: Bantam Books.

Bumiller, Kristin. 2008. *In an Abusive State: How Liberalism Appropriated the Feminist Movement against Sexual Violence*. Durham, NC: Duke University Press.

Chauncey, G. 1994. *Gay New York: Gender, Urban Culture, and the Making of the Gay Male World, 1890–1940*. New York: Basic Books.

Coontz, S. 2015. "The Evolution of American Families." In *Families as They Really Are*, edited by B. J. Risman and V. Rutter, 36–55. New York: W. W. Norton.

Corrigan, Rose. 2013. *Up against a Wall: Rape Reform and the Failure of Success*. New York: New York University Press.

Cowan, Philip A., and Carolyn Pape Cowan. 2015. "Beyond Family Structure." In *Families as They Really Are*, edited by B. J. Risman and V. Rutter, 358–379. New York: W. W. Norton.

Davis, Angela. 1981. "Rape, Racism and the Myth of the Black Rapist." In *Women, Race and Class*, 172–201. New York: Random House.

De Vries, Brian, and David Megathlin. 2009. "The Meaning of Friendship for Gay Men and Lesbians in the Second Half of Life." *Journal of GLBT Family Studies* 5(1–2): 82–98.

Dozier, S. 2015. "The Power of Queer." In *Families as They Really Are*, edited by B. J. Risman and V. Rutter, 458–474. New York: W. W. Norton.

Filipas, Henrietta H., and Sarah E. Ullman. 2001. "Social Reactions to Sexual Assault Victims from Various Support Sources." *Violence and Victims* 16(6): 673.

Finkelhor, David, and Larry Baron. 1986. "Risk Factors for Child Sexual Abuse." *Journal of Interpersonal Violence* 1(1): 43–71.

Fish, Jessica N., and Stephen T. Russell. 2018. "Queering Methodologies to Understand Queer Families." *Family Relations* 67(1): 12–25.

Fisher, Bonnie S., and Francis T. Cullen. 2000. "Measuring the Sexual Victimization of Women: Evolution, Current Controversies, and Future Research." *Criminal Justice* 4: 317–390.

Garcia-Roberts, Gus. 2017. "Bryan Singer Rape Accuser Says Fear of Being Outed Kept Him from Going to Police In 2003." *Los Angeles Times*, December 18. www.latimes.com /business/la-fi-ct-bryan-singer-20171208-story.html.

Guadalupe-Diaz, Xavier. 2014. "Same-sex Victimization and the LGBTQ Community." In *Sexual Victimization: Then and Now*, edited by Tara N. Richards and Catherine D. Marcum, 173–192. Thousand Oaks, CA: Sage.

Guadalupe-Diaz, Xavier L., and Elizabeth Whalley. 2022. "Queering #MeToo: Working toward Queer and Trans Inclusion." In *#MeToo and Beyond: Perspectives on a Global Movement*, edited by Cristina Alcalde and Paula-Irene Villa, 163–182. Lexington: University Press of Kentucky.

Hammack, P. L., D. M. Frost, and S. D. Hughes. 2019. "Queer Intimacies: A New Paradigm for the Study of Relationship Diversity." *Journal of Sex Research* 56(4–5): 556–592.

Heiner, Brady T., and Sarah K. Tyson. 2017. "Feminism and the Carceral State: Gender-Responsive Justice, Community Accountability, and the Epistemology of Antiviolence." *Feminist Philosophy Quarterly* 3(1): https://doi.org/10.5206/fpq/2016.3.3.

Kaba, Mariame. 2021. *We Do This 'Til We Free Us: Abolitionist Organizing and Transforming Justice*. Chicago: Haymarket Books.

Lonsway, K. A., and J. Archambault. 2012. "The 'Justice Gap' for Sexual Assault Cases: Future Directions for Research and Reform." *Violence against Women* 18(2): 145–168.

Lorenz, Katherine, Sarah E. Ullman, Anne Kirkner, Rupashree Mandala, Amanda L. Vasquez, and Rannveig Sigurvinsdottir. 2018. "Social Reactions to Sexual Assault Disclosure: A Qualitative Study of Informal Support Dyads." *Violence against Women* 24(12): 1497–1520.

Malloy, Lindsay C., Allison P. Mugno, Jillian R. Rivard, Thomas D. Lyon, and Jodi A. Quas. 2016. "Familial Influences on Recantation in Substantiated Child Sexual Abuse Cases." *Child Maltreatment* 21(3): 256–261.

McCloskey, Laura Ann, and Jennifer A. Bailey. 2000. "The Intergenerational Transmission of Risk for Child Sexual Abuse." *Journal of Interpersonal Violence* 15(10): 1019–1035.

Moraga, Cherrie, and Gloria Anzaldúa. 1981. *This Bridge Called My Back: Writings by Radical Women of Color*. Watertown, MA: Persephone Press.

Rice, Marnie E., and Grant T. Harris. 2002. "Men Who Molest Their Sexually Immature Daughters: Is a Special Explanation Required?" *Journal of Abnormal Psychology* 111(2): 329.

Russell, Diana E. H. 1982. *Rape in Marriage*. New York: MacMillan.

——. 1984. *Sexual Exploitation: Rape, Child Sexual Abuse, and Workplace Harassment*. Beverly Hills, CA: Sage Publications.

Simmons, Aishah Shahidah. 2019. *Love with Accountability: Digging up the Roots of Child Sexual Abuse*. Chico, CA: AK Press.

Stoltenborgh, M., M. H. van Ijzendoorn, E. M., Euser, and M. J. Bakermans-Kranenburg. 2011. "A Global Perspective on Child Sexual Abuse: Meta-Analysis of Prevalence around the World." *Child Maltreatment* 16: 79–101.

Stroebel, S. S., S. L. O'keefe, K. W. Beard, S. Y. Kuo, S. V. Swindell, and M. J. Kommor. 2012. "Father–Daughter Incest: Data from an Anonymous Computerized Survey." *Journal of Child Sexual Abuse* 21: 176–199.

Struening, Karen. 2015. "Families 'In Law' and Families 'In Practice.'" In *Families as They Really Are*, edited by B. J. Risman and V. Rutter, 116–136. New York: W. W. Norton.

Tillman, Shaquita, Thema Bryant-Davis, Kimberly Smith, and Alison Marks. 2010. "Shattering Silence: Exploring Barriers to Disclosure for African American Sexual Assault Survivors." *Trauma, Violence, & Abuse* 11(2): 59–70.

Ullman, Sarah E. 2010. *Talking about Sexual Assault: Society's Response to Survivors*. Washington, DC: American Psychological Association.

Weston, Kath. 1997. *Families We Choose: Lesbians, Gays, Kinship*. New York: Columbia University Press.

Whalley, Elizabeth. 2020. "The 'Bait and Switch' of Sexual Assault Response: Expanded Carceral Power at a Rape Crisis Center." *Affilia* 35(2): 200–217.

Whalley, Elizabeth, and Colleen Hackett. 2017. "Carceral Feminisms: The Abolitionist Project and Undoing Dominant Feminisms." *Contemporary Justice Review* 20(4): 456–473.

Index